MARSHALL LOEB'S
1993 Money Guide

MARSHALL LOEB'S
1993 Money Guide

by Marshall Loeb
Managing Editor of Fortune *Magazine*

LITTLE, BROWN AND COMPANY
BOSTON • TORONTO • LONDON

FIRST EDITION

The Library of Congress has catalogued this serial title as follows:

Marshall Loeb's money guide. — [1984]– — Boston: Little, Brown,
  c1983–
      v.; 24 cm.
    Annual.
    ISSN 8755-1586 = Marshall Loeb's money guide.
    ISBN 0-316-53073-5
    1. Finance, Personal — Periodicals. I. Loeb, Marshall. II. Title:
Money guide.
HG179.M342   332.024′005 — dc19   84-646730
                                                        AACR 2   MARC-S

10 9 8 7 6 5 4 3 2 1

MV-NY

*Published simultaneously in Canada
by Little, Brown & Company (Canada) Limited*

PRINTED IN THE UNITED STATES OF AMERICA

For my family
Peggy, Michael, Margaret, Gail,
Michael II, Kate — and more TK

Contents

Preface

WELCOME to the 1993 *Money Guide*. I have been writing these books since 1983, but this one is quite special. It is greatly revised, substantially expanded and thoroughly updated to take account of the many changes in the law, in the marketplace and in the world of finance. My goal is to provide the most comprehensive, accurate and immediately useful book that you can read on your personal finances.

I hope that I can help you answer five basic questions:
—How can I earn more money?
—How can I invest it more profitably?
—How can I save it more prudently?
—How can I spend it more sensibly, and more pleasurably?
—How can I enhance my career?

This book is based largely on the work of my distinguished present and former colleagues — the writers, reporters and editors of *Fortune* and *Money* magazines. To them it is dedicated. One part of my job as Managing Editor of *Fortune* is to choose articles from the magazine, abridge and reedit them and then present them on the CBS Radio Network in daily broadcasts titled "Your Dollars." Previously, I did the same as Managing Editor of *Money*. I have relied greatly on these scripts in creating the 380 chapters in this book.

Special thanks belong to Susan Pearson, who served as chief researcher, managed other researchers who worked on the Guide, supervised the checking and made many useful suggestions. My appreciation also goes to the other researchers, Therese Eiben, Ani Hadjian, Anne Hopkins, Alice Kantor, Anne Murphy (who deserves credit for the new section on long-distance phone service) and Sara Solberg (who revised the sections on computers). Thanks additionally to Bobby McFarland for his help in typing the manuscript.

Helen O'Guinn, Editor in Chief of *Endless Vacation* magazine, expertly added many new insights to the chapter "Your Vacation." Jerry Cobb of the CNBC network and Hratch Alexanian of Morningstar Securities gave their time and professional help. Joel Dreyfuss, my former *Fortune* colleague and now Editor of *PC* magazine, made countless contributions to the chapter "Your Computer." My thanks to them all.

Warren M. Bergstein, a senior manager with the accounting firm of Ernst & Young, and his associates Sandra Price and Gwenn Selzer were surefooted guides through the maze of tax law. I am very grateful for their expert insights and suggestions.

Robert Klein, editor and Certified Financial Planner, expanded upon a number of chapters, made significant contributions and gave excellent counsel.

My deepest appreciation as well to Anne Gut, my highly talented and dedicated administrative assistant, who has been so exceptionally helpful in so many ways.

Ray Roberts of Little, Brown, an editor and a gentleman, worked wonders to bring this book to publication. Dorothy Straight did a smoothly expert job of overseeing the copyediting.

James B. Hayes, *Fortune*'s superlative publisher, gave the project enthusiastic support. Marilyn Sahner and Patricia A. Straus, invaluable colleagues at Time Inc. Magazines, made it possible for me to broadcast material from *Fortune* and *Money* on the CBS Radio Network. At CBS, my particular thanks go to Frank Murphy and David Kurman.

Let me express my gratitude to Jason McManus, Editor-in-Chief of Time Warner Inc., a brilliant journalist and a deeply caring man; to Richard Stolley, Editorial Director of Time Inc., and Gilbert Rogin, Corporate Editor of Time Inc., who have been sources of inspiration; and to Edward L. Jamieson, longtime Executive Editor of *Time*, my friend and colleague for the better part of thirty years.

MARSHALL LOEB'S

1993 Money Guide

Introduction

Ten Ways to Preserve and Protect Your Money and Make It Grow

People enjoy more personal freedom and can make better choices about their lives if they learn to handle their money sensibly. Just as a financially sound company has more opportunity to do great things than a strapped and worried organization does, so a financially sound person has more opportunity to act imaginatively and expansively. Certainly, money is not an end but a means: a means to help make the most out of ourselves by being able to pay for education, travel, medical care and a worry-free retirement. The more we earn, quite obviously, the more we can spend to enhance and secure the lives of ourselves and of our families, to enrich our communities, to aid our favorite causes. The more we save and invest, the more we also provide the seed capital that helps create new enterprises and jobs.

Each and every one of us has the opportunity — and the obligation — to preserve and protect our money, and make it grow. This book speaks to our opportunities — our opportunities to earn more money, to invest it more profitably, to spend it more sensibly and more pleasurably, to save it more prudently and to improve our careers.

We have better chances than any other people at any other time to do all that. Chances to put our money into forms of investments, savings, insurance that did not exist just a few years ago. Chances to build our careers or start businesses in fresh forms of industry, services or commerce, in newly expanding regions of the country. Chances to borrow capital through rather novel means.

The trouble is that chances mean choices, and making choices is hard. We have new freedoms to decide whether, when, how and how much to invest, save, spend. Tough choices. Many people dodge such decisions. They take life as it comes and then lament their missed opportunities. That is practically always a mistake. Almost invariably, it is better to make some decision than no decision. A bad decision can be reversed; making no decision leaves you in limbo, uneasy, frustrated.

Thus, my aim is to outline your money choices and to urge you to seize your opportunities. Let me start by explaining 10 ways in which you can act immediately to preserve and protect what you have and help it to grow. Many of these steps will sound familiar, but few people have taken advantage of all of them, and they provide a sound base on which to begin. All of them — and many more — are elaborated upon in later chapters of this book.

STEP ONE: *Build up a cash cushion to protect yourself against emergencies.*

That way, if you unexpectedly need money, you will not have to borrow at exorbitant interest rates or sell off investments at what may be unfavorable prices. Try to accumulate and maintain easily tapped liquid savings equal at least to three months of your after-tax income. Put that money into a money-market deposit account or a savings certificate at a federally insured bank or savings institution. Another sound choice is to place your savings in a money-market fund.

STEP TWO: *Start investing regularly and faithfully, come rain, come shine.*

According to Towers Perrin benefits consulting firm, a 45-year-old person with an annual household income of $83,000 will need a ton of money if he or she wants to retire at age 62 with an undiminished living standard. Bear in mind that with normal salary increases and inflation that person will be earning considerably more than $83,000 by the time he or she reaches 62. Towers Perrin estimates that he or she will then need about $3.1 million, half of which would be the assumed value by then of government pensions and other benefits. If he or she cannot produce the other half out of savings and invest-ments, then retirement at that age would be something of a squeeze. Even if Towers Perrin estimates prove to be on the high side, the point is indisputable. You have to accumulate substantial funds for retirement.

So, after you have established your necessary liquid savings, begin deploying your money into a diversity of investments. Your insured savings are secure; they grow at a measured pace, depending on the level of interest you collect, and you can tap into them at any time. Your investments carry some risk, but they can grow at a faster rate than your savings.

You reduce your risks by diversifying. Markets have become so volatile that you no longer can buy only one stock or bond and confidently hold it for a lifetime. Thus, it is wise to start investing by buying into a diversified, professionally managed mutual fund; then branch out into some stocks and bonds, and later perhaps some real estate investment trusts (REITs) and precious metals, in the form of gold bullion or a mutual fund that invests in gold and silver mining companies.

Resolve to invest the same amount of money every month or from every paycheck. That's known as dollar-cost averaging, but you can think of it as investing on the installment plan. When your investments rise in value, you can congratulate yourself for having earned some paper profit. When they fall, at least you can take advantage of your new opportunity to pick up some bargains: a short while ago, your regular monthly investment could buy perhaps only two shares, but now it can buy three!

Above all, don't despair; all investments decline sometimes. Wise investors position themselves for the long term. If you believe that the country and its economy will do well over the long term, then your investments will do well. That is, they will do well if you don't become greedy and rush to buy when markets surge to their tops, and if you don't panic and rush to sell out when markets plunge to their bottoms. The discipline of dollar-cost averaging helps you avoid those two common errors.

STEP THREE: *Act now to further reduce your taxes for this year — and future years.*

For money earned in 1992, higher-income people face federal income tax rates of 31%.

Probably nobody takes all the deductions to which he or she is legitimately entitled. So resolve now to use your tax-saving opportunities and to keep better records of your deductible expenses. Remember: Pack rats always save more, and organized pack rats save the most.

Here are a few of many money-saving steps you can take:

Buy municipal bonds. The federal government does not tax the interest you collect on most of them, and if the bonds are from your home state, you will probably escape state and local taxes, too. Also invest in supersafe U.S. Treasury securities or U.S. Savings Bonds, the yields on which are exempt from state and local taxes, or in U.S. government bond funds if your state exempts them from its taxes.

Deposit money in your company's profit-sharing or stock purchase plans; taxes are deferred on any contributions made by your employer and on any earnings made by those contributions and by your own deposits. Take advantage of a so-called 401(k) salary-reduction plan if your company offers one; of the income you earned in 1992 you can contribute up to $8,728 tax-free. The saving for someone in the top tax bracket is more than $2,700. And many big corporations add 50 cents for each dollar of employee contributions up to a maximum of 6% of pay.

Deduct expenses incurred for charitable work, such as making phone calls or driving your car to and from the place where you do volunteer work (the allowance for your 1992 income taxes is still 12 cents a mile). Give your old clothes, books or furnishings to charities and collect receipts for the gifts' estimated value. You can also donate shares of stock or other securities. Note: You must itemize your return in order to take charitable deductions.

STEP FOUR: *Open an Individual Retirement Account* (IRA).

Even though one of its most important tax-saving features has been limited or eliminated for many people by tax reform, an IRA can be a valuable device both for reducing your taxes and for increasing your capital. Everyone who earns money from a job can have an Individual Retirement Account, and almost everyone should.

The dividends, interest and capital gains on your investment compound tax-free until you withdraw the money, probably after you retire. When that time comes, you can arrange for gradual withdrawals over the course of many years. It's remarkable how fast your money will grow when it is unencumbered by taxes. If you put away $2,000 every January and it grows 8% annually, you will have some $31,300 after 10 years, $98,800 after 20 years, $244,700 after 30 years and $559,600 after 40 years. Of course, withdrawals and taxes on them are inevitable, starting gradually no later than age 70½, but you'll still come out way ahead.

Anyone who is not covered by an employee pension plan can deduct the full IRA deposits from his or her taxable income. So can anyone who meets certain income limits. In 1991, of the 44.8 million joint returns, more than 30 million were eligible for at least a partial deduction, and 54.6 million single filers were eligible for the same, according to the U.S. Joint Committee on Taxation.

If you are covered by an employee pension plan — whether or not you are vested — you will be able to deduct your contribution only if you earn a rather moderate income. Under the law as of 1992, if you are a single person covered by an employer, you can take the full deduction if you earn $25,000 or less annually in adjusted gross income. Married couples filing jointly keep the full deduction if their combined income is $40,000 or less. Singles who earn between $25,000 and $35,000 and joint filers who earn between $40,000 and $50,000 can deduct part of their contribution. The deduction tapers off as you earn more money. It vanishes altogether when your income tops $35,000 or $50,000.

As described later in this book, you can put your IRA money into almost any form of savings or investment except for art and other collectibles. My own favorite repository for an IRA, particularly for young people who are confident of the future and willing to take sensible risk, is the no-load growth mutual fund that invests in stocks and other securities. Funds with the best performance records are named in the mutual-fund chapters of this book, and you can get an updated list of the top performers in the "Fund Watch" column of *Money* magazine.

STEP FIVE: *If you are eligible, also open a Keogh account or a simplified employee pension, called a SEP for short.*

Keogh plans and SEPs work much like IRAs, but you can put much more money into them and deduct it all from your taxable income. You can open one if you are self-employed full- or part-time. It's surprising how many people are eligible for Keoghs or SEPs but don't know it — or don't take advantage of this large and liberal tax shelter. You qualify just so long as you work for yourself. You can work full-time, part-time or free-lance. You can work at one job for an employer but still contribute your earnings from a second, self-employed moonlighting job. Among those eligible for Keoghs and SEPs are most small-business people and many lawyers, doctors, dentists, carpenters, plumbers, actors and directors, free-lance writers, waiters, taxi drivers and the like.

You can contribute about 18.5% of your income from self-employment to a Keogh or about 12% of your income to a SEP, up to a maximum contribution of $30,000 a year. Also, you can have both an IRA and a Keogh (although most probably you may not be able to *deduct* your IRA contribution). Between them, some high-income individuals can put away as much as $32,000 a year. If both spouses are self-employed, they can shelter up to $64,000 annually. There's even a special kind of Keogh, called a defined benefit plan, to which older high-income professionals can contribute much more than $30,000 a year.

One warning: Unlike an IRA, which you can open as late as April 15 of next year, you have to open a Keogh plan by December 31 of this year in order to contribute any of this year's earnings to it. However, you can make those contributions up to the time you file your income taxes — as late as April 15, or August 15 if you get an extension. Or you can open a SEP, which follows the rules for IRAs.

In any case, it is wise to make your annual IRA contribution to these plans as early in the year as possible. Let's say you deposit $2000 every year for 10 years and earn 10% annually on it. Put that money in every January 2, and in 10 years you will have $35,000. But if you regularly wait until April 15 of the following year, your money will have grown to only $29,000. Over a period of 20 to 30 years, the compounding of tax-deferred earnings on early contributions can add tens of thousands of dollars to your account. Don't forget, however, that if you withdraw your money before age 59½ you usually have to pay a 10% penalty in addition to postponed income taxes.

STEP SIX: *Be sure you have a will — a sound, valid, hard-to-shake and up-to-date will.*

There is no way without a will to make sure that whatever you leave goes to whomever you wish. If you do not have a will, your heirs could be clobbered by taxes and your children could be raised by someone you don't want. Yet it is shocking how many adult Americans do not have this basic document — almost two-thirds of them do not.

Estate laws change fairly often and sometimes radically, so it is important to review your will regularly. The last major change was in 1981; if you made out your will before the end of that year, your money may not get distributed the way you wish it to be. Therefore, check right now to see if your will is current. If it is not, make an appointment with a lawyer to prepare a new one as soon as possible. It is best to have your will drafted by an attorney and updated at least once every three years.

STEP SEVEN: *Save money on your life insurance and make sure you have the right kind of policies.*

For basic insurance protection, the least expensive policy is still annual renewable term. If you are a nonsmoking man, say, 40 years old, $100,000 of coverage at Prudential will cost you $187 for annual renewable term and $1,694 for traditional whole life. But if you want to protect your family and simultaneously build up tax-deferred savings, your best means may well be whole life. And if you are 55 years old or older, the premiums for annual renewable term will approach or equal those for whole life bought when you were younger.

Another strategy: you might be wise to buy term insurance and then put the money you save into mutual funds or some other sound investment. You can save still more by buying only the life insurance you need. How much do you need? Remember this: If no one is relying on you for financial support, you probably don't need any life insurance at all.

STEP EIGHT: *Save money by giving it away.*

If you think income taxes are high, you should look at death taxes. They start at 37% on the federal level and go all the way up to 55%. Instead of leaving all that to Uncle Sam, give it — while you're alive — to those whom you want to have it. You don't have to pay tax on gifts of money paid directly to a college to help cover your children's or grandchildren's tuition and fees, and none on payments made directly to hospitals or nursing homes to pay the bills of less fortunate family members or friends.

Generous donations to your favorite charity or cultural institution, whether the local symphony or your alma mater, can also help to save you money now. Just make the gift to a charitable trust. While endowing a worthy cause, you can reduce your current income taxes on gifts of appreciated stocks. In one form of charitable trust, you get the investment income from your gift for the rest of your life.

STEP NINE: *Buy a personal computer and learn to use it.*

If you invest your money — and, more important, your time — in purchasing and mastering a computer, it will pay you dividends many, many times over. With the vast range of new and sophisticated programs available, the computer has become an essential household and business tool. The tasks it can help you with include storing (and easily retrieving) huge amounts of information, preparing your taxes, and picking out the best stocks. For example, from the thousands of issues, you can segregate those few that are priced well below their book value or that have especially modest price/earnings ratios or that are selling far beneath their recent peaks. A computer also can help you chart and graph the movements of specific stocks.

It can keep track of the investments you have and alert you to any that are starting to go sour. Not least, new programs that employ simple question-and-answer procedures can help you mightily to plan your tax strategy, keep the records that will simplify the chore of paying taxes, and legitimately reduce what you have to pay.

STEP TEN: *Keep up with the news that affects your money.*

The world changes rapidly, and almost every event of consequence close to home or in some distant corner of the world influences your investments, your savings, your personal balance sheet. A referendum in Denmark, a move toward peace in the Middle East, continued regional conflict in the former Soviet Union, abusive treatment of dissidents in China — not to mention events at home, such as urban unrest, the passing of a bill in Congress or a policy shift by the Federal Reserve Board — can alter the price of everything from chocolate bars to new cars. Such events also can lead to sharp gyrations in the values of your investments and the levels of the interest rates you pay or collect. It is important, then, to become an avid reader of the daily financial pages and of business magazines. One rather immodest but heartfelt comment: I think you will find *Fortune* to be particularly valuable and enjoyable.

So there you have the 10 initial steps. There are more, many more, that each of us can take in order to seize the moment, make the right choices and take advantage of our opportunities. For an explanation of them, read on.

— MARSHALL LOEB

Your Personal Finances

How to Become Financially Independent

FINANCIAL independence means having the wherewithal to say to yourself: "If I wanted to, I could quit what I'm doing today and live comfortably for the rest of my life."

Millions of Americans can achieve that dream.

You do not have to marry well or choose your parents wisely to reach financial independence. More likely, you will gain it by investing — shrewdly and boldly. Or by starting your own business. Or by working for a generous company and taking advantage of all the corporate savings plans, stock purchase programs and profit-sharing plans that you can.

The sooner you start saving, the easier and faster you will be able to accomplish independence. And you will have help along the way. Banks and a bewildering variety of investment firms are all clamoring for your money, and offering reasonable real rates of return to get it. In many cases, the government will even let you shelter your savings from taxes. One of the smartest ways to begin is to put the $2,000 maximum each year into a tax-deferring Individual Retirement Account. If you start doing that in 1993 and earn 10% compounded annually on the money between now and the year 2013, you will have $126,000.

Even if you cannot deduct your contribution, an IRA is still a great tax saver. Your money can grow at a surprising clip. Thanks to the law of compound interest, you earn returns not only on your original stake but on your accumulated gains as well. At a 10% rate of return, the average for stocks over the past 66 years, your investment would double in just over seven years.

As a step toward financial independence, pick the safest high-growth investment you can find — and then give it your undivided attention. Probably it will be in the stock market. Choose growth stocks or undervalued companies, including some blue chips, scattered in several industries. Your best investment is probably a mutual fund that automatically diversifies your portfolio. Over the last 10 years, the growth funds have had total returns averaging slightly under 15.9% a year.

According to the compensation and benefits consulting firm Hewitt Associates, Social Security and a pension will replace roughly 36% of pre-retirement pay for today's $100,000-a-year employee. Social Security will replace only a small slice of pre-retirement income; today's maximum individual payout is only $13,056 a year. It is critical, therefore, that you take advantage of the liberal employee-benefit plans offered by many corporations. Job hopping from company to company is not the way to build a reserve of capital. Most programs do not go into effect until you have been with a company for at least a year. But an employee earning, say, $50,000 who stays with the same firm for 20 years can amass as much as half a million dollars from generous benefit plans.

The most important capital-building corporate benefits are profit-sharing and savings plans. In both, your employer usually contributes money above and beyond your regular salary to an account that is turned over to you when you quit or retire. In a profit-sharing plan, the contribution depends on the company's annual earnings — and in the best years usually amounts to about 10% of your salary. In a typical savings program, the company will match each dollar you invest with 50 cents of its own. And remember: Everything the company tosses into the pot, plus all the earnings on both your own and the company's contributions, will get the huge boost of tax deferral. The money grows free of taxes until you withdraw it.

A relatively new kind of savings program — called a salary-reduction, or 401(k), plan — offers a great tax break. You put part of your pay in the plan and it is not considered immediate income — so it is tax-deferred and can grow with extra speed. One drawback, though: You cannot take out any of your money before you leave the company, except in times of hardship. Even then, if you withdraw money before age 59½, you may have to pay a 10% penalty on top of any income tax you owe.

Most employers, however, let you borrow against your 401(k) plan. A 1991 survey by Hewitt Associates showed that 67% of companies offering 401(k)s had loan provisions, and an additional 3% were considering them. It is possible to borrow at least some of your untaxed contributions and often the employer's contributions as well. You can borrow up to $10,000 on a balance of $20,000 or less, and on higher balances, up to $50,000 or 50% of the amount that is vested, whichever is less. The interest rate is likely to be lower than you would pay a bank or other commercial lender. It is a fixed rate based on a money-market index such as the prime rate or the five-year Treasury note. You repay the loan with payroll deductions that can be spread over five years — or longer in some instances. Another advantage of 401(k) loans is that they do not reduce the balance in your retirement fund. All of your money there keeps earning tax-sheltered income, sometimes at a higher rate than you are being charged for the loan.

Probably the most common way to try to become financially independent is to start your own business. You are likely to find the widest range of opportunities in the Pacific Coast region and the Sunbelt.

Before you launch any business, take a hard look at its real market potential. Do not try to start too big. The safest course is to create a firm small enough for the money you have and then make it larger. A small success is better than a big failure.

Be sure you start with enough money. Underfinancing is as bad as overborrowing. It can choke a promising enterprise or force you to give up control to your backers. A little financial help from your friends and relatives is fine, but treat such loans as strictly business deals, complete with signed legal agreements. Handshake deals often lead to bitter quarrels.

To launch and maintain almost any enterprise, you need a credit line from a bank. When you first go to a bank and begin to establish a relationship, do not rush to the highest officer. Instead, find a younger manager who has time for you. Ask him or her to review your ideas and refer you to a lawyer or accountant who can help you to write an intelligent business plan. In at least three or four pages, it should describe your product or service; the staffing, space and equipment you will need; and the reasons that your business should succeed. The plan will help you to define your objectives — and to get a line of credit. Draw from it as you need the money, not in a lump sum that would saddle you with unnecessarily large repayments.

Still another way to gain financial independence is to go to work for a start-up company and persuade the founders to give you some stock in the firm in lieu of a large salary. But before you count your gains, bear in mind that one-quarter of start-ups fail to survive even two years. They tend to be undercapitalized and shorthanded, so you often work long hours for little pay.

You can find many start-ups among deregulated businesses, in fields such as airlines, trucking and other transportation; fast-food services; real estate and personal financial services; health services, especially geriatric care; and in software and other computer-related businesses. To locate start-ups, watch the help-wanted columns in trade periodicals and newspapers. You also can learn about new ventures in national magazines such as *Inc.* and in regional business magazines and newspapers. High-tech ventures cluster around universities, so a business school professor may know of some. Another source is the management-assistance officer at your district Small Business Administration office.

Before you join a new venture, be sure to consider certain questions: Is the new product or service really worthy? For evidence, read the founder's business plan. What is the founder's business record of past success? For information, consult his or her business associates and rivals. Who is putting up the money? A token of an entrepreneur's commitment is the amount of his or her own money invested in the new venture.

The more complicated your employment arrangement, the more you will want a contract or at least a letter of understanding. Get as much down on paper as possible, then show the agreement to your lawyer.

Defining Your Financial Goals

FEW PEOPLE know what they really want their money to do. Several years' accumulation of savings or a sudden inheritance or other windfall leaves them with money to invest and no idea of how to make it work best for them. The first step toward taking control of your personal life is to calculate your net worth. That is what you own minus what you owe. Once you figure out what you are worth, you can set your goals — for example, to take a vacation, buy a house or secure a comfortable retirement. Then you can devise strategies to reach those goals.

Anyone with a simple pocket calculator can figure out his or her net worth. Add up the current value of all your assets. Start with your checking and savings accounts and money-market funds. Don't forget the current market value of any stocks, bonds or other securities you may own. Your insurance agent can supply the current cash value of your life insurance if it is not stated in the policy itself. To find out what your house or condo is worth, consult a real estate broker or note the asking prices of similar homes for sale in your neighborhood. When adding up, do not overlook the current worth of your employee benefits, such as profit-sharing and thrift programs and unexercised stock options. Often these assets are second in value only to your house.

If you own some art, antiques, jewelry or other collectibles, you may need to call in an appraiser to give a good estimate of their current resale price. No matter what kind of collectible you have, you can expect to pay an appraiser an hourly fee of $100 to $300. If you do not have many collectibles, you do not need an appraiser. Just ask a knowing dealer what he or she thinks you could sell them for.

You should recalculate your net worth at least once a year. Some debt counselors urge their clients to take their financial reading immediately before they start Christmas shopping.

What is *your* financial goal? For example, are you saving for college tuition, or future security? A necessary first step to accomplish your goal is to estimate just what you want your money to do and how much you will need to do it. The next step is to figure out how much you must put away each week — or month — to reach your goal.

Follow through on your goal: Many victims of fiscal irresponsibility are plagued by inaction. What they really yearn for is someone who will make their financial decisions for them, and as a result they often get stung by following unsound advice, or — often more disastrously — by not acting when they should. The cost of not making investment moves immediately can add up. Say that, after a check of your personal finances, you decide to shift some money from your low-paying savings account into higher-yielding Treasury bond mutual funds. If you delay just a few months, your procrastination can cost you a bundle of money.

Maintain careful records: You have to keep — and keep updated — lists of your investments, your bank accounts and any financial advisers you might have. Your personal financial file should list names and amounts of all your securities, money-market funds, hard assets and life insurance policies. It also should give the location of your safe-deposit boxes and contain your tax records and credit-card information, as well as wills and deeds.

Maintaining it is not only a wise precaution in case anything happens to you; it is also a constant reminder of your financial position. If you are always aware of where your money is, you can take advantage of tax changes and map out new investment strategies. Keeping such information complete and correct makes it easier for you to switch around your investments and eases the burden on your family if you become ill or injured.

Don't be greedy: Some people are so obsessed with making tax-exempt or tax-deferred investments that they often miss much more lucrative, if taxable, investments. You should look for good, sound economics in an investment before you weigh the tax benefits. This is especially true now that changes in the law have eliminated or reduced the tax advantages of many investments.

Get advice from professionals: It is a mistake to heed advice from people who are not qualified to give it. Amateurs — like your next-door neighbor or your cousin's son-in-law — can do more damage than good. You are better off soliciting and then carefully considering professional advice from brokers, bankers, attorneys, accountants or financial planners. Fees should be agreed on in advance, but sometimes the advice is free. Don't be afraid to ask questions.

Keep your investment knowledge up to date: Another common mistake is a failure to keep an open mind about investment opportunities. Many people invest in just one thing and stick with it. Huge sums of money are still locked away in passbook savings accounts, which these days typically pay interest of less than 4%. Short-term bond funds or tax-deferred annuities from the strongest insurance companies are safe as well as rewarding, but many people are — in the words of one savings bank president — too lazy or afraid to move their money.

One of the biggest mistakes most people make with their money is not hedging their assets and not diversifying their investments. If you have a variety of investments, you stand a better chance of riding out any financial storm.

Organizing Your Financial Files — At Last

WHERE record-keeping is concerned, almost everybody belongs to one of two groups: those who hang on to everything until their house resembles the Collyer brothers' mansion, and those who jettison everything that looks even vaguely financial, often without reading it.

You wouldn't knowingly discard a certificate of birth, baptism, marriage, military discharge or death, nor would you trash your divorce decree, the deed to your house, the share certificate for your co-op apartment or your life-insurance policies. But plenty of people mislay such documents or carry the secret of their whereabouts to the grave. According to the Securities Information Center, investors lost — physically misplaced, accidentally discarded, had stolen — nearly $2.6 billion of stocks and bonds in 1990. So make a list of your vital papers and where they are kept, have the list duplicated and give copies to your next of kin, your lawyer and the executor named in your will.

Permanent records of life's landmarks are best kept in a family safe or bank vault. You should not only know where such documents are stored but also have ready access to them. One exception: Keep your insurance policies and your last will and testament in a file drawer or strongbox at home, lest your bank safe-deposit box be sealed by the state.

Less basic but mighty important documents seem to arrive with every mail. Statements rain down monthly or quarterly from brokers, mutual funds, insurance companies, banks and other financial institutions. Together these write the history of each investment: when you bought it, what you paid for it, what it paid you in dividends or interest or capital gains, when you sold it and for how much. Only in rare instances, however, should you preserve every statement.

Many mutual funds send periodic cumulative reports showing each transaction in your account during each calendar year: new investments, redemptions, fees, dividends, capital-gains distributions and reinvestments, if any. The bottom line on each statement is a running total of the shares you own.

You can tell whether fund statements are cumulative by reading the date of the first entry. If it is the same on each successive statement throughout the year, keep only the latest one. But if the statements start with different dates, save as many of them as you need to preserve a complete record of each year's transactions. That way, you will be able to figure your gain or loss when you sell some or all of your shares.

Keep money-market-fund statements as well. There is no capital gain or loss with money funds, but in case of an IRS audit, money-fund statements can provide vital evidence of cash deposits and withdrawals that might pique the auditor's curiosity. So keep complete records of each year's transactions.

Brokerage statements are not cumulative. Each month is a new story, even if you made no trades. Collect the statements as a record of dividends and interest received and securities bought and sold. Transaction slips showing the purchase or sale of securities arrive, usually in duplicate, a few days after you put in the order. Keep all such slips on file for tax purposes. You will need them to document your capital gains and losses.

For IRA, Keogh and other retirement accounts, which are not subject to immediate taxes, it is still important to keep transaction slips. They constitute a record of the prices paid for each investment so that you or your adviser can occasionally check your overall rate of return. Purchase prices will also be a factor in decisions about when to sell a security.

Brokerage statements often come punched for insertion in a three-ring binder. Take the hint and put them in one. Some investors create a separate compact file for each individual security, mutual fund and retirement account owned. Using vertical file folders or durable brown business-size envelopes, they label each file with the name of the account or security and arrange the files in alphabetical order in a filing cabinet or a desk drawer. Other people keep all of their transaction slips in one file. The important thing is to be systematic and consistent about where you put such documents.

Stash in these files the fund statements or transaction slips showing the price paid for and the date of purchase of individual securities.

Store in their proper files the latest prospectuses and annual financial statements for your mutual funds, and at least the latest annual report for your stocks. If you take physical possession of stocks or bonds, however, don't put them in the same file; store them in a safe or, preferably, a bank vault. Replacing lost or destroyed securities is a long and costly process.

Retain investment records for two years after you have sold a particular security or all the shares of a mutual fund. Many of these documents will migrate to your tax files, where special rules of retention apply. (See "Your Taxes: Keeping Records.")

Canceled checks and monthly bank statements are worth keeping for six years on the remote chance of a really exhaustive tax audit, which the IRS uses to spot-check for general compliance with the tax code. Keep the latest 12 months' worth handy and older batches in long-term storage. Canceled checks are a great budgeting aid as well as proof of purchases and tax-deductible expenses.

After sorting out the year's checks and putting the deductible ones in your tax file, truss up the rest in a rubber band, wrap them with the year's statements and keep them in your dead file. Old checks, stubs or registers can help you track down the cost of things and the names of tradespeople whom you might hire again if only you could remember their names. They also document what you paid for valuables such as furs, jewels, art objects and antiques.

What's that? Your bank no longer returns canceled checks? Then your only ready references are smudgy checkbook carbons or your check stubs or register. Get in the habit of filling out complete register or stub entries, including the category of expense (plumber, pathology lab, taxi to airport). Don't forget to record the number of each check and the date and year it was written.

People who write only a few checks a month may find enough space for the current year's batch in a vertical file or an envelope. As the year winds on, though, your wad of canceled checks can get bulky. People devise many different means of storage. A couple of suggestions: the box that your last batch of new checks arrived in, or a low-rise brown accordion file.

Unless you plan to write your financial autobiography some day, there's seldom any need to hoard canceled checks and bank statements for more than six years. But make an exception for checks evidencing the purchase of items of lasting value such as jewelry and art objects. Find a permanent place to keep them in case you have to file an insurance claim for their loss, theft or destruction.

Household papers of another sort should be filed to document fire and theft insurance claims and to buttress warranty claims against manufacturers and retailers. The best evidence to back such claims is invoices or bills of sale for major purchases. Whenever you lock horns with a company over a defective product or service, set up a temporary file for what may develop into prolonged correspondence. Keep copies of all the letters and invoices of factory-authorized attempts to remedy the defect.

Also keep your credit-card vouchers and statements, with a separate envelope or vertical file for each active card. Set up a miscellaneous file for vouchers from stores, gasoline stations, airlines and other vendors with which you have charge accounts. As bills arrive, check off the vouchers against the statements, and if they match, throw out the vouchers.

This file is your defense against false and unauthorized billings, your primary record of finance charges and a great budgeting tool. When household spending gets out of hand, credit cards are often to blame. Evidence of purchases of major items should remain on file for as long as you own the items. Save warranty-correspondence files until the dispute is settled to your satisfaction. Hang on to credit-card statements for six years.

Facing Up to Your Fears

LET's admit it: Many people's personal finances are a mess. They don't keep records, their savings are scattered and not earning nearly as much as they could and their family budget is all bull and a yard wide. But you *can* get your personal finances together.

Your greatest obstacle is fear. Yet when people recognize their fears of finance, they often choose to confront and conquer them. Fortunately, the three most common fiscal fears are easy to identify. They are fear of responsibility, fear of risk and fear, believe it or not, of wealth.

Victims of fiscal irresponsibility are plagued by inaction. What they really yearn for is someone who will make their financial decisions for them. So, often they unquestioningly invest in what some broker or banker — or even some fairly successful friend — advises them to invest in. And often they get stung.

Then there is fear of risk. Victims are afraid to do anything with their assets for fear of doing the wrong thing. So they keep their money in low-yielding bank accounts when they could easily earn a little more interest in money-market funds or U.S. Treasury securities or federally insured bank certificates of deposit.

As for fear of wealth, people sometimes feel undeserving of increased incomes or substantial inheritances. If they have investments, they're afraid to change them even when a security plummets. They feel guilty about earning more than their parents did. Their guilt translates into immobility.

Facing up to your fears about money and then taking steps to act and put your finances in order is one way to sleep free of worry or guilt. And, in a world where so much seems to be sliding out of control, it's reassuring to know that, if you're willing to make the effort, it's still possible for you to determine your own financial destiny.

Making — and Sticking to — a Budget

O NE of the surest moves to financial security is to create — and stick to — a budget. You need this all-important personal balance sheet whether you are a student whose money runs out long before the month does or an executive with a comfortable income. A budget will quickly tell you whether you are spending too much and how you can save. Having a real budget — not one that you pretend to keep in your head — allows you to sleep at night without agonizing over how you are going to keep up with ordinary expenses and pay for the unexpected.

If you do not have a budget, start one now. In just three months' time you can win the battle of the budget. If you devote only a few hours during each of those months to considering and correcting your income and outgo, you can reduce overspending, free up money for savings and investments and build a cash reserve for that sudden urge — or need — to splurge. There are many products on the market — ledgers at stationery stores and computer software programs at electronics stores — that can help you to organize your expenses.

During the first month, figure out precisely what you earn and what you spend. Add up your salary and any other money you receive, such as dividends, interest, allowances or child support. Then examine how you spend your money. You do not have to exhume all records dating back for years. It is more than enough to analyze your expenses — and your income — for, say, the last 12 months. This will enable you to calculate routine monthly expenses as well as sums that you must pay at irregular intervals, such as insurance premiums, school tuition and gifts. One purpose of your analysis is to help you plan for these irregular but necessary expenses so that you will never again have to invade your investments to pay for unexpected bills.

You may find that you just cannot account for a large share of your spending. To get a handle on that, try to keep a journal and jot down all expenses as they hit you, day by day, for a week.

Devote the second month of your budget program to figuring out how you can trim any excesses in your spending so that you can build savings and investments. Calculate what percentage of your total income goes to each expenditure, from clothing to commuting costs to mortgage payments or rent.

Some financial advisers recommend that you allocate no more than 65% of your take-home pay for regular monthly expenses, including food, utilities and rent or mortgage payments. Of course, that can be difficult for young people living in expensive urban areas. But, ideally, try to find a way to stick to that two-thirds of monthly income figure, and then allow another 20% for occasional outlays such as household repairs, recreation and clothing. Put aside 10% for necessary expenses that hit at different intervals, such as insurance premiums and property taxes, and the last 5% — or more, if possible — for savings.

Take a close look at your monthly installment debt. You are in good shape if 10% or less of your after-tax income is spent on car payments, department-store and credit-card installments or bills for furniture and appliances that you bought on time. In a difficult economic climate, you may be tempted to buy more items on installment, and to keep onetime expenditures to a minimum. But beware: The last thing you want is to be laid off and to find yourself saddled with many bills. If the amount of those bills is 10% to 15%, you are creeping toward the danger zone. If those expenses stretch beyond 15% to 20% of your income, you are losing the battle of the budget.

To correct that, allocate a set amount of money each month for debt repayments. Pay as much as you possibly can afford. Figure out what indulgences and luxuries you can sacrifice — temporarily. It may be sensible even to raid your savings to pay your debt. You will never get rich keeping cash in a passbook account paying only 3½% while your credit-card or other installment debts cost you 15% to 20% and, in some cases, even more.

Particularly if you have a checking account that pays interest, you may be inclined to wait till the last minute to pay your ordinary bills. After all, the longer you delay, the more interest you earn. But be careful! If you cut it too close, you could end up paying finance charges. They probably would cost you far more than the interest you would earn on your checking account. Interest-bearing checking accounts in mid-1992 paid 2.8% annual interest or less, but credit-card charges typically are 18.6% annually. Despite recent "wars" among credit-card companies to win customers, the charges have not fallen significantly. Paying out high finance charges never helps to create a healthy budget.

How can you make sure your bill payments will be on time? Keep this in mind: It is the day of *receipt* that counts, not the postmark. Federal law requires creditors to mail bills to you at least 14 days before you are supposed to pay them. But companies have to rely on the Postal Service to deliver them on time. And then you have to allow enough time for your payment to arrive by the due date. Postal delays do not entitle you to an extension.

In the third month of your budget-making schedule, carefully re-evaluate your income-and-outgo statement and make any changes so that you can live on your budget. Do not get carried away. Everybody needs some luxuries, so you and each person in your family should be allowed to keep at least one indulgence. If you are passionate about movies and want to see three or four films a week, then adjust your spending in some other area. Successful budgeting depends on being neither too rigid nor too loose. If your budget is too lean, you will not stick to it. Your purpose is to make a budget that you can keep.

Once you have created a workable budget and conquered your debt problems, you should start saving a fixed amount each month. Deposit that sum in a money-market fund, a bank money-market deposit account, short-term bank certificates of deposit, U.S. Treasury bills or other liquid savings. Put that cash away as regularly and as faithfully as you meet your mortgage payments or rent. Aim to build up savings that eventually will amount to three months' worth of your living costs, not counting income and Social Security taxes.

One of the surest and simplest ways to save is to have a regular amount automatically deducted from each paycheck. If your employer offers a company savings or investment plan, grab it. You frequently can arrange for a fixed amount of each paycheck to be deposited in a bank savings account, a money-market fund or a credit union. To find out how you can best accomplish that, just ask an official of your payroll department or the financial institution where you want your money deposited.

Automatic saving does not have to rely on the plans available through your employer. Comparable thrift routines are available at most banks and mutual funds. As a bank depositor you can have a fixed monthly amount automatically transferred from your checking account to a savings account or, better, a higher-yielding money-market account.

Eventually, the new saver emerges from the chrysalis as a full-fledged investor. Mutual funds send out pollen in the form of automatic investing plans. By sending in a form and a voided copy of your check, you authorize the mutual-fund company to draft a fixed amount from your bank account at specified intervals — usually twice a month, once a month or once a quarter. On those investment days the company buys as many shares as your regular payment will cover and immediately credits them to your account. The same day, the fund submits a draft for the money to the nearest Federal Reserve bank or branch, an outpost of the Automated Clearing House. Via this interstate highway of electronic funds, the investor's bank instantly transmits the money to the mutual fund's account.

Another way to save is to bank each pay raise until the next one comes along. Or sock away any minor windfalls, such as bonuses, gifts, tax refunds, profits from your investments or free-lance fees.

Sticking to a budget requires work. Primarily, you will have to continue keeping sound records. You can do that by paying for all items over $25 with checks and letting them serve as your expense ledger. Put an asterisk on a corner of each check that you later might charge off as a tax deduction. If your bank doesn't return your canceled checks, fill out your checkbook registers or stubs as if they were your expense ledger, which indeed they should be.

You also will have to keep working to hold your spending in line.

Figure out what are your biggest expenditures, and how to restrain them. Probably most formidable are your income taxes. You may be able to cut them by setting up an IRA — plus a Keogh plan or SEP if you have some self-employment or moonlighting income — and by switching from some taxable investments to tax-free ones, such as municipal bonds. Make certain that you are using all legitimate deductions, notably those in the Introduction and under the heading of "Your Taxes: How to Cut Your Taxes."

Your second major expense is housing. It varies greatly, depending on where you live. If you buy a house in or around New York City, for example, you probably will pay twice as much as you would for a house in Phoenix. If you are spending as much as 40% of your take-home pay on your home loan, check with a banker or some other housing lender to see if it makes sense to renegotiate your loan. Usually it pays to do so if you do not plan to sell your property soon and can get a longer-term mortgage or one with a rate one or more percentage points below the loan you now have. With a favorable new mortgage, you may be able to recoup the closing costs in a year or two and reduce your monthly expenses by more than $100.

The Charms of Asset Management Accounts

To PULL your personal finances together and make the most of what you have, you can get considerable aid from a relatively new service offered by brokers, bankers and mutual funds: an asset management account. It is a combination money-market and bro-kerage account that usually lets you earn interest on your spare cash, buy and sell securities, borrow more money than you otherwise could and write an unlimited number of checks at no extra charge. You also get a single monthly statement listing all your financial transactions, and that can be a convenience.

So what's the catch? You generally need cash or securities worth $10,000 or more to get into the tent. And you have to pay an annual fee, which can range from $25 to $120. But here are two notable exceptions: The Schwab One Asset Management Account at Charles

Schwab & Co. discount brokerage doesn't charge any fee; its initial deposit is $5,000 in cash or securities. The Fidelity Plus Account, at the Fidelity mutual-fund and discount brokerage house, also asks for a $5,000 opening deposit and requires no annual fee.

Your first decision is to choose where you want your asset management account to be. A broker and a banker are equally safe: they offer plenty of insurance for your assets. If you are primarily interested in investing, you want a broker's advice and you see the account as a way to simplify your investing paperwork, you should find an excellent full-service broker. If you pick your own stocks and bonds, or if you prefer no-load mutual funds, choose a discount brokerage. And if you want mainly to organize savings and checking transactions, you will be best off with a bank.

Look carefully at the standard features these accounts offer. One of their greatest charms is the so-called sweep. It automatically reinvests dividends and bond income in a money-market account. So your cash earns decent interest from the day you get it until the day you spend it. Find out whether the sweep is done daily or weekly, and whether it includes all your cash or just the amount above a certain minimum.

Asset accounts let you write checks against your money-market deposits. Checking typically is free, and you can write as many drafts as you wish with no minimum checking amount. The big issue here is whether or not you will get your canceled checks at the end of the month. Banks generally return asset-account checks, but most brokers simply note the payee, amount and date on your monthly statement.

Most asset accounts include a MasterCard or Visa card at no added charge. But unless you pay extra, this plastic works more like a debit card, with the disadvantage of immediately deducting your charges from the cash in your account. Shearson Lehman Hutton offers an optional American Express Gold card, at an annual fee. With this card and the extra-fee versions of other cards, you don't get a monthly bill that lets you pay after some delay; rather, the balance due will be deducted from your money-market fund at the end of every month.

You can borrow against your securities in an asset management account. Shop around to see where you can get loans with the lowest interest rate. Often that is from a broker. With a brokerage asset management account, you can borrow as much as half the value of your stocks at the so-called margin rate, which is usually much lower than consumer loan rates charged by banks.

When picking an asset management account, also study the kind of brokerage service you can expect. An asset account with a bank or a mutual fund gives you access to discount brokerage service, with commissions as much as 90% lower than the fees charged by full-line brokers. But traditional brokers will give you something for their extra charge: investment advice.

Take a close look at the monthly financial statement you will get with your asset management account. Some are jumbles. Make sure you can understand the statement.

Also find out exactly who will service your account. Many banks promise that if you open an asset management account with them, you will be assigned a personal banker. With a brokerage asset account, you will be assigned an account executive to handle securities trading. But he or she most likely will be underjoyed when you call about a lost check or a statement error, since an account executive doesn't earn commissions by solving such problems.

In sum, a bank may offer you better personal service and lower brokerage commissions, but a broker may offer you lower interest rates on loans and more investment advice.

Where to Get Help

Does the thought of organizing your personal financial affairs still overwhelm you? Take heart. You need not — indeed, should not — do it all by yourself.

Help in getting your finances together ranges from books that can motivate and educate you to professional financial planners who can compile voluminous studies of your economic life. Or you can enroll in courses, attend public seminars and ask the advice of a stockbroker, an insurance agent, attorney, accountant or banker.

There is no reason why you cannot at least decode the basic ciphers of money management in a few weekends of dedicated reading. One of the best books is *Personal Financial Planning* by G. Victor Hallman and Jerry S. Rosenbloom.

For tax planning, it is hard to beat the Ernst & Young *Tax Guide*, which is updated annually.

Finding a useful guide to investments is harder, because there are so many bad ones around. Your top choice for a broad-ranging work is *The Complete Guide to Investment Opportunities*, edited by Marshall Blume and Jack Friedman. Each of the book's 58 chapters is written by a specialist in a particular type of investment, be it Art Nouveau furniture or Treasury notes. An outstanding guide to Wall Street is Charles Rolo and Robert Klein's *Gaining on the Market*, which explains in layman's terms the strategies of professional investors. If you plan to buy a house or invest in property, *The Real Estate Book* by Robert L. Nessen will tell you just about everything you need to know.

Courses on personal finance are offered by more and more colleges, universities, community service organizations and other sponsors of adult education programs. The charge is often $75 or less, or even free for senior citizens. The chance you take is that your teacher is merely a salesperson in the guise of an educator, so check his or her credentials closely. Avoid instructors whose expertise is limited to selling stocks, bonds, insurance or other so-called investment products.

Finally, you can get an inexpensive education by enrolling in one of the thousands of investment clubs. (See "Your Investments: Starting an Investment Club.")

What a Financial Planner Can Do for You

IF YOUR only financial plan is to stay one jump ahead of the bill collector, and you hardly have time to balance your checkbook, you may need help from a planner. This professional may sell everything from general advice on your taxes, budgeting, retirement and estate planning to specific investments, such as mutual funds, life insurance and real estate, energy and other limited partnerships. Most planners work independently in a solo or group practice. Others are on the staffs of accounting firms, brokerage houses, banks, insurance companies or mutual funds.

The majority charge an initial fee to devise a written comprehensive plan diagnosing your financial ailments and prescribing monetary medications to achieve financial health. The plan generally will cost from $500 all the way up to $10,000, depending on three factors: your net worth or income; the planner's reputation; and whether the planner also charges a commission on any investments you buy from him or her. After you get the plan, you and your planner should review your finances at least once a year. This will cost you 30% to 50% of your original bill. However much you pay a planner, the cost is relatively modest compared with the potential long-term rewards — and risks — of following his or her recommendations. Planners' fees are usually tax deductible. As a rule, don't spend more than 1% of your investment assets on a plan. Exceptions: You have complications caused by divorce, multiple pensions, tax shelters that make the IRS gasp or the like.

What can you reasonably expect from a financial planner? For starters, he or she should be able to calculate your net worth and help you devise a workable budget to meet your goals. After that, a planner should make sure you are properly insured against sickness, disability and death, and that you, your cars and your house are well protected against damage, injury and damage suits. Next should come a sizing-up of your income-tax status, a retirement plan and a review of your will and other provisions for passing along your wealth.

A planner should coordinate the specialized help you will need from such other professionals as a securities broker, an accountant, an insurance agent and a lawyer. Any adviser should guide your choice of long-term investments according to a strategy that matches your needs — and your nerves. Some planners will even take responsibility for running your everyday finances. But that's usually still your job.

A planner will advise you to direct your investments into broad areas. For example, he or she may suggest that you put half of your capital into stocks or stock mutual funds, one quarter into bonds or bond funds and one quarter into safe and predictable savings certificates. Because most financial planners are not stockbrokers or securities analysts, they tend to shy away from recommending individual stocks. Instead, they often suggest mutual funds, which are professionally managed, and other "packaged" securities. But any financial planner these days who steers you into limited partnerships deserves at least preliminary suspicion.

A planner suggests what you should do, but first he or she has to ask you several questions. How much risk are you willing to take? How important to you is it to reduce your taxes? How do you feel about borrowing to invest? As you answer, you often begin to realize that your attitudes toward money may not square with the way you actually spend and invest it.

Once the planner has a fix on your goals and how you want to reach them, he or she begins to make recommendations. At that point, you are free to head for your nearest insurance agent or mutual-fund dealer to do your buying. Or you can allow the planner to sell you the financial "products" he or she thinks you need. On such sales, the planner collects commissions of 1% to 10%, and sometimes more.

How to Find a Good Financial Planner

THERE are no licensing requirements or laws to protect the consumer, so anyone can hang out a shingle and call himself a financial planner regardless of education, experience or ethics. The Securities and Exchange Commission requires financial planners to register as investment advisers, referred to as RIAs, and can put them out of business for breaking securities laws. But almost anybody can register by sending the SEC a $150 fee and filling out a form. Even planners admit that many who claim the title are incompetent or worse. While a few seem to be charlatans, many are simply salesmen of financial products, worried more about their own commissions than about your wealth. The proliferation of pseudo-planners began a decade ago, when thousands of stockbrokers, insurance agents and tax-shelter floggers renamed themselves financial planners.

But first-rate financial planners are increasingly available — if you know how to identify them. You can find some by asking for recommendations from an accountant or lawyer, by attending the free seminars that planners often hold to recruit clients, and by requesting names from planners' professional societies or trade associations: The Institute of Certified Financial Planners (800-282-PLAN), The International Association of Financial Planning (404-

395-1605) and the National Association for Personal Financial Advisors (800-366-2732).

Good practitioners usually have credentials as Certified Financial Planners from the International Board of Standards and Practices for Certified Financial Planners (IBCFP). Most CFPs have taken correspondence courses from the College for Financial Planning (4695 South Monaco Street, Denver, Colorado 80237-3403) in preparation for examinations designed, administered and graded by the IBCFP. The exams cover taxes, estate planning, investments and other subjects. Many accredited colleges also give courses that prepare planners for the exam. Roughly 200,000 people purport to be financial planners, but only 32,000 are CFPs. Another respected certification is that of Chartered Financial Consultant (ChFC), awarded by the American College (270 Bryn Mawr Avenue, Bryn Mawr, Pennsylvania 19010).

Cross off any candidates who have not bothered to get at least this much training. And be sure to check the planner's credentials with the organization that issued them. Remember, though, to feel free — in fact, smart enough — to check on a financial planner's background yourself. None of the planners' organizations are ferocious watchdogs when it comes to policing standards, or even in confirming that a member's education or employment background is accurate. As a former head of the SEC's Division of Investment Management explains: "These are essentially volunteer trade organizations."

The Institute of Certified Financial Planners and the rival International Association for Financial Planning have compiled separate registries of practicing financial planners who have met the organizations' rather similar requirements. These include appropriate college training, the passing of an exam and full-time experience in planning or a related profession. Once admitted to either registry, planners must put in a prescribed number of hours of continuing education each year to retain their membership. Call the ICFP or the IAFP at the numbers listed above to find out whether any of their members work in your area.

You should assemble a short list of prospects, and be sure to interview each one. Ask for samples of plans each has prepared, and the names of clients you can call.

If a plan is all you want, there is a flourishing and inexpensive plans-by-mail industry. You fill out a questionnaire and back comes a computer-generated report with some recommendations. For generic advice but not specific investment recommendations, the

Personal Financial Services Division of Price Waterhouse (55 East Monroe Street, 30th Floor, Chicago, Illinois 60603) charges from $200 to $350 for its Personal Financial Products. Major brokerage houses and some large banks and insurance companies also offer these canned plans.

Questions to Ask Your Financial Planner

B EFORE you hire a planner, ask some tough questions. That's the best way to separate the crack advisers from the quack advisers.

Be sure to ask how the planner earns his or her money. As mentioned, many planners charge fees of $75 to $200 an hour. Others give free advice but earn commissions by selling you mutual funds, insurance or other financial products. So ask him or her to state in writing how he or she will be compensated.

Members of the National Association of Personal Financial Advisors (NAPFA) are fee-only planners and have pledged to accept no commission in any form. The advantage of hiring a fee-only planner is that you know he or she will not recommend an investment to you just to collect a commission. But fee-only planners are costlier than those who accept commissions. Most planners combine fees and commissions. As a compromise, some planners charge fees but subtract from them the commissions they earn by putting a plan into effect. Planners should be Registered Investment Advisers. As such, they must initiate disclosure of their fees and other compensation.

Always ask how much money a planner makes on everything he or she tries to sell to you. If you know that someone stands to pocket a 10% commission on one investment and only 3% on a less expensive alternative, you will have reason to ask why you are being steered toward the costlier one.

Most consumer complaints about planners involve those who earn their keep solely by commissions, especially those who peddle just one line of goods. The biggest beef is against salespeople who call themselves financial planners to disguise their true calling.

A conscientious planner should channel your assets into a variety of investments so that your returns will be stable despite market or interest-rate fluctuations. Ask your planner to draw up a pie chart of his recommendations. If one type of investment swallows more than a quarter of your pie, request an explanation.

Ask the planner how much wealth you can reasonably accumulate in five years. Most investors do well if their returns consistently outpace inflation by 4% or 5% a year. If your planner claims to be able to top those rates, he or she may be misleading you or steering you into high-risk ventures.

If you are within 10 years of retirement, ask your planner to estimate how much money you will need to meet your retirement goals. He or she will get estimates of how much you can expect from Social Security and company pensions, and will make projections of the nest egg that you can put aside in savings plans and your own investments. Then the planner will factor in an inflation rate so that your living expenses will not outrun your means. With this information in hand, he or she should tell you whether you will need to save more or work longer to meet your objectives, and what rate of return your nest egg should earn to keep you ahead of inflation. He or she should also show you the sources from which your income will flow — interest, dividends or the sale of assets.

At this point in your life, a planner should concern himself or herself as well with planning your estate — largely a euphemism for reducing death taxes. He or she should total up your net worth and ask to see your last will and testament. The heirs of people who leave assets in excess of $600,000 must share 37% to 55% or more of that excess with federal and often state tax collectors unless something is done to head them off.

For married couples the refuge involves rewriting their wills. And it may require a reshuffling of their assets. Each spouse should own in his or her name a large enough share of the family wealth to take advantage of that $600,000 limit on untaxed bequests.

Ask how much time the planner will spend with you, and who will write your plan. In large firms, your case may be consigned to junior staffers, and you may not get the experience you want. Expect a planner to spend three or four hours with you, gathering facts and discussing ideas. Take time to consider the planner's recommendations before you buy any financial products. And do not feel you have to buy anything. What you need may well be insights instead of new investments.

The final clue to a financial planner's caliber is commitment. Your planner should be ready to work over the long term with other professionals you may hire, such as a lawyer or tax accountant. No one person can master all of the technical information that goes into preparing a well-designed financial plan. Have your planner arrange for you and all your advisers to sit down together at least once. That way everyone will know what everyone else is supposed to do.

The Separate Role of the Investment Adviser

SOME people, particularly active investors and recipients of six-figure rollovers from retirement accounts, find it worthwhile to hire an investment adviser. This professional may be a financial planner, a money manager recommended by a planner or broker, or a specialist whom you find on your own.

An investment adviser recommends stocks, bonds or mutual funds that, in his or her judgment, are suitable to your goals and taste for risk. With a discretionary account, you may give this adviser the power to buy and sell securities for you without first consulting you. Or you may give him or her discretion only to sell your holdings or to do nothing without your permission.

Until recently, investment advisers wouldn't even look at you unless you could give them custody of $250,000 or more. Competition and loss of business after the market crash of October 19, 1987, have forced many advisers to accept much smaller accounts, sometimes starting at $10,000 or less for firms that manage mutual-fund accounts. Usually, however, an initial outlay in the six-figure range is required. Annual fees generally start at 1½% to 2% of assets up to $500,000, with a sliding scale of lower fees on larger accounts. An adviser might charge from 0.75% to 1.25% of a million-dollar stock portfolio, 0.5% to 0.75% for a more easily managed portfolio of bonds. But many firms charge a minimum of $1,000, which can be prohibitive if you have $25,000 or less to invest. Clients also pay brokerage costs, which are likely to add 1% a year to the total freight.

The latest money-management wrinkle combines brokerage costs with a percentage of assets into a single rate called a wrap fee. Brokers and financial planners marketing wrap-fee accounts point out that this form of payment removes any incentive the money manager might have to "churn" the account — that is, to trade stocks excessively for the sole purpose of generating commissions. This is true enough, but the typical wrap-fee account costs a flat 3% of assets. By comparison, no-load mutual funds seldom charge more than 1½% for essentially the same services.

Financial planners and brokers often use talent scout services to match you with the right investment adviser. Firms including CDA Investment Technologies of Rockville, Maryland, Mobius Group of Atlanta, Investment Management Institute of New York City, and Stolper & Co. of San Diego calculate the total returns, risk factors and other gauges of performance for hundreds of advisers. This information is updated quarterly — or, in Mobius's case, for some clients twice quarterly — and piped to subscribers' computers over telephone lines or via a diskette. Stolper & Co. is the only talent scout that deals mainly with individuals. It will choose a manager for you from among 1,500 in its files for a sliding fee starting at $3,000. Then, for $1,500 a year, it will monitor your results.

To determine for yourself whether an adviser measures up to your needs is no simple task. The performance statistics that money managers hand out may be more inflated than the Goodyear blimp. Nevertheless, ask for figures going back at least 10 years. If they have been audited by an outside accounting firm, so much the better. Check the results in years when stocks fell as well as when they soared. A first-rate manager preserves your capital in bad years. You can't expect him or her to beat Standard & Poor's 500 stock average every time, but he or she should have turned in a superior long-term record.

Find out an adviser's investment philosophy before making your choice. It should harmonize with your own. A growth manager tries for capital gains by picking companies whose earnings will go up more than the average for their industry. A pursuer of aggressive growth leans toward riskier small-capitalization stocks. A conservative growth seeker looks for blue-chip stocks. A market timer tries to get you into the market near the bottom of the price cycle and out near the top, while a value investor ignores market trends but buys neglected stocks of well-managed companies and holds them indefinitely. A contrarian takes the same approach but doesn't make long-term commitments to the stocks he buys.

Once you have contracted with an adviser, be patient. In general, wait at least a year before you judge the record — but sometimes less than that. If the value of your holdings drops 20% while the market is rising or holding steady, the adviser should take corrective action. If he or she does not, it may well be time to fire him or her.

Windfalls: Handling Unexpected Wealth

M ANY people joke about it, some even cry over it, but, in fact, the odds are improving that one day you will receive a windfall. Thirty-four states and the District of Columbia had lotteries in mid-1990, and the jackpots are huge. Most sudden money comes less spectacularly, from estates and court settlements; this year alone *millions* of Americans will inherit some wealth. If you are one of them, you face a nice problem: What do you do with your fresh fortune?

Unless you already have considerable money and know how to manage it, sudden wealth will require a new financial strategy. Your goal should be to preserve that hefty capital and make it work for you. Taking large risks with your riches is not only unnecessary but also unwise.

When that first check arrives, stash the cash for six months or so in a money-market fund, a Treasury bill or some other short-term investment. There it will remain, liquid and safe, while you sort out your options.

You may need a tax accountant right away. There is no income tax on inheritances or gifts, no matter how large, but there certainly is on lottery winnings and other prizes. Twenty percent of your lottery loot will be withheld for the U.S. Treasury, and you will almost surely owe more than that. Most million-dollar lottery winnings come in 20 annual installments, which means you will have to pay quarterly estimated federal income taxes. Your state may also require quarterly estimated tax payments. Some states, though, do not tax their lottery winners unless they move to another state.

Dream a little. You have hit the jackpot for $5 million, which will come to you in $250,000 installments, before taxes, for the next 20 years. Your annual net windfall is $200,000. Welcome to the 31% tax bracket. You'll be losing most of your personal exemptions, too, and at least $3,000 worth of your deductions. You'll need to put away $27,500 to cover taxes not being withheld.

So you have $180,000 to spend, save or invest. Enjoy part of it, but budget at least half for investments, and you will convert your 20-year windfall into a lifetime income. While there is no shelter from taxes on the winnings themselves, you surely can ease Uncle Sam's bite on what they earn for you.

Start by building a portfolio of municipal bonds rated A or higher. The interest you earn will be tax exempt. Also put a fixed amount each year in a flexible deferred annuity. You will postpone taxes on the earnings inside this remarkable retirement vehicle until you withdraw them. After you are 59½, you can collect monthly lifetime income from your annuity, part of which will be *un*taxable. Or you can retrieve the entire cash value without penalty, though you'll owe income tax on the total earnings.

Or suppose your windfall is an inheritance that comes all at once. The main rule then is to diversify, so that you do not blow the whole wad on a single mistake. Consider a mix of a no-load mutual fund that invests for growth and income; a single-premium deferred annuity, in which you can invest as much as you want, all at one time; Treasury securities; and municipal bonds or unit trusts. Such trusts are sold by brokers, and they invest in a variety of municipal bonds. In mid-1992 they were yielding about 6.25% interest. You do not pay federal income taxes on that income. Consider the state tax implications as well.

Seek professional help. You probably will need an accountant for tax advice and a financial planner to devise a strategy for conserving your money and making it grow.

Many of the suddenly rich feel uneasy, not to say guilty, about their new wealth. Others make the mistake of quitting their jobs in euphoria, and some suffer by altering their life-styles, changing too much about their lives too soon. A windfall can catapult you from one economic position to another, but attitudes, values and behavior change more slowly. So ease into your enviable new status gradually.

Your Investments

How to Start Investing and Do It Right

M ANY people who have not done it before are wondering how to start investing — and do it right. If you are in that position, you need an investment strategy.

Start by analyzing yourself. Define your financial goals and how you plan to reach them. Is your goal to pay for college or for a house or for a comfortable retirement — or all of the above — and just how much money will you need to achieve that objective?

Before you invest in anything that has the slightest risk, be sure you have enough insurance and savings to protect yourself against an emergency. It is smart to hold savings equal to three months' worth of your living expenses. Do not worry if it takes you two or three years to accumulate that amount.

It is also important to assess your tolerance for risk. If your fear of losing money is stronger than your desire to make large profits, stick with a conservative investment philosophy. Conservatives invest for safe and steady returns including growth and income. More adventurous types put the accent on growth.

All investors must contend with two risks. The first is the risk of down markets, which reduce the value of securities. The second is that of inflation, which diminishes buying power. Short-term investors — those who will need their money in five years or less — should worry more about down markets. Longer-term investors should worry more about inflation.

Short-term money should go to work in investments that guarantee all of your money back when you're going to need it: bank accounts, certificates of deposit, money-market mutual funds, Treasury bills and Treasury notes or tax-free bonds maturing in less than five years. But to defeat inflation, investors should put some of their money in investments that come with no guarantee but can grow in value.

Primarily, growth calls for stocks and real estate. Over the years, both will surely fall as well as rise, but their general direction throughout modern times has been up.

If you are over 50, you will probably want to put a large share of your spare cash into income-producing assets. If you want steady income payments, consider Treasury and top-grade corporate bonds. You can get instant diversification by investing in a bond mutual fund or unit trust.

But inflation is no respecter of age. Even after your retirement, your money must last twenty or more years — perhaps *many* more. So plan on owning stocks all your life.

Whether you buy bonds or stocks, do not get too caught up in the race for quick profits. Most investors do best by picking several stocks as a way of cushioning the loss of one flier that takes a dive. And be prepared to live with the rule of five. It says that out of every five stocks you own, probably one will be a loser, three will do nicely and one will do much better than you expected.

Stocks and bonds are, of course, your basic tools of investing. Before you invest, you should determine just what you want your tools to accomplish and which ones to use to reach your goals.

When you buy common stocks, you become part owner of a corporation. A stock can increase your wealth in two ways: by paying you regular dividends and by rising in price. If it does indeed rise, you can sell out at a profit. It is this growth, not the dividends, that gives stocks their investment edge. The past 66 years of carefully documented financial market performance reveals the long-term superiority of stocks over any other type of investment. Since 1926, the 500 stocks in the Standard & Poor's index have produced an average return — from price appreciation plus dividends — of 10.22% a year. That is almost double the average 5.3% annual return that investors got from corporate bonds. In other words, a dollar — one dollar! — invested in the S&P 500 in 1926 would have grown to $500 in 1990, assuming no taxes and the reinvestment of all dividends. Under the same assumptions, a dollar invested in intermediate-term U.S. government bonds would have grown to only $22, and a dollar in Treasury bills to a meager $10, barely enough to beat inflation.

You can choose from different types of stocks depending on your investment goals. Growth stocks are shares in companies that often expand faster than the overall economy. In rising markets, the stocks of young and growing companies tend to do at least one-third better than the broad stock indexes. But when the market falls, they are also likely to plunge faster.

Income stocks place an emphasis on dividends, so their prices are more stable. In a prolonged market rise, income stocks do not climb as fast as growth stocks. Utility shares are a foremost example. In the 12 months after the bull market began in August 1982, the Dow Jones Utility Average rose 24%, which was less than half the gain of the Dow Jones Industrial Average. But top-rated utilities pay high dividends — 8.11% to 8.17% in mid-1992.

Most investment advisers believe the stock market should do well over the long term. But if you are unsure of how to start an investment program that will take advantage of a favorable future, you should consider buying shares in a mutual fund. Funds offer just what beginning investors need: professional management and instant diversification. You can get in with an investment of $1,000 or less. Once you own shares in a fund, you typically can add as little as $50 or $100 at a time. You can find the addresses and phone numbers — often toll-free 800 numbers — of various funds in advertisements on the business pages of newspapers and also in financial magazines.

What if you want to start investing, but you have only a small stake, say $100? Will any brokerage houses or mutual funds welcome your business?

Yes indeed, many will. At least 150 mutual funds will accept an initial investment of $100 or less — and in some cases there is no minimum at all. For a description of more than 1,650 funds, look in your public library for a book called *Wiesenberger Investment Companies Service*. Another source is *Winning with Mutual Funds* by the editors of *Money* magazine.

As for stockbrokers, many have such large minimum commissions — at least $25 every time that you buy or sell — that it does not make sense to start an account with just $100. As an alternative, you can try

Merrill Lynch's so-called Blueprint Program. It charges $12.50 on trades up to $125, and 10% on trades to $200. After that, commissions decrease on a sliding scale. Trades exceeding $7,500 are charged at Merrill's regular rates.

If you find it hard to set aside money regularly, try this: have a mutual fund automatically deduct a set amount from your checking account every month. Many employers also let you have a specific amount taken out of your paycheck and invested in a company-sponsored profit-sharing or thrift plan. Such programs usually let you choose from at least two types of funds. You can put your contribution in a stock mutual fund or a fixed-income bond-and-savings fund.

The drawback is that you may have some trouble if you want to withdraw the whole amount before you leave the company. But that is balanced by the nice fact that all the earnings on your money compound tax-free, until you withdraw it — which won't be required until you are 70½, even if you change jobs.

Some employers will match part of your contribution. This gives you an immediate profit. If that is the case, be sure to accept this company offer — and save or invest as much as you possibly can.

After you have built up some mutual-fund shares, you may get the itch to start picking stocks on your own. You will have an advantage over major financial institutional investors, those who tend to buy conservatively for bank trust departments, corporate investment plans and pension programs. The institutions' investment managers generally stick to the shares of 500 or so fairly substantial companies, but you can choose from 8,229 stocks. It is easier for small investors to buy shares in young, unproven, fast-growing firms. If the business becomes large enough to attract big investors, the stock's price — and your profits — may jump dramatically.

Anyone with more than $2,000 to invest in stocks should put it in two or more companies. You will want to diversify among industries too. That will help protect you. If, for example, mortgage rates rise and you own nothing but housing stocks, you could be pummeled. Countless academic studies larded with complicated formulas have shown that diversification lowers your risk without crimping returns, and the three U.S. economists who established the importance of diversification as an investing tool won a 1990 Nobel Prize.

Ultimately, you should aim to own five or more stocks. That is a small enough number to be manageable and large enough for diversity. When you reach that point — and you want to strike a balance somewhere between the young, daring investor and the older, conservative investor mentioned earlier — you may want to aim for the following division of your money:

A quarter of your stock portfolio should consist of small and promising companies producing goods and services that are unique or stand to be in strong demand even in periods of recession. Another quarter should be invested in the largest, most conservative companies; they can offer stable growth. The remaining half should be in medium-size concerns that are growing faster than the economy as a whole.

You will have to do your homework. Before buying a stock, look up its record in *The Value Line Investment Survey* or *Standard & Poor's Corporation Records* or *Moody's* manuals, available in many public libraries. You also can ask a broker to send you a copy of the company's annual report and the even more detailed 10-K statement that must be filed every year with the Securities and Exchange Commission.

Finally, deciding when to sell your shares is as important as choosing when and what to buy. Do not rush to dump a long-term growth stock just because it hits a temporary sinking spell. In fact, that is when smart investors consider buying even more shares — at bargain prices.

If you are a working couple in your mid-20s, much depends on whether you own your own home. If you don't, many advisers still suggest applying your money toward the down payment on a house or condominium. Real estate values are not expected to rise as fast as in the past, but they should keep pace with inflation. In many cities and suburbs, real estate values have tumbled, creating a rare buying opportunity. And switching from rent to house payments will remain a good deal, since you get a tax deduction for your mortgage payments and property taxes.

Dual-income couples who have no tax-sheltered savings plans at work should try to put $4,000 every year into his-and-her Individual Retirement Accounts, even if not all of it is deductible. A sensible buy for your IRA or any other investment might be a growth-stock mutual fund. To cite just one example, the Twentieth Century Investors fund, headquartered in Kansas City, has gained an average 19.76% a year over the last 10 years.

Couples with fairly young children should aim to build up a major sum for college tuition. Tax changes in the 1980s made saving for your child's education more difficult, in part because the rules are just so confusing to follow. But if you plan wisely, you can still find ways to reduce your taxes and increase the size of your college fund. Two possibilities are to buy tax-exempt securities or stocks in fast-growing companies.

You might also consider series EE U.S. Savings Bonds. Any EE bonds that you bought in 1990 or later may be redeemed tax-free after six months to pay college or vocational-school tuition for the bondholder or the bondholder's child or spouse. To qualify, you must be at least 24 years old when you buy the bond. Parents must buy the bond in their own name. And when you redeem it, you must have a modified adjusted gross income below a certain total, or else the amount of interest that you can collect tax-free starts to decline. For money earned in 1992, the decline starts for couples filing jointly with incomes above $66,200, and $44,150 for singles and heads of households. There is no tax benefit at all for people filing jointly who earn $96,200 or more, or for singles and heads of households who earn $59,150 or more.

But these brackets will rise in step with the Consumer Price Index, so even if you earn, say, $70,000 today, your EE Bond interest may be tax-free when your child enters college. If you don't qualify for the federal tax exemption, you can still save on taxes with EE Bonds. Their income is exempt from state and local income taxes. And you need not pay federal taxes on their interest until you cash in the bonds.

Focusing too closely on tax avoidance can be a mistake, though, even for an education fund. Until a child is within five years of entering college, investing in a well-managed stock mutual fund gives you the best chance for high returns without high risk.

The same is true for couples in their 50s. Trying to enlarge their retirement nest egg without increasing their tax bill can lock them into investments that lack the growth potential to keep them ahead of inflation.

Retired couples should invest around half their money conservatively for income. Depending on current yield, they might consider Treasury notes as well as CDs. In mid-1992, two-year Treasuries yielded 5.23%; two-year CDs paid 4.95%.

In sum, here are three sensible rules for investors, beginners and veterans alike:

First, put aside a fixed amount of money each week or each month, no matter how small. Then save or invest it regularly, come rain, come shine. When markets fall, you can figure you are at a bargain sale because you will be able to buy more shares for your money. And when markets rise, you can congratulate yourself, because your investments will rise too.

Second, diversify. No longer can you buy just one stock or bond and confidently hold it for a lifetime. The world changes too fast for that. So, even if your investments are modest, spread out to several kinds of stocks — or into a widely diversified mutual fund.

Third, do not wait to buy in at the very bottom of the market and do not try to sell out at the very top. Nobody — but nobody — is smart enough to do that. Remember: Bulls make money and bears make money, but hogs never make money.

Finally, sit back and let the power of compounding work for you. A nice, sedate 9% annual rate of return will double your money in eight years.

The Prospects for 1993

WHERE, more specifically, should you put your savings and investment money in 1993, a year many forecasters expect to be marked by a slow-growing economy? Stay calm. No matter what happens over the next year, or few years, the worst thing any investor could do is to panic and sell everything or, in the case of a beginning investor, stuff his or her greenbacks under the proverbial futon.

Take a deep breath and look ahead: Adjust your portfolio to capitalize on the coming economic and demographic changes. And quit listening to your neighbors who keep boasting about how well they did back in the 1980s. Sure, they enjoyed the second-best bull market in stocks, and the best bond market on record. That was then. This is now, and they are facing the same uncertain market that you are.

For them, and for you, stocks continue to be the best investment, with the market edging upward more than downward and yielding a total rate of return at about the average historical rate, 10% or so a year. Growth stocks are in. Takeover plays — gone the way of Donald Trump's fortune — are out.

Since most economists expect inflation to remain moderate, bonds should prove to be a reasonably sound investment in the long-term. Real estate will most likely be an iffy buy in 1993, if you are thinking in terms of making money. If you are looking for a good deal on your first home, however, then the real estate market will be attractive. Gold hasn't been a bright buy for several years, and unless inflation shoots up, probably isn't worth considering. One lesson of the 1980s and early 1990s will continue to hold true: technological developments will most likely drive growth. Investments in such industries as fiber optics and computer imaging, biogenetics and other emerging technologies may well boost any wisely chosen portfolio.

Strategies to Meet Your Own Goals

INVESTING is as much an art as a science. That's especially so if you are trying to pick the right mix to pay you a rather large sum at a time that is far off. Many forecasters with eminent records predict relatively moderate inflation and relatively slow, stable growth between now and the year 2000. That would provide a climate in which stocks and bonds should do well.

If you are a conservative investor looking for a place to put money you may need some years from now, you might divide your cash into three equal parts and then apportion it this way: put one-third of it in two- to five-year Treasury notes; another third in short-term corporate bond funds and adjustable-rate mortgage funds; and a third in mutual funds that buy U.S. and foreign stocks. Remember: The first aim of safe investing, even in good times, is to hold on to your principal. Money lost is not so easily regained. The example is a hoary one, but if your stock or bond declines 50% in value, it will have to double in price just to get you back to where you started.

So much for a portfolio for the conservative investor. What if you are willing to accept more risk in hopes of earning more profits? Then put 50% of your investable cash in growth stocks or the mutual funds that buy them. Place 10% of your money in two- to five-year Treasury notes, 10% in a money-market fund and 20% in intermediate-term corporate bonds rated AA or higher. The remaining 10% of your moderate-risk portfolio might be in real estate, which is a sound hedge against inflation.

Let's say you know you will need retirement income in five years or so. Or you will have tuition bills to pay. Or perhaps you are looking for a sensible long-term investment for your IRA or some other tax-deferred account. What then should you buy? One investment to use as a base may well be zero-coupon U.S. Treasury bonds. You might put as much as 90% of your IRA money in them. With "zeros," you don't collect your interest payments in semiannual installments but in one big lump sum when the bond matures or comes due. (See "Your Investments/Bonds: Zero-Coupon Bonds.")

A potential problem is that you are liable for income taxes on that interest even though you do not collect it right away. So zeros belong only in a tax-deferred account such as an IRA or Keogh plan, or in the hands of a lightly taxed person such as a child over 13.

If you want high yields outside of a tax-sheltered account, you might carve up your money this way: 40% in short- to intermediate-term municipal bonds that are exempt from federal taxes; 50% in no-load municipal bond funds, also short- to intermediate-term (3 to 10 years) and tax-exempt; and 10% in real estate.

What if you have already put away enough money for emergencies, your children's education and your retirement? Congratulations! Now you have a bit of excess cash you want to invest. Why not go for maximum growth?

You might start with stocks in small companies. They're riskier than large-company stocks from year to year, but over decades they have outperformed the biggies. Or invest in depressed industries. Some of the most successful investors do just that, figuring that stocks in battered businesses have nowhere to go but up. For example, shares of many securities brokers and investment companies, which had plunged deeply in 1990, made a remarkable recovery in 1991.

To some extent you can have it both ways: the stock market's superior return without all the price gyrations. New York's Neuberger & Berman investment firm looked at the many asset mixes to calculate how they would have performed since 1960. Neuberger found that if you had put half your money in one-year Treasury bills and the other half in stocks, you would have achieved 89% of the total return of the S&P 500 with only 52% of its price volatility, the most appealing trade-off of any that was studied. While the S&P 500 has yielded a compound annual return of 10.4%

since 1960, this 50-50 mix would have grown at a very respectable 9.25% rate.

Investments for Different Stages of Your Life

You need different strategies for investing at different stages of your life. Say you are a young, single adult. Now is the time to start saving to build a cash cushion to protect yourself in case of emergency. Now is also the time to begin investing to make your money grow for the future.

If you have all your money tied up in a passbook savings account paying only 3½%, try to shift some of it into a higher-yielding certificate of deposit (CD). You can get a federally insured CD for a minimum of $500 at most banks, savings and loan associations and stock brokerage firms.

Aim to build up your insured savings until they amount to three months' worth of your after-tax living expenses. Once you have that security blanket, you can take some measured risks and begin investing. A sensible way is to put aside a fixed amount every month. You might invest in a growth mutual fund or a few conservative stocks.

There are many good mutual funds, of course, and you can get their names and toll-free 800 numbers in financial publications. Three funds that had average total returns of 15% or more a year over the past five years are AIM Weingarten, Janus Twenty and Financial Industrial Income.

If you are willing to take a bit more risk in hopes of getting more reward, consider buying shares in a real estate investment trust from a broker. These trusts invest in buildings, land and mortgages, and they are like mutual funds of real estate. Their shares trade just as stocks do and they pay dividends.

If you are married and do not have children, you have a special opportunity to build up some savings and investments. Financially, a married couple can be more than the sum of their parts. When you have only each other to look after, you have an obvious edge over singles and parents. One spouse can work steadily while the other goes for a college degree or launches a promising business. Or if both spouses hold jobs, you can try to live on the income from one and save or invest the other paycheck.

But couples do face financial problems. While you have more investment opportunities, you also confront more complex choices than ever before. Above all, avoid making devastating mistakes. The worst disasters often involve high-risk investments that crash. If you want to be safe, don't put too much reliance on any one investment. Here's a list of financial dos and don'ts for married couples without children:

— Do buy life insurance and disability insurance to protect both spouses in case anything happens to one of you. But don't buy more insurance than either mate will really need; your employers may already provide enough. If you do buy, your best bet is probably term insurance.

— Do build up your savings. But don't keep money in a low-yielding passbook savings account. As mentioned above, you are better off with a money-market fund, which you can find through a mutual-fund company or a brokerage house, or with a certificate of deposit which you can get at a bank or savings and loan association.

— Do put money away in savings or investment plans that your employer offers. Not only do such programs give you tax breaks, but often the employer kicks in 50 cents or so for every dollar you put in, and that's "found money."

— Do be financially nimble enough to change course suddenly when baby makes three.

Financial planning for parenthood is a bit like preparing for a long siege. As parents, you may have to stretch your budget to accommodate pediatrician bills, piano lessons and pilgrimages to summer camp. For a middle-income couple, the cost of rearing a child until the age of 18 will be over $100,000. And that estimate does not include the special parenting costs faced by two-income couples: they must choose either to pay for day care or to lose a paycheck while one parent stays at home with the child. Nor does that figure include the towering burden of college. In the 1991–92 school year, the average total annual bill for a student at a private university was about $16,336, up almost 7% from the prior year.

When negotiating the route from diapers to diplomas, your first financial need is to establish an emergency cash reserve. Next, you can turn to your long-term goal of building capital. You might want to consider investing in a steady-performing growth mutual fund and, for diversification, in growth-oriented real estate or a high-yield income mutual fund. Also keep in mind that money or investments in your child's name may become a barrier to financial aid at college — more so than if you keep the assets in your own name. Under the aid formula, 5% of your liquid assets must be used each year for your child's college expenses, whereas the child must use 35% of his or hers.

When your children are grown and leave home to strike out on their own, you are suddenly relieved of a great financial burden. No more bills to pay for everything from food and clothes to visits to the dentist. Your immediate temptation may be to spend all your new extra money on yourselves, on many of the things you have been waiting so many years for. Purge that urge to splurge! Instead, now is the time to put money away in a savings and investment plan. After all, you will need it soon enough for retirement.

Figure out just how much those tuition bills and other child-rearing expenses have cost you. Then aim to save and invest just about that much for at least the next several years.

It's also wise at this stage of life to re-examine whether you are taking full advantage of all your opportunities to reduce your tax bills. You will want some additional deductions because you will have fewer dependents to claim.

Perhaps you have put off opening up an Individual Retirement Account because you felt you did not have enough funds to do it while you were still supporting your children. Consider opening an IRA now. And if you are self-employed or earn some free-lance income, seriously consider also opening a Keogh plan, which allows you to shelter much more money than an IRA alone.

Reducing Your Risks

A N INVESTOR, by definition, is a person who takes risks — but only sensible risks, the kind that will not endanger his or her financial health. And there are ways that you can reduce your risks in the market.

When you invest, as the late Wall Street writer Charles Rolo has observed, there are seasons for courage as well as for caution. So a strategy for all seasons must be one that decreases or increases your exposure to risk, depending on what kind of investment weather you expect. Managing risk does not mean dumping all stocks or other investments when you see storm clouds — or rushing in to buy at the glimpse of a rainbow. Controlling risk usually calls for making a few adjustments in your investments rather than for a sweeping change.

To develop a strategy for all seasons, you first must ask yourself a basic question about your investment goals: Are you more interested in seeing your investments grow in value for the long term, or in collecting immediate income from dividends and interest payments? Obviously, betting on future growth is riskier in the short run than collecting fairly well-assured dividends and interest payments. But over the years the greater risk is inflation, so you need growth to keep up with it.

The degree of risk that you choose to take should be determined by your family situation, current and prospective earning power, net worth, tax bracket — and temperament. A single person with bright career prospects may be more inclined to take large risks than a couple with children or retired persons living on their savings.

When calculating how to manage risks, it pays to bear in mind that there are three kinds of investment risk:

First, the risk that is related to the overall behavior of the securities market is called, not surprisingly, *market risk*. The standard yardstick of a stock's market risk is its volatility — that is, the extent of its price fluctuations in relation to those of the Standard & Poor's 500 stock index. A stock that historically has risen or fallen more sharply than Standard & Poor's index is considered riskier than the market as a whole. To find out a stock's historic record of volatility, ask your broker to look it up in *The Value Line Investment Survey*. (For more on *The Value Line Investment Survey*, see "Your Investments: Choosing Advisory Services.") When you think it's time to be cautious, you can cut your market risk by reducing the portion of your assets that is invested in common stocks, eliminating the most volatile issues.

Second, stock prices also fluctuate because of industry and company developments. This type of risk is called *diversifiable risk* because you can reduce it if you diversify your investments. Small investors can achieve good diversification by owning only five stocks, provided they are in different industries that are exposed to different types of economic and political risk. For example, some stock groups that are not likely to behave in the same way at the same time are: airlines, banks, computers, cosmetics, energy exploration, gold mining and hospital management.

Third, investors also face what is called *interest-rate risk.* It stems from changes in interest rates and it applies primarily to bonds. But it can also affect the shares of corporations whose earnings are hurt when interest rates rise — and helped when they fall. The stock market as a whole often sinks when interest rates soar, because stocks must then compete with high bond yields. Some firms are especially sensitive to changing interest rates: utilities, banks, finance companies, savings and loans and others.

Ideally, you would buy interest-sensitive stocks just before interest rates started to turn down — and then switch into money funds or Treasury bills just before the next uptrend began. Calling the turns on interest rates right on target is an impossible dream, but anybody who reads the financial pages carefully should be able to get a handle on which way rates are likely to head.

Before you make any decisions about your investments, watch the relationship between short-term and long-term interest rates. The stock market always has trouble making headway when short-term rates, such as those available on Treasury bills, are higher than long-term rates, the kind offered on bonds. When short-term rates fall significantly below long ones, a bull market quite often follows in a few months.

However, if unexpected bad economic news sends the market down, then be sure to avoid companies with big debts. Look instead for stocks of large growth companies with low price/earnings ratios that are selling at low prices. Because of their low base, even a modest rise in price would mean a big percentage gain for you.

Your Safest Investments

A LMOST all investments have some risks, but don't let that stop you from investing. Sometimes the riskiest strategy of all is to do nothing. If you had just let your cash sit in an ordinary savings account in the 1970s, inflation would have drastically cut the value of your money. Smart people analyze their own situations and decide which risks they are willing to take, and which they want most to avoid.

Above all, you will want to protect your principal — that is, to make sure that you don't wind up with less cash than you start out with. One safe haven that conserves your principal is a money-market fund or a money-market deposit account.

Finally, you will need safety against inflation. When inflation kicks up, tangible assets, such as real estate or gold, tend to rise in value. So if you put some money into them, you will be protected if hyper-inflation strikes again.

Putting your money in a variety of investments is the safest approach. If some of them tumble, the others may well stand up — and you won't lose everything. As a rule, place no more than 10% of your investment money into the stock of any one company. And don't sink more than 20% into stocks belonging to any one industry. That way, trouble in any single stock or industry won't derail your holdings.

Base your choice of stocks on their value, not on their price alone. Begin by comparing a stock's price against a measure known as its book value per share. You can find that figure in the firm's annual report, or ask a broker. Stocks that sell *below* their book value may well be bargains.

Next, check the stock's price/earnings ratio. You can find this number in the financial pages of most major newspapers. If the price/earnings ratio is below 10 to 1, and the company's earnings are rising, you may have found solid value.

Other relatively safe stock-market strategies include buying so-called convertibles. These are hybrids — part stock, part bond. They offer higher profit potential than is typical with conventional bonds. They are also less risky than common stocks. (See "Your Investments/Bonds: Convertible Securities.")

When looking for a mutual fund, keep in mind performance rankings by Lipper Analytical Services and their weekly roundups of the top-yielding funds. If safety is a prime concern, look to *Money* magazine's Fund Watch. All funds listed under "Investor Choices" are notably low-risk, having cleared their own risk-adjustment screen.

Two outstanding examples of all-weather stock funds are the United Income Fund and the Phoenix Balanced Series. Over the past 10 years, investors gained an annual average of 19.71% in United Income and 18.75% in Phoenix Balanced. Others that have provided strong returns are AIM Weingarten and SoGen International. Over the years, AIM Weingarten averaged an annual gain of 21.29% and SoGen International had an average annual gain of 17.31%.

One way for a fund to minimize risk is to move its money between the securities markets and the money market as the economy goes through its cycles. Two funds that successfully employ this flexible approach are the Mathers Fund and the Janus Fund.

In the decade ahead, the single most important determinant of investor success will be asset allocation — how you distribute your assets among the various classes of investments, such as stocks, bonds and real estate. Ibbotson Associates and Brinson Partners, two firms based in Chicago, did an elaborate study of asset allocation, based on the actual performance of 91 huge pension funds over time. Analysis of the results indicated that allocation among assets accounted for — get ready for this — 93% of the difference in returns among various portfolios. Selection of particular assets within classes accounted for no more than 7%.

You can be sure that your money will be protected if you put it in one of the money-market deposit accounts. You get them at federally insured banks or savings institutions, and most require that you keep a minimum balance of $100 to $500. All your deposits up to $100,000 are guaranteed either by the Federal Deposit Insurance Corporation or by its subsidiary, the Savings Association Insurance Fund.

If you have less than $1,000 to put away, look into one of the money-market funds. They are sponsored and sold by mutual-fund companies, and they put your money into an array of so-called money-market instruments, including Treasury and government agency issues, bank certificates and short-term corporate debt. They are not federally insured, but only one fund has failed to pay off in full in their 19-year history. Many money funds require an initial minimum investment of $500, but in most cases you need not maintain any set balance to earn the fund's full yield.

The safest short-term investments are Treasury bills. As long as you hold these federally backed issues until they mature — in either 13, 26 or 52 weeks — you will get back your entire principal. The interest, which is paid in advance, is exempt from state and local taxes. The trouble is, the price of admission is steep. You need $10,000 to buy a Treasury bill.

Buying on Margin

B ROKERS are only too happy to lend you money to buy stocks and bonds if you open a so-called margin account. You have to put up only part of the securities' price and you borrow the rest from your broker.

You just sign a couple of forms and your broker runs a routine credit check on you. Brokers are eager to approve your application because margin accounts lead to additional business and higher profits for them. You can come out ahead in rising markets because you put up only 50% of the cost of your stocks, and 25% of your bonds. So your money works at least twice as hard for you. The interest that you pay on your margin loan is not only low, but it is also deductible from your taxable income up to the amount of your net investment income for the year.

In mid-1992 the interest rates charged for margin loans ranged between 6.75% and 8.25%, compared with about 9% for personal secured loans at a bank. Sound easy? Maybe too easy. Margin accounts can be a lot more risky than you might expect.

Let's say you want to buy 100 shares of a stock that costs $40 per share. Normally you would pay $4,000 plus commissions. But with a margin account, you must put up only 50% of the purchase price, or just $2,000. Your broker would lend you the remaining $2,000, and the stock that you bought would act as the collateral for your loan.

If the value of your stock rises — great! If it rises enough, you could sell some shares, pay off the loan and come out ahead. But if the gains in your stock do not cover your net interest payments, then you lose money. And if the stock price falls, you could suffer in two ways. Not only would your investment dwindle, but you could receive a call from your broker — a so-called margin call.

A margin call occurs when the value of your collateral falls below a certain percentage of your total purchase — usually 30% to 35%. If the worth of your holdings drops below that level, your broker will demand that you deliver enough cash or other securities to bring your collateral back up to the required amount. If you can't deliver — sometimes by the next day — the broker will sell your stock, take back what he lent you and collect interest.

Before you decide to borrow on margin, the key question to ask yourself is: Do you believe in the shares so wholeheartedly that you would be willing to borrow money even from a bank in order to own them? If not, a margin account is not for you.

If you do invest on margin, keep a close watch on your stocks. Check the closing prices at least twice a week, or more often if the shares tend to fluctuate widely. You don't want a margin call to take you by surprise.

To protect yourself, you can buy what's called a put option. It is the right to sell a stock at a specified price to the seller of the put. If the price of your stock drops enough, the put option will become more valuable. Then you can sell the option to offset the losses on your stock.

For extra insurance, you can instruct your broker to sell your stocks automatically if they fall to a certain price, by using a so-called stop order. Choose the price at which you would no longer want to own the stock and advise your broker to sell at that level. Then, if your shares fall without your noticing, your broker will sell them anyway to prevent you from losing more money.

One little-known tip: You can use margin loans to buy more than stocks or bonds. Say you want to purchase a house or apartment that costs $100,000. If you are fortunate enough to own $200,000 worth of stocks, your broker will lend you $100,000 against them. You continue to own those securities, and you avoid the up-front costs that you would have to pay on a mortgage loan. For a $100,000 mortgage, those so-called closing costs — for taxes, origination fees, lawyers' fees, title search and the like — can easily run $3,000 to $5,000. Just remember that you ultimately have to pay off your margin loan, and you will have to pony up more securities if their price drops in a falling market. And check with your tax adviser: margin interest has limited tax deductibility.

How to Act When Interest Rates Move

NOTHING affects the prices of your investments more than changes in interest rates. Here are answers to some common questions about consequences of those changes — and how to act on them.

Can you make profits on bonds when interest rates fall?

Yes, you can. Since bond prices rise when interest rates decline and vice versa, a skillful trader can make money by buying bonds at the top of the interest-rate cycle — and then selling at the bottom. The trouble is those once-steady interest rates have been bouncing down and up quite quickly — and this new volatility makes bond trading riskier than ever.

When interest rates fall, does it make sense to buy stocks?

Yes, it often does. Lower interest rates reduce a company's costs and thus lift its profits — and often its stock price.

What stocks do best when rates fall?

Many stocks do well at those times. Among them are the shares of banks and savings and loan associations, because they can pay lower interest rates to depositors. Utilities are big borrowers, and so they stand to gain when their interest costs decline. Lower rates also help boost the housing market, so real estate investment trusts, lumber companies and appliance manufacturers also prosper.

Do any stocks perform well despite high interest rates?

High rates reflect expectations of steep inflation, and investors turn to natural resources as inflation hedges. So oil, gas and mining company stocks tend to rise.

Should you buy stock on margin when rates are high?

Not unless it's a very promising stock. The interest you pay is tax-deductible up to the amount of net income you earn from your investments. But when rates are high, your stock still would have to rise quite a bit for you to break even.

If you want to play absolutely safe, where can you invest your money when rates are high?

Four financial instruments offer a safe return at close to top interest rates: money-market funds; bank money-market deposit accounts; six-month certificates of deposit; and U.S. Treasury bills with maturities of 90 days to a year.

But do these four have any disadvantages?

Yes, they do. Since these investments are short term, you can't lock in high rates for very long. Also, remember that the minimum investment for Treasury bills is $10,000.

Should you borrow on your life insurance to invest when rates are high?

Probably not. Even if you have an old whole life policy that you can borrow against at a rate between 5% and 6%, you would not earn more than that after taxes unless short-term financial instruments were yielding 9% or more.

Which Economic Indicators to Watch

WE'RE always hearing about the latest change in this or that economic indicator. Unemployment is up, say. Or, the prime rate is down. But which economic weather vanes will really help you understand the direction of the economy?

First, to predict the direction that interest rates will take, look at the interest rate on *three-month Treasury bills*. The three-month Treasury bill rate is especially sensitive because it is based on the rate that investors demand in return for putting up their own money — and on the direction of Federal Reserve monetary policy.

To figure out whether inflation will rise or fall, keep a close watch on *major labor contracts*. Steep increases in wages are, of course, a signal that inflation could soon begin to climb. In the first quarter of 1992, wage increases covering more than 125,000 workers averaged about 3% — a modest increase in line with the current inflation rate.

Another gauge of future inflation is the relative strength of *the dollar*. When the dollar drops in value against other currencies, prices for foreign goods rise. This stirs up inflation.

An excellent indicator of the economy is the *payroll employment* figure. This counts the number of employees currently on company payrolls around the country. As this figure rises, so probably will consumer spending, and, along with it, the stock market. The much-discussed unemployment rate can be a misleading economic indicator. It can go up just because more people become hopeful of finding a job and resume looking for one.

Probably no statistic is more closely watched as an indicator of the financial future than *the stock market* itself. When the market rallies, it's a good sign for the economy in general. People and companies become more willing to invest and create jobs. To read the market, look at the Standard & Poor's 500 stock average. Because it samples 500 companies, it is more useful than the Dow Jones industrial average, which is based upon the stock prices of only 30 companies.

Beware of Boiler-Room Scams

D ID you recently get a phone call from a smooth-talking salesman who promised you could win a license in a federal cellular telephone lottery? Or perhaps he gave you a chance to invest in a gold mine, with a promise to sell you the gold at two-thirds the market price? Watch out. You could be getting a snow job straight from America's sunny capitals of fraud.

Much of the selling that goes on over the telephone is legitimate, but you should be wary of get-rich-quick schemes, a remarkable number of which originate in California and Nevada. Florida has its share too. Boiler-room operations generally depend on a corps of salespeople working out of a cramped office — hence the term "boiler room." They may reach you on specially rigged telephones that filter out the background din to give you the impression of someone calling from a quiet suite. Sometimes the voice seems to come from Davy Jones's underwater locker. And when you hear it say, "Hi there in Philadelphia, we have prizes for you from here in Los Angeles," you should know that this is a caller you can hang up on without feeling impolite.

The pitch is always smooth and grabby and sounds as though it's read from a carefully prepared script. You may be offered certain profits with no risk or loss. Often the salesperson will falsely claim that you'll be able to deduct the entire investment from your income taxes. Sadly, this last claim might come true. If you lose your entire investment, you may be able to deduct that amount as a capital loss.

You wouldn't be alone. The Alliance Against Fraud in Telemarketing estimates that such scams rob Americans of as much as $15 billion a year. The Alliance publishes a brochure that offers tips to consumers on how to avoid being taken by such con artists. The brochure, titled "Swindlers Are Calling," is free. Write to the Alliance, c/o National Consumers League, 815 15th Street, NW, Washington, D.C. 20005. One of the most common scams is the promise of prizes, for buying anything from a water purifier to vitamins. Then comes penny stocks (see "Your Investments/Stocks: Penny Stocks"). Also among the favorites are offers of vacations and fine art at prices too good to be true.

The prices *are* too good to be true. Boiler-room victims rarely get their money back. So *never* buy *any* investment that is pitched to you over the phone unless and until you carefully — very carefully — check out the company making the offer. The place to begin checking is with your own state-government securities department, or the attorney general's office.

Starting an Investment Club

INVESTMENT clubs are becoming more popular than ever among the people who want to learn about the stock market — and make a little money while they are at it. New clubs are being formed in college classrooms, corporate offices, condominium living rooms and even church basements. The National Association of Investors Corporation, which helps the new clubs get started, estimates that there may be well over 25,000 of them across the country, with around 400,000 members.

Typically clubs have about 16 members, and for them the monthly meetings are an opportunity to learn about investing and dabble in stocks at an affordable price. Clubs require members to ante up an average of $37 a month.

At some meetings the atmosphere is relaxed and informal; at others it's almost as intense as a session of a billion-dollar mutual fund's portfolio committee. In successful clubs, members usually do their own research rather than rely on brokers or investment analysts. The members spend long hours poring over annual reports and such resources as Standard & Poor's *Corporation Records* and *The Value Line Investment Survey*. Both of those are often available free in public libraries. Some clubs even send members to interview the chief executives of local firms that look like promising investments.

Only a few clubs determine by majority rule whether to buy or sell a stock. Most use a weighted voting system so that long-term members with the most money at stake have the biggest say. No one seriously expects to grow rich solely through a club. According to the National Association, the average club's portfolio contains 15 to 20 stocks with a total value of less than $55,000 — meaning about

$4,000 a member. But some clubs have impressive growth rates on their investments.

Because most investment clubs are partnerships, individual members must pay capital gains taxes on their share of any profits. New investment clubs with only small amounts to invest may find brokerage costs running more than 10% of their trades. As a result, some of them use discount brokers, who charge considerably less but give you no advice on where to put your money.

Most investment clubs do not want new members, and a few have stiff entrance requirements: you sometimes have to put in as much money as the other members have. Therefore, if you want to become a member of an investment club, you are probably better off starting a new one than trying to join an existing group. The majority begin simply, with two friends deciding to start a club, and they each sign up two or three other friends, and the chain grows. If you want to create a club of your own, you can get valuable help from the National Association of Investors Corporation, which sponsors more than 7,600 clubs. It will send you a handbook with advice on organizing a club, and for $17 a primer on the fundamentals of stock analysis. Write to: The National Association of Investors Corporation, 1515 East Eleven Mile Road, Royal Oak, Michigan 48067. The NAIC's annual dues are a modest $30 per club, plus $10 for each member.

The NAIC recommends that all clubs, especially new ones, follow these conservative principles:

— Invest regularly, preferably monthly, no matter where you think the stock market is heading — because a club that tries to predict broad stock trends is often wrong.

— Reinvest all earnings so that your club's portfolio can rise faster through compounding.

— Invest in growth companies. The association defines them as firms with both earnings and dividends outperforming their industry average.

Clubs should aim for 15% annual growth in their investments. To start you toward your goal, the association will send you a model portfolio, which is updated quarterly by its professional stock selection committee. The organization also provides work-sheets to help members analyze stocks on their own.

Investment clubs tend to do well, but when they fail it is often because they allow a trading attitude to sweep away the more reliable accumulation attitude. When the market moves sideways or down, impatient members often urge the club to follow an in-and-out strategy. It is much wiser — and more profitable — to hold on to sound investments for long-term growth.

STOCKS

The Long-Term Case for Stocks

THE stock market may be hitting new highs, sinking fast or treading water. It doesn't matter which. *Any* time is the right time to invest in stocks. History teaches that you take a worse risk by staying out of the market than by staying in. That lesson is just as true whether you are young, middle-aged, nearing retirement or already out to pasture.

The lesson does not apply to all of your investments, only to money that you won't need for the next five years. Stocks can kill you in the short run. Since 1926, the market as measured by Standard & Poor's 500 stock index has lost as much as 43% of its value in a calendar year. By comparison, long-term bonds have lost no more than 9% in any year.

But time is the ally of the investor. Since 1926, stocks have returned an average of 10.22% in annual price appreciation and dividends combined, about twice as much as corporate bonds and nearly three times as much as Treasury bills.

Naturally, you wouldn't have earned that much every year. In 20 of the 67 years from 1925 to 1992 the market would have handed you a loss. But the longer you hold stocks, the more favorable the odds become. Over successive five-year periods (1925 to 1930, 1926 to 1931, etc.) — in spite of the Great Depression, periodic recessions, wars and political upheavals — stocks were winners all but seven times and at worst were down no more than 12.5%. Over successive 10-year periods, stocks had just two down periods and never gave up more than 1%. Finally, over 25-year periods, stocks never showed a loss and always beat inflation. So, while in October 1990 the Dow Jones industrial average declined 11% from its summertime high, by April 1991 the average had broken the 3,000 barrier, and by January 1992 the 3,200 mark had been passed. The secret to investing wisely in the stock market, it seems, is to chant over and over again: "Think long-term, think long-term."

Beginning in the Market

MORE and more young people are setting aside part of their paychecks to invest in the market. That is partly because they can no longer assume that Social Security and a company pension will ultimately take care of their retirement needs. They also recognize that when you begin investing while young, you can still afford to take some risks in search of great profits. But, regardless of your age, how can you best get started in the stock market?

Your first decision is whether to aim for income (that is, for high dividends) or for growth (that is, for stocks that pay little or no dividends but have good reason to rise in price). Most investment counselors agree that young people should choose a strategy of capital growth.

As a start, you might consider investing in a mutual fund. For $1,000, or sometimes less, you can buy shares in a pool that is invested by the fund's professional managers in a wide range of stocks. That way you get a diversified investment that you probably could not afford on your own. Many funds grow nicely and, on the down side, few conservative funds lose very much. When it comes to average performance by category during the period 1987–91, conservative funds performed far better than others.

There are two basic types of funds: load and no-load. You buy load funds through brokers or financial planners, and they charge you a sales commission, as much as 8½%. You buy no-load funds by mail, telephone or through a handful of discount brokers, and you pay no commission for them. Since both kinds of funds perform about the same, it often makes sense to save the commission by buying the no-loads. (For more, see "Your Investments/Mutual Funds.") Another way to begin is to join an investment club as mentioned in an earlier chapter.

Once you strike out on your own, you probably will be able to afford only one or two stocks at first. But ultimately you should aim to own five to 10. That is enough diversity but not too much for you to keep watch over.

Which stocks are safest? Though there are thousands of listed stocks, your choices narrow basically to two types: growth or value. Growth shares are those of companies with above-average profit increases. Because of their superior growth rates, the stocks sell at higher price/earnings multiples than the average share even though they pay little or no dividends. Value stocks, on the other hand, often lack the panache of high-growth stocks, but they make up for it with bargain-basement prices.

Balance is important. A quarter of your investments might be in small companies that give you a chance for big gains — and, of course, the possibility of big losses. Another quarter could be in the largest, most conservative companies for stable growth. The remaining half might be medium-size concerns that are growing faster than the economy. In every case, try to spot companies whose share prices are relatively low compared with their current earnings and future prospects. Also, learn to watch for companies whose earnings surpass research analysts' expectations. In the first two months of 1991 alone, stocks of companies that reported earnings that were higher than predicted beat the S&P 500 return by up to 41%.

Keep your eye on investing's early-warning system. The market as a whole usually moves about three to six months *ahead* of changes in the economy. On average, the market begins to rise about six months *before* a recession ends. Typically, the climb lasts 2½ years, followed by about 1½ years of downturn.

Bear in mind that business conditions affect various stock groups differently. Basic industries such as autos and housing rise and fall along with the economy. So they prosper when an economic recovery begins. But when the recovery is a year or more old, the strongest companies tend to be consumer-goods firms such as retailers, clothing makers and home-furnishing manufacturers. That is because consumers finally feel secure enough to spend freely.

In picking stocks, you probably can benefit from buying some sophisticated market information guides. A popular one is Standard & Poor's *Security Owner's Stock Guide,* which gives the vital statistics on over 5,300 common and preferred stocks and more than 500 mutual funds; it costs $118 a year. You can get still more in-depth information from *The Value Line Investment Survey* for $525 a year. To save money as well as earn it, just remember that these advisory-service guides often are available at your public library. (See "Your Investments/Stocks: The Best Market Newsletters.")

When you buy stocks or bonds, you can choose either to hold the certificates yourself or keep them in so-called street name. That means they are held by your broker. Which is better for you?

There is one clear drawback to holding your stocks in street name. If the brokerage firm runs into severe financial troubles, your holdings could be tied up for months. You will, however, get them back eventually, because they are insured by the Securities Investor Protection Corporation.

But keeping your stocks and bonds in street name has many advantages. It is certainly convenient. You do not have to worry about losing your certificates or sending them through the mail. If you want to borrow on margin — that is, take out a loan from your broker — your securities in street name easily serve as collateral. Brokerage houses also maintain up-to-date records on the value of your holdings, and will reinvest your dividends automatically in, say, a money-market account.

How to Pick Them

ARE you tired of hunting frantically for tomorrow's hot stocks? If so, you should consider investing in *undervalued* stocks — and waiting patiently for their market prices to rise.

Many of the professional stock pickers who have done best in fair markets and foul alike are known as value hunters. They believe that the only sound investment strategy is to buy a stock when it is selling below the company's true value. Then they wait — perhaps for years — for other investors to recognize this value and bid up the stock's price. To succeed with such a strategy, you will need discipline and a willingness to buck the prevalent opinion of the Wall Street herd. But value stocks are so cheap to begin with that they have less distance to fall — and while you are waiting for them to rise you can sit back and collect dividends.

As a small investor, you might think you just cannot compete in a stock market dominated by large financial institutions. But there is a sound reason why amateurs like you can humble the institutional investors. Because so many of them have to concentrate on safety and the ability to sell out quickly if they have to, they choose their stocks largely from among 500 or so of the nation's biggest and best-known companies.

Professional managers are reading and hearing the same good or bad news about the same stocks at the same time, so they often buy and sell in a pack. This makes investing in the institutions' relatively few favorites increasingly risky for the rest of us: the bottom could drop out of stocks that fall from favor. But individual investors do not have to worry about causing market turbulence or justifying their stock picks to a fickle clientele. They can go prospecting in a market of some 8,000 or so stocks that most of the institutions ignore and few, if any, analysts bother with. As a class, these shares produce the biggest profits. The Leuthold Group, a research firm that follows the historical performance of financial markets, tracks such "neglected" issues in its study of stocks with less than 30% institutional ownership. It also follows "royal blues," stocks most heavily owned by institutions. For the years 1985 through 1989, Leuthold's overlooked issues rose 92%, while the institutional favorites climbed 54%.

Before you make your stock selections, learn what investment analysts — the ones who have the best records of forecasting and picking winners — think will happen in the market. You can get a reasonable idea of that by reading the financial press and investment advisory newsletters.

If you want to develop winning stock strategies, it is wise to follow certain guidelines:

Scout for stocks owned by fewer than five big institutional investors. These shares, while risky, often tend to rise faster than others. You can find out how many institutions hold an issue by looking it up in Standard & Poor's *Stock Guide,* which all brokers and many libraries have.

Keep in mind that low stock prices don't automatically mean value, as buyers of commercial bank stocks in 1990 learned to their sorrow. The median decline in 1990 of the shares of the 50 largest banks was 36%, despite the fact they began the year at depressed levels. Your margin of safety will come from buying healthy companies at attractive prices. "Healthy" means low debt with returns on equity of more than 15%. "Attractive" means that the stocks are selling at or below the market's price/earnings multiple, and a 25% to 50% discount to book value.

Also, search for stocks whose prices are low relative to their earnings. Newspaper stock tables show the price/earnings ratios based on the *previous* 12 months' earnings. For a better guide, use the ratio based on analysts' estimates of *future* earnings. You can find such estimates in *The Value Line Investment Survey*. Or ask your broker to send you Standard & Poor's stock reports for specific companies.

Look also for shares of well-established firms that have high dividends relative to stocks in general, notably relative to stocks of companies in the same industry. The recession has taken its toll here, too. Dividend payouts were hit in 1991. According to Standard & Poor's, the number of companies increasing dividends was down 14% in 1991, while the number cutting dividends was up 30.8%, due to too little profit and too much debt. For the long-term investor, therefore, current dividends may not be as sound an indicator of health as they were in the past.

One popular strategy among small investors is to concentrate on issues selling for $3 or less. These cheap thrills can be fast-growing small companies. Another tactic is to try to catch a fallen star, a stock that has fallen victim to bad news. You can spot these unfortunates in daily newspaper lists of stocks reaching 52-week lows.

To find out whether the company is reeling from only a temporary setback instead of a terminal problem, look for long-term debt that is not greater than 40% of the company's total capitalization and less than 10% of annual sales. Aggressive new management, significant cost reductions and the introduction of potentially profitable products are other signs that the corpse may be coming back from the grave.

Sometimes you can find hot stocks on Wall Street by making a cool evaluation of the people, products and services you encounter on Main Street. Many successful small investors discover that personal experience leads them to stock-market winners. For example, your children might direct you to a new fast-food chain that is packed with hungry youngsters. Perhaps the firm's stock is worth a nibble. Or you might detect a changing pattern in sales at your job. An investment opportunity may be behind it.

Investing in what you know firsthand lets you exploit two of your best assets — your experience and your own good judgment. But do not invest without first finding out more facts. Superb products and services can come from poorly run, unprofitable companies. And a close encounter with a single product tells you nothing about a firm's other lines of business. They may not be so terrific. In other words, use your experience, but do not let it overimpress you. You should do the same kind of research you would do with any investment. For example, does the company have cash hoards, real estate, oil reserves or other assets that might catch the eye of a takeover artist or make the market take a second look? The most convenient source of answers is usually *The Value Line Investment Survey*.

Ask a stockbroker for a copy of the firm's latest annual report, or write the company for one. Look for steady growth in revenues and net income over a five-year period. See how current assets compare with current liabilities, and hold out for close to a two-to-one ratio in favor of assets.

Also, see how the company measures up to others in the same industry. You can find reliable comparative data in Standard & Poor's annual industry surveys. One of the key figures to compare is return on equity. If your firm's return is lower than that of its competitors, beware. The company probably is not being managed as well as it might be.

Strategies for Buying

ALTHOUGH nobody can be sure whether the stock market will go up or down over the next few months, you should aim to recognize in advance the few really major, long-term turning points in the market, such as the huge rebound that began in August 1982 and the crash of October 1987.

Stocks generally move in expectation of changes in the economy and in corporate profits. The market is always looking ahead. If both inflation and interest rates are heading down, that's bullish news. But when the consumer price index and interest rates on Treasury bills show sustained increases, watch out. It's a clear and present danger signal.

Fortunately, your own decisions about the stock market do not have to be perfect to be profitable. Just watch for the major turns in the market. You can buy somewhere *above* the bottom and sell out some time *after* the market has hit its peak — and still make more money than the investor who ignores the market's long-term gyrations.

One old belief about the stock market is called the "efficient market theory." It holds that all new information about any stock spreads too quickly for ordinary investors to profit from the news before the stock rises. But that's not really so, according to a study by the Institutional Brokers Estimate System, a service of the brokerage firm Lynch Jones & Ryan. It found that after several stock-market analysts sharply increase their earnings estimates for a company, its stock probably will do *better* than the major market averages for the next six months. In other words, you can benefit from good news.

Over ten years from March 1980 to March 1990, if you put money into the 20 stocks with the highest upward revisions of earnings estimates, and then sold them a year after you bought them, you would have earned 35½% a year. That's far more than the 16.6% annual rise during the same period in the Standard & Poor's 500 stock index. The moral: It pays to shop around for stocks of companies on which several stock-market analysts have recently increased their future earnings estimates.

At the other extreme, you also can do well buying stocks that recently have plunged as a result of disappointing earnings or other sour news. A number of them become good bargains. In fact, some of the shrewdest investment professionals study each day's stock-market tables just to find shares that have hit new lows. They figure that if these stocks have intrinsic values, they may have nowhere to go but up.

If you decide to buy stocks, you must determine their basic values, as previously discussed. To help you gauge that, you would be wise to look at four measures:

Number one is the stock's *historic trading range*. You should consider buying on bad news when a stock nears its lowest price in the last three to five years.

Number two is *earnings*. Look at how well a company has done in the last 10 years for an idea of what it is capable of earning. If the most recent results are at the low end of the range, ask a broker for his firm's estimate of earnings for the next six or 12 months. If a turnaround is expected, you may consider buying the stock.

Number three is *book value per share*. That is the company's net assets divided by the number of shares. If the stock is selling for less than book value per share, it may be underpriced — and thus a good buy. If the price is less than half the book value, you have little to lose.

Number four is the *balance sheet*. Be suspicious of an unusually large amount of long-term debt. The ratio of a firm's debt to the market value of its stocks should not be significantly above the average for its industry.

Once you have picked out some undervalued stocks, don't buy right away. It is axiomatic that turnarounds generally take longer to materialize than anyone expects. So spend some time watching those stocks. But also don't plan to wait until a stock hits its very bottom. Nobody is smart enough to discern that. Instead, set target prices, and buy if and when the stock reaches them. By doing that, you might do well buying bad-news stocks.

Strategies for Selling

ANYONE can buy a stock, but the real test of smart investing is knowing when to sell it. Almost from the moment you purchase a stock, you should be thinking about what will be the right time to unload.

For many investors, however, selling a losing stock is like shaking some bad habit. It's a painful step you know is good for you, but you keep putting it off. In fact, deciding when to sell a stock is harder — and more important — than deciding when to buy. If you do not buy a stock and the price rises, all you lose is an opportunity. But if you fail to sell a stock and then the price falls, you lose real money.

Here are some guidelines to help you decide what to do when the stock you love no longer loves you back:

Set a goal. You might aim to sell if a stock rises 50% above the price you paid — unless you have sound reason to believe it will climb a lot more.

Cut your losses. Never hesitate to sell because you are behind. You could wind up further behind. Consider dumping a New York Stock Exchange issue if it declines 15% from the price where you bought it. American Stock Exchange and over-the-counter stocks are more volatile, so give them more rope. But sell them if they decline 20% to 25%. You can instruct your broker ahead of time to sell a stock automatically if and when it declines to a certain price. You do this by placing a so-called stop-loss order every time you buy a stock.

If you bought a stock expecting favorable developments that then do not occur within a reasonable time, bail out. And if the expected does happen, but the price of the stock does not move, unload promptly.

Another sell signal is a sudden spurt in the price/earnings ratio of a stock. This means that buyers are becoming too wildly optimistic. In falling markets, stocks with price/earnings ratios that have soared are likely to come tumbling down if earnings are at all disappointing.

Some advisers suggest you consider selling if a stock's price/earnings ratio rises more than 30% above its average for the past 10 years. For example, if the price historically is about 10 times earnings per share but suddenly jumps to 13, that may be the time to clear out. You can get these figures from a broker or from *The Value Line Investment Survey*.

If you learn of a significant deterioration in a company's sales growth or profitability or financial health, then it is time to kick the stock out. The same applies if the prospects for the industry that the company is in no longer seem so bright, or if the company itself loses its competitive edge.

It pays to read through the proxy statements that begin to clog your mailbox just before annual shareholder's meetings. While the purpose of proxy statements is to explain proposals to be voted on at the annual meeting, including such routine items as reappointing a company's accounting firm, they also often disclose a wealth of information, including how much top management is paid as well as any special deals benefiting management and directors.

Sometimes the behavior of the stock itself will tell you that your love affair with it is getting too hot not to cool down. One sign is if the stock market is rising and trading volume in the issue is heavy, but still it fails to advance in price. Another is when a stock is not making gains similar to those of others in its industry.

Many people put off selling when it's time to sell because they don't like the idea of paying taxes on their gains. But it's much wiser to take a taxable short-term gain than wait and suffer a long-term loss.

Losing some money is inevitable. No investor buys only winners. But as Martin Zweig, a top investment adviser, says, "You can be right on your stocks only 40% of the time and still do fine — if you cut your losses short."

How Technicians Spot Trends

SOME professional stock watchers called technical analysts have several theories worth knowing about. To judge when the market is ready to make a major move, technicians study a number of indicators.

One is called *momentum*. This means the speed with which market averages, such as the Standard & Poor's 500 stock index, rise or fall. If the index continues rising, but at a slower and slower rate every day, it may be heading for a fall.

Another technical measure is *trading volume*, the number of shares changing hands. It is a good sign when volume is large on days that the market rises and small on days that it sags.

Yet another measure is called *on-balance volume*. For example, if the market rises on volume of 100 million shares one day and then falls the next day on only 60 million, the on-balance volume is plus-40. That is a bullish omen. But when the on-balance volume turns down, watch out. It could be a signal that the pent-up buying power is nearly exhausted and that stock values are about to sag.

Then there is the *advance/decline line*. Very simply, it is a daily count of the number of stocks that rise and the number that fall. When the gainers outnumber losers, the advance/decline line goes up; that is a sign that the market is getting stronger. When losers predominate, the advance/decline line goes down. That is a sign of weakness in the market.

One sign that a rising market could be heading for a fall is when different stock-market indexes say conflicting things. For example, if the Dow Jones industrial average is rising at the same time that the Standard & Poor's 500 stock index is falling, that is a cautionary indication.

Another so-called technical indicator is how much money mutual-fund managers are keeping in cash instead of in stocks. Traditionally, if they have more than 7% of their assets in cash, it is a favorable sign for the market: the money might go into stocks.

Market peaks also are marked by clear signs of speculation. Two of the surest occur when small investors start borrowing heavily to buy on margin and when small-company stocks all seem to be scoring huge gains.

The Wisdom of Dollar-Cost Averaging

IT NEVER fails. Every time you plunge into the market, you find yourself buying in at the top. Then, stocks stumble and you get so discouraged that you sell — precisely at the bottom. You can avoid these expensive errors by investing a set amount of money each month — regardless of whether the market is heading up or down. This is a canny and often profitable investment strategy called dollar-cost averaging.

Dollar-cost averaging begs the question of which way stocks are heading. It follows the simple expedient of investing fixed amounts at regular intervals. When the market is high, your dollars buy fewer shares than when the market is low.

Think of it as investing on the installment plan. You regularly invest, say, $50 or $100 each month. If stock prices then go up, you can congratulate yourself for having earned some profits. But what if prices go down? Well, you congratulate yourself on your new opportunity to pick up some bargains. Several months ago, your $50 monthly investment could buy, say, only two shares; now it can buy three!

Many people find that a sound way to practice dollar-cost averaging is to buy the shares of a mutual fund at regular monthly intervals, particularly a no-load mutual fund with a record of having done better than the broad market averages over the last several years. No-load mutual funds give you professional management of a diversified portfolio of securities for a small fee.

Investing a fixed amount per month or per quarter is the traditional form of dollar-cost averaging, but a lesser-known version called value averaging lowers the cost even more, according to Michael Edleson, assistant professor at the Harvard Business School. Value averaging works best with a no-load fund. Each month you invest only enough money to add a set amount to your fund's total value. In months when your fund has risen, you add only enough to round out the market gain to your preset monthly target. In months of sharp price rises you might actually sell shares.

For example, if you are value-averaging at the rate of $100 a month, and the market during the previous month has lifted your holdings by $60, you add only $40. But if your fund has lost $30, you invest $130. And if your fund has gained $150, you sell shares worth $50. In hundreds of computer simulations using the Vanguard S&P 500 Index Fund, Professor Edleson found that value averaging outperformed dollar-cost averaging 90% of the time.

But even if you dollar-cost average into an index fund — one that clones the 500 stocks in the Standard and Poor's index — your results could be terrific. For example, in the 18 years to January 1, 1991, a stock fund that duplicated the S&P 500 would have rewarded semi-annual purchases with an 11.5% average annual return. Investments of $1,000 made every six months over that period totaling $36,000 would have grown to more than $104,000. The market value of the account would have fallen only three times, including a decline in the second half of 1990.

Mutual-fund companies offer to make the traditional strategy an automatic process for their investors. By pre-arrangement, they will move a fixed sum every month from your bank or money-market fund to the stock fund of your choice. Or they will send you 12 postage-paid envelopes, each printed with a different month of the year.

Dollar-cost averaging also can be used to buy shares of individual stocks, but brokerage fees on small transactions can be prohibitively high — often at least $25 to $35 a trade. And because mutual funds have diversified portfolios, they tend to bounce back from market disasters — when the market ultimately recovers. But an individual stock can fall through the floor and stay in the cellar for years.

True enough, if you sink all of your money into the stock market in a lump sum, and then the market proceeds to rise like a rocket and continue climbing for many years, you will do better than if you put in your money bit by bit, month after month. But look at dollar-cost averaging as a defensive strategy. It will keep you from getting crushed in the wild up-and-down market swings.

The discipline of investing fixed amounts in regular installments helps you to avoid two common errors: putting all your money into the stock market at a time when it might be getting ready for a sharp tumble, and selling out at big losses when stocks are deeply depressed.

Watch the Insiders

Do you want an inside tip on the stock market? Then watch for those times when high executives buy or sell shares in the company they work for. Information on such insider trading is easy to find and simple to use.

When officers of a company trade its stock, they often know something you don't know, and their deals have to be reported to the Securities and Exchange Commission. When they *buy* a lot of their own stock, it usually does much better than the market averages. When insiders *sell*, watch out. Heavy sales by insiders preceded many of the market's disasters.

Thus, when you see heavy significant insider selling of a stock, consider cashing in your own shares in the company. The situation is particularly dangerous when insider selling suddenly increases after a stock has started to decline. You can protect yourself with a stop-loss order. That way, if disaster does strike, you can escape with limited damage. That doesn't mean you have to stay out of the market. It's a good time to look at the stocks those knowing insiders have been *buying*.

You can follow the trading of high company officers by subscribing to newsletters that follow the subject. A top letter is *The Insiders*, a biweekly (3471 North Federal Highway, Fort Lauderdale, Florida 33306; $49 a year).

Buying What the Big Winners Buy

Have you ever heard of a 13D filing? No, it is not something that you would find in a dentist's office or on a clerk's desk. It is one of those obscure government reports that might give you a clue to making some money in the stock market.

For that clue, recall what Damon Runyon used to say: "If you rub up against money long enough, some of it might rub up against you."

Some of it might rub off on you — if you follow the purchases of the handful of billionaire investors who make audacious bids in the stock market to take over whole companies. Their names are often in the headlines, names like Warren Buffett, Carl Icahn, Robert Bass, Marvin Davis and others.

Quite a few smaller investors closely study this smart-money group. One who does is Kiril Sokoloff, publisher of the newsletter *Street Smart Investing.* In one five-year survey, he measured the investment results of 150 of these big capitalists and found that of nearly 300 stocks in which they took major positions, 95% rose in price. Sokoloff maintains the study's conclusions are still valid today.

You can follow the trades of these large investors fairly easily. Many of their deals are a matter of public record because of the size of their purchases. By law, any investor who acquires more than 5% of a company's shares must report that transaction to the Securities and Exchange Commission within ten days on a form called 13D. The SEC publishes a daily summary of these so-called 13D filings in the *SEC News Digest,* which you can study at the SEC's public reference rooms in New York and Washington, D.C., as well as at libraries of universities with strong business departments. Or for a fee, you can get this information more conveniently from several computer services and investment newsletters. In addition to *Street Smart Investing* (Southeast Executive Park, 100 Executive Drive, Brewster, New York 10509; $350 per year), newsletters include *SEC Today* (655 15th Street, NW, Washington, D.C. 20005; $600 the first year, $575 thereafter); and *Special Situation Report and Stock Market Forecast* (P.O. Box 167, Rochester, New York 14601; $230 a year). *SEC Today* is the only newsletter to include the entire *SEC News Digest.*

The Best Market Newsletters

MORE than 400 newsletters claim to tell you which stocks to buy to make money, and the editors of some of them have done amazingly well over long periods. But such advice does not come cheaply. Newsletters typically cost about $150 a year, though the price ranges from $18 to $895 or even more.

If you don't know much about the market and have a few hundred or few thousand dollars to invest, you might be better off letting mutual funds manage your money. But a good service might be helpful if you have, say, $15,000 to invest.

Of course, many newsletters also have performed poorly. Almost anyone can do some research and put one out. The Supreme Court has ruled that newsletter publishers no longer must register with the Securities and Exchange Commission as investment advisers. They can publish anything as long as it is not misleading or fraudulent information. In fact, the publishers have included high-school dropouts, an electrician and a hairdresser. Some of the investment services are addicted to self-congratulation, often making ambiguous forecasts and then boasting that they have been "right on target." Published performance records often overstate gains and understate losses because they don't take buying and selling commissions into account. For example, if a service advises buying a stock at $10 and then decides it should be sold at $11, the service credits itself with a 10% gain. After brokerage commissions on a trade of 100 shares, the investor's real gain might be closer to 3%.

Thus, the need for weeding the good newsletters from the rotten is more important than ever. To find the best, you can read services that keep score on them. *The Hulbert Financial Digest* (316 Commerce Street, Alexandria, Virginia 22314; $37.50 for a five-month trial) rates about 120 advisory services on their performance. Another service, *Timer Digest* (P.O. Box 1688, Greenwich, Connecticut 06836; $175 for 18 issues every three weeks), monitors 80 to 100 newsletters that claim to call the major turning points in the market and reports on the 10 best. These publishers may give you a free copy if you call or write, or you can probably see a copy for free at a stockbroker's office.

It's wise to sample as many advisory services as you can before committing yourself. Most offer a one- to six-month trial subscription for a low price, and some will send you a sample copy at no charge. The best way of getting to know a variety of services is to write for the free catalogue published by Select Information Exchange (2315 Broadway, New York, New York 10024). It describes hundreds of services and offers a trial subscription to 20 of your choice for $11.95.

The major advisory services that focus mainly on fundamentals often are the most useful. They provide earnings estimates, industry and company analyses, investment strategies, stock recommendations and model portfolios — a package of investment materials that you cannot find assembled elsewhere in one place.

One of the largest advisory services is *The Value Line Investment Survey* (711 Third Avenue, New York, New York 10017). This weekly service costs $460 the first year, or you can try 10 issues for $55. For those who learn to use the vast amount of information and guidance it offers, *Value Line* can be very valuable. Every week its staff of about 100 analysts, economists and statisticians evaluates 1,700 stocks. Each issue also includes a comprehensive overview of the market.

Another major service is *The Outlook,* published weekly by Standard & Poor's Corporation (25 Broadway, New York, New York 10004); a year's subscription costs $280. *The Outlook* is cautious. It's easy to read and digest, does not encourage taking great risks and is backed by the large analytical staff of Standard & Poor's. It lists the best- and worst-acting stock groups and gives a weekly updating on some 800 issues with recommendations for buying or selling graded on year-ahead appreciation potential.

For a quick scan of economic and market indicators plus computer-based forecasts and lots more, a popular publication is the twice-monthly *Market Logic* (3471 North Federal Highway, Fort Lauderdale, Florida 33306; $95 a year). It counsels subscribers on almost every aspect of investing, from stocks and mutual funds to options and gold.

Charles Allmon, noted for finding growth stocks ahead of the crowd, publishes the twice-monthly *Growth Stock Outlook* (4405 East-West Highway, Suite 305, Bethesda, Maryland 20814; $195 a year). His is one of a handful of publications whose recommended stocks have made money every year since 1975. Allmon also publishes *Bank Stock Analyst,* a listing of smaller American banks — none of them in New York — which are making money for their investors. It comes out twice yearly and is $50 if you don't subscribe to *Growth Stock Outlook.*

Finally, the *Dick Davis Digest* (P.O. Box 9547, Fort Lauderdale, Florida 33310; $140 a year) reprints excerpts, including specific recommendations, from 450 market letters.

Beyond looking into the advisory services, you would profit from reading several books on investment. A pair of classics are *The Intelligent Investor* by Benjamin Graham and *The Battle for Investment Survival* by Gerald M. Loeb (no kin, incidentally). A modern companion to these is *Gaining on the Market* by Charles Rolo and Robert Klein.

Also for information on specific stocks, you can call almost any corporation's shareholder-relations department for information. Request the annual report, the 10-K form that public corporations file with the Securities and Exchange Commission, all recent corporate reports to shareholders and transcripts of presentations the firm has made to brokerage societies or analysts' groups.

The Merger Market

IN THE 1980s, when debt was widely perceived to be a magic elixir, stock prices levitated as management borrowed heavily for takeovers and leveraged buyouts. Today, with banks holding back on the credit that fuels deals, merger mania is history. According to Merrill Lynch, the dollar volume of mergers and acquisitions dropped 44% in the first two-thirds of 1990 alone. But just because the sheriff has thrown Drexel Burnham's junk-bond carnival out of town doesn't mean there will be no more big deals. Investors still need to know how to react to an offer for their stock. Suppose you wake up one fine morning, turn on the radio or look in the business pages of your newspaper, and find that a company in which you own stock is supposedly a takeover target. What should you do?

The primary rule is: Don't chase rumors. There are far more false stories out there than real deals. But if a stock you own does become an active takeover target, your choices are many.

You may be asked to consider what is known as an equity buyback plan. If so, break out the bubbly and hold on to your shares. Maybe even buy some more. When a company announces that it is buying back its own common stock, chances are strong that the price of the shares will rise.

Another form of corporate maneuver that investors often must ponder is the leveraged buyout. This basically means that the firm's own management or an independent investor proposes to buy up the shares owned by the public and take the company private. If a leveraged buyout proposal comes your way, do nothing until you have read the official offering statement. Then see what you are really getting for your shares.

Do accept the deal if you figure that over the long term the transaction will yield you a substantially higher return than would selling at the current market price. But be wary of offers in which you will be paid in low-quality junk bonds as well as cash. Often the bonds in these deals are riskier than the stocks you are holding. Many LBOs have come to grief.

If a company whose stock you own decides to spin off one of its divisions, you have to answer a couple of questions:

First, should you hold on to your shares in the parent firm, or perhaps even buy more? The best answer is that the parent firm is often worth keeping — if the spin-off rids it of unprofitable, debt-laden divisions, or if the deal unloads businesses that the parent lacks the expertise to manage.

Second, should you dispose of the stock you receive in the spun-off enterprise? The answer is: Don't automatically sell those shares. Give the company a year or so to prove itself. If it does not do well within that period, then sell.

A more difficult deal to decipher is a hostile takeover bid. Basically, you have to decide whether to hold on to your shares or to sell out. The primary piece of advice is: Don't get greedy. Sell out if the stock rises to within 10% of the price the raider proposes to pay.

But say the shares have not risen quite that high yet. Then you still might consider selling and taking whatever profits you have earned as a result of the takeover bid — if the management seems to stand a fighting chance of beating back the takeover offer. It usually does so if it owns more than 10% of the firm's stock. If management seems too weak to resist, you would be wise to hold on to your stock, wait for the raider's last offer, then get out.

You also want to delay selling if the target firm actively seeks a so-called White Knight to pay a still higher price or if it announces an offer to buy its own shares. A bidding war could result and kick up the price of your stock. Of course, do not sell if you think the price of your shares will eventually rise anyway, with or without the takeover.

Although most analysts agree that the last years of the 1980s were aberrations, takeovers are still occurring, and acquiring companies still pay 30% or more over the market price for each share of a company they want to acquire. It's worth investigating those firms that you think might be candidates for takeovers. According to the late Wall Street writer Charles Rolo, here are some guidelines for finding them:

First, look where the bargain-hunting corporations shop. Acquirers prefer companies that have large cash holdings. The buying company then can recover part of the purchase price by using the selling company's very own cash. Acquisition-minded corporations also look for stocks selling appreciably below book value — that is, total assets minus total liabilities per share.

Second, look where owners may want to sell. Deal makers often search out companies whose principal owners have reasons to want a merger — for example, if they are elderly, own the controlling interest and have most of their eggs in that one corporate basket. A sellout would enable them to diversify their holdings and perhaps get some stock that is more readily marketable.

Third, look where takeover and merger activity is already strong. It has been intense in the broadcasting, publishing, oil, insurance, health care and software industries.

Investing in Tomorrow's Products

THE classic way to grow rich is to get in on the ground floor of a new product — not necessarily by making it or selling it, but by investing in it. You do not have to be an Eli Whitney or an Alexander Graham Bell to invest profitably in the products that will create the fortunes of the future. What you *do* need is information, patience and an eye for the products and processes that can make life easier, more efficient, longer or more enjoyable.

Which fields are most likely to produce the next generation of successful new companies? If you ask venture capitalists, business school professors, bankers and owners of small enterprises for their list of the potentially fastest growing areas of the economy in the coming years, they most likely will recommend these:

First, data processing: Bruising competition has brought a series of failures, but many survivors of the shakeout should do well. The future looks bright for those companies that manufacture or service computers and software — provided they bring unique products or special capabilities to this crowded field. A number of computer companies, for example, are working on "artificial intelligence" software systems that would enable machines to make decisions, diagnoses and conclusions beyond a human being's capability. Any company that develops such a system would be hugely promising.

Second, health: Americans spend almost $540 billion a year on personal health and medical services, a figure amounting to 12% of

the gross national product. One reason for this high bill is that it costs
so much to stay in a hospital. So there will be plentiful opportunities
for making, selling or servicing medical equipment for use in the
home.

Third, genetics: Some of the best possibilities for smaller firms in
this area are in support fields — for example, manufacturing lab
equipment or producing enzymes for use in genetic research.

Fourth, communications: Opportunities can be great for entrepreneurs who make, sell or service cable TV and satellite transmission
equipment.

There are, of course, still more opportunity areas: for example,
extracting valuable metals from material before disposing of it, or
helping companies become more productive and efficient. For a
really far-out investment, you can put some cash in space companies.
Private firms are beginning to launch extraterrestrial projects. You
can buy stock in companies that already have earthbound businesses
but are planning space ventures. Or you can contemplate investing in
one of a few space-only companies that are now privately held but
plan soon to go public. Most opportunities are in the dozens of space
firms that seek money directly from individual investors, and promise
in return a share of future profits.

In *all* these areas, you have to be particularly careful when
selecting stocks. Few investors know enough about technology to
judge whether or not any wildly trumpeted product represents a
genuine profit-making opportunity.

The worst method for investing is to be seduced by hot tips from
unknowing in-laws and friends. As one top mutual-fund manager
warns, there is no faster way to the poorhouse, other than pursuing
slow horses and fast women, than following tips in the new technologies.

But a sober and sensible way to invest is to first pick out an
emerging field in the new technology and then follow it carefully.
Subscribe to specialty magazines and trade journals. Some good ones
are *Electronic News* (P.O. Box 1051, Southeastern, Pennsylvania
19398; $45 a year); *Electronic Business* (275 Washington Street,
Newton, Massachusetts 02158; $64.95 a year); and *California Tech-
nology Stock Letter* (P.O. Box 308, Half Moon Bay, California 94019;
$270 a year; California residents add tax).

Once you have done some homework, you can consider putting
cash into those companies that are most effectively pioneering new
products. Conservative people might wager 10% or so of their

investment money on such ventures; more aggressive types might put in 30% or even 40%.

The most glamorous way to invest in the companies that are turning out revolutionary new products is to buy the shares of firms that are going public for the first time. That is not always easy. Since supplies are often limited, most new issues are offered first to a broker's best clients. But do not despair if you cannot get the crisp new shares on the initial offering. If you like a company, there is no reason not to buy its stock later on. You may even get it cheaper. Many new issues drop below their initial offering price sometime within a year.

Before you buy, learn all you can about a company that is going public. Ask your broker for copies of newsletters that discuss new issues. Among the leading letters, one is *New Issues* (3471 North Federal Highway, Fort Lauderdale, Florida 33306; $95 a year); and another is Standard & Poor's *Emerging & Special Situations* (25 Broadway, New York, New York 10004; $223.50 a year).

Look to see if responsible analysts say the company's product has the potential for capturing a 20% share of a market that itself could grow very large within a decade. Favor concerns that have 20% to 30% annual growth in both sales and earnings over the past several years and that are plowing 10% to 15% of annual revenues into research and development.

Above all, read the prospectus. You owe it to yourself to slog through it before you put up a penny. Check out who the company's officers are — they're listed in the prospectus — and how much experience they have had marketing other products in the same or related fields. Make sure that the underwriters and the venture capitalists who are backing the firm have sound records of success. If the venture capitalists are not selling their entire stock holdings in the offering, that could be a favorable sign that they think the company has a strong future. (For more, see "Your Investments/Stocks: The Pleasures and Pitfalls of New Issues.")

You also can invest in tomorrow's products by buying shares of one of the mutual funds that concentrate on purchasing the stocks of small, promising companies. A sound method of choosing among the funds is to get a subscription to one of the many newsletters that rate mutual-fund performance. Two of the best letters are *United Mutual Fund Selector* (101 Prescott Street, Wellesley Hills, Massachusetts 02181; $125 a year), and *NoLOAD FUND*X* (235 Montgomery Street, San Francisco, California 94104; $114 a year).

Among the most successful funds that invest chiefly in small stocks are the Twentieth Century Ultra, Kaufmann, Brandywine, Acorn and Baron Asset funds. If you want funds that specialize in high-tech issues, you might look at Alliance Technology Fund or Kemper Technology Fund.

Another way to invest is to buy into publicly traded venture capital companies and small-business investment companies. They often sell shares that are traded over the counter or on exchanges and use the money to invest in promising new ventures. When you are evaluating them, the best measure of their performance is their net asset value per share — of course, it should be rising. (For more, see "Your Investments/Stocks: SBIC and Venture Capital Shares.")

Fast-Growth Stocks

O NE route to profit in the market is to find fast-growth companies while they are still too small to attract wide attention. But before buying, examine growth stocks by five important measures:

First, there's earnings. Ideally, they should have increased an average 20% or more a year for the last five years.

Second, check into the capitalization — that is the value of all common shares. If the capitalization is under $100 million, the stock often sells for a bargain price.

Third, consider the price/earnings ratio. Usually, a stock should sell for no more than 20 times its earnings per share.

Fourth, look at return on equity. It shows how effectively management is using the money it has received from shareholders. A return of 15% on equity is good; 30% is extraordinary. You can arrive at the figure by dividing a company's net income by its net worth, but it's much easier just to ask your broker.

Your final test is a low ratio of debt to equity. Usually a company's long-term debt should be no higher than the total market value of its common stock.

Some of the most sought-after growth stocks, of course, are those of companies on the cutting edges of technology. High-tech stocks were bid to crazy heights after the market surged in August 1982. The inevitable day of reckoning came in mid-1983, and the overpriced shares went down in smoke. By mid-1984, the price/earnings ratios of high-tech stocks were back to where they had been two years earlier, before the market exploded. But these stocks still carried price/earnings ratios about 50% higher than that of the market. That was because investors continued to believe high technology would be the economy's major source of long-term growth. They still have sound reasons to do so, even though young companies in over-crowded, highly competitive fields are especially risky.

The human side of high technology is the speculative but exciting biotech or health-technology industry. Biotech stocks are *not* for the timid. In 1991 they surged an average 142%. But by mid-1992 prices of biotech shares fell 25% to 30%. Health-tech stocks usually under-perform the market for about six months following a recession. And because of a large supply of new public offerings, these stocks can be especially vulnerable. Often, profits are a long time coming because years of clinical testing are required before a medical product can be sold. Ask a stockbroker for firms whose products are well along in the clinical testing phase.

Over-the-Counter Stocks

IF YOU are willing to buy stocks that are risky but may offer some outsized rewards, you might want to shop on the over-the-counter market. Shares on the OTC market tend to be those of companies that are too small and too new to be listed on the major exchanges. They also have fewer shares, so even a small amount of buying or selling can cause sharp moves, up or down.

Thousands of OTC issues are listed on what's called NASDAQ, which stands for the National Association of Securities Dealers Automated Quotations system. That's a computer-linked network of about 500 competing broker-dealers who electronically post the prices at which each of them will buy or sell certain OTC stocks. The NASDAQ listings are loaded with small, glamourless companies, some of which are selling for a bargain price of only 10 times earnings — or even less. They may be undervalued simply because few people have bothered to look at their financial statements.

If you want to invest in this market, swear off hot tips. Think instead about small companies that have caught your eye — say, by selling a product or service you admire or by expanding in a market you understand. Candidates might include new firms that are major competitors in emergent fields and seasoned concerns that are prospering in otherwise troubled sectors, such as computers or savings banking. For guidance, you can turn to newsletters. One with a high batting average is *OTC Insight* (1600 School Street, Suite 105, Moraga, California 94556). It costs $39 for two monthly issues and $195 a year.

Also popular are mutual funds that specialize in over-the-counter stocks. One of the best is Fidelity's OTC Portfolio (82 Devonshire Street, Boston, Massachusetts 02109; 800-544-6666 outside the state). It got started only in December 1984, but as of mid-1992 it had gained 333%.

SBIC and Venture Capital Shares

ONLY rich people used to be able to ante up the venture capital that got new companies going. But you can invest in beginning businesses too, and you don't have to be a millionaire to do it. One way to get in on the ground floor is to find a promising firm that is just starting out and put money directly into it. In exchange you will be given some of that company's stock, and you can call yourself a venture capitalist.

Trouble is, you have to search hard for these opportunities because they are rarely publicized. Your best leads will come from local bankers. Ask them what ventures are just beginning and need some cash. Look for companies in businesses you know something about. It is also wise to start with ventures that are near your home so that you can maintain close contact with the people running the company.

But let's face it: Most people who sink their money directly into start-ups will lose at least part of it. Even successful ventures rarely show a payoff within five years. Arthur Lipper III, author of *Venture's Guide to Financing and Investing in Private Companies,* recommends that you place no more than 20% of your investment cash in such companies.

You can improve your odds by buying shares in small-business investment companies, or SBICs, that are open to public investment. These companies raise capital and invest it in businesses with a net worth of $6 million or less. There are 268 all-purpose small-business investment companies and another 133 that specialize in enterprises run by what they define as socially or economically disadvantaged people. Most are owned by banks or groups of private individuals, but a few have public shares that can be bought or sold over-the-counter or on the American Stock Exchange.

SBICs concentrate on small business that creates jobs. They are licensed by the Small Business Administration, which guarantees repayment of up to 90% of their loans. Some of the money is invested in start-ups that offer little more than potentially workable concepts. The rest is in second- and third-round financings to help spur the growth of companies that are already marketing a product or have moved solidly into the black.

A number of SBICs prefer to cut out as much risk as possible. They invest only in companies that are mature enough to provide them with some current income, which they in turn pay out to their shareholders in dividends.

What kind of SBIC you invest in depends on whether you want immediate income or longer-term capital gains. But whatever kind you select, ask yourself two questions: Do you think that the companies supported by the SBIC are sound businesses? And what is the investment record of the SBIC's manager? You can draw much of this information from the SBIC's quarterly and annual reports.

Another way to get in on start-up businesses is through a venture capital company. This is essentially a mutual fund that invests in nonpublic concerns. Venture capital firms tend to put their money in riskier enterprises. But some of them have produced big winners. For example, Boston's Nautilus Fund is best known for its investment in Apple Computer back in 1979. Apple soared and made many shareholders happy — notably those who took their profits near the peak before it eventually plunged. Venture capital companies are traded over-the-counter or on the American Exchange.

Before you buy shares in a venture capital company, read the annual and quarterly reports carefully. You want to know what new companies they are financing and how well — or poorly — the investment manager has performed in the past.

You also can try to buy the shares of new companies when they first go public. It is not easy to get in on a popular new issue. And the price may shoot to the stratosphere when all the people who could not buy it try to pick it up from those who could. Within a year, however, many new issues slip back to their offering price — or go even lower. Investors who wait for such a decline usually have gains as big as those who got in early.

If you want to buy a company that is going public, ask a broker for a prospectus. See who is doing the selling. If all the original backers are now backing out, beware. The public offering of stock may be rescuing them from a bad investment. But if the original investors are hanging on to their shares, that could be a sign the company has a very bright future.

The Pleasures and Pitfalls of New Issues

INVESTORS seem to be passionately eager to get in on the hot new issues of stocks that are coming to market for the first time. But before plunging in, examine them closely. Offering prices are often inflated, and companies that are too questionable to win the financial support of blue-ribbon underwriters have little trouble finding unexacting sponsors. As one long-established underwriter warns: "Anyone who ventures into new issues needs to be rigorously selective. A lot of junk is being brought to market, and that's scary."

On the other hand, quite a few companies of real substance are selling their issues to the public for the first time. According to Ernst & Young, the public sales of stocks and convertible notes by biotechnology companies totaled $3.7 billion in 1991 and more than $1.8 billion in the first half of 1992. Those figures are amazing when compared with the $777 million raised in 1989 and 1990 combined.

The new-issues market is presenting the public with a chance to invest in some youthful companies that are trailblazers in applied technology. Out of such companies will emerge the top growth firms of the 1990s. Again, the key is selectivity, and its importance is shown by the performance statistics.

Getting information about new public issues is not difficult. Some brokerage houses publish weekly calendars of forthcoming offerings. Most brokers subscribe to *Investment Dealers' Digest,* a weekly that covers the new-issues market. The prospective investor should ask his or her broker for the stock's prospectus, the so-called red herring, and scrutinize it carefully.

Look for the passage that lays bare the holdings of the top officers of the company that is selling its stock to you. To repeat, if they are unloading a lot of their own shares, you should shun the issue.

Check the prospectus to see that the underwriter of the issue is a well-established firm. Even the best underwriters make errors of judgment, but they will not knowingly market the stock of a company that is likely to damage their reputation. Some of the highest-quality new issues are brought to market by such blue-chip investment firms as Ladenburg Thalmann; Alex. Brown & Sons; and Morgan Stanley. Yet these companies, too, can fall victim to cyclical downturns in the market or unexpected competition from lesser-known firms and suddenly find their deals and reputations souring. The bottom line is to be careful not to depend too heavily on any one underwriter.

See who is providing the venture capital financing. Strong backing by venture capital entrepreneurs suggests that the new company has been well groomed to go public and probably has genuine promise. You can breathe easier if the prospectus lists such respected venture capital firms as Kleiner Perkins Caufield & Byers, DSV Partners, Sutter Hill Ventures or Venrock Associates.

Examine the balance sheet in the prospectus. Are the new company's finances strong enough to keep it going even if profits do not meet expectations — or, if profit growth is on target, to provide capital for continued expansion? If you don't trust your own judgment on these matters, don't invest in new issues without reliable professional guidance.

Penny Stocks

H AVE you been told that you can make easy money by investing in penny stocks? Well, you might, but it's highly unlikely.

Penny stocks are high-risk securities that are issued at $1 a share, or much less. Sometimes they quadruple in price on the first day of trading, possibly because they have been manipulated by unscrupulous securities firms. Penny stocks usually trade not on an exchange but in markets made by some 300 regional brokerage houses. Many penny-stock brokerages use fraudulent sales pitches to promise investors gains that don't materialize. According to some estimates, penny-stock fraud costs U.S. investors $2 billion a year.

The Securities and Exchange Commission has issued a list of the three warning signs of penny-stock fraud: unsolicited phone calls, high-pressure sales tactics and the inability to sell the stock and receive cash. And in 1990 the SEC created a penny stock cold-calling rule requiring stockbrokers to determine in writing that penny stocks are suitable investments for you. You must provide your written approval on the statement until you have bought the securities of three companies covered by the rule. If you want to report a potential violation of the SEC rule, contact your state's division of securities regulation or write the Securities and Exchange Commission, Office of Consumer Affairs, Mail Stop 2-6, Washington, D.C. 20549.

If you are still lured by the chance that your penny stock will really take off, make sure your brokerage is registered by the National Association of Securities Dealers. Then if it should be liquidated, you can get back whatever money is in your account and the stock you bought, whatever it is worth. Trying to recover the money you originally put out for the stock is another matter.

Buying Shares of Bankrupt Firms

Business failures do happen, and that's a shame. But many investors are finding bargains in bankrupt firms. They buy up the stocks and bonds of big, bankrupt corporations at distress prices. These speculators hope that the companies will come out of their court-directed reorganizations slimmed down and comparatively debt-free, and that the increased value of their securities will amply reward investors for the steep risks they are taking.

Investors' eyes glisten at memories of the huge fortunes that were made on such bankrupt companies of the past as Penn Central and Interstate Stores, which later became Toys "Я" Us. Of course, many investors in bankrupt firms have lost considerable money: Global Marine is just one example.

The potential for gain springs from the nature of the bankruptcy laws. They are designed to give moribund companies a new lease on life, to let them work out a plan to pay off creditors. Among those creditors, bondholders have the first claim on a company's assets. Common stockholders' rewards are much less assured. They are entitled to whatever assets are left — if any — after the bondholders and other debt holders are paid.

So, bankruptcy investors tend to stick with secured debt. At times they will venture further down the pecking order to buy preferred or common stock. But usually they will do that only after a company has just come out of reorganization, shining with such virtues as a clean balance sheet, an accumulation of tax losses that can be carried forward to offset future earnings and a talented management with definite ideas about where it's heading.

Investing in bankrupts is not for the faint of heart or short of pocket. Even situations that look promising often do not pan out. Since the bankruptcy investment game is dominated by the professionals, it would be foolhardy to sit in without coaching. One mutual-fund manager with a flair for profiting from bankruptcies is Michael Price, head of the Mutual Series funds. Most were closed in mid-1991 to new investors, except those who wanted to open an IRA. For help in picking your own stocks on the rocks, you might consult the experts at Bear Stearns or another of the brokerage firms that invest in bankrupt companies. Another source of advice is the *Turnaround Letter,* edited by bankruptcy investment specialist George Putnam III (225 Friend Street, Suite 801, Boston, Massachusetts 02114; $195 a year). It reports on the prospects for securities of companies in trouble, including a list of 30 stocks to buy or hold.

Foreign Shares

A S THE the economy becomes increasingly global in nature, more and more Americans are investing in foreign stocks. In recent years, many overseas markets have risen even faster than the U.S. stock markets. Foreign shares also stand to do well if the dollar experiences another drop against the currencies of Japan, Germany, Britain, Switzerland, the Netherlands and other countries. Even if the stock you pick doesn't rise but the dollar declines against the currency of that country, you will come out ahead when you sell. The reason: the foreign currency you collect from the sale will convert into more dollars than it cost you to buy the stock. And if the stock rises, you will get a double lift.

On the negative side, Americans who invest in foreign stocks run the risk that a foreign currency decline will cut into any stock gains. In the specific case of Japan, that country's currency rose so fast against the dollar, and Japanese stocks soared so high relative to corporate earnings, that they were destined to crash, as they did early in 1992. Also, different accounting standards make it hard to evaluate foreign companies, and information is not as quickly available as it is for U.S. stocks. For those reasons, money managers believe you should probably limit your international investments to at most 25% of your stock holdings.

One important reason for investing abroad is — here's that word again — diversification. Furthermore, while the U.S. stock market did very well for investors in the 1980s, with a total return of 325%, eight overseas markets topped that figure by substantial margins. Britain's stock market had a return of 431% for the decade, and Sweden offered investors total returns of more than 1,100%.

You can buy individual foreign stocks yourself. Most Canadian shares are traded in the U.S. just like American securities. So are the stocks of about 700 other foreign companies. They are sold in the form of American Depositary Receipts, or ADRs. Each ADR is issued by a U.S. bank and represents one to 10 shares of a foreign stock held abroad at a custodian bank. ADRs generally trade over-the-counter, though a few are listed on the New York Stock Exchange.

Experienced investors seeking a wider choice can buy and sell shares directly on foreign stock markets. Your U.S. broker should be able to handle the transactions. But don't expect him or her to offer expert advice on which foreign stocks look particularly attractive.

An easy way to get your feet wet is with American mutual funds specializing in foreign stocks. Among them, Merrill Lynch Pacific and G. T. Pacific concentrate on Far Eastern stocks. For stocks of companies in Europe and elsewhere, you might consider Alliance International, T. Rowe Price International, Scudder International, EuroPacific Growth and Harbor International.

Seeking Safe Utilities

PARTICULARLY if you are looking for high yields, electric-utility stocks may have a place among your investments — provided you realize that the dividends are not certain and the stocks' prices are subject to swift change without notice. That is because volatile oil prices and the debate over nuclear power cause many electric-utility stocks to be as risky as some high-tech issues.

In the past, if you were shopping for utilities stocks, you might have been advised to avoid companies with plans to build nuclear plants. Today construction of nearly all power plants has halted. Building has been deterred by overcapacity at both nuclear and fossil-fuel plants and by the increased regulations and costs for the building and maintaining of nuclear facilities as a result of the Three Mile Island accident.

Even though the last order to build a plant was placed in 1979, many power companies have at least some ownership of nuclear facilities. Some analysts recommend screening out those companies. Among the utilities that do *not* have nuclear plants are Sierra Pacific, Brooklyn Union, Atlanta S&L, Energen, Idaho Power, Southern New England, Southwest Bell, Ameritech, People's Energy and Pacific Enterprises.

Then there are the utilities that operate nuclear plants safely and conscientiously. Several that analysts have been recommending include Consolidated Edison in New York, Northern States Power, Wisconsin Energy, Wisconsin Public Service, Duke Power and Houston Industries.

Dividend-Reinvestment Plans

YOU rarely get something for nothing, particularly when it comes to buying stocks. But one exception is the dividend-reinvestment plan. It lets you buy shares *without* paying a broker's commission — and sometimes at a discount price.

When you buy stock in certain companies, they offer you these reinvestment programs. They automatically let you use your cash dividends to buy more shares in the company free of a brokerage commission. Almost 800 companies have reinvestment plans. Better yet, more than 60 of them also give you discounts on the price of the stock. Discounts range from 3% to 5%.

Once you are on record as a shareholder, you simply sign a form authorizing the company to put all of your dividends in additional shares. For example, if you reinvest $100 of dividends in a company that also offers a 5% discount, you get $105 worth of stock. When you don't have enough to buy a full share, the company credits you with a fractional share. You also can buy additional shares for cash, thus sidestepping a broker's commission.

In short, dividend reinvestment is an easy, money-saving way to build up more stock. A good broker can give you the names of companies that offer reinvestment plans, or you can get a list of more than 700 of them — all those listed on the New York and American stock exchanges — by sending $39.95 for a single issue or $70.00 for two issues a year to Standard & Poor's Direct Marketing Department, *Directory of Dividend-Reinvestment Plans*, 25 Broadway, New York, New York 10004.

Keep accurate records of the prices at which you bought shares through dividend reinvestment. When you ultimately sell the stock, you will need to know its original cost basis in order to determine your taxable gain or loss.

Index Options

WHEN you invest in only one or two stocks, you are taking the chance that *they* might not go up when the market does. Most people cannot afford to buy a variety of stocks wide enough to fluctuate with the entire market. But now there is an investment designed to let investors profit from the rise or fall of the total market: index options.

Index options are like stock options. They give you the right to buy or sell securities at a predetermined price any time before the option expires. An option to buy is a call; the right to sell is a put.

When you buy such an option from a broker, you place a bet that some broad index of stocks will rise or fall, usually within the next 90 days. An index option usually costs only a few hundred dollars, but you could reap the same profits as if you had invested $15,000 to $20,000. That is because a small move up or down in the index can cause a much bigger change in the value of the option. This enormous leverage accounts for the thrills of index-options trading. And the chills. Because if you wager wrongly you lose everything you had invested. That happened to many sad investors in the crash of October 1987.

The most popular index option is called the Standard & Poor's 100. It is a weighted average of the current market value of 100 blue-chip stocks selected by the Chicago Board Options Exchange. Twelve other stock indexes are also used for options trading, including the New York Stock Exchange composite and the American Exchange's major market index.

If you are optimistic about the market, you buy a call option. It surges in value when the market goes up. If you are pessimistic, you buy a put option. It surges when the market goes down.

Remember, investing in stock index options is tempting but very chancy. One top brokerage officer recommends this strategy: First, determine how much capital you are willing to risk. Then, invest it all in supersafe one-year Treasury bills — except for an amount equal to the interest that you will collect on your Treasuries. Next, place *that* amount into stock index options. Even if you lose it all, the interest you collect on your Treasuries will cover your losses.

You also can use puts to protect any profits you already have made on the stocks that you own but do not want to sell just now. If the market should fall, your stocks also would probably fall, but your put option would rise. That gain would offset at least part of the losses on your stocks.

BONDS

Sizing Up the Market

B ONDS used to offer secure income from interest, a safe harbor for your money and no excitement whatever. Oh, how that has changed. Jagged rises and falls in interest rates have sent bond prices plunging and leaping like a bronco with a burr under its saddle. Rates now fluctuate more in a day than they once did in a year. Since bond prices move as fast as interest rates, but in the opposite direction, the bond market is no longer a calm haven for the faint-hearted. Even bond newsletters are having a difficult time keeping up with the business. According to Mark Hulbert of the *Hulbert Financial Digest*, the current volatility in the bond market has made it nearly impossible for any newsletter to beat the Shearson index. "It is always tricky," he says, "because the bond market is so difficult to time. Cumulatively, over the past five years, none of the bond newsletters beat the index."

The huge wave of corporate takeovers and leveraged buyouts in the 1980s had its own unsettling effects. Takeover artists raised the money to buy the outstanding stock of a target company by getting Wall Street firms to underwrite huge bond issues secured by the assets of the corporation being acquired. In the ensuing financial restructuring, borrowings in the form of bonds replaced equity in the form of stock, leaving the company far more heavily in debt than before. Takeover bonds therefore have low quality ratings. With less and less affection, investors call them "junk bonds." If the company being acquired happens to be a blue chip like RJR Nabisco, its old top-rated bonds suddenly descend, price-first, into the junk pile.

Despite the uncertainties in the market, Americans have gone on a bond-buying binge. But many of the professionals who manage investments for banks, insurance companies and pension funds are apprehensive about buying long-term bonds. They are afraid to commit money for decades ahead at fixed rates. What has the bond market on edge is worry that the U.S. Treasury must borrow so much to finance 12-digit federal budget deficits that interest rates may surge once again, causing bond prices to plunge. Of course, many other forecasters believe that the deficits will soon narrow and inflation will subside permanently, thus pushing interest rates lower.

Business cycles often create bond profit opportunities. When investors sense the onset of a recession, they start bidding up bond prices in expectation that the Federal Reserve Board will start pumping money into the economy. Boosting the money supply forces down interest rates. At the other end of the seesaw, bond prices go up. Such a year was 1991–92. From April to April, interest on 30-year Treasury bonds fell from about 8.12% to 7.85%. Investment-quality corporate bonds went from 9.23% to 8.81%.

In 1992 interest rates continued to drop, making bonds a less attractive proposition. With interest rates nearing bottom, the likelihood of further decline diminishes. When rates rebound, as they tend to do during an economic recovery, all bond prices fall in value.

At almost every phase of the business cycle, bold investors who are willing to trade actively may be able to profit handsomely from volatile interest rates. The principles of trading in fixed-income investments are simple: To get the highest yields you should invest for as short a term as possible when rates are rising. Once you are convinced that rates have peaked, you should move into longer-term securities — to lock in those high yields and to reap any capital gains.

Prudence dictates caution in the bond market. But you can make sound use of bonds provided you understand the risks. For in-and-out speculators seeking quick capital gains, trading can be as attractive in bonds as in stocks. If you seek steady income, you can still find that old-time safety, perhaps by buying the bonds of reliable, major corporations that are selling at deep discounts from their face values. For even greater safety, stick with Treasury bonds. No takeover onslaught can downgrade them, and they cannot be called in before their due date. Whether you choose corporates or Treasuries, however, if you are willing to take a risk with your principal, you should grab the next opportunity to lock up 10 or 20 years of reasonable yields by buying long-term bonds.

How They Work

IF YOU are thinking about investing in bonds, you have a vast smorgasbord of choices. You can buy ordinary, individual bonds, just like Mother and Dad did, or you can buy into whole portfolios in the form of a bond fund or a unit trust.

A bond is a long-term IOU, and it pays a fixed rate of interest. Usually, you collect your interest checks every six months. Then when the bond comes due, your capital is repaid in full. So you can choose to tuck your bond away in a safe-deposit box and collect regular interest payments until the bond matures. But it is precisely those far-off maturity dates and the fixed interest rates that make bonds risky.

Say you buy a new 30-year corporate bond at its face value of $1,000. Say also that it pays 10% interest, so you collect $100 a year every year until the date when the bond matures, or comes due. But if long-term interest rates in the meantime rise — say, to 20% — your bond will fall in value. It will be worth only about $560 in the open market, because that is the amount that makes your $100 annual return, plus a $500 profit when the bond comes due, equal a 20% yield. The bond is said to have an 18% yield to maturity. If you had to sell it to raise cash before it matured, you would lose money. And while you owned it, your $1,000 would be tied up earning only 10% when it might have been yielding 20%.

On the brighter side, however, if interest rates fall below 10%, your fixed-interest bond is obviously worth more than $1,000. That is because an investor would have to pay more than $1,000 in the market to buy a bond that would yield the guaranteed $100 a year that you collect. You may want to speculate in bonds if you think that interest rates will fall, thus pushing prices up.

When you buy a bond, you should consider seven factors: First, there is the so-called coupon rate. That is the fixed dollar amount of interest you collect. Second is the maturity date. That is the date when you will be paid the face value of the bond, usually $1,000. The third factor is the current yield, which is the coupon rate divided by the current market price. For example, if the rate on the face of the bond is 9% and the bond is selling for $900, the current yield is 10%.

Fourth is the yield to maturity, which combines the current yield with the price you paid for the bond if it was more or less than the face value. Fifth is the yield to call, which assumes you may have to turn in the bond at face value, or a bit more, as soon as it is callable. Sixth is the tax status. The interest paid on bonds issued by government bodies is usually exempt from certain taxes. Finally, there is the quality rating — AAA or B minus, for example — which tells you the financial soundness of the issuer.

Most investors should stay with bonds that have a quality rating of AAA or AA. Indeed, U.S. Treasury securities, which are guaranteed by the federal government, are even safer than AAA corporate or municipal bonds.

But adventurous buyers might consider lower-quality issues. A bond rated BBB offers a yield one and a half to two percentage points higher than one rated AAA. And yields for so-called junk bonds — which are rated BB+ or lower — are still richer. These low-rated bonds have heavier risks. Interest payments could be deferred or the bond's quality rating could be lowered further, and that would depress the price.

Your Choices

I T WOULD take a bleak forecast indeed to make bonds seem as tempting in 1993 as they were a short time earlier. Only a prolonged and deepening worldwide recession would be likely to drive interest rates much below their mid-1992 levels. Anyone who bought in *before* that was likely to do well because, of course, bond prices *rise* when interest rates fall.

But interest rates at any time are impossible to predict with great accuracy. If you wish to invest in bonds, the wisest course is to spread your money over a range of maturities, from as short as two years to no longer than 10 or at most 15 years. There is seldom much of a reward in terms of extra income for tying up funds any longer than that. By staggering your maturities over time in this fashion, you will soon have money coming due that can be reinvested if interest rates go up. And if rates fall instead, you will have the satisfaction of owning bonds that lock in higher yields than might then be obtained for the same risk.

You will probably do best buying U.S. Treasury issues or perhaps AAA-rated corporate bonds. Yields on 10-year Treasuries in mid-1992 were about 7.39%. That compared with the 8.28% available on top-rated corporates. This was a spread that made T-bonds the wiser choice of the two. Corporate bonds yield more to reward you for taking a chance that the company that issues the bond might get into trouble and be unable to pay the interest or principal when it comes due. Not only are Treasuries safer — the U.S. government would have to fall before they default — but also the interest they pay is exempt from state and local taxes. Sorry, you *do* have to pay federal taxes on it.

There is another important difference: when interest rates drop, private companies often "call" — that is, buy back — their high-yielding bonds. By contrast, 30-year Treasury bonds are "noncall-able" for at least 25 years, and some are protected for the full 30 years; all other Treasury bonds are totally "noncallable." So you can hold on to these high-yielding bonds for a long time —usually until they mature — with no fear that the government will force you to sell out. When you buy any kind of corporate or municipal bond, you should check to see how soon it can be called in by the issuer. Some corporate bonds guarantee against calls for up to 10 years.

Municipal bonds are hard to buy in units smaller than $5,000. They are equally tough to sell without paying a high commission if you own fewer than 25 bonds. So the best way for most people to buy these securities is through one of the tax-free bond municipal funds. (See "Your Investments/Bonds: Tax-exempt Municipals.")

Deep-discount bonds should not be confused with low-quality bonds, those rated BB+ or lower, which are known as junk bonds. They reflect weak spots in the issuer's financial armor and behave more like stocks than bonds. Their prices tend to rise in line with improvements in the economy or in the fortunes of the issuing company.

Speculators who aim for maximum capital gains — but are willing to take maximum risk, too — might consider convertible bonds. They are called "convertible" because they can be swapped for a stated number of shares of the issuer's stock. A convertible's price swings not only with interest rates, but also with the issuing company's underlying shares. When share prices rise or fall, so do convertible prices.

Many individual investors may wish to use Treasury Direct, a seven-year-old program that allows you to buy securities without paying a commission. Such purchases could save up to $20 to $70 a trade. But Treasury Direct covers only new issues. For more information, call the Treasury's Bureau of Public Debt, 202-874-4000.

Bond Funds and Unit Trusts

B ECAUSE prices of individual bonds are so unsteady, investors are looking for less risky ways to get into the bond market. You can spread the risk of default by buying bond mutual funds and unit trusts, which give you a small share in a large number of bonds. Professional managers relieve you of worries about which bonds to buy and sell, and when to purchase or unload them, by performing those tasks for you.

A bond mutual fund will always redeem your shares at the present worth of the underlying bonds. If the prices of bonds in the mutual fund's portfolio go up, then your shares immediately go up. Of course, it works the other way around, too. Brokers sell bond funds and collect commissions of 4% to 6% from you, but you easily can buy commission-free, no-load bond funds by mail.

As an alternative, of course, you can buy individual bonds. And you can sell them back in the market at any time. But whether you are buying or selling, you will usually take a beating on the price because commissions are high unless you are dealing with very large amounts. So you stand to get a better deal on commissions with no-load bond funds than with individual bonds.

Individual bonds do have some advantage over funds. If interest rates rise and a bond's price drops, you know that your bond eventually will be paid off at its face value — when it matures, or comes due. But bond funds never mature. So, if interest rates surge and stay high, your bond fund shares may never again be worth what you paid for them.

Unit trusts are usually huge bond portfolios assembled and sold by brokerage houses in small slices of $1,000 to $5,000. They give you the combined benefits of diversification and fairly good prices. After you have paid commissions, you generally get about $950 to $960 worth of securities for each $1,000 you invest. The yields are slightly bigger than those of bond funds because there is no management fee.

The trust's sponsor almost always will buy units back from you at a price equal to their net asset value. The advantages of liquidity and diversification, however, come at some cost; you run a risk that interest rates will rise, and the price of your units will decline. Also, the sponsors usually buy long-term bonds maturing in 30 years and do not sell any of them unless the issuer is revealed to be in imminent danger of default. By then, of course, it is usually too late.

True, you will not be too badly clobbered because the trust owns many different bonds, and it is highly unlikely that more than a few bond issuers would default at any one time. Still, the way to safeguard yourself against turkeys in your trust — before you send in your money — is to read the trust's prospectus. It lists each bond in the portfolio along with its credit rating and tells you about any provisions that the bonds may be called in early by the issuer if interest rates fall.

You also can buy tax-exempt unit trusts. Such trusts, which offer you an opportunity to buy into an almost unchanging portfolio of municipal bonds, were born in the 1960s and peaked in the 1980s, when they took a backseat to municipal bond mutual funds. In mid-1992, investors had about $102.8 billion in these trusts, compared with $163.1 billion in muni mutual funds, and the trusts were paying interest of about 6.4% — tax-free.

Investors who are especially safety-minded can put some money into an *insured* tax-exempt trust. The bonds are backed by an insurance company guarantee that interest and principal will be paid on schedule, but the cost of the insurance reduces the yield to a shade less than you would get on an unsecured trust. (See "Your Investments/Bonds: Insured Municipals.")

Taking all the factors together, the easiest and safest way for most persons of moderate means to buy a diversity of bonds is to invest in a no-load bond mutual fund. The interest income is reasonably steady, there are no commissions when you buy or sell and the annual fees are modest. Unlike unit trusts, bond fund portfolios are actively managed. The issues in them are constantly being traded, and presumably the managers know enough to escape from a troubled situation and sell out well before a bond encounters the danger of default.

Tax-exempt Municipals

MUNICIPAL bonds have become the tax shelter for everyone. The federal government does not tax the interest you collect on most of them, and if the bonds are from your home state, you probably will escape state and local taxes, too. This exemption is not the only reason to buy munis. They also yield high interest. Often they pay about 80% to 85% as much as U.S. Treasury bonds do, but your income from Treasuries is not exempt from federal taxes. In mid-1992, AAA general obligation municipals were paying around 6.7%, which was substantially higher than the annual rate of inflation.

To love tax-free bonds, merely compare the interest rates with those of other bonds before taxes. For example, if you were in the 31% federal tax bracket for your 1992 income, a top-rated municipal yielding 6.7% would have paid you the equivalent of a 9.6% taxable yield. If you were in the 28% tax bracket, your equivalent yield would have been 9.2%.

Municipals have the usual risk: if interest rates climb, the prices of the bonds fall. Then, if you had to sell off your investment to raise money, you would get less than you paid for it. Another risk is that the state or city agency that issued the bond could go broke and default on its payments of principal and interest. To avoid this danger, small investors should stick with the highest-quality bonds — those rated AAA or AA by Moody's or Standard & Poor's.

You can buy individual bonds from a stockbroker; he or she usually will require you to purchase at least $5,000 worth. But it is unwise to buy them unless you plan to hold them until they mature and the issuer pays you back the full face value. If you sell out earlier, you could lose as much as 5% of the value of your bond on the spread between the higher "asked" price at which the broker sells you the bond and the "bid" price at which he will buy it from you. You are at the broker's mercy for what he will pay because the vast majority of municipal bond prices are not even published in newspapers.

One new investment is a tax-free municipal bond that has no certificate. Buying or selling this bond is merely a computer transaction, and your record of ownership is a monthly brokerage statement. An advantage to it is that the interest is paid directly into your brokerage account on the day it is due. You do not have to wait for a check to arrive or clear. And there are no worries about certificates' being lost or stolen.

Another fairly new wrinkle in tax-exempt securities is the single-state municipal bond fund or unit trust. You usually pay no federal, state or local taxes on the interest from this investment — provided that you live in the state in which the securities are issued. Residents of high-tax New York and California have been buying single-state funds for years, and investor demand has been rising throughout the country. Arkansas, Maine, New Mexico and Washington are the newest states to be included among the 37 states where single-state funds or trusts are available.

Such funds give you the advantage of diversification: you get different bonds, all issued by agencies within one state. The higher your tax bracket, of course, the more you can benefit from a single-state tax-exempt fund.

You can reduce your risks as well as your costs by buying shares in a municipal bond fund or a unit trust, whether single-state or not. Bear in mind that you will have to pay state taxes on your earnings from multi-state funds.

Probably the best tax-exempt investments for most people are the shares of no-load tax-exempt bond mutual funds. For annual management fees and expenses of only about one-half of 1% of your investment, the funds give you a share of a professionally managed portfolio of bonds that you can sell at any time. Based on total returns for the five years ending May 1992, the top no-load municipal bond funds recommended by Lipper Analytical Services include UST Master Tax Exempt Funds, Inc.: Long Term Portfolio; Alliance Municipal Income Inc.: National Portfolio; United Municipal Bond Fund Inc. and General Municipal Bond Fund Inc.

The funds with the highest total returns for the 12 months ending May 1992 were Strong Municipal Bond Fund, with a total return of 13.39%, and GW Sierra National Municipal Bond Fund, with a total return of 12.74%. You can buy funds directly from mutual-fund companies. Their toll-free numbers and addresses are found in advertisements in the financial press. (For more, see "Your Investments/Mutual Funds: Tax-exempt Bond Mutual Funds.")

Insured Municipals

IF YOU are thinking about investing in municipal bonds, you may be worried that many states and localities are severely troubled by federal budget cutbacks and shrinking tax revenues. But there is a way that you can invest in municipals and insure yourself against any losses from defaults.

You can profit from the oversize yields and still be able to sleep at night by investing in *insured* municipal bond funds or trusts. The portfolios of insured bond funds and trusts are backed by a number of private insurance companies, and all are rated AAA by the authoritative Standard & Poor's rating service. Though prices still fluctuate, the insurance guarantees investors full payment of interest and principal when due, and costs about $1.25 a year for every $1,000 you invest. This has the effect of reducing your annual yield from a fund or trust by only one-eighth of 1%.

Insured trusts are sponsored by many brokerage firms. You can buy units through your broker, who will deduct a sales commission of roughly 5%. That means that if you put up $1,000, you get about $950 worth of bonds. Such bond insurance, available since the early 1970s, has become a major marketing tool and is important to investors. According to the Public Securities Association, insured munis accounted for more than 30% of the $46.9 billion of long-term tax-exempt issues sold in the first four months of 1992.

Merrill Lynch's Municipal Bond Fund Insured Portfolio is insured principally by AMBAC Indemnity Corporation and Bond Investors Guaranty Insurance Company. The fund offers an extra: you can write checks of $500 or more against your money.

Beware of Unwelcome Calls

YOU MAY have an unpleasant surprise in store if you own high-paying bonds that were originally issued in the early 1980s: those securities could soon be called in and paid off. Yes, you would get back all the money you paid for the bonds, but you would lose those nice, high regular interest payments.

Interest rates on municipal bonds, for example, hit their highs of more than 13% in 1982. When yields fell, state and local government agencies paying those 13% rates redeemed their older bonds as soon as they could and sold new bonds at lower rates. These early payoffs are known as "calls."

Investors generally are protected from calls for at least 10 years after the bond is issued. But some bonds may be redeemed within five years, or even less. A stockbroker or a financial planner can tell you whether your bond is among the ones at risk of an early redemption.

If you are considering buying a new bond, it's probably wise to pick one that offers you call protection for at least 10 years. That way you can lock in today's interest rates for well into the future. This would become especially valuable if and when interest rates decline.

Investors in bond unit trusts also need to watch call provisions, especially if the trust touts an extraordinarily steep yield. Such trusts often are invested in many of the older high-interest bonds, which may be called. You would be wise to check the call dates on bonds listed in the prospectus of the trust to see if you are adequately protected. Otherwise, you could end up in a few years with most of your money back — and the need to find another high-yield investment.

Variable-Rate Option Municipals

ONE investment that allows you to earn tax-free income without tying up your money for more than a year is the variable-rate option bond. It is a long-term municipal bond, but the interest rates it pays are adjusted annually — up or down — to whatever the current market rate is. On a daily, weekly, monthly or yearly basis, you will have the option to cash in the bond and collect what you paid for it.

According to Kenny S&P Evaluation Service, one-year variable-rate option bonds, sold by many brokerage firms, were paying approximately 3.4% in mid-1992. True, the variable-rate yield was more than one point below the rate available on AAA long-term municipal bonds. But if investors in those regular bonds sell out early, they have no assurance of getting back the full amount they have invested.

If you plan to hold on to your tax-free bond for many years, you are probably best off buying a regular municipal bond. But if you think you will need your money back in a year, you might be well advised to consider variable-rate option bonds.

The Glories and Dangers of Junk

B ANKRUPTCIES of companies that went through leveraged buyouts, and the collapse of Drexel Burnham Lambert, the investment banking firm that engineered so many buyouts, temporarily took the gloss off junk bonds. Many of them defaulted in 1989 and 1990, while the rest sank dismally in market value. By the end of 1990, the junk bond market was virtually nonexistent. But in the next two years it came back. Investors busily bought up junk bonds and junk funds, feeling that the bonds were yielding a return adequate to make up for the risk: a big 4.25 percentage points over Treasuries. Consequently, there were some spectacular gains.

Junk bonds either have no ratings or are rated low by the official bond rating services: BB+ or lower by Standard & Poor's, BA1 or lower by Moody's. If you are eager to get into the junk bond market, though, there is another path to take. In 1991 a new market began to emerge for lower-rated corporate debt, or so-called near junk bonds, those nonconvertibles rated in S&P's "Triple-B" category or lower. Over 80 such bonds were issued in the first quarter of 1992, with a volume of $21 billion of that debt. Such bonds offer investors higher yields and the potential for higher returns than higher-rated fixed-income securities.

You can lessen your chances of getting wiped out by a default if you diversify, buying a bond mutual fund. Look for a fund that has the term "high-yield" in its name — that means junk. Most junk bond funds cut their dividends in 1989 and 1990 after they were forced to sell bonds to redeem the shares of panic-stricken investors. Some analysts then began looking at them as promising speculations.

Along with towering yields, junk stood to produce huge capital gains if investors ever regained confidence in them. And despite the 1990–91 recession, they did. In 1991 they returned a high 36.3%, and in the first half of 1992 they gained 11.36%.

When you shop for junk, you should distinguish between two types: genuine trash and quality junk. Some bonds may be diamonds in the rough. The companies that issue the bonds may be simply too young to have a long and favorable credit history. In other cases, the ratings services may not yet have recognized turnarounds in the issuing companies. And still other bonds may be quality junk because they are found in out-of-favor lines of business. So you may do well by scouting for glitter amid the junk.

To be on the safe side, avoid junk bonds issued in connection with takeovers and buyouts. Some of them may be sound, but it's almost impossible for amateurs to evaluate. Also, diversify your holdings to reduce your risk. The best way is to invest in a corporate bond mutual fund that actively manages 70 to 140 issues. Some of the top performers in the first half of 1992 were Dean Witter High Yield Fund (43.46%), National Bond Fund (39.45%) and SunAmerica Income Portfolios: High Yield Portfolio (35.78%).

Convertible Securities

CONVERTIBLE securities are part bond and part stock. In today's uncertain financial climate, they can be a sensible buy — provided you are an experienced investor.

A convertible is a bond or preferred stock that pays a fixed rate of interest or a preset dividend. And it has a unique advantage: it can be exchanged for the issuing company's common shares — if and when they rise to a certain price. So an investor in convertibles might have it both ways. He collects high interest or dividend income now — and maybe he pockets big profits later on by converting into the common stock.

But you must pay a price for this flexibility. The cost of a convertible is higher than the value of the stock you can exchange it for. Also, the interest or dividends you collect on a convertible are usually three or four percentage points below what you can get on the same company's bonds or preferred stock.

If the issuing company's common stock rises steeply, a convertible reaches what is called its conversion price. It then is smart for you to switch into those common shares — and earn a profit. But what if the stock market goes down? The convertible is still attractive because it usually holds its value better than the common stock will.

To many investors, the ideal convertible is one that costs about $1,000, pays you 7½% to 8% in interest and costs you only 10% to 12% more than the value of the common stock that you can switch it into. Such a convertible will tend to keep pace with the common stock in an up market and fall only half as fast as that stock will in a down market.

You might also consider convertible bond funds. They usually pay about as much interest as money-market funds do. But since you can trade in the bonds in a fund for stocks, you can still reap big gains when stocks start to rise again.

Convertible bond funds are less risky than stock mutual funds, in part because bonds are safer than stocks. The total returns of convertible bond funds for the year ending May 31, 1992, as tracked by Lipper Analytical Services, averaged 15.15%. Two funds that did well were the low-load Rochester Convertible Fund (annual return 27.05%) and the no-load Fidelity Convertible Securities Fund (25.63%).

U.S. Savings Bonds

THE Treasury Department has overhauled good old U.S. Savings Bonds to make them more enticing. Are the bonds better investments than before? They certainly are. The low interest rates used to fight the 1990–91 recession and to combat the economy's erratic sluggishness in 1992 transformed the humble series EE bond into the Miss America of fixed-income securities.

While returns on Treasury bills and money market accounts withered to 3.5%, EE bonds as usual guaranteed 6%. To earn that rate, all you have to do is hold them for five years. But even if you turn them in after six months, you are assured of a 4.2% return.

What's more, the guaranteed rates are mere minimums. EE bond interest can rise with rates in general.

The return on EE bonds held five years is 85% of the average yield of five-year Treasury notes and bonds. The rate changes each May and October. It is to protect you against sharp interest-rate drops that these bonds are guaranteed to pay at least 6%.

The interest is exempt from state and local taxes. And by letting it pile up in the bond, you pay no federal tax until you cash in the bonds. Even then, you can defer the tax by swapping series EE issues for series HH bonds, which you can get for $500 all the way up to $10,000. The interest on series HH bonds — 6% paid twice a year — is taxable annually, but you are still postponing payment of taxes on your series EE bonds' interest and using tax-deferred dollars to earn interest on series HH bonds.

You can buy EE bonds for $25 to $5,000, with small denominations tailor-made for payroll savings plans offered by thousands of employers.

Zero-Coupon Bonds

YOU might think that zero-coupon bonds are the real nothings of the investment world. They pay you no interest now nor will they do so for years to come. Worse, *you* are liable for income taxes on the interest you have not even received. What kind of an odd investment is this — and who would want to buy it? Well, *you* might.

Zeros are not without their attractions. With a zero-coupon bond, you can invest as little as $50 and be assured that it will grow to a specific sum when the bond comes due. The term generally ranges from six months to 30 years. These securities sell at really deep discounts. Example: For only $680 you could buy a U.S. Treasury zero-coupon bond in mid-1991 that would pay you $1,000 in 1996; for $285 you could get one that would pay you $1,000 in the year 2006.

When the bonds mature, you collect all the accrued interest. If you own a zero-coupon, you are not confronted every six months with the problem of reinvesting the interest income — at unpredictable rates — to maintain the high yield. That is the zeros' strong point: they eliminate reinvestment risk.

And you can escape the necessity to pay taxes on the phantom interest year by year. Just buy zero-coupon Treasury or corporate bonds for your Individual Retirement Account or your Keogh plan or some other tax-sheltered account. Or invest in tax-free municipal zero-coupon bonds.

Watch out for brokers' hidden markups. They can cause the prices — and yields — of zeros to vary. Many brokers don't disclose the commissions you pay. Take, for example, a "Triple-A"-insured $1,000 zero-coupon bond maturing in the year 2009. One regional broker, A. G. Edwards & Sons in St. Louis, quoted the bond in mid-1991 to sell for $237.21. But another broker, Butcher & Singer in Philadelphia, would have charged $223.95. In the former case, you would collect a yield of 8.6%. In the latter, you would collect 8.8%. So, shop around among brokers to make sure of getting your very best deal.

Ginnie Maes

MEET my friend Ginnie Mae. She's quite attractive, not a racy type at all, but safe and most rewarding for those who know and love her.

Ginnie Mae is really a security, issued by the Government National Mortgage Association and backed by the mortgages that the wholly owned U.S. government corporation holds. When you invest in one, you are buying a share in a pool of fixed-rate home mortgages insured by the Federal Housing Administration or the Department of Veterans Affairs. You also get your principal returned in monthly installments because homeowners pay off their mortgages monthly. You will probably want to reinvest that principal right away, so you do not deplete your capital. Since you get both interest and principal paid in installments, you collect higher regular payments from a Ginnie Mae than from a bond or a certificate of deposit or some other interest-bearing security.

One problem with Ginnie Maes is that you can never be certain how much money you will receive each month and how long these installments will last. That's because homeowners often pay off their mortgages ahead of schedule. Prepayments are so common that Ginnie Maes backed by 30-year mortgages actually have an average life of only 10 to 12 years. To compensate investors for the uncertainty, Ginnie Maes offer a higher interest rate than Treasury issues of comparable maturities. For example, the "bond equivalent yield" on Ginnie Maes backed by 10% 30-year mortgages in mid-1991 was 8.62%, versus 7.5% on the 10-year Treasury bonds with which they are most often equated. The bond equivalent tells you how much you would have to get from other bonds that pay interest only twice a year to equal the yield of a Ginnie.

Ginnie Maes are as safe as U.S. Treasury securities because the government protects you against late payments and losses on foreclosures on the loans backing the securities; so they are particularly attractive for conservative investors. But, as mentioned, Ginnie Maes will give you only about a point or two more yield than comparable Treasuries will. Many investors find that such a low spread is not enough to compensate for the risk that the mortgages will be prepaid by homeowners if interest rates fall.

Another trouble is that Ginnie Maes cost a bundle — $25,000 each. But for $1,000, and in some cases as little as $100, you can go to a mutual fund or a stockbroker and buy Ginnie Maes in the form of bond mutual funds or unit trusts. The mutual funds produced an average total return of 13.46% for the year ending August 31, 1991. But beware: If mortgage rates fall a point or two, Ginnies won't shoot up in price as much as bonds will. Instead, more homeowners will prepay their mortgages, and you will have to reinvest your capital at the lower rates.

Some Ginnie Mae mutual funds let you write an unlimited number of checks against your money; the minimum check is usually $500. You also can reinvest your monthly payments of interest and principal. That allows your money to compound and keep continually working for you. And you can cash in your shares at any time, without fees or penalties.

Fannie Maes and Freddie Macs

A NOTHER way to park a good bit of money in mortgages that earn safe, high yields is to invest in securities known as Fannie Maes and Freddie Macs.

Fannie Mae is the nickname of the Federal National Mortgage Association, and Freddie Mac stands for the Federal Home Loan Mortgage Corporation. Both issue mortgage-backed securities similar to the more famous Ginnie Maes. The difference is that when you buy a Fannie Mae or a Freddie Mac, you invest in a pool of conventional home loans, and not the Federal Housing Administration and Veterans Administration mortgages that you get with Ginnie Maes.

Like Ginnie Maes, Freddie Macs and Fannie Maes pass along to investors on a monthly basis the interest and principal payments made by homeowners on mortgages in the pools. Even if homeowners do not meet their obligations, Fannie Mae and Freddie Mac guarantee that you will receive your fair share of interest and principal every month.

Newly issued securities from Freddie Mac and Fannie Mae require a minimum investment of $1,000. But these securities are usually not available to the individual investor. You can, however, buy into a mutual fund that invests in them. One is USAA Income Fund of San Antonio.

Both Freddie Mac and Fannie Mae are corporations chartered by Congress, though they are not officially part of the federal government. In mid-1992 Freddie Macs, Fannie Maes and Ginnie Maes were yielding 8.07%.

SONYMAs and Sallie Maes

I F YOU are in a high tax bracket, SONYMA can help you. SONYMA stands for the State of New York Mortgage Agency, which issues bonds that are backed by fixed-rate mortgages. It uses the proceeds to subsidize housing loans at below-market interest rates for first-time home buyers.

SONYMA bonds are exempt from federal income taxes for most investors. But if you are subject to the alternative minimum tax, you will have to pay taxes on a SONYMA. For residents of New York State, these bonds are also exempt from state and local taxes. In mid-1992, a SONYMA maturing in 2017 was yielding 7.35%.

Many other state housing agencies issue similar mortgage revenue bonds. Check to see whether your state offers double- or triple-tax-exempt issues at an attractive price, selling at or below face value.

Then there is Sallie Mae. That is the nickname for the Student Loan Marketing Association, a government-chartered, publicly owned corporation that buys and otherwise finances education loans, primarily federally sponsored student loans. To bankroll these activities, the corporation issues debt securities. For steady income, you might consider buying Sallie Mae bonds. They are rated AAA by Standard & Poor's and Moody's and are exempt from state and local taxes. Minimum investments are as low as $1,000. You might prefer Sallie Mae stock, which is traded on the New York Stock Exchange. Sallie Mae shares were first issued in September 1983, at $20; in mid-1992 they were trading at the equivalent of more than $150 — in fact, $60 to $65, after a 2½-for-1 split in 1989.

MUTUAL FUNDS

How to Make Money in Them

JUST as there is no perfect person or painting or poem, so there is no perfect investment. But the one that comes closest for most people is the mutual fund. From 1981 to 1989, investment in mutual funds increased more than 400%. By mid-1992, more than $7 trillion was invested. The reason for this popularity is simple: What you get from a mutual fund, at relatively low cost, is professional management of your money. Your investments are handled by people who devote their full time and attention to them.

You also get diversification. A fund buys a wide variety of securities and then sells its own shares to the public. The price of a share rises or falls every day, along with the rises and falls of the total value of the securities the fund owns. And you can sell your shares back to the mutual fund at any time.

Funds offer you an increasingly broad range of investment choices to meet your specific objectives. You can buy anything from aggressive but risky funds that aim for maximum capital gains to more conservative funds that hold bonds or tax-exempt securities and aim to pay you high regular interest. Then there are money-market mutual funds, which give you an escape hatch once readily available only to the rich professional investors. If you think there is trouble ahead for stocks, you can switch out of the stock market and into the safe money market, just by making a phone call to the mutual-fund company. To have this flexibility, just be sure that the company you choose offers a variety of stock, money-market and other mutual funds.

But mutual funds as a group don't often keep pace with the broad market indexes. According to *Money* magazine, from 1969 to 1991 the unmanaged S&P 500 stock index handily outgained the average stock fund, rising 680% versus 551%. That means $10,000 invested in a portfolio that matched the S&P 500 would have grown to $78,000 by January 1, 1991, while the same amount in the average stock fund would have grown to $65,800. The expense of running a mutual fund accounts for the difference — or most of it. *Short-term* investments in mutual funds can be very risky, particularly in declining markets. Too many people learned that lesson in the crash of 1987, when many funds — though by no means all of them — plunged.

Once you invest in a fund, you may receive dividends every quarter and capital-gains distributions semi-annually, or annually if the fund has earned either. A fund earns and distributes capital gains if and when it sells securities at a profit. Almost all mutual funds offer to reinvest your earnings automatically in additional shares. You can also use mutual funds for your Individual Retirement Accounts and Keogh plans.

What kind of mutual fund should you choose and how should you choose it? The answers are explored in later chapters, but in sum the choice depends on your objectives and on how much time you are prepared to spend regularly studying the stock market. Perhaps you follow the financial news but you certainly do not want to reexamine and make changes in your investments as often as every week. What you need is a mutual fund that over the years consistently climbs at least as much as the stock-market averages during good times while not falling more than the averages in bad times. Quite possibly that will be one of the so-called growth funds, which invest in the stocks of expansive but well-established companies, or growth-and-income funds, which favor bonds and the stocks of large companies that yield big dividends. Pick with care because many of these funds have *not* done as well as the market averages. Those that have are usually managed by people whose records of success go back five or 10 years.

On the other hand, what if you are willing to pay really close attention to your investments and try for spectacular gains during bull markets? Then you are a candidate for so-called maximum-capital-gains funds. They are aggressive funds that search for the fast-moving stocks of small, potentially rapidly rising companies. But be ready to bail out of such a high flier quickly. Maximum-capital-gains funds tend to climb fast — and then tumble fast when the market starts to turn down.

You can specialize — and hedge your bets — by buying so-called sector funds, which concentrate on specific areas of the economy. Let us say you are essentially optimistic about stocks but also a bit wary about a possible resurgence of inflation. In that case, you can invest part of your assets in a technology-stock fund, which buys into promising though risky technology companies. But simultaneously you would keep another part of your money in a natural-resources fund that buys into mining, forest-products and energy companies, which offer more stability.

A major decision is whether to buy a fund from a stockbroker or a financial planner — or directly from one of the mutual-fund companies. The broker or planner will charge you a load, or commission, usually 2% to 8½%, which is the legal limit. In some cases, instead of the initial load, there is an annual fee of up to 2%, which pays for the costs of attracting new shareholders. In addition, stock funds charge an average of 1.3%, taxable bond funds 1.02%, and municipal funds 0.78% to cover their expenses. Instead of a load or commission up front, some funds charge an exit commission as well. There are two kinds of back-end loads, one for early withdrawal and one simply for redemption no matter what the timing. Whatever the load is, it will be explicitly laid out in your prospectus. What's more, the fees on new shares will decline as your assets grow. An 8½% load on $1,000 might become 4½% on $50,000 and 3½% on $100,000.

Many investors were initially lured to mutual funds because the high returns justified the fees. In 1980, according to Morningstar, Inc., a Chicago mutual-fund rating service, annual expenses for growth stock funds averaged 1.16%. By mid-1992 they had risen to 1.40%. Asset growth over that period should have lowered costs, but a surge in promotional expenses pushed the fees up.

If you feel you need investment counsel, it makes sense to buy a load fund. But if you do not need hand-holding, you might as well buy a so-called no-load fund directly from a fund company and save the commission. For a directory of 550 no-load funds, send $5 to the Mutual Fund Education Alliance, 1900 Erie Street, Suite 120, Kansas City, Missouri 64116.

Even with the commission taken into account, the strong long-term performers tend to be split fairly evenly between load and no-load funds. However, if you want to put your money in a mutual fund for only a short time — three years or less — you should go with a no-load fund. A load fund always has to earn a higher total return to perform as well as a no-load. And three years is seldom long enough for a load fund to do that.

Some previously no-load funds are charging fees of 1% to 3% when you buy, and others impose exit fees. More than 1,000 funds are using yet another method: under what is called the 12b-1 plan, fund managers take money directly from shareholders' assets to pay for advertising, marketing and distribution. Funds charge anywhere from $\frac{1}{100}$ of 1% to 1.25%. To discover if you are paying a 12b-1 levy, look in your fund's prospectus for the table that itemizes all expenses in a standard format and shows the hypothetical total costs over at least one and three years.

Management companies sometimes pay the fees themselves for brief periods, temporarily increasing returns to lure new money. A few funds, such as Dreyfus U.S. Government (10.4% average annual compounded return over the past three years), have high gains in part because they boast zero expenses. But be forewarned that the deal may not last forever. Footnotes in the fund's prospectus should tell you the amount likely to be tacked on once the promotion ends.

Whether you choose load or no-load, market professionals advise that you not necessarily buy the hottest fund of the moment. As mentioned earlier, the funds that do spectacularly well when the market is rising often do spectacularly badly when it begins to fall. In short, this year's heroes can easily turn into next year's bums.

So it is wise to look for funds that have been consistently profitable over the years, those that have outperformed the broad stock indexes in both up and down market cycles. This provides the best test of fund managers' ability to handle money over the long term. To compare the performances of mutual funds consult listings that appear annually in business magazines and *U.S. News & World Report.*

Funds that replicate the S&P 500 portfolio outperform most human managers. One such fund is the Vanguard Group's Index Trust 500 Portfolio. Both the Vanguard Fund and the S&P index have beaten the human managers for years.

Nine Top Long-Term Performers

MONEY magazine has identified nine funds among the roughly 1,200 stock mutual funds trading today that have made money for their investors in every calendar year from 1978 to 1991. They remained winners in the difficult first quarter of 1992. One way to make money in the stock market is never to lose it. These nine funds certainly accomplished that. What's more, the top five placed in the upper 25% of all equity funds in the ten-, five- and three-year periods to April 1, 1992. Here they are, in order of their records for the full 14 years, not counting the deductions for sales loads.

Phoenix Growth (800-243-4361; maximum load, 4.75%). This classic growth fund seeks out stocks with faster-than-average profit increases. Since 1978 it has served up a spectacular 20.2% average annual rate of return.

Merrill Lynch Capital Class A (800-225-1576; load, 6.5%). Outperforming the average growth and income entry, this fund has made money at an average annual rate of 16.9%.

Investment Company of America (800-421-0180; load, 5.75%). With its own unique management system, this 123-stock fund is maintained by 10 different managers. Guided by its emphasis on bargain-priced blue chips, it produced an average annual return of 16.6%.

John Hancock Sovereign (800-225-5291; load, 5%). This $375 million fund limits itself to picking up companies that have increased dividends every year for the previous 10 years. Average annual return: 15.6%.

CGM Mutual (800-345-4048; no-load). The biggest gainer in diversified stock funds since 1978, CGM has returned an average of 15% a year. In mid-1992 it cut its stock market risk by moving 40% of portfolio into long-term Treasuries.

Nationwide Fund (800-848-0920; load, 7.5%). The $675 million growth and income fund outgained the average entry in its category over the ten- and five-year stretches, 17.1% to 14.9% and 10.6% to 8.3%, respectively. Since 1978 it had an average annual return of 13.8%.

Eaton Vance Investors (800-225-6265; load, 4.75%). With $207 million in assets, this balanced fund gained an average of 13.2% a year. In mid-1992, the 31-stock portfolio had 51% in equities, 8% in cash and 41% in intermediate-term bonds.

Pax World (800-767-1729; no-load). This socially responsible fund shuns the weapons, liquor and tobacco industries. It has not had a losing year since 1974. Since 1978 it has had a compounded annual return of 13%.

Mutual of Omaha Income (800-228-9596; load, 4.75%). Even though this fund has been the slowest grower of the nine, with an average annual return of 10.6%, the editors of *Money* consider Mutual of Omaha to be the most likely of the nine funds to extend its streak of positive yearly returns.

Choosing the Best Ones for You

B EFORE you invest in a mutual fund, write or phone the fund company for its prospectus and its latest financial report. You can find the addresses and phone numbers of most widely available funds in advertisements in financial magazines or the business pages of newspapers.

Read the latest report to learn how much the fund has gained — or lost — not only over the past year but also over the past five or 10 years, and how well it has held up over periods of major market downturns. The report also lists the securities the fund holds.

Meanwhile, the prospectus should clearly define the fund's investment objectives. Make sure you are comfortable with them. Look also for the section that says whether the fund's managers are allowed to shift out of stocks and into, say, U.S. Treasury bills or certificates of deposit as market conditions change. This flexibility to switch into fixed-income investments gives you added protection against losses when stocks turn down. The prospectus will also tell you whether the fund carries a load, up to 8½%, or is a no-load. Some funds also charge fees of 1% to 5% when you sell your shares; be sure to check in advance whether the fund you are considering levies such redemption fees.

You typically buy a no-load fund directly from a mutual-fund company and a load fund from a broker or financial planner. In return for the commission, the broker or planner should be able to give you investment advice and tell you the fund's objectives, what it invests in and how it has performed in both up and down markets. If he or she does not know or refers you to the prospectus instead, find another salesperson. Better yet, particularly if you do not need ongoing advice from a broker or planner, buy a no-load fund and save the commission.

A load fund's strong performance over time can make up for the commission. But there is no evidence that load funds as a group outperform no-loads. Above all, remember this: A far more important consideration than the size of the commission, if any, is how well the fund has performed compared with others.

Be aware that funds on a roll are sometimes swamped with new shareholders and more money than they can wisely invest. Make sure you note the size of a fund's total assets. Generally, smaller funds are nimbler than their larger brethren. That is because funds managing less than $100 million of capital are better able to invest a significant portion of their assets in a promising company with a slim amount of outstanding stock. The larger a fund, the more difficulty it has buying a lot of those thinly traded stocks of small companies. If the fund's total assets have risen to $500 million or more over the past several years, chances are it will move away from emerging growth companies. Many mutual-fund firms manage a "family" of funds. They let you switch your money from one fund to another, usually just by making a telephone call. This convenience can be important if you buy into a fund that invests aggressively for maximum capital gains. When the fund is rocked by a declining market, you can quickly switch to a steadier income-oriented fund.

Whichever types of funds you choose, you should consider following a strategy called dollar-cost averaging. You just put an equal amount of money into the same fund at regular intervals. That way, you buy most of your shares when stock prices are down, and you avoid the temptation to invest heavily near a market peak.

The choices you make among funds will depend on your financial and family situations. You need to ask yourself what your financial commitments will be in the future for college costs, retirement or other necessities. Can you afford to take some risks now, or is preserving your money supremely important to you?

Once you have answered such questions, look for a package of different mutual funds that suits your needs. Many strategists recommend putting 20% to 40% of your investment money into corporate or tax-exempt bond funds. That's because bonds, despite their ups and downs, perform in a less volatile manner over time than stocks do, and they do better than stocks during recessions. It's also a comfort to know that temporary losses in bonds' market value show up only on paper, while the income that bonds pay continues to flow to the people who must depend on it.

Among the top-rated corporate bond funds for the year ending June 1, 1992, were Merrill Lynch Corporate–High Income A (27.6% gain), Vanguard Fixed Income–Inv. Grade Corp. (15.8%) and FPA New Income (13.8%).

Depending on your tax bracket, municipal bond funds may be the right choice for investments that are made outside of retirement accounts and are therefore exposed to current taxes. Muni funds' dividends are usually exempt from federal taxes. For a list of the top-performing high-yield tax-exempt funds for the year ending April 1, 1992, see "Your Investments/Mutual Funds: Tax-exempt Bond Mutual Funds."

You also have to decide how much money to put into the different types of funds. If you are young and confident and have few obligations or dependents, you might want to emphasize aggressive funds that aim for maximum capital gains. But if you are saving for college bills or an approaching retirement, you probably would be more comfortable with so-called growth funds, which are less volatile, or still more conservative growth-and-income funds.

Always remember that you will make the wisest selections if you consider such changing personal factors as your family situation and your financial responsibilities. Take a fairly young couple, earning comfortable salaries from their two jobs. They would be smart to aim for long-term growth of capital. To get it, they might put one-third of their mutual-fund assets into aggressive-growth or long-term-growth funds. Another third would go into a growth-and-income fund, and the last third into a bond fund.

A couple with two or more teenage children would take a different approach. College costs probably would be on their minds. So such a couple would want to start moving that tuition money from stock or bond funds into a money-market fund, where they could withdraw it swiftly and without fear that their shares had lost value. Our mid-life couple would also be concerned about building a nest egg for retirement. Thus, they probably would want to put half of their remaining money into growth and growth-and-income funds, a third or more into bond funds and perhaps 5% in a gold fund as a hedge against inflation.

Older couples intent on preserving whatever wealth they have built for their upcoming retirement might put 20% of their fund assets into growth funds with strong records in weak stock markets. Another 35% might go into growth-and-income funds, and still another 35% would be put into bond funds, including one that invests in tax-exempt bonds. The remaining 10% should go into a money-market fund.

Managing a Team of Funds

A SUPERB way to invest in mutual funds is to buy the shares of not just one but several different funds. This increases your chances of scoring consistent gains. For example, over the three years to 1992, you would have done well if you had put money into international funds, growth-and-income funds and capital-appreciation funds. Those that specialize in foreign-owned companies showed impressive gains while the dollar was decreasing in value relative to foreign currencies. Later these funds tumbled, due in part to the strengthening of the dollar. But growth-and-income funds have remained sound even though investors lost faith in them after the 1987 crash. Capital-appreciation funds have tracked the continuing strong economy.

You can get even greater diversification by investing in other kinds of funds that specialize in single industries or specific geographical regions. But because these so-called sector funds concentrate on one economic area, you should limit your investing in any one of them to about 10% of your assets. That way you will not be hurt too badly if that sector turns down.

It is often wise to put money in several mutual funds whose managers excel in different investment specialties. You would want a champion at picking growth companies, for instance, and another who has proved to be outstanding at identifying undervalued companies. You would want a specialist in finding large corporations and a wizard at spotting small companies. Your job, says Thomas Ebright, co-manager of Pennsylvania Mutual Fund (average annual return over ten years ending May 31, 1992: 18.16%), is like that of a baseball team's manager. You find the best player for every position — the one with the best long-term record of success — and let them all do their best for you.

Money magazine's July 1992 list of superior funds — all of which were among the best in their investment style — lines up like this:

— *Growth stock funds:* Janus Twenty, AIM Weingarten, Nicholas II, SoGen International.

— *Total return:* Financial Industrial Income, United Income, Investment Co. of America, Phoenix Balanced Series.

— *Overseas:* Ivy International, T. Rowe Price International Stock.

The Specialty Funds

PERHAPS you think a certain sector of the economy is about to surge, and you want to cash in on its rise. Then you might want to consider buying into a specialty mutual fund that invests in that part of the economy.

About 400 funds buy stocks in particular economic sectors. They may concentrate investors' money in specific industries, such as health services, high technology or banking. Or they may focus on individual commodities, such as gold or oil and gas. They may buy foreign stocks or shares of companies operating in a particular region of the U.S. or the world.

Some mutual-fund companies, such as Fidelity, Vanguard and Financial Programs, Inc., have funds that offer investors the choice of several sectors. Fidelity's Select portfolio, for instance, contained separate mini-funds for 36 different sectors in mid-1991. An investor can switch money around among the sectors simply by phoning the company and requesting the change. Other companies may offer only one sector, but almost all will give the investor a choice of switching out of it and into a money-market fund. That way, whenever you sense danger in the sector, you can immediately move your investment to a safe money fund.

Unlike regular mutual funds, specialty funds are not for beginners. Since they concentrate on a single type of stock, they can be highly volatile and risky. Some specialty funds tend to be quite stable, but the prices of others move up — and down — much more sharply than the market as a whole.

Gold and precious metals funds, for example, are mercurial. During 1980, when inflation was in double digits, they rose faster than all other mutual funds, soaring as much as 64%. Later, when gold prices fell, they plunged. But they rose again, and were the biggest gainers among funds in 1987. According to Wiesenberger Investment Companies Service, these funds climbed 75.3% during the first nine months of 1987, and ended the year with a gain of 37.4% despite the crash. In 1988 they fell 16.8%, while in 1989 they rose 28.9%. In fact, two of the top five mutual funds in 1989 were gold funds. They were the United Services U.S. Gold Shares Fund, with a total return of 64.73% for the year, and the Strategic Investment Fund, with a total return of 61.21% for the year. But in 1991 gold funds plummeted again. Talk about a roller coaster!

If you think inflation will get out of hand once more, and are willing to take big risks for the possibility of big gains, you might put some money into gold funds. On the other hand, if you believe that inflation will not run away and the economy and the stock market will do well for the next few years, now may be the time to invest in mutual funds that aim for aggressive growth.

While these aggressive growth funds are not specialty funds, they do concentrate their investments in a particularly incendiary area: small companies that have large potential. Such firms tend to be involved in high-tech, biotech, health care and other services. Like the companies they invest in, the funds usually jump, and tumble, faster than the market itself. In 1992, two aggressive growth funds that bought into small companies were Montgomery Small Cap, with a twelve-month gain of 42.5%, and Massachusetts Financial Lifetime–Emerging Growth, with a gain of 42.3%. But even the most optimistic analysts stress that you must be prepared to move out of highly speculative aggressive-growth funds at the first sniff of decline.

Tax-exempt Bond Mutual Funds

FOR a sound investment on which you will not have to pay federal income taxes, consider buying shares of a tax-exempt bond mutual fund. Caution: You will have to pay state income taxes on at least a portion of the interest you earn, unless the fund invests only in bonds issued by state or municipal agencies in the state where you live. You will not have to pay any sales commission if you purchase shares in a no-load bond fund directly from a mutual-fund company. But all the sponsors charge fees, which range from 0.29% to 2.08% a year and average 0.85%.

Managers of these funds invest in a large variety of tax-free municipal bonds, and this diversification will help protect you against loss. The managers watch their holdings closely, aiming to unload any bonds that may be going sour. And they can make gains through trading. The risk, as with all bonds, is that your shares will lose market value when interest rates surge.

The top high-yield tax-exempt bond funds, ranked by one-year return for the period ending April 1, 1992, were Putnam Tax-Free–High Income (12.1% gain), Vanguard Muni–High Yield (11.9%) and Fidelity Advisor High Income Muni (11.8%).

"Humanistic" Funds

IF YOU are concerned about social issues such as the spread of armaments or pollution, should you apply your ethical standards to your investments? That's your decision, of course. Many people think that trying to do good with your investments will keep you from doing well. But in fact, you *can* profit both financially *and* spiritually. Self-professed "socially responsible" investment managers were in charge of $625 billion in stocks, bonds and mutual funds last year, up from only $100 billion in 1985. Over the past 10 years, some of the mutual funds that are guided by their own ethical criteria have performed better than stocks in general. Other such funds have not done as well, so you have to be particularly selective.

Naturally, picking investments to match your ethics limits your choice. If you want to avoid arms makers, as well as alcohol, tobacco and gambling enterprises, you will not be able to invest in 60% to 70% of the stocks listed on the New York Exchange. You can achieve reasonable results, but you may not get the highest return possible.

Then too, choosing stocks to meet your standards can be troublesome. Consider the question of South Africa, in which drawing lines between specific companies may be difficult. For example, a corporation that has closed its operations in South Africa may still do business there through a middleman. And a company that has chosen to continue in South Africa may well be providing jobs and opportunities for blacks.

The first question to ask yourself is what you really hope to achieve. If you want to influence corporate or government policy, you may be disappointed. Chances are your investments just will not be big enough. You would probably be better off investing for maximum returns and donating some money to an action group. But if your goal is to keep a clear conscience, social investing can work for you.

If you want advice, an organization called the Social Investment Forum (430 First Avenue North, Suite 290, Minneapolis, Minnesota 55401; 612-333-8338) will send you a list of brokers who use social criteria. The Forum estimates that there are 25 mutual funds dedicated to making only investments that they deem to be socially responsible.

For example, the Dreyfus Third Century Fund (800-645-6561) avoids corporations that have operations in South Africa and favors companies that endorse environmental protection, occupational health and safety, purity of consumer products and equal employment opportunity. Dreyfus Third Century rose 6.43% in the twelve months to mid-May 1992.

Both the Calvert Ariel Appreciation Fund and the Calvert Ariel Growth Fund (800-368-2748) keep their money away not only from companies that do business in South Africa but also from those involved in nuclear power or weapons systems. For the year to May 31, 1992, these funds rose 1.88% and 2.85%, respectively.

If you are concerned about energy development, you might want to try the New Alternatives Fund (516-466-0808). It searches for firms that conserve and produce alternative sources of energy, excluding nuclear power, and it will not invest in arms makers, companies doing business with South Africa or companies with poor environmental records. The fund gained 3.27% for the year to May 31, 1992.

The Pax World Fund (603-431-8022) also avoids arms makers, companies with gambling, alcohol or tobacco interests and those that it believes discriminate against minorities and women. It was the first fund to adopt social criteria. A so-called balanced fund, Pax World holds its money in about 67% stocks and 33% bonds. Its annual return over the past ten years averaged 15.17%.

The Parnassus Fund (415-362-3505) is both a socially conscious and a contrarian fund. It invests in out-of-favor companies that its managers think make quality products, treat their employees well and are community-minded. It rose 16% for the year to May 31, 1992.

A money-market fund that applies very strict rules is the Working Assets Money Fund (415-989-3200). It avoids companies doing business in South Africa and shuns U.S. Treasury securities as part of its antiweapons policy. The fund also searches for firms that have waste-reduction and recycling programs, do not violate Environmental Protection Agency regulations or show a pattern of discrimination and have a record of good labor relations. Its yield for 1991 was 5.47%.

To find out about more such funds, you may wish to subscribe to *Investing for a Better World* (monthly; $19.95 a year; 617-423-6655).

Environmental Funds

THE 1990s have been called the Green Decade, and that is only tangentially a reference to the color of money. Our earth has become the focus of soaring public concern that is bound to increase as the nation heads toward the next millennium. This concern has already been translated into policy and law, and corporations, too, have jumped on the bandwagon, if only to avoid being overrun by it. Analysts project annual spending on clean-up products and services to double by 1995, to $200 billion. From this sky-high vantage point, environmental cleanup looks like a growth industry of the 1990s.

Several major mutual-fund companies have already caught on to the environmental-services industry and its prospects for long-term growth. Fidelity was the first to devise a sector fund that invests in waste-management, toxic-waste-disposal and pollution-control firms. From its start on June 29, 1989, until May 31, 1992, Fidelity Select Environmental Services (800-544-6666) earned 15.37% (no-load) for its investors, while Standard & Poor's 500 stock index rose 30.61%. Three other funds begun since 1989 are Alliance Global Environmental Fund (800-247-4154), Freedom Environmental Fund (800-225-6258) and Oppenheimer Global Environmental Fund (800-525-7048). Kemper's Environmental Services Fund (800-621-1048) has been around since 1990.

Another, smaller group of mutual funds avoids waste-management and -disposal companies, citing their waste-disposal and water-pollution violations and voicing concern over toxic-ash disposal. The monthly newsletter *Investing for a Better World* recommends three of these funds:

The New Alternatives Fund (see "Your Investments: Mutual Funds/'Humanistic' Funds"), known as the greenest of the green, is the oldest social mutual fund (started in 1982) devoted exclusively to investing in companies with positive records in environmental protection and energy conservation. Over the past three years (May 1989–May 1992), New Alternatives produced a total return of 23.5%.

The Progressive Environmental Fund (800-826-8154), launched in February 1990, also has tight environmental screens and will donate a portion of its marketing fees to environmental groups. Alas, its total return from inception through May 31, 1992, was a negative .8%.

The Eco-Logical Trust was created by Merrill Lynch with help from Progressive Asset Management, an Oakland-based brokerage firm for socially responsible investing. It is unlike mutual funds in that its 29 securities are not actively managed and the trust itself will be dissolved in April 1995, after donating a portion of its profits to the Environmental Federation of America. The trust avoids investment in environmentally controversial businesses such as waste-to-energy. For information call your broker or Progressive Asset Management (510-834-3722).

Switching Among the Funds

SINCE today's fast-rising mutual fund can easily turn into tomorrow's loser, one way to make money in funds is to be a fair-weather friend. You get out of the losers and into the winners by switching from fund to fund in an ongoing effort to be in the groups or sectors offering the best returns. Reading widely in the business press may help you to anticipate big up and down swings in the stock market. When the market is advancing rapidly, you invest in the speculative funds. Then at the merest flutter of danger, you can switch to the safety of a more secure conservative fund or a money-market fund. Investors also quite often have the option of moving to tax-free municipal bond funds or corporate bond funds within a group managed by the same fund company.

But you need to know when to switch and more specifically which fund to switch to. For this reason it probably pays to subscribe to a monthly newsletter advisory service that tracks the performance of the various funds and may recommend the best buys or timely sells. Among those newsletters are *United Mutual Fund Selector* (101 Prescott Street, Wellesley Hills, Massachusetts 02181; $125 a year); *Growth Fund Guide* (P.O. Box 6600, Rapid City, South Dakota 57709; $89 a year); *NoLOAD FUND∗X* (235 Montgomery Street, San Francisco, California 94104; $114 a year); *Mutual Fund Strategist* (P.O. Box 446, Burlington, Vermont 05402; $149 a year) and *NoLOAD FUND∗ Investor* (P.O. Box 283, Hastings-on-Hudson, New York 10706; $105 a year).

The letters rank the mutual funds according to how much the prices of their shares rise or fall in value over a period of time: one-month, three-month, six-month or one-year periods. One strategy of switching is to (1) buy into the mutual fund that is on top of the rankings for performance over the past year, and (2) keep your money in that fund as long as the advisory service tells you it is among the top five in its category for the past year. The categories that the funds are divided into are growth and equity-income.

When your newsletter arrives — usually a week to 10 days after the end of the month — a quick glance will tell you if the fund you are invested in is still on top. If it is not, you replace it with the new number one. But since this strategy calls for frequent switching, confine it to no-load or low-load funds.

You must be willing to go to the trouble of closing your account with one mutual-fund company and opening a new account with another company that offers the currently best-performing fund in its category. According to one study, if you had followed a *NoLOAD FUND*X* switching strategy with "class 3" high-quality growth funds between early 1989 and mid-1990, you could have gained 31.3%. But if you had chosen this strategy with the newsletter's riskier funds, you would not have done as well as with Standard & Poor's 500 stock index.

Leapfrogging from fund to fund in search of the best return does require a bit of work. The first step is to call the toll-free 800 number of the new fund you want to invest in. You can get these numbers from mutual-fund newsletters or mutual-fund companies' ads or merely by dialing toll-free information at 800-555-1212.

When you reach the mutual-fund company, ask for shareholder services. Tell the person with whom you speak that you want to open an account and then request an account number for yourself.

Next, write to the head of the shareholder services at your old fund, that is, the one you are currently invested in. Your letter should say, "Please sell all full and fractional shares in the account of . . ." and then give your name and your old account number. Ask that the redemption check be made payable to, and sent to, the new fund you are moving to. And be sure to request that the words "for the benefit of" appear on the check, followed by your name and your new account number.

Probably it will take one to two weeks for your money to arrive at your new mutual fund. You can short-circuit this process if you have a money-market account with the mutual fund that you are leaving. Tell that fund to switch all your assets to your money-market account. Then write a check for the full amount you have in the account and mail it to your new mutual fund.

Fortunately, there is one way to skip that paperwork. All you have to do is open an account at any office of Charles Schwab & Co., the San Francisco-based discount broker. Then, by making a single toll-free phone call to Schwab, you can switch in and out of over 500 no-load mutual funds. Schwab will charge a fee based on the size of your order — for example, $36 on a $1,000 swap and $74 on a $10,000 swap. So this will cost you more than if you shift assets on your own.

Borrowing Against Your Mutual Funds

THE Securities and Exchange Commission not long ago repealed a long-standing ban on using mutual-fund shares as collateral when you borrow money from a stockbroker. That means you now can use your mutual funds to get a personal loan from your broker or to buy securities on margin.

Should you take advantage of this opportunity? Probably not — if you are a conservative investor who likes to buy steady and sound securities and just put them away in a safe-deposit box without trading them. But if you have a high tolerance for risk, margin buying can increase your potential rewards.

Federal rules limit borrowing against securities and funds. To borrow $4,000 to buy *stocks*, you would need to pledge fund shares worth at least $4,000. However, to borrow $4,000 as a *personal loan,* you would also have to put up $8,000 in such shares. Either way, you would pay a variable interest rate, usually one-half to two and a half percentage points above so-called broker loan rates. As with broker loans, the interest rate decreases as your account balance increases. You do not have to make regular payments on the interest or the principal. You can repay whenever you want, just as long as the market value of the fund shares you pledge as collateral remains above a certain percentage of the loan amount. Usually it's 30% or 35%.

As a margin buyer you will be at greatest risk when interest rates are rising. That means you will have to pay higher rates on your loan. Also, the value of securities tends to fall at such times, so you may get a margin call from your broker and thus have to put up additional collateral. The good news is that mutual funds are less volatile than many stocks and bonds. When markets turn down, fund shares are not likely to drop dramatically in price and trigger a margin call.

BROKERS

How to Choose One

B ACK in the bullish periods of the 1980s, it almost did not matter whether your stockbroker was a genius, a guru or simply somebody's smiling son-in-law. The momentum of the market was so strong that you were fairly well assured of making money.

That's no longer true in today's volatile market. So, choosing a brokerage firm for the first time, or switching to a new one, becomes a key decision. It isn't easy, particularly for small investors. Some firms don't want to bother with accounts of less than $15,000. Not many will turn you down flat, but your account is likely to get serious attention only if it can generate sizable commissions.

If you are a small investor, you will find that big, national brokerage houses generally are more hospitable than lesser outfits. These large companies stand to make a bit of profit from the sheer volume of their small accounts. Look for the major firms that offer special services, such as cut-rate commissions.

But if you want to concentrate on investing in companies located in your own area, you might do better with well-established regional brokerages. Their traditional strength has been in spotting small local companies that have gone on to become great winners. True, they also have a disadvantage: they often are less familiar with companies located far away, and with complex stock strategies, than are the larger national houses.

If you follow the market very closely yourself and feel you do not need regular, professional advice, then consider using discount brokers. They generally offer no frills and no hand-holding, but they often charge commissions of less than 1%.

Once you have picked the brokerage house that you like, how do you select the salesperson in that firm just right for you? Choosing the right broker is not quite as important as selecting the right spouse or the best boss, but since the broker will do much to determine whether you are affluent or financially uncomfortable in the future, it is a decision to be taken seriously.

The first thing to do is to solicit recommendations. Ask friends who are themselves successful investors. Ask accountants and tax preparers. They have inside knowledge of how well their clients are doing in the market, and legally and ethically they can tell you who some of the winning brokers are.

If referrals don't produce enough candidates, write letters to the branch managers of some brokerage firms listed in your local Yellow Pages. Set forth your financial situation and investment goals. When replies come in, interview not just one but several brokers. Ask each one: How long has he or she been a broker? Where does he get his information? In what areas have his greatest successes been? What does he think is his biggest weakness? At the time he suggests buying a stock, does he also prudently recommend a price at which you should sell out in the future?

You are generally better off with a veteran, well-experienced broker — one who has been through a few market reverses, who knows that stocks can go down as well as up — than with an eager newcomer who will learn his lessons with your money.

Instead of looking for a broker who will tell you what to do, search for one who can use his or her knowledge and experience to help you make *your own* decisions. Read financial publications and perhaps subscribe to an investment advisory service. Get various research reports from your brokerage house. Use them to learn the factors that professional analysts employ to evaluate stock.

Before doing business with a broker, don't be shy about asking him or her for the names of people whose accounts he or she handles. Then call up two or three of them. You might uncover some unexpected blemishes, such as a tendency to overtrade. Too much trading may produce high commissions for your broker but very small returns for you.

Be sure to evaluate your market performance coldly after you have been with the broker for six months. And then do it yearly. Compare your gains and losses with the Standard & Poor's index of 500 stocks. If your portfolio's performance, before commissions, falls below the Standard & Poor's, don't hesitate to take your money and run — to another broker.

Several firms, including Merrill Lynch and Shearson Lehman Brothers, offer "wrap" accounts. Instead of charging a commission each time a trade is made, the broker charges a flat annual fee of 3%, which is shared by the broker and an independent money manager who handles the account. Brokers justify the high commission by noting that in-house analyst research is part of the package, and that they spend a lot of time monitoring the account — in short, they are engaged in customized money management.

Be Careful of Securities Analysts

I F YOU are like many investors, you buy stocks because your broker recommends them. But did you know that most brokers get their tips from someone called a securities analyst? How reliable is his or her research?

Securities analysts are highly paid investment sleuths who work for brokerage houses, banks and other financial institutions. They spend their time finding stocks that they think will make a profit. But many analysts are too often bullish on the wrong stocks. Michael O'Higgins, president of his own investment counseling firm in Albany, New York, and author of the book *Beating the Dow*, compared the records of professional analysts. He checked their forecasts from 1973 to 1989 on the 30 stocks that make up the Dow Jones industrial average. O'Higgins found that you would have earned almost three times as much money investing in the 10 firms that analysts predicted would have only slow earnings growth as you would if you had taken their recommendations of the 10 that they expected to have faster earnings increases.

Analysts often fall in love with their stocks, just as novice investors do. And they occasionally fear that gloomy forecasts will alienate the managements of the companies they follow. Sometimes an analyst is under pressure to give a company a good report because the analyst's parent firm is acting as the well-paid underwriter for that company's new stock issues. Therefore, it is smart to ask any broker who recommends a stock to you if his firm has an investment banking relationship with the company he is pushing. If it has, you should be extra careful.

Analysts also tend to pass news along first to big, institutional customers and then to the retail brokers who do business with smaller investors. This puts you at the rear of the information line and, in many cases, that is too far back to take any profitable action on the tip. In general, it is wise to patronize brokerage houses that freely publish their analysts' recommendations and keep track of the resulting profits or losses in those stocks.

The Discounters

YOU can save as much as 90% on commissions by dealing with a discount broker. But you pay some penalties for these price cuts. So, should you use a discount broker?

If you do, you will have plenty of choice. There are more than 100 independent discount brokerage firms plus perhaps 3,000 discount offices associated with banks. You can find discounters through ads in newspapers and financial magazines, and you can reach them over toll-free phone lines.

The appeal of discount brokers goes well beyond thrift. More and more of them offer special customer services, and a few even supply that most touted of full-commission services — stock-market research. But don't be misled by the assumption that all discount brokers are alike. Indeed, Mercer Inc., a company that follows the discount brokerage industry, points out that there is a surprising range in commission prices among the discount firms. In a trade involving 500 shares at $10 a share, for example, the average discounter would charge $65 but the most expensive discount rate would be $100, possibly more. The fee nevertheless falls short of the $160 commission an average full commission brokerage would charge.

Whether or not you decide to use a discount broker should depend on your investment behavior. If you are fairly new at investing and don't know your way around Wall Street, a traditional broker is the right choice for you. He or she will advise you what to buy, what to sell and when to buy or sell it. Just one winning stock recommendation from a full-service broker's research staff could more than make up for his higher commission. If you want cut-rate commissions but feel hesitant to end your relationship with a full-service broker, try asking for a discount. Your broker probably can offer as much as

30% off the typical full fee on any substantial transaction. According to Lipper Analytical Services, three-quarters of the $6 billion in annual retail sales continue to be handled by full-service firms.

On the other hand, you might do well to move to a discount broker if you feel confident enough to make your own stock-market decisions. In choosing the discounter, it is paramount to select a company that can weather precipitous ups and downs in the stock market. If a firm has at least eight years of service, then it already has survived two market downturns, and you are probably safe.

Your chief consideration may well be commission rates. Generally they vary with the kind of trading you do.

So-called value brokers charge rates that are a percentage of the dollar value of each transaction. This usually works out best for you if you deal in low-priced stocks.

Then there are the so-called share brokers. They offer bigger discounts when you trade large numbers of shares. Share brokers work to your advantage if you buy or sell 500 shares or more and if you deal in high-priced stocks.

To cite a couple of examples of the wide variances in commissions charged by discounters:

If you wanted to buy 100 shares of a $10 stock, Marquette de Bary in New York City would charge you $25. But Whitehall Securities in New York City would charge $50. That's about the same as a full-commission broker.

If you wanted to buy 500 shares of a $50 stock, Whitehall's commission of $62.50 would be less than half the fee charged by Marquette. And a full-service broker might charge about $400.

The major discount brokers are licensed to do business in most states and have nationwide toll-free numbers that you can find in newspapers and financial publications. All have Securities Investor Protection Corporation insurance of $500,000 per client and usually additional commercial insurance. They are subject to the same regulations as are traditional brokers. In sum, discounters are safe.

Many offer specialized services that set them apart. For example, Charles Schwab & Co. insures the value of its securities up to $2.5 million. And when you phone in an order to buy or sell, Schwab will execute it immediately. Before you hang up, you will learn the price you paid or received. That is information you normally don't get as fast from regular brokers.

When picking a discounter, choose on the basis of not only the size of the commissions but also the scope of the services. You should be free to trade more than just stocks, or to buy stocks on margin — that is, to borrow up to 50% of the cost from your broker. You also should expect a discounter, like a full-service broker, to pay you interest on cash in your account and to give you stock quotes during market hours.

In the past, discounters have provided impersonal service. Now they increasingly offer you the choice of dealing with one representative or a team of them. Many discounters will take custody of your Individual Retirement Account or Keogh plan. And a few offer the combination of credit-card service, margin trading and free checking available in a full-fledged asset management account. So read the financial press closely to see the various deals and extras being dangled by discounters, and shop around.

While national firms like Schwab and Fidelity Brokerage Services will charge you less than half the rate of a full-service shop, you could save even more — up to half again as much — at several dozen smaller firms around the country. Known as deep discounters, they are able to offer such low rates because they have found ways to cut costs even more than the well-known discounters. They spend far less on advertising and marketing and they offer fewer services, unlike the "premium" discounters that provide customers with checking accounts, a variety of funds and 24-hour availability. Some such brokers include K. Aufhauser (800-368-3668), which charges $40.99 for 500 shares at $20 per share, and Pacific Brokerage Services (800-421-8395), which charges $45 for the same kind of transaction.

Using Your Bank as a Broker

C AN your banker also be your stockbroker? Well, he or she could not until the government began to allow such double duty a few years ago. Now some 3,000 bank holding companies and savings and loan associations have either bought or linked up with stockbrokers. Just about every large bank in the country has brokerage operations. And it's almost impossible to find a city where some bank doesn't sell stocks. So, the one-stop financial shop may be right down your block.

At a number of banks, the brokerage is nothing more than a

self-service computer terminal with a telephone. Sometimes it's a counter with a bank clerk to help you fill out applications and phone in orders. At others, it's a fully staffed mini-brokerage office, complete with trained broker.

Most banks sell stock through their own or an affiliated discount broker. So their commissions are usually lower than those at full-service brokers. But the banks' discounters often are 10% to 20% more expensive than independent discounters are. In a 1990 study by Mercer Inc., banks charged an average of $88 on a $9,000 trade, while discount brokers charged an average of $73 for the same trade. The reason is that only a handful of banks execute their own trades. The rest just take your order and must hire — and pay — another company to do the buying and selling of securities.

Still, banks are more likely than independent discounters to offer a wide range of so-called financial products. Bank-affiliated discounters often sell everything from bonds to gold bullion, while some independents confine themselves to stocks and stock options. On other counts, bank-affiliated brokerages score well too. They can execute trades almost as swiftly as any discounter — and perhaps get the money to you even faster.

But if you want detailed investment research or advice, your best bet is still a full-service broker. Most banks will give you only current stock quotes and basic investment information.

Regional Brokers

JUST about everyone is familiar with Merrill Lynch's thundering herd, and you may recall that when E. F. Hutton talked, you were likely to get the soup in your lap because your waiter was listening. But a growing number of investors are turning their ears to lesser-known regional brokerage houses. They can get you into the stocks of small local companies that are among the fastest growing in the country.

Regional firms often specialize in fairly small companies with strong managements. Some firms limit their bailiwick to a single city; others specialize in regions — for example, growth companies of the Midwest or Southwest. Analysts read the local papers, understand the local economy and continue to follow local companies even if they temporarily fall out of favor with investors.

These brokers tend to have strong and deep ties to their region. Many began as municipal bond houses handling underwritings for towns and small cities too insignificant to be noticed by national firms. Gradually, the regionals branched out into selling common stocks as well.

If you think the economic prospects are bright for companies in a specific part of the country, a long-distance call to a regional broker will get you a sampling of current research reports. If you like what you see, you can open an account, also by phone, and start receiving monthly market letters with regional economic forecasts and lists of recommended stocks.

Many regional brokerage houses have notable records of performance. In the East, for example, are Advest in Hartford, Connecticut, and Alex. Brown & Sons in Baltimore. In the South are J. C. Bradford in Nashville, Tennessee, and Robinson-Humphrey in Atlanta. In the Midwest are Cleveland's Prescott, Ball & Turben, and Milwaukee's Robert W. Baird & Co. In the West and Southwest, there are Rauscher Pierce Refsnes of Dallas, Boettcher & Co. of Denver, and Bateman Eichler, Hill Richards in Los Angeles.

To find other regional firms, one good source is a Standard & Poor's guide called *Security Dealers of North America*. It lists securities firms, their addresses and phone numbers, by city and state. The two-volume set for spring and fall costs $475, but it is available in most libraries.

When these firms venture out of their regions, it usually is to cover the competitors of local companies. Their analysts keep turning up small companies that have fast-expanding markets and earnings. Gradually the glitter of these little stars will attract attention by national firms. That is the regional analyst's dream: finding stocks, getting clients into them early, then waiting until a big national firm discovers them, recommends them — and sends the price up.

Questions to Ask Your Broker

S TOCKBROKERS are salespeople, and so they can sell hard. If you feel uncomfortable when a broker urges you to buy a stock, be sure to ask some pointed questions.

One of the first should be: How has that stock done lately? A more important question, particularly if you are a long-term investor who plans to buy and hold: What are the long-range earnings forecasts for the stock? If your broker doesn't have the answers immediately, tell him that's all right — that he can call you back when he gets them. Patience pays.

Did your broker or an analyst at his or her firm do the research on the stock? If it was an analyst, ask to see his or her report on the company. And find out how well other stocks that this analyst has recommended have done.

Is the stock undervalued? One sign that a stock could be a buy is that its price is near the bottom of its trading range of the past few months. But a stock could be cheap because the company faces serious problems. Ask what makes the stock such a bargain.

What is the company's profit margin? If it is above its industry average, the company is probably well run.

Why should you buy this stock *now*? Obviously you don't want to bother with a concern when its business cycle is about to turn down. Most industries have predictable cycles of earnings declines and recoveries. Ask when to expect the next longer-term upswing or downswing and when the stock price is likely to reflect that change.

What are the chances that, near-term, the stock will go down instead of up? Ask if the company faces strong competition, is involved in expensive litigation or is laden with debt. Heavy interest payments may cut into earnings. Get your broker to help you set a price at which you might be wise to sell and cut your losses. The price he names will help you gauge the risk he sees in the investment.

How does this stock fit in with your overall strategy? Make sure that your broker knows whether your investment objective is long-term growth or high-dividend income or a quick killing. Tell him or her how much risk you are willing to shoulder to achieve your aims.

If you are a buy-and-hold investor and your broker keeps suggesting ideas suited to frequent traders, then trade brokers.

Who are the large shareholders in this company? What you would like to hear is that some wealthy private investors have just bought a lot of the stock and are thinking of attempting a takeover. Or that the firm's management owns a sizable portion of the shares. Top managers who are also substantial stockholders have an added incentive to see that a firm does well.

Is this stock better than the one the same broker urged you to buy last week? Most brokers have several stocks to sell, so get yours to compare some of the other issues on his or her list with the ones he or she is flogging now.

Remember: If you invest in a stock and its price plummets, you will lose money but your broker will still pocket a commission. Unlike you, he or she is guaranteed to profit if you follow his or her advice.

And a final word: If you feel your broker has steered you in a ridiculously wrong direction, you can always take him or her to court. One Manhattan attorney, Lloyd Clareman, suggests that unhappy investors should learn to use the arbitration system as a means to recoup losses. According to the Hearings Department of the American Stock Exchange, investors who have gone before an arbitration panel of any of the exchanges — the panels consist of one securities representative and one or two public arbitrators — won awards on 68% of their claims in 1991.

How Safe Is Your Brokerage Account?

W HENEVER a stock brokerage firm fails, investors start wondering, "What happens if *my* broker goes broke?"

Despite the market collapse in 1987, only four brokerage firms went under. Six failed in 1989, and eight in each of the two following years. So it is very unlikely that your brokerage will go bust. But if it does, your stocks, bonds and money fund shares are protected by the Securities Investor Protection Corporation against losses up to $500,000. This government-chartered private corporation — nick-named "Sipic" — oversees liquidations of brokerages and restores securities to clients. To do this, SIPC has a fund of more than

$700 million, raised by assessing the brokerage firms. It also can tap a $1 billion line of credit at the U.S. Treasury and a $1 billion credit line with private banks.

Commodity futures contracts are not covered by SIPC, nor is cash left with a broker specifically to earn interest. Options are covered, but when a firm fails, they are closed out as of the date SIPC files for trusteeship in court.

One problem is that providing customers with access to their accounts usually takes from one to six months. In the meantime, customers cannot sell any securities in their accounts. Customers first receive any securities held in their own names. If their stocks or bonds are in the firm's name — that is, in "street name" — clients will be given a prorated share of any street-name securities that the firm can produce. SIPC then will make up the difference between what the clients got and what they are owed, up to the limit of the statute.

If you are worried about your broker's financial health, there are signs of trouble to watch for. Does it take a long time for your broker to execute your orders to buy and sell? Do confirmation slips fail to square with transactions? Are your monthly statements inaccurate? Problems like these suggest the firm could be having back-office snarls, and it might be time to move your account.

Even if you are confident of your broker's stability, you should take steps to protect yourself. Certainly, don't hold more than $500,000 worth of securities at any single brokerage house. If you are really skittish, you can hold securities in your name instead of the firm's name or even keep the certificates at home or in a safe-deposit box. In a liquidation, you will get the shares in your name back faster than shares in a street name. And you will have them back in no time if they never leave your possession.

Selling Without a Broker

D ID you know that you can sell stock that you own without using a broker? That way, you can save the money that you would normally spend for the sales commission. As mentioned earlier, you can also buy and sell Treasury bills without using a broker, although the actual transfer of funds must go through a bank or a brokerage.

The procedure for transferring ownership of stock is not all that hard. First, sign the back of your stock certificate and have your bank guarantee your signature. That is to protect you against forgeries. Then, fill in the new owner's full name, as well as his or her Social Security number and address. Next, get the name and address of the transfer agent of the company in which you own stock. To obtain it, simply write to the corporate secretary of the company. Finally, send the stock certificate by registered mail to the transfer agent. Attach a letter explaining that you are selling the shares. The transfer agent then will issue a new certificate in the new owner's name.

And what is the charge for this? Nothing at all.

PRECIOUS METALS

Gold

I T IS hard to think of an investment that has performed worse in the last dozen years than gold.

How does it fail us? Let us count the ways.

First, gold pays no dividends. That may seem trifling when its price is streaking ahead, but over many decades it matters a lot. Since 1926, dividends have accounted for almost one-half of the return from owning stocks. A further shortcoming of gold is that it cannot compound investors' gains as a company can when it retains earnings and uses that fuel to grow.

And gold has lost much of its allure as a safe-haven investment. Just after the Iraqi invasion of Kuwait, the commodity didn't even maintain a 10% increase in price. While some advisers say that an all-out war might have sent more investors scurrying for bars of bullion, others feel that different, higher-yielding investments — such as government money-market funds — have become much more appealing.

Even gold buyers who want to hedge against inflation may get less than they bargain for. Though an ounce of gold today still has the same purchasing power as it did hundreds of years ago, gold's shorter-term record as an inflation hedge is poor. Since 1980 inflation has reduced the purchasing power of a dollar by nearly 40%. Not only has gold failed to offset that loss, but its price has actually fallen some 59% during that period. Silver has done even worse, dipping to a 17-year low of $3.53 an ounce in February 1991, before recovering slightly to $3.82 in the autumn of 1992.

Still, if you believe that double-digit inflation, oil-supply interruptions and world monetary crises will strike yet again, you might be inclined to invest in precious metals. You then would have a series of choices of how and what to buy.

Extreme pessimists who have no faith in any country's currency probably would prefer gold bars. But owning such bullion can be a nuisance. You have to pay for storage and insurance, and you also may have to transport the metal to and from dealers, and perhaps lay out more money for assay costs when you sell.

A simpler way to invest in gold — or silver and platinum — is to buy certificates of ownership. They signify that you own a specified amount of the metal stored in bank vaults. When the time comes to sell, a phone call is all that is necessary. Your minimum initial purchase might be $2,500. After that, you make subsequent investments for as little as $100. Commissions range from 1% to roughly 3% when you buy, depending on the quantity. You also pay an annual storage charge based on weight when you buy and 1% to 2% when you sell. Choose your dealer carefully: a couple of metals certificate programs have been exposed as scams.

Instead of certificates, many people prefer to buy one-ounce gold coins, such as South African Krugerrands, Canadian Maple Leafs, Chinese Pandas, and the American Eagle, which the U.S. Mint introduced in October 1986. Although you pay 3% to 6% more than their gold content is worth, and sales tax on top of that, coins are easier to resell than gold certificates or bars. The easy portability and worldwide acceptance of coins appeal to the so-called refugee mentality. Again, you should bear in mind that neither gold coins nor bars nor certificates pay any dividends.

Shares of high-quality South African mining companies do offer high dividends and a chance at capital appreciation. But mining stocks are typically more volatile than bullion. That's because mining profits balloon once the price of the metal moves above the cost of extracting and refining it. A price rise of a few percentage points can double the earnings of a mining company. When gold prices decline, however, shares also drop more sharply than the metal itself.

This volatility also carries over to the dividends that the companies pay. In mid-1992, when gold was selling for about $342 an ounce, the dividends were roughly 7% to 9%. At $600 an ounce, dividends would likely be 12% or 14%. One warning: Buying South African gold stocks still subjects your investment to political and economic risks. Even though white South Africans voted in March 1992 to support an end to apartheid, the country's future remains uncertain.

You can minimize the risks of gold stocks by diversifying. For example, you can balance South African mining shares with North American ones such as Placer Dome, a company listed on the New York Stock Exchange.

If you do not wish to make a big investment but you want broad diversification, you could buy into one of the gold mutual funds. They acquire the shares of diverse gold-mining companies. But they're as volatile as nitroglycerin. These funds soared in the early 1980s, then slumped, recovered strongly and took a nosedive in the crash of 1987. They led other fund groups for a brief period in 1989, only to slip again in 1990 and 1992.

For the five years ending May 31, 1992, Morningstar Inc. has identified the top four gold mutual funds: Freedom Gold and Government (with a 6.54% annualized return); Oppenheimer Gold and Special Minerals (5.34%); Franklin Gold (−.18%); and Vanguard Specialized Portfolio–Gold and Precious Metals (−3.62%). The disparity in performance among the leaders in gold indicates the risk in gold investment.

Before you buy, remember: Just as gold stocks generally rise faster than gold when the market is up, so too they usually plunge faster than the metal when its price falls. Whether you choose to purchase gold funds or gold stocks or the metal itself, the amount you buy should be only a relatively modest share — perhaps 5% — of a well-diversified investment portfolio.

Platinum

W HEN people think of investing in precious metals, they usually consider buying gold or silver. Platinum rarely comes to mind. But in the mid- to late 1980s, platinum's price often topped that of gold. The price has since slipped from its high of more than $500 an ounce, due in part to political upheaval in producing countries, particularly South Africa and the former Soviet Union. In January 1992 it dropped below $359 an ounce, almost converging with the price of gold.

Demand for platinum rose 5.5% in 1990, to record levels, but supplies increased 9%, also to a record, producing the first platinum surplus since 1986. Another surplus occurred in 1991.

For long-term investors, now may be a good time to buy. Prices are low, and some industry analysts believe that they are nearing bottom. Platinum's use as an anti-pollutant will rise as emission-control standards tighten in both the U.S. and Europe.

Future platinum prices will also be influenced by industrial and consumer demand in Japan, the world center of platinum purchasing. Demand will probably climb throughout the 1990s as the Japanese continue to buy more platinum jewelry. Jewelry accounts for 35% of the metal's total market, and the Japanese are responsible for 90% of that. Some studies show that nearly every woman in Japan owns at least one piece of platinum jewelry. The Japanese increasingly give platinum coins as graduation and birthday gifts, further lifting demand.

The coins sell for 3% to 8% over market value for the metal itself, due to both fabrication and distribution costs. In mid-1992 the popular one-ounce Isle of Man Noble coin was selling for $375. The limited-edition Australian Koala, which carries a different depiction of a koala bear every year, was $385, and the Canadian Maple Leaf was also $385.

People who invest in the metal often choose to buy so-called platinum futures, which bet on future price trends. But futures are extremely risky. You can lose many times your stake if the market goes against you. The safer approach is to purchase the metal outright. The least expensive way is to buy one- or ten-ounce bars from refiners such as Johnson Matthey of London.

COMMODITIES

Playing the Riskiest Game

FOR those who yearn for the fastest, toughest, highest-risk financial game of all, there are commodities. As many as 90% of all amateur traders lose money and drop out within a year, and the only consistent winners are the brokers who charge you commissions. Still, if you crave excitement and have a cast-iron stomach, commodities trading can offer impressive gains for that tiny portion of your investable funds that you are willing to put completely at risk — your mad money. But unless you are an expert, and have pockets as deep as an oil well, never put more than a nickel or dime out of every investment dollar into commodities.

The reason that commodities futures trading offers both outsized losses and outsized gains is leverage. When you buy commodities contracts, you do so on margin. The contracts give you the right to buy a specified commodity at a set price for a limited time. Let's say the price of gold is $400 an ounce, and you think it will rise in the next six months. Then you can invest in a contract to buy 100 ounces of gold at about $400 an ounce. That's $40,000 worth of gold. But speculating in gold futures costs less than 10% of the price of the metal. If gold goes up to, say, $450 an ounce by the time your contract expires six months from now, you win. On an outlay of less than $4,000, your profit will be $50 an ounce, or $5,000 — minus commissions.

But if prices move strongly against you, your broker will demand that you put up still more money. Unless you produce the cash immediately, the broker will sell out your position, at a potentially bone-chilling loss. To avoid that, give your broker a stop-loss order on each futures contract. That way, you establish in advance a price at which you will automatically sell out a position rather than take further losses.

In the early 1980s, some commodity prices suffered their longest decline in 15 years. Blame Mother Nature. She gave us bountiful harvests, which lowered prices of many farm commodities. Also blame the sluggish economy, which curbed demand for metals, and high interest rates, which lured investors out of commodities and into money-market funds. Commodity prices revived slowly as the economy pepped up and interest rates returned from their trip to the moon. Then the drought of 1988 drove grain prices high for a long period; in 1991 and 1992 they eased.

It cannot be stressed too much that commodities are risky. Small investors who speculate in commodities make two major mistakes. Many of them operate on the basis of tips; they are often wrong, and the amateurs cannot hope to match the professional traders for access to updated, accurate information about markets. Small investors also tend to be undercapitalized. To stay in this game, you should have five dollars in reserve, ready to commit, for every dollar you put up. You might also read one of the dozens of market letters on the subject. *Commodity Traders' Consumer Report* (1731 Howe Avenue, Suite 149, Sacramento, California 95825; 800-999-2827) tracks over a third of these while providing helpful articles, interviews and trading tips. A subscription costs $198 a year.

You can make do with less money by buying mini-contracts on the Mid America Commodity Exchange, which is located in Chicago. Mini-contracts control smaller quantities of commodities than do regular futures, but they are just as volatile as full-size contracts, and you will still get margin calls. But because you put up proportionately less money, you have less to lose.

A reasonable way for some sophisticated small investors to get into the market is to invest in one of the 180 or so publicly traded commodity futures funds. The advantage is that the funds are professionally managed and diversify your investment among many types of commodities. More important, any losses are limited to the amount of money you put up; you are never subject to a margin call. But before you invest, you should know that average annual costs take 20% of the fund's equity. Also, you should make sure that the trading advisers of the fund have proved that they can make money. If you are interested in commodity funds, you can follow them in a newsletter called *Managed Account Reports* (5513 Twin Knolls Road,

Suite 213, Columbia, Maryland 21045; 301-730-5365). A subscription costs $265 a year.

Financial Futures

E VEN for the experts, the commodities futures market has always been a gamble. But now there are futures contracts for people who don't know beans about soybeans. The so-called commodities in this case are good old stocks and bonds, and they are traded in the fast and furious financial futures market.

The financial futures include contracts in Treasury bills, bonds and notes, bank certificates of deposit and a variety of other interest-bearing securities. When you buy one of these contracts, you are betting that, for example, interest rates will go down in the future and thus the prices of the bills, bonds or notes covered by the contract will go up.

You can buy financial futures through commodity firms or through brokers who specialize in commodities at large stock brokerage houses. But if you are a would-be buccaneer in the financial futures market, take a tip from the experts and do your trading on paper for a while, until you get your sea legs. If and when you are ready to start wheeling and dealing for real, then pick active markets, such as those trading in Treasury bill and Treasury bond futures. The more trading that is going on, the more likely you are to find a buyer or a seller for your contract at the price you want. And don't forget to place stop orders with your broker. They instruct him to close out your position when the price reaches a certain level — and they can help you limit any losses.

Any way you play it, futures is a highly leveraged business. So this kind of investment — while increasingly popular — is not for those who aren't prepared to take substantial risks.

OTHER INVESTMENTS

Art

IT REQUIRES artistry to invest intelligently in paintings, sculpture, photographs and prints. The key is to avoid fads and have patience. Even when you buy with extreme selectivity — and with the close advice of a reliable dealer — you may not make a profit for five years or more, unless you are able to afford one of the few sought-after masterpieces. But this is a good time for newcomers to the art market.

Prices are down at the high end, the glamour sales of Impressionist and contemporary art. At the spring 1992 auctions at Sotheby's and Christie's in New York, contemporary art that was expected to bring about $35 million sold for a total of $23.5 million. Even Andy Warhol's *210 Coca-Cola Bottles,* billed as the star at Christie's, fetched only $2.1 million — just under the auction house's low presale estimate. "Serious collectors were looking for high-quality works fresh on the market," said Sotheby's David Nash, noting also that drawings and works on paper were bucking the down trend. In June 1992 Sotheby's sold a watercolor by the Austrian artist Egon Schiele for a world-record $1,086,800.

But if you're a fledgling collector, chances are your sights aren't set on breaking world records. If you have limited funds along with adventurous tastes, watch for events like Christie's 1992 sale of paintings by Haitian artist Hector Hippolyte; prices ranged from $75,000 to an affordable $1,000. Generally speaking, experts advise novice collectors to investigate paintings and sculpture by little-known contemporary artists.

If you hanker for big names, however, don't overlook prints and photographs. Christie's Kathleen Guzman notes that prints by a contemporary superstar such as Robert Rauschenberg can be found for as little as $5,000, and photographs by a giant like Ansel Adams for $3,000 to $5,000. A caveat: Insist on top condition. A Rauschenberg in less-than-perfect shape won't increase in value.

In fact, all three fields are particularly promising and reasonably inexpensive for beginning collectors: prints, photographs and contemporary works of painting and sculpture by little-known artists. Some of them may become tomorrow's great stars. Fine pieces in these fields may be had for as little as a few hundred dollars. Buyers on limited budgets no longer have to settle for obscure artists. For example, some of the 4,000-plus lithographs by 19th-century French social satirist Honoré Daumier can be had for less than $100 each.

A factor that has nothing to do with an image's beauty can boost the price of a print or photograph. People regularly pay 100% more for a work that has the artist's signature on it. For less affluent collectors, the absence of a signature is a small price to pay for the opportunity to acquire a superb print for little money.

Among the most reputable sources of prints are major auction houses and the galleries that belong to the Art Dealers Association of America. For their names and addresses, write to the Art Dealers Association at 575 Madison Avenue, New York, New York 10022.

To find the best sources of photographs, write to the Association of International Photography Art Dealers at Suite 200, 1609 Connecticut Avenue, NW, Washington, D.C. 20009. You can order its $5 booklet, *On Collecting Photographs,* or, for $20, its illustrated catalog and membership directory.

In assembling a collection of contemporary paintings and sculpture, it is sometimes fun to try to discover new talent on your own. But the safest path for the neophyte is to develop long-term relationships with professional dealers who are closely associated with emerging artists. These dealers can offer much expertise and advice.

The major galleries and auction houses are concentrated in New York City, still the undisputed capital of the U.S. art trade. If you cannot make fairly regular trips to New York, then seek out local dealers as your agents to establish relationships with other dealers and auction houses.

The place *not* to buy works by lesser-known contemporary painters and sculptors is at an auction. Auction houses rarely offer such works anyway because they sell poorly there.

By contrast, auction houses are often excellent sources of prints and photographs. First, go to dealers to see what the prices are.

Then, if something you want comes up at an auction, you may be able to get a better price.

When you are ready to buy, deal only with galleries and auction houses whose directors and employees have well-established reputations for honesty. Make sure they're willing to disclose all the facts about the art they sell. No reputable dealer should object to your consulting other experts before you make a purchase. You also can consult the Art Sales Index at an art dealership or at a university library. It will help you to determine what a piece of art should be selling for. The index lists 120,000 auction results and dates back to 1969; it costs $198. Remember, too, that buying art is like seeking out the best doctor for an operation: feel free to get a second, even a third, opinion.

In the course of buying from a dealer, it's customary to *negotiate* the prices. Many dealers routinely add 10% to their asking prices for bargaining purposes. But don't badger a dealer who insists that his price is firm. Quite a few dealers allow buyers up to a year to pay, interest-free, and sometimes even longer than that.

Even though you are buying art on a low budget, there are some so-called bargains you will want to avoid. Stay away from World War I and World War II posters that are more interesting as historical curiosities than as art objects. Also avoid any contemporary prints that were produced in huge numbers and photographs that are neither rare nor of high quality. And remember: Nothing is a good buy, unless you really want it and have a passion for it.

Folk Art

NOT even the experts agree on what domestic folk art is, and nobody can say for sure what it is really worth. Generally, as writer Gus Hedberg has observed, American folk art can include any tangible rudiment of daily life in the 18th, 19th and 20th centuries that has been enhanced by a touch of art — everything from a gravestone to an old rag doll. Indeed, some 19th-century weather vanes can cost more than the average meteorologist earns in a year, and some patchwork quilts are so rare and valued that nobody would dream of sleeping under one. And there are folk art paintings, portraits and landscapes by talented individuals who, in many cases, lacked formal training.

You can find plenty of investment-grade American folk art for less than $1,000 — and even more that is just fun to own for much less than that. Above all, the best folk art buy is something that delights you aesthetically and personally. It should figure as a wise investment only secondarily.

Prices for folk art, which a couple of years ago seemed to be dropping through the barn floor, are on the rebound. In October 1991 a version of Edward Hicks's famous *Peaceable Kingdom* fetched $1.2 million at Sotheby's. Below that dizzying level the market has been resilient and stable, with prices ranging from $2,500 to $45,000, depending on the size and condition of the painting and the subject matter. "In this field, children are irresistible," says Sotheby's Nancy Druckman.

A reliable guide to the shops, auctions and regions where a fledgling collector might begin looking for American folk art is the *Maine Antique Digest*. It costs $29 a year, and its address is P.O. Box 1429, Waldoboro, Maine 04572-0645. You might also check *Antiques and the Arts Weekly*, also known as the *Newtown Bee*, for the newspaper it once was part of. It costs $38 for a 52-week subscription, and its address is 5 Church Hill Road, Newtown, Connecticut 06470.

If you want to buy folk art, it is wise to concentrate on a particular category. That will help you to establish a sense of confidence and expertise.

Among the most enduring investments are quilts. That is partly because there is a growing international demand for them. When buying for investment, look for a visually appealing quilt with small, disciplined stitches and with unusual features, even a one-of-a-kind pattern. Top-quality old examples range all the way from $1,000 to $20,000, and the exceptionally beautiful and rare ones have gone at auction for $100,000 and more. However, handsome contemporary quilts that you can actually sleep under without depreciating your investment are available for less than $500.

When buying a basket, check the bottom to see if it is still strong. But if the rest of the basket looks well-worn, yet the bottom has hardly been scuffed, that's a sure sign of a forgery. The best investments in baskets are those with unusual forms or those with handpainted decorations. It's hard to find one in sound condition for less than $150. To get bargains, avoid shops with expensive business cards, and head for stores and auctions in the back hills. There you sometimes can come across an oak splint basket from the late 19th century for as little as $75.

With a weathervane, older is considered better. If wood, it should be dulled and weathered; if gold leaf, it should have lost much of its gilt; if copper, it should be green. A vane with a beautifully aged patina is worth considerably more than one that has been repainted.

If you buy a painting as an investment, be wary of heavy restoration. And an anonymous folk painting may be just as valuable as one by a recognized artist.

If you are buying furniture, rely on the eye of an experienced dealer to avoid counterfeits. Once you get home with your piece of furniture, stifle any ambitions that may arise in you to fix it up. One woman who bought an 18th-century painted chest a few years ago for $25,000 then proceeded to refinish the piece. As a result, it's now worth no more than a few hundred dollars.

Collectibles: Plates, Books and Medallions

ADVERTISEMENTS breathlessly proclaim that limited editions of porcelain plates, books, medallions and china dolls offer terrific investment opportunities. In fact, companies that make and sell these purportedly limited editions of collectibles tend to exaggerate their investment value. Still, a careful collector can come out ahead. If you are tempted to buy, you would be wise to follow four rules:

First, buy only what you love. If it takes 20 years to sell your four Finnish Christmas plates, at least you will enjoy looking at them in your china cabinet.

Second, make sure that a manufacturer announces how many items constitute an edition before he begins taking orders. Avoid companies that will sell to anyone who orders within a fixed period, usually six months or a year. That means everybody who wants the item will get it, thereby killing the potential for a resale market.

Third, buy the finest material and craftsmanship that you can afford.

Finally, keep your collectibles in mint condition. You can't dine off collector's plates or let your children play with limited-edition porcelain dolls. If you eventually try to sell them, such factors as how clean they are or whether or not you can provide the original box they came in can make all the difference.

Each type of limited edition has its own characteristics and peculiarities. For example:

Plates: More than seven million Americans — more than for any other limited-edition item — collect plates made of porcelain, pewter, crystal and even silver. About 150 manufacturers, including Royal Doulton and Rosenthal, bring out some 500 new issues a year. Single plates generally cost between $25 and $125, although some go for as much as $350. But if you ever try to sell, you may not get what you paid. Only about 30% of the bids ever find buyers.

The most publicized place to buy and sell plates is the Bradford Exchange in Niles, Illinois. The toll-free number is 800-323-8078. Sellers phone in their asking prices and buyers call in bids. If a trade is made, sellers pay a 30% commission, and buyers pay a minimum of $4 if the plate is under $100, 4% on plates that cost $100 or more. All transactions are guaranteed by the Exchange.

Books: With a complete set of Audubon's *Birds of America* bringing a record $4.07 million at Christie's in 1992, investors are learning the value of a good book. And you don't have to pay seven-figure prices to get pleasure from buying books and profit from selling them a few years down the line. But be careful. Buy only top-quality volumes with handmade paper, hand-set type and illustrations commissioned for the book.

Bibliophiles scorn many mass-produced reprints of classics. Though they claim to be limited editions, thousands of such books are printed, and their quality is often mediocre. But serious collectors admire and have bid up the prices of volumes published by some quality limited-edition presses. Among them is the Limited Editions Club in Manhattan. For example, its edition of Joyce's *Ulysses* sold for $10 in 1935; recently it brought $2,200 at auction. Contact the club at 39 E. 72nd Street, New York, NY 10021; 212-737-7600.

A few hundred small presses irregularly publish well-crafted books in editions of fewer than 500 volumes. You can find reviews of small-press books in a quarterly magazine called *Fine Print* (P.O. Box 193394, San Francisco, California 94119; $36 for an introductory one-year subscription).

Medallions and commemorative coins: In 1992 the U.S. Mint was busy issuing commemorative coins: one set for the Olympic Games, another marking the White House bicentennial, and a third for the 500th anniversary of Columbus's epochal voyage. (For ordering information, call 301-436-7400.) These '92 specials should prove attractive to collectors. But if you're just getting into the field, beware of buying gold and silver medallions that are minted not by governments but by private companies. Interest in these novelties peaked in the 1970s, when private mints rushed to capitalize on gold fever. They turned out tokens commemorating all sorts of events and personalities. But collectors' ardor for them has cooled along with gold and silver prices. Even in the best of times, such ceremonial wampum has been hard to resell. For example, one 12-medallion sterling set honoring the poet Robert Frost was issued in 1974 for $275; today, coin dealers will pay only about $55 for it.

Perhaps 10% of the medallions can be resold at more than the intrinsic value of the gold or silver in the piece or set. With very few exceptions, those issued by private companies in so-called limited editions are actually mass-marketed and thus are worthless as either investments or collector's items. And unless you are an expert at evaluating the age of those issued by a government, it is best to stay away from them also as investments. They are rarely dated, and thus the buyer has no way of knowing whether the piece was minted in the early 1920s or 1990 — the government often uses the same mold over and over again, perhaps with time lapses between mints.

Richard Doty, a numismatic curator at the Smithsonian Institution in Washington, warns: "When you sell them, limited-edition medallions tend to be worth no more than the silver and gold they contain. Your only hope of selling them at a profit is if you have a very dumb brother-in-law."

Coins

MANY of us first became captivated by coin collecting when we were children. While helping to count up all the pennies and nickels in the kitchen cookie jar, we hoped to find a valuable old coin among them, or, at the very least, an Indian-head penny. But coin collecting is no longer simply a gentleman's sport. In the past few years it has become a $5-billion-a-year industry, dominated by Wall Street–backed limited partnerships, auction houses and large-scale dealerships. In 1989, the rare coin market handed investors a 50% return — no small change. Alas, the other side of the coin is that in 1990, profit-takers sold, recession struck and prices flipped down 50% to 60%.

Wall Street's interest in numismatics arose after 1986, when the Professional Grading Service started "slabbing" graded coins. That is, once the condition of a coin had been graded, the coin was then encased in a grade-labeled tamper-resistant plastic holder called a slab. Investment-graded coins are judged on a scale from MS-60 to MS-70, the highest mint-state grade. Until slabbing began, few dealers would buy a coin sight unseen. Many current investors in the numismatic market haven't ever seen — and probably won't ever lay hands on — a rare coin.

Some independent dealers still won't buy a coin sight unseen, and many will de-slab a coin in order to submit it for another shot at a higher grading. The grading of a coin depends in part on its age. But while age is important, condition is even more so: an 1892S silver dollar in good condition is worth about $13, but the same coin in top uncirculated condition can be valued at $65,000. Grading alone doesn't mean that a coin will attract high prices; the rare coin market, just like other art-related markets, is fickle and subject to the rapidly changing whims of investors. For example, in the mid-1980s, Morgan silver dollars (graded about MS-65 or higher) were hot. These coins, minted between 1878 and 1904 and again in 1921, could command more than $1,500 in 1989. But that market has since taken a dive, high grading or not.

If you are new to the game, your first step should be to find a dealer you can trust. Look for one who has been in business at least 10 years and belongs to the Professional Numismatics Guild or the American Numismatic Association. Ask him for references from customers and from a local bank. Be particularly wary of mail-order offers and telemarketers.

Dealer markups range from 10% to 15%. So if you try to sell a coin back, expect to get about 15% *less* than its stated market value at the time. Usually, you will have to hold a coin at least five years, and possibly 10 years, before turning a profit. That's why dealers and financial planners recommend that you commit no more than 10% to 15% of your investment money to your collection.

You will stand a better chance to profit if you concentrate on coins of a particular period or country. U.S. Government mintages are the only reasonable choices for novices because they have the broadest appeal to investors and collectors. With experience, you can reach for the exotic. For example, so-called ancient coins — those minted before the fall of the Roman Empire in the fifth century A.D. — have appreciated about 10% to 20% annually in recent years. You can still get some bargains on ancient coins sold in the U.S. and Europe. Prices range from about $10 to $20 for common, fourth-century A.D. bronze coins to many thousands of dollars for rare gold or silver pieces. Two magazines that publish current prices are *Coin World* and *Numismatic News,* available at most larger newsstands.

In a 1984 ruling the IRS decided that coin dealers must report purchases of South African Krugerrands, Canadian Maple Leafs and Mexican gold coins. The government wants to be sure that any profits that collectors make on them will not go unreported and untaxed.

But the rule generally does not include numismatic coins, scarce or rare coins that usually are worth far more than the gold, silver or bronze they contain. Because sales of them still do not have to be reported to the IRS, goldbugs have been trading in their Krugerrands for numismatics. There is, however, a caveat: sales tax is due on these purchases in some states and capital gains have to be reported to the IRS when numismatic coins are resold.

Gems

DIAMONDS, rubies, emeralds, sapphires — ah, what romance! But as investments, those luscious gems are quite chancy. Before you try to profit from your jewelry box, remember that gems that have been bought to wear are seldom of investment quality. When you buy them, you rarely pay wholesale prices. The dealer takes a substantial markup — sometimes as much as 100%. And if you ever try to sell the stone, dealers usually will offer you even *less* than wholesale prices.

Unlike stocks and bonds, there is no easily quoted market for gems because no two stones are identical in quality or value. Diamonds are evaluated by four measures: carat (or weight), color, clarity and cut. Even the color of white diamonds is graded from D for the whites, to Z for dingy yellow. The difference of just one letter grade can amount to thousands of dollars per carat in the price.

If you do invest in diamonds, insist on receiving a certificate from an independent laboratory that has graded the stone within the last 12 months. Even with that, you also should get a recertification by having your jeweler send the stone, insured, by registered mail, to the Gemological Institute of America. It has offices in New York City and Santa Monica, California.

The diamond market has lost a lot of its luster due to the recent recession. One third of the world's gem-quality stones are sold in America, and polished diamond imports to the U.S. were down 11% in 1990. But that hasn't translated into bargains for jewelry lovers have. A top-quality one-carat D flawless stone sells for around $13,000 wholesale — or some $20,000 or more retail in a Tiffany setting — just as it has for most of the 1980s.

In short, if you are acquiring jewelry for pleasure, fine. But don't deceive yourself into believing you are making a sure-thing investment. Unless you are an expert, gems are for buying, not for selling.

With occasional exceptions, colored stones are less costly than diamonds — but more risky. That's because a world diamond cartel usually keeps a floor under prices, but there are no cartels to hold the prices of rubies, emeralds or sapphires.

Among the colored stones, fine rubies have risen the fastest lately. Supplies are short because few rubies are being exported by Burma, the source of the richest and reddest stones. The next most valuable rubies come from Thailand, while the lighter Sri Lanka rubies are less coveted. Sapphires are almost as rare as rubies, and some of the best and the bluest are from Kashmir. Emeralds may be a safer investment because they are easier to resell than sapphires.

The steep price of precious stones is stirring interest in much more speculative semi-precious stones, notably aquamarines and topaz stones, which come in shades of orange and yellow. The finest opals are too fragile to be a solid long-term investment; they can crack fairly easily.

There is no universally accepted grading system for colored stones, as there is for diamonds. But before buying, an investor should insist on independent written appraisal of the gem's quality, weight, color — and, of course, its dollar value.

Toys

Toys of the 1950s and early 1960s aren't kid stuff anymore. Now they are called contemporary collectibles, and many command precious prices. Collectors are paying hundreds — and sometimes thousands — of dollars for toys that sold for a few dollars when new. The buying and selling is done at antique toy auctions. You can find auction locations and dates advertised in a monthly magazine called *Antique Toy World* (P.O. Box 34509, Chicago, Illinois 60634. A year's subscription costs $25).

Collectors covet dolls of the 1950s and early 1960s for their beauty and wardrobes. Among those that have appreciated the most are the eight-inch Madame Alexander Brand Romeo and Juliet dolls. They cost $3.50 each when they came out in 1955. Now a pair in good condition can fetch up to $3,000. Barbie can bring you bounty, too. An original Barbie, first sold for $3 in 1959, today can command as much as $2,500 in pristine condition and preserved in her original box.

The 1950s-era techno-toys, such as robots and satellites, also can command high prices at auction. Other valuable toys include small metal trucks and cars of the 1950s. Some of the tiny matchbox vehicles that sold for 39 cents now sell for more than $40. And the Hot Wheels versions of America's so-called muscle cars — Chevrolets of the late 1950s and Mustangs of the early 1960s — go for as much as $50 and are expected to rise even further.

So-called character toys, often from cartoons or kids' TV shows, are popular. A wind-up tin Popeye doll from the 1930s brings nearly $550.

You may be able to find toys that have more than nostalgic value and sell them for high prices. Where to look? Garage sales are one place. Before you buy, inspect the toy carefully. Make sure it functions properly, has no missing parts, peeling paint or other signs of corrosion. With toys, condition is everything. Top bids are reserved for toys in mint condition and with their original boxes. The best place to find toys worth a bundle is at home. Just think: The joys may be in your attic.

Pop Collectibles:
Rock 'n' Roll and Movie Stars

SOME of the hottest collectors' items now are rock 'n' roll memorabilia. They are bought and sold at auction houses that deal in collectibles.

Rock 'n' roll collectibles include original recordings, posters, souvenirs, clothing and guitars. At a Sotheby's New York auction in June 1989, an electric guitar that Roy Orbison played sold for $8,800. More recently, Christie's in London sold five of Elvis Presley's bedsheets — plain white percale, but adorned with the King's laundry mark — for $1,200. Also at Christie's, you could have bought John Belushi's bee antenna for a mere $320 or, at the other end of the scale, one of Marilyn Monroe's poured-on *Some Like It Hot* gowns for $35,000.

If you want to collect goodies like these, be disciplined. You should specialize in items related to a single band, or in a particular category of items, such as backstage passes. The most valuable collectibles are likely to be those associated with musicians who marked a turning point in rock history. At the above-mentioned Sotheby's auction, a suit that John Lennon wore on concert tours fetched $3,575. A year later, at a Sotheby's London auction, one of Jimi Hendrix's electric guitars sold for over $300,000. And for those who want a bit of Hendrix without tossing around a lot of notes, a poster might be the next best thing. According to *Fortune*, rock 'n' roll poster prices are rising quickly. New York City gallery owner Jay Kastor bought a Hendrix poster for $100 in early 1990; less than nine months later he felt confident enough to consider offering it for sale at $4,000. But keep in mind that assets like these are not very liquid. As with most collectibles, you are best off buying an item because you want to own it, not because you expect to make a profit.

REAL ESTATE

Your Prospects for Profit

R EAL ESTATE has been the source of more great fortunes than any other investment, but its future is clouded because of overbuilding and reductions in its once lavish tax benefits. At the extreme, alarmists prophesy that property values will continue to plunge and that so many investors will walk away from their buildings they will need a parade permit.

Don't be taken in. If you adjust your investment strategy, you should come out all right. Buy real estate investments for income and capital appreciation, but don't insist that every nickel you spend is a deduction. Here's why:

You are no longer allowed to deduct so-called passive losses from other income, such as your salary or income from stocks and bonds. You can use passive losses only to offset income from passive investments. Generally, limited partnerships and rental real estate investments qualify as passive investments. Thus, if you own rental property, you will be allowed to deduct your mortgage interest, property taxes and expenses only up to the amount of your rental income plus your income from limited partnerships.

The wise choice for real estate investors is to acquire property that, because of location and other attributes, has intrinsic value above and beyond the tax benefits. The key to success now is patience, with an eye toward long-term gains and consistent annual income.

That advice holds true whether the investment you are considering is part of an office building, a shopping center, an apartment house or even your own home. In fact, do not count on making any profit from buying a house or condo now for your own use if you are likely to move within three or four years. The increase you can expect in the value of your home probably will not offset the cost of borrowing and the real estate commissions you will have to pay when you sell.

The increase in property values is expected to average 5% or so annually, though it will be much higher — or lower — in some regions and neighborhoods than in others.

If you want to own and manage property directly, your best investment today would be a single-family house or, if you can afford it, a multi-unit apartment building. But for a lot less money, you can become a limited partner in a real estate syndication or a shareholder in a real estate investment trust, or REIT. You can buy limited partnerships from stockbrokers and financial planners, and you generally have to put up at least $5,000. (See "Your Investments/ Real Estate: REITs and Limited Partnerships.")

The Tax Benefits

THOUGH you may still qualify for a host of deductions as a real estate owner-manager, be aware that being a landlord is not for everyone. Many busy people simply do not have the time or temperament to cope with tenant complaints and broken boilers. Instead these people can buy into REITs or limited partnerships.

Within the limits of the tax law, landlords can deduct not only mortgage interest and property taxes but also fire and liability insurance premiums, expenses for finding and screening tenants, commissions for collecting rents, the cost of traveling to and from the property and, best of all, depreciation.

Tax reform has stretched out the depreciation of residential rental real estate from 19 years to 27½ years for property placed in service after 1986. And you can use only what is called straight-line depreciation. To get your annual depreciation allowance, divide the cost of the property by 27½.

Investors who fix up old buildings also can do well. You can get a tax credit for rehabilitation expenditures made on buildings at least 50 years old in 1986 and buildings that are certified historic structures. The credit is equal to 10% of your cost of renovation, subject to some limitations. To qualify for the tax benefits, you must sell or rent out the building for nonresidential commercial or industrial use, which does not include apartment rentals. Also, the improvements must cost at least $5,000, or more than the price you paid for the building.

If the building is a certified historic structure or is located in a historic district, you get a tax credit for 20% of the renovation costs, again subject to limitations. In this case, however, you can also take the credit for apartment buildings.

To find out whether a building qualifies, check with the U.S. Department of the Interior or your state's or city's historic-preservation office. And to learn what your tax credit might amount to, be sure to consult your tax adviser.

The Ideal Property Investments

YOU no longer can assume that just about any real estate will automatically increase in value, but property still can be a terrific long-term investment — if you know what to buy. Novice investors should avoid commercial properties such as stores and office buildings. Managing them requires special expertise such as, for example, knowing how to handle business leases. Stick with residential properties; they are easier to handle.

Experts consider three-bedroom, two-bath houses to be particularly desirable investments. They are large enough for small families, which tend to be the most stable tenants. There is great demand in many communities for these single-family homes. That means they usually can pay you enough in rents to cover your mortgage and maintenance costs — and give you a nice profit. They are also relatively easy to sell if you need to cash in your investment in a hurry.

If you are a first-time investor, you would be wise to stick close to your own community. The market will be familiar, and the travel time will be less than if you buy a far-off building. By investing in your backyard, you are in a good position to anticipate what will happen to real estate prices. Wherever you buy, talk with other property owners and visit many properties to get a feel for real estate values. Make sure the neighborhood is economically stable. There is no quicker way to lose your money than to purchase a house on a block that is about to be engulfed by crime. Look for solid construction and sturdy appliances before you worry about charm.

If you do not have much time to spend on repairs, buy real estate that is in ready-to-rent condition. But if you do have hours to spare and are handy with a saw and paintbrush, look for structurally sound houses in less than sterling condition that can profit from a moderate amount of fix-up.

One sensible rule is to buy the *worst* house on the *best* block. A property that can be pulled into rentable condition with a fresh coat of exterior paint could be an excellent investment. Bringing this home up to par with its neighbors by later adding a room or doing some landscaping can pay big dividends in rental profits. It also can produce a fat gain when the property is sold.

Another choice is to look for a deteriorating house in a turnaround neighborhood. You will stand your best chance of locating such a property by searching in a community that you know well. As mentioned, you can save taxes by renovating properties that are considered to be historically significant. But use caution. Such investments require rehabilitation skills and a sharp sense of timing. If you are too early, you will not get enough rent to pay for its upgrading.

How to Buy

O NCE you decide to invest in rental property, you probably will be eager to buy something quickly and put your money to work. *Resist* the temptation. Many new real estate investors underestimate the complexity of the field and overestimate how much they know about it.

Immerse yourself in a study of real estate as you would any new business venture. Talk with other investors and brokers; that will help you pinpoint the neighborhoods with the best investment potential. Seek out areas that have begun to gain favor among young householders as an alternative to more expensive established neighborhoods. Look for good transportation, shopping and schools and a strong, diversified employment base.

Then you can narrow your search to specific properties. Your best ally is likely to be a broker who is knowledgeable about your chosen area. Check his or her reputation with local bankers and attorneys. Discuss with the broker your debt limits and investment standards. Other obvious sources of sale properties are newspaper real estate sections, posted "FOR SALE" signs, auctions of buildings in arrears and word of mouth. Plan to inspect dozens of buildings before you make a bid.

If you find a property that approaches your standards, investigate it thoroughly. Unless you are versed in building construction and mechanics, take along a construction engineer whose judgment you trust. The $175 to $400 fee will be worth it. You also can use the engineer's report to negotiate a better deal.

Look for a modern furnace and a water heater that has a capacity of at least 40 gallons for each family. And ask when that water heater was purchased. Be alert for signs of trouble. Stains on ceilings might mean plumbing or roof leaks and sagging floors could indicate structural defects. Your biggest worry will be the condition of the roof — replacement costs are high. Particularly with a large building, check the condition of the central air-conditioning plant and that of the asphalt parking lot, if there is one. You can confirm the stated age of a building by looking inside the toilet tank; most are stamped with their date of manufacture. Or look for a city building inspector's sticker.

Before investing in a rental house or apartment building, always ask yourself: Does it make financial sense for you? Can you *really* afford the initial cash outlay? Rental units may cost about $100,000, and of course, many are much costlier. You will have to put 10% to 25% of that down — or $10,000 to $25,000. Legal fees, advance property taxes and mortgage surcharges will add another $3,000 to $5,000 on the medium-priced home.

Make sure the property can pay you enough rental income to cover mortgage payments, taxes, utilities and maintenance costs. A property that does not is especially risky in low-inflation periods. You cannot count on its price to rise steeply enough to make up the losses.

When calculating the economics of a property, pay particular attention to financing. Do not go to just one bank or other lender, but shop around to several of them to get the largest possible mortgage at the lowest interest rate.

In many cases, the best source of financing is the seller. If the owner is anxious to unload the property, he or she may offer terms that are far more attractive than those at the banks. Many real estate ads will mention the availability of owner financing.

If the price of the property is more than you can afford, you may want to look into a type of cost splitting called a shared-equity financing agreement. With it, you will not buy the property for yourself, but you will share the ownership — and the cost — with the occupant. (For more, see "Your Home: Shared-Equity Mortgages.")

How to Be a Landlord

POSSIBLE tax breaks and potential capital gains might well tempt you to consider becoming a landlord. But be warned: The migraines are multiple, and the investment is not the instant winner it once was. Whether the property you rent to outsiders is a vacation cottage or the home you have lived in, to succeed as a landlord you need patience.

Don't expect to turn a quick profit. In some cities, you will have to wait for rents to rise, and that could take years. And remember that in many parts of the country values for existing homes are expected to increase only 5% or so annually — and in some cases even less — for the next several years.

Before you leap into landlording, be sure you can afford to tie up your money for as long as it will take for the investment to become profitable. The restrictions on deducting losses virtually require that the building you buy produces a positive cash flow — that is, its rents must exceed your maintenance and financing costs. If it does not do so immediately or at most within a year, the property will merely wring cash out of you. For this reason, when you are stalking the positive-cash-flow property, confine your search to a tight rental market where the vacancy rate is 6% or less and rents reasonably could be increased.

Take a hard look at the troubles of being a landlord. Do you really want to hunt for tenants? How do you feel about being rousted out of bed by a phone call telling you that a pipe has burst? Of course, you can hire a management firm to take care of those chores. Its services will cost you 6% to 8% of the rent and could go as high as 20% if you have a single-family house.

If you are new at managing property, take a tip from experienced landlords: Use great caution in screening prospective tenants. The hours you spend can save days of grief later on. Check each applicant's references. Call his or her employer to confirm job tenure. Ask the applicant's present landlord if he or she would gladly continue renting to the applicant. You may want to run a credit check, and you would be wise to get a security deposit of two months' rent.

Once the tenant has moved in, inspect the premises often, looking for little problems that could cause big troubles later on. Then fix them. If you do not want to be bothered by frequent minor repairs, you can offer the tenant a rent break to do his or her own maintenance. Your periodic checks will let you know whether the work is being done properly.

All in all, landlording has its rewards. It just takes longer now than before to realize them.

Renting to Your Parents or Children

I F YOU have older parents who need shelter, there is a superb way for you to help them and at the same time enjoy the tax benefits of being a landlord. You can buy a condo or house, lease it to your elderly parents and take deductions for maintenance, mortgage interest and depreciation — provided, of course, that your deductions are within the limits set by the new tax law. The IRS insists that you charge your kin a fair market rent. You can easily document that by asking a local real estate broker for a written estimate of what rent the property should command.

In fact, if you have parents who are 55 or older, you may want to buy their house. That way, you *both* can get tax breaks. Your folks do not have to pay any federal income taxes on their profits from the sale — up to $125,000. And now that you own the house, you can deduct the property taxes, mortgage interest payments and depreciation from your rental income and perhaps as much as $25,000 of your net losses, if any, from your ordinary income. (See "Your Investments/Real Estate: The Tax Benefits.")

The same tax breaks apply, of course, when you buy a house in a college town and rent it out to your son or daughter, the student. Many parents are managing to make money on their children's college education by buying houses for them — and perhaps a few classmates — to live in. Be sure you charge a fair market rate in order to get a passing grade from the IRS. But if you hire your child as the building superintendent, you can give him or her a 10% rent rebate.

Just one real-life example: When Bill Nelson was a sophomore at the University of California at Santa Barbara, he and three of his classmates could not find a house to rent. So his mother bought one. The boys got a nice deal. For a four-bedroom house, they paid $450 a month — exactly what they had paid for a rather cramped three-bedroom apartment the year before. The $450 almost entirely covered Mrs. Nelson's monthly mortgage payments, and the boys also promised to handle the repairs. After Bill Nelson graduated, he rented the house out for $775 a month. The house originally cost Mrs. Nelson $85,000; five years later, in the then-booming Santa Barbara area, it was worth $250,000.

Buying a house in a college town can be an excellent investment, but it does present risks. Not all students are really cut out to be landlords. Some are too immature, or may see their parents' real-estate venture as an opportunity to shelter friends. These youngsters may be reluctant to collect rent from their pals. Besides, owning a house requires constant attention. Occasionally the student landlord has to make a tough choice between mopping up a flooded basement and studying for an exam.

If you like the idea of buying a house or condominium for your college-bound youngster, you may be wise to let your child spend freshman year getting used to his or her surroundings before you commit your money. If you then decide to buy, choose a larger, five-bedroom house over a smaller, two-bedroom one; the extra rental income is often worth the additional expense.

Some other tips:

— Avoid a rattletrap house that needs a lot of work — unless you are prepared to spend considerable money to fix it.

— Pick a property as close to the campus as possible. But if housing demand is really high, do not rule out anything up to five miles away.

— Think twice about buying in a small town that does not have many year-round residents. After all, you have to find people who will be temporary tenants during the summer vacation.

Buying — and Selling — Condominiums

As MENTIONED earlier, real estate investments can offer a mix of rental income, tax benefits and capital gains. But ownership of a condo — that is, a dwelling unit in a group-owned building or on group-owned land — has additional advantages. Condos generally require less capital and have fewer maintenance problems than single-family houses do.

You can start by buying a unit for personal use. Condo owners can deduct mortgage interest and real estate taxes from their taxable income. People who rent out units also can deduct monthly maintenance and depreciation — up to the limits set by tax laws. In 1990, about 15% of the condos in the U.S. were held as investments.

Some investors convert whole apartment houses into condos. You can invest in one of these deals either directly, by buying a building and converting it, or indirectly, as a limited partner who supplies some of the capital but stays on the sidelines. Of course, if you buy into a limited partnership, you will be able to use any losses only to offset income from passive investments.

If you are a tenant in a building that is being converted, you generally will have to pay twice as much per square foot to buy your apartment as the converter did. Even so, that "insider's" price may be well below the market value of similar homes. Some tenants make a profit by immediately reselling. That's known as flipping.

Tenants who buy and stay on commonly have to pay more per month in maintenance fees and mortgage expenses than their previous rent, but much of that extra cost may be offset by tax deductions.

What do you do if you own a condo and want to sell in the current slow market? Above all, don't panic. In mid-1992 the National Association of Realtors saw signs that the condo market had bottomed out, and that prices were beginning to increase at normal, nonrecession rates. So wait a few months, or if there's a condo glut in your area, wait about a year to see how much prices rebound. A cutback in condominium construction in some places should eventually balance out an oversupply.

Besides waiting, another choice for a condo owner is to move and rent out the unit. You might consider offering a tenant a lease with an option to buy at a prearranged price in, say, 12 months. That way, if real estate values rise, the tenant will be delighted to buy your condo at what will then be a discount.

If you must sell now, list your condominium for 10% to 20% less than the price of a single-family house in a comparable location. Historically, that's the difference needed to attract buyers to condos. Also, put some buzzwords in your newspaper classified ads. The words "overlooking pool" appeal to singles. Young couples might be lured by the opener "Can't Afford a House?" And phrases such as "safe, no kids" and "carefree living" might attract empty-nester parents in their 50s or 60s.

Buying Vacation Homes

S ECOND homes are bought primarily for recreation, relaxation and retirement, but they can be profitable real-estate investments, too. Generally speaking, if you buy in the right place at the right time, there's a good chance that the value of your vacation retreat will rise. Granted that in many areas the recession years haven't been the right time: from the start of 1990 to mid-1991 vacation-home prices in places such as Nantucket and Hilton Head plunged by more than 35%. By mid-1992, however, there were some signs of a turnaround: with consumer confidence helped by such factors as low interest rates, the vacation-home market began to pick up.

In any kind of market, you have the best chance of getting a good price if your second home has two characteristics. First, it has to be fairly easy to get to. The choicest turf is no more than a gas tank away from a big population area. If you can afford it, buy on or near the water. This is the surest bet for both high rentals and capital appreciation.

Second, the land surrounding the property should have limited potential for development. That automatically limits the supply of houses. Environmental laws that put a lid on construction have made waterfront properties especially attractive, though costly, investments. The state of New Jersey, for example, stopped a developer from filling in and building on some wetlands. In the three years after that ruling, prices of second-home plots in the area surged 300%.

Stay away from idiosyncratic vacation homes. The dwellings that hold their value best are those with exteriors that are in keeping with the area. And look for communities that have stable growth, strong zoning and a distaste for go-go construction projects.

If you are considering a development that is under construction, grill the developer and the real estate agent about the timetable for installing such amenities as recreational facilities, community water supplies and sewage disposal. Get guarantees in *writing*. Check with the local real estate commission or with an office of the federal Department of Housing and Urban Development to see if the developer has registered for interstate land sales and has posted a substantial bond to pay for anything he inadvertently omits.

When you have located a property you are interested in, bargain vigorously. Bid at least 20% less than the asking price — especially in areas where the market is sluggish.

Timing is critical in both the purchase and sale of vacation real estate. Because it is a discretionary purchase, prices fluctuate more widely in economic booms and busts than the prices of other houses do. Lately, buyers with cash in hand have been finding tremendous bargains in some areas. The reasons include overbuilding and the new tax laws.

Finding a mortgage should be easier than it's ever been. Both the Federal Home Loan Mortgage Corporation (Freddie Mac) and the Federal National Mortgage Association (Fannie Mae) now buy vacation-home mortgages held by banks. That helps make credit readily available. Also, many sellers will take back the mortgages themselves. This means they, in effect, agree to receive payment for the house over a period of 10 years or so.

But it is important to shop around for financing. Many banks demand not only a ½% premium for such loans but also 20% down, plus points and fees that can amount to at least 3½% of the total mortgage. Check with a local real estate agent or title company to find which banks grant the best vacation-home mortgages.

One way to beat the cost of second houses is to divvy up the ownership — and expenses — with several families. For example, four couples share a $100,000 ski condominium in Keystone, Colorado. Each couple arranged their own financing and borrowed from private sources, since banks do not give mortgages on a quarter of a house. Under a legal agreement, if one couple wants out, the others get first crack at buying their share.

To help pay for the mortgage, taxes and upkeep, more and more owners are renting out their second homes. Local real estate agents find tenants, and keep an eye on the property once it is rented. The agents' fees range from 10% to 20% of the rent. For higher fees, managers of some resort communities not only find tenants but also collect the rent and take care of repairs.

Like owners of any house, you can deduct the mortgage interest and property taxes on your vacation home — as long as the IRS deems your pleasure palace a second home. If you do not use it for more than 14 days a year, the house may qualify as rental real estate. Then you must meet the requirements of any rental real estate owner in order to deduct up to the maximum $25,000 allowed beyond the amount of any passive income you may have.

REITs and Limited Partnerships

F EW small investors can afford to spring for an office building, a large apartment house or a shopping center. Yet you can get in on these potentially lucrative investments, and it is easier than you might think. You can become either a limited partner in a real estate project or a shareholder in a real estate investment trust, commonly known as a REIT.

Limited partnerships are sold by brokerage houses, insurance agents and financial planners. You generally have to put up a $5,000 to $10,000 minimum. That entitles you to shares, or units, in a major real estate investment. Remember that under the tax law all limited partnerships are passive investments. That reduces their tax benefits and enhances the appeal of income-oriented partnerships. Limited partnerships therefore emphasize investments for income and the prospect of capital gains when the partnership's properties are sold.

But by mid-1992, limited partnerships were a shaky investment. Some investors who had attempted to withdraw before the properties were sold found that their holdings had fallen to 20% or less of their asset value. For most investors who don't have the skill to do the necessary research, limited partnerships are just too risky. If you do have enough assets to diversify into limited partnerships, discuss them thoroughly with a qualified investment adviser before buying.

Real estate investment trusts are very different from limited partnerships. A REIT operates somewhat like a closed-end mutual fund, but one that invests in a diversified portfolio of real estate or mortgages instead of stocks and bonds. Shares of REITs are traded just like those of closed-end funds or common stocks, on the exchanges or over-the-counter. This means you can sell your REIT shares in the open market. REITs thus offer the advantage of being a liquid form of investment in real estate, which is traditionally an illiquid asset.

You can buy REIT shares from stock brokers and financial planners. Shares typically cost from $2 to $35 each, with no minimum purchase required. You then collect the income that the trust earns from rent and other sources. In fact, REITs are required by law to distribute at least 95% of their taxable income as dividends to shareholders. Because they pay out so much of their earnings, they pay no corporate income tax. That means that their earnings, unlike those of companies that issue stock, are not taxed before they are distributed. Thus, investors get a bigger share of the profits than they do with stock. When you collect those dividends, you also may be able to defer paying taxes on a portion of them.

When the trust sells off the properties it owns, you get the profits from the sale. You collect them in the form of either special dividends or, if the proceeds are reinvested, increased earnings per share, which often boost the price of your REIT stock.

If properties owned by an REIT rise in value, the market probably also will bid up its shares. REITs soared in the early 1970s, then crashed when a number of construction and development loans failed. The boom-and-bust pattern has continued, though the industry profile has changed. REIT investments in actual property (rather than mortgages) have steadily increased; in 1992 more than two-thirds of the industry was composed of equity REITs.

Such REITs took their lumps in the savings-and-loan debacle: in the first eight months of 1990 their value plunged 16.3% after adjusting for dividends — twice the decline of the S&P 500 stock index. When federal regulators started dumping foreclosed commercial properties on the market at distress prices, real estate investors got the shakes. The onset of recession only made matters worse.

Funny thing, though. Plenty of REITs were prospering in 1992, with fully rented properties. The strongest sign of health showed up in growing cash flow, a figure that adds back the depreciation that lowers taxable profits. Few REITs carried heavy debts. If they had a weakness, it was strictly in the stock market's aversion to real estate investments.

In mid-1992, institutional investors were concentrating on the larger REITs. The largest, New Plan Realty Trust, was capitalized at $1 billion. The runner-up, Meditrust, was worth $725 million. More typically, the market values REITs at $100 million to $400 million. Market capitalizations that size are not liquid enough for some large investors such as pension funds and insurance companies. But the REIT market has ample liquidity for individual investors.

The most successful REITs are regional and often specialize in one type of property, such as shopping centers or apartment buildings. In picking REITs, as in picking mutual funds, hitch yourself up with skilled managers with long records of success. Some of the best companies thrive on buying rundown properties and putting them back in the profit column, says Kenneth Gregory, president of Litman/Gregory & Co., San Francisco investment managers. He cites as an example New Plan Realty. New Plan buys poorly managed strip shopping centers in small mid-Atlantic cities with no competing malls. It fixes them up, improves the mix of tenants and finds ways to attract shoppers. Many analysts also recommend health-care REITs: they are recession-resistant and are expected to benefit from the aging population. Two small no-load mutual funds specialize in REITs and other real estate stocks. Fidelity Real Estate Investment Portfolio, a no-load fund, was paying a 4.4% dividend in mid-1992. United Services Real Estate Fund was yielding 3.8%.

REITs can also offer a tax advantage: as much as half of their cash distributions may be sheltered.

Buying Into Second Mortgages

ALMOST everybody complains whenever mortgage rates rise to daunting levels, but those rates are a cause for rejoicing for one kind of person. He or she is the sophisticated investor who is willing to take the risk of putting his or her cash into second mortgages.

Second mortgages are loans made to homebuyers whose down payments and primary mortgages still don't add up to the appraised value. Anyone with a fairly large sum to invest can grant such second-mortgage loans and earn an annual return of 10% or more.

With most second mortgages, the borrower makes monthly payments only on the interest. The investor — that is, the lender — gets his principal back in a lump sum when the loan expires; typically, that is in three years. The interest rate is negotiated by the lender and borrower. As a rule, it is about two percentage points above the rate local banks charge on first mortgages.

Recently there has been an alternative to the second-mortgage formula called a shared-equity financing. Here an investor puts up part of the down payment on the house. Technically, this is not a loan; the investor becomes a co-owner. (For more, see "Your Home: Shared-Equity Mortgages.")

Say that you want to invest in a second mortgage or a shared-equity deal. You can get leads to people who need such financing by asking builders, real estate agents or mortgage loan brokers. Beware, however, of shady brokers, who lure investors with promises of suspiciously high returns of 18% to 24%. In New Mexico, two mortgage brokers recently were sentenced to prison for, among other things, failing to tell investors that one-third of their borrowers defaulted.

With either a second mortgage or a shared-equity investment, it is easier to get in than get out. If the investor in a second mortgage needs his money before the term of the loan is up, he can sell the note. But if interest rates are higher than at the time the loan was made, he will have to sell the note at a discount.

So if you are prospecting for high annual returns, you may want to consider the second-mortgage investment market. But be prepared to keep your money locked up for the length of the loan.

Making Tax-free Exchanges

IF YOU hold some land or a house for an investment, there may come a day when you will want to sell it for a profit. You would get a better deal if you do not sell it, but swap it for another piece of property. That way, you delay paying any taxes on your capital gains. You do not pay until you ultimately make a sale. This rule applies to all kinds of real property, so long as you use it as an investment. It could be a house or a condo, a plot of land on which you plan to build or even barren land that you are holding for possible future development.

For example, one couple living in Utah long owned 100 acres of idle farmland way off in North Carolina. Because they bought it many years ago, when prices were cheap, they would have a big profit if they sold it — and they would have to pay large capital-gains taxes. But they can avoid that if they find someone with whom to make a tax-free exchange for other property, perhaps closer to home in Utah.

The properties you exchange do not have to be identical or even of the same value. You could swap farmland for an apartment building or a condo. But you would be taxed on any additional cash you received at the time of the deal. And the swap has to be almost simultaneous. You have to receive your new property no later than 45 days after you transfer ownership of your old property.

How do you find some other property owner to swap with? Just write to your state board of realtors for a list of brokers who are certified commercial investment members. That means they have received special training in real estate transactions and passed state exams. Be sure to seek the help of a tax attorney who is knowledge-able about real estate to make sure that your swap contract meets all the requirements of a tax-free exchange.

Your Home

The Outlook for Housing Prices

A S AMERICANS, we grow up expecting nothing less than life, liberty — and a house that appreciates in value year after year. But now young homeowners don't automatically anticipate that they will someday own a home larger than the one they grew up in. Median prices of existing houses have increased less than the Consumer Price Index in six of the past ten years. Housing prices have remained flat in Denver and Phoenix, and in 1990 and 1991 plummeted as much as 20% in New England, metropolitan New York, and San Francisco — before recovering slightly in 1992.

The housing boom of the 1980s, of course, couldn't last forever. Demographics were bound to reverse or at least slow the trend. Coming up behind the 75 million baby boomers are 48 million baby busters, the age group now 18 through 28 and approaching their thirtysomething household-formation stage of life. Many experts reckon that houses in general will appreciate only about as fast as the inflation rate.

The prospect of modest gains has broad implications for mobile Americans who have come to depend on their houses as their best overall investments. For example, you would be wise to refrain from stretching for a second mortgage or home-equity loan on the expectation that the eventual sale of your house will bail you out.

Also don't count on appreciation of a recently bought house to provide collateral for your children's college loans. Still worse, unless you live in a house for at least three to five years, closing costs, brokerage fees and other expenses may wipe out any profit you can expect when selling.

Looking at the positive side, many new homebuyers will find that lower mortgage rates will make financing their new home possible. Mortgage rates dropped to single digits in mid-1990, and have remained there as of mid-1992 — lower than they had been for most of the past decade.

Cities Where Prices Are Highest — and Lowest

FOR HOMEOWNERS, real estate prices have not been cause for raising the roof. Median prices for existing homes rose a little more than inflation in 1990 and 1991, but 1992 has shown a slight recovery, although the picture varies from city to city. The market has softened considerably in some places, particularly those that boasted high rates of return in the 1980s. For example, in Bergen County, New Jersey, prices in the last decade rose by as much as 59% in a single year. But from mid-1989 to mid-1992, median prices dropped 8%.

The National Association of Realtors reports that the median price for an existing single-family home in the United States ranged from a low of $46,200 in Cedar Falls, Iowa, to a peak of $339,500 in Honolulu. In the twelve months through June 1992, the nationwide median price for previously occupied homes rose 2.3% to $103,600. Cities where housing costs hovered around the median included Baltimore, Las Vegas and Raleigh-Durham. Some of the most reasonable housing — with median prices of around $70,000 or less — could be found throughout the Midwest, as well as in San Antonio, Toledo and Louisville.

When Is the Right Time to Buy?

I**S NOW** a good time to buy a house? The answer is yes — if you really need a house to live in and if you have found one that you like. Contrary to popular wisdom, the National Association of Realtors reports that it is easier now to buy a house than it has been for many years. In July 1992 the NAR's "affordability" index for first-time buyers showed that anyone earning $37,000 a year — the median income for young families who currently are renters — had *more* than enough income to buy the median-priced starter home costing $103,600. In 1981, by comparison, most young renters had less than half of the necessary income.

How much of your income can you afford to spend when you are buying a house or an apartment? A little less than you used to. Some years ago, it was sensible to reach financially to get the biggest house in the best neighborhood that you possibly could manage. Inflation then was running away, meaning that your house was likely to spurt in value, and you would be paying off your mortgage debt in ever-depreciating dollars. Now that inflation is moderate, real estate professionals advise you not to buy more house than you can handle. They say you may spend a little more than you are comfortable with because real estate stands to remain a sound — although not a runaway — investment. Beware, however, of buying a house well beyond your means. Once you own it, you will not be able to keep it up, and that will hurt you when you are ready to resell. If you don't have the money to paint your house or otherwise repair it, you will never get top dollar for it.

When should you trade up to a larger house? Homeowners have been afraid to make a move in the depressed market, worrying that they will have to sell their home at too painful a discount. But many who have been willing to take the chance have found that they ultimately got a great deal on a new residence.

How Much House You Can Afford

House hunters' eyes are usually bigger than their wallets. That's as it should be. Your job is to find the house you want to live in. When it comes to financing the place, though, it's the banker's job to measure you for size.

Lenders usually follow guidelines laid down by the Federal National Mortgage Association, better known as Fannie Mae. Mortgages, you see, have become commodities in a resale market, where investors trade in mortgage securities. Fannie Mae and the other secondary mortgage companies need uniform products to sell.

Following these guidelines, here's how lenders judge your ability to pay back a loan:

First, they calculate your housing expense ratio, which is the highest percentage of your gross income that bankers will let you spend on monthly payments. They add up your salaries, investment income and other steady streams of income, such as alimony or child support or disability benefits. That's your gross income. Then they tabulate the basic costs of ownership. The main items are mortgage interest and principal, real estate taxes and homeowner's insurance. Other possible expenses might include mortgage insurance guaranteeing payment to the lender or special tax assessments on the property, such as for use of the sewer system or fire protection. In a condominium or a special housing development, there might also be association dues for maintaining a pool and other amenities.

Divide your monthly housing expenses by your monthly gross income and multiply the answer by 100 to arrive at your housing expense ratio. If the answer is more than 28%, you probably won't get a conventional mortgage. If it's above 29%, you won't usually qualify for an FHA loan, the type insured by the government.

The lenders' second measure, called the total-obligation-to-income ratio, equals the percentage of your gross income that will be needed to pay both your housing expenses and other long-term obligations. To your housing expenses, the loan officer will add your monthly payments on any other nonbusiness mortgages, installment loans, credit-card balances with terms longer than ten months and regular payments to an ex-spouse for alimony or child support. You are probably over your head for a conventional loan if your total obligations equal more than 36% of your gross income — or more than 41% for an FHA or Veterans Administration (GI) loan.

Let's presume that you can clear those hurdles. Congratulations! But don't order furniture just yet. You still have to satisfy a lender that you are a worthy risk. Banks and mortgage companies will check out your credit report to make sure you haven't missed payments on other loans. They will make sure your salary and employment history jibe with your answers to loan-application questions.

Oh, and one more thing: the down payment. More often than housing expenses, this obstacle will sour the deal. Fannie Mae generally wants you to put at least 20% down on a house. Cash-shy buyers may get by with 15% or even 10% down if their income is hefty enough. But they will have to add about three-eighths of a percent to their loan rate to cover commercial mortgage insurance.

Folks with shallow pockets and small salaries should investigate FHA or VA mortgages. The minimum down payment on an FHA loan starts at a minuscule 3% of the first $25,000 borrowed and rises to 5% on the rest of the loan. On a $100,000 mortgage, the down payment is an affordable $4,500. FHA, however, puts a ceiling on the loan size. It cannot exceed the median house price in your county. If you're a vet who qualifies (yes, Gulf War veterans do), no down payment at all is necessary. And anyone who served in the Armed Forces for as few as 180 days in peacetime or 90 days in wartime qualifies.

Choosing a House to Purchase

AMERICA'S favorite investment is still the family house. It is also by far the biggest investment that most people make. Mid-1992's median price of $119,000 for a new house represented a slight dip from 1991 figures, although the reverse was true for one that had been previously occupied — $103,600 in 1992, up from $100,200 the year before. In fourteen years, those figures had jumped from, respectively, $55,700 and $48,700.

Prices will not soar in the early 1990s as they did a decade earlier. Still, today's smart buyers can expect to earn a profit when they sell.

You probably *will* sell your home at some point, unless you feel sure that you will remain in it for the 30 years it will take to pay off the mortgage. Thus, when choosing a house, you should select one that not only appeals to you but also stands to be a worthwhile investment. Whether it's a small starter home or a spacious family dwelling, the same factors affect the resale value of a house:

Medium-sized houses are better long-term investments than very large or small ones. Those with three bedrooms are easier to sell than those with four or more. Houses in the strongest demand also have at least two full baths.

Houses are better than condominium apartments. Most people prefer single-family detached houses. Consequently, you'll find a buyer's market for condos or co-ops in popular areas of many cities, including New York, Miami and Stamford, Connecticut.

Conventional styles sell more easily — and for higher prices — than do unconventional ones. In the East, conventional means split-levels and colonials; in the South and West, contemporaries are more common; in the Heartland, a style known as Midwestern traditional is most appealing. Remember: Today's trendy style may be tomorrow's out-of-fashion oddball.

Standard interiors attract more buyers and higher prices than unusual configurations do. If you want to sell a pink Cadillac, you will have to find someone who dotes on pink Cadillacs. Two rooms add the most to resale value: the kitchen and a second bathroom. The kitchen should have plenty of light and modern appliances. It does not have to be equipped for Julia Child, but it should come with a dishwasher and a garbage disposal. And even if you live in the Deep South, buy a house with a fireplace. Though wasteful of energy, fireplaces are romantic accessories that usually hold their value in all parts of the country.

The houses in a neighborhood should be of roughly equal value. Stay away from places where there is a wide disparity, because smaller, cheaper dwellings depress the prices of their more elaborate neighbors. If you do find yourself in a neighborhood where house values differ substantially, look for the ugly duckling on a street full of swans. Even if you do not improve the property, the neighborhood will lift its value. So remember: The least expensive house in a neighborhood is a much better buy than the most expensive one. The former will be pulled up by surrounding values; the latter will be held down by them.

Location is paramount. It's hard to beat a house in a neighborhood where the homes and lawns are well cared for. Check the zoning laws. You don't want to see auto body shops or mobile homes springing up among standard single-family homes.

One way to pick the right neighborhood is to see how other buyers are voting with their dollars. A second gauge is the variation between asking and selling prices. In choice neighborhoods, the difference is small, often only 3% to 5%.

Another measure is how quickly houses have been selling. For years, the rule of thumb has been that if the average length of time on the market is less than three months, the area is strong and in demand. Similarly instructive is the percentage of houses put up for sale that are actually sold within 90 days. In an undesirable place, or in an overpriced market, two-thirds of all the homes listed with real estate firms might not change hands within that period or might even be taken off the market without being sold. In 1989, however, it took an average of 97 days before a house was sold, and by 1991 that number was up to 105 days, according to the Better Homes and Gardens Real Estate Service 1991 Housing Cost Survey. To get this information, call either a local board of realtors or a home builders' association. It's best to call at least three or four sources.

A smart way to start your search is to look for a community or part of the city that has superb schools, whether or not you have school-age children. Parents are willing to pay premium prices to move to an area that offers excellent education. Check to see how much the community budgets for school expenses *per child* and compare that figure with other school districts in the area. Also find out what percentage of the high-school graduates go on to college; 80% or more is excellent. Before you buy, be sure to visit a local school and speak with the principal. Simply by asking him or her what distinguishes the school, you can gain some valuable impressions. For example, if the principal boasts, "Our school is almost as good as Smithville's," you might then want to search for a house not in that school district but in Smithville's.

You also can make a sound investment by putting your money in a brand-new tract house. Builders are very anxious until they get those first few houses off their hands and see that the development will sell. Savvy buyers can capitalize on those fears to knock down the asking price or squeeze such extras out of the contractor as better-quality kitchen fixtures.

Before you buy a house anywhere, you may want to find out about the record and reliability of the firm that built it. One way to gather information is to call an organization called Home Owners Warranty and get a list of its members to see if your builder is one of them. (To find the nearest HOW council, phone 800-CALL-HOW.) More than 10,000 builders belong to HOW. They are required to build according to approved standards and to carry a 10-year protection against major structural defects in the houses they construct. You can also get free brochures on how to protect your biggest investment, and what to do to maintain it or remodel it, by writing to Home Owners Warranty, P.O. Box 1214, Malvern, Pennsylvania 19355. In addition, it's a good idea to investigate other homes constructed by the same builder to see how they have held up over time.

How you buy can be as important as what you buy. The success of an investment depends largely on getting favorable financing. Put down as little of your own money as possible and try to get as much financing as you can from the seller. Ask for as long a term as the seller will accept. Assume the seller's mortgage if you can. You will normally be able to do so if it is a Federal Housing Administration– or Veterans Administration–backed loan, or if the mortgage has been in effect for many years.

In summary, here are some tips for the purchase and sale of your home that will pay off:

— The best way to buy a house is to buy the neighborhood. Look for a superior school system. That is what potential buyers will want when you sell your house.

— If your house has one bathroom, one of the best improvements you can make is adding a second bathroom. Another profitable remodeling project is redoing the kitchen.

— You stand to earn more profit in a new dwelling than in an old one. From 1980 to mid-1992, prices of new single-family homes rose 84%, versus 66% for old ones.

— If you want to build onto your house, do not plan an addition that raises the value of your property more than 20% over the value of other houses in the neighborhood. It will not pay in the end, when you sell your house.

— When it comes time to sell, try to make the sale before you buy and move into another house. Empty houses seldom command their asking prices.

How to Get the Most from a
Real Estate Agent

B EFORE you search for a house or apartment, you should hunt for a real estate agent. Do not rely on luck and newspaper ads but start with recommendations from friends who have recently moved. Call the board of realtors in the community you are moving to and ask for names of several former Realtors of the Year; agencies earn this designation because they sell a lot of houses and know much about the market. If the board of realtors is not listed in the phone book, a local realtor should be able to direct you to the nearest board. Also, go to open houses where the public is allowed to view some of the homes listed for sale with various brokerage firms.

The agent you choose should have access to the local multiple listing service. It is a computerized network that gives him or her a complete rundown of all the houses listed for sale in the area. He or she also should know the local mortgage market and help you figure out how much house you can carry based on your income and expenses. Once you have found a house you want to buy, the agent will help you negotiate the price and close the sale.

A brokerage firm usually earns a commission of 6% or 7% of the selling price of the house for listing it — that is, putting it on the market — and selling it. If your agent works for another firm, the commission is split 50-50 between the firm that lists and the firm that sells. But the bottom line is that the seller of the house, not the buyer, generally pays the commission.

Almost all agents really work for the seller. For this reason, when you have found a house you would like to make a bid on, never tell your agent: "Let's offer the Smiths $200,000 — but we'll go as high as $220,000 if we have to." The agent is obliged by the custom of the trade to repeat that information to the seller. So wait until the seller refuses your offer before you volunteer that you are willing to pay more. And remember: It is generally in the broker's interest to downplay whatever faults lie in a house or neighborhood.

Some agents, however, have set themselves up to represent only the buyer. The buyer often pays this kind of broker a flat fee or by the hour. That way the broker will not steer the buyer to more expensive houses in order to get a fatter commission. If the buyer does not find a house he or she likes, the broker usually refunds part or all of the fee.

The broker who works for a buyer will examine houses listed through agencies as well as those advertised directly by owners. He or she will also inspect the house for flaws in construction and check the neighborhood for potential changes in assessments or problems in the schools. Such a broker is likely to strike a much tougher bargain for his or her customer, the buyer, than a conventional broker. The broker might demand, for example, that the seller guarantee the integrity of the roof or the plumbing for a period of up to one year. When serving the buyer, some real estate agents submit question-naires to sellers requesting specific details about a house's condition. This tends to flush out the costly little surprises.

What if you are selling your house? You will find that the competition among real estate brokers for your business has become fierce, partly because nationwide companies are fighting to expand in the market. Thus, you can make some particularly good deals now.

The large, national organizations claim to offer more tempting services than small, independent agencies can. For example, one national agency, Electronic Realty Associates (ERA), promises to buy your house if it can't make a sale within 210 days *and* if you buy another house from ERA.

Independent real estate brokers have been fighting back, some-times offering to work for less than the prevailing commissions. But the kind of deal you get from any agent depends overwhelmingly on how desirable your house is. If you have a sound, attractive structure in a sought-after location, you might be able to offer a broker a commission of 4% or 5% instead of the conventional 6%.

Occasionally you can persuade a broker to give up part of his or her commission just to get a stalled deal moving again. If a buyer and a seller are only a few thousand dollars apart, the broker may agree to cut his or her fee if the seller accepts a lower price. In effect, the broker absorbs some of the seller's loss.

Some brokers have unbundled the traditional package of services and provide, at an hourly rate, only what customers need. Other brokers — the discounters — are charging commissions of about 2%. But these agents use color slides to let the potential buyer screen properties in their offices, and then they expect sellers to show their own houses to prospects.

Count On Those Extra Costs

WHEN you buy a home, you will discover that the price is much bigger than what the seller is asking. Behind the down payment and the mortgage installments lurk nettlesome expenses known as closing costs. They can amount to 4% to 8% of the size of the mortgage. On a typical $80,000 mortgage, that means you will have to pay an additional $3,200 to $6,400.

Among the extras you have to fork over are loan origination fees and points. Origination fees are typically figured as 1% of the mortgage amount, or one point. In addition, your lender is likely to demand one to three points — all up-front interest. Other typical mortgage costs are an application fee ($75 to $300), an appraisal fee ($150 to $300) and a survey ($125 to $300).

And buyers who cannot put down 20% or more of the purchase price in cash are required to buy private mortgage insurance to protect the lender against default. For this insurance, you typically will be charged a onetime fee of one-half to one point plus annual premiums of a quarter-point or more.

Mortgage lenders also want proof that the seller has a clear title to the property you are buying. That is why you will have to pay for the cost of a title search. You also will have to buy insurance to cover the possibility that the search missed something. Figure on the two fees running you $500 to $650.

It is up to you to insure the house. At the closing you must show that you have a policy and that the first year's premium has been paid. That will come to between $350 and $600 for a single-family house and slightly less for a condo.

Of course, many towns, counties and state governments also muscle in on the closing, demanding their due in the form of sales or transfer taxes. These are usually based on the selling price of the house or the size of the mortgage and can run a couple of points or more.

Just when you think you have paid every conceivable tithe, tariff and tax, a few more bills will crop up. If you need an attorney to represent you at the closing, for example, that will be $300 to more than $1,000. But you will know you have finally reached the end of the line when you have to pay to have your deed recorded. That cost usually will be only $40 to $60.

Raising Money for the Down Payment

E VEN IF you are struggling to come up with a modest down payment, you can still buy a home. Do not automatically assume you have to raise 10% to 20% of the purchase price in cash.

If you have served with the armed forces, you may be able to get a mortgage insured by the Department of Veterans Affairs for 100% of the cost of the house or apartment — with no down payment. You do not have to be a vet to qualify for a Federal Housing Administration–insured loan that can cover up to 95% of the purchase price. You can apply for VA and FHA loans at banks and savings and loan associations.

You also can qualify for a 90% to 95% loan without government backing if you take out private mortgage insurance. A lender will be most likely to insure you if your income is high and your credit rating is impeccable. A good repayment record on auto and student loans is essential.

If your employer allows it, you can borrow against your contributions in a corporate profit-sharing program or a salary reduction plan. You will be charged interest at a rate that is often lower than a bank would charge.

If your parents want to help you out, they can give as much as $40,000 each year to a married child and spouse without having to pay federal gift taxes. Or in return for making the down payment, your parents could become co-owners of the house. That way you could buy a more expensive place than you could otherwise afford. And you won't be alone in seeking such help. According to a 1990 Chicago Title & Trust Co. survey of homebuyers, only 78% of the average first-time buyer's down payment comes from his or her own savings.

The seller of the house you want to buy also can be the source of the down payment. One possibility to explore with him or her is renting the house for a period with an option to buy. A portion of your rent could go to building a down payment.

As a last resort, consider dipping into your own IRA. If you're not yet 59½ years old, you'll have to pay ordinary income tax and a 10% penalty on the amount of your early withdrawal, but these costs may be outweighed by the tax deductions your new house will generate.

Finding the Best Mortgage

THE excitement of home buying involves not only the hunt for the right house but also the search for the right mortgage. Lenders have a large supply of cash, and they are so eager to lend it that they are offering many new kinds of loans. You will find analyses of different types of mortgages in the following sections. Here is a quick guide:

If you value predictability and need a guarantee that your mortgage payments will not rise, you may well want a *fixed-rate* mortgage. The rate you pay will be higher at first than you would get with other kinds of mortgages, but it will remain constant. In mid-1992, fixed-rate 30-year mortgages were available at 8.56% — the lowest level since 1978 (except for a brief period in 1987). Among the reasons for the modest rates are the prospect of moderate inflation and the 7.32% yield on 10-year Treasuries, which traditionally influence the direction of mortgages. On a $75,000 loan, for example, the monthly payments worked out to $580, excluding taxes and insurance.

Then there is the initially more affordable *adjustable-rate* mortgage, or ARM. It is inviting for younger buyers who expect their salaries to grow rapidly. The interest on it goes up or down, usually every one to three years, in line with an overall index of interest rates that you and your lender agree on. To draw customers, lenders generally offer adjustable mortgages at interest rates below fixed-rate loans. This enables you to start off paying low rates. But after the first interval, usually one year, the monthly payment will change.

If you cannot decide between an adjustable-rate or a fixed-rate loan, the solution may be a *convertible* mortgage. It starts out with an adjustable rate that is lower than that on a fixed-rate mortgage. But if, for example, interest rates drop in the future, you can convert to a fixed-rate mortgage at close to the then-current rate for such loans.

Say that you took out a convertible mortgage on which the interest rate might have started at 8.85%, which was far lower than the available 10.3% on a fixed-rate loan. After three years your adjustable rate drops to 7.5% but your lender is offering fixed-rate mortgages at 7%. You would be able to convert to that 7% fixed-rate loan. There is a price for convertibility, of course. If you convert, lenders commonly charge a fee of between $100 and $250. Often, too, their conversion interest is a shade higher than the going rate.

When you go shopping for a mortgage, start by looking in your newspaper to see what local lenders are offering. Then look for a real estate broker who uses a computerized service, which can make comparison shopping a lot easier and faster. In many cities and suburbs, a broker will punch into a desktop computer the size of the loan you are looking for, the amount of your income and other details of your finances. The computer then displays on its screen descriptions of different mortgages that are available from various lenders. It also displays the latest interest rates being offered and tells you if you are likely to qualify for a particular loan. In some cases, these services permit you to apply for the mortgage electronically. You never deal with the lender in person and the papers are simply mailed to you for signing.

The most valuable matchmaking services are clearinghouses for mortgages from many lenders, including those in faraway places where money may be more easily available and interest rates more competitive than in your own area. One big computerized service is the American Financial Network in Dallas. The service enables local, regional and national lenders to display their mortgage plans in real estate brokers' offices and allows you to make an application directly with the chosen lender. Currently, the Network is available at more than 100 real estate brokerage firms throughout the United States. For information call 800-275-3994.

Another such matchmaker is HSH Associates (1200 Route 23, Butler, New Jersey 07405; 800-UPDATES, or 201-838-3330 in New Jersey), a mortgage-search service that you must contact directly. For $20, you can get a kit for homebuyers that includes the booklet *How to Shop for Your Mortgage* and the latest HSH weekly reports on the terms of loans from dozens of institutions in your state. HSH publishes regional editions for 36 states and 50 major metropolitan areas. Before you send your check, call and see if HSH covers your area.

Adjustable-Rate Mortgages

I F YOU'RE young, have a good salary and face prospects that your pay will get even better, investigate adjustable-rate mortgages, or ARMs. The initial rate you pay is generally about two and one-half percentage points lower than on a fixed-rate loan. That discount usually disappears in the second year, when the lender adds a markup to your rate. After that, the rate goes up or down periodically along with interest rates in general.

It pays to get an ARM if its lower monthly payments help you to qualify for a loan on the house you truly desire. Just make sure you can really afford the house. An ARM also makes sense if you expect interest rates to rise long-term or if you plan to remain in your house or condo no more than three years before you sell out. The benefit you get from your first-year discount should more than make up for any rises in interest rates in the next few years.

What's the ideal adjustable mortgage? First, the loan agreement should include caps that limit the interest rate changes to no more than two percentage points a year and five to six points over the life of the loan. Second, your initial interest rate should be about two to three percentage points below that of fixed-rate loans. Third, when you get your mortgage, you should have to pay no more than two points in loan fees — a point being equivalent to 1% of your mortgage principal.

Unfortunately, the perfect mortgage is rare, but you should be able to trade some features for others that are especially important to you. For example, to get a lower interest rate, you can agree to pay additional fees up front. Whatever horse trading you do, however, never accept a cap on your monthly payments. When interest rates rise but your payments don't, the size of your loan grows because the unpaid interest is added to your mortgage.

The Federal Reserve Board and the Home Loan Bank Board have produced a booklet to help you understand adjustable-rate mortgages and read behind the fine print. It is called *The Consumer Handbook on Adjustable Rate Mortgages*. You can get it from mortgage lenders and real estate agents or by sending 50 cents to Consumer Information Center–P, Department 4237, Pueblo, Colorado 81009.

Shared-Appreciation Mortgages

A YOUNG couple in Phoenix spotted a house they wanted to buy. The price: $98,500. They figured that after putting 20% down they could get a $78,800 mortgage at interest rates then at 13½%. But monthly payments would have come to $950 a month, and that was more than the couple could afford. Their solution was to go to a mortgage company that offered them what is known as a shared-appreciation mortgage.

This type of loan lowered their payments by one-third. In return the buyers promised to give the lender one-third of the profit they make whenever they sell the house. Because housing values have risen so dramatically in the past, offering to share your appreciation might sound like a pact with the devil. But by agreeing to share profits, the Phoenix couple were able to buy as their first house one that otherwise might have taken years to acquire. And when they do sell, even though they will have to give the lender a third of the profit, they still stand to come out ahead. That's because their two-thirds share will probably amount to just as much as the full profit on a cheaper property.

Generally, these shared-appreciation mortgages help not only first-time buyers, but also elderly buyers who cannot afford to make big payments and who expect to own their houses for the rest of their lives.

If you consider a shared-appreciation mortgage, be aware of the risks. Under some agreements, a lender can collect his share of the appreciation after 10 years, even if the homeowner has not sold. If the homeowner does not have the cash to pay, he will have to borrow and perhaps take out a new mortgage. This could zap him with exploding monthly payments.

The shared mortgage is also a poor choice for a do-it-yourselfer. If you make home improvements yourself, the value that you add to your house is shared with the lender.

Shared-Equity Mortgages

WOULD you like to help your grown child buy his or her first house? Then you might want to consider a so-called shared-equity arrangement. It allows you to split the costs of buying and maintaining a home and combine two incomes to qualify for the mortgage.

A shared equity deal works like this: Two people purchase a house, but only one lives in it. The other partner is solely an investor. The occupant of the house must pay a fair market rent to his or her partner but keeps the proportion of the rent that represents his or her ownership. Meanwhile, the partner who does not live in the house typically pays a portion of the monthly carrying costs, including the property taxes and first-mortgage installments, and does not collect monthly interest payments. He or she gets to split the deductions for interest and taxes with the co-owner who occupies the house. Eventually they divide the value of the property, including any appreciation. Usually after a period of three to 10 years, the owner-occupant must buy out the investor.

Unfortunately, the investor who wants out of a shared-equity arrangement is really stuck. There is no secondary market at all for such investments — not yet, anyhow. But if you want to set up such an agreement, have a real estate lawyer with experience in this field draft a contract. The fee is typically $300, depending on what your lawyer charges per hour.

Still More Mortgages

A POPULAR method of reducing your early mortgage payments is the so-called buydown. A standard type, according to HSH Associates, is the 2-1 buydown that reduces the rate for two years at the beginning, 1% each year. In the first year, you would pay 2% less than the mortgage rate; the second year, 1% less. In the third year, you would begin paying the full rate and continue to do so for the remaining life of the 30-year loan. The overall cost of the mortgage would be higher than what you would pay for a straight 30-year fixed mortgage, but the reduced starting rate may be worth the extra cost.

Another type of buydown, usually offered by banks and S&Ls, requires you to deposit money in a non-interest-bearing account that the lender draws on each month to make up the amount of the monthly payment that you are, at first, unable to meet. For example, you give the lender $800 a month on a $1,000 per month loan the first year and $900 the second year. Accordingly, the money in the account is reduced $200 a month for the first year and $100 a month in the second year. After that, you cover the entire $1,000 payment each month.

Perhaps the most popular buydown of all is done with points, which are a prepayment of interest. The more points you can pay, the lower the rate.

A different type of loan, popular lately, is the balloon mortgage. It is structured like a 30-year mortgage, yet the interest rate is from ¼% or ¾% less than that on a typical 30-year fixed-rate loan. This is because the mortgage is due in only three, five or seven years. Often the loan will have a built-in refinancing option, offering you whatever the going rate is at that time. In any case, you *must* refinance.

You could save much money over the life of your loan with a so-called biweekly mortgage. This is actually not a mortgage but rather a way to ensure that your mortgage payments are made steadily and automatically. You ask your bank to deduct your house payments every two weeks from your checking account. Each payment is half of what you would turn over every month under a conventional mortgage. But you make 26 payments annually, not 24 — in effect amounting to an extra month's payment every year.

This could produce a big savings. Take a $100,000 mortgage at 11%. Your biweekly payments would be $476, and you would wind up paying $952 more a year than if your payments were monthly. But you would be able to retire your mortgage in about 20 years rather than 30. That works out to a savings in your interest payments of $95,000.

Particularly if you are a first-time homebuyer or are returning to the housing market after many years, you will need to educate yourself further about the myriad types of mortgages and real estate terms. A sensible way to do this is by reading a booklet called *How to Shop for Your Mortgage,* published by HSH Associates. It defines the most popular types of mortgages (without endorsing any one of them) and helps prospective buyers understand the fine print in mortgage contracts. It also contains an easy-to-read page of mortgage payment tables and a prequalification table that lets you calculate the mortgage you can afford. To get a copy, send $9 to HSH Associates, 1200 Route 23, Butler, New Jersey 07405.

The Profits and Perils of Swapping Your Mortgage

I F YOU are one of the boatload of people who still have not refinanced the high-interest mortgage you took out in the early 1980s, this may be the time to switch to one that lets you lower your monthly payments. In the first months of 1992, a walloping 70% of mortgages applied for were refinancings.

You may be carrying a mortgage with rates as hefty as 14% or more, perhaps because you have just not bothered to look around to see what's available. Although lenders have been offering a bewildering array of loan choices, they have done away with sharply discounted "teaser" rates on ARMs. And no sooner had the refinancing wave begun in early 1991 than rates temporarily edged up a bit. So swapping a peak-interest loan may or may not be a smart move. Everything depends on your up-front costs and how long you plan to keep your home.

Looked at over the full term of the loan, a saving of even one point in the interest rate on a 30-year, $100,000 mortgage saves you nearly $13,000 in total payments. But unless your new arrangement brings your monthly payments down enough over the time you plan to stay in your house to offset the out-of-pocket costs of refinancing, it's probably not worth the hassle and the immediate expenses. For example, if there is a prepayment penalty clause in your mortgage, you will have to pay plenty to get out of the loan agreement — as much as 3% of the unpaid balance. That's on top of the usual costs of refinancing, which often can be almost as much as the closing costs on the original mortgage.

So check carefully to see what these real costs will be, after you figure in your income tax deductions for them. Then compare them with the immediate and long-term savings you can expect by refinancing. You also should be planning to live in your house for at least three more years. Otherwise, the costs most likely will exceed the amount that you would save in monthly payments.

One quick way to see how long it will require for refinancing to pay off is to divide your closing costs by the reduction on your monthly payment. The result will equal the number of months it will take you to break even. For example, if your closing costs are $6,000 and your monthly saving is $150, you will need to keep your home 40 months to break even (6,000 divided by 150 equals 40).

For still more information, read a booklet published by the Federal Trade Commission, *A Consumer's Guide to Mortgage Refinancing*. It outlines what the costs are and how to tell if the time is right to refinance your home. You can get it by sending 50 cents to Consumer Information Center–P, Department 425Y, Pueblo, Colorado 81009.

Buying a Bargain House by Hotline

O NE way to find affordable housing is to phone 800-553-4636. On the other end will be Fannie Mae, the mortgage purchaser that would like to sell you a repossessed house at an attractive price. If there are residences available in your state of choice, you will receive a list of the properties in the mail, with their location and the name of a local agent.

The Department of Veterans Affairs has similar lines in Houston, St. Petersburg and Denver. Following electronic commands, you punch in the zip code of your chosen area, then the desired number of bedrooms and baths. If such homes are to be had, you listen to a list of houses identified by address, list price and square footage. Contact your local VA office for the hotline numbers.

The largest owner of foreclosed properties today is the Resolution Trust Corporation, the federal agency that has taken over the assets of failed savings and loans. As of mid-1992, the RTC had tens of thousands of properties for sale — one-third of them in Texas. The agency cuts prices 20% to 50% on homes that do not sell within specific periods. Call 800-RTC-3006 for a printout of what's available in any region, state, city or zip code.

A hotline is just one innovation that both private and government agencies are using to sell the many single-family homes that are foreclosed each year. Freddie Mac, another mortgage buyer, has five regional offices across America. They will send you a list of foreclosed homes in any area but must refer you to a broker if you want to buy.

As of September 1992, the U.S. Department of Housing and Urban Development had more than 30,000 homes for sale. Owning such properties is not the business that mortgage institutions want to be in — and that is good news for prospective buyers. You can be sure they will give you the best deal in town.

Whatever the location of foreclosed houses, their prices vary widely. Many are in the medium range for their area, while others are obviously at the low end. For a real bargain, consider the "handyman's special," the diamond in the rough that can be brought to brilliance with your own time and energy — and money. Every mortgage institution has some of these to sell. Fannie Mae prides itself on installing new fixtures and carpeting along with painting and replacing appliances. Freddie Mac also refurbishes. The Federal Housing Administration, the Department of Veterans Affairs and the Federal Deposit Insurance Corporation, on the other hand, all sell a house pretty much as is. These agencies are insufficiently funded to make many improvements.

Hotlines and special programs aside, sale procedures are standard. You can easily spot newspaper ads placed by real estate brokers as well as by agencies holding properties. Repossessed houses are sold through local brokers at fair market prices. Agencies also take sealed bids from any number of hopefuls who submit a price at a prede- termined time and place. Highest bids win. If houses languish on the market, agencies may accept lower-than-list prices, and they occa- sionally hold formal auctions.

A warning from David Kaufman, owner of Kaufman Lasman Associates, a real estate auction firm in Chicago: "Some people come away from auctions with a steal, and others get butchered."

Here's how to survive and even prosper at a real estate auction:

Avoid the auctions and sheriff sales held by court order. They are aimed strictly at real estate pros. Watch for auctions operated by national, regional or local companies on behalf of lenders and developers.

Prepare for an auction by finding out all you can about the

property for sale and the price of comparable houses in the area. Tour the house with a professional inspector. If possible, talk to a real estate broker familiar with the place. Get a professional appraisal to help you determine what your maximum bid should be. Remember that a house in a deteriorating neighborhood won't offer much investment potential. Hire a lawyer to make sure there are no other claims on the property. You want to buy it free of liens and disputes.

Arrange financing before the auction. You will have to submit a certified check for between $1,500 and $3,000, depending on the auctioneer. If your bid is unsuccessful, you get the money back. If your bid wins, the check goes toward the down payment. But if you can't qualify for financing, you lose the deposit.

Both the Federal Housing Administration and the Department of Veterans Affairs are prepared to give individual assistance to potential homebuyers at their regional offices throughout the country. The Department of Veterans Affairs will provide 100% financing, and you needn't be a veteran to qualify. Just reduce the VA's foreclosed houses by one.

Assembling a House from a Kit

YOU can buy almost anything from a catalogue today. But did you know that you can buy a new house from a catalogue? And it could be a much better deal than you think.

Some 15,000 people bought so-called kit houses in 1989. The basic components are pre-cut and marked in the manufacturer's factory. Then they are shipped to you with instructions for assembling by you or your contractor.

The cost of a kit house is about half that of a custom-built home. One four-bedroom, two-bath kit house that was recently built in Minnesota carried a base price of $45,000. That did not include the cost of putting it together or the land.

Kits also let you put up a house faster than you could by hiring an architect and a contractor to design and build a house. And we are not talking here of a shack in the box. The materials are usually as good as — or even better than — those in a standard home.

You can order kits that are complete — right down to the poles in your closets — but most include only the materials to construct a weather-tight house shell. That means the framing, lumber, roof, walls, exterior siding, windows and doors. You then pay a general contractor to buy and install everything you want to finish the house, such as the wallboard, wiring and plumbing.

You can save as much as 10% to 15% on construction costs by acting as your own contractor. Then you would have to find the various subcontractors needed to finish the house, and you would monitor their work schedules. That, of course, takes a lot of your time.

There's a list of 215 kit makers in *The Complete Guide to Factory-Made Houses*, available for $11.95 from the Building Institute, 127 South Broadway, Nyack, New York 10960. Advertisements for kit homes also appear in housing and building-trade magazines.

The first step in buying a kit is to steep yourself in manufacturers' catalogues. When you see something you like, phone the company to find its local dealer. Check with your local Better Business Bureau or state consumer-affairs office to see if any complaints have been filed against the company. Also ask the firm for names of local builders who have assembled its kits and for homeowners who have bought them. Interview them and visit their houses.

Once you know that you are dealing with a reliable company, you are ready to sit down with its representative to discuss the details of the house you want. Most buyers choose log houses. They are a far cry from Abe Lincoln's boyhood home, and they are sold by such firms as New England Log Homes (2301 State Street, Hamden, Connecticut 06518), Rocky Mountain Log Homes (1883 Highway 93 South, Hamilton, Montana 59840) and Southland Log Homes (P.O. Box 1668, Irmo, South Carolina 29063).

Many people work up their own designs. Of course, the more you depart from a standard plan, the more you will have to pay.

Selling Your House

B EFORE you buy a house or apartment, be sure to sell the one you now live in. Otherwise, you can run the risk of paying two mortgages and being forced to sell out at fire-sale prices. Do not assume that your present house will sell as quickly or for as much money as you think it should, especially if you are in a soft real estate market. Get an appraiser's estimate of its value and ask a real estate agent how rapidly homes in that price range are turning over in your area.

If houses stay on the market for more than two or three months, do not even look for a second home until you have a firm contract of sale on the first. And continue living in the house, if possible, while it is on the market. Untenanted houses give buyers the impression that the owners are desperate to sell.

To put your house into shape for selling, figure on spending several weekends of your time for a minor cosmetic facelift. Start with your home's so-called curb appeal, or how it looks from the street. A househunter's first impression can make or break the sale. You do not need to spring for a major paint job unless the outside walls are blistering and peeling. But touch up the trim. The $100 or so you spend on paint for outer doors and window trim often makes your house look freshly painted.

Do not forget to wash the windows, inside and out. When the glare of the sun hits dirty panes, you can see the streaks from the street. Patch cracks and potholes in your driveway. Finishing touches such as a bright red mailbox or tubs of pink geraniums flanking the front door sometimes can do more for the house than any major expenditure.

You also should spruce up the interior. Thin out your possessions before you show your house. The fewer things you have in a room or closet, the larger it will appear. Repaint rooms that need it, such as those that your kids have graced with unusual colors. Kitchens and bathrooms always must be immaculate. A rusty sink or a ring around the toilet bowl can scare off prospective buyers who might think the plumbing needs repair. All homebuyers are conscious of energy costs, so your heating system must appear to work well. Wipe the boiler and the area around it to remove soot or oil stains.

You are probably better off not trying to sell your house yourself. Real estate agents can market it through a multiple listing service, which alerts nearly every agent in the area that your home is up for sale. If you are still eager to help, some experts recommend preparing a fact sheet that includes a floor plan, utility and insurance costs and maintenance fees. Such a fact sheet would answer most buyers' questions while emphasizing the most attractive, or marketable, features of your home.

Before your house goes on the market, make sure it is correctly priced. It is worth hiring a professional appraiser, but shop around because fees vary. To find several candidates in your area, write or call the Appraisal Institute (875 North Michigan Avenue, Suite 2400, Chicago, Illinois 60611; 312-726-6888). Or you might solicit opinions from up to three brokers to ensure a competitive price.

While you are awaiting the sale, investigate the area you will be moving to. Drive around and see what neighborhoods best suit you. Survey the prices quoted in real estate ads in the Sunday paper. But do not actually househunt. You could fall in love with a new homestead while you are still wedded financially to your old one.

By selling first, of course, you may have to move out before you have found another house. Try to avoid that possibility in your negotiations with a prospective buyer. For example, you might be able to postpone the closing date to give yourself time to find a new place.

Such an extended closing period also gives the buyer more time to change his or her mind. So, a better solution, if the buyer is amenable, is to close the deal as soon as possible but rent your house back from him until you find another one. If the buyer balks at such a provision, resign yourself to renting elsewhere, preferably in or near your future neighborhood. Though a temporary inconvenience, this strategy will acquaint you with the market and make you a smarter buyer.

Financing Your House Sale

A RE you trying to sell your house or apartment but just cannot get rid of it? Then consider lowering your asking price rather than offering to lend some of the money to a buyer. So-called seller financing should be your last resort.

Sellers typically make loans at rates as much as two percentage points below market rates. But you should not subsidize the buyer unless you cannot sell your house any other way. Most people do not have the time or skills to manage such an investment successfully.

Say that you decide to help provide the financing for the buyer of your house. Your first problem could be neglecting to do a thorough credit check on him or her. Although you might be planning to get tough the moment your buyer misses a payment, there is not much you can do.

You might figure you could threaten to foreclose — that is, take back your house. Just try it! Foreclosure can drag out for months. All the time, your debtor can enjoy the comforts of your old home — and you cannot exactly expect him to treat the house with tender loving care during the whole nasty affair.

Even the best-referenced buyer can go belly-up. Whatever you can do to make that option as unpleasant as possible for him or her will stand to your advantage. So demand a healthy down payment, at least 10% and preferably more. For an insolvent buyer, it is a lot less painful to walk away from a mortgage contract with nothing to lose but a good credit rating than to lose both his credit rating and, say, $10,000.

If you want to finance the sale of your house yourself, you can enlist help from officers at your bank or savings and loan association. For a fee of ½% to 1% of the loan amount, they will service, or collect payments on, the mortgage you give to a buyer. For additional fees, the banker will do a credit check on the prospective buyer and handle a foreclosure — if one becomes necessary. Finally, the bank or savings and loan can sell you insurance against default. Typically, the cost is $400 for a $40,000 loan.

Once a mortgage contract is signed between seller and buyer, it is usually too late to make adjustments. So a mortgage contract always should be drafted by a professional — usually a lawyer — to meet the specific needs of both buyer and seller. Real estate agents, who are often involved in arranging owner financing, generally use blank forms that are filled in by the buyer and seller and later checked by the agency's lawyer. If the contract turns out not to be what you want, too bad.

In many states, for example, if a mortgage contract does not say that the loan you give to the buyer of your house is nonassumable, it is legally considered to be assumable. Thus, by simply promising in writing to make a loan in these states, you have agreed to make it assumable.

If you ever need money before the note comes due, you will have to sell the loan to a mortgage banker for less than its face value. But you will get a better price if you arrange the loan at the outset through the Federal National Mortgage Association's Home Seller program. A Fannie Mae–approved bank or savings institution processes your buyer's application. The fee, which is negotiable, is usually paid by the buyer. To get the names of participating lenders in your area, write to the Federal National Mortgage Association (3900 Wisconsin Avenue, NW, Washington, D.C. 20016).

One form of seller financing that some buyers find attractive is the so-called balloon mortgage. With a balloon, repayment of a large part of the principal is deferred. So monthly payments are low until the loan period ends, when you, the lender, get one big payment. A common problem with giving the buyer a balloon mortgage is that it ties up your money until the note matures and he or she has to pay you back. But an arrangement known by the dismaying name of hypothecation allows you to negotiate a way around that grim obstacle to liquidity. Essentially you use the money owed you as collateral for a new but smaller loan that you get from a bank or savings and loan association. Then you can use the loan money to add to the down payment on your new house.

With hypothecation, you might well work out the figures so that the homebuyer's monthly payment to you will be exactly the same as what the bank asks you to pay on your smaller loan. Your buyer could send his or her check directly to your bank and, in one stroke, be paying an installment on both your loan and his or hers. In any case ask your bank or savings and loan about the possibility of using hypothecation.

If you are thinking of financing the sale of your own house, here is what you should do:

— Get a lawyer to write *all* your contracts — even if you use a real estate broker.

— Cover in writing everything that could possibly happen.

— Do a property credit check on the buyer.

— Make sure you get a big enough down payment to keep your buyer from hightailing it.

— And insure your loan.

Giving Your House Its
Semi-annual Physical

E VERY spring and autumn is the time to save some money, and protect what is probably your biggest investment, by giving your house its semi-annual top-to-bottom physical examination. No matter how invulnerable your home may look, hazards to its health lurk almost everywhere. So it pays to head off problems in the early stages by practicing preventive maintenance. If you take care of your house, it will take care of you. In sum, you will get more for it when you sell it.

The best way to handle maintenance chores is to put them on a schedule. For newer houses and those in mild climates, an annual inspection tour should suffice. But if your house is more than 10 years old or has to weather ice and snow, you are wise to make quarterly checkups.

In most parts of the country, the worst enemy of your house is water. The place where it does its earliest damage is the roof. The most vulnerable roof areas are the flashings — the metal sheeting that covers the joints where chimneys and vent pipes rise through the roof. Cracks and gaps in the sheeting sealant should be recoated with tar or latex sealer, which will cost you only about $10. Other trouble spots include gutters and downspouts. A handyman usually can clean, patch and adjust them in an hour or two for about $60.

If you have shingles, make sure they are well maintained. If your shingles are loose or cracked, leave any repairs to a professional. Ask your neighborhood hardware dealer for the best caulking compound and fill any gaps in the seal around windows and doors and the junctures between the foundation and patios and walks. Such steps can save you hundreds, even thousands, of dollars in emergency repairs later on.

It is tempting to postpone brick, concrete and asphalt repair jobs. However, you should not underestimate the damage that can be done by water freezing in masonry cracks. The repair work is often back-straining, but the consequences of not doing it promptly can be costly.

You also can save both time and money by repairing your house in stages rather than all at once. The south side usually needs painting every three to six years. The other sides require it only every eight to ten years.

The indoor preventive maintenance you should perform most often is to change or clean the filters in air conditioners and hot-air furnaces. Tend to furnaces about three times a year and central air-conditioning systems twice as often. Filthy filters can reduce their efficiency 10% to 25%. An oil-fired furnace should be professionally cleaned and serviced once a year. The charge should be about $60. You may be able to save up to 25% of your energy costs simply by caulking windows and putting weather stripping around doors.

It is prudent to inspect your smoke detectors and any burglar alarms once a month. And check your electrical panel every several months. If you detect a burning odor, you may simply have a blown fuse, which you can take care of yourself. But you may have loose wires or a power overload. When in doubt, call an electrician.

You do not need a professional, however, to fix your dripping faucets. Usually you can do that with just a wrench and a 10-cent washer. Your subsequent savings on water can be surprising.

Fortunately, there is a wealth of books that can help you do many repairs yourself. One way to choose among the wide variety is to focus on a project you know something about. Say it is repairing a faucet; then check that section in several books and get the one that describes it most clearly.

Among the best is *The New York Times Complete Manual of Home Repair* by Bernard Gladstone. The 36-volume Home Repair series published by Time-Life Books also gets high marks from do-it-yourself advisers. Each volume concentrates on a particular subject — for example, masonry, plumbing or wiring. For $11.99 you can buy the specific volume you need.

Which Improvements Pay Off?

IF YOU own a house, you may get back what you spend if you remodel a kitchen or add a bathroom. But do not install a swimming pool solely to enhance resale value. If you choose the right home improvement projects, you will find that some of them will pay off dramatically better than others when the time comes to sell your house. In a 1991 Americans and Their Money poll by *Money* magazine and the Gallup Organization, 29% of respondents said they intend to renovate their home in the next few years.

Energy efficiency improvements have begun to pay for themselves — but only since the oil price shocks of the 1970s. Earlier, homebuyers often could not care less about insulation or energy-saving windows. Now, most people are concerned about saving on their energy bills. But trendy innovations — for example, solar heating panels — offer a less certain return.

The more personalized a project, the more chancy the return. Remodeling a kitchen usually adds sales appeal. But if you put in a deluxe gourmet kitchen and wind up with a buyer who is a canned-soup cook, do not expect to get your money back.

An extravagant improvement can make your home harder to sell. Not every prospective homebuyer will love a $15,000 pleasure center with a custom-made whirlpool, hot tub, steam bath and built-in stereo system. Indeed, it could be a turn-off. So do not spend too much on your home improvement, especially if you are thinking of moving in a few years.

The limits on what a house can sell for are well defined in any neighborhood. If the houses range from $90,000 to $120,000, your top resale price still will not be much more than $120,000, no matter how many rooms, baths, hot tubs or skylights you add. You are not likely to recover any costs that raise the value of your property to more than 20% over that of similar homes in your neighborhood. People tend to want the *least* expensive house in an area. If yours is the *most* expensive, it will be less marketable.

Just as you should not invest too much in improvements, you should not make them yourself, either. Hiring professionals to do the entire job usually gives you the soundest investment. If you are less than craftsmanlike, your botches can subtract from the value of your house. Now is a particularly good time to hire someone to help you renovate. With new-home starts at their lowest since 1946, building contractors are eager to make up for lost income from the recession.

The most profitable interior home improvement is to remodel your kitchen. That is because the kitchen again is the nerve center in many homes, a combination family room and workplace. So it should be sunny and spacious. It also should have new appliances, plenty of storage and a step-saving layout that positions the stove, sink and refrigerator close together. But try to confine your remodeling expenses on it to 10% of the estimated value of your home. As mentioned, if your renovation is sensible and not extravagant, there is a strong chance you will recoup your entire investment when you sell.

Another project that should return almost its entire cost is to add a second bathroom. A third bathroom is popular, too, but most prospective homebuyers consider more than three unnecessary. Since decor is so much a matter of taste, elaborate bathroom *remodeling* is less likely to pay for itself. But do not skimp on finishing touches. An elegant ceramic tile floor creates a far better impression than vinyl.

Fireplaces can be one of your best investments. That is rather surprising; people know that fireplaces usually waste more heat than they provide but figure they can afford it. A fireplace that you install will return much of what you paid. As for central air conditioning, it helps you sell your house if it is in the Sun Belt. But in colder regions buyers are reluctant to pay extra because air conditioning is so expensive to operate.

Since people crave a comfortable place to lounge outdoors, another worthy investment is a deck or patio. Yours could return 40% to 70% of its cost. When you sell out, you also can get back 40% to 70% or even more of the cost of adding a conveniently located family room. But an addition that disrupts the traffic pattern, or fundamentally clashes with the style of the house, can detract from its worth. If you convert the garage to a game room, you eliminate all the buyers who want a garage.

As investments, swimming pools do not add much to the market price of a house in cooler regions of the country. Many people worry about the time and trouble it takes to maintain a pool, as well as the potential danger to children. Even in warm areas, recovery of your outlay is uncertain.

If you make big, important improvements that add to the value of your house, you can subtract the costs from your profit when you sell your house. That will cut your tax bill. Beware, though: Ordinary home repairs and replacements do not qualify.

Tax-saving Home Improvements

A RE you spending money to improve your house? Be sure to keep track of exactly how much you are paying. When the time comes to sell your house, you should be able to get significant tax deductions. Not only can some renovations boost the price of your home, but the Internal Revenue Service might count them in the total cost of your residence.

When you sell your house, you usually have to pay a tax on any profit — the difference between what the house originally cost you and what you sell it for. But the IRS will let you include in your cost the price of major improvements made after you bought the home. And the higher your total cost, the lower your profit — and the lower your taxes.

For example, if you have put in some new shrubs or trees or a lawn, a new fence or a porch, you can list any or all of them as part of the total cost of your residence. Many internal improvements count as well: storm windows, lighting fixtures, air conditioners — even wall-to-wall carpeting is recognized by the IRS. So are termite-proofing and waterproofing. The key word is *improvement*. The tax people will not let you count things that are normal repairs and upkeep.

It pays to keep accurate records of *all* your improvements and renovations. That way you can avoid having to guesstimate when the time comes to pay the IRS.

One more tip: You can also add to the cost of your house any legal fees you paid when the house was purchased. Your legal fees and commissions on the sale of the house will decrease your sale price.

Raising Capital for Home Improvements

L AST year alone, Americans spent almost $60 billion on major improvements and additions to their homes. How did they raise all that money? For the most part, they did it the old-fashioned way: they *borrowed* it.

Your best deal when seeking money for a major home improvement project is a second mortgage or a home-equity loan. You'll pay a low interest rate, and that interest will be tax-deductible. The next best rate may be the one you get by borrowing from your company profit-sharing plan or against the cash value of your whole life insurance policy. You will pay below-market interest rates. If you cannot tap these sources, you can apply for a variety of loans offered by banks, credit unions and finance companies. Interest rates are lowest at credit unions, higher at banks and highest at consumer loan companies.

Most homeowners finance their remodeling projects by taking out either a home-equity loan or a second mortgage. Some simply refinance their existing first mortgage. The right choice depends on the circumstances.

Home-equity loans (HELs) are best for improvements whose cost will be spread over a number of months. HELs are lines of credit, which can run as high as 75% or 80% of the appraised value of your house, minus the unpaid portion of the mortgage principal. Then you simply write your own loans by writing out checks as you need the money.

You can get HELs from brokerage firms as well as banks, savings-and-loan associations and some credit unions. The interest rate is usually adjustable, varying monthly. Most lenders peg the interest to the prime rate, adding one and a half or two percentage points to that bellwether rate, which stood at 6% in mid-1992. But you pay no interest until you actually tap into your credit line, and then only on the amount that you borrow. You do have to pay closing costs on most HELs, but many lenders keep those costs to a minimum. An estimated 15 million homeowners have taken out HELs, and not just for home improvements. You can use the borrowed money for any purpose.

Second mortgages are a better choice than HELs for money you need all at once. You can spread the payments over as long as 30 years, and you can get a fixed interest rate, making the payments predictable for all those years. You'll pay a higher rate, though, than the current home-equity loan rate — typically one to two points over the first-mortgage rate — along with hefty closing costs.

That big rate differential makes refinancing advisable if, as in recent times, mortgage interest rates have fallen sharply. (For more on refinancing, see "The Profits and Perils of Swapping Your Mortgage.")

The interest that you pay on a mortgage or home-equity loan remains deductible under the new tax rules. But Congress has put on some limitations. These restrictions apply primarily to affluent people and are quite complex. So they take some explaining:

Since the 1988 tax year, you can fully deduct only the interest you pay on your first $1,000,000 of debt whether you are single or married. (If you're married and filing separately, you may deduct interest on the first $500,000.) This covers debt that you incur when you acquire, construct or substantially improve your principal and/or second residence and that is secured by such property. But wait: There's a further wrinkle. The million-dollar limit applies only to debt taken out after October 13, 1987. Interest on all debt that you had taken before October 13, 1987, will be deductible even though it exceeds the limit. However, the amount of this previous mortgage debt will reduce the $1 million limit on all new debt.

Say you had bought a house or apartment with an $800,000 mortgage two years ago and you want to buy a vacation home this year with a $400,000 mortgage. Then you will not be able to deduct the interest on your entire debt of $1,200,000 but only the interest on your first $1,000,000 of it. But if you already had incurred the $1,200,000 in debt before October 13, 1987, you could deduct the total interest on the mortgage debt.

Also, you can fully deduct the interest incurred on $100,000 of a home-equity loan regardless of the purpose of the loan or the original cost of your home. This applies to all home-equity loans taken out on or after October 13, 1987. A home-equity loan taken out before October 13, 1987, is subject to the tracing rule — that is, a taxpayer must trace how the proceeds of the loan were used.

Finding Repairmen You Can Trust

FINDING craftsmen to repair or remodel your house calls for almost the same degree of care you would employ in looking for a family doctor. To do otherwise is to jeopardize the value of your most cherished investment.

For small home-repair and remodeling jobs you can get by with the name of a craftsman plucked from the phone book. But make sure your nominee has been in business locally for three years or so and will supply references. Be certain to call these people and have them give you an account of the person's workmanship, prices, reliability and character.

If you are planning a project that calls for superlative craftsmanship, ask for referrals from building materials wholesalers, such as plumbing supply houses and lumberyards.

For major remodeling jobs, you will probably need a general contractor. He or she will assume command of the entire project. That means finding designers to draw up your plans, hiring subcontractors to do the work and arranging for building permits and inspections. The fee: roughly 10% to 25% of the entire cost.

Coping with Contractors

A MAJOR home improvement project is not likely to be a tranquil experience, but it should not be a calamity either. Your satisfaction with the job may depend more than anything else on how skillfully you choose and deal with the carpenters, plumbers, electricians and any other contractors you hire to work on your house.

To get the best deal from a contractor, first of all be careful whom you hire. You can get names of financially sound workmen from bankers and storekeepers who deal with them. Local chapters of such trade groups as the National Association of Home Builders and the National Association of the Remodeling Industry also can point you to reliable contractors. And the Better Business Bureau keeps files on tradesmen who have drawn complaints.

Once you have located several candidates for a substantial job, evaluate them carefully. One consideration is rapport. It's a mistake to hire a workman just because he is engaging; yet it's also wrong to dismiss personal chemistry. Pick someone you can communicate with. And visit one of his job sites. If the place is messy and disorganized, it is reasonable to wonder whether the tradesman takes meticulous care of his work.

When picking a contractor, ask yourself the following questions:

— Was he recommended by a trustworthy source?

— Has he supplied the names of previous customers whom you can check for references?

— How long has he been in business under the same name? More than 10 years is a definite plus.

— Will the contractor give you his home address and phone number?

— Has he agreed to include starting and completion dates in the contract?

— Does a check with his bank indicate that he is financially sound?

— Did he offer you a *written* guarantee?

Finally, if you answer yes to the next two questions, perhaps you should look for another contractor:

Has he made oral promises that he will not put in the contract? And, did he offer you a discount for signing up at once? If so, those are danger signals you cannot afford to ignore.

For your big home improvements, try to get at least three bids. When all have come in, discard any astronomical ones. But you may want to choose the contractor who comes highly recommended even if his bid is *not* the lowest.

No bid is set in concrete. So negotiate with the contractor you really want. Contractors expect their profit to be 10% to 25% of a project's total cost. But if they need work, they will accept less.

Whether you are renovating your whole house or simply adding kitchen cabinets, following some basic rules will help you get the most from your contractor:

Before hiring any workmen for a major project, write a tight contract that cites the details of the job practically to the last nut and bolt. In remodeling a bathroom, you should designate the brand name, model number and color of appliances and fixtures. You should also specify materials for cabinetry, countertops and hardware.

Start with a standard form, called an owners and contractors construction agreement, to spell out your expectations. The forms are available at many stationery stores. You can also write to the American Homeowners Foundation, 1724 South Quincy Street, Arlington, Virginia 22204. For $5.95, the foundation will send you an eight-page model agreement. Be sure to put down the particulars of your job, including the following: a precise list of all work to be done and appliances and fixtures to be installed; the starting and approximate completion dates of the work; a stipulation that all work must be done to the highest standards and a guarantee to provide replacement materials and additional labor, if necessary; and, finally, a provision that the contractor is responsible for obtaining any required building permits.

Pay the contractor in stages. Turn over 10% at the start and 30% as each third of the job is finished. Hold off paying the last installment until two weeks after the project has been completed. This way you can make sure there are no surprises. (Also, expect to pay between 8% and 12% of estimated construction costs for working drawings, and another 5% if you want the architect to supervise the work.)

Do not skimp on materials or workmanship. As one Houston stonemason remarks: "Cheap workmanship is like cheap wine. The price is right, but you'll regret it later."

Putting Your House in the Movies

I F YOU have always dreamed of being in the movies but never made it, consider making a star out of your house. Putting your home in pictures — or on TV or in a full-color magazine ad — can be fun and fairly lucrative, and it's easier now than ever. More and more film and TV producers and advertising agencies are looking for real-life settings for their extravaganzas. In New York City, your house could earn you $1,500 for a 10-hour commercial shoot and $2,000 or more a day for a movie.

Your chances are best if you live in or near areas where most commercials, TV shows and movies are filmed, meaning New York or Los Angeles. But many production companies and advertising agencies are also active renters in Atlanta, Boston, Dallas, San Francisco and other cities.

If you would like to make your home a star, first list it with your state and local government film commissions. They help producers find locations. Also register with at least one of the nationally known location services, such as Judie Robbins Locations or Great Locations in New York City. Some of these services are listed in the Yellow Pages under "Motion Picture Location Service."

Some services will list your house at no charge; some may charge a fee for taking their own photographs to show your place off to best advantage. Firms like Cast Locations in Los Angeles work out special arrangements for each big "shoot," taking 30% or 40% of the total fee for their services, which may include negotiating the contract and stationing someone on your premises to keep a watchful eye on the proceedings.

This last is no small consideration. Putting your home in pictures may mean that a cast and crew of up to 100 people — with countless pieces of equipment — may be trooping over your property and upsetting family routines. They might want to repaint or even completely redecorate your house. So make sure the producers sign a contract that spells out the filming dates and makes the company responsible for any damages.

Your Taxes

How to Cut Your Taxes

Almost anyone now can reduce his or her taxes by using some techniques that the rich have been employing for years. You do not have to be wealthy to take advantage of them. But do not wait until the eve of April 15 to think about ways to save. Start looking today for deductions and credits that will cut your tax bill for this year — and well into the future. The earlier you act, the more you stand to save.

As you read this chapter, you may recognize tax savings that you failed to consider when you filed your most recent tax return. You can correct these omissions by filing an amended return. (See "Your Taxes: The Best Time to File.")

Of course, it will not pay to increase your write-offs if you do not itemize them or unless you have a business of your own where the deductions can be taken as a direct offset against income. So the first thing to do is add up any expenses that you can write off for the year. The standard deduction is indexed to the consumer price index, meaning that the deduction will rise with inflation. For income earned in 1992, the deduction is $3,600 for single individuals, $5,250 for heads of households (such as single parents), and $6,000 for married couples filing jointly. If your total deductions top the standard deduction, then it pays to itemize. Check the standard deduction amounts carefully if you are over 65 or blind, because you get an increased standard deduction at that age or for that handicap.

The following chapters elaborate on the major ways to reduce your tax liability, but here is a summary of some of them:

You can give money and other assets to your children. Children under 14 years of age are taxed at their parents' rate on investment income above $1,100. But children who are 14 and over pay taxes on all their income at their own rate, which is probably much lower than your own.

Congress also has provided that some investments legally and quite effectively shelter you from taxes. Municipal bonds yield tax-exempt current income. Real estate investment trusts can provide tax-deferred income. But anyone mulling over investments that will save taxes is a little like a teenager pondering marriage: You had better be sure that the lust to avoid taxes is not leading you into a disastrous long-term commitment.

Also, check the implications for your state taxes, particularly on municipal bonds. Usually you have to pay state and sometimes even city taxes on the interest you earn from them, unless the bond was issued by a community or agency in the state where you live. In addition, the alternative minimum tax can wipe out the federal tax benefit on some types of munis.

It's worth repeating that the surest and simplest way for many people who have earned income to reduce taxes is to contribute to an Individual Retirement Account. You can deduct the full amount from your taxable income if neither you nor your spouse is covered by an employer retirement plan or your adjusted gross income is under $40,000 if married or under $25,000 if single. You will be allowed a partial deduction provided your adjusted gross income is between $40,000 and $50,000 if you are married and between $25,000 and $35,000 if you are single. No deduction will be allowed if your adjusted gross income is over $50,000 if you are married and over $35,000 if you are single. In any case, IRA savings grow tax-deferred.

If you want to set up an IRA for last year's income, you can do it any time before you file this year's tax return — that is, as late as April 15. But self-employed people who want to establish a tax-saving Keogh plan have to set it up by December 31 of this year — or their Keogh contributions this year will not be tax-deductible. You can make contributions to your IRA as late as April 15. If you ask the IRS for an extension, you can contribute to a Keogh until the extended due date of the tax return, as late as October 15 when you get a valid extension. This is not true for the IRA. However, the earlier the contribution is made, the earlier tax-deferred interest begins to be earned.

Taxpayers can take write-offs for rooms in their homes that are used exclusively for a profit-making business. (But the IRS rules for home office deductions are quite specific and limiting. You should thoroughly read them before taking any deductions.) You also can take some deductions for the purchase of home office supplies, phone bills, utilities, repairs and even maid service and other operating expenses. You can depreciate such assets as file cabinets, desks and typewriters. Instead of depreciating property, however, you can elect to treat all or part of the cost of qualifying property as a currently deductible expense. The total amount that can be expensed for a single tax year cannot exceed $10,000, and is limited to the amount of taxable income that is derived from the active conduct of any trade or business. Any part of the deduction that cannot be taken because of this rule can be carried over to the following taxable year.

If you have a home computer that you use half or more of the time for your business, you can either deduct that portion of the cost from your taxable income in one year or depreciate it in installments over five years. Your business software and other expenses of an office at home also may be deductible.

You can deduct a number of unreimbursed business and job-related expenses and miscellaneous expenses. But you must lump all these expenses together, and you can write off only the amount by which they exceed 2% of your adjusted gross income. Deductions in this category include union dues, tax preparation and investment advisory fees, job uniforms, job-related educational expenses and the cost of business publications — including this book.

If you use your car while on the job, you can write off your operating expenses as part of the miscellaneous deductions. Your regular commuting costs to and from work are not deductible. But if you drive your car on business — say, to make sales calls — the IRS lets you deduct 28 cents a mile for all miles of business use. Unfortunately, this can fall far short of what it costs to keep your car running. Remember, however, that instead you can deduct your *actual* auto expenses — as long as you have the proper documentation. In short, you can fatten your deductions by maintaining thorough records. Start by keeping a log of the miles you drive for business purposes and note your total mileage for the year. Also, keep track of your outlays for gas, repairs and insurance. Then figure out what proportion of your driving is for business. You can deduct that percentage of your costs.

Resolve to keep better records of all your tax-deductible expenses this year. As mentioned, at tax time pack rats always pay less. Silly little deductions have a way of becoming impressive big ones. Keep even your grocery receipts when the purchases are for business entertaining.

You no longer can deduct interest on consumer loans such as auto or college loans or any nonmortgage debt. Nor can you deduct credit-card finance charges or interest on tax deficiencies. However, interest on home-backed and investment-related loans remains deductible within certain limits. Investment-interest expense is deductible to the extent of your net investment income.

Since no deduction is allowed for your consumer interest, you should consider restructuring your debt through a home-equity loan.

Frequently overlooked write-offs include the fair market value of property you give to charity, such as clothing (you must itemize your return in order to deduct charitable gifts). If you are itching to change jobs within your current field, you can deduct most travel and other expenses connected with your job search — as long as you itemize your return. And do not forget to deduct this year any capital losses from previous years that exceeded the $3,000 annual limit. Always eager to squelch too much of a good thing, Congress in 1990 began taking away deductions for high earners. Single or married, if you earn more than $105,250, you now lose 3 cents' worth of deductions for every $1 of income in six figures. The new tax-the-rich formula applies to all itemized deductions except medical expenses, investment interest (this includes income from any property producing interest, dividends, annuities, royalties or gains) and theft and casualty losses. If your salary is high enough, the tax code will take away as much as 80% of your other deductions.

Tax credits — which you can get for child-care expenses and certain investments, among other things — are much better than tax deductions. Deductions reduce only the adjusted gross income on which your taxes are calculated, but credits reduce your actual taxes, dollar for dollar. So if you have a chance to gain any credits, take it.

Remember: There is nothing wrong with employing legal tax-reduction strategies. Every one of them was put into the tax code by an act of Congress or a judicial decision for some purpose — at best to encourage Americans to save, invest and become homeowners, which in turn enables businesses to start, to grow and to expand employment. As the late Judge Learned Hand said in a 1947 tax decision, "Nobody owes any public duty to pay more than the law demands: taxes are enforced exactions, not voluntary contributions."

Stop Lending Money to the IRS

I F YOU get an income tax refund this year, there is no reason to feel smug. You just gave the government an interest-free loan last year. And it was probably no piddling loan. The average refund is about $900. Had you invested that yourself over the years, you could be hundreds of dollars richer by now. One advantage is that if you would otherwise have squandered that money, receiving an income tax refund acts like a forced savings plan.

You can reduce your withholding by going to your employer's payroll office and changing the number of so-called allowances on your W-4 form. Each allowance exempts $2,300 of your 1992 pay from withholding.

The amount rises from year to year in step with inflation. You get an automatic exemption for yourself, for your spouse and for each child who is either under 19 years old or a full-time student under age 24. If your full-time student is 24 or older, he or she must earn less than $2,300 to count as an exemption. If you cannot claim the exemption, the child may claim the exemption on his or her own return.

Caution: Personal exemptions have been phased out for certain high-income taxpayers. In 1992 the phase-out will be calculated before you arrive at your taxable income. The new phase-out will be equal to 2% per $2,500 of adjusted gross income (or fraction thereof) over $105,250 for single taxpayers, $157,900 for joint returns, and $131,550 for heads of households. The phase-out stops at adjusted gross income over $227,750 for singles and $280,400 for married filers. Consult your tax preparer.

To jump-start a recession-bound economy President Bush decreed a lower withholding-tax schedule starting in March 1992. The effect on most households was to bump up take-home pay immediately but slash tax refunds due in 1993. The boost in paycheck bottom lines goes to joint-tax-return filers earning less than $90,200 and single filers earning less than $53,200. The extra spending money doesn't amount to much. A single worker making $25,000 might get an extra $3.32 a week, and a couple earning $50,000 might take home an additional $14.00. But the cumulative delay in tax collections forms a mighty ocean of uncollected revenues. Through September 1993 the Treasury will take in $25 billion less. Nor will this shortfall be replaced in future years, because the lower withholdings are permanent.

Of course, people who are addicted to their refunds and don't mind lending the government money need not accept the extra cash. Instead, they can go to their payroll office and fill out a new Form W-4, the Employee's Withholding Allowance Certificate. The simplest way to assure yourself of getting your usual refund is to multiply the extra take-home dollars you're getting in each pay envelope by the number of paychecks you receive per year — 52 if you're paid weekly, 26 if biweekly, 12 if monthly, etc. Then, on line 6 of the form, request that an equal amount be withheld during the rest of the year.

But here's a much better idea: Have the extra money withheld from your pay (if you haven't reached the maximum allowable), either for your 401(k) retirement savings plan or, if you have no such plan, for the purchase of Series EE U.S. Savings Bonds in your company's payroll savings program.

To find out how many exemptions you can claim, use your tax return for last year to estimate your deductions for the current year. Then check the table on the W-4 to calculate the number of allowances your deductions generate. But do not go overboard. Your withholding and any estimated tax payments have to total at least as much as your actual tax liability last year, or 90% of the ultimate tax liability for the current year. Otherwise, you could be liable for an underpayment penalty.

Be reassured that you won't be penalized if the new payroll withholding schedule leaves you owing taxes at the end of the year. But doctoring your W-4 to underpay withholding taxes can get you fined $500. And if the IRS really wants to get rough, it can charge you with tax fraud, which is punishable by a fine of up to $1,000, a prison sentence, or both.

In certain situations, however, paying in at least your prior year's tax will not be sufficient to protect you from underpayment penalties. There are new estimated tax rules for taxpayers with incomes over $75,000 who expect their incomes to increase by more than $40,000. They must pay in based on 90% of their ultimate tax liability.

Keeping Records

A CCOUNTANTS often complain that their clients' idea of record-keeping involves tossing all sorts of papers into a shoe box or shopping bag and handing over the unsorted mess at tax time. To save heaps of time when doing your taxes, or heaps of money when your tax preparer does them, emulate Brer Squirrel. Save everything.

As editor and Certified Financial Planner Robert Klein writes, the best and safest place to keep tax records is a well-organized, fire-resistant filing cabinet. Set up several headings that make sense to you, but be sure to provide a place for any slip of paper that could conceivably save you tax money or headaches, either now or in the distant future.

There are a multitude of computer software programs that you can use to put together the numbers and save you or your tax preparer lots of time, but you will always need to retain the original supporting documentation for some years. A list of vital documents would include the forms W-2 and 1099 that arrive in your pay envelope or in the mail after the first of the year, brokerage records of capital gains and losses, records of retirement-plan payments and withdrawals, doctors' bills and health-insurance reimbursement statements.

If you earn enough from investments or moonlighting to require payment of estimated quarterly taxes, reserve a filing slot for your Form 1040-ES, its accompanying work-sheets for the current year and a record of each quarterly payment made. Medical bills must equal 7½% of your adjusted gross income before you can start deducting them, but you never know when your turn will come for an avalanche of surgical, dental or drug costs. So tuck away in their own special filing slot receipts for prescription and over-the-counter drugs, health-insurance premiums and notes on mileage driven to visit doctors, hospitals and other treatment centers. Also store there the reimbursement records that come with health-insurance checks.

The list of things to file goes on: receipts for real estate taxes, charitable donations, job-hunting expenses and relocation costs and child-care services; the Social Security numbers of nannies and other domestic employees; year-end pay stubs showing cumulative deductions for health insurance, retirement plans and charitable contributions. If you are divorced, keep records of alimony and child-care payments made or received, and also your ex-spouse's Social Security number and a copy of the divorce decree.

Label other manila folders for statements of interest on mortgages and home-equity loans, K-1 tax forms and financial records for limited partnerships, S corporations and estates and trusts. Keep a log of unreimbursed business expenses, such as mileage driven in your own car, along with receipts for car rentals and fares for public transportation, including taxis.

Canceled checks and old bank statements are essential documents for tax files. Keep the latest 12 months' worth handy and older batches in long-term storage on the remote chance of a tax audit. Save all mutual-fund monthly statements. They are vital when a mutual fund is redeemed. Past statements help determine the cost basis of the shares you redeem. This information is necessary to determine your capital gain or loss.

After you have sent in the year's tax returns — federal, state and perhaps city forms as well as small-business or corporate forms — there is more filing to be done. Stuff all the supporting documents and records in a large envelope or container and label it with the year. Keep last year's package in or near your current tax file in case you get a query about the contents from the IRS, the state taxing authority or your tax preparer. Find a storage place for earlier years' records — always keeping each year's data separate.

In some obscure place safe from weather, make room for deep tax-file storage. The American Institute of Certified Public Accountants advises holding on to tax records for six years. Clean out your files after that. "Don't fall into the trap of saving unnecessary documents," says the accounting group.

Some papers, however, should be held on to permanently. Among them are real estate records.

The average single-family home is owned for only seven or eight years. That means you will probably have a capital gain to report, though not necessarily a tax to pay, at fairly frequent intervals. Each time you sell your principal residence and buy another for the same amount of money or more, you can postpone paying the tax. But to minimize the eventual taxable gain, you must accumulate records that trace the financial history of every house you have owned. For this purpose, store in a safe place, such as your bank vault, all the documents that were generated when you bought each home. These include the property survey, the real estate broker's itemized invoice showing the sales commissions and other selling costs, and the many receipts that changed hands at the title closing.

As a further aid to figuring eventual gains, keep a separate but permanent file at home, where you can conveniently add to it receipts for any work that might qualify as a capital improvement (see "Your Home: Tax-saving Home Improvements"). Anything that adds to the value of your home or prolongs its life is an improvement, from a built-in barbecue grill to weather stripping, from shrubs to laundry appliances. When in doubt about a home-improvement expense, file the receipt.

Again, to protect these irreplaceable records, it's best to store them in a fireproof strongbox. Keep duplicate records in a ledger of home improvements in your bank vault. Once a year, and after major projects, update your capital-improvements ledger. When you sell your home, you will need a complete record of the improvements you have made to it and to earlier properties and, above all, the receipts from contractors, home-improvement stores, nurseries and such. By carrying forward these costs, you will cut down your eventual taxable gain. Remember, however, the burden of proof is on the taxpayer.

Until a few years ago, it seemed unthinkable that homeowners might face a capital loss when the time came to sell. But in the 1990s, with real estate prices well below their peaks in the 1980s, losses are no longer uncommon. Unfortunately, Uncle Sam refuses to share the pain. You cannot deduct such a loss from the sale of your personal residence from your ordinary income. If the property becomes rental property before you sell it, however, you may be able to deduct a loss from sale.

Another item to store in a permanent file is the purchase prices of stock. These figures become important when stock is sold.

Your FICA Tax:
Social Security's Big Bite

THREE out of four Americans now pay, directly and through their employers, more Social Security tax than federal income tax.

Payroll deductions for Social Security, labeled FICA on most paychecks, have skyrocketed over the past 20 years. For 1992 the maximum FICA tax for employees has risen to $5,328.90. That includes a flat tax of 6.2% on wages up to $55,500 (that money goes to a fund to pay old-age, disability and retirement benefits) and 1.45% on wages up to $130,200 (that money goes to pay for Medicare insurance). Matching employer taxes double the bill, to $10,657.80.

If you have your own unincorporated business, you must pay both halves of this tax out of your own pocket. This is known as self-employment tax. But you can deduct one half of it on a special line on Form 1040 where you calculate your adjusted gross income.

What do Social Security beneficiaries get for the money? Pensions, life insurance to protect their dependents, disability insurance for themselves and their families and help with hospital and other medical bills if they're disabled or over 65. (See "Your Retirement: How Much Social Security Contributes.") All told, more than 40 million people collect Social Security checks. The total they will receive in 1992 is about $291 billion. Quite a sum. Yet it's lots less than we're paying for. In 1992 the annual surplus will grow to about $56 billion, and by the turn of the century it will hit $117 billion.

The balance in the Social Security Trust Fund by the year 2025 is expected to swell to the inconceivable total of $5.5 trillion. After that the fund will start to decline as baby boomers hit retirement age. In the meantime, by law, the Social Security Administration must invest the money in U.S. Treasury securities. So 1992's $56 billion surplus and the larger and larger surpluses to come are really helping to finance the federal budget deficit. Come 2030, our kids or grandchildren will be paying still more payroll taxes to help see the baby-boom generation through old age.

The New Tax Rates

UNDER the tax law that took effect in 1987, most people got a drop in their federal income tax bill. But reformers who spoke of simplifying the tax code must have been humming "The Impossible Dream." Today's tax law is anything but simple. Still, one thing is easier to figure: your tax rate. Now, all people who pay income taxes fall into one of three brackets: 15%, 28% or 31%.

For the 1992 tax year, married couples who file jointly will pay 15% if they have up to $35,800 in taxable income. From $35,800 to $86,500, the rate is 28%. Above $86,500, the rate is 31%.

Single taxpayers will pay 15% if they have taxable income up to $21,450. From $21,450 to $51,900 the rate is 28%. Above $51,900, the rate is 31%.

Heads of households will pay 15% on taxable income up to $28,750, 28% on amounts from $28,750 to $74,150, and 31% on amounts above that.

Married taxpayers filing separately will pay 15% on taxable income up to $17,900, 28% on amounts from $17,900 to $43,250, and 31% on amounts above that.

However, the tax on capital gains may be special. The Revenue Reconciliation Act of 1990 imposed a maximum tax rate of 28% on net capital gains. Net capital gain means the excess of net long-term capital gain over net short-term capital loss. (Long-term applies to property held over a year, short-term to that held one year or less.) Any net short-term capital gain would be taxed at ordinary income rates, including the 31% rate. In fact, the effective tax rate may be somewhat higher than 31%. The Revenue Reconciliation Act of 1991 reduces itemized deductions by 3% of the amount of a taxpayer's adjusted gross income in excess of $100,000. Medical costs, casualty and theft and investment interest are excluded.

One further note of caution: Some taxpayers, mainly wealthy ones, may be subject to a special set of rules known as the alternative minimum tax (AMT). If so, certain tax strategies and some deductions may be disallowed or worth less than before. Your accountant or tax lawyer can advise you on this.

Company Thrift Plans

WHEN bureaucratic-sounding memos come around explaining your company's savings, stock purchase or profit-sharing plans, do you just toss them? Then you are making a money-wasting mistake. If your employer offers you a chance to get into such a program, seize it.

You get two big tax breaks on company thrift plans. Taxes are deferred on all contributions your company makes to your account *and* on all the earnings on the money put in by both you and the company. You do not pay any taxes on the dividends, interest or capital gains until the income is distributed to you.

One type of company thrift plan is the profit-sharing program. The company makes annual deposits in employee accounts. These may be based on the size of each year's corporate earnings, but they don't have to be. On top of that, employees may be able to add voluntary contributions of their own.

Usually you have a choice of investing the money in stocks or bonds and perhaps an interest-paying savings account. Happily, some companies now offer a family of mutual funds as an alternative, giving employees a wider choice of investments. You can divide your stock money, for example, among large and small companies.

Another type of company plan is the stock purchase program. In this, you might have the option of contributing between 3% and 6% of your pre-tax salary. Often the company will kick in one dollar for your two. All that money goes to buy stock in the company itself. You may have to wait three years or more to become vested — that is, to have title to the stock bought by the company matching funds.

If you have a choice of several company plans, the best place to park your voluntary contributions is where the company puts in the highest proportion of matching funds. That is "found money." But how much you want to contribute to a company stock plan will also depend on how optimistic you are about your employer's future. Beware of buying your company stock so heavily that most of your assets wind up in that one issue. A reverse in the firm's fortunes could jeopardize both your nest egg and your job.

Whichever plans you select, you generally cannot withdraw your money until you quit or retire or reach age 59½. Otherwise, you may have to pay a 10% penalty on top of the ordinary income tax you will pay. But many plans allow you to borrow against your accumulated balances at market interest rates.

When you leave the firm, you may be able to use a tax-saving maneuver on your lump-sum distribution, provided that you were a participant in the plan for at least five years. Favorable treatment of lump-sum distributions under the tax reform of 1986 is generally limited to a one-time election of five-year forward averaging after you reach age 59½. If, however, you reached 50 before 1986 and you receive a lump-sum distribution, you can elect five-year forward averaging under the new tax rates or 10-year forward averaging under the 1986 rates, and you do not have to meet the age requirement of 59½. On lump sums of up to $250,000 or so, averaging puts you into a lower tax bracket.

Or you can roll over your lump-sum distribution into an IRA and postpone any tax until you are 70½. Your IRA funds won't be eligible for averaging, but that seldom matters because your earnings can keep on compounding with no tax to drag down their growth. Remember: In certain circumstances a rollover must be made within 60 days after you receive a lump-sum distribution from a retirement plan, and you must put the money into another qualified plan or IRA. If you change jobs and your new company has a qualified plan, you can put into it all or part of your IRA savings from your previous employer's qualified plan. If you put only part of your money into the new plan, only that portion will be tax-deferred. The rest of your money — that is, the amount you do *not* roll over into a new plan — will be taxed at your ordinary income tax rate.

401(k) Plans

I F YOU like your Individual Retirement Account, you may love the misleadingly named "salary-reduction plan." Actually, it reduces your income tax bill while helping you save and invest some salary for retirement.

The salary-reduction plan is like a super IRA. Yes, you can have both an IRA and a 401(k). But the IRA contributions may not be deductible. And you can put more into a 401(k) — up to $8,728 in 1992 income. None of the money is taxed until you withdraw it. Meanwhile, all the dividends, interest and capital gains that you earn on the money grow untaxed until withdrawal.

Many companies offer these plans to their employees. Instead of collecting all your pay, you can choose to put part of it into a 401(k). Often, for every dollar that you put up, your employer kicks in another 50 cents — and that is a bonus nobody should pass up.

A similar but more generous plan is usually available to employees of schools, colleges, hospitals and other not-for-profit institutions. It goes by various names — tax-sheltered annuity, supplementary retirement annuity and 403(b) plan, among others. But whatever it's called, its upper limit is a $9,500 yearly contribution, with larger "catch-up" amounts for late starters.

As with an IRA, you must pay income taxes on any amounts withdrawn from a salary withholding plan, plus a 10% penalty in most circumstances if you are younger than 59½. Under a new law starting in 1993, employers are required to deduct 20% for income tax on all withdrawals. You'd have to pay the tax anyway, plus the 10% penalty if you are under 59½. But now there's a trap ready to spring on you. Suppose you are leaving the company and intend to redeposit your 401(k) money in an IRA. This maneuver, called a rollover, ordinarily preserves the tax-deferred status of your investments. But the new law makes rollovers taxable. Fortunately, another change in the law lets your employer transfer 401(k)s directly to either an IRA rollover account that you can establish for yourself or your new employer's 401(k) plan. So be sure to arrange a transfer unless you really need the money right away.

There are better ways to get at your money in a pinch. You can generally borrow as much as 50% of your savings up to $50,000 and still earn income on the money, though you do pay interest on the loan.

You can't borrow from an IRA. In rare instances, you can withdraw funds from your 401(k), or 403(b), without penalty. An example is borrowing for medical expenses. The penalty is waived if you use the money to pay medical expenses that exceed 7½% of your adjusted gross income.

The trouble with 401(k) and 403(b) plans is that most people choose overly cautious investments for their money. One survey of more than 400 large companies found that employees put 60% of their contributions into bonds, money-market funds, and guaranteed investment contracts, or GICs. Stocks are riskier than those investments, but over the long run they have far greater growth potential.

The pity is, many employees have little choice but to be cautious. Ideally, a 401(k) plan should have at least half a dozen investment options. Some employers limit you to three or fewer options. In addition to GICs and bond funds, a 401(k) should offer a large- and a small-company stock fund and an international stock fund. Small stocks have outperformed large-company stocks over the years, while foreign markets beat the U.S. markets in some periods. There should also be a stock index fund, which mirrors the performance of the total stock market.

If your plan falls short, don't hesitate to complain to your benefits department. Meanwhile, get as much information as possible about the investment options your company *does* offer. Employees have the right to examine the annual reports of their 401(k) plans. Such reports list the assets and investments in the plan, some of the expenses, and the performance figures for each fund.

Use this information to allocate some of your money to the highest-performing fund. Unless you expect to retire in the next seven years or so, you'd do well to put just about all your 401(k) money into stocks. If that strategy seems risky to you, remember that you may already have one low-risk nest egg in Social Security, and perhaps a second in your company pension plan.

Keogh Plans and SEPs

Two marvelous tax-saving devices are available to most doctors, plumbers, movie directors, taxi drivers, lawyers, architects, actors, artists, authors and moonlighters of all kinds. The money-sparing pair are the Keogh plan and the simplified employee pension, an oversized type of IRA better known as a SEP. Many people who are eligible to start a Keogh or SEP do not even know it. If you own a business or work for yourself, or just do some moonlighting as an independent contractor, you may be one of them.

By starting a pension plan and funding it with as much money as they can afford or the law allows, the self-employed can postpone taxes for decades on their pension contributions and their investment earnings as well.

People whose tax return includes Schedule C, "Profit or (Loss) from Business or Profession," are almost universally eligible for a Keogh or SEP. They can shelter income in much the same fashion as corporate employees and schoolteachers do.

Most Keoghs and all SEPs come under the heading of defined contribution plans. That is, you can take a defined amount of money out of your net earnings each year, untaxed, and invest it in a retirement account.

Examples of defined contribution plans are profit-sharing Keogh plans and money-purchase Keogh plans. The maximum allowable contributions to a profit-sharing plan are the lesser of $30,000 or 13% of your earned income for the year. The maximum allowable contributions to a money-purchase plan are generally the lesser of $30,000 or 20% of your earned income. Profit-sharing-plan contributions can vary from year to year, but money-purchase-plan contributions must be the same percentage every year. You probably have heard higher figures mentioned, 15% and 25%. These are percentages of what is left after the contribution has been deducted.

In another kind of Keogh, called a defined benefit plan, there is no dollar limit at all. This plan is more like a pension than a savings plan. It allows some people the flexibility to put away just about all the income generated by their enterprise. Under a defined benefit plan, you promise yourself a retirement benefit of some fixed amount each month for the rest of your life. The annual contributions are based on the amount that would be needed to provide you that size pension at normal retirement age.

The tax law puts a limit on the size of the pension rather than on the size of the contribution. The maximum annual benefit that could be funded in 1992 at retirement age was $112,221. Obviously, this is a plan for people with lots of surplus income. They are likely to be people in their 50s and 60s. And if they employ others, they must put enough money away to finance a pension for anyone (except their spouse) who's been on the payroll for a year or more.

The deadline for setting up any kind of Keogh plan for 1993 income is December 31, 1993. Once the plan is established, future contributions to the Keogh may be postponed until tax-filing time — or later, if you apply for an extended deadline.

SEP stands for Simplified Employee Pension plan — "simplified" because it is easy to set up. Basically, a SEP resembles an oversized

IRA. Instead of $2,000, the maximum allowable yearly tax-deferred contribution to a SEP is the lesser of 13% of self-employment income or $8,721. SEPs have a special appeal for procrastinators. In contrast to the deadline for a Keogh, the last date for starting a SEP in time to make deductible contributions for 1993 is the same as the tax-filing deadline, including extensions.

In choosing the right self-employment plan for you, ask yourself how much of your earnings you can really spare. If 13% or less is a comfortable limit, open a SEP. It does the least to complicate life. Keogh plans are more complex as well as more potent.

But, of course, nothing is truly simple where taxes are involved. The wrong kind of Keogh plan can put you in a financial bind by requiring larger contributions than you can afford in a tough year. Up to the set limits, you can put in as much or as little money each year as you please in a profit-sharing plan. But you must *always* kick in the same percentage to a money purchase plan.

The solution: Open one plan of each kind. Commit yourself to only 7% contributions to the money-purchase plan. And whenever possible, also put the full 3% in your profit-sharing plan.

How should you invest your Keogh money? Your strategy should mesh with your needs and goals. If you are a professional or an entrepreneur and you figure that your Keogh funds will be a main part of your retirement income, you will want to put a premium on safety. So, diversify to reduce your risk, and stick to top-rated bonds and stocks. If you are financially secure and willing to take some risks in hopes of higher gains, you might buy speculative growth stocks and perhaps some high-yielding, low-quality bonds.

If you eventually plan to take all the money out of your retirement fund in a lump sum, your Keogh may be less heavily taxed than your IRA or SEP because only the Keogh is eligible for forward averaging. After you reach age 70½, you *must* start withdrawing funds from your Keogh. But you can continue to contribute to your Keogh or SEP for as long as you earn self-employment income — even after you begin withdrawals at 70½. You can't do that with an IRA.

Saving from Sideline Businesses

PARTICULARLY if you are a young adult, you should be looking for ways to increase your income rather than merely avoiding taxes. One familiar way is to start a small sideline business of your own. It can be both a tax haven and a nice investment that eventually may turn into a profitable full-time enterprise. You might look to your hobby for something you really enjoy doing — and turn it into a spare-time occupation. As tax expert Paul Strassels notes, "It could be anything: chartering a fishing boat, dealing in antiques, selling real estate, catering parties."

If you have your own business — or a part-time business — you can take some of the juiciest tax deductions the IRS will allow. You may be able to deduct all *business* expenses for your car, equipment, travel — even any magazines or books that you could demonstrate were necessary for research in your field of business, or the expense of attending out-of-town seminars directly related to your enterprise. You also may deduct 80% of your business-entertainment expenses.

A sideline business has another major tax advantage. If it loses money, the loss is deductible from income that you earn elsewhere, say from your full-time salaried job, as long as you were an active participant in the business. The IRS will let you deduct such losses if you report a profit in just three out of five consecutive years. For the breeding, training, showing or racing of horses, the activity must result in a profit in at least two out of seven consecutive years. But be careful. If you report only minuscule earnings, the IRS could assume that you are not serious about making the business succeed. So keep meticulous records that document the place and purpose of all business expenses. They will help you show that you spend considerable time and effort looking for clients and making the business work.

Unfortunately, the IRS audits the owners of small businesses more than any other taxpayers. Do not get carried away and deduct too much for your sideline. Deductions for what the IRS deems unnecessary or unreasonable business, travel and entertainment expenses come in for close scrutiny. And the taxmen are especially watchful for such cardinal sins as failure to report income or neglect in paying withholding taxes.

Saving by Giving Money Away

U NLESS your child is a rock star, his or her tax bracket probably is lower than yours. So it pays to shift assets from your name to your minor child's, where the income may be taxed less harshly. But wait for the child's 14th birthday. After that, the interest, dividends and capital gains earned on that money may have many years to compound at the youngster's modest tax rate.

Children who are under age 14 are taxed on any investment income over $1,100 at their parents' rate. Similarly, an adult who owns stocks or bonds that have appreciated in value and sells them to pay for a child's education is just plain foolish. Instead, *give* the securities to the child over 14, and let him or her sell them. Profits from the sale will be taxed at the child's rate instead of your much higher one.

The easiest way to give money to your child is to set up a custodial account under the Uniform Gifts to Minors Act. You just get a Social Security number for the child, then ask a banker, a broker or a mutual-fund manager to open an account in the child's name. (Unless the child has a Social Security number, you cannot claim the child as an exemption or later set up a custodial account to receive gifts for him or her.) You can give each of your children up to $10,000 a year without incurring any federal gift taxes. Couples can give away $20,000 a year to each of their children. Whoever is custodian of the account — usually a parent — can spend the money and the earnings on it for any purpose that benefits the youngster. This commonly includes private school, summer camp or violin lessons — but not some frivolous activity like a trip to Disney World. You also lose the tax break if you spend the child's money on anything that constitutes an ordinary parental obligation, such as clothing or food or shelter, except in the case of college room and board. (For more, see "Your Education: How to Save for College.")

Investment Deductions

INVESTMENTS can give you some of your best tax breaks.
Municipal bonds will pay you tax-exempt income. You will not pay
any federal tax on the money, and if you invest in bonds issued in
your own state, you will not pay state or local taxes either. You can
get municipals from brokers, or you can buy them indirectly as
shares in mutual funds or unit trusts.

You also can get some partially tax-exempt income by investing in
supersafe U.S. Treasury bonds, notes or bills. You will have to pay
federal tax on your earnings, but states and localities cannot touch
your income. To buy these securities, simply call the nearest Treasury
Department regional office or Federal Reserve Bank.

Even old reliable U.S. Savings Bonds can provide tax benefits.
Your interest is exempt from state and local levies, and no federal tax
is due until you redeem the bonds. Series EE bonds held five years or
more return at least 6% a year — or 85% of the average yield on
Treasury securities with five years remaining to maturity, whichever
is higher. In mid-1992, this worked out to 6.8% for an EE bond that
had been held for five years.

The Technical and Miscellaneous Revenue Act of 1988 (TAMRA)
offers an exclusion of interest income on U.S. Series EE savings
bonds issued after 1989. The income is excluded from gross income
to the extent that the redeemed principal and interest are used to pay
for higher education tuition expenses during the year of redemption.
The exclusion is available if you or your spouse have bought these EE
savings bonds, are at least 24 years old at the time of purchase and
don't have too high an income. The exclusion originally phased out
gradually for couples reporting an income between $60,000 and
$90,000 and for single parents earning $40,000 to $55,000. But those
figures are raised each year to adjust for inflation. In 1992 they are
incomes between $62,900 and $92,900 for couples and between
$41,950 and $56,950 for single parents. In short, this amounts to a
nifty break for parents of youngsters heading for college.

Capital Gains and Losses

L ONG-TERM capital gains continue to have favorable treatment. Under the 1990 tax act, the maximum on net gains from assets held over one year is 28%, even if you are in the 31% bracket. Net capital gains means the excess of net long-term capital gain over net short-term capital loss. Any net short-term capital gain would be taxed at ordinary income rates, up to 31%.

You can deduct from your salary and other ordinary income up to $3,000 a year in net long-term or short-term losses that you have suffered from the sale of stocks, bonds or other assets. If you have had a larger loss than that in any previous tax year, you can save the excess, carry it over to later years and then use it to offset future capital gain income.

You should be keeping track of your "basis" price on all your investments in order to determine your capital gain or loss. Remember, basis can mean more than your original purchase price. For stocks, dividend reinvestments add to your cost basis. On the other hand, returns of capital reduce your basis — and raise your capital gain. Real estate investment trusts and utility stocks sometimes pay "dividends" that are untaxable returns of capital.

Medical and Dental Deductions

I N ORDER to take tax deductions for your medical bills on your 1992 income taxes, they have to total more than 7.5% of your adjusted gross income for the year. That is quite a lot, of course, but you may have more deductible medical expenses than you realize.

Are you paying to support a child in college? Then your medical costs include any portion of college fees that covers his or her prepaid group health care. Among other frequently overlooked expenses are your travel costs on your way to visit a doctor, a hospital or just about any place you go to get medical services. If you buy or rent equipment that your doctor prescribes, such as a whirlpool or dehumidifier, that cost, too, is a deductible expense. And do not forget to count in your expenses for insurance premiums on policies covering dental care, or for replacement contact lenses. Deduct only expenses for which you are not reimbursed by your insurance plan.

Remember to add to your medical expenses those you also pay for adult dependents, such as elderly parents or relatives. You can claim these bills if you provide more than half of the dependent's support. A lump-sum payment for lifetime medical care of a dependent can be claimed in the year you made it. The annual cost of institutional care for a mentally or physically handicapped dependent qualifies — so long as the care is medically necessary. By this measure, nursing-home fees can qualify as deductible expenses.

The 1990 tax act eliminated the deduction for unnecessary cosmetic surgery. Such procedures are deductible only if they are necessary to ameliorate a congenital abnormality, personal injury or disfiguring disease.

Some procedures and programs that improve your well-being can be claimed as medical expenses, especially if your doctor prescribes them. Paying for them in one year will enhance your chances of exceeding the 7½% medical deduction threshold. Be sure to keep statements from your doctor and maintain accurate records of your expenses.

Participation in a cafeteria plan offered by your employer may enable you to increase your tax benefits. If you make contributions to your plan (in pretax dollars), you can then be reimbursed by the plan for some medical benefits. The reimbursement is not taxed. Cafeteria plans can also be used to pay for dependent care.

In addition, a self-employed person can deduct 25% of his or her health insurance premiums without regard to the 7.5% threshold. The remaining 75% of premium costs are considered part of total medical expenses, which then have to exceed the 7.5% threshold.

Home Office Deductions

THE Internal Revenue Service is tough on tax returns that include deductions and depreciation write-offs for home offices. If you want to set up a home office that the IRS can live with, you should do so for business-related reasons first and tax benefits second. Before you can claim any deductions, you must be able to prove that the area of the house or apartment you work in is used regularly and exclusively for enterprise. But you need not devote an entire room to your business. If you can prove a part of a room was used just for work, that will do. Partitioning the room with a divider will help support your case, but it is not necessary.

You also must make certain your home workplace meets at least one of two IRS tests:

One, the office is your primary location for any trade or business.

Two, you must spend substantial time at the office, and there should be no other location available to perform the office functions of the business.

Once your home office passes either one of these two tests, you can start counting your deductions. In fact, you can claim deductions for a part-time business operated out of your house even if you work full-time somewhere else in another job. A deduction is also allowed if the taxpayer maintains a structure separate from the residence used exclusively and regularly in a trade or business. An employee is allowed a deduction if use of the office is for the convenience of his or her employer. But there is a limit to the generosity of the IRS in becoming your silent business partner. You cannot deduct more than your *net* income. And you usually are not entitled to deductions if you use your home office just to manage your investments.

Starting with the 1992 tax returns, you must include the actual square footage of your workspace and the total area of your home. Dividing total space into workspace gives you the percentage of maintenance costs you can deduct.

Your list of allowable deductions should begin with your direct business costs — those solely attributable to your work space. They include expenses as diverse as painting or repairs and supplies that have a useful life of less than a year. If you rent an apartment and use one room as an office, you can deduct the portion of the rent that is equivalent to the size of the work area.

Homeowners and renters can deduct a prorated portion of their utility bills, including electricity, gas, oil, telephone, water and trash collection. Also deductible are insurance premiums paid to protect your home office from a casualty loss or theft. But you cannot deduct the cost of landscaping around your house.

Your juiciest write-off may be depreciation. If you own your house or condo or co-op apartment, you can depreciate the part used as an office over 15 to 30 years, depending on when you bought your home. If you bought your home on or after January 1, 1987, you can depreciate the office over 27½ years. Better yet, you can depreciate over five to seven years any office equipment and furniture, from a personal computer to a coffee table, or write off up to $10,000 in one year within net income limitations.

The IRS does not give any guidance on how lavish a home office can be and still be deductible. As a rule, however, writing off a Persian carpet or a crystal chandelier is out. But you can depreciate, say, a $15,000 computer system if it is necessary for your business.

Last-Minute Deductions

A S CHRISTMAS approaches, taxpayers eagerly if belatedly start shopping for deductions they can take before the year draws to a close. Normally, the golden rule of such year-end tax maneuvering is to claim all the sensible exemptions, credits and deductions you can in the current year and, simultaneously, to delay receiving as much income as you can until next year. That way, you quite legitimately can put off paying taxes on it for a full 12 months. Self-employed people often delay billing their customers or patients until the very end of December so that the money will not arrive until early the following year. Companies put off paying their year-end executive bonuses until January.

You, too, can follow the same tactics. If you make estimated payments of state income or local property taxes, send in your fourth-quarter installment in December, instead of January when it is due, and you will be able to deduct it from your tax bill for the current year. For the same reason send in your December home mortgage payment before January 1. You might consider squeezing two years' worth of charitable contributions into this year to increase your deductions. Watch out, however, for maneuvers that may make you eligible for the alternative minimum tax.

You can get extra write-offs for business expenses by prepaying next year's subscriptions to business publications and dues to professional groups. But remember that, unless you run your own business, the IRS counts these as part of your miscellaneous deductions

— which must equal more than 2% of your adjusted gross income in order to qualify for a deduction.

If you are self-employed, open a Keogh account at a bank, brokerage house or mutual fund before December 31, or open a Simplified Employee Pension plan by the following April 15. A Keogh is like a super IRA and will save you taxes. (For more, see "Your Taxes: Keogh Plans and SEPs.")

One warning: If income tax rates go up next year, you may well be better off collecting income this year — and then paying the lower rate on it. The information in the previous paragraphs is applicable to those years in which tax rates are stable or decreasing.

Here are a few more tips, which are useful regardless of changes in tax rates:

If you need a tax loss and are willing to boot out a few dogs among your investments, there is a way to do it without altering your basic investment strategy. Swap lagging bonds for similar ones. You can do the same with stocks, but it's harder to find shares that are almost identical to the ones you already hold. Generally you carry out the swaps late in the year. But do not wait until late December to make these exchanges. It may be difficult then to find just what you want. Also, watch out for the wash sale rules, which may disallow your loss.

Mutual-fund investors can consider taking a few losses as well. What you do is redeem only those shares that are worth less than you paid for them. You will need to review carefully your records of purchase, with their dates and prices, and it is drudgery. Pick out the losers, and send a list of them to the bank that serves as the fund's transfer agent, instructing the bank to redeem only those particular shares.

The Best Time to File

WHEN should you file your income tax return? The earlier the better after January 1 — if you expect to get a refund. If you file by the end of February, you should receive your check in the mail within six weeks. But if you delay and file in April, when the Internal Revenue Service is deluged by forms from other last-minute taxpayers, you could face a 12-week wait for your refund.

As mentioned earlier, do not congratulate yourself too enthusiastically if you are in line for a refund. That just means you gave the government free use of money that was rightfully yours. If you want to put that extra cash to work for you instead of for Uncle Sam, simply reduce the amount withheld from your paycheck. You do that by asking your payroll department at work for a W-4 form and increasing your number of allowances on it.

If you have the money to pay but just cannot complete your tax return by the April 15 deadline, the IRS will extend your day of filing to August 15. What you have to do is send in an extension form — IRS Form 4868 — and an *estimated* payment of your taxes by April 15. Just estimate your income for last year and subtract any deductions and credits you expect to take. Then refer to the tax tables in the 1040 instruction booklet for the amount you owe.

If you still cannot complete your tax return by August 15, you may apply for an additional extension using IRS Form 2688. The IRS may extend your day of filing to October 15. This is the last deadline to file your return.

Some states require extension requests. Some will accept a copy of the approved federal extension form. Send a state extension form if taxes are due.

If you underestimate the bill, you may have to pay the ½%-a-month penalty — plus interest — on your balance outstanding. But if you send in your return late without having filed for an extension, the IRS will be much less forgiving. (See the next chapter.) Another matter to watch: Even if you file an extension form, you must make your past year's contribution to your IRA by April 15.

But, as long as your Keogh was opened by December 31, you have until the extended due date to make the balance of your Keogh contribution. If you have a SEP plan you may also take an extension.

If you have omitted information or would like to add information to your tax return after you have filed it, you may prepare amended federal and state returns. Generally, the IRS allows you up to three years from the original filing date to amend your return.

What If You Can't Pay on Time?

A LMOST one out of four people who owe the government taxes on April 15 cannot pay. What should you do if you come to the cold discovery that you owe the government more than you can possibly raise in cash?

Don't panic. What you should do is file your *tax return* on time and send in whatever amount you can. Otherwise, you will be stuck with stiff penalties.

First, you will be liable for a fine of at least 5% and not more than 25% of your tax liability *each month* up to 25% for late filing of your form plus ½% *each month* for late payment. Second, you may be charged annual interest, compounded *daily*.

You can avoid tax fines by filing a timely extension and paying 100% of your total projected tax liability. You still will have to pay interest on any balance due.

If you do not have the money to meet your tax obligations, you need to tell that to the government. The IRS can attach your paycheck and seize your bank accounts and house. But it almost never takes such drastic action — if you earnestly try to pay your debts.

The key is communication. If you do not enclose a check when you file your return, you eventually will receive a letter demanding payment within 10 days. Do not ignore this notice: the IRS gets tougher with every passing day. Just be sure to telephone or visit the IRS office listed on the delinquency notice. Do that immediately after receiving the first notice instead of waiting for the fourth and final one about three months later. If you have a professional tax adviser, bring him or her along to the tax office. Your adviser probably will charge you, but he or she can get the IRS to agree to better terms than you can.

Several hundred delinquent taxpayers each year manage to persuade the IRS to reduce the amounts they owe. But such deals are reserved for people who the tax collectors think will never be able to pay their bills in full. For example, an elderly person with few assets and little chance of earning much might be a candidate for such a compromise.

Once this ordeal is over, make a point of preventing it from happening again. If you are a wage-earner, take fewer withholding allowances at work so more money for taxes will be deducted from your pay. If you are self-employed, increase your quarterly estimated tax payments.

How the IRS Sizes Up Your 1040

I T IS always a bad idea to try to cheat on your income tax, and it is even worse now. Thanks to their powerful computers, the tax collectors are checking up on much more of your income than ever before. Until recently, about the only lines on your tax return that the Internal Revenue Service could check and verify without an audit were those for interest income, dividends, salaries and wages. But the list is growing fast.

Since 1983, the IRS has been corroborating against other sources such income as any state and local tax refunds you may have received, proceeds you collected from any sales of investments, your Social Security benefits and IRA and pension payouts. With your return for 1985, the IRS also began verifying mortgage interest deductions and alimony income. By law, companies, banks, broker-age firms and government agencies that pay various types of income must fill out IRS forms stating the amounts distributed to you during the year. Banks and other institutions have to declare how much interest they collect and any IRA contributions they receive from you.

It may take about 18 months for the IRS to finish matching the information it gets from these sources with what you declare on your 1040 tax forms. When there is a discrepancy that does not look like a harmless error, an IRS computer will fire off a letter demanding that you explain the difference or pay up. If you under-report interest or dividend income, the letter also will say that you owe a 20% penalty. Other discrepancies do not produce an automatic fine, although the IRS could try to prove in court that you intentionally tried to misrepresent your earnings or deductions.

You should check the IRS notice that you receive before sending in the amount shown as due. In certain situations, you may have listed the income under another name on the return, or in a different income category. If this is the case, you should write a letter to the IRS explaining the reason for the discrepancy and asking the IRS to adjust its notice. The IRS is not always correct.

How to Avoid an Audit

L ITTLE more than 1% of all personal income tax returns are audited. So, chances are you are safe. But if you are called in by the IRS for one of those troubling and time-consuming procedures, you can take some comfort from these facts:

One of every eight audited taxpayers emerged from the process in 1991 owing no more than when he or she filed. Indeed, five in one hundred people who were audited came away with refunds averaging about $3,800. And many thousands of others negotiated settlements with the IRS that left them paying more taxes, but less than the agency originally had demanded.

Generally the IRS begins sending out audit notices in July of the year in which the returns in question are filed. If you receive a letter saying your return will be audited, you typically have up to six weeks to get ready for a meeting at a local IRS office. There is one exception: If the deductions in question can be easily documented, you can respond by mail.

Who gets audited? Anyone can, of course. Whether or not your return will be audited depends mostly on how closely your tax data compare with the average deductions, exemptions and credits claimed by taxpayers with your income. The bigger your income, the more likely you will be audited. High-income people who make the greatest use of sophisticated tax breaks are the most likely to claim the kinds of debatable write-offs that the IRS likes to challenge. Also prime candidates for audits are people who are paid mostly in cash, such as waiters, taxi drivers and beauticians.

How to Survive an Audit

I F YOU become one of the million or so unfortunate taxpayers who are audited each year, keep cool. The damage probably will be minimal, unless you have engaged in outright fraud.

After the audit notice arrives in the mail, try to get some idea of how extensive the examination is going to be. One way is to phone the IRS and say you want to schedule an appointment on a day when no one will be rushed. If the IRS agent responds that the interview should not take longer than a couple of hours, relax. It is likely to be a hasty one-hour job. That is the kind most people get. But if you are told to set aside a week, then you know it will be a serious review — and you have trouble.

If you find that you are repeatedly audited for the same deductions — say, higher-than-average dental bills — and these deductions have been allowed in the past, have your tax preparer write to the IRS to ask that the latest audit be canceled. When he points out that in past years these deductions have been allowed, you have a better than 50% chance of avoiding an audit this year. Alas, this is not the case with an audit of taxes on your business if you are self-employed and report on a Schedule C.

Before you go into any audit, be sure you are well briefed. Confer in advance with your tax preparer. You probably will have to pay his or her usual fee for the strategy session, but getting him or her to explain the reasoning behind any challenged deductions, exemptions or credits is well worth the expense.

Always bring a tax professional along to help explain your return. Your preparer can even appear instead of you, though only if he or she is a CPA, an attorney or someone who has passed a tough IRS test to become a so-called enrolled agent. That rules out most storefront preparers. Insist that the audit take place at the IRS or at the office of your preparer, but not at your own home or office. There is no point in giving the tax collector a more complete picture of your economic situation than he will get from your written return.

The most important factor in deciding the audit's outcome will be the evidence you present to support your deductions. A dossier of receipts, bills and diaries will help you document your write-offs. You will do best if you offer a sound defense without appearing defensive. You might even ask for additional deductions at your audit. If you can document them, you may improve your overall bargaining position.

Your attitude will do a lot to determine how tough or lenient the auditor will be, so be polite. Answer all questions simply and directly, but never volunteer any information. If the auditor assigned to you is abusive, you have the right to demand another. But do not act belligerently toward your IRS examiner. Do not speak loudly. Do not smoke, and do not wear clothing or jewelry that might cause the auditor to think that your income is higher than you reported.

If you are not satisfied with the outcome of your audit, you can appeal on the spot to the examiner's supervisor. That person will come to his or her own conclusion. If you then are still dissatisfied, you have 30 days to ask that an IRS appeals officer hear your case. You might find him or her more willing to concede some or all of the issues than your auditor was. Unlike auditors, appeals officers are allowed to weigh the cost of a possible court battle in determining how much, if anything, you should pay.

You can appeal further to the U.S. tax court, district court or Claims Court. But before you take that step, you should decide whether the battle is really worth it. Tax court cases are typically long, often expensive and rarely successful. (For more, see "Your Taxes: How to Complain to the IRS.")

How to Get the Tax Adviser Who Is Best for You

SUPPOSE you are salaried, earn less than $40,000 a year, perhaps own a little stock and pay a mortgage. Chances are your tax profile is simple. If so, you should be able to handle your own forms with the help of a do-it-yourself tax preparation book. Or you can take your forms to one of the national storefront chains such as H&R Block or Beneficial Income Tax Service. They all charge set fees, depending on the complexity of your form. In 1992, the average price of a Block preparation came to $53.32.

If your personal finances are more complex — say that in the past year you have sold a house, started a business or had active stock trades — you will find that no professional is better trained to handle your taxes than a certified public accountant. It is best to hire a CPA who specializes in taxes, rather than one who does general accounting. Accountants charge $70 an hour and up. Merely having your forms filled out probably will cost at least $300.

If your income is large enough to warrant an accountant's help, you probably will need tax planning, too. At one of the major accounting firms, that could include estate planning, several meetings with a personal adviser on tax strategies and shelters, updates on relevant IRS rulings, quarterly projections of your taxes and an array of tax reports. The cost is generally more than $3,500. But an experienced CPA in a small firm should be able to approximate this royal treatment for $1,000 to $1,500.

A group of professionals who offer expertise in areas where even accountants fear to tread are tax attorneys. They are great for handling specialized tax problems such as those related to divorce and the sale, purchase or start-up of a business. These lawyers usually work for taxpayers in, or close to, the top tax bracket who want to shelter part of their income. Tax lawyers can argue your case before the IRS and into tax court. Their rates can be $250 an hour or more.

Whomever you choose to prepare your taxes, he or she should sign your return, and should be willing — unequivocally willing — to appear along with you at the IRS in the event you are audited.

Before you sign the completed return yourself, read over each line and check to see the figures correspond with your records. When you do not understand how your preparer came up with a certain number, ask. If the IRS finds an error, it is you who will have to pay any back taxes, interest and penalties. So do not just dump your financial records on your accountant's desk and run.

Also make sure your return will be completed before April 15. Recently, one taxpayer's attorney had prepared his forms but sent them in three months late because of a clerical oversight. The Supreme Court ruled that the taxpayer was indeed liable for a late-filing penalty. You should ask your preparer "early and often" how work is coming along on your return. And if you think there is a chance he will not finish on time, file for an extension.

How can you evaluate the quality of help you will get from an accountant or tax lawyer or storefront tax preparer whom you are contemplating hiring? Start by asking what kind of clients his or her firm handles. See if its members are experienced with people in your shoes. Beware of firms that operate on a "pool arrangement" in which your tax forms float among a number of accountants, each of whom handles a few lines.

Listen to the questions the tax adviser asks *you*. If he or she neglects to inquire about the basics of your tax situation — whether you own a home, have a pension plan or contribute to an IRA — you have drawn a dud.

The vast majority of tax professionals are competent and honest, but the number of incompetent, negligent and fraudulent tax preparers is much higher than the Internal Revenue Service's estimate of only a few thousand, out of roughly 200,000 in the country. According to the government's General Accounting Office, the IRS is not doing enough to find or penalize the wrongdoers.

How can you tell if your tax preparer might be a problem? Watch out for one who demands a percentage of your tax refund as payment. Especially steer away from a preparer who guarantees you a refund. Also, avoid anyone who says he or she will give you a refund right away and will later endorse and cash your IRS check. That is illegal — and subject to a $500 penalty.

If after looking for a professional tax adviser, you still choose to prepare your forms yourself, there are many good books and software programs to guide you. Among the best are the *Consumer Reports Books Guide to Income Tax Preparation* (Consumers Union, $12.95), *The Ernst & Young Tax Guide 1993* (Wiley, $12.95) and *J. K. Lasser's Your Income Tax 1991* (J. K. Lasser Institute, $12.95; they also offer a free 24-hour staffed hotline). If you don't have any interest in an explanation of the current tax code, J. K. Lasser offers another book, *Your 60-Minute Tax Return 1992* ($8.95). Among the software programs are *Personal Tax Preparer* (Parsons Technology, $49) and *Andrew Tobias' Tax Cut* (Meca Software, $59.95).

How to Get Quick Answers

WHOM do you call when you have a question or two about your taxes? Try the IRS. It provides recorded tax information that is accurate, reasonably clear and free.

For the number to call, turn to pages 77 and 78 of your 1040 instruction booklet. Then look on pages 78 and 79 for the list of some 140 tax subjects and their corresponding three-digit codes. Once you place the call, you punch these codes on your touch-tone phone to get a tape-recorded discussion of the selected subject. If you have a rotary-dial phone, wait until someone answers and then state the code for the tape you want to hear.

In most cases, the recordings also refer you to free IRS publications for more information. If you want to talk directly to an IRS staff member, you can find the appropriate phone number on page 77 of your 1040 booklet. Trouble is, according to tests by the General Accounting Office and *Money* magazine, the live answers are often wrong. You stand your best chance of getting through to IRS staffers if you phone early in the morning or late in the week. But recorded help is available around the clock seven days a week for taxpayers with touch-tone phones. (All the page numbers given above come from the instruction booklet for 1991 income and are subject to change.)

How to Complain to the IRS

SAY that you are entitled to a tax refund but it does not arrive, or it is smaller than expected, or you receive a bill to pay additional tax. If you have a complaint about your taxes, there are a few secrets for getting action — and satisfaction — out of the IRS.

Taxpayers have the right to be treated fairly, professionally, promptly and courteously by IRS employees. To help insure this treatment the IRS has a new publication that explains these rights.

You also can get in touch with one of the agency's specially designated problem-resolution officers, or PROs. There are 73 of these merciful missionaries, one in each IRS district office and service center. If you call a PRO, he or she usually can sweep away weeks or months of potential bureaucratic frustration.

If your complaint isn't settled in five working days, the problem-resolution officer is supposed to advise you of the status of the case and give you the name and phone number of the person down the line who can solve it. And if you don't get satisfaction even then, you can ask that your case be sent to the IRS appellate division. If you lose there, you have 90 days to take one of three further steps:

First, you can withhold payment on a claim of less than $10,000 and take your case to the small-claims division of the U.S. tax court.

Second, you can pay a disputed tax of any amount and file for a refund with your IRS office. If it's disallowed, you then can sue in a U.S. district court or the Claims Court.

In 1990 the government won 75.8% of the cases brought in the district courts; taxpayers won complete victories in 17.4% of the cases and partial victories in 6.8% of them.

In the Claims Court during 1989 the government won 89.1% of the cases, while taxpayers won 2.7% and gained partial victories in 8.2%. The Claims Court has several drawbacks for aggrieved taxpayers. Fighting a case there requires you to make a trip to Washington. Before your case is even heard, you must pay not only the taxes in dispute but also any interest and penalties. Yes, you do get a refund if you win. But only when you can afford the cost and inconvenience should you resort to the Claims Court.

Finally, you can sue in the U.S. tax court without paying the tax in advance. In the past several years taxpayers had full victories in only a small percentage of cases.

You probably can avoid the courts if you have a legitimate claim. Indeed, if an IRS problem-resolution officer cannot help you, go to your congressman. Often, he or she or an aide can break a logjam in your case in a matter of hours.

Your IRAs

How They Work

I F YOU were limited to just one investment a year, what would it be? For many people, a sound choice still would be a tax-saving Individual Retirement Account, even though 10 million IRA holders stopped funding theirs after the 1986 tax reform.

True enough, tax reform took away from many people one of the two major benefits of IRAs: your ability to deduct from your taxable income every dollar you invest. But even if you can't cash in on that benefit, IRAs still offer what could be a more important advantage: you will pay no taxes on the interest, dividends and capital gains you earn on your contributions as long as the money remains in your account. Therefore, the whole account can benefit from the marvels of compounding interest until you start making withdrawals, presumably after you retire. Then you will pay income tax at your ordinary rate — but only on the taxable part of the cash you remove. It is even possible that your tax rate at that time will be lower than it was when you were working — but don't count on it.

Employed people and their spouses who are not covered by a pension plan can deduct all contributions to an IRA. But if you are in a company plan — whether you are vested or not — you can deduct your contribution only if you meet certain income requirements. Married couples who file jointly can deduct their full IRA deposit if their adjusted gross income is $40,000 or less a year, regardless of whether either spouse participates in a pension plan. Single filers can deduct up to $2,000 if they earn $25,000 or less. Couples who earn between $40,000 and $50,000, and singles who earn between $25,000 and $35,000 can write off part of their contribution. The amount you can deduct tapers off as you earn more money. Unfortunately, these amounts are not adjusted, as income tax brackets are, to account for rises in the cost of living.

Even if your earnings put you above the $35,000 to $50,000 ceilings, you may be able to claim at least part of an IRA deduction. Another way is to take advantage of a 401(k) plan if your company offers one. With a 401(k), you can instruct your employer to put away part of your salary — up to $8,728 in 1992 — toward your retirement. For each dollar you contribute, some employers add 50 cents or more to your account up to a predetermined maximum.

Because the money you put away under a 401(k) is not considered taxable income (but it is subject to FICA), your contributions lower your adjusted gross income. Say that you and your spouse earn $52,000 and thus are not eligible for an IRA deduction. But if you put $8,728 into a 401(k) plan, your adjusted gross income would decline to $43,372. In that case you would be able to make a partially deductible contribution to your IRA. Similarly, you may qualify for a full or partial IRA deduction if you put money into a Keogh plan or a Simplified Employee Pension and you are within the income limitation.

The fact that IRAs compound tax-free means that they are government subsidies to investors. If you put the maximum $2,000 a year into an IRA each January for 20 years and it earns 10% annually, your $40,000 in contributions will turn into $126,000. By contrast, if you put the same amount of money into nonsheltered investments and earned 10% on them but withdrew the amount needed each year to pay taxes, using an average federal and state tax rate of 32%, your account after 20 years would total just $85,000.

IRAs do not have many drawbacks. Yes, you may have to pay between $10 and $30 a year in fees to the bank, savings and loan association, brokerage firm, mutual-fund or insurance company where you keep your account. (Charles Schwab & Co., the discount broker, now has free IRAs.) Plus, you cannot ordinarily withdraw the money before age 59½ without being assessed a 10% penalty by the tax collectors. But both are small prices to pay for what can be a really terrific tax shelter.

You have until the time you file your income taxes — as late as April 15 — to open or fund your IRA and put some of your previous year's pay into it. You can invest your money in bank certificates of deposit, stocks, bonds, mutual funds, annuities, limited partnerships, stock options, futures contracts, real estate, Ginnie Maes and U.S. Treasury securities. Off limits are life insurance, precious metals, gems, art and other collectibles. But you are allowed to buy U.S. Treasury gold and silver coins as well as state-issued coins.

The further you are from retirement, the more an IRA's tax-deferred compound earnings can do for you. If you are 35 and start depositing $2,000 a year for the next 30 years and your money earns 10%, you will be richer by $362,000 when you turn 65.

Your IRA will grow much faster if you put in your contributions as early each year as possible. Let's say you make the maximum $2,000 contribution, but you wait until the very last minute — that is, until every April 15 — to make your contribution for the prior year. If your investment earns 10% annually, in 20 years you will have $114,500. But if you make that same contribution as soon as each new tax year begins, on January 1, you will end up with $11,450 more in the same amount of time. And after 30 years, you will have $33,000 more than you would have if you waited until the last minute.

Remember that you do not have to put the maximum $2,000 in your account every year. Legally, you can open an IRA with as little as $1, but most banks require at least $25. Your contribution need not be made all at one time. You can make periodic deposits, as with any other account — as long as you meet the April 15 deadline. You can even skip a year, but you cannot make up for it by putting in more than $2,000 the next time. You also can open as many IRAs as you please and divide deposits among them, just so long as your total contribution in one year does not exceed $2,000. Watch out, though, for multiple fees. You also can switch your IRAs from one financial institution to another without forfeiting the tax benefits. Note that you can no longer contribute to an IRA once you have reached age 70½.

Once you have made an initial contribution, you can leave your account at that level or you can build it up with weekly or monthly deposits. Even small deposits grow nicely. Put away just $9.60 a week, for instance, and in 12 months you will have a tax-sheltered nest egg of $500 — plus whatever interest, dividends and capital gains you have earned on it.

Some employers offer payroll-deduction plans for IRA contributions. These periodic deductions are a convenient method of forced savings. One disadvantage of any installment-style pay-ins is that they do not let you accumulate the maximum amount possible in your IRA, because your total allowable contribution is not made in one lump at the beginning of the year and is not working for you the entire year.

As mentioned above, your IRA money will be taxed as ordinary income when you start withdrawing it. Unless you are disabled, you may face stiff consequences for *permanently* withdrawing any money too early in life. The IRS will claim as a penalty 10% of the funds you take out, and you will also owe income tax on the total withdrawal at your regular rate. The earliest age at which you could avoid the penalty used to be 59½, but tax changes in 1988 liberalized that rule. You can now start taking out money much sooner by scheduling annual withdrawals as lifetime income. At 50, for example, a man can begin tapping a $100,000 IRA for as much as $11,000 a year or as little as $3,000, depending on a wide range of permissible assumptions about his life expectancy and the rate of return his money will earn. You can even change the assumptions from year to year.

The new rules also cover other retirement plans, such as Keoghs and SEPs. So parents can use tax-deferred retirement money to help pay for their children's college education or even for a wedding. But once withdrawals start, they must continue for at least five years or until you reach 59½, whichever comes later. Stopping them too soon will cost you retroactive 10% penalties on all the money previously taken out, plus interest. You'll need guidance from an accountant or financial planner on how much you can safely siphon off, and for how long.

There's one other escape hatch in the early-withdrawal rules. You can *temporarily* withdraw money from your IRA once a year, without paying any tax or penalties. You just have to roll over and replace the money within 60 days. So, if you are careful, you can use your IRA money for a short-term emergency loan. The only extra cost may be a fee imposed by some banks or mutual funds when you withdraw and replace your IRA funds this way.

You are allowed to start permanent withdrawals anytime after age 59½, but you *must* begin making them soon after you turn 70½ — to be precise, by April 1 of the next calendar year — taking out at least the minimum amounts decreed by the IRS on the basis of life-expectancy tables. For instance, if you are a 70-year-old man, you are expected to live 12 more years, so you must withdraw at least one-twelfth of your funds in the first year. If you are dependent principally on the IRA income, it might be safest when you retire to transfer the entire sum into an annuity that provides lifetime payments for you and your spouse. Then at least you can't outlive your money.

When you die, the money or annuity payments from an IRA go to any beneficiary you have named. A spouse may reregister the IRA in his or her name and continue enjoying tax deferrals. If the beneficiary is not a spouse, the money must be withdrawn and the tax paid in no more than five annual installments.

If only one spouse is employed or if one spouse has a very small income, the couple can contribute a total of $2,250 annually under the "spousal" IRA provision. But each partner must have a separate account. The $2,250 spousal IRA can be divided as the couple wishes, so long as no more than $2,000 goes into either account in a given year. For example, one partner may contribute $2,000 and the other $250; or each may contribute $1,125. You can contribute the full $2,000 to your spouse's IRA based upon your earnings even if you are over 70½, as long as your spouse is under 70½. In case of divorce the ex-spouses keep individual control of the funds already in their separate accounts except for settlements in community property states, where the IRAs must be divided 50-50.

If you own a small business, you can increase your nonworking spouse's IRA deduction. Just hire your beloved part-time. As long as the service he or she performs is legitimate and the compensation is reasonable, you can put up to $2,000 of the spouse's salary in the IRA every year. But you also will have to make other federally mandated tax payments for your spouse, such as for Social Security.

True enough, some people should not open IRAs. As a rule, children ought not to put earnings from summer or after-school jobs in an IRA, because they are already in a very low tax bracket or pay no taxes at all. And if you think you will need your savings in a few years to buy a house or start a business, that money should not go into an IRA. The penalty for early withdrawal will probably exceed what you would gain in tax-sheltered earnings on several years of IRA contributions. But almost anyone else who has earned some income from a job, and can afford to put aside savings that he or she will not need anytime soon, should think seriously about opening an Individual Retirement Account.

Where to Invest Your IRA Money

I NVESTING the cash you put in your Individual Retirement Account is like shopping in a well-stocked financial supermarket. You can choose from many thousands of securities, bank instruments, mutual funds, annuities and income-producing limited partnerships. But your decision will be considerably easier if you answer these four questions:

First, how old are you? The closer you are to retirement, the less risk you may wish to take. The stock market might be a terrific investment for most of the savings of someone under 50. But at age 63 you might be asking for trouble, since a market slump could leave you shortchanged at a critical time.

Second, what other investments do you have? You want to diversify. If your non-IRA assets are mostly in common stocks, you might balance them by filling your tax-deferred account with high-yielding fixed-income investments, such as bond funds and bank certificates.

Third, how daring are you? If an investment is going to keep you awake at night, it is not for you. One fairly painless way to learn your tolerance for risk is to put a small part of your IRA money into a growth stock or an aggressive growth mutual fund. As the price swings, the lining of your stomach will tell you how much risk you feel comfortable with.

Fourth, what do you know? Do not invest in something you do not understand. Avoid limited partnerships in real estate, oil and gas or other areas unless you are expert enough in such investments to tell a good deal from a bad one. Other investments that demand extreme caution include options and commodities futures.

Over the years your IRA should grow — and change — just as you do. The younger you are, the more you should go for growth. Let's say you are 30 and have some safe investments outside your IRA. In that case, you might do well to place almost all of your IRA money in long-term growth mutual funds.

By contrast, if you are in your 50s and plan on dipping into your IRA within five years or so, you would be well advised to start moving out of stocks and into such safer staples as money-market funds and short-term bonds. Specifically, you might be wise to invest 50% of your money in certificates of deposit, U.S. Treasury securities, Ginnie Mae funds and short-term or intermediate-term corporate bonds. Another 20% might be in money-market funds. The remainder could comfortably stay in a portfolio of solid stocks with growth potential.

To repeat, if your IRA investment strategy emphasizes safety, fixed-income securities are hard to beat. Short-term certificates of deposit are the best-known type. However, rates are currently extremely low. Other fixed-income investments offer comparable returns. Among them: Ginnie Maes, which are home mortgage securities backed by the federal government.

You can take more risk — and possibly earn a bigger return — by buying shares in a mutual fund. There are over 2,795 stock and bond funds, and you can choose one whose strategy fits your own.

If you have accumulated at least $10,000 in your IRA and are willing to do your own investment research, you may want to open a self-directed account at a bank, a brokerage house or a mutual-fund company. Such accounts let you trade stocks, bonds, funds, certificates of deposit and other securities at will. Self-directed IRAs can cost about $25 to open, $25 a year to maintain and $50 to close.

If you are undecided how to divvy up your IRA funds between stocks and fixed-income investments, consider the new breed of mutual fund that will make the decision for you. Known as asset allocation funds, these funds strive to get the best return by dividing their assets among stocks, bonds, foreign securities, gold and money market securities.

No one asset is ideal for an IRA, despite what its sponsor might say. By contrast, some investments are truly unsuitable for the accounts.

Question any rate of return that seems seductively high. There is probably a reason for the steep yield, such as excessive risk. Be especially wary of CDs that offer split rates — a lofty one for 60 days and a lower one for the duration of the term. Insist on having the annual yield calculated for you. It is the best basis for comparison. The new truth-in-savings law requires this.

In evaluating an IRA investment, first consider how it scores for preservation of principal. Ask yourself how great a chance there is that you could lose some, or even all, of the money you invest. But remember that you generally pay for high safety by accepting relatively low returns.

Another key characteristic to watch for in your IRA account, once you are 59½, is liquidity. The more quickly you can convert an investment into cash, the more liquid it is. The more liquid your IRA assets, the easier it is to plan cash withdrawals and adjust your investments in response to economic changes. You can always withdraw securities from an IRA without selling them.

Also consider volatility. If investments that jump and fall sharply make you nervous, play safe. But if you have a strong gut, go for growth and don't worry too much about volatility.

Consider also how well an investment will stand up to inflation. A locked-in 8% interest on a long-term Treasury bond looks nice enough when inflation is around 3%, but that unchanging rate loses much of its luster if inflation rises toward double-digit levels. The message: Include in your IRA some investments, such as stocks, whose long-term growth can keep you ahead of inflation.

Mutual-Fund Plans

THE best place to invest your IRA money may well be in a large mutual-fund group — that is, a company that operates several kinds of mutual funds. When you put your cash in one or more of these groups, your fees are low, your investment choices are numerous and at many fund families you can move your money around from one investment to another simply by making a telephone call. What's more, several major fund companies now offer discount brokerage services, including Fidelity, T. Rowe Price and Vanguard.

A great many mutual-fund companies have funds that invest in stocks, bonds and the money market — plus, in some fund families, an astonishing array of permutations and combinations of the three — and let you switch your money among them. One big mutual-fund company, Fidelity, offers more than 130 choices, ranging from a money-market fund that invests exclusively in federal government securities, to a fund that buys stocks of fast-growing high-tech companies, to a highly specialized fund that buys into companies in a specific line of business. The primary advantage of such variety is that you are not locked into one type of investment.

That is important when you are putting money aside for a retirement that is possibly decades away.

The three discount brokerage firms of Charles Schwab & Co., Charles White Inc. and Waterhouse Securities have a special deal. With your IRA money, they let you buy, sell and switch among some 500 no-load and low-load mutual funds as well as stocks, bonds, options and government securities. The brokerage fee at Schwab, for example, for a $2,000 IRA transaction is $29 for a mutual fund, $39 for a bond purchase and $64 for a stock purchase.

When you buy a so-called load mutual fund, you pay a commission — as much as 8½% — most of which goes to the salesman or broker who sells it to you. But you can save a lot by investing instead in a no-load fund family. In that case you will generally pay only an annual IRA maintenance charge of $5 to $10 per fund. That can add up, however, if you spread a few thousand dollars over several funds. No-load funds, like load funds, also charge annual management fees, normally ½% to 1½% of the value of your account. The difference is that you buy directly from the no-load fund group instead of from a broker. There is no evidence that either load or no-load funds outperform the other.

Bank and S&L Plans

IF WHAT you want is a worry-free and very nearly decision-free Individual Retirement Account, then you may be wise to open your IRA at a bank, a savings and loan association or a credit union that is federally insured. An IRA account at any of these institutions has several advantages. You deal face-to-face with your banker; the fees are modest to nonexistent; you can get started by depositing as little as $25 at some institutions; and the federal government insures your CD and money-market account balances up to $100,000. When your account gets near the insurance limit, just open *another* IRA at a different banking institution. More and more banks also sell mutual funds, usually load funds.

But there are reasons why not everybody is beating a path to his or her local banker. One is the very low rate CDs have been paying. Also, if you need to withdraw your money for some emergency, you may have to forfeit at least three months' interest on bank certificates of more than a year, and one month's interest on those of a year or less. However, if you are 59½ or older, most banks will waive this penalty when you cash in certificates of deposit on your IRA.

The closest equivalent to a bank or credit union savings account is a money-market fund. Money funds are considered quite safe, although they are not federally insured. Banks and savings and loans attempt to compete with money-market funds by offering money-market deposit accounts that have federal insurance up to $100,000. But the interest rates on both have fallen to the 3% range, with bank deposits generally paying less than money funds.

Banks and S&Ls also offer two types of longer-term IRA savings certificates:

First, there are fixed-rate certificates. They guarantee you both preservation of capital and predictable returns. This they do by locking you — and the bank — into the same interest rate for anywhere from three months to 10 years. The shorter a CD's life, the lower the rate, although rates have been dipping at the long end. You would want a short-term CD if you believe interest rates will rise in the future; then you fairly soon could cash in your CD and buy a new one that pays the higher rate. But if you think that interest rates will decline in the future, you would want a certificate with a fairly long-term fixed rate. That way you would continue to enjoy today's relatively high real rates. Better yet, divide your CDs into maturities from six months to 30 months or more. This is called "laddering," and it covers some of your money whichever direction rates take.

Then there are variable-rate certificates. The initial yield is a percentage point or so lower than on fixed certificates, but the yield moves up or down every few weeks, in line with interest rates in general. Consequently, you would choose variable certificates if you think rates will rise.

Stock brokerage firms also sell — or, rather, resell — CDs that they have bought from a bank or savings and loan association. Most brokerages sell them without charging a commission, and the interest rates they pay you are often higher than at banking institutions. That's because brokers can scour the market for the steepest returns. Then again, brokerage CDs don't reinvest your interest. It goes into a money-market fund, where it is likely to earn less than the CD was yielding.

The interest rates that banks and S&Ls pay on IRA accounts vary widely from plan to plan, from bank to bank and from state to state. So be sure to shop around. The only accurate rate comparison is between the compounded annual yields, also known as the effective annual yields.

When shopping for CDs, be wary of advertising hype. A "bonus of 2%," for example, may turn out to be exactly what it says it is — a premium of only 2% of the base rate, not a bonus of two percentage points above the base rate. Another lure is the split-rate CD. It pays an extraordinarily high rate for a millisecond or two before reverting to a rate that may be lower than prevailing ones.

Insurance Company Annuity Plans

YOUR friendly insurance agent can tell you all about his company's annuity plans for your Individual Retirement Account. It might be wise to listen.

An annuity that you take out with an insurance company is two things at once. First, it is a contract promising to pay you income for a specified time, usually from the day you retire to the end of your life. Second, it is an investment that pays either a fixed return (like a CD) or a variable return (like a mutual fund).

As investments, annuities simply duplicate the tax advantage of nondeductible IRAs. The earnings are tax-deferred, with or without IRA protection.

Fixed annuities should produce higher interest than competing CDs. Variable annuities, which many insurance companies are now offering, fluctuate along with the ups and downs of the stock or bond market. So, you get a crack at capital gains, which you don't get in a fixed annuity. Of course, you can also suffer capital losses if the market goes down. Variable plans allow you to move your money at will from one type of investment to another, typically into a stock investment fund, a bond fund or a money-market fund.

On fixed annuities, some insurance companies have been guaranteeing relatively high effective one-year yields, after management fees. But watch out: A number of insurance companies announce a guaranteed rate on your *new* IRA contribution each year, but say nothing about the rate that they will pay on your deposits and reinvested earnings from previous years. So make sure you ask the insurance agent which rate he is quoting: the new money rate or the so-called portfolio rate, which applies to your recent contributions *and* all the money in your account.

The disadvantages to annuity plans are the high sales charges you will face if you want to withdraw more than 10% of your funds during the first few years. These charges come on top of the IRS penalties for early withdrawal. And yearly management fees on variable annuities can run high. But annuities offer you the largest choice of payout plans once you do retire, including a lump sum. Just be sure to pick an insurance company with a high rating for its ability to keep its promises. (For more, see "Your Retirement/Annuities: Savings with a Tax Shelter.")

Bond Plans

IT IS easy to see why bonds have proved seductive to IRA investors. They offer steady, fixed rates of return. Plus, if you hold a high-quality bond until it matures, you are almost certain to get back every penny you put in.

Bonds are issued by corporations, by the federal government and by state and local authorities. But for your IRA, you should consider only bonds issued by Uncle Sam or by companies. That is because interest on municipal bonds is tax-free. So if you spend your IRA money on a muni, you would be paying for tax breaks you cannot use. Worse than that, you would pay tax on the interest when you withdrew it from the IRA. All withdrawals from IRAs are fully taxable by the federal government and — if they have income taxes — by your state and city.

Unless you are willing to take chances with your money, you are best off picking bonds rated A or higher by the major bond-rating services. There is little risk that the borrowers will not be able to pay your interest and return your principal.

The safest bonds, bar none, are issued by the U.S. Treasury and other federal agencies. If Uncle Sam gets into a pinch on his debts, he simply raises taxes, prints new dollars or issues new securities. But safety has its price. Treasury bonds usually yield a percentage point or two less than do corporate bonds with comparable maturities.

You generally buy corporate bonds and government agency certificates from brokerage firms. Banks and brokers sell Treasury securities. Be sure to shop around for the lowest commissions. Zero-coupon Treasuries are best. They lock in a compound return.

Real Estate Plans

REAL ESTATE can play an important role in your IRA. True, it may not be the very top investment for your Individual Retirement Account this year. But eventually nearly everyone should have some real estate investments in his or her tax-saving IRA. That's because tangible assets such as land and buildings provide a good hedge. If inflation rises again, they will tend to jump in value, while such paper investments as stocks and bonds usually slump.

The best way to get real property into your IRA is to buy shares in real estate investment trusts, commonly known as REITs. Their shares are publicly traded, just like stocks, and you can buy them from brokers. REITs invest in such projects as apartment complexes, office buildings and shopping centers. Some REITs also make mortgage loans.

By law, REITs must distribute at least 95% of their taxable income to their shareholders. So, shareholders can collect high regular payments if the trust performs well. In mid-1992, yields ranged from 7% to 8% for so-called equity REITs — the kind that invest in property. And yields were 12% to 14% for REITs that exclusively make loans.

Equity REITs are usually best for IRA investors. The reason is that they are the ones that will grow in value when commercial real estate recovers from its prolonged slump or when inflation kicks up.

Before you buy, study the annual financial statements of several equity REITs and look for those that actively try to improve their properties. Shares in such REITs are more likely to outperform inflation. For safety, lean toward REITs that have bought their properties outright with all cash. That means they will not be saddled with tough-to-meet mortgage payments in hard times. It is wise to stay away from REITs that own mainly urban office buildings. Such properties have been overbuilt in many areas throughout the U.S.

Better yet, invest your IRA in no-load real estate mutual funds. Fidelity Real Estate Investment Fund holds a diversified portfolio of REITs. In mid-1992 it was yielding 4.4% and had a 12-month total return of 19.43%. Another such fund, United Services Real Estate, has done well recently with single-family home stocks. Its yield in the same period was 3.8%, and its total return was 17.07%. Or invest in a closed-end fund, Real Estate Securities Income Fund, a diversified REIT assemblage that trades, often at a discount, on the American Stock Exchange. With an 8.6% yield and a 12-month total return of 13.68%, this fund may reward you well for waiting until real estate turns around.

Self-directed Plans

Some 42 million taxpayers have Individual Retirement Accounts, but only a quarter of them actively manage their money. The rest just hand their IRA money over to banks or other financial institutions. But if you just tried, perhaps you could make your IRA grow faster than the big boys can. Particularly if you read the financial press and take the time to study investment markets, you should consider opening a self-directed IRA, for it will give you a nice variety of investment choices.

Of course, you can buy stocks for your IRA, selecting either shares that pay high, dependable dividends or growth stocks that offer the chance for fat profits — along with, alas, the risk of big losses. You also can fill your account with mutual funds, ordinary bonds, zero-coupon bonds, bond trusts, Ginnie Mae unit trusts, commodity funds, promissory notes, certain kinds of options and income-producing limited partnerships. About the only things you cannot do through a self-directed IRA are invest in life insurance or such tangible items as gold, silver, Oriental rugs or diamonds. U.S. Treasury gold and silver coins came off the forbidden list in 1987 and state coins in 1988.

You can open your self-directed IRA at almost any brokerage house. It usually costs at least $25 to start such an account. Besides that, you will have to pay commissions on any trading you do. For example, they will run to $70 or so on a $2,000 transaction with a full-service broker. So if you plan on heavy trading, consider a discount broker who will trim a few dollars off relatively small transactions — and as much as 75% off the posted commission rate on trades of $10,000 or more. But some discounters limit their business to stocks and bonds. If you want to invest in, say, limited partnerships or commodities, you may have to go to a full-service broker.

When weighing whether to open a self-directed account, consider how aggressive you want to be with your investments. If a conservative strategy appeals to you, one of the best ways to invest IRA money is in ultra-safe corporate or government bonds. AA-rated long-term industrial bonds in mid-1992 were paying roughly 7.8% interest, and corporate bond unit trusts very nearly that much.

But there is another way to look at IRA funds, especially if you are in your 20s or early 30s. Over the long run, conservative investments such as bonds and bank certificates of deposit probably will not grow nearly as much as stocks in well-managed companies. If so, you stand to earn higher profits from such shares, even after taxes.

Consequently, an investor who will not be needing cash for five or 10 years most likely would do better to invest in a diversified portfolio of the shares of innovative companies than to tie up money in fixed-interest securities. Indeed, almost anyone who feels optimistic about the future of the stock market should keep at least some IRA money in growth-oriented stocks or mutual funds that invest in them.

Comparing the Fees

DEPENDING on where you invest your IRA money, you can pay practically nothing in start-up fees and annual maintenance — or quite a lot. Generally, banks and savings and loan associations have the lowest fees — from nothing to only a few dollars a year. The banks often sell you a certificate of deposit for your IRA. If you decide to transfer your money to another kind of investment, there is only a modest charge, provided you do not switch out of your

CD before it matures. At most banks, if you cash in your IRA certificate early, you will forfeit at least three months' interest.

No-load mutual funds also charge minimal fees, usually $10 a year. These funds are the kind that you buy directly from the mutual-fund company rather than from brokers. But if you choose a so-called load mutual fund, the kind that is sold through brokers and some financial planners, add a fat onetime 4% to 8½% sales commission.

You can set up your own self-directed IRA at a brokerage house. Both full-service and discount brokers may charge a small fee to start one, plus around $30 a year or more to maintain it. Charles Schwab & Co. allows you to open an IRA at no charge and will bill you $22 annually to maintain it. Wherever you open your account, you will have to pay commissions on all of your securities trades for the IRA.

Annuities that you buy from insurance companies tend to have the heaviest fees. If you put $2,000 into an annuity plan, and then withdraw it in less than a year to switch to another form of IRA investment, the experience could cost you about $140.

Most institutions subtract your fees from your account. But if you do not want to drain assets from your IRA — and if you want the maximum tax deductions it offers — you can arrange to make separate payments of your fees. Then, on your income tax return you can itemize them under "miscellaneous" and, if your total deductions amount to more than 2% of your total adjusted income, Uncle Sam may share the cost with you.

How to Switch Your Account

MANY people who have put their IRA money in a bank, a brokerage firm or a mutual fund figure that they have to keep it there until they retire, many years from now. But that's really not so. You can move your Individual Retirement Account from one financial institution to another quite easily.

Say you have your IRA invested in stocks but you figure that the stock market is in for a tumble. What to do? Simply switch your account out of stocks and into a money-market fund or some other investment that pays a safe, fixed rate of interest or preserves your capital.

You just tell your broker to sell the stocks. Then you can reinvest the money through the broker, in one of its money-market funds or in CDs or short-term Treasury securities. Or you can take all the proceeds yourself and deposit them in a bank IRA. This is called a rollover.

Similarly, if you already have your IRA money in a bank but figure the stock market will go up, you can switch your money into stocks or mutual funds. This also is a rollover. Usually, you can roll over an IRA only once a year. If, however, you have three or more separate IRAs in your name, you can make one rollover annually from each of the accounts.

To make a rollover, you can write for withdrawal instructions or go in person to the institution that now holds your IRA and just take out the funds. Then you deliver them to your new custodian.

One big caution: Be sure that you transfer all the money to your new account within 60 days of withdrawing it from your old account. Otherwise the money will be taxable and you may have to pay a penalty. To answer any future IRS challenge, always write "IRA rollover" on the back of the check or security.

You can avoid this problem by making a so-called direct transfer. Just ask the institution to which you want to transfer your IRA money to have it sent directly from the institution that is now holding it. The new custodian will send you a transfer form to fill out and return. For example, if you have your IRA invested in a mutual fund, you can ask the fund to transfer it to a bank or vice versa. This is often the better way to handle the transaction. You can move your IRA as often as you wish.

Although major banks whisk millions around the globe in seconds, they typically require 30 days' prior notice for IRA transfers. Why do they take so long? Chiefly because many financial institutions are inundated by more accounts than they can efficiently handle. Yet mutual funds manage to execute transfers smoothly and quickly.

Rolling Them Over

You can save a bundle of taxes on the lump sum of cash or stock that you collect from your company savings or profit-sharing fund when you leave the firm. You do that by opening a special tax-deferred Individual Retirement Account, called a rollover account, at any bank, brokerage firm or mutual-fund company. Then you instruct your company to transfer the proceeds directly to that account. You thus postpone paying taxes on your contributions and earnings in these company plans, and on your employer's contributions, until you start withdrawing the money from the IRA.

The direct transfer becomes imperative in 1993 because of a change in the law. Previously, employers always paid out the money. You then had 60 days to put it in an IRA rollover account. Later, if you joined another company that offered a 401(k) salary-withholding retirement plan, you could move your rollover account into that plan.

But starting January 1, 1993, employers are newly authorized to transfer these retirement savings accounts directly to your IRA. If they issue you a check instead, they must withhold for tax purposes 20% of previously tax-deferred lump-sum payments. You can still roll over the whole lump sum within 60 days, but first you will have to scrounge up an amount equal to the 20% that has been withheld. On $500,000 worth of retirement money, that's a staggering $100,000. Or you can roll over the 80% and pay tax on the rest. Later, when you file your tax return, you can apply for a refund of the amount withheld.

Another caution: The taxman won't let you roll over any after-tax contributions that you made to the company plan, since these are not subject to income tax when you leave the company. Be sure to have your employee benefits consultant or your tax adviser spell out your tax liability before you accept any lump sum subject to withholding tax.

Some Better Alternatives

ALTHOUGH Individual Retirement Accounts are a worthy way of saving money and reducing your taxes, they are not the only way. You might do better not only with a company savings plan but also with a nonprofit-group annuity, a 401(k) salary-reduction plan or a Keogh plan.

If you are self-employed and don't earn too much, you can have *both* a Keogh plan and an IRA, so you need to decide which to contribute to if you cannot afford both. The Keogh wins hands down because you can shelter much more income in it than in an IRA.

Another nice shelter is the nonprofit-group annuity. It can be bought by teachers, hospital nurses, social workers and other employees of nonprofit organizations. If you work for an eligible group, you can tell your employer to put as much as 20% of your pay into an untaxed annuity or some other investment. You get all the advantages of an IRA but usually can shelter up to $9,500 of your salary per year. There is no tax penalty for withdrawals.

As noted earlier, many companies are offering their employees 401(k) plans. Again, a portion of your salary is withheld — untaxed — and the money is invested in your choice of a CD-like guaranteed-investment contract, in the company's stock or in some type of mutual fund. (See "Your Taxes: 401(k) Plans.")

To repeat: If your employer has a savings plan, chances are you will be able to accumulate more money, after taxes, by contributing to it than by opening an IRA.

Your Family

Wedding Costs:
The New, Sensible Sharing

Nowadays couples are back to marrying, or remarrying, in old-fashioned ways, even if they have been living together for years. This return to basics, alas, makes a considerable dent in the family's finances.

Traditional weddings, with white satin gowns and three-tiered wedding cakes, are in style again, but it is expensive to let them eat cake. The cost for food, drink and dancing — along with flowers, invitations, clothing and church or synagogue fees — comes to a national average of $16,500. Of course, prices can vary greatly, according to region and extravagance, ranging from $1,000 to six figures. One-third to one-half is spent at the reception. The dinner or buffet, including liquor and champagne, ranges on the low end from $7 a person in small Midwestern towns to an average $85 a head in Boston or New York. Add 5% to 10% for kosher catering.

Sensible planning can reduce the bill. Some couples getting married on the same day agree to share the cost of flowers at the scene of the ceremony. Others save a few hundred dollars by skipping such reception giveaways as printed matches and napkins. Friends can contribute their photographic or musical talents, or even their cake-baking and flower-growing abilities. Traditionally, members of the wedding paid for their own dresses and formal wear. In some cases, couples and their families sensibly handle these bills instead of giving their attendants expensive gifts of jewelry as keepsakes of the wedding. And now you can rent bridal gowns and bridesmaids' dresses, instead of buying them.

It used to be that the wedding bills were paid by the father of the bride, but that old etiquette is giving way to the new economics. Today, families of the bride and the groom commonly split the costs. Often the expenses are divided four ways — among both sets of parents and the bride and groom.

Splitting the costs seems natural to many of today's career-minded brides. After all, their parents paid for educations that were intended to prepare their daughters to pay their own way — or at least a good part of it. So parents of the bride can take heart: you may be losing a daughter, but at least you are not obliged to pay the whole bill.

Even pre-wedding festivities are more practical. Gone are the days of a group of women giggling over a sexy negligee at a bridal shower. Today friends often give "couples showers." Guests are encouraged to bring gifts that both members of the pair can use, like gardening tools. Couples who start out willing to share gardening chores can probably count on sharing many years together.

The custom of the bridal registry is "in" again, but it is a registry with a twist. Many brides circumvent the suburban department store in favor of museum shops, antique shops and upscale catalogs such as Williams-Sonoma's. In fact, in 1991 California-based Home Depot stores opened their own bridal registry. The preferred gift of many of today's young brides and grooms is money. A check is also the gift of choice for more mature newlyweds who already have fully stocked households. At some weddings, regional or ethnic custom dictates that you give cash to the bride or groom at the reception. Or you can mail your check to the couple's home within a week after the ceremony. Although the actual figure is dependent on the economic standing of the guest, the average expenditure on a wedding gift is $50.

For up-to-date, innovative tips on how to scale down wedding costs, read *Bridal Bargains: Secrets to Throwing a Fantastic Wedding on a Realistic Budget* (Windsor Peak Press, $9.95), by Denise and Alan Fields, who offer a money-back guarantee on the price of their book if you don't save at least $500 on your wedding. Or call them on their wedding hotline at 800-888-0385.

Prenuptial Agreements

FOR many modern couples who plan on marriage, only one deeply intimate, often embarrassing subject remains taboo: money. It seems indelicate, if not downright greedy, to ask "What's your net worth?" before saying "I do." Nevertheless, more and more engaged people are overriding their inhibitions and writing prenuptial contracts. These specify who owns what property and what should become of it in various contingencies.

You may be wise to prepare and sign a prenuptial contract. You spell out in advance just who owns what — and which financial obligations each partner has to the other. Such an agreement is particularly important in cases where the bride as well as the groom has a career, with her own income, assets and obligations, or if one partner has children from an earlier marriage and wants to protect their inheritances. Love may be lovelier the second time around, but marriage finances are messier. If one mate-to-be is studying for a profession, a contract can help you pin down how much the other partner's working contributes to his or her future earnings. Finally, an agreement can clarify who owns what property and how pooled assets would be split if the marriage dissolves. A doctor or accountant, for example, may stipulate that one's spouse accept a lump-sum settlement instead of a share in his or her practice or business.

Courts in most states now recognize a contract that tries to head off a battle in the event the marriage breaks up. Such agreements can save hundreds of hours of fact-finding and testimony and thousands of dollars in legal and other fees. More important, a prenuptial agreement can help you set the financial ground rules for a fair and lasting marriage and resolve ahead of time any mismatched expectations over money.

You can work out the details of your prenuptial agreement on your own, of course. Each partner should have his or her own lawyer review the contract, however, because judges often suspect that without an attorney to protect the interest of each side, one party may too easily sway the other. One sign of the effectiveness of prenuptial pacts is that not many of them have had to be tested in court.

What Finances to Settle Before Marriage

WHETHER or not you sign a prenuptial agreement, you and your mate-to-be should thoroughly discuss the subject of money before you step up to the altar. Take inventory of your separate assets and liabilities. Decide what property you want to keep in your own name and what you want to merge. Most financial advisers suggest that you keep separate as well as joint bank accounts.

Be sure to familiarize yourself with the law. Each state has its own laws governing marital and separate property and stipulating what happens if the two are mingled. One tip: If you want to put property in your spouse's name, avoid the federal gift tax by transferring ownership *after* the marriage. The marital gift tax deduction is unlimited.

You and your intended should discuss the advantages and disadvantages of joint ownership. An accountant or financial adviser can explain the nuances. For example, in one form of joint ownership, the title specifies that if one of you dies, the property goes automatically to the spouse. In another form, however, each of you owns half of the property, and you can leave your share to whomever you wish, such as a child from an earlier marriage. If a married couple takes title to a house as *tenants in common,* then either partner can leave his or her share of the house to whomever he or she names in his or her will. (For more, see "Your Family: The Perils of Holding Your Assets in Joint Name.")

Be certain to update your will. If you die without a will, your spouse generally receives only one-third to one-half of your separate property. The rest is distributed among other relatives.

Consolidate or coordinate your medical insurance. If you both have group plans where you work and you are paying part of the premiums, you may be able to save money by dropping one plan and having the other cover you as a family. Or you may be able to keep both policies, naming each other as dependents, and get more of your medical costs covered. And do not forget the obvious: Be sure to change the name of your beneficiary on your IRA, life insurance, pension, profit sharing and annuity.

One of the best approaches for divvying up household bills when both spouses hold paying jobs is to have three bank accounts — his, hers and theirs. The common pot might go for food, maintenance of the house or apartment, recreation and joint savings.

What Every Spouse Should Know

IN FINANCE, as in love, it is what spouses do not tell each other that hurts. Talking to your mate about what you own and what you owe seems such a simple thing to do. Yet many people are reluctant to do it. Some husbands still assume their wives do not understand finances or are not interested in them. And some married partners do not trust each other. But keeping your mate in ignorance can be dangerous to your wealth.

A sensible time to review your assets is when you are writing your will — and *both* spouses should have wills. Use the occasion to make or update lists of all the valuable possessions you own separately or in common. Include all real estate, bank and brokerage accounts, cars and boats, precious stones, works of art and life insurance policies. Keep the separate lists of your assets in the same secure place you keep your wills.

You should know the names and addresses of the financial professionals in your mate's life. This includes any stockbroker, accountant, personal banker, attorney and financial planner. You also should learn the details of your spouse's job benefits and work history, such as whether you have survivor's rights to his or her pension. If your mate held a previous job long enough to earn a pension, you could be eligible for additional retirement funds.

Military service often endows survivors with financial rights in the event of a spouse's death. If your husband or wife was in the armed forces, you might be eligible for G.I. life insurance, a pension, burial expenses, even a VA mortgage loan. To apply for these benefits, you will need the veteran's discharge papers.

That is one reason why couples should exchange written lists of documents and where they are kept, including military discharge papers, birth certificates, marriage license, wills and insurance policies.

Rent *two* safe-deposit boxes and put in your own box the papers you will need if your spouse dies. Banks in some states will seal the box of the deceased upon notification of death, and you may have to wait weeks or months for a court to grant permission to open that box. Also leave copies of all necessary documents with a lawyer, an adult child or some other trusted third party.

The Perils of Holding Your Assets in Joint Name

AT SOME point in your life you will almost certainly want — or need — to own an asset jointly with your spouse or with your parents, siblings or friends. But before you make that very important decision, you should know a few things about the complex laws of ownership. Sometimes, even for the happiest of married couples, joint ownership is not so smart.

True enough, joint ownership can simplify estate planning and the eventual disposition of your wealth. On your death, your share of jointly held real estate, stocks or other property usually passes *automatically* to your surviving co-owner. That means it bypasses probate — the often lengthy and expensive process by which a will is proved valid in court.

Yet joint ownership can lead to feuds among co-owners and heirs and daunting tax bills. For example, a childless couple may think they can do without wills because they hold all of their property jointly. Not so. If the husband dies, everything passes to his wife without complication. But if the wife then dies later without a will, every cent would go to her relatives under state laws known as laws of intestacy. The husband's relatives would be left with no legacy at all.

You can avoid such problems by writing a will that describes how you want the assets disposed. Trouble is, you would not avoid probate this way.

But you can sidestep probate if you set up what is called a *revocable living trust.* For several hundred dollars to several thousand dollars, an attorney will draw up the trust. In it, you agree to transfer ownership of your assets, while you are still alive, to a trustee. That person then manages the property on behalf of the people whom you name as beneficiaries. In every state but New York you can name yourself the sole trustee. Then you retain control of the assets in the trust, and, if you also name yourself as a beneficiary, even receive income from them.

You can have the trust written so that, after your death, its assets go automatically to your heirs. Or the assets can remain in the trust, with the income from them going to your beneficiaries. Either way, the assets avoid probate.

Joint ownership is also dangerous for individuals who own highly appreciated assets — such as a house that has jumped substantially in value — or whose estate is worth more than $600,000 this year. They would be vulnerable to heavy estate taxes.

Take a couple who bought a house for $50,000 in 1970 and held it jointly until the husband's death. At that time, let's say the house was worth $200,000. Half of the house's value would pass automatically to the wife, leaving her with both her husband's $100,000 share plus her own equal share. If she then sells the house for $200,000, the IRS would tax her on a $75,000 capital gain on her share. But she could have avoided the tax if her husband *alone* had held title to the house and had passed it to her in his will. The reason: Married couples can leave estates of any size to each other tax-free. Because she inherited a house worth $200,000, she would not have any taxable gain if she sold it at that price.

There is, however, a serious problem with this strategy. You can seldom be sure whether the husband or wife will die first. If the wife dies in the above example, the husband would own the whole house and would have to pay taxes on the entire capital gain when he sold it.

Many spouses also object to putting the house in one partner's name. They fear that their mate might divorce them and keep the house. But contrary to popular belief, you usually cannot keep goods out of your spouse's reach simply by registering them in your own name. Judges simply will not stand for it.

Despite the tangles that can occur, there are times when joint ownership does make sense. You might elect to own property jointly if you want to shift income to a family member in a lower tax bracket. If, say, a mother and her young child owned stock together, the child's share of the earnings might be lightly taxed — if at all. That is because the child presumably would have little or no other taxable income. The tax reform act makes this harder to do because investment income over $1,100 is now taxed at the parent's rate if the child is under age 14.

Joint ownership also can help you shield assets from creditors. And it can have psychic rewards for a mate who feels happy just holding half of the family's riches. But remember: While joint ownership can give you or your spouse a warm feeling, it can give you or your heirs the chills when it comes time to settle up with the almighty IRS. If you die with assets above $600,000, the excess will be subject to federal estate taxes, beginning at 37% and going as high as 55%, and your heirs will be hit with state estate taxes, too. Yet a husband and wife together can shelter $1,200,000 from estate taxes by dividing most of their assets between them, owning the assets individually and establishing what are called estate tax credit trusts in each of their wills.

Protecting Your "Significant Other"

NEARLY three million American couples fit the Census Bureau description of POSSLQ. That stands for Persons of the Opposite Sex Sharing Living Quarters. They and other co-habitating unmarried couples have special financial problems, which they can solve by taking some sensible steps.

The facts of unmarried life are that the law is muddy about the financial rights of two people living together without a marriage license. Take inheritance, for example. When one member of a *married* couple dies without a will, state laws typically assure that the bulk of the person's property will pass to the surviving spouse. But when an *unmarried* person leaves no will, all of his or her earthly goods can be claimed by the next of kin. Even a loathsome great-aunt thousands of miles away stands before a live-in partner in the inheritance line.

The message is clear: If a person is living with someone to whom he or she would like to will his or her worldly goods, that person had better put his or her intentions in writing. That may sound unromantic, but the harsh fact is that putting your financial intentions in writing is the best way to protect a joint venture of the heart. Written contracts can protect your interest if disputes arise with your partners — or with an ex-spouse or government authorities — over such matters as insurance, inheritance or debts that you have to pay.

Couples with few major assets can get by with the fill-in-the-blanks legal forms usually found in books on living together. If your finances are more complicated, you may need a lawyer's assistance to draw up a financial agreement. If you choose to do it yourself, your agreement at least should be notarized. Contracts between unmarried couples generally are recognized by the courts as long as they violate no laws and both partners enter into them freely.

Unmarried couples should always own things separately. For example, he buys the car, she buys the computer. They should acquire as little as possible together and keep receipts or other records of what each buys. Doing that will prevent bitter battles if and when they split up.

For much the same reason, unmarried couples should not have joint bank accounts or credit cards. In joint charge accounts, each person is 100% responsible for debts incurred by the other, and creditors can seize bank assets that are deposited in either name.

The tidiest way to split household expenses is down the middle. Many POSSLQs simply put their initials on receipts of bills they pay, toss them into a drawer and square accounts once a month. An exception, of course, is if one partner is enrolled full-time in college or is too ill to work. Then the other, working partner pays the bills. But records should be kept and, ultimately, he or she should be paid back — at least in part.

For example, a young woman in Raleigh, North Carolina, returned to college. Her live-in partner underwrote her expenses with a 7% loan. She signed an agreement to repay him, whether or not the two continue living together.

Unmarried partners also should be sure to do the following:

— Buy medical insurance if either partner isn't covered by a group health plan.

— Name your long-term POSSLQ as a beneficiary of your life insurance policy.

— Sign a so-called medical power-of-attorney permitting your POSSLQ to visit you and to make medical decisions if you're seriously ill.

— And, perhaps most important, write a will leaving to your POSSLQ what you want him or her to have.

Financial Planning When You Are Expecting a Child

M ANY young two-career couples do not worry excessively about their financial future. But once they are expecting a baby, they find they have a compelling reason to think ahead. They need investments that will help them build up their net worth as quickly as possible.

If you are expecting your first child, you should open a money-market account at a bank or in a money fund and try to build a cash reserve equal to at least three months' worth of living expenses. Only after you have this secure cash cushion should you think about investing — because all investment involves some risks.

One of the best ways to start investing is to put money in a growth mutual fund. It invests in stocks of solid companies that offer better-than-average opportunities to multiply money. If you choose a no-load fund, you will avoid paying a sales commission, which can run as high as 8½%.

A sensible way to invest in a mutual fund is to put in the same amount each month, whether the market rises or falls. That is known as dollar-cost averaging. Your money buys fewer shares when the market goes up, and more shares when it goes down. By signing a form provided by the fund, you can have it withdraw the money automatically from your checking account every month.

Be sure to review your insurance — preferably before your baby is born. You may need more coverage than your employer offers. Hewitt Associates, the benefits and consulting firm, found that in 1991, 66% of 666 major employers offered some sort of child-care aid and 51% granted parental leave. In all, 76% of those providing paid leave and 86% of those providing unpaid leave extended it to fathers as well as mothers.

Your total disability insurance coverage should replace about 60% to 70% of your salary. Each working parent also should buy enough life insurance to replace most of his or her earning power at least until the child has finished school. An insurance agent can help you figure out how much you'll need.

If you do not have a will, sit down with a lawyer and have one drawn up. It may cost as much as $700 for each parent. Make sure you carefully choose a guardian for your child in the unlikely event that both of you die before your heir apparent reaches the age of 18. Most lawyers advise that you choose a brother or sister instead of your aging parents.

The Real Cost of Kids

FOR most married people in the baby-boom generation, having children is not just a fact of life but a matter of choice. Often they are postponing children because they worry that kids cost too much. What is the real cost of raising children?

Bringing up baby is more expensive today than at any other time in history. That is partly because the luxuries of a generation ago are considered middle-class birthrights today. The U.S. Department of Agriculture estimated that in 1991, the national average cost of raising a youngster aged 15 to 17 was $9,410 a year.

If Mom stays home until Junior toddles off to kindergarten, her lost income from a job could amount to another $100,000 or more. And that dollar cost may be compounded by atrophying skills and evaporating seniority.

Knowing when the expenses of childhood rise and fall can help you prepare for them. Newborns enter the world at considerable cost. Routine hospital and delivery fees run an average $5,000 in a metropolitan area, and an untroubled cesarean birth adds some $3,000. But from age one to five or six, the costs of child-rearing are relatively low. This is the time parents should put away cash in deep-discount bonds, zero-coupon bonds, U.S. savings bonds and other investments to pay for the expenses that start moving up as soon as the child goes off to school and skyrocket during the teenage years.

Puberty is pricey, due in part to dating and all its accoutrements. The annual insurance premium on your car can more than double with a 16-year-old son at the wheel. At 18, child-rearing costs are exponentially higher than costs incurred in the birth year. Welcome to the groves of academe and the most expensive years in a child's life.

If you have — or plan to have — children, you can prepare now for those predictable costs ahead. Start by checking what your health insurance covers. A good maternity package in a group policy will pay at least two-thirds of the hospital and physician's fees for the birth of a child. Later on, most policies do not cover the routine examinations of a healthy baby. So, unless you belong to a health maintenance organization, you may have to budget as much as $600 for those monthly visits to the pediatrician during a baby's first year.

Where to Adopt a Child

I F YOU are childless — and not by choice — you have many new options in adoptions. Today almost anybody can adopt a child, but it may be a rather special one.

Two decades ago public and private adoption agencies had many more healthy American-born babies than they do now. The reason, of course, is the wide availability of birth control devices and abortion. Also, unmarried mothers are more willing to keep their children. You can get a directory of agencies that place healthy American-born children by writing to the National Committee for Adoption, 1930 17th Street, NW, Washington, D.C. 20009-6207. The Committee also publishes *The Adoption Fact Book,* a comprehensive 300-page guide that includes a list of adoption resources, a summary of state regulations and a discussion of the major issues involved in adoption today. It is available through the same address for $39.95 plus $4.50 postage.

Would-be parents are becoming increasingly interested in adopting children from other countries and kids whom social workers categorize as "hard to place" or as having "special needs." They include youngsters with physical, mental or emotional disabilities, as well as older children of all races and brothers and sisters whom adoption agencies do not want to split up. Youngsters with special needs account for nearly half the children now available for adoption in the U.S.

Agencies are finding it easier than ever to place them, often with people who formerly did not qualify as adoptive parents. Single, disabled and low-income people — even couples in their 50s and 60s — are now allowed to adopt.

About two-thirds of all parents adopt through agencies; the rest get children through doctors or lawyers. Public adoption agencies, operated by state and local governments, generally do not charge fees. Private agencies, commonly sponsored by religious and charitable groups, charge an average of $9,000, which often includes lawyer's fees. If it doesn't, you will usually have to pay $1,000 to an attorney for preparing adoption papers.

The fees are often reduced or waived for parents who adopt children with special needs. Almost all states also have subsidy programs for parents who adopt such youngsters. In conjunction with federal reimbursements created by tax reform in 1987, the subsidy could amount to $2,000, for use toward adoption costs.

A small but growing number of corporations are granting maternity leaves and other benefits to employees who adopt children. For example, Procter & Gamble and Johnson & Johnson give unpaid leaves plus up to $3,000 for adoption-related expenses. Time Warner Inc. gives up to one year unpaid parental leave plus up to $5,000 in reimbursed adoption expenses. So, if you are an adoptive parent or are considering becoming one, check to see if your company will provide any benefits.

Your city or state department of social services can give you a list of licensed adoption agencies in your area. For help in finding special-needs children in states beyond your own, write to the National Adoption Center (1218 Chestnut Street, Philadelphia, Pennsylvania 19107; 215-925-0200). Or call 800-TO-ADOPT.

If you want to adopt a healthy child quickly, you can seek help from American agencies that specialize in international adoptions. The wait is usually no more than 18 months. Most of the children come from Asian countries, especially the Philippines and South Korea, as well as from Latin America and Eastern Europe. Babies available for adoption in Western Europe are as scarce as in the United States.

Adopting a child from another country usually costs between $4,000 and $15,000, and the investment is not without risk. There have been more than a few recent cases of fraud. In some instances, children have been illegally smuggled out of their native countries. And in 1983, 31 Americans lost about $2,500 each when a Chilean attorney fled his country without honoring his promise to locate babies for them. If a private international adoption goes awry, you will have small chance of recouping any money you handed over in advance. However, international adoption is better regulated than it used to be; the U.S. Immigration and Naturalization Service works diligently to assure that children coming into the U.S. have been adopted properly.

In any event, it is best to work only through well-established organizations. You can find many of their names and addresses in *The Report on Foreign Adoption,* which costs $20 and is available from the International Concerns Committee for Children (911 Cypress Drive, Boulder, Colorado 80303). For a list of lawyers, social-services agencies and orphanages in Central and South America, you may write to the Latin America Parents Association (8646 15th Avenue, Brooklyn, New York 11218; 718-236-8689). Holt International Children's Services (P.O. Box 2880, Eugene, Oregon 97402; 503-687-2202) is an agency specializing in placing children from all over the world.

The U.S. government used to publish a booklet on foreign adoption titled *The Immigration of Adopted and Prospective Adoptive Children.* Although no longer in print, it is a good thing to know about; you may be able to get a copy from attorneys or adoption agencies.

Another way to avoid waiting years to adopt a child is through private placement known as independent adoption — that is, adoption without an agency's help. People who use independent placement find the birth mother on their own and take the baby straight home from the hospital. Many consult relatives, friends, clergymen, teachers, social workers, lawyers and doctors — any person who might help locate a pregnant woman who chooses not to keep her child. This way, you can bypass the demands and restrictions that adoption agencies may impose on your age, religion, and marital status *and even* the adoptive mother's employment. Sometimes agencies also demand proof of infertility. Independent adoption is often faster than using an adoption agency, which might take four years or longer. The cost of an independent adoption is anywhere from $3,000 to $20,000.

Independent adoption does have drawbacks. It is not permitted in Connecticut, Delaware, Massachusetts, Michigan, Minnesota and North Dakota. Even where it is allowed, you must find a pregnant woman willing to give up her child and then, typically, pay her medical and legal expenses. There is always the chance that the mother will change her mind and try to reclaim her child in the courts.

To find out more, write or phone the adoption office of your state's department of social services. You also can contact local adoption groups through the Adoptive Families of America in Minneapolis (612-535-4829) or, for special-needs adoption, the National Adoption Center in Philadelphia and the organization RESOLVE (5 Water Street, Arlington, Massachusetts 02174; 617-643-2424).

Finding Reliable Child Care

TRADITIONAL households, those with a working husband and a wife at home, are at an all-time low. At least 65% of all mothers work outside the home; more than 50% of new mothers enter or re-enter the work force before their child's first birthday. According to a University of Maryland study, in 1985 American parents spent an average of only 17 hours a week with their children. Today, people continue to find themselves away from home more often than not, and many have trouble finding decent care for their kids. Trained, full-time nannies are expensive; they can cost $250 to $600 a week plus benefits. Baby-sitters are less costly but not always reliable. Increasingly, parents are concluding that the best solution is to put their children in a day-care center. In 1990, 46% of working moms' preschoolers were enrolled in such facilities.

Many new centers have opened in recent years, but the number still has not kept up with demand. Shortages are critical in urban areas that have high concentrations of low-income people; the need is particularly great for centers that will accept children under the age of two. Day-care centers just cannot find and hire enough capable staff members at fees that are within most parents' reach.

About half of the licensed day-care centers in the U.S. are run by churches and other nonprofit organizations. For-profit operators make up the rest. They range from small independent centers to larger chains. Burud & Associates, national child-care benefits consultants, estimated that in 1990 at least 1,250 employers sponsored child-care centers or shared a center with another employer. About 3% of all major corporations now do so, and the number is growing.

Revelations of child abuse at some day-care centers are appalling, but it would be a sad mistake to write off *all* such centers. Many of them offer quality, convenience and affordable prices. Happily, reported incidences of child neglect or abuse are quite rare. Still, providers of group care vary widely.

People who operate small group-care programs in their own homes usually are not subject to — or do not bother with — state licenses. But centers that look after more than 15 kids are almost all licensed. State licenses help ensure that the centers meet minimum standards for health, fire safety and staffing.

The other advantages of large day-care centers over the small home-based programs are greater stability and broader curricula. The operations that allocate a higher percentage of their budget to attract better teachers and reduce staff turnover are often able to provide a higher level of quality in their programs. Staff is the key to quality. Many corporations offer employees a free child-care referral service; IBM uses 250 different organizations. The company also has pledged $22 million in recent years to improve the quality of day care available in the towns and cities where most of its employees live.

Some smaller companies are paying attention as well. American Bankers Insurance Group, based in Miami, maintains a day-care center for employees' children aged six weeks to five years. After that the child can attend a Dade County public "satellite" school for an additional three years. The school takes care of the child from 7:15 a.m. to 6:15 p.m. and keeps its doors open during school holidays and summer vacations.

The cost of group care depends largely on a child's age and on the size and experience of the staff. Monthly fees for children under age five average about $330, but monthly fees of $600 to $800 are not unusual. Uncle Sam helps to defray day-care expenses with a tax credit for working couples and single parents. Depending on your income, the annual credit may be worth as much as $720 for one dependent and $1,440 for two or more. The least credit is $480 for one dependent and $960 for two or more. An alternative fringe benefit, if your company offers dependent-care accounts, is to put up to $5,000 a year — with no tax taken out — into such an account for day care.

The employee does not have to pay any income taxes or Social Security taxes on such reimbursements up to a maximum deduction of $5,000. And the employer can deduct them as regular business expenses. For example, Johnson & Johnson supports an on-site day-care center at its headquarters in New Brunswick, New Jersey. The company subsidizes part of the cost, but employees using the center still pay $110 to $130 a week, depending on the age of the child. Alternatively, the company can pay an employee directly for child-care costs until the employee's children reach the age of 16. Care for disabled dependents of any age also can be covered. Since it costs less for a company to pass out child-care subsidies than to build and run a day-care center, many firms may be inclined to adopt them. If you are a working parent looking for help with child-care costs, you might ask your personnel office to consider sharing your payments.

Selecting a good center is not child's play, but your task will be easier if you ask a few important questions of fellow parents and of the professionals who provide child care.

Question one: How large are the classes? Big groups tend to be too confusing for babies and toddlers. The maximum number of babies under two years should be eight per group, with at least two staff members. Toddlers aged two to three should not be placed in groups larger than 12.

Question two: What is the ratio of staff to children? There should be at least one adult for every three or four babies — or for every six toddlers.

Question three: Can you meet with the teachers easily and often? Most centers encourage parents to drop by anytime for a visit. Be wary of those that do not. And formal conferences to evaluate your child's progress should be scheduled at least twice a year.

Question four: Is there a wide variety of toys designed for your child's age group? Infants like colorful mobiles, mirrors and plastic boxes. With preschoolers, look for musical instruments, games and costumes.

Question five: Are teachers conscientious about sanitary conditions? Kids under age three in day-care centers are more likely to contract gastrointestinal ailments than those who stay at home.

Question six: Have arrangements been made for medical emergencies? A nurse or doctor should be available nearby, ready for a call. Parents should be informed promptly when there are outbreaks of illnesses such as chicken pox or measles.

Once you have settled on a day-care center, keep monitoring it for changes in its programs or personnel. But your best indicator of quality may be your child's enthusiasm. If your son or daughter hates to leave the center at the end of the day, chances are you made the right choice.

Parents often assume that all branches of a day-care chain meet uniform standards of quality, but this is not always the case. The difference between sound and sloppy centers is determined mainly by the quality of the local director and staff.

Sometimes parents overstress the importance of teaching academic skills in a day-care center. In fact, teaching everyday living skills to children may be more important than drilling them in the alphabet and numbers. But the main point is this: Before placing a child in any center, parents must check it out thoroughly, by visiting it and by speaking both with staff members and with parents of other children who attend. For further information on child care, call the Child Care Action Campaign (212-239-0138), which provides free guide-books for the public.

Another form of child care, at-home care, is often handled by an au pair. The U.S. Information Agency has authorization from Congress to issue special one-year visas to young women from 17 European countries. They must live with American families and work up to 45 hours a week as nursemaids. The cost is $9,000 to $10,000 a year, or $175 a week — far less than you would pay a truly qualified nursemaid. The figure covers transportation, training, health insurance and perhaps $300 in tuition at a local college, which is part of the deal. An au pair also gets two weeks of paid vacation, which most young people use to tour the U.S.

For au pair hosts, the major disadvantage lies in their having to entrust their children to a youthful foreigner whom they have never met or interviewed. But au pair candidates must be 18 to 25 years old and must have at least one year of child-care experience, a secondary-school education and fluency in English. Screening and interviewing are done by offshoots of well-known student-exchange organizations with uniform requirements: AuPairCare (800-288-7786), AuPair/Homestay U.S.A. (202-408-5380), Au Pair in America (800-727-2437), EF Au Pair (800-333-6056) and Euraupair (800-333-3804). Each group can issue visas to 2,840 au pairs each year.

The one-year limit on an au pair's stay puts off those parents who hope for a long-term relationship between child and nanny. But on the other hand, 68% of participating families reapply for a new au pair.

If you judge an au pair under the USIA program to be incompetent or incompatible with your family, a program coordinator will try to arrange a swap with another family who also finds its au pair unsuitable. Failing that, a new candidate may be flown in. About 85% of the original matchups succeed, however.

Using an au pair from one of these five sponsors simplifies your tax life because you are not required to withhold any tax from the weekly stipend.

Setting Your Child's Allowance

WITH ice-cream cones costing $1 and more, children are being pinched by high prices, just like Mom and Pop. So they are getting jobs at younger ages, doing their own comparison shopping for toys and clothes and turning to a price-fighting tactic as time-honored as the tooth fairy. Kids are clamoring for increases in their allowances.

What principles should parents follow when giving an allowance?

Experts in child-rearing suggest that children should start getting allowances early, along with some basic lessons in cash management. Even preschoolers can figure out that a quarter is worth more than a dime.

The amount of the allowance should grow along with the child and his or her spending needs. According to a 1991 survey of 1,440 households by Dr. James McNeal of Texas A&M University, children aged eight and nine received an average weekly allowance of $6.95, 10- and 11-year-olds $8.50, and 12-year-olds $15.04. McNeal expects those figures to rise more than 15% a year through the 90s. He says children begin to handle money at the age of three and a half; by age four or five, kids are full-fledged "penny-candy purchasers who exhibit mastery of the purchase concept." McNeal also believes that we as a society are growing more concerned with our children, creating a "filiarchy" in which parents are spending less money on themselves and considerably greater amounts on their children. More and more, children are emerging as central decision-makers regarding household expenditures.

A youngster's spending money should be enough to cover regular expenses and still leave something to save or spend as he or she chooses. If he or she blows it all, parents only hurt the child by giving more, except in very special cases. A child must be taught to manage well and live within his or her income.

Child psychologists also warn parents to beware of inadvertently causing children to confuse money with less tangible family gifts, such as love and attention. Sometimes divorced parents pay their kids hefty allowances to compensate for their absence — and that does the youngster no good at all.

But children can profit from a special clothing allowance as soon as they are old enough to spend large sums wisely, usually by age 12 or 13. How much to give? One guideline is what the government figures a middle-income family spends to clothe a child — about $46 a month for a 14-year-old, $59 for a 17-year-old.

The recent inflation-age psychology of many adults — buy now, save later — seems to have permeated children's minds, too. By many measures, teenagers are saving less than they ever did. So, to encourage thrift, many parents open bank accounts for their kids. Wise parents also believe that just as kids must be taught to save, they must learn to give to charity. As a small child, David Rockefeller, retired chairman of Chase Manhattan Bank, was required by his father to give 10% of his $1 a month allowance to charity. His childhood financial training served him well.

Teaching Your Child to Invest

D O YOU have a child who is curious about the stock market? With encouragement, your budding T. Boone Pickens can learn the ABCs of investing and perhaps earn a little pocket money.

Some children fare quite well managing their own investments. Take Trevor Nelson, the son of a Merrill Lynch stockbroker in Washington, D.C. Trevor has been an avid stock-picker since 1982, when he was 11 years old. Among his early winners was Coleco, which he bought at $14.25. After a stock split that turned his four shares into eight, Trevor sold at $44.50. That was a good move, because the stock later went sour.

Like Trevor, most kids who are keen on the stock market get their inspiration from investment-minded parents. To be soundly schooled in the market, it is best that your children invest real money — yours or theirs. Investing is not child's play. And it is hard to capture a kid's imagination with hypothetical stock picks.

Investing can be fun when kids buy into companies they know, such as fast-food chains or computer makers. You also can tap your youngsters' enthusiasm by suggesting that they follow and select stocks of highly visible firms in your hometown.

Of course, investing real money means real money may be lost. One of Trevor Nelson's pals, Byron Schulze, was excited about the stock market until he lost all but $10 of his $180 investment in Pizza Time Theaters. The company went bankrupt, and Byron now keeps his money in a bank account.

Despite such risks, children are usually best off investing in individual stocks rather than a mutual fund. Funds offer diversification and professional management. But they are not necessarily well suited to teaching your youngsters about the market. With stock, children are introduced to the idea of owning a piece of a company. This concept will become increasingly important to them as they grow older. You, however, will have to buy, sell and register the stock in your name as the child's custodian. Under state laws, a minor legally can own securities — but not trade them by himself or herself.

Kits and publications are increasingly available for the child who shows a leaning toward lucre. The Consumers Union publishes *Zillions*, a bimonthly magazine aimed at 8- to 14-year-olds and patterned after *Consumer Reports*. A subscription costs $16, and you can order one by calling 800-234-2078. Fidelity Investments, the mutual fund and discount brokerage house, will send a free kit called "You and Money," aimed at fourth- to sixth-graders. Anyone can get the kit by calling 800-544-6666. And the Federal Reserve Bank of New York offers several colorful and informative comic books about money, banks and credit. You can get them free by writing to the Public Information Department, 33 Liberty Street, New York, New York 10045; or call 212-720-6130.

How to Choose a Legal Guardian

CHANCES are your minor children will never need a guardian, but you should make provisions for their future in case anything happens to you and your spouse. Most people put off the grim chore of selecting someone to look after their children if they become orphans. Yet if you should die and there is no one ready to assume responsibility for them, the surrogate's court or the probate court will appoint a guardian. Often it is a relative. The judge will not be able to grant your wishes unless you have expressed them in print.

The way to avoid this potential misfortune is to name a guardian in your will. There are two kinds of guardianships: first, guardianship of the person; and second, guardianship of the property or the estate.

A guardian of the person handles the children's day-to-day upbringing, while a guardian of the property manages whatever money or property you have left for the kids. A guardian of the property must submit an annual accounting to the court of how he is managing the assets and often must request permission to make various expenditures on behalf of the kids.

Although this system protects the children's interests, the guardian gets tangled in red tape. He also must post a bond to protect the estate in case he absconds with the money. A bond on a $250,000 estate would run about $1,300 a year, and the estate foots the bills, somewhat diminishing what you leave for your children.

To avoid these complications and expenses, lawyers recommend that you nominate only a guardian of the person and pass any assets along to your kids in a trust. The trust document, which should be drawn up by a lawyer, should spell out how you want the money spent — on schooling, clothes, music lessons and so forth. A trustee then can write checks up to limits set by the trust without having to ask the court for approval. Some lawyers recommend that the guardian not be the same person as the trustee; if two individuals are chosen, each can oversee the other. But others recommend that the nominated guardian also be the trustee, for convenience of administration.

The hard part about selecting a guardian is picking the right person. Choose someone who is about your age and, preferably, related to you. If you are not close to your relatives, pick a person who would bring up your children in the manner you would. Make sure you ask the people you have in mind whether they would be willing to take on the responsibility of guardianship. Discuss with the guardians the financial arrangements you have made for the children and how you want them brought up.

A guardian named in the will is under no legal obligation to accept the responsibility and can refuse it. If he does, the court will have to find another person, who may not be someone you would choose.

For that reason, attorneys recommend that you also name at least one back-up guardian in your will.

Where appropriate, children, too, have the right to know who their guardian is going to be. So consult at least your older children before you make a decision.

Every few years, or whenever personal or financial circumstances change, review the guardianship provisions in your will. The brother you have named may have been divorced or your best friend may now run a head shop in Malibu. If you think you should name a new guardian, tell the current one and draft a new will.

If someone asks *you* to be a guardian, think hard about whether you should accept. Find out what the parents expect of you and whether the children are to live with you. Ask how the parents want the children educated and if there are any restrictive conditions, such as a statement in the will that the children cannot be moved out of the country. Inquire about money. You should be told what funds are available for the kids' day-to-day upkeep and to carry out any special wishes, such as sending Junior to Harvard.

Ask your lawyer or the lawyer who drew up the will to explain your obligations and rights. And, if you have children of your own, find out how they would feel about having other children in the household.

Discussing Finances
with Your Aging Parents

IF YOUR parents are approaching or beyond retirement age, there are certain sensitive subjects that you should broach now to help ensure their well-being. Raising matters of money and mortality with them requires delicacy. But it is crucial that you have an understanding of your parents' financial affairs in the event you are called on to manage them.

Start by asking your parents to make a list of their assets and liabilities. They should note whether these assets are held in joint tenancy, tenancy in common or in one parent's name. Then a lawyer who is expert on estate and tax matters should evaluate whether their forms of ownership are the most advantageous ones for estate purposes. If your parents refuse to discuss their finances, suggest that they draw up the list in private and keep it in a sealed envelope or a locked box at home. Make sure you know where it is.

Next, you should determine whether your parents' income is sufficient to meet their retirement needs. For example, do they have low-interest-bearing passbook savings accounts and World War II–vintage savings bonds that could be cashed in and used to buy bank CDs paying more? Their house also could be a source of income even while they live in it. Ways to unlock this equity include so-called reverse mortgages, sale leasebacks, charity life agreements and home equity credit lines.

If your parents are 65 or older, they qualify for Medicare. But they also need supplementary health insurance that pays the deductibles and the percentage of doctor and hospital bills not reimbursed by Medicare. Discourage your parents from piling on one policy after another. They cannot be reimbursed more than once for the same bill.

Most nursing-home costs are not covered by Medicare or private health insurance. But your parents may be eligible for government programs designed to supplement income and cover the medical costs of the needy, such as Medicaid. Be sure to check whether your parents are eligible, and if they are not, find out how they can become eligible. The rules vary from state to state, the most important factor being how low your parents' own assets must go in order for them to qualify for Medicaid. To qualify in some states they have to spend almost every last penny that they possess. This is particularly tragic when only one spouse requires nursing-home care but the other spouse has to exhause practically all of his or her remaining assets as well. Fortunately, a number of states are becoming more liberal, allowing the elderly to hold on to more than before. To repeat, check up on the rules in the state where your parents live.

Do *both* of your aging parents know how to handle financial matters? Often in marriages one person manages the money. If that spouse dies first, the survivor may be at a loss to assume the task. While both parents are alive, you might suggest that the partner who is unaccustomed to balancing the checkbook take over the bill-paying for one month a year. Both your parents should know where important papers are kept.

Senility, illness or accident could leave one or both of your parents unable to manage. If no provisions have been made, a court will appoint a guardian, committee or conservator — even if one partner is still competent. So each of your parents should have a durable power-of-attorney agreement. This is an inexpensive way to ensure that people whom your folks trust will manage their affairs when they cannot. Your parents should give the power of attorney to each other — and also name a successor, either your or one of your brothers or sisters.

Ask your parents how they feel about life-prolonging hospital procedures. To protect against extraordinary measures to keep your parents alive, an advance directive for health care, such as a living will, may give you charge over their health-care decisions. In a living will your parents themselves may declare just which "heroic," life-extending procedures they do — or do not — want, and under what circumstances. Almost all states provide legal standing to living wills, health-care proxies, durable powers of attorney for health care or other similar health-care decision-making documents for this purpose.

If your parents' wills are over five years old, or if your folks have moved to another state since their wills were written, these documents probably should be reviewed. A lawyer can update the wills to take into account such changes in estate tax law as the increased marital deduction.

Finally, you should know where your parents keep their important papers. The best place is in their attorney's office. They and the executor of their estates should have copies as well. Your parents should keep these papers in triplicate — with one copy in a safe-deposit box, one in a fireproof box at their home and another at one of their children's homes.

Ins and Outs of Powers of Attorney

WHEN aging parents — or anyone else, for that matter — fall ill and cannot handle their own financial affairs, their families can run into frustrating barriers to acting on their behalf. In cases of prolonged disability, you must ask the courts to appoint a guardian, sometimes called a conservator or committee, to handle the stricken person's finances. This is a time-consuming and expensive process, which might result in the appointment of a stranger. Still worse, while the legal process unfolds your hands are tied. The prices of the stricken person's stocks may be falling, or a great offer may come in on a home he had up for sale. But you can do nothing.

The way out of these and other impasses is for everyone who owns valuable assets to give a durable power of attorney to someone trustworthy and wise. A document prepared by a lawyer and properly signed and witnessed will do the job. The fee shouldn't normally be more than $200. You can even create your own durable power of attorney, although it is not recommended. Stationery stores carry standard forms, but many financial institutions may refuse to comply with boilerplate forms. Each state has its own laws and court rulings about how to execute a durable power of attorney. So it's best to go to a lawyer.

In addition, ask your banker and stockbroker to let you execute their own company's durable-power-of-attorney form. Financial institutions can be balky about acknowledging outside attorneys' documents even though they are perfectly legal.

What if it goes against the grain for your parents to let anyone, even their own child, mess with their investments while they are in their right mind? Then there may be another way to protect them. They might be willing to give you something called a springing power of attorney. This document specifies the conditions in which you can act on his or her behalf. It might say, for example, "This power of attorney shall become effective upon the disability or incapacity of the principal." Springing powers of attorney are legal in most states.

In either a durable or a springing power of attorney, Sanford J. Schlesinger, a member of the law firm Shea & Gould in New York City and a national authority on elder law, recommends listing specific powers. For example, the person being appointed should have right of access to safe-deposit boxes, power to sign tax returns and settle tax disputes and power to collect money due from Medicaid, Supplemental Social Security and other government entitlements, and possibly even power to make gifts.

When a Parent Needs Your Money

A S PEOPLE live longer, more and more grown children will be called upon in the future to give financial help to their aging parents. But how much support should you provide, and how can you do it without making grave sacrifices yourself?

A wrenching dilemma arises when the financial needs of the older generation conflict with those of the younger generation. Nobody has developed a formula for resolving it. Even clergymen provide varying responses.

Rabbi Stanley Schachter, former vice-chancellor of the Jewish Theological Seminary of America, says: "Children have an obligation to maintain their parents at a level of their *highest* dignity, ideally in the manner to which they are accustomed."

John Rhea, a Presbyterian minister who is an expert on the subject, has another view: "The top priority for an adult child is not to make the parents happy but to make them comfortable, to make sure their *basic* needs are met."

And Monsignor Charles Fahey, a former chairman of the Federal Council on Aging, says: "There is a strong responsibility to care for and love your parents, but that does not necessarily equate with economic support. Your primary responsibility is to your *own* children."

These different outlooks mean that each individual has to decide for himself or herself. Still, you *can* get guidance from a trained social worker or other professional. A hospital, nursing home or senior-citizen center can refer you to such a counselor.

Most people want to take care of their parents, and they do an admirable job of it. In approximately 80% of cases, any help the elderly require comes from family members. And the National Council on Aging reports that up to 30% of the American work force is involved in providing care for elders — a figure expected to jump dramatically as the number of people over 65 surges in the next decade.

Helping to support an aging parent need not mean the end of your dream of educating your own children or retiring comfortably or leading a reasonably good life. What you need is to give in ways that cut the burden on you by sharing it with Uncle Sam.

The key is to transfer assets from you to your parents *temporarily*, by lending them the funds rather than giving them away. Then have your folks invest the money in *their* names, so that any dividends, interest or capital gains are taxed at *their* rate, which is presumably lower than *your* rate. In fact, a couple 65 or older filing jointly paid no federal tax if their taxable income in 1992 was $11,300 or less. An individual 65 or over was exempt on sums of $6,400 or less.

Giving direct financial aid is not the only way to help your aging parents. A whole new network of sources has sprung up to provide care and support for the aged. To find out what is available locally, consult your city or state department of aging, listed in most phone books. Also try Family Service America, a nonprofit group representing 280 accredited family-service agencies. It will direct you to its local agency. Write to Information Center, Family Service America at 11700 West Lake Park Drive, Milwaukee, Wisconsin 53224, or call FSA at 800-221-2681.

How and Where to Get
Good Care for Aging Relatives

JUST about everyone has heard an aged parent or grandparent plead, "Whatever you do, don't send me to a nursing home." Take heart. You have several new steps along the path to the old nursing home.

Getting your elder involved in outside activities is one way to prolong his or her interest in staying well in the first place. Family Friends, in Omaha, Nebraska, has elderly volunteers visiting regularly with chronically ill patients, and the University of Pittsburgh's Generations Together organizes phone links between older people and so-called latchkey kids — children who return to empty homes after school. Such programs are available in most major metropolitan areas through your state's local office for the aging, your community's family-services bureau and various religious organizations. You might call a neighborhood senior citizens' center; its employees can guide you to programs for older people.

When your elder is impaired — that is, in need of some supervision — the least painful venue for all concerned is usually the geriatric day-care center. There are now more than 2,100 adult day-care centers in the country, giving respite to the caregiver and providing health maintenance and monitoring for the elder. At minimum, adult day-care centers offer elders a place for interaction, exercise and a hot noontime meal. Other activities include games, craft and cooking classes, musical shows and field trips. These centers are located primarily in nursing homes, but you'll find them in churches, community centers and hospitals as well. In 1990, the Stride Rite Corporation completed the first intergenerational day-care complex, accommodating aging relatives as well as children of its employees. This has sparked interest from state agencies, private hospitals and other corporations, and the complex has become a model for others of its kind.

Costs for adult day care vary, but the average daily figure is $32. Your best source for further information is the National Council on Aging (409 3rd Street, SW, Washington, D.C. 20024; 800-424-9046).

Services available to the elderly in their own homes are expanding rapidly, and so is the number of government, charitable and for-profit agencies that provide such care. For example, a state-sponsored program in Florida, Community Care for the Elderly, has been successful in helping more than 39,000 older people, providing them with extensive at-home services. These elders can have meals delivered to their homes, get assistance for personal care and homemaking and in some districts get transportation to needed medical services. Your local Department of Aging will know of other similarly innovative services in your area.

When medical care is needed, the caregiver or elder should look into home medical care. Limited services by a registered nurse are 100% reimbursable by Medicare if they are related to a hospital stay, and this care may extend for an unlimited duration as long as the necessary qualifying conditions are met. Medicare will also pay for the services of a home health aide in conjunction with skilled nursing care. Sometimes, even if an older person doesn't require skilled nursing, private health-insurance policies will pay for personal care and home health services.

To determine whether the agency providing home care is a good one, you can review the checklist in *How to Choose a Home Care Agency,* a free publication from the National Association for Home Care, 519 C Street, NE, Washington, D.C. 20002. Be sure to ask whether or not the agency is certified by Medicare; if it is, it means that it has complied with federal guidelines.

If home care is not an option, check into apartment buildings designed specifically for the elderly. So-called residential care facilities provide room and board, limited health care and social and recreational programs. The continuing-care retirement communities look like college campuses and offer up to three living choices: apartments for people who are well enough and desire to live alone; intermediate-care facilities for those who need some medical attention; and sometimes yet another facility that offers around-the-clock skilled care. Continuing care can be ideal for the elderly person who is independent but realizes that the day of infirmity inevitably will come.

Still, nursing homes may be the only choice for some families with elderly relatives. In general, those homes have improved significantly since the mid-1970s. The best tend to be nonprofit institutions sponsored by religious, union or fraternal organizations.

You can get names of such nursing homes in your area by asking your doctor or hospital social worker. Also, you can inquire at a senior citizens' center, your state affiliate of the American Health Care Association, or the American Association of Homes for the Aging, 901 E Street, NW, Suite 500, Washington, D.C. 20004.

You should visit any homes you are considering at least twice — once on an official tour and once as a surprise, if possible. Supervisors of a well-run home will welcome you and your questions. Make sure the residents seem content, clean and neat. Taste the food. To get brochures on choosing a nursing home and finding financial aid, send stamped, self-addressed envelopes to the American Health Care Association, 1201 L Street, NW, Washington, D.C. 20005.

Inescapably, nursing homes are expensive: from $1,500 a month to $6,000 or even more, depending on the locality and the kind of accommodations. The national average is $30,000 a year, or $82 a day. Medicare, which is commonly thought to cover the costs of care, in fact pays for less than 5% of nursing-home costs nationwide. Among the many stipulations: The patient must have been in a hospital for at least three days, the patient must enter the skilled-care facility within 30 days of his or her discharge from the hospital and the facility must be approved by Medicare.

If all conditions are met, Medicare pays in full for the first 20 days; from the 21st to the 100th day, the patient shares the cost by paying a nationally set daily rate of $81.50. Still, the average length of stay paid for by Medicare is 26 days. To find out if your elder is automatically covered for this because of credits for quarters worked in his or her lifetime, call your nearest Social Security office. If your elder is interested in Medicare medical insurance, which may help pay for covered services received in a nursing home from a doctor, the Social Security office can assist you with that as well. But remember that you can sign up for the insurance only in the first three months of the calendar year.

Long-term-care insurance, which accounts for less than 1% of nursing-home payments, is available in every state from the American Association of Retired Persons, from some employers and from increasing numbers of insurance companies. According to the Health Insurance Association of America, if you are 50 years old, a policy offering $80 per day in nursing-home benefits and a 20-day deductible period costs about $483 per year. The same policy costs $1,135 annually if you are 65, and about $3,841 if you are 79.

Make sure any long-term-care policy you consider has no hidden obstacles to collecting claims. Reject any plan that makes even a day or two of hospitalization a prerequisite for the payment of benefits. Look for a policy that covers three levels of nursing care — skilled, intermediate and custodial — and that pays an amount equal to at least half the nursing-home benefit for any home care your elder may need. The policy should explicitly cover Alzheimer's disease, Parkinson's disease and other mental disorders that are organic in origin. It should pay for care needed because of preexisting diseases. The daily benefit rate should climb from year to year to protect against fast-rising nursing-home costs.

Medicaid, the program for patients who have no money, is now the major financer of long-term care, covering about 42% of nursing-home bills nationally. Eligibility depends on need, and "need" is defined differently by Medicaid programs in different states. Some states not only require the impoverishment of the patient but also place a limit on the assets of the patient's spouse.

However, federal law allows spouses who remain at home to retain a "maintenance needs allowance" of up to $1,500 a month. The new law establishes new rules for the transfer of their assets to children or other relatives. In doing so, the spouses disqualify themselves for Medicaid, but only for a limited time. Under the new federal guideline, they can become eligible for Medicaid in 30 months or less after applying for it and after transferring assets to others.

Children of applicants who anticipate a long nursing-home stay should consider suggesting that their parents do this: Give to their potential heirs all of their assets except the amount of money needed to either pay for or insure the next 30 months of care. A family entering this process should seek the advice of a lawyer knowledgeable in this field. In addition, all should be aware that federal law prohibits nursing homes from requiring large cash registration deposits from those who qualify for Medicare.

The New Economics of Divorce

M ARRIAGES may be made in heaven, but more and more divorces are being negotiated in accountants' offices. Because of a revolution in property settlements, splitting up a marriage is becoming much like the dissolution of a business partnership. Alimony is going out, a concept called "equitable distribution" is in, and court decrees are so unpredictable — and so expensive to obtain — that couples should go to extreme lengths to avoid trial.

Instead of fighting bitterly over who did what to whom, smart couples now are more likely to concentrate on tallying all the dollars and cents that were acquired during their life together so that they can be split equitably. State legislatures and courts across the country are acknowledging that both parties put effort into a marriage, so both are entitled to their fair share of the assets if they divorce. Both the spouse who pays the bills and the partner who works as a homemaker or who earns less are credited with their contributions.

Since 1970, most states have adopted new concepts of what marital property is and how it should be split. The new theory is that any property accumulated during a marriage should be divided not only fairly but also *finally* so that each partner can move on to the next stage of life, unencumbered by leftover financial ties. This is based on the two modern realities that many marriages do not last and that women are increasingly able to support themselves.

A dozen years ago, women could not count on receiving any assets that had not been held in their own names. Recently, though, more and more women have been getting at least half of the marital assets, even in the 41 states without community property laws on the books.

Now most states hold that all assets earned during a marriage, no matter by whom or in whose name they have been held, go into a common pot to be divided in whatever way a judge decides is fair. The only exceptions are anything that a spouse owned before marriage or received as an inheritance or a gift during the marriage. Such property continues to belong to him or her.

At the same time, though, women are getting less alimony. Just 16% of divorced wives receive these payments, and short-term alimony is becoming more common than long-term. In sum, courts are more reluctant to burden a husband with an ex-wife's maintenance until she remarries — if ever — and with an obligation to support the children until they are grown. It is expected that most women will work for pay and support themselves. So rehabilitative maintenance usually is awarded just long enough for them to re-enter the work force or train for a better job. And support of children is considered the responsibility of *both* parents.

What are really on the rise are lump-sum, one-shot settlements. They are based on an analysis of the couple's financial assets. Figuring out the size of those assets, and just which partner is entitled to what, can mean lengthy litigation and high legal fees. Property judgments by a court are unpredictable at best, and sometimes downright unfair. If the couple cannot decide for themselves who gets what, the judge will. But these decisions are only as equitable and intelligent as the judge himself or herself.

Divorce is becoming so prevalent that more and more couples make an inventory of their assets every several years, just in case. They evaluate what they own, from cars and carpets to stocks and bonds. Then each partner outlines his or her individual contributions to this joint balance sheet, including the value of the wife's services if she is at home caring for children. Such written tabulations can save hours of high-priced legal time and help ensure a fairer division of property if a couple ever separates.

Because of the radical changes in the economics of divorce, anyone thinking about dissolving a marriage is well advised to do some serious financial planning first. Divorce lawyers now orchestrate elaborate financial settlements, and they often call in help from property appraisers, accountants, tax specialists and the like. The cost of divorce varies according to the size of professional fees in different localities. It can easily run to $10,000 for a middle-class couple with children, a house and other assets — and that is when they settle *out* of court. If they insist on going to trial, the fee easily doubles or triples.

The Virtues of Divorce Mediation

D IVORCE does not belong in the courts. That puts the couple into an adversarial position, and it tends to drive them further and further apart. You can reduce the cost and pain by using a professional mediator to help determine who gets what. Mediation, of course, is not for every couple. Sometimes differences are too sharp and hurtful for the estranged couple to sit down and reason together. The first chore of a mediator is to search for common ground.

If the three parties — husband, wife and mediator — agree that the mediation can work, the couple then faces a tough homework assignment: to bring budgets, balance sheets, tax returns, pension information and other financial reports to their next meeting. It may take anywhere from two to a dozen or more sessions for a couple to reach an appropriate financial agreement. The eventual settlement may involve payments for child support and alimony, division of pension and retirement funds or simply a divvying-up of the spoils of a lifetime — including the dog and the cat.

One reason for lopsided divisions of marital property may be that despite a generation of women's liberation, wives still typically come to the divorce table ill informed and therefore ill equipped to negotiate. In many cases, the woman has not taken an active role in handling finances other than the household budget.

Under the guidance of a competent mediator, divorce becomes an educational process for both spouses. In sharp contrast, a divorce hammered out between lawyers for each party tends to stop the flow of information. Still worse, says Robert Coulson, president of the American Arbitration Association, lawyers often widen the gap between couples. In his or her proper role as an advocate for one party in a dispute, a lawyer may instruct a wife, for example, to pull all the money out of a joint bank account, or advise a husband to close his wife's charge accounts.

Strictly in terms of dollars preserved, a meeting of minds offers opportunities to keep enormous sums out of the tax collector's reach. Take the sale of a house. Let's say she's 55 and he's 57. The house they have owned and lived in for 30 years originally cost $30,000. The house is now debt-free and worth $500,000. Neither spouse wants to live in it any longer. In the throes of an adversarial separation, a couple will often sell their house and split the proceeds. As joint owners over 55, they can *together* claim a once-in-a-lifetime $125,000 exemption from taxable capital gains. That way, each might net about $180,000 from the sale.

Under a mediator's patient tutelage, however, the couple might agree, while still married, to change title of the house from joint ownership to tenants-in-common, giving each a separate one-half interest in the property. Then, by waiting until after the divorce to sell his or her share, each ex-spouse would become eligible for a *separate* $125,000 capital-gains exemption. Instead of netting $180,000, they would each take away $200,000 or more.

Some divorce mediators are attorneys; others have backgrounds as social workers, teachers, clergymen, financial planners, psychologists or therapists. Where their financial competence is limited, they may call in actuaries, accountants and attorneys to complete the job; in some cases they may even refer overwrought clients to psychotherapists.

How much does divorce mediation cost? Anywhere from $80 to $170 an hour is the typical fee for drawing up a separation agreement, which will probably go through several revisions. Responsible mediators advise their clients to review the settlement with their own attorneys.

If the divorce mediator is also a lawyer and draws up the formal settlement, there will be additional fees: perhaps $1,500 for the agreement and $1,000 for filing it in court. In most cases, the entire cost of a mediated divorce is less than $5,000. Although that is far less than the usual charge for an adversarial divorce, few practitioners recommend mediation strictly as an economy move. Rather, they say, mediation is a less traumatic and more effective way of reaching a fair settlement.

How to locate a trained divorce mediator? The Academy of Family Mediators (P.O. Box 10501, Eugene, Oregon 97440) requires members to meet certain standards, and can provide names of those in your area. Or try the American Arbitration Association, listed in the Yellow Pages under "Mediation Services." It has offices in 40 cities and, for a $125 fee, will recommend a mediator who meets its professional standards. For a free pamphlet titled *Family Mediation Rules,* write to its Publications Department at 140 West 51st Street, New York, New York 10020-1203.

Undoubtedly, the best divorce settlements come about when both partners are able to put aside personal squabbles and concentrate on what might be called enlightened self-interest. In such cases they accept the fact that neither will come out ahead but that both will be able to make a clean break and to start anew. Just remember: A peaceful divorce settlement is almost always better than a trial, because it is much cheaper and is less stressful to family life.

The Tax Consequences of Divorce

I F YOU are estranged from your spouse, you may take comfort in the federal laws affecting the tax consequences of broken marriages.

It is much simpler than it was several years ago for a divorcing couple to divide ownership of their property, such as houses and stocks. In the past, if a man transferred a house to his ex-wife upon their divorce, he would owe capital-gains taxes on any estimated appreciation in the property's value. Under the new rules, though, the man owes nothing. In fact, neither the man nor his ex-wife owes any taxes until the house is sold — perhaps many years from now. But when the ex-wife eventually sells the home, she will be liable for taxes on any rise in its value since its original purchase by the husband, although there are two ways she can avoid or defer paying Uncle Sam.

First, if she is over 55, she can take advantage of a once-in-a-lifetime exclusion of up to $125,000 in capital gains on a primary residence. Or, she can purchase another home of equal or greater cost within two years of the sale, allowing her to save her exclusion for the future. Unfortunately, these special provisions do not apply to other property that one spouse transfers to another in a split-up, such as stocks. The ex-wife must still pay capital-gains taxes on these assets when she sells them.

An example: Say a man owns a house that he bought for $100,000 but now is worth $150,000. Say, too, that he gets a divorce and puts the house in his ex-wife's name. He owes no tax on the gain. On the other hand, his ex-wife stands to end up owing taxes if she sells the house, on all its appreciation since her ex-husband first bought it.

The basic rule on the tax treatment of alimony shapes many divorce settlements. If you receive alimony, the IRS considers it just like any other income, and you have to pay taxes on it. Similarly, if you pay alimony to an ex-spouse, the IRS considers it an expense, and you can deduct it from your taxable income.

The federal law says that alimony in most cases is what goes clearly to the ex-spouse alone. Here is how the current rules work: Say you pay $1,500 a month to your ex-spouse, and she uses $500 of it for the children. You can deduct only $1,000 a month from your taxable income, but you cannot deduct the $500 that is spent for the children. This money is considered child support, and you have to pay taxes on it. There are some instances, however, when money that benefits *both* the ex-spouse and children can be considered alimony. One tax break for a nonworking spouse who receives alimony lets him or her shelter as much as $2,000 of it annually in an Individual Retirement Account.

It is also possible to claim a share of your former spouse's pension. You can start collecting as soon as your former mate reaches early-retirement age, normally 55. Or you can demand your share in a lump sum if the company pension allows it. You can postpone taxes on the lump sum by rolling it over into an IRA.

Another point: Deadbeats who miss child-support payments are in big trouble. Strict child-support enforcement rules in every state provide for withholding refunds and placement of liens. Frequently delinquent parents may be required to post a bond and could have their poor payment history reported to credit agencies. Furthermore, if a parent fails to pay the specified support, any federal, as well as state, tax refunds that he or she is entitled to could be diverted to help provide for the child.

Your Spending

How to Get Bargains

IF YOU plan your shopping carefully, you can buy the best of nearly everything at the top stores in the country for 15% to as much as 75% off the original prices. Everyone knows that department stores, specialty stores and manufacturers have sales from time to time. But the smartest shoppers track the sales systematically to learn in advance just which products and services will be discounted when.

Seasonal markdowns now are likely to start earlier and last longer than they have in many years. The traditional white sale of household linens, for instance, often winds on for two months several times a year. Stores are under heavy pressure to turn over their merchandise constantly because high real interest rates make it costly to carry it on the shelves. Retailers estimate that less than 25% of the total sales of high-fashion clothes in department stores are made at the original retail prices. In a 1990 survey of 4,000 households by Management Horizons, 68% of respondents said they considered sales the single most important reason to enter a store; that number was up from 45% only four years earlier.

If you want to cash in on bargains, make a calendar of sales in your area. Very often stores have sales at the same time, year after year. For example, fall is a good season to check for promotional sales of brand-name china, glassware and silver. Storewide clearances of all kinds of merchandise regularly occur after Thanksgiving, Christmas, the second week in April and Independence Day. In the better department stores, men's clothing sales begin in early December and early June, and last four weeks. Men's specialty stores schedule sales quite predictably — just after Christmas and Father's Day.

The most expensive brands of perfume, skin cream and cosmetics rarely go on sale in department and specialty stores, although some discount stores such as Manhattan's Cosmetics Plus do sell these high-ticket items at slightly lower prices. But promotional sales — for example, giving away packaged samples with a purchase over a certain price — are common before Mother's Day and Father's Day, at Christmas as well as in the spring and in the fall, when cosmetics houses introduce new products and colors.

One cautionary note: Do not assume everything in a sale has been marked down for clearance. Even fine stores stock special sale merchandise of inferior quality.

Luxury Goods

I T IS a great time to find bargains on high-priced goods — *if* you have the cash to pay for them. Now that the eighties are behind us and times have gotten tougher, conspicuous consumption is out of style. That's helped drive the price of many luxury goods down, down, down.

Take, for instance, boats. Thanks in part to the new luxury tax on boats and yachts that cost more than $100,000, many of them are going for only about half what they would have fetched a few years ago, and sometimes less.

Then there's jewelry. Gold prices are relatively low, and jewelry production has become more efficient. So, an 18-karat gold chain that sold for about $1,500 two years ago now might run you about $1,300. Now is also a good time to trade in your old watch for something better. Prices of brand-new timepieces are relatively stable. But a strong collectors' market for vintage watches has pushed up the value of some that are only a few years old. Demand for old

Rolexes, for instance, is so strong that some models are worth five times what buyers paid in the eighties.

The New Discounts

A NEW kind of suburban mall is burgeoning across the country as shoppers increasingly look for bargains. A 1991 *Money* magazine poll of 300 subscribers revealed that 54% were more concerned about finding bargains than they had been just a year earlier. The outlet malls — now over 275 in number — are quite different from dumpy, depressing bargain basements or earlier, unadorned off-price discounters. Enthusiastic developers have created Colonial clusterings in the East and casual Western decor for California. Most of the stores belong to manufacturers who clear out surplus designer and brand-name merchandise — at a profit. But their profit is your reward. You often can find clothing, housewares, electronic goods and even furniture at steep discounts. At a mall in Chattanooga, Tennessee, you can buy Ralph Lauren suits, Coach leather bags, Perry Ellis shoes and Wamsutta sheets, all at 25% to 60% below regular retail prices. Other manufacturers at malls include Liz Claiborne, Joan Vass, Harvé Benard, Bass, Gucci, Van Heusen, Lenox and Oneida. A word of warning: There are apt to be limited selections and a frenetic atmosphere, especially if you shop on Sunday.

You can find these malls in a directory published by Value Retail News. *The Joy of Outlet Shopping* provides lists of the manufacturers and maps to the nation's outlet shopping centers. To order, send $7.45 to *Joy*, P.O. Box 17129, Attention Customer Service, Clearwater, Florida 34622-0129.

You also can pick up appliances and furniture at big discounts at special warehouses or stores that many major retailers maintain in or near large cities. Prices are low — because items are often discontinued, slightly damaged or overstocked. For example, a Sears catalogue surplus store outside Seattle offered a Kenmore electric oven for $300, which was a $180 saving. And at a Macy's clearance center in San Jose, California, a slightly damaged $4,000 bedroom set sold for half its department-store price. To find off-price outlets near you, telephone such major chain stores as Sears, J. C. Penney and Macy's. And don't forget to check out the prices at Kmart, Wal-Mart and Dayton-Hudson's Target stores. The fight among these three to be America's number-one retailer will create more bargains for shoppers. Even the upscale Nordstrom's department store chain now has an outlet store, Nordstrom Rack, which offers significant discounts on name-brand goods. Other off-price chains include Filene's Basement, Marshall's, and T. J. Maxx.

In addition, many cities now have huge megastores called membership warehouse clubs. Two of the largest clubs are Price and Costco. To find them, look in advertisements and the phone book for retailers with words such as "warehouse" and "wholesale club" in their names. Clubs carry thousands of products, including appliances, automotive supplies, clothes, food, furniture, liquor and toys, all at prices 20% to 40% below those in regular retail stores.

Membership is restricted. To qualify, you must either own your own business or belong to or work for a designated organization. Such groups generally include labor unions, credit unions, hospitals, banks, savings and loan associations and local governments. Most customers own a small business and pay a yearly membership fee of about $25. There is usually no membership fee for nonbusiness customers, but they must pay 5% over the store's so-called wholesale price. Most stores allow members to bring along a guest.

The key to success for warehouse outlets is volume. Their gross profit margins are thin — from 8% to 11% compared with 50% or more for department stores and 20% to 35% for discounters. Clubs have a no-nonsense decor. Towering banks of unadorned metal inventory racks rise from concrete floors. Most merchandise remains in the suppliers' cartons; only one sample of each is on display. You commandeer a wide-body shopping cart or a six-wheel dolly and wend your way through carton canyons of goods. At the checkout, you pay with cash or check. Credit cards are not accepted.

You can get further bargains on furniture by buying from discount stores in the big furniture-making state of North Carolina. Quite a few stores there will ship anywhere in the country, and your savings will pay many times over for the freight charges. A velvet wingback chair that retails nationally at $349 costs only $197 from a Winston-Salem discounter named Hickory Tree. You will find comparable furniture deals at other North Carolina retailers. Many of them advertise in home-related magazines and on the cable shopping networks and take telephone orders on toll-free numbers. Avoid any dealer who asks for a deposit of more than 50%. Otherwise, you surrender your leverage if your order is long overdue or damaged in transit.

For many types of goods, some top stores and catalogue retailers have taken a tip from the airlines and are offering freebies to frequent buyers. Purchase a certain amount in a year on several major department stores' credit cards and you will qualify for special services such as free gift wrapping. The more you charge, the more you get. Frequent buyers from the J. Crew catalogue often get $5 and $10 gift certificates. In general, mail-order shopping is a smart way to save. *The Wholesale-By-Mail Catalogue* by Lowell Miller and Prudence McCullough (HarperCollins, $14.95) is a good sourcebook, with multiple listings of retailers that offer savings through mail-order purchasing.

But remember: No matter how much you love an off-price item or how much you stand to save, a bargain is not a bargain under the following circumstances:

— If it does not fit you or the space it is intended for or your life-style. For example, no matter how low their price, massive, heavily carved end tables will never look right flanking a light, graceful Louis XVI sofa.

— If you have to buy something else at full price to make use of it. A perfect plaid skirt marked down 70% is no buy if most of your blouses are prints.

— If it is not complete. Designer skirts or slacks missing their normal linings, top-notch camera bodies supplied with inferior lenses or furniture missing shelves can be fixed, but adding in the extra costs raises the ante sharply.

As a rule, never buy something just because the price is low.

The Fine Art of Haggling

Many shoppers find it hard to look a salesperson in the eye and ask a legitimate question: "Can you give me a break on the price?" The mere mention of the word *haggling* makes Americans cringe or recall some quaint foreign bazaar where matching wits with shopkeepers is an official tourist sport. But bargaining for the best price is also a respectable stateside tradition, especially in individually owned stores and dealerships for big-ticket items such as cars, furniture, jewelry and appliances.

The key to successful haggling is comparison-shopping to find out the fair market value of what you want to buy. You will also need an idea of the markup to see how much leeway you have to bargain. The typical markup on a new subcompact car, for example, is around 10%. On appliances, it is about 20% to 28%. Clothing is commonly 100%, while antiques dealers tend to build in breathtaking profits.

After asking for a break on the price, resist making the first offer yourself. If the price tag is $175, do not leap in with a $125 bid. Let the seller make the first offer. Then you can come in with a still lower one. It often pays to offer to buy several items at discount; many sellers are eager to reduce inventory and will give you a much better deal on bulk purchases.

Do not make your bids in round numbers. If an item costs, say, $700, it is better to offer $485 than $500. Round numbers beg to be negotiated up by the seller. Odd numbers sound harder and firmer.

And take your time. If the seller quickly gives you a small price reduction, do not succumb to the natural tendency to breathe a sigh of relief and accept the offer. When you feign indecision or voice a need to consult with your spouse, the merchant may be only too eager to sweeten the deal for fear of having no deal at all.

Smart Buys at Auctions

SHOPPING for artworks, antiques and other collectibles, more and more people are turning up at auctions in search of bargains. You don't have to be a high-roller or a big-time collector to get them. But the growing number of auction buyers has made those bargains harder to come by. Besides the regular sales held at big-city auction houses, two places where you can still find bargains are at the charity auction and the old-fashioned country auction.

People who attend auctions held for charity or political fund-raising are often more interested in the cause than in the merchandise. As a result, bidding seldom becomes heavy, and you can get some real buys. Similarly, most of the bargain hunters who show up at country auctions of estates are local folks interested in the land, the stock or the machinery on the block. That leaves the field clear for you, the seeker of antiques and other collectibles.

Wherever you go, the rules are fairly simple. All auctions display the merchandise before the bidding begins, so don't bid unless you have inspected an item thoroughly. You can get an idea of what an item will go for by studying the auction catalogue, if there is one. It gives high and low estimates of each item's worth, and bidding usually starts at about 70% of the lower figure.

It's best *not* to bid at the first auction you visit. Newcomers often get caught up in "auction fever" and bid too high. You would be wise to begin by observing the auction process. Visit the pre-auction exhibit, decide how much you would pay for an item, and then see what it actually goes for. Watch who the other bidders are and keep track of the winning prices in the auction catalogue. That way, when you spot something you might want at a future sale, you will have the price history of a similar item for reference. Put that together with some knowledge of regular retail prices, and you will know how far to go in your bidding.

At some auctions you will be given a paddle or a paper plate with a number on it. When the auctioneer calls out the price, just hold up the paddle, the plate or your hand if you want to bid. If you don't like the price, you can holler out a lower figure. Don't worry that you will wind up owning some larger expensive whatnot because you scratched your nose or tugged your earlobe. That just doesn't happen.

Try to arrive early at an auction. Bidding at the start often is on the low side as the audience and the auctioneer try to get the feel of each other. Before you bid on anything, set a mental limit on what you'll pay. And be careful that you don't bid against yourself. That is a mistake some beginners make. When the auctioneer calls for a higher price, they forget that the last bid was theirs.

Auctions, Government-style

YOU can get some exceptional deals when the government auctions off its surplus property. In fact, you can buy just about anything at cut-rate prices, from a bronze statue of a Buddha to a seaside house, a down vest to a private plane.

A government auction probably is going on in your area every week. Several thousand auctions are held throughout the country each year by the General Services Administration, the Department of Defense, the Postal Service and the Internal Revenue Service. The sales raise money for the Treasury and clean out the government's attics. Meanwhile, you can save an average 50% off the retail price, and often much, much more. And the government doesn't charge state or local sales taxes.

Virtually any item the government has ever bought, used or confiscated goes to the auction block. The Pentagon offers more than 400 classes of property, from used guided-missile launchers to guard dogs. The GSA traffics in office and hospital equipment, cars from the government motor pool and even Coast Guard lighthouses. A stream of civilian property that has been abandoned, confiscated or lost goes under the hammer at Postal and IRS auctions.

The quality of the offerings varies radically. Goods at GSA and Department of Defense auctions usually have seen better days. But the property at Postal and IRS auctions is newer.

The savings and loan crisis has created one positive thing for Americans: the Resolution Trust Corporation auctions of the failed thrifts' assets. The RTC in 1991 had for sale such items as a red 1960 MG roadster, a five-foot-tall bronze of John Wayne on horseback, and $1.2 billion worth of business and residential properties valued at less than $100,000 each — in most cases requiring no minimum bid. In 1992, the RTC sold the Mulholland Library Collection of Magic and Allied Arts, which contained, among other things, Houdini artifacts.

To find out about sales, write or phone the agency whose auctions you want to attend and ask to be put on the free mailing list. The government can pack your mailbox every day with its sales catalogues and auction notices, so be selective. Some mail-order firms advertise that for $20 they will notify clients of forthcoming sales. But all they do is pass your name along to the appropriate government agency.

Government auctions often pit the amateur against the professional dealer. You can avoid competing with dealers if you look for the odd item in an auction that is dominated by another category. Wholesalers and retailers are not as likely to show up for a few pieces of jewelry or some fishing gear if the sale consists mainly of electronic parts. And if you are willing to travel, you are likely to find better buys because fewer people show up for sales at hard-to-find warehouses and military bases. For the same reason, you should try to attend the auctions that are held on weekdays rather than weekends.

A sparse audience, however, does not mean that the government will part with its property to the lowest bidder. It sets a so-called upset price, below which the property will not be sold. That price is usually at the low end of what the bureaucrats who run the auction figure the property would be worth on the open market. But such people are not always the best judges of value. So you might be as lucky as the sharp-eyed bidder who for $15,000 bought an entire lot of 94 miscellaneous furs at a GSA auction. She kept one of the sables she found in the lot and sold the others for $50,000.

To learn when auctions and sales of government-surplus property will take place, here is where to write:

— General Services Administration. For personal property, primarily manufactured goods, write to the General Services Administration, Federal Surplus Personal Property, in the region nearest to you. The regions are Atlanta (30303); Auburn, Washington (98002); Boston (02222-1076); Chicago (60604); Denver (80225); Fort Worth (76102); Kansas City, Missouri (64131); New York (10278); Philadelphia (19107); San Francisco (94105) and Washington, D.C. (20407). Each regional office has its own mailing list.

The GSA also has a monthly catalogue listing all its real estate sales. Write to Properties–C, Consumer Information Center–J, Pueblo, Colorado 81009, and request a free publication called *U.S. Real Property Sales List*. If you want to be notified of real estate sales in a certain price range and location, write for an application form from the General Services Administration, Centralized Mailing Listing Service–9KS, 525 Market Street, San Francisco, California 94105.

— Department of Defense. Write to Bidders Control Office, Defense Reutilization and Marketing Service, Box 1370, Battle Creek, Michigan 49017-3092, for a copy of *How to Buy Surplus Personal Property from the Department of Defense*. It lists items from hand tools to motor vehicles and tells how to get on a bidders' list.

— U.S. Postal Service. Postal auctions take place in five cities. For information about the sales nearest you, call or write to the U.S. Post Office, Dead Parcel Branch, Atlanta (30304-9506); New York (10099-9543); Philadelphia (19104-9597); St. Paul (55101-9514) or San Francisco (94105-9501). Include a self-addressed, stamped envelope.

If you are interested in surplus postal equipment, inquire at a local post office for the address of the nearest Procurement Services office where these sales are held. Postal vehicles, such as the jeeps used by letter carriers, are sold at fixed prices by the vehicle maintenance facilities of local post offices.

— Internal Revenue Service. If the seizure of his property does not lead a recalcitrant taxpayer to pay his back taxes, the IRS auctions it off, although this rarely happens. Write to Chief of Special Procedures, Collection Division, at whichever of 63 IRS district offices is nearest you.

Your Charities

Guides to Sensible Giving

INDIVIDUAL Americans gave more than $103 billion to thousands of charities in 1991, amounting to 82.7% of total charitable contributions that year. The sum represented 2.13% of pre-tax personal income. That's much less than the biblical tithe of 10%, but much more than people in other countries contribute. If you want your donations to have the most effect, you should make a careful analysis before you give. Charity begins with homework.

The typical donor scatters relatively small contributions among a large number of charities. Yet it would make more sense for you to give fewer but bigger amounts. The smaller your gift, the larger the share that will be spent on fund-raising and overhead.

Make sure that your contributions to individual charities are tax-deductible. The IRS will allow you to claim gifts to most religious, educational, social welfare and health groups. But several that solicit widely for funds — such as Handgun Control, Incorporated, and the Moral Majority — are classified as lobbying groups. They are tax-exempt themselves, but your donations to them are not tax-deductible. If you are in doubt about any group, just ask the IRS for a copy of a so-called determination letter, which will state whether or not your donations will be taxed.

The United Way scandal of 1992 brought accountability issues sharply into focus. High executive salaries and lavish perks for its president prompted many givers to question how their money was being spent. And rightly so. Donors *should* scrutinize their favorite charity before writing a check.

Certainly most charities are legitimate and worthy of your support. True, to be competitive, the pay of their CEOs has gone up in recent years. According to a survey by Towers Perrin, a human resources consulting firm, the average compensation of CEOs of health and welfare organizations was $122,500 in 1992. And while questionable practices were discovered in the national United Way headquarters, local affiliates of the organization are separate entities, and considered aboveboard.

You can write to any charity and request both an independently audited financial statement and an annual report of the programs that the charity sponsors. If any group fails to respond, you probably will not want to give money to it.

Once you get the data from a charity, a couple of independent watchdog groups can answer questions you may have. One is the National Charities Information Bureau, which has thorough reports on hundreds of charities that solicit nationwide. The reports include analyses of balance sheets, income and other financial statements.

By mailing a postcard to the National Charities Information Bureau, you can get a copy of its *Wise Giving Guide,* which lists the groups that meet its standards, fail to meet them, have not responded to its requests for information or are too new for a full evaluation. In a recent guide, for example, almost 400 groups — as disparate as the Sierra Legal Defense Club and the Puerto Rican Legal Defense and Education Fund — met the bureau's standards. If you request them, the bureau also will send you, free, up to three extensive reports on separate charities. The address is National Charities Information Bureau, 19 Union Square West, New York, New York 10003; 212-929-6300.

Another watchdog group is the Council of Better Business Bureaus' Philanthropic Advisory Service, or PAS. It maintains files on thousands of national charities, and thoroughly reviews more than 300 each year on the basis of such characteristics as public accountability, use of funds and fund-raising practices. For $2 and a self-addressed, stamped envelope, the PAS will send you *Give But Give Wisely,* its bimonthly guide to organizations that do or do not meet its standards. Write to the Philanthropic Advisory Service, 4200 Wilson Boulevard, Suite 800, Arlington, Virginia 22203.

The Tax Benefits

To GET tax benefits for your charitable contributions, you must itemize your deductions. In the eyes of the tax collector, not all your charitable contributions are created equal. Some will save you more than others.

You can deduct all your donations when you give to organized charities such as churches, educational institutions and tax-exempt hospitals — just so the total does not exceed 50% of your adjusted gross income. You also can deduct all your contributions to veterans' organizations, fraternal associations and certain private foundations, just so they do not exceed 30% of your adjusted gross income. Don't worry, you probably will not top those limits unless you are a really big giver.

But you may be in trouble if you give to a foreign charity. You cannot take any deduction for that.

You can deduct only a limited amount when you stand to benefit from your contribution. For example, when you buy tickets to a theater benefit, you can deduct only the difference between what you actually paid and what you would have paid for the tickets at a regular performance.

Be sure to write down and take advantage of all the tax deductions you are entitled to. You can deduct not only your cash gifts but also the value of property you donate. That includes clothing, magazine subscriptions, stocks or other investments.

If you did volunteer work for a church, a synagogue or some other charitable organization, you can deduct the cost of traveling to meetings, fund-raisers or other events. The IRS permits you to write off 12 cents for every mile you drove to or from such charitable activities, plus parking fees and tolls. Bus, taxi and train fares are also deductible — if you have receipts to verify them. You also can deduct all your out-of-pocket expenses. They include the cost of telephone calls, stationery, stamps and uniforms. But you may not deduct the value of your work for charity.

Cash is almost never the smartest thing to give. If you have a choice between sending a $1,000 check or donating the same amount of stock or property that has appreciated, you will do more good at lower cost by giving the property. That way you will avoid paying the capital-gains taxes that would be due if you sold the property. You will need to plan more carefully if you want to donate tangible personal property, such as an art collection, instead of financial assets, such as stocks or bonds. For one thing, your gift must relate directly to the purpose of the charity in order for you to receive the largest tax benefit. The rules are complex, so it's wise to consult an accountant or some other professional tax adviser before making a significant gift. Large gifts of appreciated property may make you subject to the Alternative Minimum Tax.

If you plan to will income-producing securities to charity, you can get the satisfaction of giving while you are still alive without losing any of the income. Just contribute the securities to a charitable remainder trust. Many universities and other charities set up such trusts. The charity agrees not to spend or otherwise use your full gift for an agreed-upon period of years, while you continue to collect the dividends or interest. Some remainder trusts sell your low-yielding securities and reinvest the money in higher-yielding securities — so you actually collect more than if you had not made the gift. Part of your income from the trust may be sheltered from taxes.

In one such remainder trust arrangement, for example, a Connecticut widow gave the Nature Conservancy $27,000 worth of stock that had been paying her only 4½% a year in dividends. The Conservancy then sold the stock and reinvested it in a government securities fund that paid over 11%, which the widow then collected. So she more than doubled her income from her securities without paying any capital-gains taxes on the sale of them. Besides all that, she took a big deduction on her income taxes for making the gift.

Remember: It is better to give than to receive, but it is best to do both at once.

How to Raise Money
for Your Favorite Cause

RAISING money for your charity of choice takes the persuasiveness of a politician and the tough hide of a door-to-door salesman. Particularly in this time of tight budgets and federal cutbacks, any volunteer fund-raiser needs one other attribute as well: the ingenuity of an inventor to concoct clever ways to get donations.

If you are a volunteer, it will pay you to stage events that go beyond the standard charity ball. People around the country are raising money by sponsoring book fairs, art shows, auctions and much more. Whatever device you choose, it has to be something quite special. You have to have a gimmick.

A very successful one is the "no-dinner dinner." Rather than ask donors to pay hundreds of dollars to dress up and spend yet another Saturday night in a dull hotel ballroom, some charities let their supporters off the hook by telling them: "Just send the check and you can stay home."

When people support a nonprofit group, they usually get a warm feeling and a tax deduction. But it will not hurt your charity's bottom line to offer them something more. One such lure is the chance to purchase what money usually cannot buy. With a little digging you can discover priceless opportunities that can be sold for a price. For example, at a St. Louis Arts Council auction, several music lovers bid for a chance to conduct the St. Louis Symphony in one of its regular evening performances.

If your charity sells donated goods and services, anything from crocheted potholders to dinner with the mayor, the money that is raised generally is not taxed. But before your charity sells anything to the public, it's smart to check with an accountant or a lawyer. You may have to pay taxes on your profits if your enterprise is not *directly* related to the purpose for which your group was granted tax-exempt status.

One other tip: Most charities follow the 50% rule — if you do not earn at least a 50% profit on the revenues from your fund-raising event, you have not done your job efficiently.

A favorite means of achieving that profit — and more — is to hold an auction. The charity gets all the proceeds from the sale of donated items. When gathering goods and services to be auctioned off, ask for donations from as many individuals and businesses as possible — and nothing is too wild. Some auctions have included enough cement to repave a driveway (that was given by a construction firm) and even a gallbladder operation (that was contributed by a civic-minded surgeon). Entertainment and vacation offerings are popular. A couple might contribute the use of their faraway vacation home for a week or two. You might persuade a travel agency to donate air fare to the destination.

Some staples at charity auctions include dinners given by restaurants. But even dinners need not be routine. Volunteers in several charities have persuaded their city mayors or other local celebrities to cook and serve a meal in the home of the highest bidder. It's amazing how often celebrities will help out a worthy charity. Yes, you will have to spend something to stage your fund-raising event, but those headlinable outsiders can help reduce your expenses. Ideally, you should keep costs to about one-third of the amount of the total receipts — by begging and borrowing as much as you can.

An excellent sourcebook for those interested in fund-raising for a charitable cause is *Securing Your Organization's Future*, by Michael Seltzer. It is published by the Foundation Center and sells for $24.95, plus $4.50 for shipping and handling. Call 800-424-9836 to order the book, or call the Foundation Center at 212-620-4230 for further information regarding grant and foundation funding. *Giving USA* by Ann Kaplan is a helpful compilation of statistics that sketches out a national picture of American charity. You can buy it for $45 from the American Association of Fundraising Council (25 West 43rd Street, New York, New York 10036; 212-354-5799).

The serious fund-raiser might want to consider hiring a consultant to design and help execute a campaign. Ketchum, Inc. (800-242-2161), based in Pittsburgh, has been counseling nonprofits since 1919, with significant results — recent Ketchum campaign yields have ranged from $600,000 to $186,000,000.

Your Services

Appraisers

A N APPRAISER can be a very important person in your financial life. If you are buying insurance to cover your jewelry or silverware, you will probably need an appraiser to certify their value. And you will want to hire an appraiser if you are buying or selling a house — or merely refinancing it. Countless people call themselves appraisers, but finding a knowledgeable and reliable one requires some effort.

To locate a real estate appraiser, ask your banker, lawyer or insurance agent for recommendations. Get the names of several candidates and then call each one. Ask him about his background and fees. Find out if he belongs to one of several appraisal associations. They include the Appraisal Institute, the American Society of Appraisers and the National Association of Independent Fee Appraisers. Members tend to be trustworthy and experienced because each of these organizations subscribes to the Uniform Standards of Professional Appraisal Practice defined by the recently formed Appraisal Foundation. That is important because few states license real estate appraisers.

A real estate appraisal fee will vary, depending on the size and condition of your house and on how long it takes to compare your property with others in the neighborhood. The cost also varies by region. The average cost of a residential property appraisal in the New York metropolitan area is $500. In other areas you might pay $300 or even less.

For personal property appraisers, once again seek advice from your banker, lawyer or insurance agent; museum curators also can suggest names. The two major associations are the American Society of Appraisers and the Appraisers Association of America. For jewelry alone, you might consider a member of the American Gem Society who is a certified gemologist appraiser.

Appraisers use two measures to establish the value of your possessions. One is the replacement cost, which is what you would have to pay to replace the item. Usually you insure the property for the replacement cost. Then there is fair market value — it's the price a willing buyer would pay to a willing seller. The fair market value is used for settling an estate, dividing property for a divorce or donating a work of art for a tax deduction.

The fair market value is usually only half the replacement cost. That is because a dealer's markup is often 100%. An appraiser might tell you to insure a Chippendale highboy for $10,000 because it would cost that much to replace one. But if you wanted to sell the highboy, a dealer might pay you only $5,000.

An appraisal must be precise and explicit to back up an insurance or tax-loss claim. For jewelry, it should note size and weight of stones and their settings, as well as clarity, purity and color. Art and antiques should be evaluated for age, condition and any special factors, such as rarity.

To assess your jewelry, artwork or furniture, you should hire only an appraiser who charges by the hour or by the job. Most professionals believe that it is unethical to base fees on a percentage of the value of your goods, since there is an obvious temptation to overstate their worth. You also should avoid anyone who offers to appraise your belongings and buy them too. In that case, the appraiser may deliberately underestimate.

The cost of a personal property appraisal depends on how long the job takes, which can be from less than one hour to several days. For simple pieces of jewelry, you may pay $50 to $150 an hour, according to the American Gem Society. Even gemologists who are not certified appraisers can charge up to $150 an hour.

When a personal property appraiser comes to your house to evaluate your furniture, silverware and other property for insurance purposes, he will check each item's condition. He may also photograph your valuables. If he does not, then you should take photos yourself, including close-ups of any significant details.

Keep your appraisals current. The prices of jewelry, antiques and other collectibles fluctuate so sharply that you should have your insurance appraisals updated every two years.

Send one copy of your appraisal to your insurance agent. Hold all other copies and photographs of your belongings in a safe-deposit box or in your lawyer's office or another place that is fireproof and theftproof. One appraiser tells of a client who stored in his dining room sideboard a list of the values and locations of his most prized possessions. A thief found the list and neatly checked off the items as he loaded them aboard his truck. He then scrawled on the list, "thanks for the appraisal." It was just about the only thing he left behind.

Caterers

E NTERTAINING can be draining, but if you are thinking of having a party, you can save time and trouble by holding a catered affair. How do you keep the price within bounds?

It pays to bear in mind that small parties may cost more per person than large ones with the same menu. A catered meal at home for fewer than 25 people approaches and occasionally surpasses restaurant prices. In New York City, a trendy dinner at home for 12 could run up to $1,000, plus an additional $300 for three people to help serve; liquor and wine will be extra. So if your group is smaller than a couple of dozen, a restaurant might be cheaper.

Still, it is possible to treat yourself to the luxury of a catered affair without paying luxury prices. Avoid large caterers and those that emphasize exotic foods. They can charge $85 a person for food alone, although a recent rise in do-it-yourself entertaining — the result of the recession of 1990–91 — has caused many to drop or agree to negotiate their prices. The national average is $30 a head for dinner. You would do well to seek out small caterers or those new to the business. They often give far better service at lower prices. And look for catering firms that will prepare dishes *you* can heat and serve yourself.

Beware of caterers who operate out of their homes; in many cases they will be in violation of health codes. And don't rent china, silver or linen. You could pay about $10 to $20 a setting. You are better off borrowing, or even buying, your own.

Another way to pare costs is to get by with less help, particularly those bartenders and waiters who collect $80 to $120 for an evening's work. Instead of the caterer's workers, waitresses or bartenders, enlist some college students or neighborhood teenagers who serve for half as much.

Don't let caterers provide drinks or setups. The markups on them are intoxicating, so buy your own — unless, of course, your caterer can purchase liquor at a discount through a wholesaler, in which case you may be able to save a few dollars. And if you want music or live entertainment, you can save a lot when you hire talented students from a local college or music conservatory to do the playing.

Cocktail parties, of course, are cheaper than fancy dinners. You also can lower food costs by scheduling your cocktail party for a time when people tend to be less ravenous. Guests may only nibble at the hors d'oeuvres at an open house scheduled from 3 p.m. to 5 p.m., but a reception from 6 p.m. to 8 p.m. substitutes for dinner for many party-goers. Caterers estimate that most guests will average two drinks at a two-hour party.

Wedding receptions introduce special expenses. For 100 guests, a wedding cake might add $200 to $1,200. Champagne for a toast could mean at least 20 bottles — at a total cost of $150 to $600 or even more, depending on the quality of the champagne. Again, if possible, try to pay wholesale rather than retail prices.

The Yellow Pages list columns of "caterers." Still, the best way to find one is to ask people who have used caterers in the past. If you work for a company, check with the person there who arranges corporate entertainment. Sometimes officers of churches, temples and fraternal organizations, as well as restored-home associations, also know the reputations of local firms that cater parties in their halls.

Once you have gathered a few recommendations, call and get a price estimate from each firm. Before you telephone, figure out what you can spend, and then try to get the best value for your dollar.

Ask any caterer you are considering if you may observe — at a discreet distance — a party he has arranged. Most caterers will agree and also let you sample the food. Once you have chosen a firm, be prepared to sign a contract that protects both sides from surprises.

For instance, taxes and tips are rarely included in the quoted food price. And the cancellation policy should be clearly stated. Once you have signed the contract, count on paying a deposit of up to 50%, with the balance due immediately before or after the party.

Book at least a month in advance for a cocktail party, and at least several months for a large wedding. You would be wise to call even earlier for a date in May, June, November or December — they are the peak seasons.

If you must cancel, call the caterer immediately. Weddings are generally nonrefundable, but with enough notice, many caterers will return part or all of your deposit for a cocktail or dinner party in the hope that you will reschedule and call them again.

Domestics

W ITH the proliferation of two-income couples, more and more people find that they can afford — and in many cases absolutely need — household help. But how can you find and screen good applicants for domestic jobs?

First of all, recognize that you will have to pay a lot. Full-time domestics in big cities earn $250 to $600 a week. New York City's Pavillion agency has placed several nannies who earn more than $1,000 a week. Day workers are paid $60 to $100 for an eight-hour day depending on their experience.

One reason for the relatively high wage is the shortage of domestics. Their numbers decreased by almost 50% in the decade of the 1970s.

The best sources for candidates are newspaper ads, friends who have household help and employment agencies that specialize in placing domestic workers. The agencies will charge you a fee ranging from $400 to $2,500, or a sum equal to four weeks' pay for the person you hire, and the workers tend to command top dollar. You can also ask at churches, colleges and senior citizens' centers for names of people looking for part-time or full-time employment.

If you advertise for help, try the small ethnic newspapers such as Chicago's Polish *Zgoda* or New York City's *Irish Echo,* as well as the large metropolitan dailies. If you live in a big urban area and are looking for live-in baby-sitters, consider advertising in small-town newspapers. Many young women and, in growing numbers, men are eager to spend a year or so in an exciting city but want to live in a secure household. (See "Your Family: Finding Reliable Child Care.")

Whether you locate applicants yourself or get them through an agency, take the time to interview them thoroughly. Rely on your common sense and intuition, but also be sure to check references meticulously. That's the only way you can guard against hiring a thief. Call three former employers on the phone and ask pointed questions such as: Did you like her personality? Did she often skip work? How was she with children? And, most important, do you have any reason to doubt this person's honesty?

Home Movers

T HE act of moving from one city or one neighborhood to another is among life's most stressful events, yet you can avoid the three major hassles of moving: delay, damage and overcharging.

How do you find a good mover? Ask friends and co-workers who have moved recently, or your real estate agent or the person who arranges transfers at your company. Consider hiring only those firms that conform to government-regulated standards. If you are relocating to another state, your moving company should be certified by the Interstate Commerce Commission. If you are moving within the same city or state, choose a firm authorized by the appropriate state regulatory agency, usually the Public Utilities Commission or the state Department of Transportation.

Also check the reputation of the moving company's local agent, because he is the one you will be dealing with. Call your local Better Business Bureau or consumer-protection agency and ask whether complaints have been filed against the agent. Avoid anyone who has had 10 major complaints lodged against him over the past year.

Then solicit and compare written bids from several reputable agents. Make sure the bids include charges for extras, of which there are many. For example, if the movers do the packing, figure on paying up to $37 a box. Carefully read the mover's contract, or bill of lading, before you sign. The contract should include the total cost of the move, an inventory of goods to be shipped, the amount of liability insurance and the pickup and delivery dates you and the mover have agreed on.

Some movers "lowball" their bids by underestimating the weight of a shipment just to land a job. You can protect yourself against lowballing by getting a "binding estimate." This means that the mover charges you whatever he agrees to charge you. So it pays to get several estimates. It also pays to read the Interstate Commerce Commission's booklet *When You Move: Your Rights and Responsibilities*. Your mover is required by law to give you this booklet.

Before the move, make an inventory of your possessions, then check them off one by one as they go into the van. When the movers unload the truck at your new house, unpack dishes and other breakables right away. Note any damages on your inventory list and give one copy to the driver of the van. If the move went well, you probably will want to tip the driver and his crew members $10 to $20 each.

If there are damages and you are not satisfied with the mover's offer to repair or replace your damaged goods, look at your contract to see if the company has an informal dispute-resolution system. If you still have questions, call your local branch of the American Arbitration Association, or write to the organization at 140 West 51st Street, New York, New York 10020-1203.

Many movers are reluctant to handle small shipments at all or will charge you as much as $2,000 to do so. One exception is Bekins. It welcomes loads as small as 500 pounds or 71 cubic feet. Bekins charges from $200 to $1,000 anywhere in the continental U.S.; distance determines the exact fee.

There are no special packing requirements to get the low rate. If you are shipping breakables, you can pack them yourself or pay the movers to pack for you. One warning about small shipments: They may have to wait for other shipments to fill the van.

Help When You Relocate

MOVING to a new city can be made considerably easier if you use some of the many sources of help. However, you will have to do a fair amount of letter writing, library reading and talking to strangers. And eventually you should visit the place where you think you would like to live.

Anyone contemplating a move would do well to read *Places Rated Almanac,* published by Prentice Hall for $16.95. This useful book compares the climates, crime rates, housing, education, recreation, arts, economic conditions and transportation systems in 333 metropolitan areas.

The Bette R. Malone Relocation Service of United Van Lines has free fact sheets, each of which describes any one of 7,000 U.S. and foreign cities. Just call 800-325-3870. The company will give you two sheets at a time. The *Book of the States,* which you can find in most libraries, gives you the tax rates of each state, county and municipality. The local Chamber of Commerce, of course, is another source of information.

To get a feel for life in a community, subscribe to local newspapers and city or state magazines and talk to people who live there. You can come closest to experiencing life in a strange city by visiting or becoming a paying guest of someone in town. One way is to seek commercial bed-and-breakfast accommodations in private homes.

Once you arrive, walk through the neighborhoods. A stroll past shuttered shops on Main Street and in nearby malls may tell you more about the state of the economy than any Chamber of Commerce brochure. Seek out real estate agents. They know the virtues of various neighborhoods and they are willing to spend a lot of time with serious sales prospects.

When Your Employer Asks You to Relocate

So YOUR employer has asked you to move to another plant or office. Resist rushing home breathlessly with the news. Instead, begin by finding out precisely what's being offered to you — and not just in terms of moving benefits. It is easy to underestimate the adjustment that a move will require. According to Eugene Jennings, a professor at Michigan State and an authority on relocation, you need to know three things.

First, the precise nature of your new assignment. Who, for example, will you be reporting to? Bad chemistry could more than wipe out any points you win by agreeing to relocate.

Second, the salary you will be making. A raise is the most sincere expression by your bosses that they really want you for this post.

Third, the opportunities for advancement that the new job will open up. The chance to make the first leap up the corporate ladder may come only once or twice in a career. Is the job being dangled before you such an opportunity?

The most serious portion of your analysis consists of exploring the possibilities with your family. If you have a two-career family, you will have to consider the job implications for your partner. You will, of course, want to look at the figures to see how the move would affect the family budget, both for the short and long haul. The company probably will cover the immediate costs of moving. But it may not be willing to cover the difference in housing prices here and there.

Your children may also be less than delighted with their prospects. To keep a move from being a childhood trauma, consult with your kids from the start.

Lawyers

WHETHER you are buying a house, making a will or filing a suit, sooner or later you will need a lawyer. Finding the right attorney at the right price can be a trial.

You are probably better off not to search in one of the large, wood-paneled law firms. Most of those partnerships specialize in corporate work, and even if their members agree to defend you in traffic court, the meter could start ticking at $100 an hour, or considerably more. Instead, scout for a general practitioner in a moderate-size firm that handles personal and small-business affairs.

To locate one, the best advice is old-fashioned: Ask people whose judgment you trust, such as your banker, insurance agent or a member of your company's legal department. Make sure that the recommended attorneys have dealt with cases similar to yours. Your neighbor may have had a Perry Mason for his auto accident case, but that is probably not the right lawyer for your landlord-tenant dispute.

If you want additional recommendations, try your state or local bar association's lawyer referral service. The number is listed in the Yellow Pages. The referral service will give you the next name up on a list of participating attorneys. Trouble is, quality can vary widely. Some bar associations add the name of any attorney who wants to be included; others charge a fee or require only a minimum amount of experience. So ask the service what screening procedures are used. Also explain what kind of legal help you need, since many services break down their lists by specialties.

You can check the background of almost any attorney by consulting the *Martindale-Hubbell Law Directory*, available at most large public libraries. It describes the lawyers in your community and their educations. Sometimes it also gives evaluations by judges and fellow attorneys. If you need a foreign lawyer — to settle a relative's estate, for instance — write to the Overseas Citizens Counsel Services at the Department of State, Room 4817, 2201 C Street, NW, Washington, D.C. 20520, or call 202-647-3666.

Lawyers typically charge $50 for an initial consultation, but many waive the fee if they do not take the case. Do not be shy about inquiring how much time and money your case will cost. Most attorneys charge by the hour; ask for an optimistic and a pessimistic price estimate.

For routine procedures, a lawyer may charge a flat rate — say, $75 to as much as $700 for a simple will. For personal injury and damage cases, you might pay a contingency fee ranging from 30% to 40% of the amount finally collected, depending on how much work is required of your lawyer. Real estate closings are often charged as a percentage of the sales price or mortgage, typically 1%.

Remember that the fee is only one factor. Some of the least expensive advice can be as sound as the costliest. But $150 an hour for a tough, experienced specialist may be well spent — if you stand to lose heavily in a property settlement or child-custody battle.

When your problem is relatively simple, you might turn to a cut-rate legal clinic for no-frills assistance. But even clinics offer low prices only on high-volume procedures, such as wills. Handling extras might be charged by the hour — at $75 per hour in some cases.

Prepaid legal plans are an inexpensive alternative. While some are organized as benefits for groups such as labor or credit unions, others are offered to the general public. For a yearly fee, a subscriber can get unlimited telephone consultations with a lawyer. Most prepaid plans will not cover criminal cases or litigation if you want to sue through the plan. But you can get valuable preventive advice that might keep down your costs. It is cheaper to ask a lawyer what your options are if you break a lease, for example, than to pay him to go to court when your former landlord sues for a year's rent.

Storefront and Prepaid Legal Services

IN SHOPPING malls and storefronts, many discount law offices — called legal clinics — are springing up. A customer who knows what legal clinics can and cannot do, and follows a few simple rules in dealing with them, usually can get a genuine bargain.

Legal clinics generally work on routine personal law problems: uncontested divorces, simple wills, real estate closings, bankruptcies, uncomplicated personal injury suits, traffic violations and similar situations. Unlike traditional law firms, the clinics often advertise, and this generates high volume. Since most of the cases are similar, secretaries and paralegals can do the bulk of the paperwork with standardized forms. This lets the clinic's lawyers handle more clients more quickly. Another good alternative is legal assistance offered by law-school law clinics. These clinics are topic- or group-specific, such as Brooklyn Law School's Elderly Law Clinic. They offer students supervised by law professors.

Prices at clinics can be much lower than those charged at traditional law firms. For example, at any of the eight Murrin Metropolitan Attorneys-at-Law offices in the Minneapolis–St. Paul area, an uncontested divorce starts at $500 and a simple individual will at $120. Old-line law firms in the area charge in the range of $150 to $300 *an hour*. In general, the prices charged by conventional lawyers are three or four times greater than those of clinics.

Most clinics are open on evenings and weekends, so they also offer convenience. And most get good marks for competence. Yvonne Weight, a Virginia attorney who studied the discounters for three years as a member of a state bar disciplinary committee, says: "I don't recall a single neglect-of-legal-matter case on the part of clinic lawyers. They're efficient. They get their paperwork done." But she gives them lower marks for courtroom work.

Clinic lawyers did even better in a study by the University of Miami's Law and Economics Center. It found that 22 clients of California's Jacoby & Meyers clinics got cheaper, faster and better deals than 52 clients of more traditional Los Angeles law firms.

To locate clinic-style practices, thumb through the Yellow Pages for ads of law firms that list several offices and boast of low or flat fees for routine services. Then call around to comparison-shop. Unlike many traditional law firms, legal clinics usually will quote fees over the phone. Check out the firm by going in for an initial consultation — usually about $30 for half an hour or so.

Of course, not every clinic delivers high quality for its discount rates. You would be wise to get a referral from someone who has used the clinic. Also check that your case fits into the limitations of the clinic's practice and ask for an estimate of the probable fee.

Another way to save is to use one of the new prepaid legal plans. They are the legal profession's version of a health maintenance organization. You pay a fixed premium each year and are assured of at least basic legal care. The American Bar Association has strongly endorsed the idea, and quite a number of firms offer plans.

Prepaid plans can be fine for simple legal matters. A landlord who refused to return the security deposit on an apartment, for example, might change his mind if he received a letter written by a lawyer on your behalf. Or say your new car turns out to be a lemon. A prepaid service lawyer can help you get the manufacturer to make good on the warranty.

Complex problems such as a liability suit, divorce, bankruptcy or sophisticated mortgage arrangement are beyond the scope of prepaid packages. Also, the plans rarely cover court appearances. To make sure a plan suits you, you have to shop warily. Prepaid legal programs vary widely in their range of services.

For example, Lawphone (4501 Forbes Boulevard, Lanham, Maryland 20706; 800-255-3352) has member law firms in all 50 states, the District of Columbia, Puerto Rico and Canada. It offers phone consultations, review or preparation of documents and unlimited phone calls and letters on the client's behalf. If court representation is needed, Lawphone has contracted with thousands of private attorneys to give discounts of 25%. Lawphone is available directly to the public as well as through trade and professional associations. It may also be available as an employee benefit. Rates vary according to the type of plan.

Legal service plans are available to individuals in every state. California has several dozen, many of them small. In other states, including Colorado, New York and Pennsylvania, you can choose from up to 10 services. Usually you have a choice of four to six. For the programs in your state, send a stamped, self-addressed envelope to the National Resource Center for Consumers of Legal Services, 1444 I Street, NW, 8th Floor, Washington, D.C. 20005.

Settling out of Court

A MERICANS seem to sue by reflex action when they believe they have been wronged. Yet, as Abraham Lincoln once noted, "The nominal winner is often a real loser — in fees, expenses and waste of time."

When your impulse is to sue, you don't necessarily have to go to court and tell it to a judge. There are better ways to settle legal disputes. For example, you can rent a judge who is sometimes called a "dispute resolver." Or you can go to a so-called dispute mediation center to have a quarrel settled. Such innovations are cheaper, faster and simpler than traditional litigation. Basically, they offer third-party mediation — help in resolving differences.

The best-known alternative to going to court is the American Arbitration Association. Its 35 regional offices handle more than 62,000 cases a year. People who seek arbitration submit their dispute to an impartial third party for a final and binding decision.

An increasingly popular device for business people is the mini-trial. The idea is to let companies settle their own fights out of court. Representatives of two disputing companies argue out their case before top executives of both of those companies. If they then cannot reach a compromise, they bring in a third party to help, often a retired judge.

Similar mini-trials also are well suited for disputes involving, say, a homeowner and a contractor over faulty bathroom plumbing; or the owner of a wrecked auto who is claiming more damages than an insurance company is willing to pay. They hire a retired judge — and often he can sit down with both sides and work out a settlement in an afternoon. The fee might run $300 to $4,000, depending on the type of dispute.

The savings are not only in money but also in damage to the disputants' feelings. An added benefit of resolving a case out of court is privacy. So is the fact that the remedy can be flexible, shaped by the plaintiff, the defendant and the dispute resolver. Although courts award money damages, they generally cannot order a contractor to fix a leaky roof.

Most out-of-court settlements involve mediation — that is, an attempt by the persons involved to resolve their dispute with the aid of a neutral third person. The savings can be large. For instance, in Denver, a mediated divorce case with no legal counsel usually costs about $800 for a settlement agreement. A court divorce involving lawyers could run well into the thousands — for *each* side. Many of the divorce mediators around the country are lawyers with training in mediation. (For further information, see "Your Family: The Virtues of Divorce Mediation.")

To handle everyday disputes such as neighbor-against-neighbor and landlord-tenant disagreements, more than 350 mediation centers have popped up in every state in the country. They are sometimes called neighborhood justice centers, and they are usually state-supported. Not only are they fast, informal and effective, but they also charge nothing to iron out such problems as dogfights, broken windows and loud stereos.

For consumer complaints, state or local courts that hear small-claims cases often serve you well. The maximum claims range from $300 in Arkansas to $25,000 in Massachusetts. These courts are supposed to be simple, straightforward and sometimes free of lawyers. They are designed to make it easier for you to get justice, perhaps even without hiring an attorney, but because most states allow lawyers to represent either side, you might find that your opponent has hired one who outclasses you or ties you up in costly appeals. Even so, you might do very well on your own — and it will cost you only a few dollars to bring your complaint to court.

For more information on how you can get help in settling legal disputes out of court, look in the Yellow Pages under "Mediation Services." Or phone an organization named EnDispute, which provides alternative resolution services worldwide, with offices in Cambridge, Massachusetts; Chicago; and Washington, D.C.

Finally, the Better Business Bureau offers mediation and arbitration services to consumers at most of its 160 offices.

Package Delivery Services

SENDING a package overnight to almost any city in the country is a cinch these days. Several delivery services can do the job for you. But which does it best?

Among the overnight package couriers, probably the most esteemed is Federal Express. It has been in the business since 1972 and gained fame offering delivery before 10:30 a.m. the next day. Federal Express recently lost by a hair to United Parcel Service as the company with the widest reach. Big Brown, the longtime ground deliverer, boasts overnight air service to every address in the United States, including Puerto Rico. Federal Express claims it serves areas containing 99% of the population. There are two other major companies: Airborne Express and Emery Worldwide.

The U.S. Postal Service has joined the race. It will take up to 70 pounds overnight between any of 26,000 post offices in the country that accept Express Mail. Like the commercial services, the postal people will make a special trip to pick up your package. But if your letter carrier works out of an Express Mail post office, you can leave a package in your mailbox stamped and ready for pickup.

In mid-1992, prices varied greatly for the overnight delivery of a two-pound package from New York to Los Angeles. The U.S. Postal Service charged $14. United Parcel Service charged $17.25 for same-day pickup and next-day delivery — or $14 if you called in your order the day before you wanted the package picked up and sent out. Federal Express charges ranged from $14 to $24.25, depending on a number of variables, including package size and zip code of delivery. Emery Worldwide, specializing in business-to-business deliveries and the delivery of heavy packages, charged $25, including pickup and delivery, as did Airborne Express. But if you were willing to have the same package delivered within two days of pickup, Airborne Express offered the best value: $9.

All of these services offer delivery of lighter-weight letter packages for lower fees than their two-pound rates, although these vary by company as well. And many also provide delivery service overseas. For delivery of an eight-ounce document package holding up to 30 sheets of paper, prices for two-day delivery were as follows: Federal Express, UPS, and Emery Worldwide, $25; Airborne Express, $32. Of those companies, only Federal Express also provided next-day service from New York to London, at no additional cost.

Whatever service you choose, if you are sending a package to some out-of-the-way place, you may have to pay an additional fee. Post offices and delivery-service agents can tell you whether a town is on their regular rate list. Even so, it is wise to phone the person on the receiving end and find out whether one courier seems more reliable than others in his or her area.

Plumbers

FINDING a reliable, affordable plumber can be one of life's little challenges, and you should not wait for the pipes to burst before you begin looking. Every householder needs a list of good servicemen, including a plumber or two. The best way to avoid panic is to have them lined up before you need them.

When checking a plumber's reputation, you should ask how quickly he responds to emergencies, if he can be reached at night and on weekends and, of course, how much he charges. But how do you find the name of a plumber to check out? If asking your neighbors does not turn up a satisfactory specialist, the first place to try is the local affiliate of the National Association of Plumbing-Heating-Cooling Contractors (180 South Washington Street, Falls Church, Virginia 22046). It has offices in 47 states, and sometimes it is listed in the phone book as the Plumbing-Heating-Cooling Contractors Association. Most members are licensed and covered by liability insurance and workers' compensation. Their records probably will be fairly clear of complaints. The association often works with city agencies to resolve disputes that arise over a plumber's work or charges.

You pay less if you use an unlicensed, unaffiliated plumber, but if something goes wrong, you are more likely to be stuck.

So-called master plumbers are the most seasoned and best trained and can handle the toughest assignments. They have at least five to 10 years' experience and must pass a state exam. When you have a major job, the master plumber gets the appropriate building department permit. He also hires the apprentices and journeymen who do simpler repairs and installations, and he is responsible if anything goes wrong.

You also may locate reputable plumbers by calling the United Association of Journeymen and Apprentices of the Plumbing and Pipe Fitting Industry of the U.S. and Canada. In plain English, that is the plumbers' union, and it is probably listed in your telephone book under Plumbers and Pipe Fitters Local Union. The voice at the other end of the line will not recommend a specific plumber but will give you names of contractors who do use union plumbers.

Still another source is the building or plumbing inspection department at city hall. Inspectors see the work of every plumber in town, so they know good craftsmanship firsthand. If they do not want to recommend a plumber, at least they will give you an opinion about any whose names you have.

What can you expect to pay a reliable plumber? You have probably heard the old story of the brain surgeon who calls in a plumber to fix a leaky faucet. The plumber tinkers around for a few minutes and then announces, "That'll be $50."

"Heavens!" exclaims the customer. "I'm a brain surgeon, and I don't get $50 for a few minutes' work."

"Neither did I," says the plumber, "when I was a brain surgeon."

Plumbers have a well-earned reputation for high prices. You can expect to pay them between $25 and $65 an hour — and more than that at night and on weekends. That $25-to-$65 charge can be deceptive; often it applies to plumbers' travel time as well as the time they spent on the job. And rather than raise their already steep hourly rates to cover boosts in the cost of insurance and their other expenses, many plumbers choose the artifice of a so-called cartage charge of $2 to $3 tacked onto the bill for each visit. Not surprisingly, the prices are highest on the East and West coasts and lowest in the South and Midwest, notably in rural areas.

You will not be able to negotiate the price on an emergency repair job. But if you have work that can be planned in advance, you should get bids from several contractors. Plumbing is highly competitive, and you would be surprised how much the bids differ.

Some people try to save money by buying parts for their plumber. That makes no sense. You will have to buy at retail, and plumbers buy at wholesale. You will not save any money, but you will run the risk of buying the wrong parts.

Do not assume all plumbing repairs require a plumber. There are many jobs you can tackle yourself. Anyone mechanically inclined can patch small leaks, warm frozen pipes, unclog drains, repair faucet drips and replace ceramic tiles.

But beware of getting in over your head. A workman who did was cleaning the filters in a Cincinnati winery one December when he accidentally knocked open a water valve connected with the vats of wine. The rising pressure of fermenting wine caused a backflow into the municipal water system. The resulting Christmas present for the people of Cincinnati: sparkling Burgundy on tap, somewhat diluted.

Home Entertainment Repairs

G ETTING your television set, VCR or stereo repaired need not be as suspenseful or traumatic as an episode from "As the World Turns." Well-trained repairers abound, and here are some tips for finding a reasonably priced one.

Although TV sets are generally sturdy, they probably will malfunction at least once during their average 10-year life span. If your set's problem is covered by a warranty, it must be repaired by one of the manufacturer's authorized service dealers. Their addresses usually come with the TV. A relatively small percentage of TVs need repairs during standard manufacturer warranty periods, which are generally 90 days for labor, one year for parts and two years for the picture tube.

The question remains: What to do when the warranty runs out? More and more dealers are offering their customers the option of buying service contracts, or performance guarantees, which extend significantly beyond the life of the manufacturer's warranty. For example, American TV of Madison, Wisconsin (414-521-1002) sells to its walk-in and mail-order customers extended warranties underwritten by IDS Nationwide, which has 4,400 service centers throughout the U.S.

For a five-year carry-in service contract covering all parts and labor, prices are: for a 27-inch television, $69.95; for a VCR,

$109.95; for a mid-priced ($500–$800) stereo system, $74.95. Chuck Bergen of American strongly encourages his customers to buy extended service contracts on their home entertainment purchases, especially stereos and VCRs, which have many delicate moving parts that may break down before their time. He says that the cost of the service contract will, in most cases, equal the cost of one service call.

Your worst-case scenario, Bergen says, is that you will break even — unless, of course, the appliance in question is an inexpensive television. In that case you might prefer to chuck it and reinvest in an upgrade rather than spend one-third to one-half of the sticker price to prolong the life of an outdated, technologically inferior product. After all, large-screen TVs and perhaps the new HD-TVs will continue to deliver bigger and better video images.

Even if your warranty has expired, it is wise to use an authorized dealer for repairs because he or she will stock parts for your set and will have experience in fixing appliances like yours. You can find authorized dealers in the Yellow Pages under "Television Service," "Television Repairs" or "Home Electronics." If you cannot locate an authorized service dealer, make sure the repairer you choose has a place of business, not just a truck and a phone number. Some elusive operators pick up your equipment and are never heard from again.

Membership in groups such as the International Society for Certified Electronics Technicians and its affiliate, the National Electronics Sales & Service Dealers Association, provides some evidence that the repairer is competent, as well as interested in maintaining a reputation for reliability.

If possible, take your TV, stereo or VCR to the repair shop to save on the house-call service charge. Ask for a written estimate of costs in advance.

When a repairer finishes work, he or she should give you an itemized bill that guarantees the work for at least 30 days. He or she should also return to you all parts that have been replaced, except the picture tube.

Above all, do not try to repair your TV yourself. For one thing, opening the back of your set can be dangerous because color picture tubes release electrical voltage for hours after the set has been unplugged.

Long-Distance Phone Service

I**T'S** BEEN a decade since a federal court decree ended AT&T's monopoly of America's telephone service, thereby triggering a fierce competition that started in the boom years of the 1980s and continues unabated in the slower-growth 1990s. True, AT&T is still on top, retaining about two-thirds of Americans' long-distance telephone business. Of its two chief rivals in mid-1992, MCI claimed about 19% of the market and Sprint had nearly 10%. But none of the companies is taking anything for granted: in 1990 AT&T spent nearly $800 million on advertising, and Sprint made its spokesperson, Candice Bergen, a household name long before Dan Quayle assailed her soundness on family values.

What does this competition mean to you? You may have noticed a drop in your monthly phone bill: according to the *Wall Street Journal*, by late 1991 overall phone rates had declined 45% from 1984 levels. But if you're one of the millions of phone users who spend less than $7 a month on long distance — over half the total, according to Gene Kimmelman, legislative director of the Consumer Federation of America — the new phone order has hardly affected you. On the other hand, if you live in Chicago and have family in San Diego or abroad, if you travel a lot, or if you own a small business, you should pay attention to all those commercials. They could help you tailor a telephone service plan that will save you serious money.

Basic rates don't differ much among the major providers. They all charge about 75 cents (exclusive of taxes) for a three-minute call from Chicago to San Diego, and about 40 cents for such a call at night. It's their many special long-distance plans that could offer you special advantages. With MCI's Friends and Family, for instance, you can get a 20% discount on all calls you make, at whatever time of the day or night, to the people you call most often. You just give MCI a list of these folks (whether or not they're MCI customers), and there's a 20% saving when one person within the Friends and Family circle calls another. In mid-1992 Sprint came up with The Most, a plan giving Sprint customers 20% off each month on calls to whomever they phone the most, even if the favored person lives in a foreign country. If that person is also a Sprint customer, the original customer's discount will come to 36%.

Don't overlook what local long-distance companies — yes, there are such — have to offer. One example is Least Cost Rating, an option offered by Cincinnati Bell, which serves Ohio, Indiana, Kentucky and western Pennsylvania. Each long-distance call is charged at the lowest rate offered by AT&T, MCI or Sprint — a real boon for Cincinnati Bell's clientele of residential and small-business customers.

You're somewhat daunted by the prospect of choosing among all these options? TRAC — Telecommunications Research and Action Center — will send you a chart, updated twice a year, showing the long-distance rates of major carriers and comparing special features such as volume discounts. Send a self-addressed, stamped envelope, plus $2 for a chart of residential phone service rates or $5 for one covering small-business options, to TRAC, P.O. Box 12038, Washington, D.C. 20005; 202-462-2520.

What kind of service can the big companies provide when you're traveling? You're probably familiar with AT&T's Calling Card: you can charge a call to your home phone number from almost anywhere in the world just by giving the local operator your Calling Card number (usually your home phone number plus four digits). That's not the only traveler's aid on offer. AT&T's USA-Direct, for example, can help you in more than 40 countries. With this option you can call a local number and reach a U.S. operator — and get quite a saving if you're staying in one of the all too numerous hotels that add big surcharges to guests' calls.

Possibly the ultimate in universal connections at home or abroad — as of mid-1992, at any rate — is a service like MCI's Personal 800. For a mere $5 a month this plan lets an MCI customer give his own 800 number to family and friends, who can then call him from anywhere in the U.S.; all calls are billed to the 800 customer at 25 cents a minute. Not to be outdone, AT&T is offering Easy Reach 700. For a one-time charge of $25, this plan will assign you a permanent 700 number, which you can give to family, friends and customers. You then can dial AT&T on a touch-tone phone — several times a day, if need be — and tell a computer to route your calls to whatever number you direct. This service, available for the moment only in the "lower 48" states, costs you $7 a month, plus 25 cents a minute at peak times and 15 cents a minute off-peak. One thing that inspired such a scheme is that AT&T's research revealed that the average highly mobile American has 11 phone numbers in his or her lifetime. For the customer who's really on the go, Easy Reach might bring that down to one.

The long-distance phone companies certainly aren't neglecting their fellow businesspeople, including those with payrolls a fraction the size of IBM's. If you run your own small company, it will pay you to keep up with what's being offered. In the spring of 1992, for example, MCI, the originator of Friends and Family, inaugurated Friends of the Firm for small businesses — those with $2,000 or less a month in long-distance bills. MCI will sort a company's bills to determine its most frequently called numbers. The company then gets a discount on calls to the 20 numbers it calls the most; it also gets discounts on fax transmissions, calls from car phones and overseas calls.

To counter its competitors at MCI, AT&T swiftly rolled out its Partners in Business program, offering discounts of up to 20% to companies spending $25 to $2,000 a month on long distance. And AT&T has other programs as well, including its Area Code Option, which gives a 20% discount on calls to the U.S. area code that a customer dials the most.

Where is Sprint in the small-business sweepstakes? Right up there with the front-runners, with a plan guaranteeing its small-business customers prices at least 20% lower than AT&T's direct-dial rates.

There's hardly a field covered in this *Money Guide* — with the exception, perhaps, of airline fares — where the competition is fiercer or the options for consumers more numerous, and more likely to change literally from week to week. Not to speak of the extra goodies: you might find a frequent-caller program that offers you discounts on car rentals or has a tie-in with one of your credit cards. But keep your head. Whether you're shopping for phone service for your home or for your business, first determine what you need and then look for a company that will give you exactly that. Chances are these days you'll soon find what you're looking for.

Your Savings

How Much to Put Away

AFTER a few years when interest rates paid on our savings ran well ahead of inflation, rates have plummeted. And with inflation at 3.2% and a 3% interest rate taxed at 28%, savers can get left in the hole.

High interest rates or low, Americans are not great savers. In the last dozen years or so, they put aside anywhere from an average of 2.8% (in late 1987) to 7.5% (in 1981) of their after-tax income. Comparisons with people in other countries are difficult because methods of measuring savings vary, but according to their statistics, the West Germans save 13.5% and the Japanese 14.8% of their incomes. By any measure, they put away substantially more than Americans do.

Saving, of course, means accumulating money for a specific purpose — a down payment on a house, a college education, a comfortable retirement — or for use in an emergency. You put your savings in secure places that promise to both preserve your capital and pay you steady income.

Investing, by contrast, involves accepting the risk of losing your money in exchange for a chance to earn richer gains. Thus, the amount that you should be saving depends on your age, your family responsibilities, your career prospects and even your outlook on life.

If you are reasonably young, have few or no family responsibilities and face strong earning prospects in the future, you can afford to save relatively less and invest relatively more. But if you have children to educate or are rapidly approaching retirement, you should save more and invest less. You also should follow this course if you are basically a conservative, risk-averse person or if you believe that the future prospects for America and it's economy are not ebullient.

How much should you put away? One good but *bare minimum* plan is this:

— Between the ages of 30 and 40, save or invest 5% of your pretax income.

— Then *increase* that amount by one percentage point a year between the ages of 40 and 45.

— After you are 45, aim to put away at least 10% a year — and preferably more.

Ways to Save More

Far too many Americans think they just cannot afford to save at all. If you are one of those who never seem to have anything left from your paycheck, examine your expenditures and see where you can cut back. If you are spending more than 15% to 20% of your take-home pay to meet installment debts beyond home mortgage payments, it is too much. Give the credit cards a rest.

Perhaps 20% of your spending money is going for food. Then you may have been eating too high on the hog. The national average is 15%. If you spend much more than 10% on clothing, consider slipping out of designer jeans and into less expensive models. Most people put about 5% of their expenditures into clothes.

But keep in mind that every family has unique needs. For example, if you live in an expensive city such as San Francisco, your housing costs may be twice what they would be in Denver. The average U.S. household invests just over 31% of its spending money in housing.

After you have discovered the budget items you can reasonably trim, concentrate on the one area that you want to augment — your savings.

The best way to build your savings is to treat them as a necessity. Put a fixed amount into savings each month. If doing that takes more discipline than you can muster, enroll in your company's payroll savings plan, which will deduct a regular amount from your salary before you ever see it. Use this amount to buy risk-free Series EE U.S. savings bonds. Or arrange with your bank or mutual-fund company to withdraw a certain amount from your checking account each month and automatically deposit it in a savings or investment account.

Aim to build an emergency cash reserve. It should equal at least three months' worth of living expenses. Since this cash must be readily available, store it in a money-market mutual fund or bank money-market deposit account. A bank certificate of deposit usually will pay you more, but you will forfeit much of that difference if you have to withdraw the cash early.

Once you have provided for emergencies, start saving for specific purposes. Saving is like dieting: it's tough to do unless you set goals. So set short-, medium- and long-range goals. Short-term objectives could include saving for a summer holiday or for Christmas. A three- to five-year target might be buying a vacation house or paying cash for a new car. The major long-term goals are educating the children and saving for a secure retirement.

What is the secret of saving more? Simply this: *Pay yourself first.* When you collect your paycheck, do not rush out and spend it all. Lay away a fixed amount every week or every month for your *own* savings or investments. That is paying yourself first — and it is smart.

Where to Put Your Savings Now

THIS is no time to be taking needless chances with your money. But it is possible to put your cash into institutions or instruments offering returns that are safe and guaranteed.

Where is the best place to put your savings now?

Among the many safe and rewarding places are money-market funds, bank money-market deposit accounts, bank certificates of deposit and U.S. Treasury securities. (All are discussed in the following sections.) Bonds hold out tempting yields, too, but they are riskier because their face value — the price you buy or sell them for — rises and falls along with the gyrations of interest rates.

When determining where to put your savings, you have to weigh and balance off three traditional concerns. They are: *yield* (How much am I earning on my money?), *liquidity* (How quickly can I withdraw my money if I need it?) and *safety* (Am I sure to get back every penny I put in?).

Considering all those factors, here are some guidelines:

The best all-around place to put short-term savings is in one of the money-market funds offered by mutual-fund companies and brokerage firms. They usually give you higher yields than banks, as well as instant liquidity and strong safety. For even more safety, consider two money-market funds that invest solely in securities of the U.S. government and its agencies: Calvert Insured Plus (4550 Montgomery Avenue, Suite 1000N, Bethesda, Maryland 20814; 800-368-2748) and GIT Insured Money Market Account (1655 Fort Myer Drive, Arlington, Virginia 22209; 800-336-3063). You must deal with Calvert through a broker, but you can contact GIT yourself. When you open an account with either firm, it will invest your money at a bank or savings and loan with which it has negotiated a variable rate of return competitive with those of uninsured money-market funds. Each depositor's account is kept separate so that it can be protected up to the $100,000 federal deposit insurance limit.

Calvert, by maintaining accounts in two FDIC-insured commercial banks, makes it possible to insure as much as $200,000. Those banks pay Calvert customers the 90-day Treasury bill rate. GIT works with four savings and loans, which together can insure $400,000 per depositor. The rate paid is adjusted weekly to equal the average auction discount rate for 91-day Treasury bills, as reported by the U.S. Treasury, less 0.6% per year.

If you prefer the convenience of a nearby bank, you can put your money in a federally insured bank money-market deposit account. You give up some advantage in yield — normally about 1.4 percentage points when money funds were paying more than 8.25% in 1990 — but when interest rates fall as sharply as they did in 1992, the differential all but disappears. Whatever you give up in yield at the bank, at least you can deal face-to-face with your neighborhood bankers there. Also, if you ever need a loan, it is often easier to get if you have some money on deposit in a bank.

If you are in a high tax bracket, you are probably best off in one of the tax-free money-market funds. They are offered by mutual-fund companies and in September 1992 were paying about 2.3% — free of federal income taxes. For someone in the 31% tax bracket, that's the same as 3.3% taxable interest.

It does not make much sense to put considerable savings into an ordinary passbook account. These days you would get only 3% interest on it — all taxable — at a commercial bank, savings bank or savings and loan association. You can earn a bit more at the very same institution merely by switching to other forms of savings. With $1,000 or less, you can open a money-market deposit account. And you can buy a bank certificate of deposit for $500 or less. Some banks hold out for higher minimum deposits, however, so shop around.

If you have at least $5,000 to deposit, ask the banker if that will qualify you for a special bonus rate. Many banks and savings and loans pay their bigger savers more. Healthy S&Ls often pay slightly higher rates than banks do.

Traditionally, the longer you were willing to tie up your money, the better yield you would get. That's another tradition that barely holds in the current low-interest environment. As of September 1992, six-month certificates yielded an average 3.2%. If you put some savings on ice for a year, you would have earned an average 3% — not much of an advantage.

Your Best Deals in Banking

THE revolution in banking set off by deregulation in the 1980s wasn't all bad. Sure, it left half the industry in ruins and saddled American taxpayers with a bill that, by one reasonable estimate, may amount to $130 billion to cover insured deposits. But it also led to better-regulated competition.

In mid-1992 new Federal Insurance Deposit Corporation rules placed limits on the rates weaker banks can offer customers, while allowing well-capitalized banks — which, happily, means nearly three-quarters of the country's commercial banks — to set their own rates. Such regulations spelled the end of the upward-spiraling rates of the 1980s, when small, undercapitalized institutions offered ever-higher premiums and made ever-riskier loans — major contributors to the S&L crisis. Though it's now a waste of time to go looking for sky-high rates at your neighborhood bank, you can feel more confident about the safety of your funds in a top-rated bank. Yet there are still differences among banks — in the variety of their services, for example, and the size of their fees. So the common-sense advice still applies: Shop around for your best deals in banking.

The neighborhood bank is probably still the best place for your checking account, but not necessarily for your savings. Passbook savings accounts are used little, except by children and senior citizens with small sums on deposit, because they don't pay as well as money-market savings accounts. You sometimes can earn more at no risk by putting your money into certificates of deposit sold not by banks but by stockbrokers. And you might be able to earn more by using the mail to put your savings in an out-of-state institution.

In many ways, it makes sense to give all your banking business to one institution. This is called "relationship banking," and in return for it, you often can get higher interest on your savings or lower fees on your checking or better terms on a loan. That's because when all your banking business is lumped together, you usually become a fairly big customer. For example, if your balance in a money-market deposit account or a NOW account exceeds $5,000, you may earn a fraction of a percentage point more interest than do customers with smaller accounts. But relationship banking does cost you something. If instead you used many different financial institutions, each for a different service, you might get still better deals.

Your Best Deals in Checking Accounts

A GREAT place to put your money is in a checking account that also earns interest. Traditionally, that's just what you get with money-market accounts and NOW accounts. But they all have limitations, and the NOW accounts can be downright tricky when it comes to figuring minimum balances and interest rates.

While the minimum deposit for opening an account varies from bank to bank, you typically need $500 to start a NOW account and $1,000 to $2,500 for a money-market account. All banks used to require that you maintain balances of at least $1,000 if you wanted to earn the interest rates paid by money-market deposit accounts. But minimums for a NOW — where Americans have $300 billion deposited — are commonly much less.

Watch out: Most banks have monthly charges that can add up, especially if you are likely to keep only a small balance in your account. According to a 1990 survey by the Consumer Federation of America, a NOW account costs small depositors an average $111 a year, *after* interest income.

Here's a sure way to save money on your checking account: Have your checks printed elsewhere. You can knock off about half the price of replacement checks by ordering checks over the phone from independent suppliers. Checks in the Mail (800-733-4443) charges $4.95 for 200 checks printed with the same name, address, account number and computer codes that appear on your current checks. Current, Inc. (800-426-0822) charges $4.95 for your first 200-check order and $6.95 for reorders.

When you shop around, the surest way to compare is to find out exactly how much money you will have in your account at the end of the year if you deposit, say, $100 on the first of the year. In any case, it's wise to call half a dozen banks and S&Ls and compare fees. When you are gathering information, be sure to ask how minimum balances are calculated and find out how much it costs if you slip under the minimum.

Your best buy in checking accounts depends on how much money you have and how many checks you write. For example, there's a non-interest-bearing account with no minimum and only a small balance required. Here are some of your choices:

If you write few checks, so-called economy checking may be for you. It costs $2 to $3 a month, plus 20 to 25 cents per check. Or there's regular checking, with no minimum to open and costs of $5 to $6 a month. Usually you have to maintain a $500 minimum balance. Some banks will allow 15 to 20 free checks a month, so shop around. These accounts pay no interest.

More advantageous — but far less so than it used to be — is the NOW account. It usually takes $500 to open and carries a $5 to $8 monthly fee — avoidable if you keep your minimum balance at $500 or more. Unfortunately, you won't get much interest. According to Hugo Ottolenghi of *Bank Rate Monitor*, the average NOW account paid annual interest of 2.80% in mid-1992, the lowest rate since NOW accounts were introduced a decade ago. But you usually get some free checks: most banks will throw in 20 free checks a month.

There are two types of money-market checking accounts, so you want to be sure to choose the one that is better tailored for you. One is a transaction account, which you have to put up $1,000 to open. It usually gives you 20 free checks a month and charges you 25 cents per check after that. A monthly fee of $5 to $10 can be avoided if you keep $2,500 or more in the account. Interest paid by this account will be about 3%; it varies according to market conditions. At certain times you may find that in some banks there is almost no difference between the interest paid by the NOW and money-market accounts.

The second kind of money-market account is often called an investment account. It is more of a savings account than a transaction account, though you'll be allowed to write three free checks a month. (Any more can cost you $10 a check.) You'll find this account more flexible than a certificate of deposit — you can deposit and withdraw money at will. It has largely replaced the old passbook savings account.

Though you will probably never bounce a check, you might be curious to know what the returned-check charges are for those unfortunate people who do. The cost now varies from $5 to $25. The average is $15. An overdraft checking account will make your account bounce-proof, but you will pay interest, lately 18% or more, for at least one month, on overdrafts. And there may be a *minimum* fee on any overdraft.

Another option to consider is joining a credit union. You can join through your place of work, through a club, even through a church. Call the Credit Union National Association (800-356-9655, extension 4045) to find out what you need to do. Mid-1992 saw credit unions paying slightly higher rates on checking accounts than banks (3.5% versus 3.1%), and fully 66% of them don't charge their customers any fees. Only 20% or 30% of banking customers manage to escape paying for the privilege of holding a checking account. The average fee for those who do pay is $2.88 a month. To be safe, make certain to ask for federal insurance, as about 5% of credit unions are privately insured.

How Safe Are Deposits
in Banks and S&Ls?

THE EIGHTIES boom years crashed to a halt in 1989. More banks and savings institutions failed in that year than at any time since the Depression. The enormous cost of bailing them out, as well as shoring up those near failure, raised unsettling questions about insured deposits at banks, S&Ls and credit unions.

S&Ls, the so-called thrifts, have suffered the greatest losses. From 1988 to 1991, more than 600 of these institutions were closed or sold. In the earlier years of the debacle, over half the failures were in Texas; more recently attention was focused on New England, where some 60 S&Ls were closed in 1991 and 1992. The Bush administration created the Resolution Trust Corporation to put insolvent S&Ls into conservatorship, which meant that the federal government would oversee their operations, closing or merging thrifts that failed largely because of risky investments and fraud. In the spring of 1992 Albert V. Casey, head of the RTC, estimated that the total cost of the bailout to the taxpayer would be $130 billion — a huge sum, but substantially less than the $500 billion that had once been projected.

Setting up the RTC was only one of the measures taken by the federal government and by banks to prevent future grand-scale disasters. For example, the federal government, not state governments or private concerns, now insures almost all banks, S&Ls and credit unions. Banks nationwide have added more than $140 billion in new capital and reserves since 1980.

For your own protection, find out what kind of insurance your institution has. The Federal Deposit Insurance Corporation guarantees up to $100,000 per depositor in 12,300 commercial and savings banks and about 2,100 S&Ls (this includes the insolvent ones). The FDIC can ask for additional money from the U.S. Treasury if it needs to — and in 1992, with its insurance reserves drastically depleted by the S&L debacle, the FDIC, for the first time in its history, expected to make such a request. Equal amounts of insurance coverage come with deposits in credit unions that belong to the

National Credit Union Share Insurance Fund — which has a much higher ratio than does the FDIC of reserves to deposits.

If you had money in one of these federally insured institutions and it should fail, you probably would not even feel the collapse. Government regulators can arrange a takeover or merger so quickly that your bank's doors would never have to be closed. At worst, you might have to wait a few days to collect your money and forgo interest payments during that period. But remember: Insurance will cover your deposits only up to $100,000 in each account. If you are fortunate enough to have more than that, open another insured account at another bank.

There are ways to expand the $100,000 limit. If you are married, you can have one account in your name, another in your spouse's name and a third joint account. Thus a married couple between them can have $300,000 in federally insured deposits. But you can have no more than $100,000 under the same name even if you have more than one ordinary account. Say you have $70,000 in a money-market account and $40,000 in a certificate of deposit, both under your name at the same bank. Your combined $110,000 exceeds the insurance limit by $10,000.

As with most regulatory matters, there are exceptions — and the first concerns your Individual Retirement Accounts. If you have an IRA at a bank or an S&L, any money-market deposit accounts or savings certificates in it will be insured separately. In this way, a married couple can have as much as $500,000 federally insured at the same institution: $100,000 in each of their regular accounts, $100,000 in their joint account and $100,000 in each of their IRAs.

The other exception concerns testamentary accounts, also known as revocable trusts. Their funds are paid directly to a beneficiary upon the death of the owner. When payable to a spouse, child or grandchild, the account is insured up to $100,000 separately from the $100,000 coverage granted to individual, joint or IRA accounts.

Bank Money-Market Accounts

U SUALLY, when interest rates in general are low, money-market deposit accounts at banks or savings and loan associations yield just slightly less than ordinary money-market mutual funds. Banks have considerable overhead — all those tellers and big buildings — and that makes it hard for them to pay more than the money funds.

If your savings are in a bank or savings and loan passbook account yielding only 3% or so, ask about an insured money-market deposit account at the same institution. In mid-1992 bank money-market accounts were yielding an average of only 3%. But more typically, the money-market accounts have the edge by about half a percent. These accounts also offer convenience. Most banks let you write checks on them for any amount, although they limit the number of checks you can write each month to anybody except yourself. By contrast, the money-market funds often restrict you to checks of $250 or $500 or more. Also, some merchants are readier to accept local bank checks than those drawn on a money-market fund in Moose Jaw.

If you are a particularly safety-minded person, then federal deposit insurance makes a bank money-market account or NOW checking account attractive.

Certificates of Deposit

SOMETIMES it pays to tie your money up for several months in bank certificates of deposit. But as we've seen, not lately. While ordinary passbook accounts usually yield only 3% at best, one-year CDs in September 1992 were paying an average 3.36% — not much of an advantage.

But you may be inclined — for reasons of convenience or safety — to invest in a CD anyway. You'll be reassured to know that as of March 1993, the new Truth in Savings law will regulate how the bank figures the interest on your CD (and on your interest-bearing checking account as well as your savings account). A major provision of this complex law requires the bank to calculate interest on the full principal in the account each day.

Nevertheless, you should always check whether the bank or savings institution will pay you simple interest or compound interest. The yield on a simple-interest CD is much lower than you might expect. Let's say you bought a $1,000 five-year simple-interest certificate paying 6%. It would pay you $60 interest every year, for a total of $300. Yet if that five-year CD paid the usual 6% compounded quarterly, you would end up with more interest — $347 — after five years.

Often you should be more concerned about the term of a CD than about the interest rate it pays, as you may wish to lock in a slightly higher rate for a longer period of time rather than the lower rate for the shorter term. For example, in mid-1989 the top six-month CD rate was around 10.70%, while the top five-year rate was closer to 10.25%. Then rates proceeded to decline. It turned out that investors who bought the five-year CDs locked in a rate that was nearly six full points higher than the rates that were offered in mid-1992. Generally, if rates are dropping, buy longer-term CDs; if they are rising, keep your maturities short.

Be sure to find out what the bank's penalties are for early withdrawal. Many banks are afraid of losing their CD funds, so they try to discourage early withdrawals by tacking on stiff penalties. Others, eager to attract investors, ease restrictions to make the accounts more liquid. In any case, thoroughly interview your banker before you buy a CD.

Also find out how you will be notified when your CD comes due. The bank should send you a reminder a few weeks before you have to decide whether to withdraw or redeposit the money.

You can usually get a little more interest by putting your money into a certificate of deposit at a brokerage house instead of a bank. Many stockbrokers buy small-denomination CDs in bulk from banks. The brokers then offer the certificates to the public in $1,000 units. Just like the CDs you get at a bank or savings and loan, brokered CDs have the ironclad backing of the Federal Deposit Insurance Corporation.

These CDs, however, don't pay compounded interest. The broker usually moves each interest payment to a money-market fund that is part of your account. There, the interest rate is likely to be lower than the rate your CD is paying. On the plus side, when you buy a CD through a broker, you can often sell it before it matures and not suffer the early-withdrawal penalty you would pay if you cashed it at the bank. And you will not be charged a commission.

Brokers trade CDs the way they trade bonds. So if interest rates rise after you buy a CD, your certificate's value falls. But if rates drop, you can sell out early at a profit. All in all, brokered CDs are usually a better deal than bank or savings and loan CDs.

Out-of-State Deposits

E VEN if banks and S&Ls in your state pay relatively low interest, you are free to get in on the highest rates, wherever you can find them. Just about every bank or savings and loan accepts out-of-state deposits. Institutions in states other than your own may pay a point or two more on your savings. You will have to deal with them by mail, but for a 29-cent stamp, you might earn an extra $100 a year on a $10,000 deposit.

To deposit your savings out of state is easy. Most banks will assign you an account number by phone. You then start the account by mailing in a check made out to your new account number. Be sure to endorse the check and write "For Deposit Only" on the back. And by all means make sure you know how long the quoted rate will be in effect. Some banks change their rates daily.

Watch out for institutions that insure themselves by pooling money in a fund. This insurance may not be enough in a pinch — as was shown in Ohio and Maryland, where some privately insured savings and loan associations briefly had to close or limit withdrawals in 1985. You are almost always safer doing business with a federally insured institution.

Federally insured banks in some parts of the country have been offering above-market rates. For example, on its money-market accounts with a minimum deposit of $1,000, AFBA Industrial Bank in Colorado Springs in September 1992 was paying an annual percentage yield of up to 4%.

If you have savings that you can tie up for a little while, consider putting them in a one-year certificate of deposit. Here too, AFBA Industrial Bank offered an attractive rate in mid-1992: 4.90% on a $1,000 deposit. Or, if you didn't need the money for five years, in mid-1992 you could have bought CDs that yielded 6.82% at Metropolitan Bank for Savings of Arlington, Virginia.

You can find out where the highest yields are now by looking in financial newspapers and magazines, such as the *Wall Street Journal*, *Barron's* and *Money*.

Two weekly banking newsletters can help you search for the best returns. One is called *100 Highest Yields* (P.O. Box 088888, North

Palm Beach, Florida 33408-8888). It ranks only federally insured institutions, and it costs $98 for one year. Another newsletter is *Rate Watch* (P.O. Drawer 145510, Coral Gables, Florida 33114-5510). It rates federally insured institutions that its publisher considers sound, and it costs $39 for three months, $59 for six months or $99 a year. Also, an information and money broker service that quotes the highest yields at federally insured banks across the country is *Banxquote Online* by Masterfund, Inc. (2001 Fairfield Drive, Wilmington, Delaware 19810; 800-325-3242). You can call and speak directly to brokers who will offer the highest CD and money-market rates in the country. There is no charge for this service.

Once you have selected several banks to explore, write or phone each of them for an application form and information on rates, minimum deposits and withdrawal penalties. To be on the safe side, request a copy of the institution's most recent financial statement.

Also ask about credit-card policies for nonresidents. Several banks offer no-fee Visa and MasterCards nationally, sparing you the usual annual fee of $15 to $45. Others generally charge a fee but keep interest rates on their cards at 11% to 19%, although Wachovia Bank in Georgia recently dropped its rates to 8.9% and plans to keep rates at 2.9% above the prime lending rate.

Money-Market Mutual Funds

MONEY-MARKET funds that are sold by mutual-fund companies and brokerage firms have been a big bonanza for small savers. They have usually returned comfortably more than the inflation rate, reaching stratospheric heights in 1982 and 1983. No longer. By September 1992, they tumbled to an average seven-day compound rate of 3.05%.

The chief measure of a money fund's safety is the quality of the investments that its managers make with your money. (Under SEC rules, all general-purpose funds take similar low risks.) In effect, the funds make short-term loans to federal, state and local governments as well as to corporations and U.S. and foreign banks. Generally, the funds that tack on the lowest charge for management expenses pay the highest yields.

Some safety-first investors have flocked to money-market funds that buy only government securities, such as Capital Preservation Fund and Dreyfus 100% U.S. Treasury. These often pay a sixth of a point to a point less than ordinary money funds. Almost invariably, you feel quite secure investing in a regular money fund, particularly if it is run by a well-established mutual-fund group or brokerage firm. But to sleep even more soundly at night, check that the average maturity of the fund's securities is 60 days or less by asking the fund or looking at IBC/Donoghue's Money Fund Tables, published in more than 70 newspapers. Longer maturities do not give fund managers enough flexibility. If interest rates rise and the fund is locked into securities that pay lower rates, disgruntled shareholders might start a drastic withdrawal of their funds.

Choosing a money-market fund only because of its high yield can be a mistake. Since most ordinary money funds make the same kind of investments, their returns are usually within a fraction of one percentage point of each other. You might be wiser to seek out money funds that let you shift your assets into *other* kinds of mutual funds when you think interest rates are nosing down and the stock market is heading up. Some money funds have such exchange agreements with independent mutual funds. Other money funds belong to one of the many fund families. These families also have funds that invest in stocks, and usually in corporate, government and tax-exempt bonds.

Once you invest in a family, as a rule you can shift your cash from, say, a money fund into a stock mutual fund merely by making a phone call. Often the transfer costs nothing, and generally you can move your money around as often as you like. But a few fund families limit the switches in various ways to protect themselves against a sudden loss of assets in any one fund.

A number of companies have good reputations for performance and offer a variety of funds. A sampling of the families that meet those criteria includes Fidelity, Kemper, Putnam, T. Rowe Price, Scudder, Stein Roe & Farnham, Vanguard — and many more.

Your own selection of a mutual-fund family should be based chiefly on how well its stock funds have performed over the past decade. The time may come when you want to transfer some assets from your money-market fund to your stock mutual fund. If you have chosen your fund group carefully, you will be able to keep it all in the family.

One newsletter that covers money-market funds as well as their mutual-fund families is *Donoghue's Money Letter* (Box 91004, 290 Eliot Street, Ashland, Massachusetts 01721; 800-343-5413). A one-year subscription is $109.

How Safe Are the Money Funds?

I F YOU have put cash in a money-market fund, not only are your savings collecting relatively high interest (the key word here is *relatively*), but most probably they are quite safe. Certainly, money-market funds have most of the convenient attributes of bank checking accounts. Almost always, you can take out, dollar for dollar, what you have put in, plus dividends. These are usually declared daily and automatically credited to your account once a month.

However, there are some risks. Although investors look upon money-market funds as reliable alternatives to the friendly neighborhood bank, even the soundest of them are a bit chancier than banks. Money-fund interest rates can plummet; as of September 1992 they were only slightly higher than passbook rates.

In 1989, two big funds catering to the general public, Value Line Cash Fund and Unified Management's Liquid Green Trust, were clobbered by losses in their holdings of commercial paper, a form of corporate IOU. They had each loaned several million dollars to Integrated Resources, a major dealer in limited partnerships. Integrated defaulted when its partnership business went into a tailspin, the victim of tax reform and the real estate recession. Fortunately for shareholders, both funds' sponsors bailed them out by absorbing the loss. Similarly, in 1990 half a dozen funds, including T. Rowe Price Prime Reserve and Prudential-Bache's Money-Mart Assets, took losses on the commercial paper of Mortgage & Realty Trust, a real estate investment trust, after rating services downgraded the firm's credit rating. Again, the sponsor absorbed the losses.

Since 1990 government regulations have limited money funds' purchases of commercial paper — their riskiest holdings — to issues in the top two rating levels, AAA and AA, and to unrated paper of equal quality. Even so, remember that no law says that financial institutions that sponsor money funds must make good on shareholders' losses. The lesson for investors is not to abandon money funds but rather to choose them with care. Here are three guidelines:

First, know the manager or sponsor. You need not entrust your money to complete strangers. You may already do business with a firm that sponsors a money fund — say, a brokerage house, a life insurance company or a mutual-fund group. A sponsor with an established reputation for financial responsibility will not jeopardize that reputation by abandoning its customers. Strong sponsorship can give investors more peace of mind.

Second, go for funds whose securities have a low average maturity. The temptation of money fund managers is to extend their maturities and lock in high returns when they think interest rates are about to fall. These days, however, a Securities and Exchange Commission rule compels most funds to stay within an upper limit of 60 days. By going longer, the funds risk having to report sharp cuts in daily dividends if they guess wrong and rates rise. That could cause their shareholders to switch to higher-paying funds. You should favor a fund that doesn't stray far from the pack. When other funds are hovering around the 35-day mark, be wary of those with average maturities in the 40s or 50s.

Third — and to repeat — don't chase after the highest possible yields, or the hottest fund of the month. Over a year's time, the difference in interest payments between one fund and another is likely to be inconsequential. The customer shouldn't be greedy. He or she should expect a reasonable rate of return.

You can look up the rating of your money-market fund in a newsletter called *Income & Safety*. It ranks the 135 largest funds from AAA+ through BBB on the basis of the diversification, maturity and quality of their investments. It also rounds up the 10 best yields for money markets and the 70 best yields for CDs and rates the banks for safety. For a free copy of this newsletter, write to *Income & Safety*, 3471 North Federal Highway, Fort Lauderdale, Florida 33306 (800-327-6720). An annual subscription costs $100 and includes access to the *Income & Safety* hotline, updated weekly.

Treasury Securities

IF YOU are looking for the safest place in the world to invest your money, look to the federal government. Uncle Sam borrows more than $200 billion a year, and if he cannot pay his debts, he can always print more money.

The government securities with the most appeal for individual investors are Treasury bills, notes and bonds.

Bills are sold in minimum denominations of $10,000, and they come in three-, six- and 12-month maturities.

Notes are usually sold in minimum denominations of $5,000 when they have maturities of less than five years — and in minimums of $1,000 when they have maturities of five years or more. You can get them in maturities ranging from two years to 10 years.

Treasury bonds also sell in minimums of $1,000 but have maturities of more than 10 years. If you were grading these bonds on a report card, their yields of 7.9% for 30-year issues in April 1992 would earn them marks of A-minus or B-plus. They paid a percentage point or so less than similar debt issues of top-rated corporations. But all government securities rate an A-plus for safety.

You can buy Treasury issues through any of the 12 Federal Reserve banks or 25 branch offices. Or you can order them by mail, using forms that you get from your local Fed bank.

The securities come to market at various intervals. For example, three- and six-month bills are auctioned off every Monday; 12-month bills are sold every four weeks, on a Thursday; two-year and five-year notes are generally sold at the end of each month; seven-year notes are sold in January, April, July and October. Three-year and 10-year notes and 30-year bonds are generally sold in February, May, August and November.

You also can buy Treasuries from a commercial bank or your broker. This eliminates much of the hassle but can cost from $30 to $60 and can wipe out a significant part of your return.

One problem: You will pay a rather stiff penalty if you ever want to sell your government securities before they mature. Just as brokers will charge a small investor substantially more than the market price if he is buying, so they will pay him substantially less if he is selling. Thus you are best off sticking to new government issues and holding them until they mature.

One big benefit: The interest you earn on Treasury securities is exempt from state and local taxes. And when you buy a Treasury bill, you get another nice extra. Let's take one example with round numbers for easy calculation: If you buy, say, a $10,000 10% one-year bill, it will cost you only $9,000 — that is, $10,000 minus 10%. A year later you will be paid the full $10,000. The real interest that you will collect is your $1,000 profit divided by your $9,000 investment. In fact, that's not 10% but a fat 11.1%.

Your Borrowing

Your Best Deals in Loans

IT USED to be that borrowing could actually save you money in the long run. When inflation was running wild, it made sense to avoid future price increases by buying on credit. No longer. Inflation has been moderate, so the real cost of some borrowing has been at one of its highest points in years.

In mid-1992 banks were charging an average 18.6% on your credit-card purchases. Well, subtract the roughly 3% inflation rate from the 18.6% interest rate, and you see that you would be paying a real rate of more than 15% on your credit-card loan. Compare that with the real rate in 1980. Back then it was only 4%!

Moreover, interest on consumer loans such as car, college and credit-card loans is no longer deductible, making much borrowing even more expensive than it was a couple of years ago. That increases the pressure on you to carefully consider your many credit choices and to shop around for the most favorable rates and terms.

There is nothing wrong with borrowing — provided that you do it wisely. Never borrow more than you can reasonably pay off. Never borrow for luxuries, such as gifts and vacation travel, if that means you will not be able to borrow for necessities, such as mortgage, medical or education expenses.

You should be sure, of course, that you are getting the most economical interest-rate deal. You may well be best off borrowing from a credit union, if you belong to one, or taking out a lump-sum loan from a bank or a savings institution and paying it back in installments. In mid-1992 major banks in New York City, for example, were charging about 9% for personal loans that you could secure with collateral such as a savings account, CDs, stocks or bonds. For unsecured loans — which you often can get if you have a good job or regular income and can afford the repayments — they were charging about 17%. The rates are sometimes a couple of points less than the average for your credit-card debts. So if you are paying interest on big credit-card balances, it may make sense to switch to an unsecured credit line and pay off your credit cards.

If you own publicly traded stocks or bonds or mutual funds, you can go to a stockbroker and take out a margin loan, commonly for half the value of your securities. He or she will charge you interest of generally 0.5% to 2.5% above a base lending rate determined by the brokerage firm itself. Your interest will be tax-deductible, provided that the securities are not themselves tax-exempt and you have investment income against which to offset the interest.

The point is that when you are looking for money, you generally should canvass several different kinds of lenders. That's because no bank, savings and loan, credit union or finance company will have the lowest rate for every type of borrowing.

The best place to start searching for a general-purpose loan is where you keep your checking and savings accounts. Many banks charge as much as two percentage points less for loans to customers than to noncustomers.

Your own bank may also be a good starting point if you need financing for a new car. True, in recent years the finance divisions of General Motors, Ford and Chrysler might have charged you less for a car loan than a bank would. But banks have wised up and are offering more competitive rates, while the manufacturers have pulled back and are doing fewer and more limited deals. So it's to your advantage to investigate both sources of financing.

If you want to finance the purchase of a house or apartment, you will find that rates on mortgages vary a lot from lender to lender. Once again, it pays to shop around, because the savings can be gigantic over the long term of a mortgage. You generally will get the most competitive rates and terms at savings and loan associations and at mortgage banking firms. In comparing loan terms, be sure to compare points. One point equals 1% of the loan paid up front.

364 | *Your Borrowing*

If you already have bought a home, you can turn it into a piggy bank. You do that by applying for either a second mortgage or a home-equity line of credit. The best place to get a second mortgage is a bank or savings and loan association. Recent rates for adjustable-rate mortgages have averaged 5.80%. You can get a home-equity credit line from banks, savings and loans and brokerage firms. The rate in mid-1992 averaged 8.25%.

Another source of cheap credit may be your life insurance policy. Whole life policies written before 1980 permit borrowing at 6% or even less; policies written after that have either fixed rates of around 8% or variable rates that in mid-1992 were also around 8.3%.

Many companies also let employees borrow from their assets in corporate profit-sharing, 401(k), stock and savings plans. You also can borrow against your certificates of deposit. Banks lend against CDs at one to two points over the CD rate. Finally, you can borrow money from your Individual Retirement Account once a year without penalty — just so long as you repay it within 60 days.

Many of these forms of borrowing are elaborated on in subsequent sections of this chapter.

Fast Ways to Raise Cash

Do you need to raise cash *quickly*? Perhaps you have a wedding to pay for, or some college tuition bills that are coming due soon. If so, you can still find loans that offer terms of endearment.

Start with your family. Loans from family members are inexpensive and need not be secured by collateral. If the loan is interest-free, it could be subject to federal gift-tax laws. But under those laws, a relative can lend you up to $10,000 without incurring any gift tax.

Of course, in exchange for cheap credit, you run the risk of straining a family relationship. To lessen that possibility, you should draw up a promissory note. You can get preprinted forms at many stationery stores. The agreement should include a repayment schedule. If interest is charged, you should agree to an annual rate that is high enough to compensate your relatives for their forgone income.

In order to borrow against your life insurance policy, you need a kind that has cash value, such as whole life. The amount you can borrow will depend on the number of years that the policy has been in effect, your age when it was issued and the size of the policy's death benefit. You do not have to disclose the reason for the loan, and you can repay at your own pace — or not at all. The interest rate probably will range between 6% and 8%. Only remember that in the event of death, the unpaid balance will be deducted from the policy's death benefit.

More and more company-sponsored savings and profit-sharing funds also let vested employees borrow against the money they have in the plans. Typically you can borrow 100% of up to $10,000 of your vested benefit in a company savings plan. Loans between $10,000 and $50,000 cannot exceed half of your vested benefit. Federal restrictions limit the maximum permissible loan to $50,000. How much interest will you pay? Companies must charge the going market rate, usually one or two percentage points above the prime rate. In mid-1992 that amounted to a fixed rate of 8%. You usually make your repayments through payroll deductions. You are required by federal law to repay the loan at least quarterly, and total repayment must be completed within five years. One exception: If you are using the money to buy your primary residence, you can get a payback period of 10 to 25 years.

Credit unions are another source, but few of them make unsecured personal loans larger than $5,000. (By contrast, many banks give their customers $10,000 credit lines secured only by a signature, but you will have to satisfy a series of income, net worth and length-of-employment requirements.)

You can join a credit union by depositing only a nominal sum — typically $5 to $25. And joining is a lot easier than it used to be. You may be eligible and not even know it. You may not have to work for the same company or belong to the same union or community organization as other members. For example, the First Community Credit Union in St. Louis, once open only to Monsanto employees, now accepts residents of three communities near the Monsanto headquarters, as well as employees of more than 150 other companies in the area. Some credit unions even permit members' relatives to join. For more information about credit unions in your area, write to Credit Union National Association, Box 431, Madison, Wisconsin 53701. In all, 63 million people belong to credit unions.

If you own stocks or bonds at a brokerage house, you can borrow on margin. You just pledge a portion of your holdings as collateral. The interest rates as of September 1992 were 6¼% to 8¼%. Interest is usually charged to your account and compounded once a month.

The size of the margin loan you will qualify for depends on the type and market value of the securities you pledge, and the purpose of the loan. If you want $15,000 to buy stocks, for example, you must already own shares or convertible bonds worth that amount. However, if you want to borrow $15,000 to buy a car, you will need $30,000 worth of these securities. Other forms of securities, such as municipal bonds and Treasury notes, may also be used for collateral, but brokerage houses differ somewhat on their margin requirements.

Now, say you have an all-purpose asset-management account at a bank or a brokerage house. You can borrow against your deposited assets by cashing checks drawn on the account. The rates vary with the size of the loan, but in September 1992 they were about 6¼% to 8¼%.

Another way to get a loan is to borrow against the equity you have built up in your home. Your choices include home-equity loans, second mortgages and refinancing.

Of the three, home-equity loans are probably the least costly. They are essentially overdraft checking accounts that you can open at a bank or brokerage firm, using the equity in your home to secure the credit. In mid-1992 the rates on such loans averaged 9.5%. (For more, see the next section, "Getting Money from Your House.")

If other lenders will not oblige, then you can investigate consumer finance companies. Such firms make high-rate loans to high-risk customers.

Finally, if you need some money for just a short time, you can even consider borrowing from your Individual Retirement Account. No, you cannot permanently take money out of your IRA without paying income taxes on it, as well as a 10% penalty, unless you are 59½ or older. But it is all right to withdraw some or all of your IRA funds once a year — if you make a rollover and replace the money within 60 days. There is no penalty on that.

Just go to the bank or brokerage house or wherever you have your IRA on deposit and take out some or all of your assets. If your IRA is invested in stocks or mutual funds, you may sell them. But be sure to replace all those assets within 60 days.

When you borrow from your IRA, you pay no interest on the loan, of course, because you are acting as your own banker. On the other hand, you will not collect any interest or dividends on your money until you repay it.

Getting Money from Your House

You can borrow against the equity in your house without suffering the hassle of securing a conventional second mortgage. Instead, many banks and brokerages offer a homeowners equity loan. An independent appraiser values your house, and then you can usually borrow 70% to 80% of your equity in it. You must borrow at least $1,000 and are likely to pay an interest rate about 1% or 2% above the prime rate, but that is lower than the usual charge for second mortgages. There is no penalty if you pay off your loan early. In addition, the interest on home-equity loans up to $100,000 is still fully tax-deductible.

Keep in mind that major brokerage houses and insurance companies are matching or beating the banks on home-equity loans. One good deal: Prudential Bank & Trust (800-426-4331) offers home-equity loans at the prime rate (6% in mid-1992). But you must pay closing costs and a fee.

This type of loan is good for financing a child's education or an addition to the house. But because the funds are so accessible, beware of using a homeowners equity account for risky investments. If you lose all your money, you lose your equity in the house, too!

If you are a retired homeowner, you can get monthly income from your property and still live in it. Look into a so-called reverse mortgage. It lets you borrow against your house and collect the loan proceeds — minus the interest — in the form of monthly payments. This goes on for a limited period, typically seven years. At the end of the term you have to pay off the loan, which can mean selling the house.

Then there's the shared-appreciation reverse mortgage. It assures you of income for the rest of your life or until you move. In one variation, you take out a loan against your house and pledge to give the mortgage company 50% or 100% of any future appreciation on the property. The more you pledge, the higher the monthly payments you collect. When you die, the mortgage company sells the house. The company then keeps the agreed-on share of any appreciation, plus an amount equal to all the monthly payments it made to you. Anything that is left over goes to your heirs.

How Much Debt Can You Handle?

O F ALL the financial mistakes imaginable, the grimmest is falling too deeply in debt. You do not have to be poor to get bogged down in excessive borrowing. Yet there is no reason to slip in beyond your means. Fortunately, there are ways to figure out how much debt you can comfortably handle.

Think hard about whether you really want to borrow at all. It is not cheap. As of September 1992, the short-term rate on personal loans not backed by collateral was about 16%. And with inflation at moderate levels, you no longer can count on paying back creditors in significantly cheaper dollars.

Most people, of course, do not have the luxury of avoiding debts altogether. Consumer installment debt amounted to 16% of personal income in 1990, up from 13% in 1980, according to a *Money* magazine survey. But when you do borrow, remember: *Necessities* come first. Next in order of importance are loans to finance *long-term assets* such as home improvements, major appliances, furniture and, most important, education for your children. Be sure to reserve some borrowing capacity for *emergencies*, such as unforeseen medical bills. Only after you have provided for necessities, long-term assets and emergencies should you even consider using credit for such indulgences as grand-luxe vacations.

Here is a test than can help tell you how much debt is too much for you:

First, estimate your current annual disposable income — that is, all your income, minus your tax withholdings as well as contributions to various personal retirement, savings and investment plans.

Next, map out the year's expenses. Calculate how many of them will require various forms of debt, notably installment loans.

Debt counselors and credit managers generally agree that no more than 15% of your disposable income should be committed to installment debt, not counting home mortgage payments. Do not necessarily consider this your own upper limit. You may become nervous at only 10%, particularly if there is only one breadwinner in the family and you have a number of dependents.

How to Pay Off Your Debts

MEMBERS of Congress are not the only ones having trouble balancing a budget. Many families, too, are struggling to trim their own deficit spending. Just ask yourself:

— Am I borrowing to pay off old bills?

— Am I spending more than 15% of my take-home pay on monthly installment debts above and beyond my home mortgage?

— Am I constantly forced to dip into my checking overdraft and rarely able to bring it down?

— Do I find it hard to save regularly even a small part of my income?

A "yes" to any of those questions could be a warning that you are living beyond your means. If so, there are sensible steps you can take. It is precisely when they feel they are overwhelmed by bills and responsibilities that many people decide to plan for the future as they never have before.

Once you have concluded that you are in trouble, your first order of business is to determine exactly how much income you receive and itemize your monthly expenses. List all your monthly bills in their order of importance. Set priorities for paying them off. Probably the first priority is to pay your home mortgage, and then your monthly utility and installment bills.

What if you find that you are still in debt over your head? Then it is wise to seek out your creditors and negotiate to stretch out your debts — that is, arrange a longer term of repayment in smaller amounts each month. Creditors have a great deal of latitude to extend the due date on bills by up to 30 days. They possibly can refinance a debt to allow lower, though longer, payment — even if you were overdue 90 days.

If you have trouble meeting your home mortgage payments, go to your mortgage lender for help. The last thing a lender wants is to foreclose on your property. He would much rather have your cash. So in most cases a loan can be rescheduled and payments reduced if necessary.

You might be tempted to sign up for a consolidation loan to pay off all your debts. That is simply not smart. The lure of a consolidation loan is that a bank or finance company will take over your many debts and you, in turn, will make payments to that one institution. The catch is that the interest rate on such a loan is likely to be high. So you could be replacing a heap of moderate debts with one big one that costs more to carry.

Even while working off your debt, you should plan to save. Setting aside as little as 3% to 5% of your monthly income after taxes will help you start considering saving as an integral part of your budget.

Credit Counselors

PEOPLE who have trouble composing a debt-repayment schedule within a workable budget would do well to seek the guidance of a nonprofit counselor. This professional will be sympathetic but firm. A counseler will ask you to provide intimate details about your total monthly income and expenses, a list of your outstanding bills and copies of any correspondence you have had with creditors about debts and loans. He or she will want to know whether you have been dunned by creditors or threatened with legal action, or whether a creditor has sought to have your pay garnished.

Next, the counselor will get in touch with your creditors. Counselors have more clout than you might, since creditors often prefer to deal with professionals. Your counselor will intercede on your behalf to reduce and stretch out monthly payments on debts while you organize your finances. The creditors may be in the mood to hold off for a while, because they simply don't want you to default or go bankrupt. They want to be sure to be repaid, and later is better than not at all. Sometimes a counselor can even knock down the total balance due. Once you have renegotiated the debt terms through your counselor, you make your monthly payments to him or her. Your counselor then manages the debt for you.

Debtors who pay off their debts with the intervention of a counseling service are on the road to rehabilitation. But the path will be rough at first. Many creditors will reject you because of credit-bureau reports of your need for counseling. But a good word from your credit counselor can help you reopen department-store charge accounts and maybe even finance a new house. Victor Shock, executive director of the Credit Counseling Centers of Oklahoma, in Tulsa, reports: "In our local area we have had great success with mortgage companies by writing letters of recommendation for successful clients."

Before you approach any credit-counseling agency for help, find out whether it is a nonprofit clinic, a for-profit company or simply a bill collector subsidized by your creditors. There are over 700 nonprofit credit-counseling organizations across the country. They are almost always better than the for-profit organizations, which charge much more. The National Foundation for Consumer Credit (800-338-2227) will direct you to community-sponsored nonprofit services near you.

Almost half of the nonprofit groups provide free service, and no one is turned away even by those that do charge a fee, currently $8 to $10 a month until the debts are repaid. All groups, however, ask creditors to contribute 7% to 15% of the monthly payments the counselors make on their client's behalf.

Scoring Points with Lenders

To DETERMINE whether or not you qualify for a loan, many lenders evaluate you according to a mysterious point system.

They keep their credit rating systems secret, so it is difficult to find out what information is worth the most points in determining whether you get the credit you seek. Almost certainly, you will be scored on the number and types of existing loans and charge cards you have. It helps a lot if you already have and use other forms of credit. The most desirable types you can have are the travel and entertainment cards, followed by bank credit cards and department-store charge cards. If you have a good record of paying credit-card bills and installment loans on time, that is a plus. But get rid of credit cards that you rarely use. Many lenders, if they see a long list of credit cards issued in your name, will conclude that you have a high potential for indebtedness.

Lenders do not like to see loans from finance companies. A significant percentage of bad credit risks have been in debt to these outfits. If your payment record with such companies is good, though, you shouldn't lose points.

Your income may help you pass the credit test, but lenders know that someone who earns $50,000 a year is not necessarily twice as creditworthy as someone who makes $25,000. If more than 35% to 40% of your gross income goes to paying off current debts, including mortgage and auto loan payments, lenders are not likely to approve your application. In general, you are better off if you own your home rather than rent, and if you already have a checking or savings account.

If at first you don't succeed, get a copy of your credit-bureau report (see the next section for details). There may be mistakes. If so, clear them up and apply again. Ask why you were rejected and offer additional information. Or go to another lender or credit-card issuer. Each one has different standards.

Checking Your Credit Rating

WHEN you apply for a loan, the prospective lender will probably check your credit record. But how can you ensure that this all-important record is fair and accurate?

Private credit bureaus are in the business of compiling the record of how promptly and fully you pay your bills. They sell this information to other companies — when you apply to those companies for a loan, for an insurance policy or even for a job.

If you get turned down for credit, the company that refused you must tell you the name of the credit bureau that it used in making its decision. You then should contact that bureau and ask for a copy of your report. The bureau is required by law to tell you what is in your file. If you request the information within 60 days of your having been denied credit, the bureau will charge you no fee. Otherwise, fees run from a low of $7.50 to as much as $200.

You can challenge any information in your file. If the credit bureau cannot confirm the disputed information, it must delete it. If you request it, the bureau also must send a revised copy of your report to any credit grantor that received the report in the last six months.

Even if the credit bureau finds that the information is valid, you can write an explanation for anything you may have done that is considered wrong. The credit bureau should then attach your explanation, or a clear summary of it, to your report. That way, anyone who receives your credit history will also get your side of the story.

But what if you have made some very late payments or other credit bloopers in the past? How soon can you start with a clean slate? Most of your mistakes will be removed from your record within seven years after they occurred. The only incident that can remain longer is bankruptcy, which remains on your record for as many as 10 years.

Finance Your Own Co-op

I F YOU operate a consumer co-op or would like to form one, there's a bank that wants to lend you money.

Co-ops are hardly new. Farmers have banded together for more than a century to market their crops, and tenants have been forming co-ops to buy and run apartment buildings in New York City. But they have not caught on in many parts of the country, partly because conventional banks are wary of lending money to them.

The National Cooperative Bank in Washington, however, is eager to finance not only traditional cooperatives but less conventional ventures as well. For instance, the bank has provided financial services to Seattle-based Recreational Equipment, Inc., the largest consumer cooperative in the U.S., which not only furnishes its million-plus members with high-quality recreational clothing and equipment but also contributes generously to the protection and preservation of endangered wilderness areas.

The bank charges market rates. For more information, call or write the National Cooperative Bank at 1401 I Street, NW, Suite 700, Washington, D.C. 20005 (202-336-7700).

What Credit Cards Do You Need?

THIS year alone, anyone with a zip code in a middle-class neighborhood could receive in the mail as many as 10 invitations to sign up for different credit cards. And each invitation probably would have preceded a half dozen follow-up letters as the credit-card companies pursued their plastic-bladed war for new customers. Few people really need more than one or two cards. Keeping them to a minimum helps check impulse spending and reduces your risk if the cards are lost or stolen.

If you do not do considerable driving or traveling, you probably can get by with just one card. Your best bet would be a bank credit card, such as Visa or MasterCard. Both cards are honored by some nine million establishments worldwide. People *use* their cards: In 1991, American consumers charged $170.7 billion on their 142 million Visa cards, and MasterCard members charged $99 billion on their 90 million cards. Approximately one-third of nonmortgage debt carried by Americans in 1992 was on their plastic.

If you travel extensively or run up a large expense account, you need a travel-and-entertainment card, such as American Express or Diners Club. Such cards have no preset spending limits. By contrast, the credit line on a bank card can be dented quickly by an airline ticket and a few nights in a hotel. So before you sign up for any card, be sure you will not be cramped by a credit limit that is too low.

Of course, not all credit cards charge you the same interest rate. The annual percentage rate, or APR, ranges from 14.5% to 22%, a spread on which heavy users — those whose balance due averages $5,000 — can save as much as several hundred dollars a year. And there are other money-saving variables as well.

For instance, you might find a lower rate at an out-of-town bank. To find the best deals, look at *Money* magazine's monthly "Banking Scorecard" or in *Barron's* "Market Laboratory" pages. For more complete details, get BHA's Low-Interest/No-Fee Credit Card List, which features 50 credit-card issuers that offer a low interest rate and/or charge no fee ($4 from Bankcard Holders of America, 560 Herndon Parkway, Suite 120, Herndon, Virginia 22070; 800-327-

7300). People who pay their balances in full each month should find some good deals at the banks on this list.

A low APR can be deceiving. There is no escaping paying interest unless you pay your bills promptly or the credit card offers a grace period. Ask for a card with a 25- or 30-day grace period that starts on the date postmarked on your bill. That means you can have as long as 55 or 60 days to pay up interest-free.

People who pay their balances in full might as well choose credit cards that charge no annual membership fee. The average fee is around $15, but more than 100 banks issue fee-less cards. Bankcard Holders of America will send you a list of them. But before abandoning your present card, phone the toll-free number on your bill and ask for free membership. Quite likely the company will cancel your fee. While you're at it, ask for a higher credit limit. You'll probably get that, too.

Once you go on revolving credit (that is, once you owe interest on balances carried from one month to the next), you generally have to start paying interest on every additional purchase. In other words, once you buy something today, you have to start paying interest on it today. But some bank cards preserve the grace period on new charges. This practice is compulsory in Maine, Massachusetts and Vermont but uncommon elsewhere.

Each month's finance charge depends not only on the APR and grace period but also on the way the card company computes the balance subject to interest. Federal regulations require disclosure of the method, usually in simplified language. The standard methods, assuming that a grace period applies, line up this way, in descending order of desirability: adjusted balance, average daily balance excluding new purchases, previous balance, average daily balance including new purchases, two-cycle average daily balance including new purchases.

The much ballyhooed access to cash with credit cards is really a type of loan called a cash advance. You'll begin paying interest on it immediately, whether you hand the card to a bank teller or write out one of those special checks that come with the card. A cash advance is an expensive way to borrow money. You get no grace period on the interest. The APR may be higher than on purchases. And many card companies charge transaction fees, which run as high as 5% of the amount borrowed.

Be careful about running up advances and charges that you cannot pay off in full within a few months. Personal bankruptcies, due in part to high credit-card balances continue to rise: the mid-1992 figure for personal bankruptcies filed was nearly 900,000, up 10% in one year.

Just about every bank offers two varieties of Visa or MasterCard: standard and gold. The gold cards come with higher credit limits and bristle with perks. (But if you want a higher credit limit, it is usually yours for the asking on a standard credit card.) According to Jim Daly of *Credit Card News*, the average annual fee charged by the 25 largest bank-card issuers for gold cards is about $34; for their standard cards, about $15.

Extras that go with the gold include insurance against theft or damage to items charged to your card; car-rental insurance that eliminates the need for an expensive collision-damage waiver; and extended warranties on products that you buy with your card. But if you own a home and a car, your regular insurance probably covers lost or stolen possessions, whether or not you paid for them with your credit card. Further, any credit card gives you the right to withhold payment on shoddy goods.

Automatic Teller Machines

THE ATM card — that handy piece of plastic that you slip into a bank's automatic-teller machine to get a quick fix of cash — is spreading out. In a growing number of regions you can slip your ATM card into machines on the counters of supermarkets, gas stations and convenience stores. Just by tapping out your personal identification number, or PIN, on a keypad, you can instantly move cash out of your checking account into that of your vendor, and in some cases into your own pocket.

ATM cards can make life a lot easier, whether you're out shopping or simply running short of pocket money. Your card gives you access to your cash whenever and very nearly wherever you happen to be. Bank ATMs remain open long after banks close for the day. Through regional and national networks, you can extract money from your checking account at banks that you have never heard of and that certainly have never heard of you. More than 300,000 ATMs are stationed in bank alcoves and outposts in shopping malls and student centers around the world. Japan has the most — almost 99,000 ATMs — followed by the United States, with about 85,000 machines as of early 1992.

With the ATM card's conveniences come some costs. Debit cards of all kinds expose you to potentially heavy losses if a thief figures out how to use your card. Under the federal Electronic Fund Transfer Act, the limits of liability increase in three steps, based on how long you wait before notifying your bank that you have lost your card. The liability can mount fast: $50 during the first two business days after you learn that something is amiss, $500 over the next 60 days, and everything taken after that, including any credit you can draw on through an overdraft account.

Safeguards make it hard for your bank to pin the liability on you. Only someone who knows your PIN can activate your card, but your bank can't stick you with liability simply because you wrote the number on the back of the card. (As foolish as it seems, many people do just that.) Most important, those stages of liability don't start counting down until you have had a chance to detect any unauthorized ATM withdrawals on your bank statement.

It pays to check out ATM costs when you shop for a checking account. Some banks charge routine fees for their cards. Relatively few charge their depositors for using the bank's own ATMs. Those that do may nick you for 30 to 50 cents a shot. A larger number of banks charge anywhere from 50 cents to $1 each for withdrawals via regional networks; many other banks charge $1 to $3 each for withdrawals using a national network.

If you ever have trouble with a bank involving your ATM card, seek relief from one of the following four federal agencies in Washington, D.C.:

If the bank you deal with is a nationally chartered bank, write to the Comptroller of the Currency. If you have a problem with a state-chartered bank, contact the Federal Reserve Board. If your bank is state-chartered but not a Fed member, call or write to the Federal Deposit Insurance Corporation. If your automatic-teller difficulty is with a savings and loan association, write to the new Office of Thrift Supervision. Give any of these agencies about four weeks to make decisions and get back to you.

Do not worry about being shortchanged by automatic banking tellers. You may be concerned that the impersonal machine will make an all-too-human mistake, that a $400 deposit will somehow show up on your statement as only $40. In a survey by the Federal Reserve

Board, 6% of the people who used the electronic banking services claimed they had been victims of a machine error. But 95% of the grievances were settled satisfactorily.

If your automatic teller blows a transaction, simply write the bank a note within 60 days of receiving your statement. By law, the bank must resolve the complaint within 45 days of getting your letter. If it takes longer than just 10 business days, the bank must credit your account for the amount in dispute until any investigation ends. If you still have a grievance, write to the Federal Reserve Board's Division of Consumer and Community Affairs, 20th and C Streets, NW, Washington, D.C. 20551.

The Deal on Debit Cards

A TM cards give you quick access to your money; debit cards are almost a substitute for it. The debit card, or point-of-sale cash card, is an electronic key to your checking account. But you shouldn't confuse it with a credit card.

If you haven't yet used a debit card, chances are you soon will. More than 120 million Americans already have such cards, and volume is rising fast. Californians are in the vanguard; in the month of December 1991 they made an eye-popping 12 million debit-card transactions. No wonder: They could use their debit cards at major California supermarket chains, many gas stations, some fast-food restaurants — and Disneyland. In Washington, D.C., the Metro Line subway has tested the sale of fare cards through ATMs in its stations. Soon to come are national debit shopping cards comparable in acceptability to major credit cards.

A cash card works like this: At the checkout counter, say, you slide your card through a slot in a machine called a card reader and press your secret four-digit personal identification number (PIN) into a keypad on the reader. The clerk's register transmits your tape total, PIN and other data to a distant processing center, whose computer recognizes your bank and relays the signal there. If your account contains enough money to pay for the groceries, the system approves your purchase. Then the money moves electronically from your account to the store's. The whole process takes about six seconds.

Cash cards are, in fact, more liquid than cash, and that can get scary. If you have shopaholic tendencies, watch out. A cash card gives you instant access to every dollar in your checking account plus every additional dollar of credit in an overdraft checking account. A card thief or a spendthrift relative entrusted with your card and PIN can drain your account, too.

All cash-card systems are not created equal. At this stage of development, most are limited to participating stores in a specific area, such as one state or a few adjacent states. Some cards are issued by banks; others are issued by gasoline companies or supermarket chains, like charge cards, for use in their outlets only. Dozens of regional networks are rapidly installing terminals in supermarkets, gasoline stations, convenience stores, fast-food restaurants, department stores and elsewhere. More than 50,000 U.S. retail establishments can now ring up cash-card sales, compared with 100 in 1983.

Universal cash cards, acceptable wherever credit cards are honored, do exist. Clients of some large brokerage houses get Visa debit cards that function like cash cards. The primary example is the nearly 3 million users of Merrill Lynch's cash-management account and related asset-management accounts.

Why the rising popularity? The major appeal is, of course, convenience. You don't have to carry much cash or worry about stores' accepting your checks. Shopping sprees based on cash-card plastic won't run up credit-card debts at interest rates that have lately been averaging 18.9%.

The great disadvantage is the loss of "float," the time-lapse between the date of a purchase and the departure of the money from your bank account. Shoppers who pay by check enjoy at least a couple of days' float. Credit-card users who pay their monthly bills in full can earn interest on spent money for a grace period lasting as long as 60 days.

Not all cash cards take away the float. For example, proprietary cards issued by Mobil Oil and Vons, a southern California supermarket chain, give two days' grace. Says Virginia Miller, vice president and treasurer of Vons: "Retaining a float helps families whose paycheck for the week has not cleared the bank by Saturday or Sunday, when most people shop. Other debit systems take the money before you get home with the ice cream." Retailers so far are picking up the cost of most point-of-sale cards.

The risk of loss if a thief raids your account is usually minor, although the law itself is not all that reassuring. As with lost or stolen

ATM cards, it makes you responsible for charges up to $50 if you notify the bank within two business days after you learn of an unauthorized withdrawal. For the next 60 days, if you still haven't called the bank, your liability rises to $500. Wait any longer and your potential loss is limited only by your bank balance plus any credit line in your account.

In fact, banks seldom try to shift any liability to their customers. To play it safe, however, take the following precautions:

Choose a PIN that you can easily remember. Cash-card issuers recognize that life is becoming a maze of numbers too long and too numerous to keep track of, so more and more of them let you pick your own number. But don't select one that is on display somewhere in your purse or wallet, like your house or license-plate number. Don't write your PIN on your card or keep it with your card. Don't reveal your PIN even to friends or relatives. Thieves can have scams for wheedling it out of you, but bankers track most challenged charges to family members.

Your Best Investment Now

MASTERING the credit-card possibilities calls for clear thinking about where to put your spare cash. When you find yourself with a bit of money to invest, your understandable first impulse is probably to tuck it away in an investment for the future. But if you are carrying large balances on credit cards, your best investment by far is to use the money to reduce those debts.

Simple arithmetic will tell you that it costs $180 a year to service $1,000 outstanding balance on an 18% credit card. Paying off that $1,000 can "earn" you the same 18%. What's more, you take no risk to get that return. To match it with an investment, you would have to take big chances with your money. If you are in the 28% tax bracket, for example, you need to earn 25% before taxes just to break even with what you would save by paying off the balance on an 18% credit card. You would have to earn 27.8% to match a 20% card, and 20% is about the rate charged on cards from major institutions such as Citibank, Chase Manhattan and Bank of America. Compare those returns with the 4.26% yield on a risk-free one-year Treasury bill.

Some card issuers are cracking down on customers who maintain high credit balances. In 1991 First Chicago, which issues bank cards nationwide, reviewed the accounts of its customers in the Northeast and pinpointed nearly 8,000 problem accounts, canceling those of outright delinquents and encouraging other customers to pay off their balances. By doing so, First Chicago sought to limit its own losses on borderline accounts.

Your Career

Defying the Common Myths

A sk a career counselor for the hottest job prospects, and you may well hear that the future lies in two areas: high technology and waste management. That's fine for those who cotton to computers and compost, but if you follow the herd to a field when your heart lies elsewhere, you may be making an expensive mistake. The wisest counsel in looking for a job is to pursue your own desires.

A surprising number of determined men and women are finding excellent jobs in fields that the career prophets have written off. They are doing it by challenging some of the common myths of job hunting. As writer Patricia O'Toole has observed, if you are determined to get into even the most glutted occupation, you cannot allow yourself to be daunted by common career myths.

Do not, for example, let Labor Department job projections be your sole guide. National labor forecasts often obscure opportunities in your own community. For example, by tuning in to *local* trends, job hunters some years ago might have spotted how Connecticut, in the slow-growing Northeast, was then making an economic comeback. The state's economy was spurred by the rise of high-tech and financial services businesses. Job projections may also underestimate the time it takes for new technologies to spread. For instance, biotechnology has produced considerably less employment than early enthusiasts predicted.

Don't worry about getting caught in so-called female ghetto jobs. For example, social workers are finding terrific corporate jobs in employee counseling. And believe it or not, the world can use another writer — in fact, many of them. They will be needed to interpret and organize the computer data flood. Newsletters, TV cable services and trade journals all will require people who can convert raw data into readable English. Many women can use their skills to start their own business. *Money* magazine reported that between 1980 and 1988, the number of sole proprietorships owned by women grew 82%, versus 47% for those owned by men.

Don't accept the myth that a high-tech boom means a low-tech bust. Far from it. There is a surge in demand for personal services. As the population ages, one of the fastest-expanding careers will be geriatric nursing. But the real sleeper among service occupations may well be teaching. Millions of computer buyers will need instruction, and so will millions of semi-literate workers. Hundreds of corporations already run remedial English and math classes.

Don't fall for the line that it is better to be a specialist than a generalist. Across the country, Ph.D.'s are broadening themselves by enrolling in intensive short-term introduction to business courses — and becoming everything from factory managers to security analysts.

Don't think you have to have an M.B.A. — a master's degree in business — to get ahead. The degree may get you in the door, but after that you may well have to scramble like everybody else.

Don't assume that big corporations offer the most opportunities. There are nearly 20 million small companies in the U.S., with opportunities in every imaginable field. Don't be afraid to start your own business. The hours are long, but working for yourself gives you the chance to do things your way. According to a 1991 *Money*/Gallup poll, three out of four new businesses survive.

Don't figure you have to go to the big city to find your fortune. From 1969 to 1987, for example, the number of manufacturing jobs in metropolitan areas declined by 8.7%, but in rural areas it grew by 12.2%. The trend is continuing in the 1990s. Nor are factory jobs all that can be found in the countryside. Communities in less populated areas rely on the same kinds of services and professional specialists that large cities have in splendid abundance. So if you want to find employment and are willing to pick up and go, small towns and rural areas may offer ample career satisfaction.

But whether you opt for a small town or the big city, keep a close watch on how the economy is faring in the area that interests you. A survey done for *Fortune* in mid-1992 by Regional Financial Associates found only modest signs of recovery from the recession in New York, New England and California — regions that rode high in the 1980s boom years. And the post–Cold War downsizing of the military stymied growth in Maryland, Virginia and Washington, D.C. On the brighter side, a moderate increase in housing starts was good news for the upper Midwest, the Mountain states and the furniture makers of North Carolina. And the need to replace elderly cars and trucks promised more jobs in the Midwest (auto manufacturing), Louisiana (petrochemicals) and Texas (petrochemicals and plastics). The Lone Star State was doing fairly well: Having survived the 1986 oil bust and taken the brunt of the S&L disaster, Texas was gaining some rewards from economic diversification; a rise in high-tech manufacturing and in trade with Mexico also augur well. But it's in the Mountain states that RFA foresees the most vigorous growth: always a magnet for people who crave the wide-open spaces, these states also offer employers a dedicated, well-educated work force and relatively low costs.

Where the Opportunities Are

WHETHER you are self-employed or work for a company owned by others, you will find that the greatest job growth in the immediate future is likely to occur in financial and business services, health care, recreation, engineering, telecommunications and some other high-tech business.

Accountants and auditors, financial analysts, human-resources managers and other business specialists can look forward to demand for their services. Jobs for accountants and auditors will grow by as much as 30% in the next decade. According to a survey by recruiters Robert Half and Accountemps, newcomers to accounting in 1992 typically earned starting salaries of $25,000 to $28,200. Experienced accountants can earn $35,000 to $42,000 — more with CPA accreditation and a graduate degree. The range for corporate accounting managers can be $42,000 to $61,000 — higher if they work in New York or some other very large city.

Other business specialties require a combination of management and technical training. A benefits administrator in human resources with five years' experience can earn as much as $40,000. Human-resources directors of major companies average more than $120,000 a year.

Careers in some financial services are expanding because of the new attitude people have toward money. More Americans are willing to invest the effort and expense to plan their savings and investments. So brokerage houses and insurance companies are strengthening their financial-planning departments. In addition, banks, real estate companies and other financial concerns will be hiring more analysts, portfolio managers, marketing specialists and, above all, salespeople. Some financial jobs will require M.B.A. degrees, but would-be stockbrokers who have sales experience in any area will be eligible for training programs at the brokerage firms.

From 1990 to 2005, according to the Bureau of Labor Statistics, as many as 4 million new sales and marketing jobs will open up; that is an increase of 30%. Meanwhile, the increase in the number of two-career couples will provide more work for the relocation, personnel and headhunting firms that will have to solve the problems of moving an executive who also has a working spouse.

Another growing area will be child care. There are nine million working mothers with young children, and many of them want day-care centers. Also, small businesses that help with time-consuming household chores should do well.

With the 65-and-over population rapidly expanding — some 35 million Americans will be in that age group by the year 2000 — there will be a need for business consultants who do retirement counseling and pension planning. To provide sufficient health care for the elderly, more and more other types of trained people will be required. Fewer than 5,000 doctors now are expert in geriatric medicine, but we may need as many as 31,000 of them by the year 2000 to serve an aging nation. That is only the beginning, and the field is by no means limited to doctors. According to some estimates, by the year 2000 there will be jobs for more than 500,000 therapists, researchers, nurses and workers in residential-care communities and group-living centers for older people.

The rising American concern with staying healthy will create still additional jobs. Of the 10 projected fastest-growing occupations from 1988 to 2000, seven are health-related. Medical centers will need technicians to run diagnostic equipment; office managers, marketing executives and accountants to handle the books; and nurses to treat patients. The two best places to set up your health-care business will be New England and Florida. By the year 2010, 14% of New England's population and 20% of Florida's will be over 65.

A severe shortage of registered nurses pushed up entry-level pay about 50% from 1979 to 1989. Salaries vary by region, of course, but on average nursing-school graduates now start at about $26,000 on hospital staffs. Head nurses earn up to $48,000. Pay is highest on the East and West coasts: in New York City a new graduate can earn $40,000 and a head nurse $60,000. A master's degree improves earnings because it offers new options — for example, in management or research. More than 600,000 nursing jobs may open up by the year 2000.

Computers will create new jobs — and not only where you expect them. More openings will come in banks, utilities and other businesses that use the mighty microchip than in those that manufacture it. Companies will be looking for programmers and systems engineers. And anyone who can develop software for micro- and personal computers probably will not have to hunt long for work.

The U.S. is in transition from an industrial society to an information society. In this new world, the individual and the computer will have to work together as a team. Everybody who wants to get ahead in this new society will need not only one skill but several skills. Humanists had better be able to communicate with technicians. Engineers should know how to read a balance sheet. In a world of expanded trade, people in business would be wise to know one or more foreign languages.

The workplace is shifting from emphasis on the narrow specialist who is in danger of becoming obsolete to the multiskilled generalist who can adapt. For people who can stay flexible in their jobs, the career paths of the future are wide open.

Here are some other ideas for careers in the 1990s:

— Administrative-services managers. These generalists oversee any number of supportive services such as information processing, conference travel and sale of surplus property. Employment projections indicate that this sector of management will grow faster than the average for all occupations through the year 2000.

— Actuaries. This occupation is expected to grow *much* faster than the average through the year 2000. People with a mathematical bent will be increasingly needed by insurance companies and pension funds to assemble and analyze statistics on the aging baby boomers.

— Water-resource experts. The water shortage of the 1990s could become severe in many places. We shall require more hydrologists, environmental engineers and others to preserve our most important of all resources.

— Environmental accountants. From a megadisaster like the *Exxon Valdez* oil spill to local disputes about garbage disposal, environmental issues have become everyone's concern. Businesses, and agencies at all levels of government, will need accountants versed in ecology, environmental regulations, damage assessment and insurance.

— Industrial relations specialists. With the new emphasis on enhancing industrial and office productivity, these experts will be called on to work out corporate agreements between management and labor. Employee training experts will also be in high demand, as many workers seek and/or require retraining. This business is expected to grow 3% annually for the next decade.

— Development economists. People with college degrees in international economics and business will help to market American products abroad.

— Technicians, entertainers and writers. They will bring entertainment into the home by means of cable television and video cassettes.

— Entrepreneurs. The U.S. needs plenty of these daring risk takers to start new businesses. For anybody who has a marketable idea — from the highly technical world of electronics and computers to the everyday realm of retailing — entrepreneurship can offer one of the best careers of the era. (See "Your Enterprise.")

And finally, what about selling your skills and experience abroad? As U.S. companies seek position and profits in the European Community market, jobs are opening up for Americans. Max Messner's *Staffing Europe* (published by Acropolis Books; $24.95) surveys the new European job scene and the opportunities it offers for enterprising Americans.

Where the Big Pay Is

How can you get the best salary — and where can you get it? Some companies have a tradition of paying well, notably those exploring the frontiers of science and the new technologies. But within any industry, salaries commonly are 15% higher than average at the most openhanded firms, according to Reggio and Associates, a compensation consulting firm in Chicago. The principal factor is size: the bigger a company's sales volume, the greater its pay is likely to be.

Many fields offer impressive rewards for accomplishment. Among the traditional standouts are law, investment banking, stock brokerage and executive recruiting. The recession, of course, hurt compensation in all of those fields, particularly investment banking. In a number of other fields, mostly those that are considered glamorous, starting salaries are small. But they climb sharply in the upper-middle to upper ranks. Television and advertising are examples.

Starting pay at law firms ranges all the way from the low 20s to the 60s. Although a handful of big-city firms offer stratospheric salaries, that remuneration has less to do with an individual's immediate performance than his or her future promise.

Market conditions also influence pay. Partly because rich oil companies in the early 1980s bid up the going rate for secretaries in Houston to around $20,000, less lucrative businesses there were forced to pay more for secretaries, too. While geography does exert an influence, companies generally adhere to a national schedule for top management and pay salaries determined by the industry rather than by location.

Bigger companies tend to pay better than smaller ones. Low-profit companies pay low or give meager raises or both. Old companies or those in established fields such as steel and autos tend to offer a larger share of total pay in the form of fringe benefits than those in new businesses do. But the new ones give more stock bonuses and options.

It is unwise to sell your skills short, even in times when the economy is sluggish. In bureaucratic corporations with ossified pay systems, employees who start out cheap may never catch up.

Second Careers for Women

FOR many wives and mothers, work resumes at 40. But any woman who wants to re-enter the job market will find that she needs some shrewd strategies to do it.

The most serious difficulty confronting re-entry women is a lack of confidence and focus: too many of them tend to undervalue their previous experience. If you are one who does, you should know that many of the skills needed to manage a household or organize a charity bazaar can be transferred to business. Are ill-defined ambitions a problem? The solution may be career-planning workshops offered by countless nonprofit agencies, individual counselors and almost every university and community college. Courses vary from two days to 10 weeks and cost about $150 to $250.

After determining your career objective, you may discover that you need to refurbish your skills before you try them out again. That's fine, but beware: Some older women are tempted to dock in the safe harbor of academe. They go to college for year after year, stacking degree upon degree, never braving the rougher waters of the marketplace. Although men tend to think that they would not want a job if they already knew how to do it, women often think that they have to be able to do a job before they can take it. Thus many women "overcredentialize" themselves and hold back from the day of reckoning.

As a first step back into the market, draft a résumé. You will want to present yourself on paper in a way that is meant to fit your specific goal. Unless your educational credentials are recent or sterling, you probably will want to downplay them and play up your volunteer and other experience. Employers often are unimpressed with degrees or other credentials older than your teenage son.

Omit the personal details. Nobody is going to say her health is *terrible*. By law an employer cannot ask your age, marital status or whether you have children. These same statistics are best left out of a résumé. When many an employer sees "children" written on a résumé, he or she thinks of "sick days."

Your instinct may be to run off 200 copies of your résumé and wallpaper the town. But, instead, you should treat this master copy as a draft and customize your résumé to correspond to the specific opening you are trying to fill.

To get a job interview, begin by telephoning friends and informing them that you are leaving the homestead for the wage-paying world. Use that grapevine of contacts you have developed — everyone from old school friends to members of clubs you have joined.

Even if you have had many years of significant but unpaid experience, your first re-entry job is likely to be on the lower rungs of the labor force. You should not be either insulted or excessively concerned if it is less glamorous, less responsible and lower paying than you expected. What is critical is that the job positions you for growth within the company or your chosen field.

One starting spot that rewards initiative handsomely is often overlooked — or looked down upon — by women. That position is sales. Insurance, brokerage and real estate firms will pay you at least a modest salary to learn the business. Commissions can quickly fatten the pay envelope once you master the skills. Most important, sales jobs provide avenues for advancement.

Part-Time Jobs for Professionals

A NEW class of high earners is working less and enjoying it more. The number of part-timers is fast expanding, and so is the list of employers welcoming them — and willing to pay them well.

In all, more than 20 million Americans work part-time — over 17% of the nation's labor force. A surprising number of these are professionals, from surgeons to sales managers. To be a professional and a part-time worker was once a contradiction in terms. But no more. Today, nearly 3 million professionals choose to work part-time. Some do so voluntarily, others are motivated by economic forces. Whatever the reason, about one out of every seven professionals forgoes full-time employment.

The part-time work that is easiest for professionals to get is in specialized skills. These include medicine, law, accounting, engineering and, especially, data processing. Professionals who have experience in these areas can find many jobs in federal agencies. The Federal Employees Part-Time Career Employment Act of 1978 opened 30,000 part-time positions, not only for scarce professionals but for middle managers as well. And all states now have policies permitting part-time positions in government.

A professional man or woman who chooses to work part-time can sometimes profit from the trend in private industry toward flexible working arrangements. Since managers offer part-time work as a way to hold on to valued employees, your chances of reducing your hours on an existing job may be better than your chances of finding a new, part-time position. One way to convince your boss to cut your hours is to keep a record for two or three months of exactly what tasks you do and how much time you need to do them. That will help you estimate how much you could get done if you worked fewer hours, and give you some idea of what responsibilities could be shifted to others.

You also should be able to show how you would keep up with responsibilities that normally require full-time hours, such as travel and staff meetings. Always stress the *quality* of your work above the money the company would save on your salary.

One company at the forefront in promoting part-time employment is Nations Bank, a large national bank in the South. Its SelectTime program not only has proved to be popular with staffers but has also drawn in professionals who need to divide their time between the workplace and home. IBM takes another approach in offering part-time schedules to its full-time employees, both professional and nonprofessional, within the framework of a three-year leave of absence. During the first-year, employees need not work at all, but for the following two years they must be available to work 20 to 30 hours a week as needed.

While both IBM and Nations Bank give full benefits to employees in these programs, companies typically provide part-timers with prorated benefits, according to a recent survey by the Conference Board. And many companies do not give them any benefits at all.

Tracking down a part-time job at another company will take considerably more time and effort than arranging one in the company where you already work. But employment agencies do find jobs for part-time professionals, and fortunately, agencies that handle part-time professionals and managers are beginning to spring up in large cities. Alterna Track, based in New York City, recruits experienced financial-services professionals for both part-time and full-time jobs. The Pickwick Group in Wellesley, Massachusetts, places a broad range of specialists in Boston and other New England communities and regards flexible work schedules as *the* issue of the 1990s marketplace.

You may wish to deal directly with a company rather than use an agency. One way to find a part-time job is to send a résumé with a brief cover letter stating your qualifications and what services you can provide — part-time. If you get an interview, be prepared to explain how you would handle specific problems that a job might present for someone working part-time. Also, volunteer to go full-time when emergencies arise. And offer to work a scaled-down schedule on a trial basis for a few months.

For more information on how and where to get part-time jobs, you can write or call the Association of Part-Time Professionals, Crescent Plaza, Suite 216, 7700 Leesburg Pike, Falls Church, Virginia 22043; 703-734-7975.

Making Moonlighting Pay

MORE and more people hold down not one job but two — or more. If you are one of these moonlighters, there are some rules you should follow to make the most of your extra efforts and stay out of trouble with your primary employer, with the taxman and with your own family.

More than 7 million Americans work at second jobs, and they put in an average of 14 hours a week at them. They moonlight for many reasons: to earn more money, of course, but also because they may feel stuck on a plateau in their primary job, or because they want to lay the groundwork for a new career, or just because they yearn to exploit some skill or hobby and have fun.

They do a countless variety of things: a Long Island pediatrician conducts wine-appreciation courses on weekends and Wednesday evenings; a Kansas City, Kansas, family therapist is a weekend auctioneer; a New York civil engineer moonlights as a cabinetmaker and resurfacer of paddle-tennis courts.

If you want to take on additional work, writer William C. Banks has suggested some rules to follow:

— Tell your boss at your primary job that you are moonlighting, but assure him or her that your other work won't interfere with your regular responsibilities.

— Be sure to charge enough for your moonlighting. Bill any clients one-third to one-half *more* than your regular daytime wage. After all, you are working overtime, and you do have some expenses.

— Schedule your time so that you have some regular hours for relaxation and to spend with your family. If you find that you are having more than the usual tension on your regular job or that you are becoming tired or irritable, cut down on the moonlighting.

No one wants you to succeed in your part-time career more than the Internal Revenue Service. It defines moonlighting as a sideline business and demands a share of your take. As a self-employed moonlighter, you also will have to pay a Social Security tax of 15.3% on your net free-lance income, unless you earn $53,400 or more from your regular job and your employer has withheld from your paycheck the maximum Social Security contribution — $4,085 on income earned in 1992.

But the self-employed can get special tax breaks as well. If you show a profit in three years out of five, you are presumed to be running a business rather than a hobby, and you will be allowed to deduct from your entire taxable income any losses your enterprise generates. You must, however, keep detailed, accurate records of the income and expenses of your moonlighting activities.

First, you can deduct the cost of all supplies used in your venture, plus the business mileage on your car and parking fees and tolls.

Second, if you have an office or work space at home that you use *only* for business, you can deduct the portion of your rent, heat and utility costs that goes into maintaining the office. But you cannot deduct more than your net income from the business.

Third, you can deduct from your sideline income a certain amount of your business equipment purchases. The maximum deductible varies, depending on how you and your spouse file your taxes and other factors. You can deduct $10,000 as long as your business equipment purchases are less than $200,000 for the year. When you spend more than the deductible amount, you then can depreciate the excess cost.

Computer Jobs

THE belief is common that computers are wiping out countless traditional jobs, but in fact some jobs created by the computer are going begging. Not enough people have the necessary skills. According to the Bureau of Labor Statistics, demand for people with the right training is expected to increase by as much as 87% from 1990 to 2005. We shall need more than 1.2 million specialists in computer fields.

Good jobs should be available for several kinds of trained workers to run computers: for systems analysts, who devise ways for computers to handle information; for programmers, who tell the machines what to do; for technicians, who maintain and repair the complex equipment. There is also some need for people who can teach others to use the machines. Thus, out-of-work schoolteachers are profiting from the new technology. After some retooling, teachers are finding jobs training employees at companies that use computers. Small wonder that John Kemeny, former president of Dartmouth College, says, "It is as unforgivable to let a student graduate without knowing how to use a computer as it was in the past to let him graduate without knowing how to use a library."

People throughout the work force can improve their job status if they learn to adapt to computers. Word processors may put some typists out of work, but secretaries can use the machines to do the dull part of their jobs while they take on more responsibility. Similarly, the fastest-moving business managers will be those who are the most creative in employing computers to streamline operations and save money.

If you do not know much about them, you can plug into the world of computers by taking night courses at community colleges that give you some experience with the machines. You also can learn to program computers by enrolling full-time at one of the schools that specialize in retraining. The price can be steep, $3,000 or $4,000. Often, however, your employer will pay for much or all of your retraining course.

The cheapest way to start learning about computers is by buying specialized magazines or books. One thorough text that is easy to read is *Overcoming Computer Illiteracy: A Friendly Introduction to Computers* by Susan Curran and Ray Curnow. It is put out by Penguin Publishing and costs $12.95.

Career opportunities continue to open up in parts of the country for computer systems analysts. They are the troubleshooters of the electronic age, working for most large companies as well as schools, hospitals and government agencies. The number of jobs in the field may grow by the year 2005 to more than 860,000 — which would be a walloping 87% increase over the number in 1990. In that year, the top 10% of computer analysts earned more than $62,400.

Systems analysts seldom work directly on computers, but they have to understand what the machines can do. Their job is to figure out ways computers can solve problems. In brief, systems analysts are the human masters behind the electronic brains. They determine how to save a company time, effort and money. The analyst can streamline billing, keep track of inventory moving around the warehouse and devise ways to pull together a company's financial records.

Suppose a company wants to computerize its payroll department. Call for the systems analyst! He or she has to spend a few weeks in the department poring over records and interviewing people who work there. Next, the analyst makes up a list of all the pieces of raw data that go into calculating the payroll. For example, if the company has employees in more than one state, the details of each state's tax code have to be on the list. Finally, the analyst turns the list over to the computer programmer and gives him or her step-by-step instructions on how the computer is to put all those data together to produce the correct paycheck for each employee.

The instructions sound like gibberish. An opening sentence might read: "Build a table in working storage to accommodate 1,000 batch numbers." But that is as good as plain English to the programmer, who translates the instructions into terms the computer understands and does the physical work on the machine. Systems analysts can spend a whole year computerizing a payroll — and then come back if a major change is needed.

Suppose you or someone you know would like to become a computer analyst. To qualify, you usually need a few years' experience in the industry where you want to work. It helps considerably if you have had exposure to the company's financial dealings.

Some analysts have never attended college. They simply learned computer programming in night school, got jobs in a company's data-processing department and then moved up to the higher-paid post of systems analyst. True, companies are looking for people with a bachelor's or even a master's degree in business from a school with a well-regarded computer science curriculum. But given a choice, employers may prefer an analyst who knows the company's business to one whose computer training is strong.

The basic skill required by systems analysts is the ability to communicate well. That is because they have to find out from a company's employees what jobs they want done. Nonanalysts often have an exaggerated notion of the wonders that computers can perform. A wise analyst has to mesh these expectations with the realities of what computers actually can accomplish.

Are there any drawbacks to this career? The one serious complaint is that there are no well-traveled paths to top management. Usually the best an analyst can hope for is to become chief of computer operations. But analysts' jobs do take them around the company, from department to department. So a fortunate analyst may catch the eye of an executive who might offer him or her jobs that would move him or her into the company's management mainstream.

Engineers

THOUGH demand for engineers has slowed in the recession, prospects for these professionals remain bright, enhanced by two factors: the computer revolution and the need to upgrade the country's aging infrastructure. The Labor Department estimates that the U.S. will need about 400,000 more engineers in the year 2005 than it had in 1990. Even the civil-engineering field, which traditionally suffers during construction slumps, is expected to prosper. The government anticipates that about 250,000 civil-engineering jobs could open up by the end of the century — some 31% more than in 1990.

Spurred by demographic changes in the work force, companies are bidding up salaries for women and blacks and other minorities in engineering. In fact, women sometimes start out at higher pay than men. In the early 1970s, only 3% of all engineering students were women; today, they make up about 17% of undergraduate engineering students. And young black and Hispanic men were beginning engineering studies in numbers close to their representation in the population at large: they made up about 10% of the entering undergraduate students in the fall of 1991.

Highly regarded engineering schools include Caltech, Purdue, Georgia Tech, Illinois, Michigan, MIT, Stanford, Penn State and Texas A&M. Of course, quality teaching is available in many lesser-known schools.

For students coming straight from college, engineering jobs offer the highest pay of the major professions — for example, about $38,000 for entry-level chemical engineers in 1992. Generally, oil, chemical and drug companies and major R and D labs pay the most, and government agencies and colleges the least. In many companies, engineering is a route to the top. Recent chief executives at Exxon, Westinghouse and Ford started as engineers.

The higher the climb, the less engineering is practiced. Some engineers who prefer the drawing board to administrative chores choose not to advance to management. So a number of companies promote pure technicians to some sort of consulting or distinguished fellow status. These jobs carry salaries of $70,000 to $80,000 and sometimes more — roughly equivalent to upper middle management.

With the rapid pace of technological change, engineers constantly have to re-educate themselves. They say that their usable knowledge has a half-life of eight years. That is, half of what an engineer knows when he starts out is obsolete in that time.

Financial-Services Jobs

THE bull market of the early eighties that led to a job boom in financial services came to an end with the Wall Street crash of 1987. After large layoffs by brokerage firms, there are fewer opportunities for stockbrokers and traders. But the job situation is not as dire as predicted. Many who lost their jobs after the crash were hired by banks and other financial service organizations. In the future, banking, insurance and real estate are expected to provide the most job opportunities in this field.

The best beginning jobs tend to go to people with a bachelor's degree in finance. There also are openings for liberal-arts grads, for professionals who want to switch careers and for housewives returning to work. They can start out earning salaries from $10,000 to $30,000. The lowest salaries are for jobs that involve selling, which many financial-services careers do. But salespeople also have the potential for the highest incomes because they collect commissions. The money does not always come easily. Starting out as a securities salesman usually requires pursuing new accounts aggressively, making many cold calls all day long and having people — from close friends to total strangers — say "no" to you. Small wonder that the chief requirement for salespeople in brokerage houses and insurance companies is personality.

Demand is plentiful for people with technical training, too. Anyone who can write computer programs has a particular advantage in looking for a job. These specialists can become securities analysts, investment managers and tax planners. They may not earn as much as top salespeople who are on commission, but analysts and managers can do very well.

So can bank executives. The Bureau of Labor Statistics estimates that by the year 2005, banks will employ more than 2 million people in entry and managerial positions — over 10% more than they did in 1990. Generally you need a bachelor's degree, and often an M.B.A., for the good jobs.

People who do the hiring are not too impressed by flashy applicants. They are looking for the ability to persuade, negotiate and collaborate. That's because most banking jobs still involve some kind of selling. Lending officers in particular are expected to drum up new business.

One way to take advantage of the market in financial-services jobs is to join the growing ranks of financial planners. These professionals analyze a client's entire financial situation and make recommendations about where he or she should invest and save his or her money. To become a fully trained financial planner, you have to pass six to 10 college-level courses. Two schools that offer the courses by mail are the College for Financial Planning (4695 South Monaco Street, Denver, Colorado 80237-3403) and the American College (270 Bryn Mawr Avenue, Bryn Mawr, Pennsylvania 19010).

Planners often start out as salespeople at brokerage or insurance companies, where they work on commission. Then they may set out on their own to become planners and charge a fee for their advice.

Sometimes they also sell mutual funds, insurance and tax shelters and collect commissions.

Another career area to consider is insurance. Life insurance sales have grown strongly over the last decade and agents' commissions are up, thanks to the renewed popularity of permanent policies such as whole, universal and variable life. Full-time agents who have been in business three years average about $28,000 in earnings. After five years, they average $50,000.

Insurance companies commonly hire people in their late 20s and early 30s who have had little or no experience selling. Salaries start at $18,000 on average and gradually decrease as the agents' commissions increase; in 1990, salaried insurance agents earned a median annual income of $26,700. Many insurance companies do not have their own sales corps but instead rely on independent agents. The independents offer customers a broad line of policies and annuities from any number of companies. The growth end of insurance now is selling policies not to individuals but to small businesses and big corporations or, through them, to large groups of employees.

Health Administrators

HEALTH-CARE administration is a flourishing profession that gives you the chance to do well by doing good. Managing a hospital or nursing home is much like managing any enterprise — except that the decisions can determine whether someone lives or dies.

What a health-care administrator does depends largely on the size of the institution he works for. A veteran administrator of an 1,100-bed New York hospital spends his days and about a third of his evenings in meetings — on how to contain costs, raise funds, recruit specialists and whether to invest in the latest equipment. His salary is around $275,000 a year.

The administrator of a 70-bed hospital and nursing home in a small town in Idaho has plenty of meetings, too, but typically they are with surgeons about improving the light in the operating room or with the dietitian about how to contain the costs of meals. She also squeezes in visits to patients. Her salary is $80,000 — but like her big-city counterpart, she also comes away with a sense of accomplishment.

As running medical institutions has become more complex, the administrative ranks have swelled to include not only the director or administrator, but also many middle managers who are skilled in accounting and market research. Some 500,000 people are expected to be working in the field in 1995.

Many will be outside the medical institution — for example, in government agencies, where administrators may analyze regional needs for health care. Some experts also are hired by insurance companies, where they may design new types of coverage. Quite a few of the best opportunities are in the fast-expanding health maintenance organizations, which sell prepaid medical plans entitling subscribers to the services of a staff of salaried physicians.

Jobs in health administration can be both exciting and frustrating. At any moment, a hospital administrator is apt to get a call: A child needs a blood transfusion but her parents forbid it on religious grounds. On the spot, the administrator must decide whether to get a court order or go ahead with treatment.

These jobs call for stamina and patience. Administrators must wrestle with aggrieved patients and their relatives, feisty community groups, unions, demanding doctors and trustees. Administrators share chronic problems: too little money, too few nurses, constant turnover among low-paid aides, and strict, ever-changing government regulations. But the emotional rewards can be rich.

To land a job in the field, you usually have to have a bachelor of science degree or, for high-level positions, a master of business administration or a master of health administration degree. Thirty-three schools offer undergraduate degrees in health-services administration; two of the best regarded are at the University of New Hampshire and at California State University at Northridge. Among the outstanding graduate programs, all two-year courses, are those at the universities of Michigan, Minnesota, Washington, Pennsylvania and California at Berkeley.

According to Hay Management Consultants' Hospital Compensaion Survey, an assistant administrator with a graduate degree can earn from $50,000 to $80,000, except in nursing homes, where the range is $30,000 to $40,000. After 10 years' experience, the figure jumps to anywhere from $40,000 to $75,000 for a nursing-home director. The administrator of a hospital with 10 years' experience earns from $100,000 to $180,000. The head of a hospital chain earns $250,000 or more.

People who want hospital careers can improve their prospects by joining chains such as the Hospital Corporation of America. And nursing-home administrators are in such short supply that a number of states allow them to head more than one nursing home each.

Management Consultants

As the 1980s wound down and corporate profits shrank, demand rose for those corporate doctors, the management consultants. Bright young business-school graduates rushed into the field, eager to help companies with the changing demographics of their work forces or the sky-high costs of medical insurance and other employee benefits. Many consulting firms have themselves been hard hit by the recession — a company faced with dwindling profits will consider carefully how much it needs a high-priced consultant's services — but the field remains attractive for enterprising generalists or for graduates with a solid background in a specialty such as accounting.

To land a job with a top outfit, you usually need an M.B.A. from a first-rate school. A few years' work experience also will get you in the door. People seeking a second career in management consulting can bring it off only if they offer solid grounding in a specialty. A product manager at a major consumer goods company, for example, could turn into a consumer marketing consultant.

It is not uncommon for high-ranking graduates of the best business schools to start in management consulting firms at $65,000 or more — sometimes much more. Since their services are so expensive, successful consultants must be able to get to the root of a problem and produce solutions quickly. A consultant must be articulate, assertive and versatile enough to sell his or her solution to the assistant plant managers, as well as the company president, without offending either.

One drawback, even for those who like consulting, is travel. Executives of big firms say their staff managers spend 30% of their time on the road. Another complaint is that consulting gives you influence but no real power to enforce decisions. But for bright young comers who are not sure where they want to work, consulting provides exposure within a corporation and a stepping-stone to a top-line job.

Military Officers

L ONG the nation's employer of last resort, the military is becoming downright upscale. To get a few good men and women, the Army, Air Force, Navy and Marines have offered increased pay, abundant fringe benefits and generous pensions. From 1980 to 1990, military compensation rose 38%. Some people, particularly college graduates, can find remarkable opportunities as officers. A second lieutenant can collect $27,000 a year, and a full colonel with 26 years of service easily commands $70,000. These earnings are made up of base pay plus tax-free allowances for housing and meals.

Then there are all the benefits: 30-day vacations, free family medical care and a retirement plan that provides pensions equal to 75% of the base pay after 30 years. Other benefits include discounts at commissaries, Veterans Affairs mortgages and postgraduate education with full pay. In addition, women are granted at least 42 days of paid maternity leave.

Although Uncle Sam may want you, nowadays he may not have much room. Military commissions that were yours almost for the asking in the early 1980s are now harder to come by: in the post–Cold War years the services see no pressing need for large numbers of junior officers, and they are even offering middle-level older officers cash incentives to retire. But recruiting hasn't ceased; it just goes on at a slower pace.

There are three main routes to earning an officer's commission. First are the most prestigious sources of commissions: the Military Academy at West Point, the Air Force Academy at Colorado Springs and the Naval Academy at Annapolis. Each pays cadets or midshipmen about $500 a month. After they are commissioned, they must spend at least five years on active duty.

Here is how to apply: In the fall of your junior year in high school, write to the academy of your choice for an application kit. Follow its instructions, then write to the U.S. Congressman for your district and to both of your U.S. Senators, asking them to nominate you. The legislators' staffs look for students with grades in the top fifth of their classes, good health, participation in athletics, leadership potential and gung ho personalities. Each academy chooses enough candidates to fill the legislator's quota of five students in a school at any given time. Nearly 2,800 students in the class of 1993 entered the academies through congressional nomination.

Second, the broadest channel to a commission is college ROTC. It produces more than 12,000 officers a year. To become one of them, you take two to four years of military-science courses, drill periodically and show up for summer training. Some 80,000 students were enrolled in ROTC in 1992. Many have scholarships, with the government picking up the bill for as many as four years of college. After they graduate, scholarship recipients must serve at least four years on active duty. (For more, see "Your Education: Financial Aid You Still Can Get.")

Third are the officer candidate and training schools of the Army, Air Force, Navy and Marines — still the fast track to a commission for college graduates who were not in the ROTC. These schools enroll enlisted people who have shown qualities of leadership, as well as a limited number of civilians. All candidates must be college graduates. To apply, contact one of the 7,500 recruiting stations that the services maintain across the country. Once you become an officer, you will be obliged to serve at least three years on active duty.

Paralegals

F OR a solid career in the law without spending the time and money to get a law degree, think about becoming a paralegal. The Bureau of Labor Statistics estimates that the number of paralegal jobs may grow 84%, to as many as 153,000, by the year 2000. The average starting salary is about $21,000.

Paralegals work for lawyers, researching cases and drafting documents. There is no standard licensing exam for them. Some law firms train their own paralegals, but many others prefer to hire graduates of certificate or degree programs. These are usually one or two semesters long, and they are offered by colleges and vocational schools. For a list of such programs write to the National Association of Legal Assistants, Inc., 1601 South Main Street, Suite 300, Tulsa, Oklahoma 74119. Or send $5 to the American Bar Association's Standing Committee on Legal Assistants (750 North Lake Shore Drive, Chicago, Illinois 60611) for a general information packet on paralegal training, the schools that offer it and the jobs it can lead to.

Secretaries

PARTLY because many women are turning their backs on traditional career roles, pleas for secretaries are increasing in the want-ads.

Not long ago, the Bank of America declared that on any given day it was advertising openings for 30 secretaries. Of those who responded, many were overqualified college graduates who could not find jobs in their chosen fields, so they were unhappy from the start. Quite a few of the rest were inadequately trained high-school graduates. The shortage of competent secretaries remains severe, and it is likely to grow worse. The Department of Labor has estimated that nearly 800,000 secretarial jobs could open up between 1988 and 2000. Employers probably will court secretaries by boosting pay and by making it easier for them to advance to better jobs.

More than 3 million secretaries are now employed, many of whom are back-to-work housewives who got their training 20 years ago and are willing to stay in secretarial positions. Their skills, employers report, tend to be superb, and their work ethic excellent.

The complaint is common that today's high-school graduates do not have the basic skills. As the women's movement has dimmed the desire for secretarial work, the number of students who want to learn shorthand has diminished. Many schools offer only a beginning course, although it usually takes three semesters to become proficient. High schools do not emphasize spelling and grammar the way they used to, so many grads have trouble writing business letters.

The average salary is about $23,000. Pay tends to be lowest in the South and highest in the West and in large cities. The range for experienced secretaries in New York City, for example, is from $25,000 to $50,000, though some earn even more. Shorthand can mean a salary premium for secretaries in law firms. And an applicant with a bachelor of arts degree can command up to $5,000 more than one with a high-school diploma.

Job aspirants who can afford $7,350 may take an 8½-month course at Katharine Gibbs, the country's best-known secretarial school. The curriculum includes the usual skills plus electronic word processing and accounting. There is also a course in poise — called "professional development" — which requires students to observe themselves on videotape as they perform their duties. A dress code prevails, too: no jeans, culottes, sneakers or clogs.

Fewer than 1% of secretaries are men, and that is not expected to increase, because most think it's a woman's job. One man who disagrees is Robert Metcalf, 37, a secretary at Satellite Network Affiliates in Salt Lake City. Competence makes the difference, not gender, says Metcalf, who has been a secretary for 17 years.

The payoff for top skills in many companies is that a secretary's career path follows his or her boss's. When the boss gets a promotion he or she takes the secretary along, a practice sometimes called "fate-sharing." Militant women complain that this reduces secretaries to appendages of their bosses. They urge management to post job openings scrupulously and to encourage secretaries to apply for higher-ranking jobs. Indeed, many of them do move into management. With demand for competent secretaries at an all-time high, opportunities to advance should become greater than ever.

Secretaries who stay in their jobs say they enjoy them for two reasons. They get to know a lot about what is going on in a company without having to take the heavy responsibility for it, and they enjoy helping their bosses be more productive. They make it easier for him or her to succeed, and when he or she does, they share the satisfaction.

Teachers

MANY teachers are finding lucrative jobs outside the schools and colleges. They are switching from the schoolroom to the corporate-run training room.

During the 1990s millions of computer buyers will need instruction. So will millions of office and factory workers. Already hundreds of corporations provide classes in English and math. And companies spend billions of dollars each year to train their employees. The person most likely to do the hiring of teachers is the director of training and development.

If you are a teacher, an essential strategy for making the switch is to develop — and use — acquaintances in business. Serve on school committees that have ties to local industry, or participate in community organizations where you are likely to meet people in business. Once you are in the corporate door, you can pick up other industrial training specialties. And from there you may be able to move to a job in management. You may also want to read *Your Career in Resource Development*. Write to the American Society for Training and Development, 1640 King Street, Box 1443, Alexandria, Virginia 22313, or call 703-683-8118.

The boom in adult education has brought a roaring demand for part-time teachers of subjects as diverse as programming a computer and finding a mate. If you have a skill, you may be able to earn some extra money by teaching it.

Men and women are going back to school by the millions to study an enormous range of subjects. They are interested in courses from the practical, such as How to Live Well Without Going Broke, to the whimsical, such as The Art of Social Climbing. The teachers whom most adults prefer are not ivory-tower academics but those who have earned their knowledge on the job and have direct experience to share.

As a part-time teacher of an adult education course, you can expect to earn perhaps $18 to $20 an hour. But if your course is extremely popular, you can make as much as $400 an hour. Most expenses connected with teaching — such as professional dues, subscriptions, travel to and from professional meetings — are tax-deductible. There are non-monetary rewards, too, such as learning more about your field and gaining potential clients and business contacts.

The most popular adult education subjects are: starting a small business, making money in stocks and bonds, and how to buy, use and program computers. Demand is also brisk for courses in physical fitness, assertiveness training, practical topics such as plumbing and bicycle repair, and affairs of the heart, from divorce to middle-age dating.

The best places to get part-time jobs in adult education are at community colleges, municipal recreation agencies or the fast-spreading, noncredit independent learning centers. If you teach through a learning center, you may function as an independent contractor, generally taking 30% to 50% of the fees. Tuition generally ranges from $20 to $75 per student per course. For its cut of your fees, the center will promote your course in its catalogues, handle student registration and give both you and your curriculum a sense of legitimacy.

Successful Techniques for Job Hunting

Job hunting is a skill, and it is fairly easy to learn how to do it right. Once you master a few techniques, you will substantially increase your chances of getting a job — whether you are entering the employment market for the first time or looking for a new position.

Take a case of how *not* to do it:

He seemed to have everything a job hunter could want: intelligence, charm and one of corporate America's prized credentials — a Harvard M.B.A. To distinguish himself, however, he wore a baseball cap as well as his three-piece suit to job interviews. He did indeed stick out — but he also struck out. Despite dozens of interviews, he got no offers.

The problem, of course, was the cap. Instead of marking him as a go-getting individualist, the hat told recruiters that he lacked self-confidence and was overly concerned with image. He had tried but misapplied the first rule of job hunting: Stand out from the pack. The way to do that is to do your own research into the company and its business, ask probing questions, and project certainty about yourself and your career goals without appearing smug.

The first hurdle in job hunting is to get an interview with prospective employers. Perhaps friends, business acquaintances or alumni of your high school or college can recommend you to employers whom they — or *their* friends — know personally. If all else fails, you might get an interview by writing directly to the employer. Send a forceful letter outlining your achievements and likely contributions to the company. But don't use such ruses as implying that you are something other than a job applicant.

Résumés are important, but they are not worth the incredibly long hours many job seekers invest in them. You probably can spend your time better in researching the company and thinking about how you specifically can be useful to it. The ideal résumé is no longer than one page. It should concentrate not on descriptions of your previous jobs but on your accomplishments: for example, "I increased sales 50% in six months." Do not exaggerate. An applicant who stretches the truth even about something innocuous will be branded as dishonest.

Though many recruiting professionals prefer the homemade résumé you write yourself, you may feel you need a helping hand. If you have a PC, look into software packages such as PFS: Résumé and Job Search Pro, the latter produced by Spinnaker Software of Cambridge, Massachusetts. This $60 package includes a résumé and cover letter as well as extra features such as follow-up letters and the wherewithal to create a database of company names and addresses. A similar program, Résumé Maker, is available for $50 from Individual Software of Pleasanton, California. Spinnaker also has a résumés-only program called Résumé Kit; it costs $30. If you're a college graduate, find out whether your school's placement office sends alumni résumés to prospective employers, either on its own or through services such as Skillsearch of Nashville, which dispatches computerized résumés to corporate employers.

Once you've landed an interview, start looking on yourself as a product for sale — cold-blooded as that may seem. First, you have to decide what the product is going to be — that is, what skills and qualities you have to offer an employer. The next step is to package your product well and to devise a strategy for selling it.

Like any salesman, you might practice your pitch on friends. But be prepared for the interviewer to throw some tough stock questions. One favorite is, "Tell me a little about yourself." A poor response to that begins, "Well, I was born on . . ." You would do much better to say something like: "Lately I've discovered that I can combine my abilities to . . ." and then go on to state specifically what you can do.

What you wear to the interview matters less than you may think. Of course, a serious applicant for a job at a traditional firm should not wear a scarlet jacket and white bucks or a diaphanous dress with a plunging neckline, not to mention a baseball cap. When in doubt, the best advice is to go conservative.

Since interviewers are impressed by applicants who ask sharp questions, it is wise to study the firm and its industry. You can read the company's annual report, ask a stockbroker for any written analyses of the firm and learn more about it in business reference books at a library.

Your sales presentation begins the moment you show up for the interview. Some personnel managers base their judgment partly on the office receptionist's reaction. If the applicant is rude to the receptionist, he will not get the job, no matter how smart he looks in the interview. It shows he is a two-class person.

Corporate recruiters recommend some techniques to help you stand out during an interview:

— Carry a folder marked with the company name — and take notes. That shows you are well organized.

— Convey enthusiasm. Try to turn your weaknesses into advantages. If an interviewer suggests that you lack qualifications, you can say that you are a fast learner who welcomes challenges — and then give an example.

— Prepare what vaudevillians used to call a "get-off line" — a parting comment that moves the recruiter closer to an offer. You might ask, for example, whether he sees any obstacles to hiring you.

Questions to Ask Your Prospective Employer

SWITCHING employers could be either the best decision of your working life — or a misstep that will make your old job seem like Paradise Lost. So, before you take a new job, you should ask a few crucial questions.

You might ask what happened to the last person who had the position you will be taking. If he or she was promoted, you will get some idea of where the job is likely to lead. If, instead, the person was fired, you may learn early on about a major stumbling block that could trip you up, too.

Ask to talk with someone at the company who is doing much the same job that you are being hired for. This person probably will be one of your soundest sources. Ask him or her whether your prospective boss is really as charming as he or she seems. Or ask about the *least* appealing aspect of working for the firm.

A good way to get general information about a company's style is by doing some research into the work histories and educational backgrounds of the top managers. Look them up in Dun & Bradstreet's *Reference Book of Corporate Managements* or in the *Standard & Poor's Register of Corporations, Directors and Executives*. They are available at major libraries. For example, if all top managers happen to have graduated from Ivy League colleges, that may tell you something about your chances for promotion. If you are a woman, you may want to find out how many women have advanced into upper management.

Find out as much as you can about the company's financial health. Is the firm growing? And where is this growth coming from? Your chances of advancement, of course, are greater if the company is expanding. Ask a stockbroker for research reports on the company. On the basis of its business outlook and strategy, consider where the company might be in five years.

Ask your prospective new boss or the person hiring you how and by whom your performance will be measured. You and your employer should agree on specific goals for you to accomplish — and a reasonable timetable for achieving them.

You will also want to know how the company will help you meet the goals you have agreed on. Your boss should stand ready to grant you powers commensurate with your responsibility. Will you have enough access to important support services, such as computers?

Ask what the salary range is for similar jobs in the organization. While you should aim to come in at the top of the range, this may still be too low. Many candidates will not consider changing jobs without a nice raise over their current pay.

What other compensation does the company offer? This might include bonuses and benefits such as health plans and pension and profit-sharing programs. Your potential employer probably will be most impressed if you try to tie your compensation to your performance in as many ways as possible. Once you have worked out an agreeable compensation package, it is often a sound idea to have your prospective employer set down the details of the offer in a written memorandum.

Employment Contracts

THE recent binge of corporate takeovers has given an urgent new popularity to employment contracts. The typical contract will guarantee you at least a certain minimum salary for two or three years, although you can be awarded raises that will increase it. A contract spells out your title, fringe benefits, bonuses, length of vacation and severance pay. In most cases, you agree not to quit during the term of the contract.

But if you are negotiating for a job, do not mention that you want a written agreement until an offer has been made and you agree to the terms of employment. In some cases it is enough to ask simply for a letter confirming the broad outlines of the terms. However, if you are dealing with complicated subjects such as stock options, you may want a more formal contract.

Pay particular attention to passages in the contract dealing with circumstances under which you may be fired. Avoid ill-defined words, such as "incompetence," which are subject to broad interpretation.

Be on the alert for contract provisions that could restrict your activities if you leave the company. Some employers may ask that you agree not to work for a competing firm. Make sure that what constitutes "competition" is defined as narrowly as possible.

And after you have struck a bargain, be sure to submit the proposed contract to your lawyer — *before* you sign it.

How to Move off a Plateau

BECAUSE of stiff competition in the job market, many people's careers are stalling at lower levels of work and at earlier ages than before. So, it takes more talent and drive to get ahead today than it has for many years. But by learning new skills and seeking added responsibilities, you can move up and off a career plateau. Several tactics:

Fortify yourself with knowledge. Take courses at a community college or specialized school to learn a new skill such as computer literacy or public speaking. It's quite possible that your company will subsidize your tuition.

Get involved in community or business projects. You can broaden your experience and increase your visibility by holding office in a professional group, writing an article in a trade journal or organizing a conference.

Look for new responsibilities to add to your job description. The delicate objective is to shine before superiors without alienating your immediate boss or co-workers. You don't want them to consider you an opportunist or a troublemaker. What you need is an idea that will make your superior's department look good and therefore win his blessing. Propose the plan to your immediate boss. With his approval, you can present it more formally to the company's higher-ups. If they let you try it and it works well, you're in a position to bargain for a new title or a raise or more authority. By showing eagerness to grow in your present job, you'll avoid being classified as deadwood.

Sometimes the best way to move a career off dead center is by trading your job for another at the same level. Many people now turn down transfers to other cities because they don't want to take on heavier mortgage costs or uproot a working spouse. Thus, it could pay for you to offer to move from headquarters to some distant branch office where opportunities may be richer.

It's harder than it once was for up-and-coming managers to find out where they stand. That's because the rules of climbing the corporate ladder have changed drastically since the days of the so-called "organization man" of yesteryear. Back in the 1950s and 1960s, every career move was supposed to be upward. Promotions for those on the fast track came every two years or so, and many felt nervous if they didn't have a new job title as soon as they could possibly get it.

Changing management techniques and restructurings at many corporations have resulted in a flattening of the traditional corporate hierarchy. So, many managers are sitting in their jobs longer, regardless of their skills. And lateral moves within a corporation are becoming routine, even desirable. You may be wise to talk to your boss about transferring to a different type of work in which you'd gain new skills. For example, an engineer who switches to a personnel job can acquire the managerial experience necessary for a higher-level technical assignment.

Another option is to continue doing the same job but in a department with room for advancement or with a specific need for your abilities. Even if such a horizontal shift doesn't lead to a promotion, the new challenges can get you out of a deadening routine.

To move sideways successfully, you need a history of creditable job performance, a sound plan and influential supporters. The first step is to zero in on the right department and job in your organization. Do not just listen for grapevine gossip. Check the employment office to find out who is hiring. Ask department heads to tell you their long-range plans. Scan trade magazines and securities analysts' reports to learn which parts of your industry are ripe for expansion.

Get help from insiders. Make lunch dates with people at your level or above. Ask about advancement opportunities and what it takes to land the job you're after. Only if every route off the plateau ends in a cul-de-sac should you look for a new employer.

Negotiating a Transfer

ACCORDING to the Employee Relocation Council, about half a million employees will be transferred away by their companies this year. If you are one of them, be careful to negotiate with your employer to get the best deal on moving expenses.

Most large companies have standard moving policies that supposedly leave little room for negotiation. But no matter how rigid the company position seems, employers are sometimes willing to make adjustments. If you know what to ask for, you can get more — and save yourself some unpleasant financial surprises.

The standard package begins with an agreement by the company to pay all the costs of transporting your household goods. If you own a house or condo, the company typically will arrange for the purchase of it at a price set by two or more local appraisers. If you sell the house yourself, your employer should pay for any real estate brokerage fees.

The company should cover any prepayment penalty on your old

mortgage and pay for one or two house-hunting trips to the new location. Also ask for temporary living expenses for up to six weeks and up to three points for mortgage origination. And companies may provide interest-free or low-rate loans for down payments on your new house.

When you are negotiating a transfer, don't be afraid to ask for a raise at least large enough to offset any higher cost of living in the city where you are bound. Ask for an allowance of $1,000 to $5,000 to cover the costs of carpets, draperies and any other items you have to leave behind. These allowances are taxed as ordinary income by the federal, state and local governments. So, most companies give you still another allowance to offset that extra liability.

You should also get help in finding a job for a salaried spouse. Try to have the company hire a relocation firm to assist with résumés and to provide job counseling. And ask for compensation for child-care costs while your spouse is job hunting.

The Perils of Job Hopping

FOR those people who wonder whether the surest way to the top is to hop from job to job within a given field, or to stay with one company, here's a good word for fidelity. Job hopping may have its short-term attractions for ambitious people, but those at the top know it pays to stay with one employer. Eugene Jennings, a Michigan State University professor emeritus, tracked the careers of corporate presidents since 1953. He found that more than half of them remained loyal to one company.

True enough, job hopping can help you gain valuable training and experience in the early stages of your career. After that, the best reason to switch jobs is to overcome obstacles in your career path, such as a hostile boss or a demotion. Yes, job hopping is the accepted way to move up the ladder in a few volatile lines of work, such as advertising, television, fashion design, marketing, publishing and retailing. In recent years, the demand for hoppers has risen especially in high technology and information processing.

But elsewhere, restless job switchers sometimes are suspected of being merely opportunistic, perhaps unable to get along with co-workers or unable to complete a job. And the rewards of job hopping can be fleeting. Professor Jennings found that though managers increased their salaries by 35% on average when they changed companies, those of equal ability who stayed on did *even better*.

Some job hoppers may sacrifice substantial benefits. For example, a sound reason to stay with one company is that your pension increases with your years of service.

Jennings calls job hopping a "high-risk maneuver" that "fails as often as it works." New jobs sometimes do not turn out to be as alluring as first perceived, or new bosses as charming. Even if the hopper succeeds at fulfilling a specific new assignment, he risks being stereotyped as fit only for that role. Job hoppers sometimes deceive themselves into thinking they have improved their position. In one survey, 85% of those who changed their jobs thought that their moves had helped them, but their new bosses reported that only 46% had actually advanced. So executive recruiters warn that job hopping *within a field* often should be a last resort.

How to Change Your Career

THE REASONS for veering off established career paths to explore whole new fields are often quite different today from what they were a few years ago. Career counselors say that midlife job changers no longer complain as much about too little advancement or too little pay. Their reason for switching now is as likely to be a desire for personal satisfaction as for money.

More and more managers are walking away from careers with big companies to strike out on their own. It's not hard to see why. Because of all the corporate cutbacks of the 1980s and 1990s, there may be fewer opportunities for ambitious executives at many companies. And some managers just get fed up with the stress of handling bigger work loads after yet another round of corporate downsizing. A number of competent, creative managers finally decide that working for a large company is just too confining.

Teachers, social workers and doctors often say they reach a burnout point of physical or mental exhaustion; they tend to seek out less demanding professions. One teacher of emotionally handicapped children contends she felt guilty when she first took a job as a tour consultant for a motel chain. Now she wonders why she did not make the change several years ago.

Above all, the successful career changers are adaptable. Many managers who have left one job to start their own business say that at first they really missed the secure sense of identity that a corporate job offers, to say nothing of that regular paycheck. People who move on to start their own businesses also find that they suddenly need to nurture skills that are not always encouraged at a big company — like creativity, risk taking and flexibility.

You can lessen your chances of making a big mistake in career switching if you turn to the right sources of information and counseling. For a good start, read a book called *Career Burnout: Causes and Cures*, which is published by the Free Press and costs $22.95. *Career Burnout* provides a thoughtful description of this increasingly common problem and ways to deal with it.

The most popular book that coaches people in career switching is Richard Bolles's *What Color Is Your Parachute?* published by Ten Speed Press. This $11.95 paperback emphasizes self-evaluation and defining your goals.

For information about specific jobs, you can start in the reference section of the public library. Look for the Department of Labor's *Occupational Outlook Handbook* or *The Encyclopedia of Careers and Vocational Guidance*. Both tell you how to break into a field, and they explain the kind of work done in a variety of occupations. Then head again for a bookstore. For $13.95 you can buy the *American Almanac of Jobs & Salaries;* published by Avon, it lists pay scales in various fields.

If the change you are thinking about requires you to earn a college degree, shop for a school that will give you academic credit for your achievements in life. A handbook called *Earn College Credit for What You Know* includes a list by state of colleges and universities that award credit for nontraditional academic work. You can order the directory for $19.95 plus $2.50 for shipping and handling from the Council for Adult and Experiential Learning, 223 West Jackson Boulevard, Suite 510, Chicago, Illinois 60606; or order by credit card from 312-922-5909.

You cannot learn everything from books, of course, so speak with people in the fields you are considering. Professional and trade associations and college alumni groups will give you names. Use your free hours to work part-time in your new job before you plunge in.

Even a pot-scrubber learns about such frustrations of running a restaurant as no-show reservations, late deliveries and long hours. And if you do better with a team than a tome, consider taking one of the courses or workshops in career change offered by community colleges and universities.

If you are thinking of making a change, some public libraries offer free courses in self-assessment and job evaluation. Universities, community colleges, YMCAs and YWCAs often have courses in career guidance for $200 or less. Private career counselors charge from $300 to $1,000 for several sessions.

Most of us also have undiscovered talents — artistic skills or money-making aptitudes — that we might not be aware of. If you want to make a career change and need help discovering a slumbering skill, consider having your abilities professionally tested. One of the oldest and best-known testers in the U.S. is the Johnson O'Connor Research Foundation. It charges $480 for seven to nine hours of testing and evaluation of your aptitudes for logical analysis, artistic or musical talents and even executive ability. The foundation has 11 testing centers around the country. To get a list of them, write to Johnson O'Connor Research Foundation, 11 East 62nd Street, New York, New York 10021. Or call 212-838-0550.

What to Do If You Get Fired or Laid Off

Y OU'VE worked hard to move up at your company. Then, suddenly you're laid off in a round of cost cutting. Managers increasingly are having to deal with sudden unemployment — and new job searches. A recent survey of 1,005 corporations by *Fortune* and the Wyatt Co. consulting firm has found that 86% of companies have reduced their managerial ranks in the past five years. Managerial downsizing has taken even deeper hold in companies with more than 5,000 employees. Fully 90% of these outfits have cut the white-collar payroll over the past five years. Two out of five of the top human resources executives polled say that the number of managers is likely to shrink further in the next five years.

In recessions, jobs are the first casualty. The phrase "reduction in force," hardly softened by its acronym RIF and used apologetically by corporations cutting back, spells unemployment for hundreds of thousands of workers, from the mailroom to the boardroom. Those being laid off can do little about saving their jobs but sometimes quite a bit about negotiating the terms of their departure.

Companies usually start with early-retirement packages. They may offer valued longtime employees a year's worth of severance pay or several years' extra credit toward pension benefits. Or they may ease you out with a consulting assignment at half your final salary. Early-retirement packages can put you in a bind unless you are only a few years shy of normal retirement age. The hard truth is that you are likely to accrue as much as two-thirds of your total pension in your last ten years on the job. But turning down a retirement offer has its own risks. The company may be telegraphing the news indirectly that your department may soon be eliminated, and your job with it.

Early-retirement offers didn't disappear with the end of the recession. They are part of a long-term corporate restructuring trend. Outright layoffs won't stop either, so you should do some research on your employer's policy on reductions in the work force.

Right Associates, a worldwide consulting firm that specializes in "outplacement" — the current honeyed term for firing — recently surveyed companies about their severance policies. About 40% said they paid a week's salary for each year of employment. But 5% said they gave a *month's* pay per year of service. In addition, around 40% continued their laid-off employees' group health and life insurance, usually for the same number of weeks or months.

Whatever the set policy, there's no harm in bargaining for better terms, especially if you are over 40. Severance packages usually come with a paper to sign, releasing the company from any further liability for your firing. But a 1990 amendment to the Age Discrimination in Employment Act gives people 40 and older a set time to ponder the deal, seek to negotiate better terms or even consult a lawyer. There's a mandatory 21-day grace period if you are being laid off individually and 45 days if your job is part of a mass reduction in force. Furthermore, after signing a release form, you have seven days to revoke it.

Robert B. Fitzpatrick, a lawyer in Washington, D.C., specializing in employee rights, has a battle plan calculated to leave a company vulnerable to litigation when it fires someone. The strategy begins at the first hint of a layoff. Employees who are warned of deficiencies during annual evaluations should take their supervisors literally by keeping a record of steps taken to improve their performance. "Bosses are lazy and they are busy," Fitzpatrick says. "So they don't give much time to evaluations and record-keeping. Prepare a work improvement plan if you're told to shape up. In it, outline the goals you expect to attain. Then attain them."

If you're let go anyway, you can go quietly or try to get yourself a fancier deal. Labor-law attorneys like Fitzpatrick advise many laid-off workers to threaten suit as a way of trying to wrangle better severance benefits. Possible improvements might include extra weeks of severance pay or its reclassification as compensation for the hardship of being fired after 40. Severance money under that label may be tax-free and can leave you immediately eligible for unemployment insurance. Extensions of group-health insurance coverage are also well worth some hard negotiating. It's true that federal law gives laid-off employees the right to continue their group health insurance coverage for 18 months. But the premium may be more than you can afford when you're out of work.

More important than squeezing your former employer for the last ounce is making preparations to get on with your career.

Starting over may require redefining what one does. A banker with 20 years experience in lending, for instance, may have to cast his or her net wider across the universe of financial services, and consider jobs in, say, marketing.

Dee Soder's Endymion Company counsels senior executives. She says it's hard to define exactly what one does in a managerial job. So, managers may want to begin a job search by taking a very honest inventory of their own strengths, weaknesses and aspirations. Before moving to a new career or field, managers should talk with people who have succeeded and those who have failed in it. They should be as open-minded as possible about career prospects. As Soder says, "The more inflexible you are, the more problems you will have."

The chances of becoming re-employed improve significantly if you proceed in a businesslike way. Keep your emotions in check and your wits sharp. Remember, there is considerable truth in those counselors' platitudes that you should devote at least six hours a day to the search, write 15 to 20 letters each week and consider job hunting to be a job in itself.

You should examine every option — such as moving to another city or changing careers. The biggest mistake some people make in their lives is to act as if they were born with a tag on their big toe that reads "I'm a middle manager" or "I'm an auto worker" or whatever.

But do not lurch into rash career decisions under pressure of finding another job. Do not switch careers out of anger at what has just happened to you. And do not go back to school simply to get away from the competitiveness of the job market.

You might browse through a book that career counselors recommend: *The Termination Handbook* by Robert Coulson, which is published by the Free Press. At the same time, update your résumé. List your objectives only in broad terms so as not to limit the kinds of openings interviewers might consider for you. A useful book is *The Perfect Résumé* by Tom Jackson, published by Doubleday.

A natural impulse is to call friends in other companies in the hope of immediately finding a new job. But that's simply trying to prove to your ex-boss and yourself that he had poor judgment in letting you go. The right time to begin calling around for leads is after you have a résumé and know where you would like to work.

Wangling job interviews is easier if you can use your friends for entrée. But if you have to start cold, one of the best devices is to write an enticing letter to the person who is in a position to hire. In four crisp paragraphs, outline why you are writing, who you are in terms of your previous titles and responsibilities, what you can do for the corporation you are writing to, and why you deserve a hearing.

Follow up your letter in a week or so with a phone call, but try not to sound too eager for the interview. If a potential employer senses that you are desperate, you've had it.

What do you say when a job interviewer asks whether you were fired from your last position? Don't hide it, lie about it or even dance around it. Being fired just does not carry the same stigma that it did 10 years ago. With so many mergers and corporate consolidations, it can mean simply that you were in the wrong place at the wrong time.

When you are looking for a new job, remember that personnel managers are impressed by someone who talks openly and honestly about himself. You can battle nervousness by rehearsing the job interview with a friend, preferably someone who personally has done some hiring. And although you want to cast yourself in a radiant light, managers really do appreciate a balanced self-appraisal. They like to hear a job applicant volunteer not just what he is good at, but where he is weak, too. Indeed, no one ever fits an employer's requirements perfectly.

It is equally important to have done your homework about the company and its field. Someone who has analyzed the firm's record and can speculate about its future impresses personnel executives much more than a job seeker who comes in asking, "What do you have open?"

Even if an interview goes splendidly, you probably will have to wait for a job to open. Without being overly pushy, the dedicated hunter finds reasons to keep in touch with potential employers. It is always wise to mail a thank-you note. You might even send along some new clippings or other information that might intrigue your interviewer.

But in the interview, don't be afraid to come right out and ask for a promising job. Like a salesman who is reticent about closing a sale, a job hunter who is squeamish can wreck his or her own carefully constructed campaign.

Time Management

IN THESE days of tough competition and round-the-clock global communication, it seems that work is never done. But somehow the heads of big corporations manage to stay on top of their jobs. How do they do it? A large part of the answer is that they have a talent for picking their priorities and concentrating on the essential questions of their jobs. Managers at all levels could greatly improve their productivity and reduce their stress level by taking the time to restructure their datebooks.

Smart people leave room on their daily calendars for the unexpected. If you have an agenda cram-packed with meetings, it doesn't necessarily mean that your career is going well: it may mean you aren't thinking straight. The worst thing that can happen with an overcrowded appointment book is that you could — and, of course, you will — start running late. As a result you will find yourself unable to keep up with your plan. In many ways, there can be nothing more devastating to a career than making it apparent that you are unable to manage your time correctly. Others may see that as translating into an inability to manage your company's business.

Technology can help you manage your time. Many executives say that their most useful tool is a good car phone. Yet plenty of high-level executives will agree with Laurel Cutler, the vice chairman of FCB/Leber Katz ad agency, who says her ultimate time-saving technique is learning to say *no* to some of the demands people would like to place on her time.

First, you should unjam your schedule by taking on less. Have the nerve to say no to those requests to head the Chip-and-Dip Committee for the company picnic or write a memo on the Misuse of Company Stationery. Then there are the tasks that you can delegate to others. That is just what a Los Angeles career couple did when they went to the extreme measure of hiring a 22-year-old person to do their shopping, pick up their cleaning and perform other household chores. The couple called him their "wife."

No matter how much or how little you want to accomplish, getting it all done usually requires following the standard practice of making a list. Writing the list just before you leave work at the end of the day helps get you off to a fast start the next day. You might even keep a second list that would detail all the foreseeable tasks you want to accomplish. Each day you pick 10 items from that list and put them on your daily sheet.

You might be wise to construct a personal time log. Write down everything you do for two weeks. That way, you can get a sense of the amount of time you typically need to perform certain jobs. Try to drop or delegate those tasks that take huge amounts of time but produce small rewards. Concentrate on the chores that produce large benefits for the time you put in.

Do you keep putting off little tasks because they are boring and have nothing to do with your real goals in life? If so, make an appointment with yourself once a week when your energy is running low to get through all the niggling but necessary paperwork that has to be dealt with.

Are you the victim of unwelcome interruptions such as drop-in visitors who plunk down in a chair and keep you from accomplishing anything? Maybe you are encouraging them — for instance, by making eye contact as a co-worker passes your desk. Some time-management specialists recommend turning your desk around so that you sit sideways to the door. That should keep you from making the first fateful eye contact without alienating co-workers.

Is your desk a mess? Just throw out the clutter, the memos, clippings, reports and monthly summaries you keep. Chances are you will never look at most of what you save. If you could readily replace a document, then why not chuck it?

As for the material you do decide to keep, try sorting it into four piles: first, items that require your action; second, papers that must be referred to other people; third, all reading material; and fourth, items that have to be kept in your files because it is part of your job to keep them.

Unfortunately, each mail delivery brings with it more paper, including a request that you do something at a future date. To organize all those new piles, take an accordion-shaped file folder and number the compartments from one to 31, for each day in the month. File the papers in them. Then, first thing each morning, run through the file for that date and act on all those notes that say what you must do that day.

If you are really in a mess, you may have to seek professional help. It is available from specialists called time managers, who stand ready to sort out your schedule and your clutter. Some may be listed in your Yellow Pages under "Management Consultants." Fees for time-management consultants vary widely. One example: the Work System course by Workability (914-764-0250) in the New York Metropolitan area costs $225 and includes a four-hour seminar plus materials.

Your Health

How to Cut Your Medical Costs

T HE price of a visit to the doctor has increased almost fivefold in
the last two decades, from an average of $11 to more than $50.
In that period, the average cost of a day in the hospital has gone up
roughly tenfold, leaping from $74 to $700. Although health-
insurance policies furnished by your employer may cover most of the
bills for your family, you may well face some sizable uninsured costs
if you or a family member become ill or injured. But you can
negotiate with your doctor, save on drugs and use other safe
strategies to trim the bills that your insurance does not pay.

One means of cutting your costs is simply to ask your doctor to
lower his or her price — if you consider it out of line or if you think
your steady patronage entitles you to a discount. Physicians' fees are
surprisingly negotiable.

Many health organizations offer discounts on the costs of fitness
checkups. The examinations range from stress tests to full-scale
physicals. To cite just a few examples from around the country: The
Health Plus Fitness and Rehabilitation Center in Kansas City will test
your fitness by checking such things as body fat, blood pressure and
heart rate. The examination will cost you only $150. At the Parkside
Sports Fitness Center in Park Ridge, Illinois, you can get a fitness
profile for $45. Plus, Parkside will give you a custom-designed

exercise plan. And for an additional $39, you can get your cholesterol count.

You also can save on drugs. Health insurance may pay up to 80% of your prescription drug bill. But you will pay 20% of a smaller amount if you buy generic drugs. They are virtually identical to brand-name drugs in all but a handful of instances. Ask your doctor to write out the generic name or indicate on his prescription that the pharmacist is at liberty to substitute a generic equivalent of a brand-name drug.

When you buy either kind of drug, remember that you will likely get a better price from a chain drugstore than from an independent druggist. That's because chains can buy in bulk. So can mail-order outlets, which are another good alternative.

Only one out of two Americans with employer group health coverage has dental insurance, so it is helpful to know that comparison-shopping for a dentist can produce significant savings. In New York, for example, you can pay as little as $20 or as much as $75 for a routine cleaning.

One way to save, at least on simple procedures, is to let dental students practice their skills on your teeth at a clinic of any of the 55 U.S. dental schools. Clinics do work at fees that are roughly half what you would pay a regular dentist. Students are in the final two years of their four-year dental-school education, and you will be relieved to know that they are closely supervised. Trouble is, they may keep you in the chair up to three times as long as experienced dentists.

A less trying way to reduce costs may be to seek out a dental clinic run by a hospital. These clinics are staffed by new graduates. They are faster, less error-prone and command higher fees than students. Still, they charge as much as one-third less than private practitioners.

As for psychotherapy, medical insurance usually does not cover more than half the cost, and psychiatrists in private practice charge $75 to $100, sometimes even more, for a 45- to 50-minute session. Fortunately, there are less costly — and equally beneficial — options.

Although they cannot prescribe the drugs often needed in the treatment of psychiatric illnesses, psychologists and specially trained social workers can treat people with emotional problems for less than what psychiatrists charge. For anything other than private, individual treatment in the therapist's office, you usually can save money. The same therapist might charge you only half as much to treat you in a clinic as in his own private office.

Another way to save is group therapy. Many therapists and clinics hold group sessions, in which several patients talk with a professional for about 90 minutes. The cost may run from $30 to over $50 a session, and group therapy is often used in conjunction with private sessions.

If you suffer from a well-defined problem, such as anxiety about a new job, so-called brief psychotherapy might be your best course. The treatment aims to accomplish a specific goal in a limited number of sessions, typically 20.

Still another expense you can reduce is that for eyeglasses or contact lenses. Ophthalmologists provide the contact lenses that they prescribe, but usually you must take an ophthalmologist's prescription for eyeglasses to an optician. He or she grinds the lenses and sells frames but has no medical training. Ophthalmologists charge $30 to $90 for a routine examination and up to $250 for a pair of soft lenses.

But if you don't have complex vision problems, investing in an exam by an ophthalmologist may not be necessary. For a routine eye exam, an optometrist may suffice. Optometrists prescribe *and* sell both eyeglasses and contacts. Including an eye exam, a pair of glasses bought through an optometrist is roughly 10% lower than a pair prescribed by an ophthalmologist and bought from an optician.

Checking Up on Your Health Insurance

Too many people who rely on their health insurance to pay their big medical bills are leaning on a rubber crutch. Even if you are among the more than 215,000,000 Americans covered by health insurance, you will find that almost no policy will pay all your medical bills all the time. That is why you should give your health insurance policy a thorough examination, diagnose its weaknesses and then look carefully for a policy that will *supplement*, not *duplicate*, your primary coverage.

Many of your policy's ills can be cured with additional coverage. If you are hospitalized, for example, most policies will pick up 80% of the cost of your stay in a semi-private room up to a certain length of time. Then policies will pay 100% for a "reasonable" period of time.

But if your plan will not do that, your best protection against bankroll-breaking bills is to buy an individual major medical policy from Blue Cross/Blue Shield or one of the big private insurance companies. Insurance counselors often advise that you sign with Blue Cross/Blue Shield because it often provides more complete coverage for less for all but the healthiest policyholders.

Whatever policy you buy should pick up where basic hospital and doctor-bill plans leave off. The majority of plans pay benefits ranging all the way up to $1 million — and many policies provide unlimited coverage.

It is also wise to buy an individual major medical policy if your current plan has limits on how much it will pay for surgery. But do not waste your money on the so-called dread-disease policies, which insure you against specific illnesses such as cancer. That's like insuring only part of your car.

Most health plans have limits on the total benefits you can collect in your lifetime. Experts recommend at least $1 million for each person covered. If you are ill at ease with your plan's maximum, you can supplement it at relatively low cost. For example, a family of four can buy a policy that pays all costs above $25,000 — up to a maximum $1 million. The average price nationally is about $800 a year.

About the only thing you cannot buy additional insurance for is your deductible for such outpatient expenses as doctors' appointments, prescription drugs, lab tests and private nurses. The deductible is the bare minimum you absolutely have to pay. These deductibles vary from $50 to $500 or higher a year, although $100 to $300 seems to be the average these days.

When you give your health insurance policy its routine physical, you will discover that some expenses just are not covered. In addition, two-income couples with different employers have two policies to scrutinize. The strengths of one may make up for the weaknesses of the other. But remember, family benefits are on the decline. According to a study by Northwestern National Life Insurance Co., while seven out of 10 employees believe their employers should provide health benefits for their families, nine out of 10 employers say they plan to reduce or eliminate coverage.

Try to avoid so-called indemnity plans — which pay no more than the fixed and specified amount listed in the policy for particular operations or for a hospital bed. An indemnity policy that pays $100 a day for your room takes care of as little as one-seventh of the cost. One exception to this is an indemnity plan that covers long-term care.

In choosing a policy, be aware that a company may cop out on you at the end of its term — usually one year — if you become undesirable. To head off cancellation of an individual policy, buy a guaranteed-renewable policy. It specifies that the company can neither cancel the coverage, so long as you pay the premiums, nor raise your rates merely because you have filed several expensive claims. Rates will increase, however, as medical costs rise overall.

You should keep your policy up to date, especially at major milestones in your life. Will you or a family member soon reach age 65? Watch out! It is *your* responsibility to apply for Medicare at your local Social Security office no later than three months after you turn 65. Most group plans stop regular coverage at 65 and offer only a supplement to Medicare. If you do not apply and then become ill, you may have to pay your own medical bills.

If you are retiring before 65, make sure you are still covered under your group plan. Otherwise, you will have to buy a high-priced policy on your own. And if you are laid off or fired, ask your employer to continue your coverage for at least 30 to 90 days. If you do not get that protection, shop around for an interim policy to insure you for a few months. If you work for a company with more than 20 employees and are laid off or get fired, you and your dependents have the right by law to be covered by the company's group plan for 18 months. You will have to pay for the coverage yourself, but at no more than 2% over the full group premiums. Be aware that this may amount to much more than you paid as an employee.

The law, known informally as COBRA, also gives a child turning 19 — or 23 if he is a student — the right to enjoy the group coverage for 36 months, again by paying for the premiums. The same period of coverage holds true for your family if you die or get divorced.

Finally, if you should end up as one of the 37 million Americans without health insurance, you might turn to your local public, voluntary or private hospital. You can never be refused emergency care and may be able to enroll as a clinic patient on a sliding fee schedule. You should also check with your state Department of Social Services to find out whether you qualify for Medicaid, government-funded health insurance for low-income persons.

How Medicare Works

SOCIAL SECURITY's hospital and medical insurance plan, called Medicare, is mainly for people 65 and over. But it also covers people of any age receiving disability benefits, after they have been out of action for 24 months.

Everyone eligible for retirement benefits gets Medicare coverage at 65 whether retired or still working. Of Medicare's two basic elements, Part A covers the hospital costs of everybody who is eligible and charges no premium. Part B covers doctor bills and many other medical services not supplied by a hospital, but it is optional and comes at a cost that is rising rapidly.

In 1992, the premium for Part B was $31.80 a month. The monthly rate is scheduled to rise around $5 each year from 1993 through 1995, when it will reach $46.10. Social Security deducts the premium from monthly retirement checks.

Even people who have not earned retirement benefits through Social Security can enroll in Medicare by calling Social Security at 800-772-1213. Their 1992 premium for Part A hospital coverage is $192 a month, $15 more than in 1991.

Here, in brief, are Medicare's benefits:

Under Part A, in 1992 the patient paid the first $652 of hospital costs. Medicare paid the rest for the first 60 days in a semiprivate room. The patient paid $163 a day for the next 30 days. In the rare case where you must stay hospitalized longer, you have 60 days of coverage that can be used over the rest of your life. For those days, you pay $326 of each day's bill. Your share of hospital costs goes up each year with the rapidly inflating rates at hospitals.

If the patient goes from a hospital to a nursing home that provides skilled care, Medicare covers all costs during the first 20 days and all but $81.50 a day for the next 80 days. After that, benefits stop. The accent here is on "skilled." Medicare doesn't pay for nursing homes or home care devoted primarily to attending to the patient's personal needs or for long-term care.

Other Part A benefits include some home medical care and hospice services for the dying.

Under Medicare's Part B, you are partly reimbursed for doctors' fees up to amounts approved by Medicare. You pay the first $100 and 20% of the rest of those approved rates and the entire difference between the approved fee and the higher amount that most physicians charge.

Because of the big gap in medical coverage (and the absence of any coverage outside the U.S.), it's usually wise to supplement Part B with a group or commercial "Medigap" policy. If you can afford it, buy one that covers the entire unapproved portion of doctors' bills. (For details see "Your Retirement: Your Medical Care.")

Prepaid Dental Plans

I F DENTIST bills are taking a big bite out of your family's budget, you may be able to chop these costs by joining a prepaid dental plan. It is a form of insurance that is typically limited to members of employee groups. But now individuals can buy into a few such plans. In exchange for your annual fees — $85 for individuals, $155 for a couple and $215 for a family of up to four members at Northeast Dental in New York — these plans usually do not charge you any deductibles. Since they emphasize preventive dentistry, they also do not charge you for checkups.

While there are charges for procedures, they are generally 25% to 50% below what people covered by regular dental insurance must pay. For example, the flat rate for a filling at Northeast Dental is $21.

All prepaid plans place some restrictions on your choice of a dentist. Some plans provide a long list of private practitioners whom you can use. Others require you to select your dentist at a dental center that has a contract with the plan.

If your employer offers you the option of joining a prepaid plan, first ask your benefits counselor how many of the plan's dentists practice close to where you live or work. And inquire whether your whole family has to go to the same dentist. This could be a nuisance if you prefer to use one near your office and your family needs one close to home.

Ask the directors of the plan whether complicated dental work, such as a root canal or oral surgery, is handled by a specialist. Any dentist is licensed to perform such procedures. So make sure you will be referred to a specialist if you need periodontal, endodontic or orthodontic care.

Find out how the plan handles emergencies. The better prepaid plans guarantee 24-hour availability for care, even when your chosen dentist is not reachable. This service assures you that you will not be forced to pay for treatments by a dentist who is not part of the plan. Also ask about grievance procedures to settle possible disputes between you and your practitioner. The plan should offer arbitration by a patient-relations administrator, or, ideally, pay for a second opinion from an independent dentist.

Prepaid dental plans are available in most parts of the country. To find one in your area, check the Yellow Pages under "Dental Service Plans," or call your city or state dental society.

How to Find a Good Doctor

ONE of your most important investments, surely, is your investment in health care. So it is smart to spend at least as much time selecting a good doctor as it is, say, picking a new car or a house. Not all doctors are created equal. You can measure them against certain yardsticks of quality, but you must be willing to do some research.

Start your search by assembling a list of candidates. Ask neighbors, friends and fellow workers for recommendations. If you are moving to a new town or neighborhood, get a few names of prospective physicians from the doctor you have been seeing in your old town and neighborhood. You also can request referrals from your company's medical department; that is the simplest way to get the names of professionals who have earned reputations among patients for reliability. In addition, you can ask local medical and dental societies for the names of practitioners who take new patients.

You can consult the *Directory of Medical Specialists,* available in large public libraries. It lists the names, education and specialties of all U.S. doctors. Alternatively, you can telephone the internal-medicine or family-practice department of the nearest university-owned or university-affiliated teaching hospital and get the names of doctors who are on the staff. Finally, you might ask your pharmacist to suggest doctors who he or she feels are well qualified. He or she is in a good position to know which ones are up to date on the latest drugs.

Once you have found two or three candidates, call their offices and speak to the doctor if you can. Ask what he or she charges for some selected procedures such as a basic physical exam. If the physician will not say, move on to the next. You can even drop by for a get-acquainted interview. Doctors often do not charge for a few minutes' talk with a potential patient.

You will want to find out whether the doctor practices alone or as part of a group or in a health maintenance organization (HMO). This is a prepaid group health plan that provides physicians and hospitalization for its members as needed. There is little evidence to suggest that your care will be any better or any worse in one type of practice or another. But many people feel that they get more individual attention — and hence better care — from a solo practitioner. (For more, see "Your Health: The Pros and Cons of HMOs.")

Studies indicate that the prestige of the doctor's medical school or its location — in the U.S. or abroad — may not, by itself, foretell the quality of care that he or she delivers. Two other criteria are far more important.

First, where did the doctor complete his or her residency? The best training programs generally are found at university-affiliated hospitals.

Second, has the doctor passed a certification exam given by the professional organization that oversees his or her specialty? Certification is no guarantee of excellence, but it is the best yardstick you have. Again, you can check the doctor's credentials in the *Directory of Medical Specialists.*

When you judge a doctor, also consider the hospitals he or she uses. You can't check into a hospital, except in an emergency, unless your doctor can admit you there. To do that, he or she must have been screened by its credentials committees and granted admitting privileges. Good doctors use good hospitals, so selecting the right physician can solve two potential problems. Conversely, if you favor a specific hospital, you should select your doctor from among those with admitting privileges at that hospital.

When you are traveling and need medical care, you should call the county medical or dental society for names of available practitioners. The Travelers Aid Society will also give you the name and address of the nearest hospital. Be sure to take along an ample supply of any medication you may need. Carry it with you — not in a suitcase that might be lost. If you run out, you probably will need to see a local doctor for a new prescription.

When you are overseas, an American embassy or consulate can provide the names of English-speaking doctors, although the U.S. government does not guarantee their expertise. Doctors' and hospital bills overseas usually must be paid in cash, but your health insurance program may reimburse you — after you return home.

How to Find a Psychotherapist

M ANY thousands of Americans make a major and most important investment in psychotherapy. But picking a therapist can itself be a source of anxiety: psychotherapy is expensive and practitioners range from geniuses to charlatans.

More than 300,000 therapists practice in the U.S. today, offering more than 250 types of treatments. Anyone can hang out a shingle as a psychotherapist, and, with a little knowledge and a lot of brass, can succeed. Consequently, credentials are critical. Accredited mental-health professionals fall into five classes: psychiatrists, psychoanalysts, clinical psychologists, psychiatric social workers and psychiatric nurses.

Psychiatrists and most psychoanalysts have M.D.'s, which means they can prescribe drugs and hospitalization; they are needed to treat severe illness. Clinical psychologists have Ph.D.'s in psychology; psychiatric social workers must have at least a master's degree, and psychiatric nurses are registered nurses who have at least a master's degree in mental-health nursing.

The best way to find a therapist is to ask your family doctor for a referral. You also can consult state offices of professional societies, which give out the names of members by phone. Other good sources for specialists are mental-health associations, hospital clinics or self-help groups such as Alcoholics Anonymous or International THEOS, which is a group for widowed people.

To check a therapist's credentials, contact the state chapter of the appropriate organization — for example, the American Psychiatric Association, your state psychological association or the American

Nurses Association. A few professionals might not belong, but it's safer to stick with those who do.

When you first meet a therapist, remember — you are a customer as well as a patient. Ask about credentials and fees. Some therapists will reduce charges if you are unable to pay the full rate. Feel free to get a second consultation or to change therapists.

Fees depend largely on the type of therapist the patient chooses. Psychiatrists charge the highest. In private practice, their sessions of 45 to 50 minutes cost $75 to $100 or even more. Psychologists with Ph.D.'s charge an average $60 to $100 for a session, while social workers bill $15 to $40.

Medical insurance coverage for psychotherapy can vary greatly, so before beginning treatment, it is smart to check with your insurer about what is reimbursed.

How to Pick a Hospital

WHEN contemplating the choice of a hospital, keep in mind that your selection is closely tied to your selection of a doctor because only a doctor with staff privileges can admit you to a hospital. It is therefore wise to consider these two factors together. (See "How to Find a Good Doctor.")

In judging a hospital, the basic gauge is whether it has the approval of the nonprofit Joint Commission on Accreditation of Healthcare Organizations. You can be sure that an accredited hospital has met national health and safety standards of excellence in 24 categories.

For most medical problems, accredited community hospitals without teaching programs may be satisfactory. Their staffs are competent, their costs tend to be about 15% lower than those of university hospitals and they have the reputation of being more hassle-free. For fairly routine treatment, it usually does not matter whether the hospital is privately owned and nonprofit or privately owned and for-profit.

However, for major surgery or serious illnesses, it just does not pay to be anywhere but in a university-affiliated hospital or a specialty center such as a children's hospital or an institute devoted to the treatment of a particular disease. Teaching and specialty hospitals tend to have doctors who are the most up to date. Another advantage of those institutions is that they generally see hundreds of patients a month. And, in medicine as in most disciplines, practice makes nearly perfect. Especially in surgery, volume is key. If the surgeons at a hospital do not perform 40 to 50 operations each year, they are probably not maintaining their skills. For heart surgeons, it should be closer to 200 or 300 operations annually.

How do you find out about a surgeon's or a hospital's volume? You have no choice but to ask. If your doctor does not want to tell you, try to gather information from local consumer groups, from insurance companies or from your state hospital association.

When surgery seems called for, a second opinion also makes financial sense. It can save your insurer money and you an operation. Many of the nonprofit insurers in the Blue Cross network have recognized the importance of second opinions. In some states, these organizations are encouraging them — and paying for them.

If you get a major hospital bill that is bigger than expected, check it carefully. In 1988, Equifax Services of Atlanta released figures from its ongoing analysis of hospital bills for selected group health insurers. Fully 98% of the many thousands of bills it scrutinized had errors. About 77% of the errors were over-charges. Among the most common mistakes are overstating services and charging for supplies and treatments that were never received.

When you or a relative is released from a hospital stay, insist on an itemized statement of charges. Ask for an explanation if you find items or services that you suspect weren't delivered. If you're still not satisfied, you can notify your insurance company, whose demands for an explanation will carry more clout. Some health insurers and employers are beginning to offer financial incentives to people who uncover excess charges on their medical bills.

Avoiding the High Cost of Hospitals

ONE reason for the rapid increase in medical costs is expensive, lengthy and sometimes unnecessary hospital stays. But hospitals have found several new ways to avoid the high price of in-patient care.

In nearly half of all surgical operations, patients now can return home the same day. Today, surgical lasers have reduced hazardous bleeding, and lighter anesthetics eliminate the hours of grogginess and nausea. As a result, many routine procedures such as hernia repair and cataract removal are being done safely, efficiently — and economically — *outside* of hospitals.

These same-day operations can be performed at hospital-affiliated clinics, in doctors' offices and at independent surgical centers. Three hundred of these freestanding ambulatory surgery centers have appeared in the past dozen years, and their success is due largely to their freedom from the tyranny of hospital schedules, as well as the savings they offer the patient. The doctors' fees are usually the same wherever an operation is performed, but *other* costs are 40% to 60% less than for a similar operation in a hospital. That's because the overhead in a clinic or office is lower and there are no room charges.

Some emergency-room treatment and many recuperative services also don't need the vast — and vastly expensive — resources of a fully equipped hospital. So entrepreneurs and hospitals have begun setting up independent emergency rooms. About 5,000 of them now exist across the country. They're staffed mainly by physicians specializing in emergency medicine or family practice. True, an emergency center is no place to go with a serious illness or injury. But for minor burns, sprains, cuts and colds, it can deliver faster, more convenient and often less expensive care.

Private business people also are offering home-care services that can be priced lower than the same care in a hospital. Some 12,000 agencies now provide home care, and about half of them are Medicare-approved. They send out nurses, homemakers and even companions to people who are confined at home but don't need hospitalization.

So, if you are ever headed toward a hospital, you might pause a moment to consider your growing range of alternatives.

The Pros and Cons of HMOs

HEALTH maintenance organizations, or HMOs, are often called the best prescription for achieving high-quality, economical group health care. They are not like traditional group health plans.

With a group plan, you pick your own doctors and send the bills to your insurance company for reimbursement. In an HMO, you — or more likely your employer — pay an annual fee, commonly about $3,756 or so for a family of any size. Then the plan's doctors handle almost all your medical needs for no extra charge. HMOs usually cover a higher percentage of surgical and hospital costs than do group policies, and you do not have to pay any deductibles. As a result, you may save 20% to 40% a year. The HMO bets that it can keep you well. If it does, it comes out ahead. HMOs do whatever they can on an outpatient basis. And they often reward their doctors in the form of year-end bonuses and profit sharing if they succeed in keeping their clients out of the hospital.

A common criticism is that HMOs are too impersonal. At some of them, members cannot always count on seeing the same doctor every time. Indeed, unless you are willing to pay extra for private services, you must use not only the doctors under contract to the HMO but also the hospitals, labs and other facilities with which your HMO has contracted. Another complaint is that too few specialists work for HMOs.

By and large, HMOs do provide good health care at reasonable prices — as their 38.6 million members can attest. A 1989 study conducted by the U.S. Health Care Financing Administration revealed that treatment provided at HMOs was as good as that available through conventional health care.

Still, they can vary widely in quality. So, before signing up, ask friends or co-workers who belong how they rate the plan. You should phone the administration office of any HMO you are considering joining and ask if it is affiliated with a well-regarded local hospital and has more than half of its physicians certified by specialty boards.

It is a favorable sign if the HMO is a member of the Group Health Association of America, a trade organization that sets medical and financial standards for its 320 member plans. Also ask directors of the HMO whether it is federally qualified. That means it provides a specific range of services; about one-half of the more than 550 HMOs in the country do.

Because many of the newer, smaller HMOs are operating in the red, you also will want to conduct a financial checkup. Phone the state office that regulates HMOs for an opinion on the one you are considering. The HMO is probably sound if it has been in operation for five to eight years, or if it is sponsored by a big insurance company or some other substantial institution.

Nonetheless, competition has become a threat to HMOs. Insurance companies, hospital chains and Blue Cross Associations are offering *different* kinds of plans. For example, big insurance companies also offer preferred provider organizations, or PPOs. They charge premium prices, but they allow you to choose not only your own family doctor but also your own specialists. And insurance companies and big HMOs are selling a so-called triple option — HMOs, PPOs and conventional policies, all in a single plan.

New Options in Births

A GROWING number of pregnant women do not want to give birth to their babies in a hospital delivery room. Those prospective parents now have several cost-saving options.

Certainly a hospital delivery room is the safest place to have a baby and the only wise choice for women who are considered to have high-risk pregnancies. But many women dislike the frequent use of anesthesia, the forbidding-looking equipment and what they see as the lack of personal attention. So they are choosing alternatives to the steel-and-tile delivery room.

For example, many women elect to have their babies in so-called hospital birthing rooms. Unlike the standard delivery room, these usually are furnished with beds, plants, stereos, and other comforts of home. Members of the family — including children — often can stay in the room with the mother. Labor, delivery and recovery all take place in the same congenial setting, where a nurse-midwife or obstetrician is in attendance. The cost for a routine delivery in a hospital birthing room involving a one-day stay is usually on a par with the average $3,233 for a traditional delivery-room birth. This compares with a cost of $4,334 for the usual two-day hospital stay.

There are also 140 birthing centers away from hospitals that are licensed by 30 states. The centers usually are staffed by certified nurse-midwives, and all have consulting physicians on 24-hour call. They also have arrangements with nearby hospitals so that a woman who suddenly develops complications can be transferred quickly to a delivery room. As birthing centers encourage a one-day stay, the average cost is much less than that of a traditional delivery-room birth — only about $2,000.

Some women want to have their babies in their own homes with the help of state-licensed midwives. A small number of the country's 4,100 certified midwives specialize in home births. They are trained to handle only routine deliveries. A home birth attended by a midwife could run $800 to $2,000. But it cannot be stressed enough that such procedures are *only* for women who have had an untroubled pregnancy and have received a doctor's fair assurance that they will have an uncomplicated birth.

Infertility Solutions

NEARLY one out of twelve young, married couples of childbearing age who try to conceive a child fail to do so. They know that the fight against infertility can be exasperating and expensive, but there are ways to hold down costs and increase your chances of success.

Thanks to modern therapies, couples battling infertility have more than a 50% chance of parenthood once a diagnosis is made. And it is possible to identify the cause in 80% to 90% of the cases. The testing and treatment can cost $15,000 to $30,000 — and sometimes more. Insurers cover only part of this. Couples usually wind up paying at least 20% to 30% of the bill themselves.

If you are trying to overcome infertility, then above all get expert medical help. Your family doctor or gynecologist may be able to clear up minor difficulties. But if your doctor's treatments have had no effect after several months, see a fertility specialist. For the name of specialists and fertility clinics, write the American Fertility Society, 2140 11th Avenue South, Suite 200, Birmingham, Alabama 35205-2800.

Closely question any fertility specialist you are considering. Ask about the tests and treatments he or she usually performs, how long he or she has specialized in infertility, how successful he or she has been in helping couples conceive.

Check into your health insurance coverage. Some companies do not consider infertility to be an illness. But even they will pick up part of the bill for tests and treatment of conditions that may interfere with reproduction. Your compensation may depend on the wording a doctor uses when filling out insurance claim forms. One infertility specialist advises: "Insurance generally covers the cost, as long as you do not state that the work is being done for infertility per se, but instead use such terms as ovulation disorder, tubular obstruction or pelvic adhesion."

When Should You Have Elective Surgery?

Every year, many thousands of Americans face a difficult choice: whether or not to have elective surgery. It can be costly, let alone painful. So when should you have elective surgery?

Aside from the usual fears, you have to consider many other factors, including lost income, uninsured medical expenses and extra outlays for convalescence. If you have any lingering doubts about undergoing a procedure, you will need a number of questions answered. Many of these should be directed to an internist or a family practitioner rather than a surgeon. That is because surgeons are oriented toward surgery. Find out the following:

— Can your condition be controlled by medication, diet or a medical device? If it can, are you likely to stay on the prescribed regimen?

— What are the chances that the disorder suddenly will get worse, resulting in emergency hospitalization?

— Will leaving your condition untreated limit your life-style, work or recreation?

If you decide on surgery, find out the chances of its success. You will also want a confirming second opinion before you proceed. Almost all health insurers will pay not only for a second opinion, but even for a third if the first two conflict. When seeking another opinion, avoid getting it from a colleague recommended by your surgeon. Instead, go to a doctor you have found independently.

To find another specialist on your own, phone the referral service of a major hospital, preferably one that has a medical school connected with it. Or call your county medical association, listed in the phone book. Pick a doctor who has diplomate status. That means he or she both has experience and has passed extensive exams in his or her specialty. The second doctor may insist you repeat the same tests you have already had, but if there is even a remote possibility that you do not need surgery, it is probably worth it.

The Costs of Cosmetic Surgery

COSMETIC surgery to fight sags, bags and wrinkles is performed on more than half a million patients a year. But what are the costs — and the real value — of those operations?

Depending on the operation and the doctor, surgical fees vary widely. They average from $1,260 for common dermabrasion to more than $15,000 for body contouring. But plastic surgery performed right in the doctor's office eliminates steep hospital expenses for many patients. A single overnight stay in a hospital for a face-lift might easily cost $3,500 to $8,000 for operating-room fees and a private room; in a surgeon's office the same patient might pay only $500 to $1,500 in fees for the room and various equipment — in addition to the doctor's bill, of course.

Operations are now routinely done in doctors' offices. An office nose job, for example, can take as little as two hours. Then the patient spends a couple of hours resting in a recovery room and goes home with a long list of dos and don'ts and a telephone number where the doctor can be reached, if necessary. In some states, such as California, there is another alternative: hotel-like recovery centers staffed by nurses to ease postoperative care.

Beware, though, of heavily advertised cosmetic-surgery clinics. In a few of these body shops, surgeons perform as many as 12 operations a day. This high-volume approach sometimes results in short-order workmanship. Make sure your surgeon is accredited with the American Society for Aesthetic Plastic Surgeons by calling 800-635-0635; also, verify that the in-office surgical facility is accredited with the American Association of Ambulatory Plastic Surgery Facilities, by calling 708-949-6058.

An estimated 13% of cosmetic-surgery patients are men undergoing procedures such as nose and eyelid reshaping and liposuction.

Some of them hope to enhance their business careers by getting rid of a receding chin or an oversized nose; others simply want to smooth away the signs of aging. But as one surgeon warns, "We can't make people into movie stars or mend broken marriages — the only way to get rid of every line and wrinkle is to embalm you."

How much do doctors charge? So-called tummy tucks are $1,200 to $8,500. Breast augmentation, which most recently cost up to $5,500, was relegated to the status of clinical trial by the Food and Drug Administration in 1992 and can no longer be performed routinely. The agency has taken this step to investigate once and for all the safety of silicone implants, which had come under question. A face-lift can cost between $1,200 and $8,000 but runs around $4,000 on average, depending on such variables as the particular operation, the qualifications of the surgeon and the geographic location. In one technique, the surgeon not only tightens the skin but also resculptures the jawline and neck by removing excess fat. Then he cuts and resews a neck muscle to form a kind of sling to support the neck and chin. Pain should be minimal, and discoloration should be gone in 10 days or so.

The news about nose jobs is that they are no longer the assembly-line reshapings of a decade or so ago. For a cost of between $2,600 and $6,000 you should get a nose that is natural and fits your face. The operation is done mostly from the inside out, so there is no visible scarring.

Hair transplantation is another growth business. You commonly will have to endure up to four or possibly five painstaking — and often painful — sessions with a plastic surgeon or dermatologist. Sometimes the plugs of hair do not thrive, or they sit in such neat rows that they often look as if they have been sowed by John Deere. The bill can reach a hair-raising $10,000 to $20,000, though minor jobs are significantly less.

Whatever the estimated cost, a plastic surgeon will not raise his or her scalpel until you have paid in full. The doctors say that since the surgery is elective, high postponement and cancellation rates mess up their busy schedules. More likely, though, doctors fear that some patients would refuse to pay after seeing the results. If you are less than pleased, your only recourse now is to sue.

Even if you are satisfied with the surgery, medical insurance probably will not pay for it unless the work is considered health-related or rehabilitative, such as breast reconstruction. Similarly, plastic surgery rarely qualifies for a medical deduction on your income tax. But no matter how much you have to pay, do not expect the moon. While cosmetic surgery can help you turn back the clock, you cannot stop it forever.

If you pick a plastic surgeon, you should do it as though your life depended on it. In rare cases of complications, it might. An alarming number of practitioners are charlatans. There is nothing to prevent an M.D. from hanging out a shingle, calling himself a plastic surgeon and making extravagant advertising claims. According to the head of a plastic surgeons' watchdog committee in San Francisco, misleading advertising has resulted in numerous catastrophes and several known deaths in California.

One way to measure a surgeon's skill is to check his or her certification. If he does all kinds of cosmetic surgery, he should be certified by the American Board of Plastic Surgery. You can get a list of board-certified surgeons from the American Society of Plastic and Reconstructive Surgeons (444 East Algonquin Road, Arlington Heights, Illinois 60005; 800-635-0635). If you tell the society what operation you are considering, it will provide the names of 10 board-certified doctors in your area who perform the procedure and can even send you information on its own financing program. A dermatologist doing hair transplants and skin peelings should be certified by the American Board of Dermatology.

Your surgeon should be affiliated with a reputable hospital or a medical school, even if he performs most of his operations in his office. Without the right qualifications, a hospital would not accept him. Moreover, doctors on hospital staffs are subject to review by their peers.

A plastic surgeon should be willing to spend plenty of time answering your questions. Some charge nothing for the first consultation, particularly if you decide to go ahead with surgery. Others ask for $50 to $100 or even more as a consultation fee. If you do not think a surgeon is right for you, it is better to write off the consultation fee and find someone better.

The stakes in plastic surgery are always big. Your best protection is to put yourself in the hands of a responsible surgeon.

Selecting a Fitness Club

IF YOU are just discovering the exercise ethic, you are probably wondering what is the most effective and least expensive way to begin. True, you can pursue most exercise without spending a penny. But if you need instruction, discipline or just camaraderie, money spent on shaping up is a worthwhile investment. It need not cost you an arm and a leg.

More than 23,000 fitness clubs operate nationwide. Often the best are one-stop, full-service fitness facilities. They offer pools, indoor and outdoor tracks and aerobic equipment. Membership costs range from $600 a year at a first-class full-service club to several thousand dollars at ones that provide the toniest surroundings for toning. It is probably wise to enroll for a shorter period — say, six months — even at a more expensive rate. That way, you can test both your compatibility and commitment.

Before signing up, review the contract thoroughly. Ideally, you should be able to freeze your membership if you are traveling, get a prorated refund if you become temporarily disabled or simply cancel within 72 hours if you change your mind.

The emphasis at the best places is on exercise, not just relaxation and socializing. Saunas, whirlpools and steam baths are extras that can make you feel terrific but will soften your wallet before they harden your stomach.

The best way to begin evaluating a club is to examine it at lunchtime or other peak hours when its staff and facilities are taxed the most. Make sure there are enough professional instructors on hand and that they are willing — and able — to answer your questions. Check that the equipment is well maintained. And be sure to inspect the whirlpool. A sparkling, ringless tub with carefully regulated water indicates proper attention.

You do not have to join an expensive health club. Instead, consider the not-for-profit YMCAs and YWCAs. More than 1,600 Ys have fitness facilities. Membership rates are set by the local Ys. Many have family memberships and lower single-parent memberships in addition to individual memberships. The price often includes a profile of your current physical condition, and a training regimen taught by certified instructors and matched to your abilities.

Another economically sound choice for anyone who plays tennis, racquetball or squash are the court clubs. Look for a club that offers not only racquet games but other fitness equipment and facilities as well. Often you can buy à la carte what you plan to use, much the way you purchase court time. Clubs charge $10 to $25 an hour for singles tennis, $5 to $9 for racquetball and $7 to $12 for squash.

Some people prefer to sign up for a series of exercise classes. The most important considerations are the qualifications of the teacher and the size of the class. The maximum should be 15 to 20 people.

If muscle-building is your forte, proper training is essential. Lifting free weights or using weight-resistant machinery can cause injury if you don't have sound instruction. You can get it at sleek Gold's Gyms, which cost $200 to $800 a year. Or you can try the drabber but equally serviceable body-builders' gyms, which charge $100 to $250 on average.

Fitness takes time: 30 minutes to an hour, a minimum of three times a week. Keep in mind that your success in achieving your personal best has less to do with the cash you put down than with the dedication you keep up.

Where to Take a Drinking or Drug Problem

MARY TYLER MOORE, Johnny Cash and Betty Ford have something in common with millions of other Americans. All have battled drinking or drug problems, or both — and won. If you or someone you know has such a problem, you can find effective treatment to fit just about every budget.

The number of treatment centers is huge and growing. Across the country, more than 46,000 Alcoholics Anonymous groups and some 7,500 rehabilitation clinics, hospitals, halfway houses and outpatient programs are offering help. The prognosis for those who seek help and complete treatment is good. The rate of recovery — defined as complete abstinence for one year — averages 60% and is much higher for those who regularly attend an after-care or peer-support program.

The costs range from nothing, in the case of AA, to $650 a day or even more. In fact, more and more people are getting the help they need at an affordable price. The reason is that treatment is increasingly being covered by health insurance.

In 1989 almost 90% of the 32 million workers in companies with more than 100 employees surveyed by the Bureau of Labor Statistics had group health insurance coverage for alcoholism or drug treatment. A 1990 follow-up survey of workers in companies with fewer than 100 employees found that 69% were covered by group health insurance plans and that 97% of these plans covered alcoholism and drug treatment. Medicare also covers up to 21 days per admission for inpatient detoxification programs and, in 1991, had no dollar limit for outpatient psychiatric care deemed medically necessary.

The first step for alcoholics and addicts who recognize their problem and want help is detoxification, the elimination of alcohol and drugs from the blood. In the most serious cases, detoxification in a hospital usually lasts five to eight days and costs $300 to $700 a day. But it is covered by insurance even when policies don't pay for other aspects of treatment.

Once a patient has banished chemicals from his or her bloodstream, the roots of the addiction can be addressed. Specialists in treating addiction often recommend group therapy. They argue persuasively that confrontation with one's peers is an effective way to break down an alcoholic's or addict's denial of his or her disease. Here are the four basic treatment methods that use group therapy:

First, *self-help groups*. The most prominent of them is Alcoholics Anonymous. Health-care professionals praise AA — and it is absolutely free. Similar associations that have borrowed AA's tenets are Narcotics Anonymous and Pills Anonymous.

Second, *outpatient programs*. About 85% of all alcoholics or drug addicts who receive treatment get it from clinics and rehabilitation centers but don't stay there overnight. Many facilities charge $10 to $100 a visit, depending on the type of counseling provided and, in some cases, what the patient can afford.

Third, *inpatient clinics*. Clinics charge an average $400 a day for typical 21- or 28-day stays. Generally, insurance reimbursement for inpatient care is limited to about one month per year. Although celebrities have gravitated to some clinics, everyone is treated as an equal.

Fourth, *halfway houses and therapeutic communities.* These provide extended inpatient care for people who would be likely to slip back into their old ways after a standard 30-day inpatient program. Room and board can cost $775 to $2,500 a month or even more in rare cases.

When you are ready to examine specific treatment programs, ask your doctor for recommendations. You also can get information from the National Council on Alcoholism. To locate one of their 200 local chapters, call 800-NCA-CALL.

You would be wise to look for therapies that are conventional and well tested. For example, you're best off avoiding any doctor who tells you that alcoholism or drug addiction can be treated with prescriptions alone.

If you are considering a treatment program, here are some points to keep in mind:

When you meet with the administrator of a program, be wary if he or she suggests admittance before taking a complete case history. Also beware of any evasiveness about costs or a willingness to shave a few days off a program to match your insurance coverage.

Think of the interview as your chance to assess a program's quality. First ask if the clinic meets the approval of the Joint Commission on Accreditation of Health Care Organizations, as well as state licensing agencies. Don't be afraid to ask what type of patients tend to use the program. Many of the best programs use group therapy. But if the other people in the program have radically different backgrounds from your own, you may find it difficult to identify with their problems. Also ask the administrator for recovery rates and inquire whether these are monitored by an outside agency, such as St. Paul's Comprehensive Assessment and Treatment Outcome Research (CATOR). A fair measure of success is one year of abstinence, but two years is better.

Your Education

Financial Aid You Still Can Get

Parents of teenagers who are heading toward college are becoming widely acquainted with a new American affliction: tuition shock. But there is some good news: Even though federal aid has not kept pace with rising college costs, you can still get much help from other sources.

Financing a college education always has been tough, and it is certainly not getting any easier. During the ten-year period from 1981 to 1991, college-cost inflation averaged 8.8% a year — more than double the general inflation rate. For the academic year 1991–92, direct charges (tuition, fees, room and board) averaged $15,382 at private colleges and $6,922 at public institutions. The fact that those are *averages* means that the charges at many universities were, in fact, higher. No wonder parents with college-bound children feel caught in a budget supersqueeze.

Fortunately, though, you still have plenty of ways to ensure that your children can get the education you want for them.

First, of course, start saving for college as soon as possible after your child is born.

Second, look for quality bargains in higher education. Many colleges manage to keep their academic standards up and their total costs down.

Third, press your hunt for financial aid. Sometimes it is available even to families with annual incomes of $100,000 or more. Many colleges recently have changed their scholarship programs to attract high-schoolers regardless of their financial need. Any high-school student is in the running for an academic scholarship if he or she has at least a B average and Scholastic Aptitude Test (SAT) scores above the national norm. Don't necessarily put off applying to a prestigious university because you think you can't afford it. Sometimes the most expensive schools give the largest scholarships.

Almost half of all undergraduates on campuses in the 1991–92 academic year received some sort of public or private assistance, as student aid reached an all-time high of nearly $28 billion. The federal government provided $12 billion; there are federal grants and scholarships that students do not pay back as well as student loans and work-study programs. The colleges supplemented the federal programs with more than $6.79 billion of their own aid. It is often from colleges that middle- and upper-middle-income families receive their help.

To find out whether you qualify, you go through a process called need analysis. Financial need is defined as the difference between the cost of undergraduate education and what your family can contribute. Sometime after January 1 in the year your child heads for college, you should check his or her college catalogue for institutional deadlines and form requirements. You will be asked to fill out a financial aid form that asks for detailed background about your family finances. It records family size, income, assets, household expenses and other information. You will complete either the FAF, Financial Aid Form, generally used by colleges that require the Scholastic Aptitude Test (SAT), or the FFS, the Family Financial Statement, used by colleges that require the American College Test (ACT).

The data then are analyzed in order to arrive at a figure known as your family estimated contribution. That is the amount colleges will expect you to pay annually out of your own pocket. If college costs are more than that — and they usually are — the school's financial aid officers try to figure out ways to make up the difference.

Financial aid officers determine how large a loan each student is entitled to. They usually base their decision on the so-called Uniform Methodology Formula, which takes into account not only a family's income but also its assets, such as the equity in the family house. Each financial aid administrator has the prerogative, under law, to make judgments in individual cases and can differentiate within the college's financial aid formula. If both parents are employed and, within a school year, one of them becomes unemployed or ill and unable to work, federal law allows them to reapply using a form for special conditions. The system *does* take into account unusual circumstances. Roger Koester, Financial Aid Director for the Colorado School of Mines in Golden, says, "A family can have an income in the $100,000 range and have five kids, three of them in college, and still show some eligibility. On the other hand, a family with one child in college, no unusual circumstances, and a $60,000 to $75,000 income will generally not be eligible for aid at most schools."

You can usually boost the amount of aid your child gets if you know how to massage your finances. There's nothing wrong with doing so, either. An advantageous application for college aid, like an honest tax return, violates no law or ethical principle. So why not take fullest advantage of the rules?

Rule number one: Don't put savings or investments for college expenses in your children's names. Under the federally legislated aid formula applied by the College Scholarship Service and American College Testing, the required family contribution to the child's education can include 2.6% to 5.6% of the parents' assets per year. That means the bulk of most families' wealth is never counted against them. But under the federal formula, students are expected to spend up to 35% of *their* assets each year.

Rule number two: Adjust and reposition your assets to minimize your wealth as measured by the aid system. In surveying your net worth, the system recognizes some forms of wealth as assets but not others. Bank accounts, stocks, bonds and mutual funds count against you, but the cash you accumulate in retirement funds, insurance and annuities does not. Financial planners therefore advise clients to move some of their investments into universal life or deferred annuities a few years before a child is ready for college.

Rule number three: Pump up liabilities that reduce your wealth under the aid formula. In general, the kinds of consumer loans that are losing their tax deduction also are disqualified as offsets to family wealth in the college aid formula. But loans secured by a home not only qualify for tax deductions but also get your kids more college aid. So it pays doubly to refinance credit-card balances and car loans with home-equity loans.

To get an idea of how much aid you might be eligible for, write for the guide *Don't Miss Out* (Octameron Associates, P.O. Box 2748,

Alexandria, Virginia 22301; $7.50). Updated annually, it provides a work-sheet for your convenience.

The cheapest money around is available through federally subsidized 5% Perkins Loans. Students can borrow up to $4,500 directly from the school during their first two years, or a total of $9,000 over their entire undergraduate career. Repayment begins nine months after the completion of studies and extends for up to 10 years.

Repayment terms apply six months after graduation to the old Guaranteed Student Loans now called Stafford Loans. They are offered through lenders such as banks and credit unions. Students can qualify for a maximum of $2,625 for each of the first two years and an annual maximum of $4,000 for as many as three remaining years, or a total of $17,250 for an undergraduate education. Interest rates are set at 8% for the first four repayment years, 10% for the remainder.

As mentioned, families applying for almost all federal financial aid must submit to a financial needs test to determine whether their children are eligible for the loans. But a federal offering mercifully free of a needs test is the Parent Loans for Undergraduate Students, known as the PLUS loan. Its fluctuating interest rate comprises the Treasury bill rate plus 3.25%, but it never rises above 12%. The maximum is $4,000 a year and you get these loans through participating banks or other commercial lenders. But repayment — again, up to 10 years — begins within 60 days after you take out a PLUS loan. The longer repayment period for PLUS, however, means smaller monthly payments than for most bank loans.

Many states offer subsidized student loans to residents. Among the most generous are Alaska, Illinois, Minnesota, New York and Pennsylvania. To apply, see your college loan officer or go directly to your state education agency. Loan programs often are limited to in-state colleges, but students from Illinois and Pennsylvania can take a state loan along with them, wherever they enroll.

Another major source of help may be close to home — in the form of scholarships financed by local communities, clubs and other private organizations. Every year thousands of students win more than $100 million worth of scholarships sponsored by many noncollege organizations.

Some 400 companies, unions and trade organizations sponsor National Merit Scholarships usually worth $500 to $2,000 or more a year and covering all four years of college. In addition, if you are a veteran, you can ask at your local American Legion post about awards available for your children. Civic organizations and fraternal groups also dispense scholarship money. Just a few examples: The Knights of Columbus gives 50 four-year scholarships, each worth $1,500 a year for tuition at a Catholic university, for children of members. Even a nonmember's child is eligible for scholarships from the Elks National Foundation (an average $1,500 a year).

If your child is willing to spend a minimum of four years after college in military service, you might consider the Navy/Marines, Army or Air Force Reserve Officer Training Corps. All three programs can pay full tuition, fees, books and $100 a month tax-free. Each year, between 3,000 and 5,000 high-school seniors are granted full four-year scholarships, but shorter-term awards are available to students who qualify after starting college. The ROTC branches fund a total of more than 15,000 scholarships a year.

Parents are not the only ones suffering from rapidly escalating tuition costs. The schools themselves must work harder to attract students. Consequently, many colleges are developing attractive financing programs. They are offering more and more academic scholarships for students with top grades. These awards can range from a few hundred dollars to full tuition. For example, among the most generous and prestigious in 1992 are the University of North Carolina's 54 Morehead scholarships and the University of Virginia's 21 Jefferson scholarships, which cover the entire cost of attending their schools.

A number of colleges also have adopted so-called guaranteed-tuition programs. With them, families can prepay all four years of tuition at the freshman rate. The University of Pennsylvania will even lend parents the money to do so — at favorable rates. Schools with guaranteed-tuition programs include Case Western Reserve University, Washington University in St. Louis and the University of Southern California. For families whose incomes are too high to qualify for existing programs, there are also new student-loan plans. Northwestern's Parent/Student Loan enables families with incomes over $30,000 to borrow up to the full tuition cost of $15,075 a year at 7.5%.

You can find out about scholarships of all kinds from high-school guidance counselors, college admissions officers and books such as Oreon Keeslar's *Financial Aids for Higher Education,* published by William C. Brown. Who knows? You might find a scholarship that few people compete for. At Harvard, for example, the William S.

Murphy Fund divides nearly $17,000 each year among needy collegians with the surname Murphy.

Do not fail to inquire whether any college your child is interested in offers an installment plan. Many do. Such programs often let you pay off a year's tuition bill month by month.

Another means of stretching your family's college dollars is to have your child substitute a job for a loan. Colleges are concerned about student debt and thus are expanding work-assistance programs. So is the federal government, despite cutbacks elsewhere. The government's college work-study programs can provide students with jobs from which they earn an average of $1,000 a year. In the 1991 fiscal year 789,000 students participated in federal work-study programs, earning a total $594.7 million.

Your child also can enroll in a school with a five-year cooperative education program that combines liberal arts with paid jobs. In the first year, the student takes a basic freshman curriculum of math and English along with courses in his or her major. For the next four years, the student alternates semesters of college study and paid work in a job. Usually the university lines up the job.

Some 1,000 colleges and universities offer co-op programs. Among the leaders are Northeastern University in Boston, Drexel in Philadelphia and the University of Cincinnati. For example, at Northeastern, tuition is about $9,970 a year and students can choose from a wide range of majors and paid jobs with more than 2,600 government agencies and private firms. Engineering students usually earn enough money from their co-op jobs to pay for tuition, room, board, books, entertainment — and sometimes a car after graduation. (For more, see "Your Education: Co-op Programs.")

Finally, see whether it might be feasible for your child to accelerate his or her studies and graduate in three years instead of four. To do that, your child will need to take advance-placement exams in high school. If your youngster passes, he or she can skip some beginning college courses — and save a good deal of money along the way. Remember: Any child who graduates in three years can save a whole year's costs, and these days that can range from about $6,000 to $25,000.

How to Save for College

CONTEMPLATING future costs of a young child's college education calls for a sound heart, a cool head and aspirin for those worries that go bump in the night.

In the unlikely event that college costs continue growing at the rate of 8% a year, as they have on average over the past ten years, a bachelor's degree in the year 2014, when today's newborns will graduate, could cost more than $323,000 at a private university and $145,000 at a public university. Assuming that the money you save will earn 5% annually after taxes, you would need to set aside about $845 a month to pay the costs at a private institution or about $380 a month for a public university. If you assume a higher-risk/higher-return strategy and earn 7% annually after taxes, you would need to set aside about $686 a month for a private college or about $309 a month for a public institution.

If college costs continue growing at the rate of 6% a year, as many economists predict, a bachelor's degree in the year 2114, when today's one-year-olds graduate, could cost more than $182,000 at a private university and $82,400 at a public university. Assuming that the money you save will earn 7% annually after taxes, you would need to set aside about $4,500 a year to pay the costs at a private institution or about $2,000 for a public university.

A convenient parking spot for savings is the custodial account that comes under the UGMA (Uniform Gifts to Minor Act) or the UTMA (Uniform Transfers to Minors Act). The tax code specifies that if your child is under 14, the first $600 of annual investment income in his or her name is tax-free; the next $600 is taxed at his or her rate (usually 15%); and any dividends, interest and capital above $1,200 are taxed at your rate. Once your child turns 14, however, the income is taxed at his or her rate.

The best strategy with custodial accounts is to concentrate initially on high-growth, low-income investments such as long-term growth mutual funds. Once the child is within five years of beginning college, the emphasis should switch to low-risk income-generating investments such as certificates of deposit, money-market mutual funds or short-term bonds.

Fidelity Investments, the biggest mutual-fund group, combines funds in a college savings plan introduced in 1990. They are Cash Reserves, a money-market fund; Blue Chip, a stock fund; Growth and Income, a dividend-oriented stock fund; and Asset Manager, a mixture of stocks, bonds and money-market securities. Investors can mix and match these funds in a custodial or UGMA account in any proportion they wish. For a minimum initial investment of $1,000 Fidelity waives the 2% sales charge on its Growth and Income Fund.

A different approach, based on the historic behavior of stock prices, lets you put more of your college money in the market. Over the past 67 years, rising stock prices and reinvested dividends have produced an average annual compound return on Standard & Poor's index of 500 stocks of just over 10%. Despite sharp declines in some years, losses over any five-year period have been rare. Going by past performance, then, a parent probably can preserve the value of college money in stocks by selling shares gradually after the student's 13th or 14th birthday and putting the proceeds in CDs or a money-market fund.

An investment program designed to do exactly that is available from Twentieth Century Investors, a no-load mutual fund company in Kansas City, Missouri. Through its College Investment Program, parents or grandparents can arrange to have fixed amounts of $25 or more a month transferred from a checking account to Twentieth Century Select Investors, a growth stock fund. Starting when the college-bound child is 12, 13, or 14 (your call), the fund company will transfer fixed monthly amounts from the stock fund to Twentieth Century's Cash Reserve money-market fund. Both are no-load funds, meaning there is no sales charge. But during this so-called "rebalancing phase" of converting from stocks to cash, there is a $10 annual maintenance charge (phone: 800-COLLEGE).

Families expecting financial aid might want to keep their college money in the parents' names rather than in a custodial account, as this could increase their aid package. Another reason is that custodial accounts come under the child's control after the age of 18. If you have qualms about leaving money in your child's name, you could consider setting up a minor's trust. The first $3,600 of its income is taxed at the 15% rate and additional earnings at 28% up to $10,900 and 31% thereafter.

Bonds have become popular with parents saving for future college expenses, as they produce compound interest over the years and can be timed to mature when the child is ready to go to college. Reflecting the concern with growing college costs, various bonds have been issued to serve the specific needs of parents.

U.S. Savings Bonds pay tax-free interest to those using them for college education, as long as the parents' joint incomes are $62,900 or less, or $41,950 or less for single parents. The interest exclusion phases out beyond that amount and disappears altogether at $94,350 for couples and $57,700 for single parents.

College Savings Bonds, also known as "baccalaureate bonds," have been initiated through legislation by more than half the states in the last few years. They are municipal bonds, which are free from both federal and state taxes, and do not ultimately have to be used for college costs. Some states offer a financial incentive if the child attends a school within the state. In Illinois, for example, parents who pay around $1,000 for a bond now will collect $5,000 in twenty years. If that money goes toward a college education, and the child attends a public or a private school in Illinois, the family collects a $420 bonus at maturity.

Baccalaureate bonds belong to the larger family of zero-coupon bonds, which get their name because you receive no income from the bond until it matures. You can buy a zero at a substantial discount and collect its face value when it matures. Although you receive no income until then, you have to pay taxes on the accrued interest — except on municipal or state zeros, both of which are tax-free. Tax-free zeros are fast becoming one of the most attractive long-term investments for college education. The risk with zeros is that their value fluctuates more than that of conventional bonds, as interest rates rise and fall.

The phenomenal increase in college costs has led to several creative means of financing, some of which are suffering teething problems. In state universities and colleges in Florida and Wyoming, a guaranteed tuition plan allows you to pay the state a lump sum to buy four years of future tuition at a discount. However, the plan faces serious snags on the tax front. The IRS has ruled that while the purchaser of the plan is not liable for taxes, the child will be taxed on the earnings when he or she collects the proceeds, and the state also must pay taxes on its earnings.

Another recent twist on college savings is the College Sure CD, created in 1987 by College Savings Bank in Princeton, New Jersey. The CDs are guaranteed upon maturity to cover at least some of the increases in college costs. The interest is indexed at 1.5% less than the college tuition inflation rate. You do not receive the accumulated earnings until the child enrolls in college, but the interest is taxed annually, like that of any certificate of deposit.

Financial Aid Consultants

To HELP determine a family's eligibility for college scholarships, grants, loans and other assistance, almost all U.S. colleges and universities use financial aid forms. But the forms are so troublesome to fill out that many parents are getting advice from academe's equivalent of tax advisers: college financial aid consultants.

This new breed charges fees from $20 to $500, depending upon how much individual attention you get. Consultants guide you through the aid application process and make sure no options and opportunities are overlooked. You may want to write to the national firm called Octameron Associates (P.O. Box 2748, Alexandria, Virginia 22301). A good financial planner will be able to advise you, and many local consultants are also in the business.

A consultant typically begins by reviewing your finances. Then, using his or her knowledge of the schools' finances, he or she can figure out what kind of aid and how much you would get from colleges you are considering. He or she will also point you to money available from sources other than the schools — for example, state loan programs or private scholarships. Of course, the consultant will help you fill out the aid forms; you have to repeat that arduous task every year.

To find a consultant in your area, ask a financial aid officer at a local college or a high school guidance counselor. Check the references of all consultants you consider. Stay away from anybody who makes big promises about how much financial aid he or she can get for you or who urges you to misrepresent yourself on the forms. The applications you file *are* checked for accuracy.

Co-op Programs

I F YOU are looking for means to pay for a college education *and* get a career off to a good head start, look into an increasingly popular program called cooperative education. It is an excellent way for a student to help finance his or her own education while gaining expertise in a chosen field at the same time. Students alternate terms on campus with terms working at a real job. Last year, more than 200,000 young adults enrolled in over 300 different curricula took advantage of such programs at some 900 colleges.

In a typical program a student takes a responsible job with a company that has agreed to participate in the arrangement. Students often work as trainees, and they earn an average of about $8,000 for a year's work. Some students earn up to $15,000 a year. Some of these earnings, minus taxes, are usually figured into the student's financial aid package back at school, and the grants and loans he would otherwise need may not be necessary.

The students commonly find that time spent on the job is a terrific boon to their careers. They usually receive no academic credit for their work, but they learn skills firsthand. Many positions become full-time after graduation, and pay a much higher salary than a less experienced applicant could expect.

Co-op jobs are scarcer, and salaries much lower, for humanities students than for technical students or those with specified job skills, such as nursing majors. Most co-op students are in business administration, computer science, other hard sciences and engineering. While the majority of students work for private business, the biggest employer is the federal government. It put 16,800 students to work in the 1991–92 school year. And the government usually keeps about 45% of its students on the payroll after graduation.

To learn more about these programs, write to the National Commission for Cooperative Education, 360 Huntington Avenue, Boston, Massachusetts 02115.

Choosing the Right College

FULLY 60% of the students who enter a college as freshmen do not graduate from that school. Most leave early because they realize they simply chose the wrong college. It is easy to make that mistake — but it is also easy to avoid it. Your decisions about what college to attend will determine where you spend several years — and many thousands of dollars. The best way to select is to visit several schools, meet with faculty members, students and administrators — and make your own evaluations of some key points. When comparison shopping, make sure your needs as a student are going to be met. For example:

Do the students share your talents and interests? To gauge the caliber of the competition you will face, compare your high-school grade point average with the average for this year's freshmen. College admissions officers will give you the data. If your scores are higher than the average for the entering class, you may find yourself underchallenged.

Consider the school's program in your planned major. If you intend to concentrate in science, for example, ask when the laboratories were last re-equipped. Find out where students who take your major go after graduation. It is a good sign if many get into prestigious graduate schools or win scholarships.

Take note of class sizes. At small colleges, the ratio of students to faculty members is a sound indicator of how much personal attention you will get. A ratio of 10 students per teacher is excellent. Ask an admissions officer to estimate the class sizes for courses in your major.

Find out about any special academic programs. You might be interested in completing your bachelor's degree in three years instead of four; almost every school in the country will let you do this. Or you might be interested in spending your junior year abroad — say, studying art in Italy. Many schools can accommodate you.

Determine what the total expenses are for the colleges you are considering, and decide whether you and your family can afford the price. Consider whether the added cost of a private college justifies itself or whether a solid state school can deliver academic excellence.

You will not spend money just on tuition, room and board. You also will make at least one round-trip — and probably more — between your home and campus each year. And you will have to pay for books, entertainment and perhaps a personal computer.

If you think you will require financial aid, ask college officials how your needs will be met. See whether the college offers most of its assistance in the form of grants, loans or job opportunities. A school that can afford to give out most of its aid as grants is more financially attractive than one that cannot.

Ask yourself if graduating from a certain college will enhance your career. You can expect a precise answer if you have a specific goal. An aspiring engineer, for example, can find out the percentage of recent graduates in his or her field who received job offers — and how much those offers were for.

Try to get a feel for how loyal the college's alumni are. Ask college officials for evidence of alumni networks. This can help you get a job when you graduate.

Finally, find out about the school's financial condition. A school that must survive mostly on tuition because of its tiny endowment may well have crowded classes, run-down dormitories and outdated labs. To compare colleges fairly, divide endowment by the number of undergraduates, and determine which has the largest endowment per student.

Where to Get a Degree in Business

WHAT is the most popular undergraduate course on college campuses these days? It's *business*. One out of four students is aiming for a degree in business, and many hope it will be a ticket to job security after graduation. It can be — if you choose the right school.

You should carefully check out the quality of the school before enrolling because strong demand for business teachers in recent years has produced a serious shortage of them. Look very closely at who will be teaching you. At the best schools, at least 70% of the teachers hold Ph.D.'s. Also, look at what they will be teaching you. Highly specialized areas are often quickly outdated by technology.

The American Assembly of Collegiate Schools of Business, the association that accredits business programs, has approved only 268 of the 1,200 or so colleges that offer undergraduate business degrees.

The University of Virginia's McIntire School of Commerce is often considered the most elite undergraduate business school. On average, over the past five years between 85% and 90% of the graduates landed jobs within three months of graduation.

The best schools attract hordes of recruiters. For example, at Indiana University, more than 500 corporations send recruiters to meet promising students. And representatives from nearly 600 companies visit the University of Texas.

If you are interested in accounting, check out the University of Texas and the University of Illinois. Their accounting departments are among the best. For courses in marketing and information systems, consider the University of Minnesota.

If you want to study liberal arts as well, the University of North Carolina is one school that offers courses in logic, writing and public speaking. Finally, the Wharton School at the University of Pennsylvania offers the only Ivy League undergraduate business major. It's known for its expertise in accounting, applied economics and finance.

Other schools with strong, selective undergraduate business programs include the University of California at Berkeley, Carnegie-Mellon, MIT and the University of Wisconsin–Madison.

Does an M.B.A. Still Pay?

TO EARN one of those cherished master's degrees in business administration costs $11,000 to $36,000 a year in tuition and expenses for a full-time student, in addition to salary lost by studying rather than working for two school years. But does it still pay to get an M.B.A.?

New studies by the American Assembly of Collegiate Schools of Business and the U.S. Department of Education show that the number of M.B.A.'s granted each year has more than tripled since 1970, to 77,200 in 1990. Almost 237,000 students, including part-timers, are enrolled in one of the more than 700 graduate business and management programs. Consequently, an M.B.A. no longer guarantees you an advantage in the race to top management positions. Tempting jobs open to graduates of even the most prestigious business schools are somewhat harder to get than they were in the late 1970s and early 1980s. On-campus recruitment has decreased and job offers have been fewer. The ratio of starting salary to tuition has also fallen. Starting salaries are still high, but many no longer seem as startling as they did in the past. The College Placement Council reports that in 1992 an M.B.A. with little work experience and a nontechnical undergraduate degree was offered a job paying an average of $36,096.

One way to gain even more benefit from an investment in an M.B.A. is to attend a first-rate graduate business school. The top ones include the schools at Stanford, Harvard, Chicago, Pennsylvania, Northwestern, Illinois, Texas, MIT, Berkeley, Michigan, Dartmouth, Columbia, Virginia and Carnegie-Mellon. The payoff of attending one of those schools can be impressive: 25% of Harvard's graduates in 1991 took jobs in management consulting at a remarkably high median base salary of $75,000.

It is also helpful to earn a degree in science or technology *before* going to business school. The M.B.A.'s with undergraduate majors in engineering or hard sciences usually get jobs more easily than those without such backgrounds. Another smart move is to work for a few years before going to graduate business school. The most successful combination for a new M.B.A. is to have a technical or scientific undergraduate degree *and* work experience. In 1992, such graduates with two to four years' work experience typically started at an average of $56,614. That was almost $20,000 higher than M.B.A.'s who majored in liberal arts as undergrads and had never held full-time jobs.

Opportunities Without Elite College Degrees

WE LIVE in what might be called a Bachelor of Arts economy. Graduates of four-year colleges have a significant and growing financial edge over other workers. The latest statistics of the Census

Bureau show that in 1990 the median income for men 25 and older with four years of college was $37,300 — 17% higher than the income of men with one to three years of college, and 31% more than the amount earned by those with only a high-school diploma. Every bit of evidence since then shows that the gap is widening.

Even so, many job openings call for skills that you are more likely to acquire in a technical school or on the job than on some ivied campus. Technical-school graduates are landing some jobs with a higher starting pay than newly minted bachelors of arts can command. Aircraft technicians fresh from a 2½-year program can earn $32,000 a year or more, which is on par with the starting salaries for most engineers with bachelor's degrees. Tuition runs to $19,000 at the College of Aeronautics, La Guardia Airport, one of about 140 institutions in the nation that offer such programs. A computer programmer who completes a six-month course can earn $22,000 a year while an English major is still home rewriting his résumé.

Technical training is expensive, but because it is condensed it costs far less than a $70,000 university degree. At one technical school, for example, an 18-month program to train electronics technicians costs $10,000. Many two-year community colleges and private junior colleges offer vocational training at considerably lower cost than do private technical schools. Tuition averages about $1,022 a year for such job-oriented studies as data processing, police science, real estate sales and auto mechanics.

What is most valuable in vocational education — whether at a community college or a technical school — is hands-on training. When choosing a program, first visit the school and ask many questions. Inquire about the school's resources as well as about the time devoted to learning by doing. Also check to see which companies hire the most graduates. Then query those companies' personnel managers on how they rate the school's courses.

A bachelor of science graduate of a 36-month course at the De Vry Institute of Technology can get a job starting at about $22,500 a year. That's a fair return on an investment of $23,490 in tuition and registration fees.

The best ideal, of course, is getting paid to learn a skill. High-tech companies that need a competent work force often educate people in specialized skills. The list of such corporations includes AT&T, IBM, Xerox, Wang Laboratories and Control Data. Competition for on-the-job apprenticeships has always been stiff, but businesses' need for trainees is growing. Some companies are helping to train students for the workplace before they leave high school. For example, Sears, lacking well-qualified repair people, is establishing a curriculum in a Chicago vocational high school that will give juniors and seniors the training they need to go to work as beginner technicians right after graduation.

The Labor Department's Bureau of Apprenticeship and Training supervises nearly 43,000 apprenticeship programs. Along with the standard apprenticeships for plumbers, pipefitters and carpenters, there are programs in hundreds of other occupations, including biomedical equipment technician, meteorologist and chef. To get more information about these programs, contact your local Office of Apprenticeship and Training at the Department of Labor or the state apprenticeship agency, which are usually listed in the new Blue Pages of the phone book.

Even without training, high-school graduates can land worthwhile jobs in marketing, retailing and a few other fields. And in some government-regulated sales fields — particularly real estate, securities and insurance — a beginning file clerk can impress a boss by studying hard and passing a licensing exam.

Cutting Costs at Community Colleges

YOU can get an effective and economical start toward earning a college degree by attending a two-year community college. Today nearly 6.2 million students attend such schools. Public community colleges cost an average $1,022 a year; that is about half of what tuition and fees alone average at a state university. And you can economize on room and board by living at home and commuting.

Check the catalogue to make sure that your college has a transfer program to a four-year school. The college should be able to meet liberal-arts requirements for transfer and offer courses in English, math, history and science that look like the core curriculums at a state university.

You can judge academic merits by consulting *Peterson's Guide to Two-Year Colleges* to see how many students go on to four-year programs. Anything over a 60% transfer is encouraging. Another sign of quality is the on-campus presence of a chapter of Phi Theta

Kappa, the honor society often considered the two-year counterpart of Phi Beta Kappa.

You also can earn a four-year bachelor's degree entirely by mail or phone. Most correspondence programs require some classroom attendance, but the Center for Distance Learning at Empire State College does not. The college is part of the State University of New York, and its correspondence program is accredited by the Middle States Association of Colleges and Schools. Through the Center you can get a degree in business, human services or interdisciplinary studies. Each credit will cost you $90 as a matriculated student, and you need 128 credits to graduate. If you have had previous college experience or other training, you can usually count most of it toward your degree. For more information, write to Center for Distance Learning, Empire State College, 2 Union Avenue, Saratoga Springs, New York 12866.

College Credit for Life Experience

You can earn college credits for learning you have acquired on your own — simply by taking a test. Quite a few accredited colleges administer such exams in what are generally called "external degree programs."

Two of the biggest and best known are at the University of the State of New York (Regents College, 1450 Western Avenue, Albany, New York 12203) and Thomas Edison State College (101 West State Street, Trenton, New Jersey 08608). Neither school has a residency requirement; both take students from all over the world.

To earn academic credit for work experience, you can take standardized tests. Or the college will tailor an exam to your special circumstances. To enroll in a Regents College degree program of the University of the State of New York, you pay $450 the first year plus a record-keeping fee of $230 each year thereafter and $25 to $125 for each three-credit exam. For more information you can also contact the College Level Examination Program (CLEP) of the College Board (45 Columbus Avenue, New York, New York 10023; 212-713-8064).

Budgeting for Students

ONE extracurricular activity that every student should master when heading off to college is personal money management. But a student's day-to-day spending is typically as ad lib and unbuttoned as a fraternity beer blast. That does not mean you cannot keep your undergraduate from overspending.

During a school year, the average college student will lay out about $2,000 for books, other supplies, transportation and personal expenses at a state university. There is plenty of room for economizing, and the first place to look is at food and phones. Two surveys have illustrated that point. At Penn State, boarding students forked out an extra $415 a year for all those 2 a.m. pizzas and their accompaniments. And at the University of Connecticut, students spent more than $50 a month each on long-distance phone calls.

While many students seem to think that it costs less to live off campus than in a dorm, they may be wrong. In college towns with a lot of demand for off-campus housing, accommodations within walking distance of campus tend to be expensive. Of course, off-campus students can save money by sharing housing and doing their own cooking. If landlords demand a one-year lease, students should hold out for subleasing privileges.

Most parents have to send money at one time or other. But doling out funds regularly by the week or month may tend to foster an unhealthy dependence. Instead, try giving your undergraduate a lump sum each semester and make it clear that the money will have to last. If you give your child spending money, be certain to sit down and discuss your mutual expectations. To avoid unnecessary strife, you need to know the student's assumptions about spending. And the student, in turn, should know when a check is coming, its amount and any rules about its use.

Ideally, college students should take full charge of a semester's spending. If the first semester seems too soon, put it off until the next term. But the parents' lives will not get any easier until the student runs his or her own finances.

Coaching Courses for the SATs

IF YOU are a high-school junior planning to take the all-important Scholastic Aptitude Test or the redesigned American College Testing Assessment, it makes sense to invest your time and money in a coaching school — particularly if a high score is crucial to your getting into the college of your choice, and if you are a woman or a member of a minority culture, according to critics of the two tests.

Test results show that coaching *can* improve your SAT and ACT scores. True enough, designers of the tests measure the kind of reasoning ability developed over a long period of time. But leaders of the oldest and largest coaching school, the Stanley H. Kaplan Educational Center, claim their students raise their SAT scores by an average of 150 points.

Among those who stand to benefit most from coaching are first-time test takers. Familiarity with instructions, types of questions and time pressures help to improve your performance. Coaching also aids those who tend to "choke." They can learn how to pace themselves, make informed guesses and take shortcuts.

The best courses last for a month or more. But stay away from the so-called cram houses that offer three sessions or fewer, no matter how many hours they run. Before you sign up for any courses, be sure you sit in on a session and find out if students are satisfied with the instruction.

The Kaplan Center has 150 branches with 600 satellite locations where classes are offered nationwide. You can call 800-KAP-TEST to find the nearest location or write the Kaplan Center at 810 Seventh Avenue, New York, New York 10019. The branches offer 40 hours of class in 10 lectures plus two workshops over eight to 10 weeks for $565 for SAT coaching. Scholarships are also available for needy students. Seven sessions of coaching for the ACT test cost $345. Another reputable school with many branches is The Princeton Review. For an office near you, call 800-333-3069.

If you do not feel the need for formal coaching, you might try examining the many workbooks available. One is *How to Prepare for College Board Achievement Tests* (each subject sold separately), published by Barron's at $8.95, and another is called *10 SAT's,* published by the College Board at $11.95.

Classes for Elders

MANY colleges are opening their classrooms to knowledge-hungry people aged 60 and up.

You can choose from thousands of week-long, noncredit courses through a nonprofit organization called Elderhostel. An average of $295 pays for from one to three courses taught by regular faculty members at U.S. colleges. That fee includes tuition, room and board and extracurricular activities such as films and parties. You can also sign up at universities in European and other countries, including Israel and Mexico. Two- and four-week foreign seminars on every continent except Antarctica range from about $1,600 to $5,000, including airfare.

Elderhostel enrolled more than 237,000 students in 1991 at 1,800 institutions. For information, write Elderhostel, 75 Federal Street, Third Floor, Boston, Massachusetts 02110.

Courses in Public Speaking

IN A SURVEY, 2,500 Americans were asked, "What are you most afraid of?" The most frequent reply was not death, illness or poverty, but speaking before a group. Yet people in all types of jobs are asked routinely to speak at staff meetings, sales presentations and trade conventions. Their success or failure at the podium often influences their careers.

More and more people are signing up for courses that promise to help make them better public speakers. Fees range from $50 or even less for a course at a community college or YMCA all the way to $3,600 for a commercial course. If you can demonstrate that the course will help you perform better on the job, your company may be willing to pay for the instruction.

The grandfather of public-speaking courses is the Dale Carnegie course. It consists of 12 weekly evening sessions for about $800 to $1,100, depending on region and is offered at more than 1,100 locations across the country.

You also can practice and learn through Toastmasters International, a nonprofit organization whose members attend a series of meetings to sharpen their public-speaking skills. You pay $25 to $50 a year at one of more than 5,000 affiliated clubs across the U.S., plus a onetime $12 fee to join. At meetings, there is no formal instruction. Instead, 20 or so members typically take turns giving five- to seven-minute speeches. Their peers then critique their performance.

Once you have picked a promising course, ask for the names of graduates in your field or profession. Call them and press for candid comments on the nature of the course, the quality of the instruction and the relevance of the program to your specific needs.

You may even become proficient enough to earn a second income as a professional lecturer. True enough, very few people can collect big money, but you can make public speaking pay.

Try approaching schools, libraries, PTAs and other civic and business organizations to offer your services. If you're good, your name will spread among local groups. At first, you may want to speak for free, and then as your reputation spreads you might start charging. When you can command perhaps several hundred dollars a speech, the smaller booking agencies may be willing to take you on.

Learning a Foreign Language

A LITTLE familiarity with a foreign language can go a long way when you are traveling abroad, whether on a weekend jaunt to Tijuana or a long business trip to Tokyo. The least expensive way to start learning is to take a self-taught course available on audio cassettes. These simple, repeat-after-me courses cost as little as $22. A company called Audio-Forum (96 Broad Street, Guilford, Connecticut 06437; 800-243-1234) markets sets of cassettes in 79 languages. There are 230 courses, each in one of three categories: tourist, refresher or comprehensive. The tourist tapes teach the words and sentences you will need for such basic things as checking into and out of hotels and getting around on public transportation.

For more comprehensive courses, consider the cassettes sold by the Foreign Service Institute. It is the branch of the U.S. State Department that trains diplomats and other federal employees in languages. Instruction in one of more than 50 languages costs $32 to $300 for a series of tapes lasting from 5 to 48 hours. You can buy them through the National Audiovisual Center (Order Section, 8700 Edgeworth Drive, Capitol Heights, Maryland 20743; 800-788-6282).

Top-quality foreign language classes are offered by many colleges and continuing-education schools. The language division of Continuing Education at the University of Houston, for instance, charges $265 to $385 for a 32-hour accelerated-learning course in languages as varied as Arabic, French and Chinese. Also check out classes at cultural institutes sponsored by foreign governments and located in many major U.S. cities. For example, the Goethe Institute is a German cultural center with branches in many places. Its Chicago branch offers German language courses that meet once or twice a week for 10 weeks. The cost is $150 for the ten-session course and $280 for the 20-session course.

If you want the convenience that cassettes afford and the personalized attention you can get in a class, consider hiring a tutor. That will cost you $15 to $40 an hour, although an instructor from a commercial school will be much more expensive. The most affordable instructors are usually foreign exchange students or foreign-language majors at local colleges. Ask instructors at such institutions to recommend tutors. You can also find teachers through the cultural institutes.

For a very intensive language-learning experience, go to classes offered by such chains as Berlitz and Inlingua. But be warned: Commercial courses can be costly. Expect to spend about $4,800 for a 12-day total immersion course in any language at Berlitz. For that price, you will get day-long private lessons from a team of instructors.

To make your vacation a learning experience, enroll in a study-abroad program run by both U.S.-based and foreign schools. You can study as briefly as several days or as much as four weeks — or more. Many of these language classes for travelers are reasonably priced.

Political changes have made it easier for both U.S. and Russian universities to set up a wide variety of inexpensive and flexible programs. Moscow State University and Leningrad State University permit foreign students to take language classes and to stay in the university dormitories. Clark Malcolm's Custom Tours (800-688-3301) specializes in setting up group study courses in the former Soviet Union and Eastern Europe. Custom Tours' courses typically include five hours of language instruction daily, as well as meals, activities and a shared hotel room for about $60 a day.

Your Vacation

Saving by Swapping Homes

You can cut your holiday costs in half if you are willing to let another family use your house while you use theirs. Many thousands of Americans trade homes every year, often with foreign families. For a few weeks, they enjoy comfortable accommodations in each other's houses, often with a car at their disposal. And all that comes without worrying about hotel reservations, restaurant bills and rental cars.

Far more Americans than Europeans are looking for swaps. So you would be wise to begin searching for a desirable swap at least three months before your scheduled trip. Summer vacation directories become available in January or February.

The best way to find out what is available is to join a vacation exchange organization. Get its directories and start writing the owners whose listings you like. Better yet, start telephoning them. You will find descriptions of houses up for exchange in places as diverse as Tasmania and Turkey.

Property owners pore over the directories for a house in the right spot and then negotiate trades with each other. Most clubs give advice on contracts, insurance and other details but otherwise aren't involved in exchanges. All allow members to advertise their homes for rent as well as exchange.

The largest of them, Vacation Exchange Club, lists about 10,000 homes in four directories published during the year. For information, contact the club at P.O. Box 650, Key West, Florida 33041; 800-638-3841. About half of its listings are in the United States and Canada, and the rest are in Europe, Australia, New Zealand, South Africa, Mexico and the Caribbean, with German and British swappers particularly plentiful. It costs $50 to get all editions of the directory and to list your house in one of them; for $12 more you get a listing with a photo.

A couple of tips: When you find a likely family to swap with, ask for references from people who have exchanged homes with that family in the past. And to avoid any unpleasant surprises, be sure to ask for a photograph of the interior of the house.

For further guidance in arranging a swap, consult Frommer's *Swap & Go: Home Exchange Made Easy* (Simon & Schuster, $10.95).

Rent-a-Villa Bargains

FOR a terrific vacation at a bargain price, consider *renting* apartments or houses in a tropical seaside resort. You can enjoy more privacy — at less cost — than at a big hotel. For a cold-weather week or two in the sun, rental apartments can be especially reasonable for a large family or several couples traveling together.

The best places go fast, so it is wise to book two or three months ahead. Hawaii and Mexico have the widest choice of medium-priced houses or condos. For example, on the Hawaiian island of Maui, six people can stay in a $500,000 beach-side condo for $50 a person per day. A luxury hotel nearby easily can cost three times as much.

The Caribbean has much to offer, too. Rents are fairly low on Barbados, St. Martin and Jamaica's north shore. You're likely to spend $200 to $500 per day for a two-to-five-bedroom house on or near the beach. Included may be a maid who cooks and a gardener who doubles as a houseman.

You can find a villa to rent through ads in two magazines, *Travel & Leisure* and *Town & Country*. Or look in such city magazines as *San Diego* or *New York*. The risks of renting someone's private home sight unseen are obvious.

The best way to make sure you don't wind up spending a week in a tropical Gulag is to find a villa through a reliable rental agency. Among them are WIMCO (West Indies Management Co., P.O. Box 1461, Newport, Rhode Island 02840; 800-932-2222); At Home Abroad (405 East 56th Street, Suite 6-H, New York, New York 10022; 212-421-9165), which visits 99% of its listed properties; and Creative Leisure International (951 Transport Way, Petaluma, California 94954; 800-426-6367), which specializes in Hawaiian properties.

Agents' fees typically are 20%, which you might pay in the form of a higher rent. But the charge may be worth it. A responsible agent won't handle a rental unless the owners have hired someone locally to maintain the place and take care of unexpected problems with plumbing, electricity or anything else that goes bump in the night.

Hideaways International (15 Goldsmith Street, P.O. Box 1270, Littleton, Massachusetts 01460; 800-843-4433) is a vacation/travel club that specializes in rental properties in the U.S., Caribbean, Mexican and Hawaiian resort areas but also rents apartments and villas all over Europe. Two directories and four newsletters a year, with some 2,000 listings, cost $79, which makes you a member; $27.50 will buy you a four-month trial membership, with a 30-day money-back guarantee. A black-and-white, quarter-page spread on your home, with photo, is $155 for new advertisers; the renewal fee is 10% of your weekly rental rate during high season. Hideaways also runs ads for weekly vacation-home rentals, as well as for yacht charters. Or you might want to consider joining an organization called Brennco Travel for $19.95 a year. Members receive the quarterly newsletter *Destinations,* which lists 1,650 hotels in the U.S. and overseas at 50% off regular rates. Membership benefits also include access to an organization called Condo Bank, which provides a weekly rental discount rate of $150–$400 to Brennco Travel members. For more information, write to Brennco Travel (formerly Club Costa), 7701 College Boulevard, Suite 200, Overland Park, Kansas 66210, or call 800-444-3998.

Time Shares

Between 1976 and 1989, the average cost of a hotel room rose almost 200%. Although prices are currently holding within 1% of the previous year's rates, Smith Travel Research projects that hotel rates through the decade will see an estimated 20% cumulative increase. In the face of this, time shares offer a seemingly attractive alternative. You pay a onetime fee for the right to go to the same place year after year for a week or two. But if you do not choose carefully, your bargain can become a burden.

More than a million Americans have been swept up in the vacation time-share boom. It began during the mid-1970s, when many builders of resort condominiums adopted the European idea of dividing expensive real estate among many buyers. Developers learned that they could double their profit by selling approximately 50 weekly shares in every apartment. The time-share concept quickly spread to hotels and motels as well as to yachts and campgrounds. Meanwhile, exchange services sprang up that enabled buyers to swap their time shares in one resort for vacation weeks at another resort.

Prices of time-share vacation units vary from $3,000 for one week every year in an efficiency unit in New England to nearly $25,000 for a week every year in a luxurious three-bedroom condominium at Lake Tahoe. The average cost is $8,500 a week. Most buyers are middle-aged, with an estimated average income of $53,800 but many resorts attract other people. For example, time shares in Aspen are popular among young professionals, and those in the Florida Keys appeal to wealthy, older couples.

During the early, rampant-growth years of the time-share industry, it was known for its fierce competition for customers and high-pressure sales tactics. Today, growth in the U.S. has slowed, and every state except Wyoming has a law governing time-share sales, and all of those laws include a rescission period, allowing the buyer to change his mind with impunity. Florida, the state with the most time shares, has the toughest law.

Outside the U.S., the picture is different. Growth is still strong, high-pressure sales tactics are common in some places, and the industry is not as tightly regulated. Before considering a foreign property, find out what laws protect you and govern the resort.

A number of the resorts where you buy time have gone under in recent years because of shaky financing and inept management. To avoid such heartaches, take the trouble to investigate the deal thoroughly before you invest. Look into new shares now being offered by four companies well acquainted with the vacation business: Disney, Marriott, Hilton and Holiday Inn.

Start by being wary of a promoter's aggressive sales tactics. Never, never, buy a time share on the spot. Instead, take home copies of the proposed contract, the schedule of maintenance fees and the disclosure statement, and study them carefully. Also, ask the salesman for customer references. It is best to buy from firms already running other resorts. The time-share owners at these locations can tell you how well the developer is meeting his or her obligations. Check the firm's reputation further with its banker or the state attorney general's office or, in some states, the special agency that regulates time-share offerings.

Look in the sales contract and other documents for a statement of your rights in the event the resort runs into financial trouble. If you are buying a so-called *right-to-use* time share, make sure the contract includes a nondisturbance clause. It obligates the developer's lender to recognize your occupancy rights in case of foreclosure. Ask the lender whether the same clause is in the mortgage or construction loan. If it is not, the clause — and your claim — are worthless.

In the disclosure statement and schedule of maintenance fees, see whether the developer is setting aside a part of the maintenance money for major repairs. If not, you could be socked for heavy special assessments in later years. And have a real estate attorney who is familiar with time shares review any documents before you sign them. Your own lawyer should be able to refer you to such a specialist. His or her fee for an hour or two of time will be money well spent.

If you buy a vacation time share but later become bored with visiting the same old resort, you have two options. The first is to exchange your time share for a share in another place at another time. Most resorts have agreements with one of two services — Resort Condominiums International (3502 Woodview Trace, Indianapolis, Indiana 46268; 800-358-3333) and Interval International (6262 Sunset Drive, Penthouse I, South Miami, Florida 33143; 800-622-1861) — that can arrange this trade. More than a million people exchanged time shares in 1991. But you cannot swap an off-season week at an unknown beach resort for a snow-season week at a top ski resort. You'll get the best trade if you own a time share in a popular place at a desirable time of year. And there is a charge for swapping.

The other option when you want to unload your time share is to sell. But selling the wrong season and the wrong resort may be next to impossible. Time shares rarely appreciate in value and should never be purchased with the hope of selling out at a profit. You're buying future vacation time, not real estate. But it's smart to think about the possibility of *having* to sell even before you buy.

More and more resort developers are handling resales, and using one of them will be your best option as a seller. If your resort developer or manager doesn't offer a resale service, ask for a recommendation. Before you work with any resale brokerage office, ask for referrals and check with the local Better Business Bureau. Never pay an upfront fee of any kind and don't work with a brokerage that demands such a fee. A reputable brokerage will work on a commission that typically ranges from 12% to 25%. But don't count on selling at anywhere near your purchase price.

So if you are thinking of buying a vacation time-share unit, be sure to satisfy this all-important test: Find a place you will love to be in that same time year after year. Here are some further guidelines to picking the right time share for you:

— If you buy a time-share unit in fee simple, which means you own it outright, brokers recommend you pay no more than 10 times the going rate for a comparable week in a hotel or rental apartment.

— If you buy the right to use, which in effect is a lease of 10 to 40 years, then divide the price by the number of years you get to use the property. If the amount is less than the cost of an equivalent rental unit, then the price is right.

— Buy one- or two-bedroom units. They are easier to resell than very small or very large ones.

— Buy time during the peak season at a popular area. This enhances your chance of swapping, renting or selling.

— Buy in a place that cannot be overbuilt because of geography, local building codes or moratoriums on further time shares.

— Buy your time share from an experienced builder. You will be less likely to wind up with poor maintenance, bad management or unforeseen liabilities. Also, big developers are more likely to help you rent or resell your time share.

— Buy from a resort that has a solid homeowners' association in place. As resorts sell all the available weeks, management is turned over to the owners, who must set up a structure for running the resort. As more U.S. properties mature, the strength of the home-owners' association becomes as crucial as the reputation of the builder.

— Buy in a place that is easy to reach. If it is not, that may discourage potential swappers or buyers.

— Buy a time share because you want a place to take a vacation. If you make the right choice — but only if you make the right choice — then you may have the double pleasure of regular access to a nice vacation spot plus a sound investment.

For a consumer's guide, write to the American Resort Development Association, 1220 L Street, NW, Suite 510, Washington, D.C. 20005.

How to Get the Best, Cheapest Plane Rides

WHEN you buy an airline ticket, you enter a bazaar of wild negotiating and sometimes wonderful opportunities for bargains. Ticket prices vary sharply, depending upon how far in advance you make your reservation, what day and which time of year you take your flight and from whom you order. The person sitting next to you on the plane may have paid much more — or much less — than you. This apparent confusion is governed by a process the airlines call yield management. Yield management takes many factors into consideration and determines how many different fares will be sold on a particular flight and how many seats will be sold in each of those fare categories. But those figures change — often daily — as the airline tracks sales on a particular flight. If demand is low for the flight, the airline will increase the number of inexpensive tickets available and may lower the cost for them.

Often you can get your lowest fares by ordering and paying for your ticket seven to 21 days ahead of your domestic departure, and up to 30 days ahead for international travel. And it pays to be flexible about your travel dates and the route you take. It may be cheaper to get from Des Moines to Dallas via Minneapolis than it is to take a direct nonstop flight. Even the airport can make a difference. For example, if you fly into Chicago's Midway, it may be cheaper than flying into O'Hare.

A few air carriers reduce their prices for night flights, usually beginning between 7:00 p.m. and 9:00 p.m. Weekend travel may cost $10 extra each way, but a flight beginning on a weekday and including a Saturday-night stay is almost always one of the least expensive flights available.

Sometimes travel agents can get better deals than you alone can, so it pays to use them. Of course, agents collect their fees from airlines, so you pay no extra charge for their service. But just as one airline can give you lower prices on the same run than another line can, one travel agent can bring a nicer bargain than another. And there will be times when you can actually get the best travel deals yourself, direct from the source. Obvious moral: It pays to shop around, among the air carriers, travel agents and discounters. Discounters offer tickets about 20% to 50% below normal prices.

As one airline executive has said, empty space on an airplane is "like overripe fruit in the supermarket — if you don't move it, it becomes worthless." When airlines cannot fill seats, they sell the tickets to consolidators at a considerable discount. Consolidators, or ticket discounters, have been legal since airline deregulation in 1978. There are about 100 across the country. Four reliable ones that have been in business for most of that time are Council Charter (800-223-8222), Travac (800-872-8800), UniTravel (800-325-2222) and Sunline Express Holidays (800-767-9776). Another discounter is Access International (101 West 31st Street, New York, New York 10001; 800-TAKEOFF or 212-465-0707). You may also be able to buy consolidated tickets from your travel agent.

In recent years, financial bumps within the airline industry have been consumer-friendly. June 1992 saw what one travel agent referred to as "suicide fares," in which all major air carriers offered domestic round-trip air fares at an average cost of $200. In this case, travel had to be completed by the following September, but there were no holiday restrictions — just limited seats per flight that needed to be bought within one week of the date that the airline "sale" began. In addition, for a charge of a mere $25, travelers were allowed to change either the outgoing or incoming leg of the journey. One can never predict, however, when fares will go up or down. But when they drop, as they did in June 1992, it pays to be prepared to act quickly and capitalize on available savings.

Other typical *round-trip* fares on U.S. and European carriers available in peak season from discounters around the country mid-1992: Los Angeles to New York for $308, versus the usual $660, and New York to London for $539, versus the standard "bargain" fare of $1,300.

Warning: A ticket sold by a discounter on one airline will not be honored by other airlines. The ticket also is usually not refundable and may carry other restrictions as well.

Once you have found the best price for a flight, buy your ticket right away. You then will avoid any fare increases before your departure date. Fares can and do go up overnight, sometimes sharply. However, should the price of your flight actually *decrease* between the time of purchase and the time of travel, the airline is required to give you a refund for the difference. It is up to you, however, to check the prices at the time of your departure.

Most travel agencies can track the very lowest airline fares through the Apollo computer system. For instance, Traveltron, operated by a travel agent in Santa Ana, California, guarantees to locate the least expensive fares on flights between U.S. cities and continues to search for a lower fare even after you've bought your ticket. Just one example: Fliers recently paid as much as $760 for round-trip coach tickets between New York City and Los Angeles. Traveltron directed callers to a rate of $308. Again, it is important to note the heavier restrictions that may attend lower-priced tickets — the penalty for changing the ticket could wipe out the savings. To use Traveltron, simply call 714-644-8766.

In the past, discounts were widely available to senior citizens and their companions and to other special groups. There is a trend toward eliminating these special discounts and offering only four fare classes: 14-day advance purchase, seven-day advance purchase, coach and first class. Check with your travel agent or the airline to see if there are any discount programs that coincide with your travel plans.

Happily, some airlines still offer special deals for passengers who meet certain age requirements, providing discounts of 10% to as much as 60%, on some Southwest Air flights, to passengers 62 or older and, in some cases, to a companion of any age. In addition, some offer programs that allow anyone aged at least 62 to buy bulk tickets at considerable discounts. For example, Delta issues senior travel books of four coupons for $568 and eight coupons for $984. Each coupon is valid for a one-way coach trip in the continental U.S. Two coupons are needed to go to Hawaii or Alaska. Flying days are unlimited, and the coupons are valid for one year from the date of purchase.

Whatever you pay, you can get the most for your money if you make some plans in advance. Wise travelers always try to reserve their airplane seats well before the flight. Although you can buy your ticket as many as 330 days before your flight, you may not be able to reserve a seat that far ahead of time. Call back at least three months before your departure to reserve your seat. You can also save time by asking for your boarding pass ahead of time.

You will have a smoother flight if you avoid the rear of the plane. Tail winds cause the most turbulence there. On rear-engine planes like the 727 or DC-9, you will escape engine noise and vibration by sitting as far forward as you can. By doing that, you also avoid the crowds when you leave the plane. Being one of the first out the door can speed you on your way — provided you have only hand baggage and do not have to wait for checked luggage.

On any plane, you will get the most leg room by taking the seat next to an emergency exit, since there must be enough space in that area to permit easy exiting from the plane. In the coach section, another desirable seat is in the first row, behind a bulkhead. You usually have extra leg room and a good view out a window that is unobstructed by the wing.

Avoid, if possible, flying at the busiest times, which are the early mornings and late afternoons of weekdays. For reasons travel experts have not fathomed, the most crowded day of the week usually is Thursday. Often the least crowded days are Tuesday and Saturday. Take direct flights whenever possible, and if you must change planes, try to avoid delay-prone airports, such as those in Chicago, New York and Atlanta. When you make your reservation, ask whether the flight you want is often delayed.

There is no foolproof way to avoid being "bumped" off an oversold plane. A wise plan is to call the airline the night before your flight and ask how full the plane is. If it is 60% full, don't worry. If it is full, and you absolutely have to make that flight, get to the airport at least an hour early.

Of the approximately 425 million people who flew domestically in 1991, nearly 650,000 were bumped. But if your plane is overbooked, you may be able to turn the situation to your advantage. Before bumping anyone, the airline must ask for volunteers who are willing to give up their seats. The carrot may be cash or a later flight at no charge — basically anything you and the airline can agree on. Less than half of all those who get bumped actually choose to do so. If only a little money is offered, you may be able to bargain for more. Generally, the airline's ticket-counter people up the ante if there are not enough immediate volunteers. A free ride can be well worth a few hours' wait.

When you are involuntarily bumped, the airline must get you on another flight that is scheduled to arrive within an hour of your original arrival time. If it cannot, it must pay you a penalty equal to your one-way fare up to a maximum of $200 and still fly you to your destination. If the airline cannot get you on a flight due to arrive within two hours of your original arrival time on a domestic flight or four hours on an international one, the penalty doubles to a maximum of $400. In cases when you are forced to make an overnight layover at a city not on your itinerary, the airline should pick up your hotel bill, although it is not legally obligated to do so.

Every airline has its own "contract of carriage," in which it spells out its responsibility to you. You can get a copy simply by asking for it at the ticket counter or by writing to the airline. The contract is also printed on the back of most tickets.

Do not check any baggage you don't have to. When you make your reservations, ask how much you are allowed to carry on and pack accordingly. One more tip: You can order a special meal by calling the airline at least a day in advance. Your travel agent can also order the meal for you. Quite a few lines offer a remarkable array, from pasta to pastrami, but many veteran fliers say that you get the best deal, and the freshest food, by ordering a vegetarian or kosher plate.

Finally, the ultimate bargain: Imagine getting a round-trip flight to Amsterdam for 50% or more off the regular fare. For such bargains, you just have to travel for one of several companies that use free-lance couriers.

Here's how it works. Some of the smaller overnight package express companies do not have their own fleet of planes. So they hire free-lancers to take commercial flights to destination cities, and use all or part of a free-lancer's baggage allowance to send their packages. The courier company pays at least half of the ticket price — and sometimes all of it. You can apply directly to one or more of the many courier companies around the country. One consistently successful company is Now Voyager (212-431-1616). For a $50 yearly fee, you can get such rare bargains as $150 round-trip restricted-stay tickets between New York and Mexico City. Or contact the International Association of Air Travel Couriers (8 South J Street, P.O. Box 1349, Lake Worth, Florida 33460) — for $35 a year, you can subscribe to its newsletter, which lists courier opportunities every other month.

Free Trips for Frequent Fliers

I F YOU travel often, it pays to become a steady customer of one or more airlines and enroll in their frequent-flier bonus programs. That way you can earn free trips, and you can even sell the travel awards that you do not have time to enjoy. In fact, it is smart to both concentrate your flying on one or two carriers so that you can accumulate miles quickly, and join every frequent flier club you can — you don't know just when you may be taking several trips on a particular line and may qualify for some of its giveaways.

The awards commonly start after you have accumulated 10,000 miles, when you get an upgrade to first class for the price of a full-fare coach ticket. The free rides usually begin at 20,000 to 40,000 miles, and the rewards grow progressively richer. At the highest levels, quite a few airlines will take you to foreign countries, either on their own planes or through linkups with most European carriers, as well as Air New Zealand, Australia's Qantas and some Asian lines.

United Airlines gives two first-class round-trip tickets to Asia or the South Pacific, plus 50% savings for up to seven nights in a Westin Hotel, and a one-week luxury car rental in the U.S., to passengers who have logged 150,000 miles. For 70,000 miles Delta will give you *and* a companion two coach tickets to anywhere in the U.S. (including Hawaii) and for 150,000 miles, the airline will give you two business-class tickets to anywhere it flies in Europe or Asia. These Delta awards include a 30% hotel discount over a weekend stay and the free use of a rental car for two to four days, depending on the award and the size of the car. At 80,000 miles on American, you get two free first-class tickets to anywhere the airline flies in the contiguous United States and Canada. Just about all other big airlines, and some small ones, have frequent-flier bonuses. Like the airline industry itself, however, frequent-flier programs are in a state of constant change, so it pays to both keep watch on your mileage and use it.

Frequent-flier bonus award systems have become as complicated as filing income tax. Each airline has its own intricacies and its own special perks awarded at different levels of accrued mileage. Fortunately, now frequent fliers have an answer to the increasing madness of getting what's theirs, flywise — the Frequent Flyer Club. Offering four different levels of subscriptions ranging in price from $50 to $150 a year, the Frequent Flyer Club provides services such as a monthly newsletter, a quarterly reference guide, a member helpline and insurance. Other services include computing your usage and mileage record on a monthly basis — the club will even let you know two months ahead of your award expiration that it is time to cash in your miles. Call 800-333-5937 for the Frequent Flyer Club, the H&R Block of the skies.

When calculating your mileage for an award, many U.S. carriers will even count flights you have taken on foreign airlines or other domestic carriers with which they have made exchange deals. You also can earn mileage credits by staying at certain hotels, renting cars from designated firms or sailing on selected cruise lines. So whenever you take a flight, stop in a hotel, rent an auto or take a sea voyage, be sure to ask whether you can earn credits toward the frequent-flier program or programs in which you are enrolled.

So read your monthly frequent-flier mailings carefully. In addition to providing your mileage statement, they will tell you all the new ways you can earn frequent-flier miles and may contain bonuses, such as passes to airline clubs and coupons for discounted — or even free — flights.

A new program allows frequent buyers to earn free trips. Through Air Miles, P.O. Box 593648, Orlando, Florida 32859-3648 (800-828-1342), participants collect miles by purchasing certain products and services — such as Clorox or AT&T's Reach Out America program — and by using designated charge cards. Collecting proofs of purchase can be a nuisance, but membership is free and mileage can accumulate quickly.

If you do not have the time or the inclination to take the trips you have won, you can sell them through middlemen known as coupon brokers. Their advertisements appear in the classifieds of the *Wall Street Journal* and many big-city newspapers under "Travel." But before you strike a deal, check out their reputations through local Better Business Bureaus.

Coupon brokering is perfectly legal, though the airlines dislike the practice. The price you will receive for your mileage credits is a function of supply and demand and the airlines' peak seasonal restrictions on bonus travel.

Special Deals in Hotels

THOSE lavish honeymoon packages at hotels and resorts are not only for newlyweds. Many times they are offered to anniversary celebrants as well — and it is a rare hotelier who will demand that you celebrate your anniversary on its true, verifiable date. Next time you book a room for two, simply ask for the hotel's anniversary or honeymoon rate. For instance, the Westin Bonaventure Hotel in Los Angeles offers a "Celebration Occasion" — one night's stay in a deluxe one-bedroom suite for $190, or about one-half the regular rate. Guests get champagne on arrival and breakfast the next morning, as well as complimentary parking.

Hit by the recent recession, many hotels have been offering terrific bargains to stay solvent. Even luxury hotels such as the Ritz-Carlton in downtown Atlanta feature weekend packages, including one in which a deluxe room goes for $99 a night, compared with a regular rate of $210. At other hotels, special weekend packages usually include a double room for two nights with extras that can range from welcoming champagne to ballet tickets to a gourmet dinner by candlelight in your room. You pay one price for all of this, and it is usually considerably less than everything would cost à la carte. In some cases, the savings can amount to 50%. Rates in top hotels for two people for two nights start at about $200 and run as high as $500.

Midweek packages are also available. Stouffer's Stanford Court in San Francisco was recently offering four days and three nights in a deluxe room for $569. The "Cable Car Package" included champagne, continental breakfast and two three-day cable-car passes, and the rooms overlooked the only cable-car crossing in the city. According to Helen O'Guinn, editor in chief of *Endless Vacation* magazine, you may also get rooms at 20% to 50% off the rack rate from the Room Exchange (800-846-7000; in New York, 212-760-1000).

A growing number of hotels are offering suites — many at prices far below those in traditional hotels. Some suites also come with kitchens, so you can save still more by doing your own cooking. For instance, the Windsor Court in New Orleans gives you a bedroom, a sitting room with either a balcony or a bay window, a full kitchen and up to *three* telephones for $235 to $325 a night. At the Embassy Suites hotel in Los Angeles, you pay $99 to $174 a night, depending on the day of the week and the occupancy rate, for a bedroom and sitting room, kitchen facilities plus breakfast, cocktails in the evening and transportation to and from the airport. Helen O'Guinn also suggests calling the actual hotel directly, as opposed to calling a central 800 number, if it is part of a chain, for further discounts off the rack rate.

In April 1992, there were more than 1,100 all-suite hotels in the continental U.S. For a complete listing of these, as well as more than 200 office suites offering space and services on a daily basis, you can get Pamela Lanier's *All-Suite Hotel Guide* (Ten Speed Press, P.O. Box 7123, Berkeley, California 94707; $14.95 plus $2 postage and handling). It is important, in the case of "all-suite" hotels, to ask ahead of time what is included. One hotel's definition of a suite could be a room with a hot plate.

And whenever you stay in a hotel, be sure to ask if it gives travel bonuses for repeat customers. For a onetime cost of $10 you can become a member of Holiday Inn's Priority Club and can stay with your family for the single-person corporate rate any day of the week, receive free morning coffee or tea, a free newspaper Monday through Friday and automatic room upgrades when possible. It doesn't cost anything to join Stouffer Hotel's Club Express. Points earned for the amount of money and time spent at a Stouffer hotel entitle you to upgrades and certificates that can be redeemed for free weekends, U.S. Savings Bonds and American Express gift checks. Hyatt's Gold Passport program is also free, and you earn five points for every dollar charged to your room. For 3,000 points, the starting level, you are entitled not only to a room upgrade for four nights but also to awards from Delta or Northwest Airlines and from Avis or Budget for car rentals. Individual hotels within a chain may have additional perks, such as coupons for free drinks, for frequent guests.

Bed-and-Breakfast Guest Houses

VACATIONERS find that staying in a big-city hotel can easily cost $200 a night or more. But there is a fast-growing alternative: guest houses that offer bed and breakfast for less than half that amount. They have the comforts of home at truly down-home prices.

More and more private houses throughout America take in paying guests. Like the well-known European homes that offer tourists bed and breakfast for nominal fees, these guest houses flourish in many cities, towns and resort areas where they cater mostly to travelers who have given up on hotels because of their champagne prices and no-fizz accommodations.

These guest houses rent out an average of three rooms. Rates for a couple can range from $100 a night at a Malibu Beach home in California to $30 in Albany, New York. There's usually a surcharge of up to 5% if you pay with a charge card. Breakfast and free parking are almost always part of the deal. There is no guilty fumbling for tips; hosts rarely accept them.

Most offer the kind of hospitality that is rare at hotels, eagerly sharing with you insiders' insights on fine restaurants and shopping bargains. But you may miss some amenities available at even moderately priced hotels. You probably won't have a TV or phone in your room. You may have to share a bathroom.

You can find a listing of more than 1,000 bed-and-breakfast hosts in a book, *Bed & Breakfast U.S.A.*, by Betty Revits Rundback. It is updated annually and costs $14.

Bed & Breakfast U.S.A. includes a chapter on how to start your own and lists over 115 bed-and-breakfast reservation agencies. They often send free brochures describing members' houses and an application asking for your itinerary, how long you plan to stay and whether you insist on comforts such as air conditioning. Sometimes you can choose your accommodation; other times you are assigned to one. These booking agencies may take a week or two to confirm reservations, so plan your trip in advance. Other B&B listings may be found in tourbooks published by the American Automobile Association and Mobil, as well as *The Innkeepers' Register* (Independent Innkeepers' Association, $6.95) and *Inspected, Rated and Approved Bed & Breakfasts and Country Inns* (American B&B Association, $14.95). Helen O'Guinn suggests that the *Consumer Reports Travel Newsletter* is the best arbiter of quality of B&Bs, which often escape the high level of scrutiny leveled at hotels and motels.

Two agencies specializing in city B&Bs are Bed & Breakfast/Chicago, Inc., a reservations service that represents about 70 private homes and apartments (Box 14088, Chicago, Illinois 60614-0088; 312-951-0085), and Urban Ventures, which represents about 700 hosted and unhosted apartments and townhouses in New

York City (306 West 38th Street, New York, New York 10018; 212-594-5650).

Dude Ranches

I F YOU are looking for a moderately priced family vacation, you might consider spending a week at one of America's 300 dude ranches. Each can offer a private cabin, three hearty meals a day and a companionable horse for the price of just a room in a big-city hotel. A week at a ranch typically costs around $450 to $1,400 per adult — less for children. The ranches are mostly in the open spaces of the West, but the East and South have a sprinkling of smaller spreads.

Many of the ranches still raise cattle for profit and let visiting dudes help round up the herd, brand a steer or lend a hand with chores. But the emphasis is on horseback riding. Ranches offer easy, medium and fast rides, and sometimes real cattle drives. Other activities can include fishing, hiking and swimming. The newest breed of ranches couples conventional resort fare such as tennis with an Old West setting. But the more frills a ranch offers, the more expensive it is likely to be.

To find a dude ranch, write or phone the tourist office in the state or states you would like to visit. For a list of dude ranches in the West, send $3 to the Dude Ranchers' Association at P.O. Box 471, Laporte, Colorado 80535. Or call them at 303-223-8440.

Figuring your budget is simple because the rates are inclusive. You need add in only your transportation and clothing costs. It can cost less than $150 to outfit you from head to toe for a dude ranch. The biggest and most important investment is cowboy boots. They start at about $85, unless you catch the annual Thanksgiving sale at the Tony Lama factory in El Paso, Texas. However, many ranches have boxes of old boots in a variety of sizes that are available to their "dudes." You'll also need a couple of pairs of broken-in jeans, flannel shirts and a warm jacket for cool morning or evening rides. A snug straw cowboy hat will shield your eyes from the sun and dust. The cheapest is about $20.

A warning about dude ranches: Do not expect luxurious rooms and gourmet meals. At all but the most expensive ranches, both rooms and meals are simple and basic.

Holding Down Costs of Foreign Travel

THE DECLINE in the value of the once mighty dollar is a tonic for the nation's trade balance but tough on American tourists abroad. Foreign travel is significantly more expensive than it was in the early or mid-1980s. Travel bargains do exist in Portugal, Turkey, and Eastern Europe, but Western Europe, for the most part, is not comfortably affordable. So to prevent any unexpected blows to your pocketbook, it pays to prepare a sensible travel budget in advance.

Before you go, read (or at least skim) one or two up-to-date guidebooks. They will help you arrive at a reasonable estimate of what your trip will cost. At least half a dozen travel newsletters also offer reliable cost information tailored to specific clients, such as retired travelers or singles. You can find out where to subscribe to them from travel agents, advertisements in travel magazines and your own special-interest groups.

After you have done your homework, sit down and make a daily budget. Add up the estimated costs of hotels, food, tips, taxis and incidentals. Then tack on at least 25% more for the unexpected.

Do not plan to spend the same amount each day. Try the "budget-splurge" method of travel. Cut back on certain days by eating delicatessen take-outs in the park for dinner. Then you can afford a really terrific restaurant the next day.

Prepay as much of your trip as you can before you leave. That avoids budget-busting surprises.

Package tours are surely the cheapest way to travel. But some stripped-down tours have more hidden costs than France has churches. Hotel and restaurant managers may ask you to pay extra for items you thought had been taken care of well in advance. You will have a hard time trying to collect when you get back home. Spare yourself grief by inquiring exactly what you are paying for before you leave. (For more, see "Your Vacation: Getting Good Value on Package Tours.")

The surest way to save money is to plan a trip as far ahead as possible. That way, you can get the cheapest air fares. If you do not want a package and are willing to lock in your plans at least seven days, but in the case of international travel, up to 30 days ahead, buy an advance-purchase excursion ticket, called Apex. That almost always gives you the least expensive round-trip fare on regularly scheduled airlines. Any change made after purchase of the ticket may be costly.

Plan to pay for your expenses abroad with a combination of traveler's checks and credit cards. Do not carry too much cash, because hotel thefts can be a problem. In a pinch, you usually can cash personal checks at top hotels and the offices of credit-card companies. But you need to have a credit card to do it.

If you enjoy train travel, one of the world's last great bargains is the Eurailpass. It allows you to travel first class as much as you want in 17 European countries for $430 for 15 days, $340 if three or more travel together. Children under 12 go half-price; under four years old they ride free. Many countries offer their own national pass; such passes are cheaper than the geographically unrestricted Eurailpass. Britain is not covered by the Eurailpass but has its own version, called Britrail, which allows an adult 15 days of first-class travel by railroads all over England, Scotland and Wales for $479; standard class is $319. Children aged five through 15 travel for half fare. Call Rail Europe at 800-345-1990 and buy the pass before you leave.

European trains are usually fast, clean, comfortable — much better than most of their American counterparts. They are also good for stretching out and sleeping in — which is a clever way of saving a bundle on a hotel room every now and then.

Just about everywhere, you can save money by avoiding the costly capital cities and trekking off to the provincial centers and the countryside. For example, rural Britain is not only charming but also far less expensive than swinging London. But wherever you decide to go, you might follow the advice of the most savvy and seasoned travelers: Take half of what you pack and twice as much as you have budgeted.

Getting Good Value on Package Tours

ALMOST every would-be tourist has heard horror stories about package tours. But you do not have to swear off those bargain deals if you want your vacation to go smoothly. You can get top value for your money provided you know how to examine your package tour in advance. Here are some of the questions you will want answered:

— Does the package include an inexpensive and convenient charter flight? Regular fares are down so much on some routes that you could wind up saving only about $25 on round-trip charters from New York City to London. When the savings are substantial, make sure that you do not have to stop en route in two or three other U.S. cities before heading for Rome — via London and Brussels.

— What do "first-class" accommodations really mean? The best European hotels are rated "deluxe." All that first class gets you is a clean bed-chamber with a private bath. You can determine if you are going first class or fleabag by looking up the amenities of your hotel in *The Official Hotel and Resort Guide,* available at travel agencies and libraries. The guide also lists the price you would pay for the room if you booked on your own. If the daily cost of the hotel on your package tour is *less* than the hotel's usual room rate, you know you are getting a deal.

— How many people will be on your tour? Having 59 fellow travelers is a completely different experience from having nine.

— Will you actually get to tour the sights listed in the brochure? Although the lineup may be dazzling, it's apt to lose its luster if you do all your viewing through a bus window.

— Will the meals consist of foie gras and roast pigeon, or tomato juice and roast chicken? Tour operators won't tell you what you will eat at meals included in the package, but they will give you hints. If you find you are to eat in hotel restaurants, remember that they seldom are great gastronomical palaces.

— What happens if you have to cancel? Read the brochure's fine print carefully. You will probably lose your hotel deposits, typically the cost of one to three nights. But most tour operators will refund the rest of your money, minus a fee of $25 to $100 depending on how close to the departure date you back out.

— One more important tip: You can check on the record of charter companies by phoning the U.S. Department of Transportation's Office of Consumer Affairs at 202-366-2220.

Shopping Bargains Overseas

WITH little effort, you can save 20% to 50% on some foreign purchases compared with what you would pay in the U.S. You are likely to get the best buys on the specialties of each country, such as lace in Belgium, ceramics in Portugal and crystal in France. England has the top bargains in clothing and porcelain; Italy is the place for fine leather goods. You can get diamonds in Amsterdam for as much as 30% less than you might have to pay in the U.S. For furs, look to Scandinavia.

Europe is not the only mecca for American shoppers. Mexican leather and silver are reasonably priced. Brazilian gemstones are as much as a third less in Rio de Janeiro than they are in the U.S. And Hong Kong is a bargain spot for jewelry, clothing, porcelain, Oriental rugs and Chinese crafts and antiques.

Some other shopping advice:

— If you have a specific item in mind, price it at home. You may pay less for a Burberry coat in your local store than at Harrod's in London.

— Look for bargains on products that have been brought in from countries outside the one you are visiting. A number of governments have lenient tax policies that make imported products less expensive than in the countries where they are manufactured. It can be cheaper to buy a Swiss watch in Copenhagen than in Geneva.

— Scout the big department stores, but only to determine the going prices for merchandise. Then buy the goods in the smaller boutiques and flea markets, where prices usually are lower.

— Shop the less-traveled streets. Often stores next to major tourist attractions have higher prices.

— Haggle, when and where you can. Small retailers often are willing to haggle. Although that makes many Americans uncomfortable, a successful negotiation can save you plenty. Generally, the farther south you travel in Europe, the more acceptable it is to bargain. Always deal with the person in charge of a store and never in earshot of other customers. The more expensive an article, the more negotiable the price.

— Offer to pay cash for a discount. Stores have to pay fees of as much as 10% to credit-card companies for purchases on plastic.

— Don't get carried away with your bargains. Each U.S. traveler is allowed to take home $400 worth of goods duty-free. You will pay 10% duty on the next $1,000, and the regular duty on items once your purchases amount to more than $1,400. But there is no duty on gemstones.

How to Survive Customs Inspections

You are just back from a grand trip overseas, and the only obstacle between you and your waiting family is a cold-eyed U.S. customs agent. How can you best survive the customs inspection of your overstuffed baggage?

Even before they leave home, smart travelers write or visit an office of the U.S. Customs Service and get two of its leaflets. One is *Know Before You Go,* and, among other things, it lists the articles you cannot legally bring home. The second tells about goods that are duty-free if they are made and bought in any of the 130 developing countries and territories. That leaflet is titled *GSP & the Traveler.* GSP stands for Generalized System of Preferences. You can also get these publications by writing to U.S. Customs Information, 6 World Trade Center, Room 201, New York, New York 10048. Be sure to include the names of the leaflets — Customs publishes many more than these two.

A few items are duty-free no matter where they are bought. Among them are paintings, antiques, cut, unset diamonds and binoculars.

Each returning traveler, even an infant in diapers, is allowed $400 in duty-free merchandise or $800 if you are coming home from the Virgin Islands, Guam or Samoa. A family can pool their allowances. For example, a family of four — Mom, Dad and two children — get a total allowance of $1,600.

Customs inspectors are not easily fooled. They have price lists for popular goods such as French perfumes and Scottish woolens. They can spot amateurishly stitched American labels on clothes — a sure sign that somebody bought the garment abroad.

Inspectors are tougher at some gateways than others. The easiest entry into the country is often from Canada, since there is less concern about contraband traffic from the North. The toughest entry points are from the Orient, the Caribbean and South America because that is where the drugs come from. So it is small wonder that Honolulu and Miami have a well-earned reputation as the roughest U.S. customs checkpoints. And customs inspection could delay you as much as a couple of hours in rare cases — all the more reason to leave plenty of time between international and domestic connections.

When you go through customs, you invite suspicion — and a search — if you act nervous or belligerent or carry something bizarre, such as a fur coat in summer. If an examiner finds an item you have not declared, he or she can charge you a fine equal to its wholesale price. On top of that, the agent can confiscate the item and charge you with a criminal offense.

So the best advice, of course, is to do your homework, keep your bills straight, tell the truth — and if you have overbought your $400 per-person limit, be prepared to pay your duty, which, after all, probably will not be very large.

Traveling Abroad with Children

You do not have to wait until your children have graduated from college to take a vacation in Europe. You can go now and take the children with you without breaking the bank at Monte Carlo. The money-saving trick is to stay away from places like the bank at Monte Carlo.

Peter Carry, executive editor of *Sports Illustrated* magazine, who has spent many summers in Europe with his wife and their children, advises that the first rule of international travel with the under-five-foot-tall set is: Don't travel. Rent a house and stay put except for family day trips and the occasional parental overnight. Hauling youngsters from one hotel to another and in and out of restaurants calls for the resources of the Aga Khan and the forbearance of Mother Teresa.

The key part of planning a family trip is finding the rental house. Avoid cities and well-known resorts. In a small town or village, your rent is likely to be relatively inexpensive, the chances will be good that you will have friendly neighbors and you can absorb local culture that isn't gussied up for tourists.

If you want to rent a house on fairly short notice, comb the classified ads in the Friday edition of the *International Herald Tribune*. You can buy it at major newsstands in large cities. The national tourist office of the country you want to visit, its consulate in your area or its embassy in Washington can also point you in the right direction.

When all else fails, get a guidebook to the country you would like to visit and select half a dozen or so towns that sound appealing. Then write to the local tourist office in each — most good guides like the Michelin include those addresses. You also can have your travel agent put you in touch with a rental agency. But once you have found your house, be sure to ask for photographs and a list of the contents before you consider renting.

Your largest single expense probably will be plane fares. But there are ways to hold down these and other costs. Sometimes the country where you will be staying is not necessarily the one you should fly to. For example, if you are traveling to the south of France, you may be wise to check to see if there is a specially inexpensive New York–to–London fare, and then pay extra to fly from London to Marseilles. Or you might want to fly to Barcelona because it is often cheaper to rent a car in Spain than in France.

But before you buy tickets on any cut-rate plane flights be sure they have reduced-cost seats for children; some of them do not. So more than ever, when flying to Europe with your family, you have to shop around.

You can carry more weight on a transatlantic flight than used to be allowed, because most carriers have replaced the 44-pound maximum with a system that limits each passenger to two bags of certain dimensions with a combined maximum weight of 140 pounds, plus a carry-on. This is a tremendous advantage if you are renting a house abroad.

Disposable plastic and paper household products are much more expensive in Europe than at home. So stuff all your leftover luggage capacity with them if you are renting a home for several weeks. And if you are traveling with infants, remember that an army duffel bag can hold more than 200 disposable diapers.

Consider springing for another plane ticket — and bring a baby-sitter along with you. That's right. If you usually have a mother's helper at home or often use baby-sitters, you probably can buy a seat to Europe for the same amount as these services cost. And because there seems to be an endless supply of bright, responsible American teenagers who will baby-sit in exchange for a chance to go to Europe, you need not pay more than expenses. A mother's helper means freedom for mother — and father — to get away, if only for an hour at the local café for coffee and a *digestif.*

If you're visiting London, you can drop off your children at Pippa Pop-Ins, a sleepover hotel for children whose parents want to go out for an adult evening. And Virgin Atlantic Airlines features a special children's section for overseas travel, replete with children's meals and movies — and a clown who entertains. Some resorts have programs for child care and activities, and some hotels, such as Hyatt, will "childproof" a room for you, plugging up exposed light sockets, covering the furniture to be "bumpproof," and in a number of cases, providing furniture built to scale for your child's comfort. So when planning your travel, always ask about special accommodations for children.

For grandparents interested in domestic travel with the grandkids, several tour operators offer group trips devoted to such pairings. The companies plan escorted tours to places such as Washington, D.C., and Hawaii, as well as dude ranches, for about two dozen grandparents and grandchildren at a time, assuring that there will be plenty of age-appropriate companions for everyone. Two companies that have seen business take off in the past several years include Maryland-based Grandtravel and Frontier Travel, located in Nevada.

How to Find a Reliable Travel Agent

IF YOU are planning a trip, a knowing travel agent can help guide you through the complexity of fares and the many package deals available. But how do you pick a good travel agent?

A travel agent, after all, is a double agent. He is engaged by you, the traveler, but he is paid by the airlines, hotels, tour operators and other travel services, which give him commissions — generally 10%. Thus, most travel agents prefer writing expensive international tours to planning a car trip to the nearest beach. Some may push hotels that offer better commissions than they do rooms, or package tours that are easier to arrange than customized itineraries. Be prepared to call a number of travel agents before you finalize your plans. A New York City Department of Consumer Affairs survey of local agents found a 60% average discrepancy among the plane fares agents quoted as "cheapest"; some of the fares varied by as much as 115%.

But many travel agents do put their clients' needs first. For one thing, they thrive on repeat business and recommendations. The problem is not how to find an honest agent. What is most difficult is discovering one who is expert and experienced enough to guide you. You might test to see if his taste is compatible with yours by asking him for his favorite hotels and sights in places that you have visited and are well acquainted with.

Just about anyone can set himself up in the business. Window decals that boast affiliations with national travel agent associations guarantee that the agency meets some standards, but not very high ones. If the agent himself has completed a two-year course given by the Institute of Certified Travel Agents and has five years of travel industry experience, he can use the initials ASTA (American Society of Travel Agents) or CTC (Certified Travel Counselor) after his name. This label at least suggests above-average commitment.

But the best guarantee to a competent agent is word of mouth. If you are trying an agent on someone else's recommendation, then tell that agent just who sent you. Agents work harder if they have to please old customers as well as new ones.

Solid professionals are interested in the outcome of trips. They usually take the initiative to call customers on their return. If you have complaints that are well founded, travel agents can help you get at least some of your money back.

Before settling on a travel agent, interview two or three on the telephone. Ask where each one has traveled in the past year. A conscientious agent can share first-hand experience of the places and services he recommends. He probably takes two or three week-long trips and several weekend excursions a year — just to keep his information up to date.

If an agent is unfamiliar with a destination, he should be willing to refer you to a colleague or another customer who has recently been there. You can tell an agent knows a place fairly well if he speaks authoritatively without continually consulting guidebooks and maps.

Do not hesitate to prod the agent to find the lowest fare. You will know he is really digging if he suggests times or dates that would result in cheaper tickets. On the other hand, be sure to investigate carefully any extremely low-priced package tours. Sometimes they cut so many corners that the hotel and meals aren't anything you would care to remember.

Travel agencies range from hometown mom-and-pop operations to the giant chains such as Carlson or Thomas Cook, although smaller agencies are hooking up with larger networks in increasing numbers. Customers who want personal service often do better with small agencies with local reputations to protect. But large chains and agencies frequently offer a wider selection of services and a staff that knows about more areas of the world. Volume also breeds influence. Agencies that send planeloads of travelers to a destination can get scarce hotel rooms more easily in peak seasons and may have greater access to deeply discounted fares. Yet while larger agents who deal in volume business may get you a good deal on standard package trips, you may get better service in planning a more complex, less conventional trip with a boutique agency. To find a travel agent, call the American Society of Travel Agents at 703-739-2782.

Customers with particular travel needs should seek out specialized agents. Some are expert in exotic travel, in rail travel or freighter cruises, still others in the needs of singles or business travelers. Travel guidebooks are the places to find such specialists. And foreign airlines or national tourist offices also can be invaluable guides to agencies familiar with their countries.

A number of travel agents specialize in family vacations. They include: Family Faire Vacations (420 Fifth Avenue South, Suite E, Edmonds, Washington 90820; 800-677-4386 or 206-774-6625); Families Welcome (21 West Colony Place, Suite 140, Durham, North Carolina 27705; 800-326-0724 or 919-489-2555); Rascals in Paradise (650 Fifth Street, Suite 505, San Francisco, California 94107; 800-872-7225 or 800-443-0799) and Rosenbluth Family Vacation Station (160 North Gulph Road, King of Prussia, Pennsylvania 19406; 800-621-8983).

What to Do If Your Baggage Is Lost

THE best-laid travel plans can be spoiled if your baggage is lost on an airline trip. One way to avoid this possibility is to carry all your luggage with you on board, as savvy air travelers have done at least since the invention of the hanging garment bag. Airlines usually place limitations on what you can carry with you, so if you must check a suitcase, don't pack anything in it you might need within 24 hours — or the only copy of your millionaire uncle's will. For tips on ways to minimize baggage loss, write the Department of Consumer Affairs, Room 10404, 400 7th Street, SW, Washington, D.C. 20590, and request its brochure *Plane Talk*.

The reassuring news is that less than 1% of all luggage is lost, even temporarily, and almost all bags that go astray are found, usually within a few hours. If you cannot locate your bag, your first step is to report the loss to the airline's representative immediately; the bag may still be on the plane you came in on. If a search turns up nothing, you will be given a form to fill out. Do not leave the airport without handing in the form — and keep a copy for your records. Be sure to ask to have your luggage delivered to you when it is found.

If you will be bagless overnight, most airlines will give you either a toilet kit or the money to buy one. The airlines are stickier about replacing clothes. Many a week-long vacation has been hampered, if not ruined, because an airline did not pay for clothes until the vacation was almost over. Even then the carrier might pay only half the cost.

When luggage is lost, the airline is liable for damages, usually up to $1,250 per person on domestic flights and $9.07 a pound on international flights. If your luggage and its contents are worth more than the airline's liability limit, you can buy excess-valuation insurance from the airline when you check in. Carriers charge 10 cents to $1.25 for each $100 worth of coverage — up to $25,000. Even so, some airlines may refuse to insure jewelry, cash and breakable items, including antiques and camera equipment. Keep in mind that most homeowners or tenants insurance covers losses above an airline's liability limits.

Once your bag has been missing for four or five days, you should file a claim form. Extensive dickering over the worth of goods is fairly common. In the end, the airlines usually will reimburse you for your wayward belongings' fair market value, not the full replacement cost. So you stand to collect less than the original cost of your property. For expensive items, you may need to show receipts to prove how much you paid. Count on waiting six weeks for the payment. If you feel the settlement is unfair, take the matter to small-claims court — before cashing the airline's check. Also, you can complain to the Office of Consumer Affairs, Department of Transportation, 400 Seventh Street, SW, Washington, D.C. 20590.

The major causes of missing bags are mix-ups when they are moved from one place to another, failure to remove old airport tags and theft — usually by someone hanging around the baggage carousel. To avoid loss, always pull old airport tags off a bag before checking it; that avoids confusion about where it is heading. Learn the tag code letters for airports to which you often fly so that you can be sure your bag is properly ticketed. Make sure your name, address and phone number are marked on the outside and inside (sometimes tags get ripped off) of any checked luggage. If you do not have baggage tags, the airline usually will give you stick-on labels. In sum, bright, clear identification is your best guarantee that your bags will get to their destination.

Protecting Yourself Against Other Losses

VACATIONERS are easy marks for seasoned pickpockets and thieves, but you can take steps to make any loss you might suffer less harmful to your holiday. Before you leave home, prepare several lists of all important ID, credit card and telephone numbers. Photocopy key documents, such as your passport and plane tickets. If you are traveling abroad, also take along extra passport photos and a certified copy of your birth certificate. And leave a second set of copies with someone back home.

If your passport is stolen, go to a U.S. embassy or consulate. An officer there will ask you to present a police report of the theft and, if possible, to show proof of citizenship — for example, your birth certificate. A photocopy of your passport, or a written record of your passport number, place and date of issuance plus any personal information — exactly as it is written on the document — will also help. You should be able to get a new passport within a day or so. The fee is $42.

An American embassy or consulate also will help you if a thief takes your cash. For a onetime charge of $40, you can arrange for family or friends to wire money via Western Union to the State Department in Washington. It will then authorize the overseas embassy to give you the money. You also can have your bank send money directly to the State Department or to a foreign bank near where you are staying. Such transactions are often completed within 24 hours.

When traveler's checks or credit cards are stolen, report the theft to the issuing companies. If you have your receipt with the traveler's checks' serial numbers, you may be able to get some of your money as fast as you can make it to the company's nearest refund location. Often it is a local bank, travel service, hotel or rental car agency. Without the serial numbers, your refund could take hours or even days, while the company tries to verify your original purchase. Credit cards are tougher to replace. Only American Express promises to issue a new card through its local office by the end of the next business day. Visa and MasterCard often can provide the same service; the time it takes sometimes depends on which bank issued your card.

While policies vary from airline to airline, losing a plane ticket can be costly. In the U.S., you may have to wait several months for a refund to come through, and there may be no refund at all if the stolen ticket is used. On the other hand, if you lose your ticket halfway through your travel, you may have to pay only a slight ticket-change fee, or in some cases no fee at all, instead of having to buy a new ticket altogether. Find out before you travel what penalties pertain to your ticket. An international passenger may stand a better chance of receiving a new ticket at little or no additional cost because all passengers have to show their passports before boarding.

What If Your Airline Is Grounded?

IT COULD happen. Eastern, Midway and Pan Am Airlines went out of business in 1990 and 1991. As of June 1992 four additional major carriers, while still operational, had filed Chapter 11 bankruptcy.

Don't worry; your chances of getting your money back are excellent — *if* you have charged your ticket to a credit card. Under the Fair Credit Billing Act of 1974, a creditor cannot force you to pay for a service that you did not receive. Most credit-card issuers will refund your money promptly when you send them the invalid ticket. If the airline in question has been acquired by another airline, you will most likely retain your frequent-flier mileage as well, although not necessarily at the same valuation. When Pan Am was absorbed in 1991 by Delta, travelers got a rude surprise — their mileage had been halved. Nonetheless, Pan Am Worldpassers still walked away with something.

You can also buy an insurance policy called Travel Guard Gold. One of its important benefits is a penalty waiver, which allows you to cancel a trip for any reason and reimburses you for 50% of your penalty, up to $400. This provides a good hedge if you buy nonrefundable tickets, in case you find you must cancel your trip. The policy must be bought within four days of any payment made on the ticket, and also covers tour cancellations, lost baggage, medical bills and accidental death while traveling. The minimum premium is $19 per trip, and the policy with the maximum amount of coverage is priced at 8% of the total trip cost. Travel Guard Gold is available through your travel agent or by calling 800-826-1300.

Your Enterprise

The Art of Getting Rich

C AN you still get rich in America? Yes, you can — if you are willing to take some intelligent risks.

The quickest path to wealth will continue to be launching your own business. Just ask Bill Gates. Or Michael Dell. Or the heirs of Sam Walton. New opportunities will arise as the economy shifts away from the huge industrial companies to small and medium-size enterprises. Both the economic climate and social attitudes have warmed to entrepreneurs in recent years. You do not have to invent a marvelous new machine or master some obscure technology. All you have to do is devise a more efficient and profitable way of performing an old job.

Studies of entrepreneurs have shown that those who succeed share certain traits. They are able to take calculated risks and learn from their mistakes. Many of them stumbled along the way but then quickly picked themselves up, analyzed their errors and were smarter for having made them. They develop detailed business plans. They are persistent and patient. Often they begin with little money but considerable determination. According to a *Money* magazine survey of entrepreneurs, after three years of operation, the typical small company had consumed about $60,000 of capital — much of it from the owner's personal savings. They are also willing to devote themselves totally to the business. Over half the entrepreneurs in the survey said they put in 60 hours or more a week in their first year of business, and almost half said they were still working that hard in their third year.

For example, Sam Chavez, a high-school dropout from Denver, started out in 1946 by leasing a gas station. He worked 12 to 15 hours a day, seven days a week, to make it profitable — so profitable that the company leased out three more stations to him. He kept on working with a vengeance and saved enough money to open his own auto repair shop. Today he is enjoying semi-retirement while his five shops bring in about $11 million a year, augmenting Chavez's net worth of more than $10 million.

Investing in real estate has been a road to fortune throughout American history. If you buy real estate now, you will probably find that giant returns will not come as easily in the years ahead as they did in the high-inflation 1970s. Still, you can make some gains if you equip yourself with knowledge by studying, and if you invest wisely in land or buildings with a future.

Take 44-year-old Tom Tinnin of Albuquerque. He started in real estate when he was in his early thirties, and it took him just 10 years to turn a $26,000 stake into more than $900,000 worth of land-holdings. He began by buying lots at tax lien auctions — because he could count on getting discount prices. He looked for properties that lay in the path of what he felt would be the city's natural direction of expansion. One of his favorite strategies has been to buy raw land and then help persuade local zoning boards to approve it for residential building. He tries to become acquainted with everyone living near his land to sound out whether there is any opposition. Tinnin also likes to buy during economic recessions because sellers then are more likely to agree to low mortgage rates and small down payments.

Starting Your Own Business

Aᴍᴇʀɪᴄᴀ is a nation of small businesses — nearly 20 million of them. Many are extremely prosperous, and so are their owners. More millionaires come out of small businesses than out of big corporations. Of course, not every entrepreneur does so well. Many new businesses fail during the first several years, usually because owners do not start out with enough capital or with a sound plan or simply because of bad management.

Still, a boom of sorts is under way in small businesses. The number of new firms with fewer than 20 employees increases by about 250,000 every year. One reason is that many big and medium-size companies are cutting costs by farming out more and more office chores to small firms that specialize in them. This has created opportunities for entrepreneurs in fields with low start-up costs, such as accounting, public relations, photocopying and credit reporting and collection services.

To start some of these service firms, you often need little more than a computer and a bank loan. For example, there is demand for firms that provide financial services. With $5,000 to $10,000, you can buy the computer equipment you need to do bookkeeping for bigger firms. And you can provide secretarial services with a word processor that costs $6,000 or less.

When starting your own business, the first two or three years are the critical period. To survive them, you will need to anticipate the problems that accompany each stage of the business. You can avoid or conquer difficulty with sound planning, ample capital, solid management skills and, of course, a well-conceived idea.

When you get that idea, it may seem so stunning to you, so can't-miss, that your first impulse will be to quit your job, remortgage the house and kiss your spouse and kids good-bye while you devote yourself to your brainstorm. But do not do anything of the kind. Instead, you should evaluate your drive, dedication and experience in estimating whether you can turn a pipe dream into a money-maker. Experience is the key.

Solid planning is also essential. You will need to draft a business plan itemizing the costs of developing your product or service, and projecting your company's share of market and sales over the next three to five years. This road map should be about 60 to 80 pages long and include weekly or monthly projections for the first two years and quarterly figures after that. Do the figuring yourself to become familiar with production, distribution and marketing. If you hire a professional firm to help you with your research, expect to pay at least $2,000.

To find out if your plan for a new business is realistic, you will need outside and impartial advice. Do not overlook your local banker or your lawyer for a critique of your business plan, but the most qualified source may be the president of a similar business. It is amazing how accessible these chief executives are.

You can get help of various kinds through the Small Business Administration. One SBA-affiliated volunteer group, Service Corps of Retired Executives (SCORE), operates about 400 chapters throughout the U.S. to help fledgling businesses. The SBA also sponsors about 60 Small Business Development Centers, which in turn direct more than 600 smaller groups.

The agency's guaranteed loan program helped more than 20,000 small businesses borrow $6 billion in 1992. It can back as much as 90% of loans of up to $750,000 (the average is $240,000) from both bank and regulated nonbank lenders such as The Money Store. The SBA caps rates at 2¼ to 2¾ points over prime, plus a fee equal to 2% of the loan. About a quarter of such loans go to start-ups.

The SBA also makes direct loans to certain kinds of small businesses, such as those run by Vietnam veterans or the disabled. Further, if you need funds for research and development, you may get help from the SBA-monitored Small Business Innovation Research program (800-U-ASK-SBA). It made R&D funding agreements of $483 million in fiscal 1991 with small businesses.

Help is also available at any one of the 530 Small Business Institutes in colleges and universities across the country. Advanced undergraduate and graduate students overseen by faculty work with a designated small business for one full term on market studies, promotional strategies, accounting systems and operation plans. The service is free for qualified small businesses.

Finally, you can get help from a business incubator. That is a support center that provides fledgling entrepreneurs with inexpensive space and services, including everything from copying equipment and secretarial assistance to business consulting and accounting. These centers often charge rents that are only a fraction of what businesses would have to pay elsewhere. Because overhead is so low, the business owners can devote more money to making their ventures succeed and grow. Around 500 incubators operate in the United States and Canada, a more than tenfold increase since 1984. For information about incubators in your state, write or phone the National Business Incubation Association, 1 President Street, Athens, Ohio 45701; 614-593-4331. The International Venture Capital Institute also publishes a directory of incubators; it costs $19.95 and can be ordered from IVCI at P.O. Box 1333, Stamford, Connecticut 06904; 203-323-3143.

You may be considering starting a new business all by yourself, but it pays to remember that teams have better odds for success than individuals do. The right combination brings more management skills and more money than you alone can.

But where do you find the right people to be your partners? Building an enterprise simply on blood ties, friendship or a shared enthusiasm for golf can be dangerous. True, your relatives and chums may have money to invest. Yet starting a company is strain enough without the added trauma of firing someone dear who does not work out. Or, worse yet, having to keep him or her.

Everyone tends to hire people like oneself, but you should seek those with complementary talents. An engineer who pairs up with a manufacturing or marketing person is better situated for success than a trio of engineers — even if their business is the next generation of computers. To ward off future difficulties, all partners should invest some capital in the business or at least forsake salary during the start-up phase. And you are much better off if you have worked with your new partners before.

Of course, money is supremely important when you start your business. Undercapitalization pits you against the clock in a losing race. To figure out how much capital you are going to need, hire an accountant — preferably one with experience in your industry. He can help show you how much money you would need either if heaven and Congress were on your side, or if Murphy's Law were in effect.

Raising cash has become increasingly difficult in recent years, due to the recession and the rising tide of bad loans. Nearly a third of banks surveyed by the Federal Reserve in January 1991 had tightened standards for small-business lending since October 1990. The situation had eased only slightly when the same group of banks was surveyed in May 1992. And U.S. venture capital funds, which invested more than $3.9 billion in 1,740 companies during 1987, disbursed only about $1.4 billion to 792 companies in 1991. The statistics for first-time financings were even gloomier, says Robert E. Mast, vice president of Venture Economics, a venture capital research and publishing firm in Newark, New Jersey. In 1987, more than $1.5 billion was provided by venture capital funds to initial financings of 712 companies. By 1991, first-time financings had shrunk to $277 million in only 173 companies.

Even if you have the perfect partners and more than enough cash in the till, your new business still can be done in by poor record-keeping. Well before the day you first open, you will need to have sound financial information keeping you up to date on operating expenses, inventory costs, accounts receivable, debt obligations and income. Accurate financial records are an indispensable warning system.

With all that, if your small business then can survive two or three years of growing pains, the odds for continuing success will be in your favor.

Doing It at Home

STARTING a business right in your own home can be most rewarding, both financially and in terms of life-style. More than 10 million Americans are working at home ventures. The fastest-growing kinds of these enterprises are computer data and word processing, direct sales for commissions and business services in general, including accounting, bookkeeping and typing.

If you want to start a business from your own home, first make sure you are allowed to do so. Zoning laws in many localities forbid it, as do some apartment leases and condominium bylaws. If you are in conflict with the rules, you can appeal for a permit or variance. Also make sure that you are operating within federal and state laws. Some laws, which were originally designed to prevent sweatshops, regulate what goods can be produced commercially at home.

Be certain to hire a lawyer who has worked with other home businesses. According to Donna Chaiet, a Manhattan attorney who works with small businesses and entrepreneurs, issues that affect a start-up enterprise are considerably different from those of an ongoing medium to large company. A lawyer who has had previous experience in this area can shepherd you through the several layers of bureaucratic formality that attend the birth of a home business.

You also have to decide what legal form your business should take. Most small businesses start as proprietorships. They require little expense or government approval to set up. One big advantage of a proprietorship is that both you and your business are taxed as individuals. Thus, if you have a full-time job and a part-time business that loses money, you may be able to write off your losses against other income. Be careful, though: Tax law stipulates that you must "materially participate" in a business in order to offset income from your full-time job. A major disadvantage of a proprietorship is that in case of a lawsuit, your personal liability is unlimited. That is just one reason why you should be sure to get adequate insurance. A regular homeowners or renters policy probably is not enough. You will need extra personal liability coverage.

Forming an S corporation provides a way of protecting your personal assets against liability. However, you then need to file corporation tax forms because the corporation is a separate entity.

The biggest potential tax advantage of your home enterprise is that you are entitled to deduct not only for regular business expenses but also for a host of household expenses that you can prove are directly related to your work. Such deductions are limited to the annual net income from the business.

Putting your husband or wife on the payroll of your home business can be a tax saver, but you will need to follow some IRS rules. By employing a spouse who has not previously been working for pay, many couples can increase their combined maximum annual contributions to their tax-saving Individual Retirement Accounts from $2,250 to $4,000. Your business can also deduct your spouse's salary, as well as any amounts it pays in for his or her pension or profit-sharing plans, worker's compensation, life insurance or health policies. Employing your husband or wife will not trigger a tax audit. But the IRS will not permit the extra deductions if it believes you hired your wife or husband solely for tax reasons.

If you are audited, you might be asked to prove that your spouse was hired for a legitimate business purpose. The more evidence you have that he or she is considered just another employee, the better. Many tax advisers recommend writing a job contract. It should cover your wife's or husband's duties, pay, benefits and the expected length of employment. Keeping a time sheet of his or her work hours and a description of the work will be useful as well.

Be certain that you are paying your spouse a reasonable salary. As evidence, clip newspaper advertisements for similar jobs. Or call a local employment agency and ask for the going wage. Try to get a letter from the agency documenting the quoted salary range, or at least keep legible notes on the conversation. One good guide for helping you create your home office is Paul and Susan Edwards' *Working from Home* (Jeremy P. Tarcher, $14.95).

How to Learn to Be an Entrepreneur

THE orthodox wisdom until recently was that the only school for entrepreneurs was the school of hard knocks. But to survive in today's economy, small-business people — like the big — require management skills that are often best acquired through formal training.

More than 600 colleges and universities in the U.S. offer courses in starting a small business. Some, including Babson, Baylor, the University of Southern California and the University of Pennsylvania, have introduced undergraduate majors in entrepreneurship. If you have neither the time nor temperament to work toward a degree, you can choose from a variety of commercial and Small Business Administration–sponsored courses.

A good new-business course will cover such fundamentals as evaluating an idea for an enterprise, raising capital and dealing with supplies and customers. Students are often asked to prepare a detailed business plan for their firm's first five years. You can size up a course's content by studying the catalogue or talking to faculty and former students. You usually can get names and phone numbers from those sponsoring the course.

The best and most accessible of the courses are those sponsored jointly by the Small Business Administration, Chambers of Commerce and community colleges. These courses meet at more than 800 community and junior colleges. They may last from four to 20 hours — typically, for two hours on two nights a week. Usually they cost no more than $100.

The SBA also offers pre-business workshops at more than 100 district and branch offices, where professionals such as accountants, bankers, marketing consultants and government officials meet to offer pointers to small-business people.

The nonprofit Center for Entrepreneurial Management offers lecture seminars on entrepreneurship at private clubs around the U.S. For information on courses in your area, write to the Center at 180 Varick Street, Penthouse, New York, New York 10014.

How to Raise the Money You Will Need

NEXT to a money-making idea, what you need most to get a new business off the ground is a talent for raising capital.

Even if your idea is brilliant, no backer will give you a dime until you have sunk in most of your own savings. So, the smart entrepreneur starts with as much of his own capital as possible, using all his sources of credit. If necessary, he will even remortgage his house. By maximizing his own stake in the business, he will impress other potential investors with his commitment. He also will retain tighter control of his enterprise.

When entrepreneurs need outside money, they begin by soliciting friends and relatives — and then go on to friends of friends and relatives. Close relatives usually are more willing than distant investors to wait for the profits to start rolling in.

Try to get this money as a loan rather than as an investment in return for a piece of your company. That way, you won't have to put up with Uncle Bill telling you how to run *his* business.

After you have approached friends and family, the best way to get names of potential investors you don't know is to ask accountants, bankers, lawyers, brokers and other business owners. They often know who has money to invest or lend. Local business groups like the Chamber of Commerce can provide more leads.

Once you have exhausted your individual financing sources, it is time to approach the institutions. If you need less than $100,000, the best sources are the banks, commercial finance companies, the Small Business Administration and business development companies. When you have to go to those outside capitalists and bankers for money, you may be rather pleasantly surprised. Though real interest rates are high, money to finance promising new businesses is fairly plentiful. Banks are making loans to small businesses again. Professional venture capitalists are loaded with cash, and they even complain they cannot find enough worthy enterprises to assist.

Venture firms like to invest close to home, and generally in amounts between $500,000 and $1 million. They rarely lend the money. Instead, they want a piece of the business. Because of the unusual success of some recent new businesses, particularly in the realm of high technology and services, financiers are willing to take greater risks than just a few years ago — if they figure that they may also reap greater rewards.

You might also get help from interested local investors. Check to see if there is a venture capital club in your area. There are about 150 such clubs in the U.S. and abroad. They hold monthly luncheon meetings at which entrepreneurs and investors can discuss ideas and funding for new products or businesses. Members include venture capitalists, bankers, attorneys and corporate executives. You can buy a directory listing the clubs by sending a check for $9.95 to the International Venture Capital Institute, P.O. Box 1333, Stamford, Connecticut 06904.

Beyond friends, family members, banks, venture capitalists and the federal Small Business Administration, there are many other places to raise money for your new venture. Among them, small-business investment companies, or SBICs, are private venture firms that borrow some of their funds under an SBA guarantee. In addition to the 220 or so all-purpose SBICs, there are about 130 SBICs that invest exclusively in concerns at least 51% owned by socially or economically disadvantaged people.

In about three-quarters of the states, quasi-public business development corporations make loans to small businesses to create local jobs. You can get the details by asking your state's economic development agency where you can find a business development corporation, or BDC. You also can turn to the little-known local development corporations, composed of local government officials and private citizens who borrow funds from the SBA and banks and then relend them to entrepreneurs in need of long-term financing.

Entrepreneurs searching for big money — say $500,000 or more for research and product development — should look into setting up limited partnerships. The people to speak with are local tax attorneys, accountants and brokers who have experience getting a group of high-bracket investors to invest money in a business in return for substantial tax write-offs.

You may even have to make a private offering of stock. The disadvantage is that it will reduce your stake in your own company. You could lose majority interest. The less you have to surrender, the more you can offer later to attract skilled managers and additional capital to your company.

In searching for financial help, be wary of firms that advertise that they are professional finders of money. Many of them charge high fees simply for sending out mass mailings to investors. But one reliable source of names of potential angels is the National Venture Capital Association. To order its membership directory, write or call the National Venture Capital Association, 1655 North Fort Myer Drive, Suite 700, Arlington, Virginia 22209; 703-351-5269.

Plan to spend at least three months acquainting yourself with the sources of financing before you try to raise any substantial amount. The bible for anyone planning to shop the venture capital firms is *Pratt's Guide to Venture Capital Sources*, published by Venture Economics Publishing division of SDC Publishing Inc., 40 West 57th Street, New York, New York 10019. Look for it in a good public library and save yourself the cover price of $195. Venture Economics also has the capability to provide "most active investor" listings in specific technology and industry fields through the Newark-based information services group (201-622-4500). *Guerilla Financing* by Bruce Blechman and Conrad Levinson (Houghton Mifflin, $19.95) is a source for finding a wide variety of financial backers.

If you need help putting together your plan to start a small business, ask an accountant, lawyer or banker to refer you to a reliable professional consultant. Expect to pay your professional adviser between $1,000 and $1,500. He may be able to show you how to use potential customers and suppliers as sources of financing and how to cut costs by leasing, rather than buying, equipment. So hiring a professional probably will be a sensible investment.

To increase your chances of raising money, start with the right source. If you want a bank loan, for example, call ahead to inquire whether the bank does the kind of lending you need. Then find out what your potential backers want — and deliver it. Ask a banker what it will take for him to lend you money. If you meet his standards, it will be hard for him to say no. Finally, if you are rejected, find out why. That way you can approach your next source with a better pitch.

How to Get the Right Franchise

You could have bought a fast-food franchise for peanuts a few years ago and sold it today for as much as a million dollars. But it is not too late to be your own boss and perhaps take a ride to prosperity. You can do that by acquiring one of the many *new* franchises.

If you get into a strong franchising system, the odds of surviving and succeeding as a small-business man or woman multiply impressively. Some of the strongest new franchises are those that provide services to businesses that themselves cannot afford to hire the people and buy the expensive equipment they need.

You could provide such services for businesses as typing, copying, telexing and mail pickup. A company that franchises these services is Mail Boxes Etc. USA, based in San Diego, California. Other promising franchise opportunities include photocopying and printing, specialized employment agencies and business brokers. These brokers bring together people who want to sell their small businesses and people who want to buy them. By doing just that, one Atlanta grandmother earned some $240,000 in commissions in only her second year of operation. Another group of franchises performs household services for people who are too busy to do them. These chores range from housecleaning to performing home maintenance when the owners are away.

Franchises for educational products and services are expected to grow 38%, to $1.1 billion, in 1995. There are franchised learning centers for children and adults, day-care centers and diet centers that "re-educate" you about your eating habits.

Service businesses have added a new dimension, but you also can find opportunities in franchising's traditional backbone — retail stores. In fact, franchisers account for just over one-third of retail sales in the U.S., or about $760 billion a year.

The potential is strong for stores that sell the more popular brands of home computers, TV equipment and inexpensive furnishings. Restaurants that serve ethnic specialties such as Greek or Mexican food are doing well, too.

You can call professional franchise brokers to help you locate the business you want. One such group is the International Brokers Association (508-369-2490).

There are also professional franchise consultants, but be careful in choosing one. According to the International Franchise Association, some people with little experience have set themselves up as consultants and promise much more than they can deliver. Before hiring a consultant, ask for the names of past clients and contact them.

When you get serious about buying a franchise, you would do well to deal with a lawyer who is familiar with drawing up franchise contracts and with Federal Trade Commission rules on franchising. For a recommendation, try a franchise operator in your area or the local bar association. Before hiring a consultant, ask for the names of past clients and contact them.

For a description of 2,400 franchise companies and information on how franchising works, get *The Franchise Opportunities Guide,* produced by International Franchise Association Publications (call 800-543-1038). The price is $15 plus $5 for shipping and handling.

Another comprehensive list of the offerings can be found in *The 1992 Franchise Annual Handbook and Directory.* It costs $39.95 including postage from INFO Press (728 Center Street, P.O. Box 550, Lewiston, New York 14092).

Before you sign a contract to buy a franchise, the parent company must give you a disclosure statement. From it you can get the names and phone numbers of several franchises. You would be wise to phone them to find out how well they are doing.

When you buy a franchise, you pay the company an initial fee and later a continuing royalty that averages 4% to 5% of gross sales but can reach 10% or higher, particularly for service businesses. In return, you can use the company's trademark and franchising services for a set period, usually five years, with renewal options up to 25 years. The basic service is to give operating instructions, often covering everything from sales tactics to the color of the office carpeting. Capable companies also help you pick a business location and buy equipment and inventory. Their representatives sit in with you when you hire your first employees. They also hold your hand through crises.

Instead of running franchises themselves, many investors hire managers to operate them. But franchisors usually feel that the owner's attention is crucial and therefore will not sell units to people who intend to be absentee owners. That is understandable: few salaried managers will put in the 60 to 80 hours of work each week that it takes to make a business succeed.

How to Get Your Invention to Market

A MERICAN ingenuity still thrives — and countless tinkerers are working in countless workshops and garages, hoping to become the Edisons of tomorrow. The lonely inventor who aims to make it big faces tremendous obstacles and risks. He also faces rousing rewards if he plays it right.

More than 100,000 patents were granted in 1991, but only 5% of all patented inventions ever make it to the marketplace, and scarcely 1% of them earn money for their originators. Still, individuals have brought forth plenty of recent products, from the CAT scanner to the laser amplifier.

Have you ever had an idea for a new product or some other invention? Not all bright ideas can be legally protected. But start by trying to get a copyright, a trademark or a patent.

For example, video or board games and computer software should be *copyrighted*. It costs $20 to register a copyright for your lifetime plus 50 years. Also, apply for a *trademark* as soon as you sell your product in more than one state. A trademark will set you back $200, but it will keep other people from using your product's name.

Does your invention have a unique graphic or pictorial design? A *design patent* will protect the product's appearance against the idea pirates. And, if your creation is a useful new device or process, you will need a *utility patent*.

For a fee of $300 to $800, a patent attorney will conduct a search to see if your idea is already covered by one of the more than five million existing patents. If it is not, you then apply for a patent. After paying roughly another $2,000 to $5,000 in lawyer's fees for the preparation of the patent application and its prosecution, and an average wait of 18 months, two out of three inventors get it. A patent protects your invention for 17 years and is not renewable. You may also need to apply for patents in other countries, at a cost of about $1,000 in attorney fees each (plus local patent-office charges), or else you could find your idea being exploited abroad.

In very special cases, you may have to build a prototype of your invention; that can cost anywhere from $5,000 to $20,000. Before making such an investment, you would be wise to have your invention evaluated for its market potential. If the invention is energy-related, you can have it evaluated free of charge by the National Bureau of Standards in Washington, D.C.

A few universities also provide evaluation services. Baylor charges $150 and the University of Wisconsin–Whitewater charges $165. They are part of a Small Business Administration program sponsoring institutes at nearly 600 colleges that aid entrepreneurial inventors with such tasks as market research and feasibility analysis.

Once you have your invention patented and evaluated and perhaps have built a prototype, you will face the really hard part: getting it produced and bringing it to market. You can accomplish that in many ways.

Arthur D. Little, Inc., of Cambridge, Massachusetts, gives marketing and technical support to selected inventions, generally in the high-technology field. The firm typically pumps some $50,000 into research, development and market studies for each such product, although the amounts can range from $15,000 to $500,000. Then the company uses its considerable connections to bring the invention to market and shares equally in the proceeds.

But beware of firms that want their money up front and often in alarming amounts. A number of so-called development companies promise to mount a marketing campaign that will turn the seed of a hopeless idea into a money tree. Such unscrupulous outfits prey on inventors' gullibility, vanity and pocketbooks. They extract $1,000 to $3,000 in exchange for little more than sending a form letter to prospective backers culled from the Yellow Pages.

Do not count on selling your invention to big corporations. They are seldom receptive to products that are N.I.H. — that is, "Not Invented Here." But small businesses are much more willing to buy a stake in outside innovations because it is cheaper than doing their own research. So roughly half of all new products and services are bought out by small businesses.

Making a Family Firm Succeed

MANY of the almost 20 million small companies in the U.S. are family-dominated. But keeping a family business alive — and the family happy — takes work.

Family businesses do not have enviable survival rates. Only a third make it to the second generation, and only a tenth to the third generation. That's because of the difficulty of transferring control of the business from the founding father to his heirs.

Sibling rivalry among the heirs is a major problem. So is indulging a beloved relative. Profits fall and nonfamily employees are driven away when kith and kin monopolize important jobs despite poor performance.

Often parents do not parcel out enough authority to their children because they fear their own authority will be diminished. Conflicts between generations typically boil over when founding fathers are in their 60s and their children are in their 30s. At that point, the children need to assert themselves by taking risks — perhaps by introducing new products or otherwise expanding the business — but parents want to protect their retirement security by keeping the business on a steady course.

Here are some tips on how to manage a successful succession in a family business:

— Heirs to the business first should get jobs outside the family firm. After they've proved themselves in these neutral surroundings, they can confidently return.

— When the time comes to pick a successor, the founder and his heirs should put family loyalty out of their minds. The big question is: Who can run the business best? It may not be the eldest son, but a daughter or an in-law or even a hired manager.

— If two or more heirs wind up sharing control of the business, they should agree ahead of time on some orderly way to settle disputes that may arise between them. They might agree to hire an independent arbitrator.

— Above all, the aging chief should gradually but steadily hand over control. The president of a family firm can do everything else right, but if he doesn't designate an heir, he has failed the business.

Profit from Your Leisure

To ENHANCE their incomes, more and more Americans are finding ways to get money from their fun. They are turning spare-time hobbies into ready cash. People are trading coins, playing the saxophone, performing magic, hybridizing plants — all for money.

Pastimes involving sports and entertainment seem most likely to turn into money-makers. One rewarding way for sports fans and aging athletes to stay close to the action is to become referees. A basketball ref can start out officiating at high schools for $25 to $50 a game. After a while he or she can graduate to college basketball for $100 to $350 a varsity match. Working just 50 nights a year, a college referee could earn nearly $20,000.

Some hobbies hardly ever work out well as profitable money-makers. Many indoor gardeners, for instance, try to convince themselves that cash can blossom on their blooms. In practice, the commercial growers offer such wide variety and low prices that you simply cannot compete with them from your home.

What is really blooming is the market for crafts. There are more than 30,000 crafts fairs a year, and most of them are markets for amateurs. A growing number of boutiques and even department stores also provide outlets, but their standards for hand-made items are high. If you want to learn about crafts shows, try subscribing to *Sunshine Artists* magazine (1700 Sunset Drive, Longwood, Florida 32750-9697; $22.50). Each month *Sunshine Artists* reviews many shows and offers helpful tips on displaying and pricing your work.

A basic guideline for any hobbyist is that only quality sells. So whether you want to weave a rug or blow a trumpet for money, you have to do it well. Even the amateur has to be professional, businesslike and original. Countless talented people fail because they never grasp the importance of such basic business principles as sensible record-keeping or promotion.

Hobbies are treated under a special section of the tax code. Any expenses you incur can be deducted, but only from the income you derive from the hobby. Deductions are limited to the income you report from the hobby. Suppose you spend $1,000 to buy yak teeth. Later you find you have overestimated the market for yak-teeth bracelets and you can sell only one of them for $8.75. Result: You can deduct from your hobby income just $8.75 of the $1,000 you spent.

This hobby loss limit is waived when your pastime becomes a business. Then you can take deductions larger than your hobby income; that is, you can create a shelter for other income.

If you manage to make a profit in three out of five years, the IRS automatically assumes your hobby is a business. Even if you cannot pass the three-years-out-of-five test, you may still be able to convince the IRS that you are seriously trying to make a profit. You can help make a solid case by keeping accurate and up-to-date records, showing you work hard at your avocation and expend a serious effort to sell. If you are convincing, the tax court may let you claim losses for a decade or more, even though you cannot muster one profitable year.

In a cash business — most craft and part-time paid activities are strictly cash — the temptation to ignore the taxman is strong. Since there is no record of the transactions, the IRS probably will never hear of them. But your anonymity will not last long if you are determined to succeed in business. Then you will become profitable, maybe even rich and famous, and you can be sure that the taxman will not overlook you.

Publishing Your Own Newsletter

DO YOU want a nice small business? Why not start your own *newsletter*? The cost is low, and the payoff can be large.

According to Howard Hudson of Newsletter Clearinghouse, there are more than 100,000 newsletters in the country. Publishers range from husband-and-wife teams to corporate giants. Start-up costs generally are less than $10,000. Lately people have created successful newsletters on highly specialized subjects as diverse as recipes and shopping tips about chocolate, prescriptions for restoring old houses, advice on child development and where to find special and unspoiled vacation spots. And many are letters on the subject of computers.

The field may seem crowded, but you can thrive — if you have an original idea. You can find out if your idea is unique by consulting newsletter directories such as the *Oxbridge Directory of Newsletters* or *Hudson's Subscription Newsletter Directory*. They are available at many libraries.

After choosing your subject, you will need to set a subscription price. They range from $5 to as much as $4,500 a year. Basically, your choice is between an expensive newsletter serving a limited audience and one with broader appeal and a lower price. Many publishers go for *limited* circulation — and *high* profit margins.

Next, you will want to test the market. Use direct mail to reach potential subscribers. It allows you to zero in on only those people you want to reach. You can rent mailing lists through list brokers. To find names of brokers, consult the guide called *Direct Mail List Rates and Data,* available in many libraries. Costs range from $45 to more than $100 per thousand names. A test mailing should cost a few thousand dollars at most. Ideally, it should yield a response of 1% to 3% and should bring in enough subscriptions to cover your direct-mail expenses.

How to Get Your Book Published

IT SEEMS that almost everyone wants to write a book. People read about an unknown author who sits down at the typewriter and then cashes in big with a best-seller — and they, too, want to get in on the money, and the fame.

Plotting to get your book published is frustrating, but talent and tenacity can lead to happy endings. Publishers receive more than 100,000 unsolicited manuscripts annually. They send nearly all of them back with the swiftness and compassion of Andre Agassi returning a cream-puff serve. It is by no means impossible to get your first work of fiction or nonfiction published. To do it, though, you need to persuade a publisher or an agent at least to read your manuscript.

Most publishers urge that you do get an agent. You can find lists of well-known agents in two books at your public library. They are *Novel and Short Story Writers Market* and *Literary Market Place.* Agents often act as informal editors and they can direct your book to a likely publisher. What's more, the fact that your book is being submitted by an agent known to the editor is a guarantee that the work will be considered.

If the publisher is interested, an agent probably will be able to get you a bigger advance. If you are not a well-known writer, don't expect anything more than $5,000. For their services, agents customarily charge 10% to 15% of whatever the writer receives.

Some agents also have a fee just for reading manuscripts. Before you agree to pay anything, find out what services you will be getting for your money. That's always a sound idea on any deal, of course. If an agent insists on a written contract, be sure you hire a lawyer to approve it before you sign.

It is perfectly legitimate for an unknown author who gets a nibble from a publisher to recruit an agent *before* proceeding further. The proper approach to an agent or to a publisher is to write a letter explaining the kind of book you have in mind. Enclose a chapter or at least a sample of your writing. Outline briefly what you have already published, if anything. Above all, include a self-addressed, stamped envelope if you want your chapter returned.

The easiest way to break into print is by writing what is known as popular fiction — that is, mystery stories, spy thrillers and adventure tales. Romances alone account for more than 40% of all fiction published between hard and soft covers. Advances on romances are relatively low. Harlequin Books, which started the boom in romantic fiction, pays an advance of about $2,500 with royalties of 4% to 6% of the book's retail price charged against the advance. Other publishers may pay higher rates, and an experienced writer who catches on and learns the formula may earn $15,000 or more a book.

In nonfiction, a fresh and sharply focused idea is more important than writing style. But the novice author had better be an expert in his subject. Readers want specific information on specific topics. Books on cooking and dieting do well, as does anything connected with ways to make money. And sex is definitely here to stay.

Beginning writers should take time to learn how books get published. Two monthly magazines often carry solid information for aspiring authors. They are called *Writer's Digest* and *The Writer*. Among the many books of advice, a good one is *How to Get Happily Published* by Judith Appelbaum and Nancy Evans ($9.95, New American Library).

Literary Market Place also lists all the publishers. Check to see which houses are putting out books in your field. And be persistent. Many a best-seller was rejected by a score of publishers before finally being accepted.

If you cannot find a publisher who is captivated by your manuscript, don't despair. For a fee of $3,000 to $15,000, a so-called vanity publisher will design, print, bind and promote your book. Vanity books, however, are seldom taken seriously by other publishers. Or, you can do what Virginia Woolf, Walt Whitman and Mark Twain did, and publish your own book.

Your Computer

Selecting a Personal Computer

WHEN the personal computer was introduced more than a decade ago — on August 12, 1981 — it seemed like something that had dropped to earth from another planet. Mysterious, expensive and difficult to use, these first machines struck more terror than awe into the hearts of consumers. Today, vestiges of that old terror still persist, but the PC has changed. It has leapt ahead in power and versatility while at the same time becoming easier to use and, even better, cheaper. Cheaper, of course, is not the same thing as cheap: many systems now cost less than $1,000, but for standard power and speed in processing, plus monitor and printer, you should count on spending at least $1,000 to $2,000.

The decision to buy a computer should be made with caution. Despite all the talk about computerizing your Christmas-card list or your address book, you may not actually need a computer. Your old typewriter can turn out the dozen or so personal letters you write each month without any fuss or bother, and you may choose to send all your electronic recreation dollars Nintendo's way. But if there are other factors to consider — for instance, if you have children whose education you'd like to supplement (a strong reason many parents decide to take the plunge), or if you want it for word processing and desktop publishing, or for personal finance and bookkeeping (especially if you have a small business) — the PC may be just the thing to get your projects off the ground.

For number-crunching, the computer is unsurpassed. Not only can it competently manage your personal finances and help you prepare your taxes (see Computerizing Your Taxes), it can also hook you into the world of high finance. Just one example: The Metriplex company has introduced a pocket-sized one-pound (one pound!) wireless computer that currency, bond and futures traders can lease for $300 a month. The system permits instant updates of more than 50 markets at once in ten radio-network urban areas, including the Boston-Philadelphia corridor, Chicago, Los Angeles, Houston and Dallas.

For word processing the PC is, of course, unexcelled for speed, flexibility and efficiency. If you need to type out long drafts of copy that you want to revise and edit and store for future use, or if you send the same kind of letter over and over again, the personal computer will shine for you. And because it is fast becoming an indispensable graphics tool, the PC may enable your small business not only to communicate with large clients through electronic mail but also to dazzle them with presentation graphics when you call on them.

Or maybe you would like to send your children off to school or college armed with a PC. Students are especially heavy computer users, and word processing is the personal computer's most popular campus use. But what kind of machine should you buy them?

Apple or IBM, or Does It Matter?

No MATTER who is going to use the computer, the first question a retailer will ask you is which computer family you wish to buy into. In spite of progress by many competitors, there are still two essentially unreconciled families: Apples and IBM compatibles (the latter includes both IBM machines and IBM-like machines or "clones"). Software does exist that enables some Apple Macintosh PCs to exchange information with IBM machines, but the process is slow and cumbersome. Also, hardware boards can be installed on your Mac that in effect produce a second computer inside — an IBM clone, but independent of your Mac. There is talk of a new product called *DOS in a Box* that will enable an IBM-type PC to read an Apple diskette directly. But for the time being, most of us still have to choose one or the other.

People like Apples. Among the winning machines are the Apple Macintosh Classic ($999), the popular Macintosh LC ($2,000 to $3,000), and the new notebook-sized PowerBook series (list prices vary, depending on how much hard-disk space and working memory you want to buy, from $1,599 to $4,599, but street prices start as low as $979). There are also millions of older Apples in use in America's schools. True, 85% of PC users throughout the world employ IBM compatibles, but Apple users tend to be almost fanatic in trumpeting that *their* machines are easier to run and much more versatile.

IBM-compatible computers run on MS-DOS, or DOS for short, which stands for Microsoft Disk Operating System and is the platform on which other software runs. This platform requires users to learn sometimes complicated strings of commands, though IBM is always working to simplify them.

Mac users, by contrast, have always had the (arguable) advantage of GUI (pronounced "gooey"), or a Graphical User Interface. In plain lingo, this refers to the mouse-driven, pull-down-and-click-on menus, which most people find much easier to handle than DOS. However, some diehard DOS fans find Apple-type menu-driven systems irritatingly slow to use and say that direct DOS commands preclude all that "mousing around." Apple and other companies are working on improving mouse-driven technology. When your mouse gets dirty, your screen cursor can get infuriatingly jumpy, but perhaps it's only a question of taking it apart and cleaning it (ask at your local computer store for the right product to use in cleaning).

But the Apple fans seem to have made their basic point — so much so that Microsoft knuckled under in 1985 and launched the easy-to-use *Windows* operating environment for IBM-compatible machines. It took a few years to catch on, but from the way in which the new *Windows 3.0* took off in 1990 (nine million copies were sold in the first year and a half), it was clear that *Windows* was a hit.

No matter which family you choose, then — Apple or IBM compatible — you will probably be looking at *Windows*-type operating systems. The choice then rests on preference. The old aphorism — that software dictates hardware — might convince you to choose IBM, since there is still more software out there for the IBM world than for the Mac world. But IBM and Apple are already collaborating on a joint venture, Kaleida, whose purpose is to create multimedia computer systems capable of combining audio, video and data displays on the same machine. In any case, you will be at no disadvantage with a Mac. Software will continue to be issued for both formats. Apples have traditionally had strong sales in schools. Although business schools and business people tend to use IBM PCs, many businesses that want desktop publishing swear by their Macs (see — And Desktop Publishing).

When to Buy

ONE other factor affecting your choice is timing. Remember that you are buying on a kind of obsolescence curve. That is, six months after you make your choice, the technology will turn itself inside out, and what was touted as the fastest and best will suddenly look as appealing as yesterday's pancakes. Basic to this process is your computer's silicon chip, the tiny wafer onto which is etched the fabulously complex semiconducting circuitry that enables all that digitizing to take place. It is this microprocessor that rules how fast your software programs will work and whether or not you will be able to run several programs at once, use parts of one program in another, or hook yourself up into a LAN, or Local Area Network of computers (good for two or more users who want to share files or communicate with each other via electronic mail). The faster your microprocessor, the more versatile your computer will be.

The corollary to this is that the older the microprocessor in a computer, the cheaper it will be. We are now, with the 486 chip, at Intel's fourth-generation silicon chip (a still more advanced class — 586 chips — will be shipped in a year or so, and 686 and 786 are in the works). So if you're looking for a bargain, wait until prices are cut on the models that have just been superseded. Prices are falling on 386s, which means that 286s are a drug on the market. If you can still find a model of the 286-generation Epson Equity 1+ (no longer produced by Epson but still in some warehouses), you'll probably pay no more than $350 for it; be warned that it will come without a hard drive. There are other inexpensive desktops of this generation. Just remember that you will not be able to run

Windows on any machine powered by less than a 386SX microprocessor.

Among the 386 generation of computers, you have a wide choice. The Leading Edge D3SX (without monitor), for example, goes for $1,099, discounted at $698. The IBM PS/1 lists at $2,000, but its street price is $1,200 or less. Some of the lowest prices belong to Compaq, formerly a high-performance, high-price computer manufacturer, which has introduced a new line of less costly machines designed for first-time computer buyers, and slashed prices on existing models. Other companies, notably Dell, are following suit. The Compaq 386SX ProLinea line of desktops — with respectable hard drives and RAMs — start as low as $899 and will soon be discounted.

Desktop or Portable?

HERE is yet another aspect of your decision: Do you want a desktop or a portable? How mobile is this computer likely to be? If you decide that you need to work on the train, or that your kids will need to be able to carry their machine back and forth from class or the library, then what should you choose — laptop, notebook, sub-notebook? (Yes, designers at Dell Computers have managed to cram both a hard drive and an attachable floppy drive into their new Dell 320SLi computer, which costs $2,149 and weighs less than three pounds, and they have announced an even lighter machine.)

How small is just right? If you just need a palmtop electronic organizer, a strong candidate is still the Sharp Wizard, which can now communicate with most personal information manager software programs for IBM (such as Lotus's *Agenda*). The 8600 model ($499 retail) fits in some pockets and contains a 200-year calendar, memo pad and thesaurus, and offers add-on cards (the size of your credit card) that will do everything from translating phrases in eight foreign languages to transferring information onto your expense report and, when hooked up, printing it out. It'll also tell you the time in 212 cities around the world and track your investments. For an additional $400, you can buy a fax modem card that enables your Wizard to hook into the phone lines and both send and receive faxes (it still, of course, has to print out somewhere — also no more complicated than another hookup).

The Wizard is not really a computer, but where it stops, the palmtop computer takes over. Atari and Hewlett Packard all make palmtops that can do spreadsheet analysis, E-mail fetching and more. There is a physical limit to how small a keyboard/keypad can be without subjecting users to intense finger cramping. So the wave of the future (at least until Xerox Corporation's "ubiquitous computing" — still top-secret — arrives to do away with keyboards altogether) seems to be in developing bantamweight machines that can plug into your bigger home or office models. Someday you'll unplug your credit-card-sized computer from your home PC, slip it into your pocket as you leave the house, continue working on battery power en route to your office, and plug it back into a network when you get to work.

There are also the new pen-driven machines to consider, the ones that can recognize handwriting. Apple is about to unveil its pen-driven Newton, a new PDA, or Personal Digital Assistant, priced at a record-breaking (for Apple anyway) $700 or so. It will be a while before this new technology comes down in price: Momenta International's pen-driven notebook computer lists at $4,995. Moreover, the pattern-recognition technology that enables the machine to "read" your handwriting works only in a limited tit-for-tat kind of way. The computer learns to read each of your longhand letters (no matter how difficult they are to read, if you're consistent, it will expect the next letter to look just the same way, or close), but you have to learn how to write your letters longhand without actually connecting any of the letters. In other words, it can't handle real cursive handwriting — yet. But students should (quite literally) take note. They can take notes during class and print them out later, just as they wrote them. They can then put the notes to use in a word-processing program — search through a year's worth of class notes, say, looking for particular information — without having to recopy them.

Moving up in size: appreciably bigger than palmtops are laptops and notebooks. They won't fit in anybody's pocket, but they are still much more compact than the big, heavy desktops of yore. Notebooks are looking very good right now. Toshiba's highly rated T2200SX laptop ($3,999 list for a 60-megabyte hard disk) weighs 6½ pounds, and its battery life tested at more than three hours, better than most. You can get some notebooks for $2,000, and prices are likely to drop further as the 386-processor generation of machines filters down into the mass market. You might like to look at a couple of lightweight systems based on the 386SX chip. They come with at least two megabytes of RAM, a 40-megabyte hard disk, and DOS (they are capable, that is, of running *Windows*). The $1,995 FlexNote 20 from USA Flex and the $1,975 Fora NBS-386/20 have both been well reviewed.

Monitors

UNTIL recently, notebook users had to do without color on their monitor screens. But a new breed of color notebooks has appeared. The first of its kind, the NEC UltraLite SL 125C, costs $5,000 or more and features the improved "active-matrix" screen, which is capable of delivering 512 colors.

A good thing to check when you study newspaper or magazine ads is whether the quoted price includes a monitor. The ProLinea models come without monitors, but what they do offer is a one-year on-site warranty, meaning that a technician will come to your house to fix anything that goes wrong (as long as you didn't drop it down a staircase), without charge, for one year. Where monitors are concerned, resolution is key. If you are a graphic designer and need great precision, and can afford it, go for a big 17-inch or 19-inch monitor ($1,300 and up), or even a 21-inch one, equipped with a Super VGA graphics card. Good monitors for the ordinary user sell for anywhere from $275 to $450. Anything costing less will still get you all 256 colors, but they will probably be fuzzy.

Expandability and
Other Expensive Options

THE most expensive IBM-compatible PCs designed for home use are the user-upgradable computers based on Intel's state-of-the-art 486 microprocessor. "Upgradable" means that down the line you can buy more powerful components and just fit them right into a predesigned slot. Computer systems have always been more or less upgradable, but only by technicians and at considerable expense; this is the first time anyone has made expandability a part of the basic design. A wonderful but breathtakingly expensive member of this family is the IBM PS/2 model 90 XP486, which lists at $11,295. You don't have to spend quite that much, though, for a 486 machine: the Touche 486/33 EISA computer by PC Pros goes for $3,800.

Another expensive-at-present option for your computer involves CD-ROM technology (CD-ROM stands for Compact Disk Read Only Memory — "read only" because on these disks you can only read, not alter, files). Computers are being made that have compact disk drives built right into them (these include IBM's high-end $6,000 Ultimedia PC; Apple will introduce a less expensive Macintosh with the same capabilities soon). But compact disk drives also can be bought — and added to your existing system — for between $300 and $400. One of the salient features of this new technology is its incredible storage capacity. DeLorme Mapping's *Street Atlas USA* ($99 list), for example, gets more than one million color maps onto one compact disk: you can call up any part of any city, town or rural area in the entire United States with just a few keystrokes. Also, compact disks are part of the great marriage of media that is taking place all around us. So far, CD-ROM technology's enormous potential is virtually untapped, and some of the existing applications — watching a CD-ROM encyclopedia play the national anthem of every country in the world, for example — may only make us ask, "So who wants it?" On the other hand, it's one thing to try and describe what "scat singing" is to your children, and another to turn on Ella Fitzgerald and let her *show* them.

A Good Choice

AN EXCELLENT compromise between the bargain 286 machines and the expensive 486s are the 386DX computers, which are the first to incorporate the new 32-bit processing — the latest transformation in speed and power in the PC world. Two examples of these are Gateway 2000's 386/33C ($1,695) and the ACT 386/33c from Automated Computer Technology (for $1,770). Both machines have at least 80-megabyte hard drives and four megabytes of RAM.

Other Options: Mail-Order and Used

T HE GATEWAY model has to be ordered over the phone, since Gateway is one of the big four mail-order houses. More and more PCs are bought this way, even though it would seem to be far riskier than shopping in a comfortable neighborhood store. Experience has shown, though, that if you stick to the tried-and-true quartet — Dell (800-426-5150), Gateway (800-523-2000), Northgate (800-548-9016) and Zeos (800-423-5891) — you are likely to get good hardware, good technical support, and good on-site repair service. The watchword, though, is to *use a credit card*, so that you have some leverage if things go awry. Some credit-card companies will charge you a fee of $50 for a canceled sale (just as they would if your credit card had been stolen), but better that than writing off the entire $1,500 purchase.

If you want a computer right now and can't wait for prices to be reduced further when the next generation of machines comes out, consider buying a used model. PCs lose up to half of their value just as soon as they are taken out of the crate. Two companies that match buyers and sellers are the National Computer Exchange (800-659-2468) and the Boston Computer Exchange (617-542-4414). You have your pick of a wide variety of next-to-new desktops, laptops and notebooks.

Printers

D OT-MATRIX printers — the fast, shrill-whine machines that offer either 9-pin or 24-pin clarity and that have dominated the field for the past decade — may be on their way out. But for routine text printing — draft- or letter-quality — you can't beat their prices (generally from under $300 to $500). Some of them aren't nearly as costly as they used to be — Panasonic's KX-P2624, for example, lists at about $650 but can be had for less at street prices. A good dot-matrix printer will print at a speed approaching that of a laser (though not as unobtrusively) for about half the laser's price. Ink-jet printers may seriously challenge laser printers for dominance: much-improved recent models don't clog or smear any more and have tested extremely well, but the machines still use expensive cartridges.

As laser prices fall, people are likely to find them irresistible. Laser printers used to cost several thousands of dollars — the Hewlett Packard HP-III still is $1,469, even discounted — but outlets now discount some models for as little as $650 to $700. Scanning laser technology offers just about limitless choice in type sizes and forms. These printers are quiet and fast, can handle just about any printing job, no matter how sophisticated, and result in a clean, sharp page. The Epson Action Laser II ($999 list), a six-page-per-minute printer, has tested extremely well, as has Lexmark International's Laser Printer 6 at the heftier price of $1,895.

Mac users have a choice among various Apple printers. They include the dot-matrix Imagewriter II (list $595); the ink-jet Style-writer (list $399), which despite its slow speed produces good print quality; and the Personal Laserwriter LS (list $1,199), essentially a stripped-down version of the older Personal Laserwriter: it prints four pages a minute at a resolution of 300 dots per inch, which is perfectly adequate for a single user. And as an alternative to Apple's own printers, GCC offers Mac users the Personal Laserprinter II and IIs, $949 and $1,299, respectively.

SOFTWARE

What — and Where — To Buy

A COMPUTER without software is like a camera without film. Software translates your commands into a digital language that the computer can understand. The software industry is a moveable feast — it is expanding incredibly fast, it keeps changing and it offers everything from the sublime to the ridiculous. Designers, taking advantage of newfound power and speed capabilities in hardware, are writing programs of ever-increasing complexity that can do more and more amazing things. These programs use ever more RAM and occupy ever more space on your hard drive.

If you're a first-time computer buyer, the computer you purchase is likely to come loaded with some kind of software — most commonly, a word-processing program and a spreadsheet. But after you familiarize yourself with the territory, you'll probably want to add some software of your own. If your needs are likely to remain basic for a while, try one of the so-called integrated software programs: these are something-for-everyone programs that include word processing, spreadsheet, and data base (a way of grouping related files to enable someone to work with just that information in a number of different ways). The price of this is often under $100. In the $100–$200 range, look at *Microsoft Works, LotusWorks*, and Spinnaker Software's *PFS: First Choice* for the IBM compatibles, and *Clarus Works* for the Mac.

Computer superstores are great places to do some window-shopping and find bargains, too, sometimes at 60% to 80% off list. At CompUSA, an enormous warehouse-type store that carries everything connected with PCs, you can even sign up for training classes in *WordPerfect*, say, if that's the word-processor you decide you want. Other franchises where you may or may not get good help include MicroAge, Connecting Point, Software City, Tandy Corp's Computer City SuperCenters and CompuAdd stores. Sears and Staples sell software too, but if you want specialization (though not always the lowest price), try Egghead Discount Software (183 stores across the country). One mail-order establishment with separate divisions for IBM PCs and Macs that gives good prices and excellent technical support: PC Connection (800-243-8088) and Mac Connection (800-334-4444). An alternative pair, with less reliable support, is Micro Warehouse (800-367-7080) and Mac Warehouse (800-255-6227).

Virus Protection

THERE is fun software, and there is useful software. Virus software definitely belongs to the latter category. Viruses — programs designed to make their way into your system when you boot up or when you activate an executable file — are more and more common, and you can get antivirus software. Two basic rules:

First, always, *always* back up what you have on your hard drive, but be forewarned that even your back-up files could be infected, as some viruses work like time-release capsules, waiting until you call up a file that activates them or allows them to spread. A good back-up program for IBM compatibles is *Peter Norton's BackUp* for $84 discount; for the Mac there's *Retrospect* for $145. *Fastback Plus*, at $125, exists for both formats, and some utility programs (see below) have back-up programs built in.

Second, never boot up from a floppy disk, since floppies are the likeliest source of trouble. If you boot up with a floppy in your A drive, the virus loads into memory and never leaves your system. Every time you then turn on the PC, the virus loads into memory and infects any other floppies. One consolation: Viruses — so far, at least — do not damage hardware. They reside, and sometimes spread, in files. Even if yours are afflicted, some help may be at hand.

The help is limited, though, and you may lose everything on your hard drive — the equivalent of going into your local library and dumping every card out of the card file. The books may stay on the shelves, but you can't get to them. And you will always be at risk, since most antivirus software only searches for known viruses, and according to one newsletter on virus prevention and removal, some 20 or 30 new viruses appear every month. Even brand-new, shrink-wrapped software has been known to come infected directly from the manufacturer, though this is extremely rare. You may worry about programs that you download from an on-line service. CompuServe checks all its programs for viruses, but local bulletin boards may not be so careful. If you download from reputable sources (rather than exchanging floppies with friends), and if you don't invite the general public in to use your PC, you are likely to be safe.

But do get an antivirus program. You'll be very glad you did if you run into trouble. Should a black box appear on your screen (the sign of the Jerusalem virus, of which there are more than 40 known variants), or should you see the message "Your computer is now stoned" (this is the Stoned virus, the most prevalent of all), or should your screen characters appear to drop down to the bottom of the display (sign of the Cascade virus), save your file and turn off your PC. Boot up from a clean write-protected floppy, and thank your lucky stars you've got an antivirus program.

A few good ones for the IBM PC: *Central Point Anti-Virus* ($129 list), *Dr. Solomon's Anti-Virus Toolkit* ($150 list), and McAfee Associates' *Viruscan* family of programs ($15 to $35 each). For the Mac, there is Symantec's *SAM* ($64 discount); the latest version of *Mac Tools* ($92 for Version 2.0) also includes antivirus software. Programs such as these can help you scan your hard disk and locate and perhaps fix the problem before it wipes out that disk. If you need more help (whether or not you have antivirus protection), someone at the National Computer Security Association (717-258-1816) can walk you through a few basic self-help steps (for free). If you subscribe to CompuServe, there is an antivirus forum (just type Go VIRUSFORUM). A program with up-to-date information on all known viruses is available, with monthly updates, from Patricia Hoffman (408-988-3773) for about $30 a year. Perhaps best of all, from Fifth Generation comes *Untouchables* ($95 at discount), a program for IBM compatibles that is not dependent on constant upgrading; it looks for certain kinds of changes that indicate the presence of a virus. This may prove to be the best way to get them before they get your hard drive.

Sharing the Wealth

COMMUNITY bulletin boards are numerous and growing, and they are an indication of how widespread the grass-roots digital community is. If you are interested in participating in a local bulletin board, call the Association of Shareware Professionals in Muskegon, Michigan (616-788-5131). Or you might have a look at *BoardWatch*, a monthly bulletin-board magazine available at some newsstands and software stores that publishes lists of bulletin boards and reviews shareware programs (call 303-973-6038). One software exchange group in New York City, The Invention Factory (212-431-5555), offers its subscribers a sort of bulletin-board shopping service. It not only offers all kinds of downloading possibilities, but it also checks out bulletin boards around the country and tests products. Fees start as low as $25 a year for one hour a day of access time but quickly mount for more time. A few other, well-known bulletin boards — which sometimes have new shareware programs even before CompuServe and GEnie — are Channel 1 in Massachusetts (617-864-0100), EXEC-PC in Wisconsin (414-789-4200) and Rusty and Edie's in Ohio (216-758-8342).

Using a Computer
to Manage Your Money

MANAGING money is largely a matter of managing numbers, and that's what computers do best. The awesome computational powers of the microchip enable even the greenest practitioner to perform dizzying feats of mathematics previously reserved for professional money managers.

Managing money additionally involves common sense, prudence and self-discipline, and in these departments the personal computer is brain dead. Also, to crunch your numbers in a PC, you have to get them into the machine to start with. This process, called data entry, can be annoying, redundant and dismally tedious.

So with these two drawbacks noted, everyone who wants to streamline his or her personal finances ought to at least take a look at how a computer might help.

All sorts of financial software is available: programs for personal financial management, for investments, for tax planning and filing. No one program does everything, and no one program is a substitute for a highly trained investment analyst or tax adviser or accountant. But an astonishing wealth of information is quite literally at your fingertips, and you can make your computer an important asset to your financial well-being. And consider this: If you put in the right numbers, there will be no arithmetical mistakes.

If you just want to know where your money is coming from and where it's going, many check-registering programs are now available. MySoftware's *MyCheckbook* ($25) does a good job. Other programs, such as the best-selling *Quicken* (Intuit, discounted at $59 for IBM, $45 for Mac and a lower promotional price for *Quicken for Windows*) and Microsoft's *Money* ($45), are capable of doing more. *Quicken* can now do more than reconcile your electronic checkbook with a broader personal budget. It does single-entry accounting; it allows you, for instance, to set up different ledgers for cash, checking, credit-card and investment accounts. Small businesses can add on a payroll program called *QuickPay* for $60. Another product aimed at small businesses is a simple accounting program, Intuit's *QuickBooks* (discounted for IBM compatibles at $89).

The very popular *Andrew Tobias's Managing Your Money, Version 7.0* (Meca's list price is $220, but you can find it discounted at $169 for the Mac, $199 for IBM), tries to do everything short of full-fledged double-entry accounting. Leading the others in sales and praises, it's an electronic checkbook, a budget program, a stock tracker and strategist, bond analyzer, tax planner and preparer, financial calculator and address keeper. The Tobias software, accompanied by a beautifully written manual and featuring on-screen tutorial wit, also serves as a word processor, based on the notion that a lot of your outgoing mail concerns your financial life.

These programs take a considerable investment of time to learn and to operate: you have to feed in all your cash-flow data. But if you use your personal finance software regularly (many people make daily entries), you will find that paying your bills and staying on top of your personal finances has never been easier. Real improvements include instant recall of repetitive transactions, such as payment of rent or mortgage and utilities, built-in reminders of payments due, and electronic payment of bills by check-free service. Do ask, when you shop for your personal-finance software, whether you can "export" information (or transfer data directly) from it to your favorite tax-preparation program or to your spreadsheet (*Quicken* and *Managing Your Money* both allow such a transfer). Some programs also provide you with a way to get personalized paper checks that feed through your printer. Just be forewarned that you'll have to buy special, somewhat expensive checks. If you want them anyway, try to get them from a business-forms dealer instead of from the software company — you'll save money.

For financial analysis, spreadsheets are more ambitious yet. If you have the latest version of *Lotus 1-2-3* or *Microsoft Excel*, you might wonder whether you need any other personal-finance software. The answer is probably yes. Spreadsheet programs, though they can be personally tailored to a high degree, were never intended as household managers; they are best at doing analysis and "what-if" scenarios. Check printing, for example, can be done in *Lotus* but is slow and cumbersome. The leading spreadsheets are versatile, though, in their ability to interface with other programs such as *WordPerfect* and *Harvard Graphics*. And they pride themselves on offering presentation-quality features: Borland International's *Quattro Pro* comes complete with visual and sound effects and even offers an electronic slide-show feature that can produce 35mm color slides.

More and more people also use personal computers to help keep track of their investments, investigate individual securities, size up buying opportunities and analyze trends in the stock market. If you just want stock price quotes, an add-on card in the Sharp Wizard electronic organizer can get you that. But if you want more and aren't intimidated by a stiff price tag, several programs from Dow Jones can help. *Market Manager PLUS* (available only from Dow Jones, at $299 for IBM and MAC) does portfolio management; it keeps records and updates holdings based on information from the Dow Jones News/Retrieval service. Two technical analysis programs, *Market Analyzer* and the more powerful *Market Analyzer PLUS* (also available from Dow Jones, at $499 for IBM, $349 for Mac), are capable of turning a pile of statistics into an easy-to-read chart.

Hundreds of investment software programs are available, most of them appropriate for portfolios of $10,000 and up. But there are less expensive alternatives. *Money* magazine's *WealthBuilder* ($99.95) is an investment program geared for family use. Its sophisticated asset-allocation program gives you a balanced portfolio of investments that should be able to weather ups and downs in different sectors of the market and still yield a handsome return each year. In addition, if you pay an annual fee (ranging from $100 to $175), you have access to a data base of more than 1,000 mutual funds and equities with descriptions, phone numbers and each fund's performance record over the past quarter, year, five years and ten years.

Or you can tap into the phone lines. Via modem, you can subscribe to an on-line information service and make use of its financial-services offerings. Here, once you've gotten the hardware you need and sometimes some enabling software as well, you pay an initial setup fee (CompuServe's is $39.95) and then pay an as-you-go fee or a monthly flat fee plus "surcharges" if you choose to make use of extra financial services. For instance, America Online, GEnie, and CompuServe all offer brokerage services through a variety of brokerage firms, including Charles Schwab Inc., the discounter. For a flat monthly fee of $10, CompuServe also offers an enhanced Executive Services Option membership, which gets you a discount on stock price quotes and the option of subscribing to some desirable financial services such as a newsclipping service (you can request, for example, a file of clips on all Midwestern companies with earnings over $2 million) or disclosure reports about a particular company.

CompuServe can get expensive ifyou use it a lot. If your financial news need is less urgent, you might be interested in subscribing to a special offering from the Dow Jones News/Retrieval service (you still need a modem, though): if you are willing to confine your stock-checking activities to the hours between 9:00 p.m. and 6:00 a.m. and if you are willing to limit yourself to five data bases (instead of a possible 67), the cost is only $25 a month.

And what about retirement-planning software? If you have questions such as whether you're putting enough into tax-deferred savings, or whether you are adjusting properly for inflation, or how long your resources will last, you may want to look at a couple of helpful programs. At the very least *Retire ASAP* from Calypso Software ($99) or *Harvest Time* from Computer Lab ($50) will encourage you to gather some information that you might not otherwise seek out until it was too late to make changes in the way you invest and save. If you start making realistic projections now, it might make a real difference to you and your family later.

Computerizing Your Taxes

BECAUSE computers are great organizers and calculators, they can save you money and time on your taxes — if you buy a tax program. You can devise strategies, do all the necessary calculations for your tax returns and then print out a completed 1040 form. Two good tax programs are *Turbo Tax* (ChipSoft, about $80) and *Personal Tax Edge* (Parsons Technology, list $49).

Several programs use a simple question-and-answer format to help you fill out your tax forms. Two of particular note are *J. K. Lasser's Your Income Tax* (Simon & Schuster, $80) and *Andrew Tobias' Tax Cut* (Meca, $90). Apple Macintosh users should consider *MacInTax* (Softview, about $80). All of these programs display replicas of this year's tax forms on your screen and then walk you through a line-by-line process of filling in the appropriate numbers. The fun begins when you punch a key and all the computations — percentages, depreciations and deductions — are figured in a flash. Many programs then run an audit check, which reviews your forms and flags any answers or omissions that are likely to trigger an investigation. *Tax Cut* even noticed, in auditing a sample return, that the cost of the tax software itself hadn't been listed among the itemized deductions. The *TurboTax* program, meanwhile, caught a mortgage-interest deduction that the IRS would consider too high relative to the filer's income.

Before buying a tax software program, be sure the manufacturer will sell you a revised version each year to keep up with the tax-law changes. The renewal price for *TurboTax*, for instance, is about $40, and for *Personal Tax Edge*, $25. Something to consider: Prices fluctuate depending on what season of the year you buy, so it is not always necessary to settle for the manufacturer's suggested retail price. In fact, it might be worthwhile to look for a tax software package in, say, late May, six weeks after the filing deadline of April 15. Sometimes retailers send software packages back to the distributor, but at least one discounter in New York City was selling *Andrew Tobias's Tax Cut* for $19.99. If you've never used a computer to do your taxes, you could thus pick up the basic package at a great discount and use the software not only to familiarize yourself with the program but also to do some basic tax planning. Then order the renewal package when it becomes available, and you're ready to go.

Remember, one of the first deductions on your computerized tax form should be for at least part of the cost of the computer as well as the cost of the software — as long as you use them for help with your taxes, investments or overall money management. Under the new rules of tax reform, this will count as one of your miscellaneous deductions. You can deduct only the amount by which your total miscellaneous unreimbursed deductions exceed 2% of your adjusted gross income.

Bringing It All Home

D URING the last decade, many houses have sprouted a new room: the home office. This can range in size and sophistication from a desk in the corner to an elaborately fitted-out suite complete with computer (one study found that home-office workers spent an average of $1,830 for their latest PC), fax machine, copier and advanced phone system. Users commonly think that as long as it is used for a profit-making endeavor — be it a sideline to a regular job or the main source of income for the household — spending on this space and its contents is tax-deductible, offsetting your net profits.

But beware of the so-called exclusive use test. If you are an employee, your home office must be maintained for the convenience of your employer and not just to be helpful in your job. In order to claim a deduction for operating expenses and depreciation on part of your home, that part must be used regularly and exclusively as a) your principal place of business for your trade or business, or b) a place to meet or deal with patients or clients in the normal course of your trade or business. The use of part of your home for *both* personal and business purposes fails the exclusive use test, and therefore you cannot deduct expenses for it.

A new class of retailer has appeared to serve the needs of the home office, supplying office machinery that has been downsized and even color-coordinated to fit the home environment. Stores such as Staples or Office Depot specialize in this gear. Mass retailers such as Kmart and Sears sell fax machines and computers a few aisles away from toasters and irons. Although you'll find little personalized assistance at these stores, warranties are honored, and more often than not if there is a problem the item will simply be exchanged for a new one.

Although this equipment is accessible, it is not inexpensive. New home-office machines are likely to cost from $100 for, say, a phone packed with high-tech features to over $3,000 for a personal computer with word-processing and accounting programs. As with all major purchases, advance planning is a good idea.

A word of caution: Home-office machinery is evolving at a rapid pace, and this year's wonder machine could become next year's mood ring. Generally, but not always, mass-marketed machinery will be less up-to-date. It's best to begin with a visit to a store specializing in office equipment, where you can see the latest developments in a particular machine. Then make your purchase based on price and service. You may find that the blue-light special at Kmart is just what you want, or you may prefer to buy from a specialist.

Briefly, here's a look at prices and features on two major home-office components, the fax machine and the personal copier. For a good fax machine, figure on paying $600 to $1,200, though you can get stripped-down models for as little as $350. Transmission speed for a single page has been pared to between 15 and 18 seconds, but thermal paper, with its unpleasant waxy surface, is still unavoidable on machines going for less than $1,000. Plain-paper fax machines cost $1,500 and up, and they will dominate the field within a few years.

You should consider compatibility and overlap. Plain-paper fax machines can double as copiers, but thermal-paper faxes really can't. Thermal-paper copies often come out unpresentably crinkled, and often you have to sacrifice a page from a book or magazine by tearing it out in order to copy it. If you send mostly text files, you might consider getting a fax modem, a combination fax and modem board that will send your fax out directly from your PC and can also receive. But if you need to send graphics too, stick to the fax machine. Once a luxury, it is fast becoming something that no business, however small, can afford to be without. (Nevertheless, one home-office newsletter published in Manassas, Virginia, included recommendations on how to *sound like* you have a fax even when you pay to use the fax in the neighborhood stationery store. When asked, "Can I fax this to you?" the proper response is, "Yes, you can. I have a fax down the way. Let me give you the number and you can send the information right now.")

Don't be wowed by — or pay more for — features you'll never use. Some big-office features, such as polling (the ability to scan several other fax machines to see if there is a transmission waiting for you) and broadcasting (the ability to have your machine send the same copy to a group of other machines) have been dropped from home-office fax machines, allowing manufacturers to build in other features more appreciated by home users. Canon, Sharp and Toshiba are leaders in this area. Don't worry if it can't automatically dial 10 or 100 other numbers from its memory chip. Consider the leasing option, too. You might be able to get a much better fax machine for your money.

Personal copiers, the suitcase-sized copy machines that sell for $400 to $2,000, have one great advantage over their office-grade big brothers: they are more or less maintenance-free. All the parts that cause trouble in the big machines, such as the toner container and the photosensitive drum, now come as sealed units that are simply tossed out and replaced when they are used up. Even the cheapest copiers made by Canon and Sharp, among others, are superb and should give years of flawless service.

Good news: home-office software is getting better and better. Microsoft's *WinFax Pro* for *Windows* is a program that makes sending your faxes (through a fax modem) as easy as printing is to your printer. As for other software that shows promise for the home-office market, one favorite in the we-could-probably-live-without-it category is a program called *WinPost* from Nobuya Higashiyama (list $30), which enables you to post electronic Post-its all over your files to remind you of appointments and the like. The electronic note will not only pop up like an alarm at a preset time ("It's 4 o'clock. Time to pick up the kids"), it will even play you a little tune. Such are the advantages of being what some have called "open-collar workers."

The Delights of Word Processing —

REMEMBER the not-so-good old days, when a few mistakes on the typewriter meant the letter had to be started all over again? We are light-years away from that now. The simple function of defining a block of text and moving it has radically changed the way we put words onto paper, and with improved mouse and stylus technologies, track-balls and voice activation right around the bend, things are only going to get better. Maybe computers still can't set margins or address envelopes as easily as an old-fashioned typewriter did, but electronic cutting and pasting surely beats the scissors-and-tape method.

If you are an executive, a student or a person who devotes more than four hours a week to writing or editing, you need some sort of word processor. The question is, what kind of word processor to buy? A personal computer is the most obvious choice. Yet what if you just want to write and wonder whether you need to spend money for the extra power of a PC? There are less expensive options, but you will have to decide whether what you gain in savings equals what you lose in performance. Besides the old tried-and-true IBM Selectric electric typewriter, there are the so-called smart electronic typewriters, which type directly onto paper, have some storage and retrieval capabilities and cost about $200. There are also dedicated word processors, computers that function only as word processors (and sometimes need to hook up to separate printers). Lower-end word processors, available from Brother, Smith Corona, Panasonic and Canon, among others, come with a range of features from backlit screens to built-in spreadsheets and usually cost $250 to $350. Canon's Starwriter 80 word processor lists at $900 but can be found at discount for $500 and comes with 30 pages of working memory, a built-in ink-jet printer and pull-down menus. It is portable — but just barely.

Even this last model represents some savings compared with a computer system and may still be a wise choice if you want to send your teenager off to college with a good machine for just typing. But when you consider that you can buy a 286-generation and soon even a 386-generation computer system for well under $1,000, you may decide to go for versatility and expandability, and that means a PC.

If you do take the PC plunge, you will have a wide range of choices for word-processing software. Two top sellers, *WordPerfect* and *Microsoft Word*, are so powerful that they can just about brush your teeth for you. These programs certainly make the PC smarter than the smartest electronic typewriter, give it infinitely greater memory (the working memory of a "smart" typewriter can handle only 7 to 11 pages), are exponentially faster (though this depends on what microprocessor your system uses) and can be upgraded.

All the top word-processing programs are now available for *Windows*, including two other highly rated ones, *Ami Pro* and *Lotus Write*. The pre-*Windows* and *Windows* versions, however, may differ in small but significant ways; it's best to test them yourself. Other support software for wordsmithing, such as *Writer's Toolkit* ($129 for *Windows 3.0*), may make reaching for reference works a thing of the past. With *Toolkit*, besides the usual spell-checking, you get electronic versions of a 115,000-word dictionary, a desktop encyclopedia,

Roget's Thesaurus, a grammar and style manual and a dictionary of quotations.

— And Desktop Publishing

THE BEST news is that although it's still not cheap, it's getting less expensive and easier to use your PC for desktop publishing (DTP). You can design and produce documents — newsletters, fliers, business forms, invitations, even four-color brochures and whole magazines — that incorporate both type and images and look as classy as if they had come from a professional printer. Among the leaders in high-end software is the *Aldus PageMaker 4.0* for Macs or *Windows* (list $795, street price as low as $540, recommended for use on a computer with at least a 40-megabyte hard disk), which is the program that along with Apple Macintosh computers is often credited with having created the desktop publishing industry. Also, there is *Ventura* (list $795), with a reputation for better handling of longer documents, and *Quark XPress*, the program favored by many magazine publishers ($795 list for Mac).

Just a few years ago, there were relatively expensive programs (overkill for most home uses), and there were word-processing programs that could process words but could barely do page layout. But there was nothing in between. Then two things happened: software publishers began offering lower-priced publishing programs, and word-processing programs began incorporating graphics features. *Publish It!* from Timeworks, for example, offers 95 ready-to-use layouts and can be bought discounted for $85. Other worthwhile programs include *Express Publisher* from Power Up! Software Incorporated (discount price $89), *Microsoft Publisher* (which sells for about $129 by mail order) and *GeoWorks* (about $125). A "smart" piece of drawing software (one that incorporates automated procedures — that is, procedures that anticipate your next move) is the new *IntelliDraw 1.0* from Aldus (list $299 for *Windows* and Mac). It is good for creating line drawings, business forms, graphs and diagrams. An even more moderately priced program is *Arts and Letters Apprentice* (list $169 for *Windows*) from Computer Support Corporation, with 3,000 clip-art images and 25 scalable fonts (meaning that you can vary the size and shape of your letters at will) and the ability to fit text to a curve (say, for a company logo).

If you need to do a spectacular four-color promotional brochure, or if you want automatic letter spacing, text rotation, vertical justification or automatic indexing (good for longer documents), you'll need the bigger-ticket hardware and software. The CAD software (standing for Computer-Assisted Design) is coming within reach. But you still need to spend some serious money to buy hardware capable of producing professional-looking results. Nothing less than a 386SX-processor-based system will do, for one thing, and a 40- or even an 80-megabyte hard drive is pretty standard. A super VGA monitor — the better the monitor, the easier it is to see what you're doing — is a good idea. A laser printer (prices are coming down) will give you the best results.

And last but not least, you'll need a scanner, the optical sensing device that converts an image, whether a photograph, a slide, a magazine illustration or even a TV signal, into digital form for manipulation by your computer's software. Hand-held scanners are available for anywhere from $150 to $500, but they are limited in what they can do. Most hand-held scanners can capture only four inches at a time, so you have to make multiple passes and electronically "sew" the pieces together, which is tedious. For small images, though, they may be your best bet. (For a real estate agent wanting to scan snapshots of houses for sale, for instance, it's ideal.) For more sophisticated results, look at flatbed scanners such as the Hewlett Packard ScanJet IIc (about $550). Ask whether the scanner can be used for OCR input (OCR stands for Optical Character Recognition and refers to whether the machine can also scan and reproduce text such as newspaper clippings). Also, inquire about its DPI ability (DPI stands for Dots Per Inch and is a measure of image resolution, ranging from 200 for low-resolution to 1,000 and up for high-resolution scanners). There are color scanners such as the Nikon LS-3510 or the Kodak 35mm Rapid Film Scanner, which cost anywhere from $1,500 to $10,000, but a word to the wise: before you buy a color scanner, make sure you have the printer to match. When flatbed scanner prices drop below $1,000, there may be a major shakeout with a resulting advantage to consumers.

If you find all of this intimidating, you could just check out someone else's DTP process. In some areas, computer retailers have found it profitable to rent out image-processing equipment — an excellent way for you to learn the ropes and better define which hardware and software will best satisfy your needs. This kind of service is getting easier to find. DTP rental storefronts are popping up around universities now, as merchants hurry to provide students with a way to produce stunning reports or eye-catching posters at a reasonable rate.

For the future: so-called "frame-grabbers" are devices that will plug into your computer expansion slot and connect your PC to anything that produces a TV image — TV, VCR or camcorder — to digitize that image and transmit it directly into your computer. This device is still in its infancy, but watch for it from Kodak and others. New multimedia software can already make a traditional slide presentation seem tame: MacroMind's *Action!* (list $495 for *Windows*) employs slidelike screens but can be operated with VCR-like controls and can incorporate animation sequences. There will be CD-ROM interfaces, of course, and any day now clients will be offered virtual-reality tours of new products.

Picking Educational Software

LUCKY parents! Your electronic-age kids find computers irresistible and need no convincing about the usefulness of computer literacy. The only problem is, with over 11,000 educational programs to choose from, which ones are best to buy?

Educational software for grade-school children used to be little more than electronic flash cards: a question appeared on the screen, the student answered it, and the computer said whether he or she was right or wrong. But in this age of "edu-tainment," educational software can be a lot more fun than flash cards. "Ssh! Don't tell them they're learning!" say designers at the Learning Company, producer of such educational software as:

— The Reader Rabbit series: *Reader Rabbit Ready for Letters*, for ages 3 to 5, sells for about $50; *Reader Rabbit I* and *II*, for ages 4 to 6 and 5 to 8, respectively, are learning programs featuring four animated games, selling for about $60. (Prices given here are for the IBM version; Mac versions often sell for about $10 more, and Apple II versions for $10 less, but you should keep in mind that discount chains such as B. Dalton's Software Etc. and Barnes & Noble's software store usually mark down the price 10% or more.)

— The popular Super Solver series, arcade action games using word problems that cover addition, subtraction, multiplication, division, fractions, percentages and decimals: *OutNumbered!* (for ages 7 to 10 (about $50); *Spellbound!*, for ages 7 to 12 (about $50); *Midnight Rescue!*, for ages 7 to 10, about $50; and the *Treasure Mountain!* program, for ages 5 to 9 (about $60), soon to be its own series.

— And for the Mac only, for ages 7 and up, *The Writing Center*, a word-processing and desktop publishing program with 220 color pictures, designed to enhance school reports in history, English, social studies, science and math.

Other word-processing software for kids includes the popular *New Print Shop* from Broderbund, for all ages, about $50 for the IBM platform, good for printing greeting cards and posters; *Bank Street Writer III*, from Scholastic Software (about $90 for IBM; the Mac version retails for about $130 and has more desktop publishing features).

For geographers-to-be, there is *PC Globe*, an atlas with 208 countries, for all ages (about $70), full of detailed maps with periodically updated currency conversions, point-to-point distances in miles and kilometers, and so on.

Broderbund produces many winners: *Kid Pix*, a paint program, and its add-on *Kid Pix Companion*, using the new QuickTime technology (or short video takes), have proven so successful that they will soon be part of an entire product line. Broderbund also produces the well-known *Where in the World Is Carmen Sandiego?* and its family of programs (*Where in Europe . . . , Where in the U.S.A. . . . , Where in Time . . .* and the latest, *Where in America's Past . . .*), all software packages that come with a reference book and feature a villainous former secret agent who steals the world's great treasures and must be tracked down by students, using thousands of clues (3,000 in the new deluxe edition of *Where in the World . . .* designed for CD-ROM). *Carmen Sandiego* software painlessly introduces, by way of a cops-and-robber chase, ideas about foreign cultures and currencies, geography and history. Most programs are available in both IBM and Mac formats and, though listed at either $50 or $60, can often be found for about $30.

From Maxis comes simulation software, popular with older children: *SimCity*, for ages 8 and up (about $60), invites players to address zoning issues, lay down roads and power lines, and solve traffic problems; *SimEarth*, for ages 12 and up (about $70), involves geology, evolution and spacefaring. Maxis's most recent program, *SimAnt*, for ages 8 and up ($60), puts students in charge of an ant colony; and the company is also working on *SimLife*, a genetic-engineering simulation program.

Davidson produces some good things: the wordplay and paint program *Kid Work*, for ages 4 to 10, retails for about $50; *What's My Angle?*, a for-IBM-only geometry program in the form of a miniature golf game, for ages 14 and up, costs about $50. Then there is *Headline Harry and the Great Paper Race* for ages 10 and up (about $60), where the player becomes a reporter traveling across the U.S. in search of the who-what-where-when-and-why of various real stories from our American past — the Los Angeles Olympics, Rosa Parks, and the Beatles' appearance on the "Ed Sullivan Show."

New from Earthquest Inc. is *Time Treks*, a history-adventure game with secret passages and booby traps ($60 for Mac). Earthquest also makes *Ecology*, featuring short takes on the rain forest, symbiosis and the food chain, jazzed up with villains and challenges. Also worth the purchase price is *Isaac Asimov's Science Adventure* ($80 for IBM), an explore-the-knowledge maze from Knowledge Adventure Inc. A word of caution: take a close look at the hardware requirements before you shell out hard cash for some of these "toys." The computing power necessary to run some of them can be very expensive.

For the launch into college, there are dozens of programs intended to help students prepare for the SAT exam. Most expensive and quite comprehensive (though critical reviews have been mixed) is the one offered by Krell at $299.95. You won't be cheating your favorite teenager, though, if you go instead for the highly rated *TestWise*, produced by the College Entrance Examination Board itself at a more reasonable $84.95 (for IBM and the Apple II). Less expensive software, with drills and sample tests, does exist (ask whether there's record-keeping and error analysis). Davidson's *Your Personal Trainer for the SAT* costs about $50; Harcourt Brace & Jovanovich makes one for about $40; and Cliffs Notes produces *Studyware for the SAT*, which retails for $49.95 but can be found discounted for as little as about $30.

Software also exists for help with other standardized tests, among them the PSAT and the GED (high-school-equivalency test), as well as for the LSAT (law boards). If you want your elementary-school youngster to get a real head start, you might consider an Apple II version of an SAT-track vocabulary game for grades 5 to 8 from J & S Software (retails for $39.50). It's never too soon to start, right?

Your Auto

Getting the Most from Your Car

Prices on many 1993 cars are only 3% higher than those for '92 models, so you may be thinking of trading in your auto and investing in a new one. But when you consider that the American family spends on average four to six months of its annual income to buy a new car, you may conclude that you will do better by holding on to your reliable old model. In fact, the best way to reduce your automobile costs is to drive your *safe* older car until just before it sputters to a permanent halt. Recognizing that moment takes skill, but here's a tip: Look for a sharp rise in repair costs.

Drivers who heed the maintenance instructions in their owner's manual usually can put 100,000 miles on their cars before facing transmission overhauls or other costly repairs. If you have been taking your car to a reliable mechanic for regular maintenance checkups, quiz him about what is likely to go wrong next.

Don't panic over a single big repair bill. Repair costs rise steadily through a car's first 10 years. The costs of *running* a car — gas, oil, repairs and maintenance — go up along with the miles registered on the odometer, but nowhere near as swiftly as the fixed costs — depreciation, financing and insurance — are going down. The dollar savings from keeping your car for at least eight years showed up in a 1989 study by Runzheimer International of Rochester, Wisconsin, transportation consultants to corporations. Runzheimer's analysts posed two choices for the owner of a mid-sized, six-cylinder 1985 Chevrolet Celebrity, then four years old and free of debt: Drive it for another four years or trade it in on a 1989 model and drive that car for the next four years. The finding: By sticking with his '85 Chevy, the owner stood to save more than $6,000.

Maintain your old car faithfully, using a knowledgeable mechanic. See that brakes, tires and steering stay in top condition. Keep the body clean and well waxed. In high-pollution areas, keep your auto garaged as much as possible. Consider renting a car for longer trips, if you are worried about pushing your old auto to its limits. Review your repair records regularly. In 1990, Americans averaged 38 cents a mile to own and operate the family car. If your costs suddenly shoot up, it's probably time to trade in.

In that case, now could be a good time to take advantage of benevolent market pricing and technological improvements, especially in American cars. Credit, too, may be easier to get — particularly if you qualify for a General Motors credit card, which offers no annual fee, interest rates 10.4 points above the prime rate and up to a $500 rebate toward the purchase of a new GM car.

How to Find a Mechanic

To ENJOY years of trouble-free driving, finding the right auto technician can be almost as important as finding the right car. The best way to discover a competent mechanic is through a growing network of reputable repair shops that are identified and appraised by the American Automobile Association. This is done through AAA's Approved Auto Repair program.

The program is the first nationwide effort to identify and evaluate reliable repair shops. It covers every kind, from franchised dealers to independent neighborhood garages. The program includes 4,000 garages in 30 states and the District of Columbia. AAA inspectors apply rigorous standards. In fact, more garages fail than pass their first AAA inspection. The repair bays, tools and mechanics' qualifications are checked. Then the AAA queries customers whose names an inspector picks from the shop's files.

You do not have to join the automobile association to take

advantage of the program. Simply look for a garage with AAA's red, white and blue sign and the inscription "Approved Auto Repair." Or phone the local affiliated auto club for names of approved shops in the area.

One of AAA's measures of a worthy shop is whether or not its technicians are certified by the National Institute for Automotive Service Excellence, or ASE. The institute supports itself entirely from examination and registration fees. To earn a certificate of competence, a mechanic or technician must have passed at least one of ASE's eight automobile specialty tests and have two years of hands-on experience.

Shops lacking AAA approval may still do first-rate work. Those that display the blue and white ASE sign have at least one mechanic certified in one of the institute's specialties. Or go one step further and have the mechanic show you if he or she has an ASE certificate that says he or she is qualified to repair the system that you need to have fixed.

New-car owners are inclined to have repairs done by the dealer because that's where their warranty is honored. The dealer usually has good facilities and makes a special effort to please a customer who has bought one car and may buy another. But dealers tend to be expensive. And a recent study by the New York attorney general's office takes a dim view of the service contracts that dealers offer to car buyers. The office concluded that dealers overcharged half of the New York customers who bought service contracts in 1989.

For specific services, such as buying and installing a muffler, you may get the best price at a discount store, mass marketers such as Sears or Montgomery Ward or a specialty shop such as Midas. You may save on a set of shocks by going to a specialist.

But don't let bargain prices take you away from an able general mechanic — if you have been lucky enough to find one. When you take a sick car to him, describe the symptoms in detail or even write them down. Request an estimate and ask him to call if something unexpected or expensive turns up. But don't offer your own diagnosis. That is *his* job.

Your Best Deals on Wheels

T HE price that a dealer quotes to you for a new car represents only the first offer in a round of haggling. To negotiate with confidence, you need to know the dealer's cost or invoice price. It may be $500 to as much as $4,500 *less* than the car's sticker price.

Information on new-car prices is widely available in automobile and consumer-affairs publications. A specialized source is *Consumer Reports' Auto Price Service*, which supplies a computer printout for each model you request, comparing invoice and sticker prices and listing the cost of all factory-installed options. One printout on a single make/model/style costs $11; two printouts cost $20. Call Auto Price Service at 313-347-5810 or write to Box 8005, Novi, Michigan 48376.

When you've done your research, total up the dealer's cost for your car, including all optional features. Then make your first offer, at $125 to $200 more than the invoice price. The dealer will bid that up, of course. But try to hold out for a price $200 to $500 over invoice for an American-made car — and at least $500 over invoice for a foreign one. Be sure you know what the rebate is and look out for extras that add to the invoice price.

For $20 plus $2 postage, a national car pricing and referral service called Car/Puter will send you a computer printout listing dealer cost and suggested retail price on all standard equipment and factory options. Then, if you wish, a personal counselor will be appointed to guide you, at no additional cost, through the car-buying process. The dealers listed by Car/Puter typically charge $50 to $150 over invoice for domestic cars and as low as $300 over invoice for imports. To use Car/Puter, call 800-221-4001. For instant auto prices, try Car/Puter's 900 number, available 24 hours a day at a cost of $2 per minute. During business hours a live operator can usually answer your questions and refer you to a dealer in two to five minutes. Call 900-903-CARS.

A relatively stress-free way to get a used car is to buy one from a major car rental company. Avis, Hertz and National operate used-car lots made up of 10- to 18-month veterans of their fleets. Prices are nonnegotiable but well below retail for used cars. A complete maintenance record for each former rental is available.

Good Deals on Demonstration Cars

A UTO dealers often offer attractive deals on demonstration models. These are cars that have been lent to salespeople for their personal use or for showing to potential buyers. After three to six months and usually between 3,000 and 7,000 miles, the autos are sold at discounts of 15% to 20%. Most demos are covered by what remains of manufacturer's warranties, and many dealers will extend those warranties for a small charge.

The cars also qualify for the special financing packages that are available on brand-new cars. Before you buy, compare the price of a demo with the price that the dealer may be offering on a *leftover* car from the *previous* model year that has not been driven at all. The leftover car will sell for less. But the higher resale value of the previously driven but still newer demo probably will provide you with a better deal in the long run.

The Advantages of Leasing

D ETROIT and the nation's auto-financing companies are luring more of us to a leasing way of life. While the price of a new car has risen about 10% a year on average for the last decade, Ford, Chrysler and General Motors have devised programs that cut the cost of leasing. Now that the interest you pay on car loans is no longer deductible from your taxable income, leasing your new car can make good sense.

Paying cash is still the cheapest way to buy a car. Of course, most people can't afford to do that at today's new-car prices. For them, financing still beats leasing if they can get the low interest rates so often used by both U.S. and foreign manufacturers to perk up sales.

But if you lack the money for a down payment or don't want to tie up your cash or plan to keep the car for only four years or less, leasing may be for you. The four-year rule applies because new cars depreciate so fast that if you buy one and sell it any sooner than that, it could fetch far less than the unpaid balance of your loan.

Under General Motors' SmartLease program, you can drive away a new $13,817 Pontiac Grand Am for a mere $275 security deposit and $255 a month (excluding sales and use tax) for three years. That's less than the $324-a-month payment on a loan with 20% down, a $500 rebate and an 11.35% interest rate. In this case, however, the advantage fades when, after three years, you would own the financed car but would have to spend another $6,431 to buy the leased one.

If you decide to lease, shop the new-car dealers first and then check rates at local banks and independent auto-leasing firms. Judge each offer by comparing information that car lessors are required to disclose. In addition to basic data such as the mileage limit and the cost of auto insurance, check out a few other crucial items:

What is the car's capitalized cost? The leasing company calculates all monthly payments from this figure. You may be able to bargain down the amount that the company has set as the capitalized cost.

Does the lease contract provide for "gap" protection? If you have an accident, gap protection pays off your contract if your insurance carrier doesn't provide a large enough settlement to cover the amount you owe on your lease.

How much do you pay up front? A deposit equal to one or two monthly payments is unavoidable and eventually refundable. But watch out for something called a "capitalized cost reduction" payment. It can amount to 10% to 20% of the car's value, due in advance.

What will it cost to get out of the lease early? To keep monthly payments down, some firms rope you into a longer lease than you need and then charge a hefty fee if you attempt to escape.

How much are the "disposition" fees? These cover the company's cost of selling the car once you are through with it. Any more than $250 is too much. Some companies (GMAC is one) do not charge a fee.

What constitutes "excessive wear and tear"? Leasing companies must state the kinds of damage charges they may impose on you after the lease ends. Make sure the description is specific.

Finally, if you might want to buy the car when the lease runs out, look closely at the terms of a "closed-end" lease. Don't settle for a vague price based on fair market value. Insist on a contract stating an exact, fixed purchase option price. Then, depending on used-car prices at the end of the contract, you can either buy at a bargain figure or walk away from the deal.

Devices That Deter Theft

PROFESSIONAL car thieves are so swift and experienced that police, insurance underwriters and even manufacturers of antitheft devices feel that it's hard to thwart them. But although alarms and other preventions are not foolproof, the right ones can save you anguish and expense. Even if nobody ever tries to steal your car, you will get a 5% to 15% discount on your auto insurance.

If you own an expensive automobile and particularly if you live in a big city, your best protection against theft is never to leave your car on the street. Professional thieves are a match for almost any antitheft equipment. However, you should seriously consider buying alarms and locks to discourage joyriders and casual miscreants.

Antitheft devices now are so varied and sophisticated that you can outfit your car to do just about everything but roll over and play dead when it is attacked. Fortunately, you can buy these gadgets at stores that sell automotive accessories.

You are probably smart to start with an alarm because it will scare away the nonprofessional thief. Typical alarm systems, such as those manufactured by Harrison Electronic Systems Corporation in Wilkes-Barre, Pennsylvania (800-422-5050), cost anywhere from $125 to $350 installed. The most expensive type sets off a siren at a variety of intrusions — for example, if someone bangs a window or jolts the car. Two other antitheft systems are the Crimestopper Stiletto ($350) and the Vehicle Security Electronics Quantum Pro ($450 plus installation). If you figure an alarm may not be enough to scare the professionals off, you probably should invest in a device that stalls the engine before a thief can drive far, like the Safestop Starter Interrupt, available for about $80, including installation, from Harrison Electronic Systems.

Less elaborate automobile protection devices also lock cars more tightly than usual. One of the best is a Medeco Super Lock, a heavy-duty ignition cylinder, made by C.E. Security Corp. of Long Island City, New York. It disengages the starter, locks the hood and sets off the alarm for $250 installed. Although professional thieves can bypass the ignition switch in most late-model cars, the Super Lock makes it almost impossible to start the car. However, a thief will not be put off by a cane lock, one end of which clamps to the steering wheel and the other to the brake pedal.

If what a thief wants is your wheels and tires, you can complicate his task by installing locking lugs. A set of four plus the special wrench needed to unlock them costs only $12 to $45, depending on where you live. Or, for about $600, you can have a vehicle-tracking system such as LoJack installed. Police cars equipped with special receivers can track down your car and the thief. Many police departments use this product to keep tabs on their own fleet.

For further information on security systems as well as the plethora of electronic devices available for your car, the FCC publishes a booklet called *All About Auto Electronic Products*. It's available for 50 cents from the Consumer Information Center, Department 405Y, P.O. Box 100, Pueblo, Colorado 81009.

Choosing Among the Clubs

WORRIED about being stranded in a disabled car on a snowy night, millions of motorists have sought reassurance by joining an auto club. If you or other drivers in your family have any doubts about coping with breakdowns on your own, the question is probably not whether you should join a club but which one to join.

All auto clubs claim to offer the same basic services, and their annual fees range from about $21 to about $68. But these charges are no indication of the quality of what they provide. In fact, two basic services — trip planning and accident insurance — should not be important considerations when you choose a club. Your choice should be dictated by the quality of an auto club's road service.

Three national clubs offer so-called dispatch service. That means members have only to call the club's number and wait for help to arrive. The three are the American Automobile Association, Amoco

Motor Club and Allstate Motor Club. If your club does not offer dispatch service, you will have to find help on your own.

Some other clubs provide a directory of affiliated service stations or a toll-free number for you to call to get the name of an approved station near where you've broken down. In most of these cases, the club pays for the emergency service, but that is usually limited to towing and minor roadside repairs, such as tire changing and battery recharging. Still other national clubs merely reimburse you for service you arrange on your own, which can be no boon to the panic-prone.

Whether the club pays directly or reimburses you later, the payments are often unrealistically low. For example, there is always either a dollar limit or a mileage limit for towing. The limit for road services generally ranges from $50 to $100, and if you exceed it, you pay the extra cost.

Be sure to read the fine print of any auto club's membership contract. Some demand an initiation fee and charge extra for a spouse, and others do not. Some clubs cover emergency service on any car you're driving; others limit coverage to cars you own or lease long-term. One tip: If you rarely travel far from home, you may find that regional auto clubs offer road service equal to or better than that provided by many of the nationals.

Neo-Classic Cars

A LMOST nothing brings out the boy in a man so quickly as acquiring the car he yearned for in his youth. Now grown men — and women — are buying the automobiles of the 1950s and 1960s that they couldn't afford in adolescence. As a result, some neo-classic cars of relatively recent vintage are becoming valuable collector's items. People who own these autos can sell them for fancy prices at auctions and through ads in car-buff magazines.

For example, the 1963 Corvette Sting Ray was a design milestone with its split rear window. It cost $4,257 when it was new but now is worth $40,000, or at least three times that if it is the ZO-6 model — a so-called big-block car, with a heavy suspension and fuel injection. Ford introduced the Mustang in 1964 for $2,368; today a convertible could fetch well over $20,000. Less sporty cars are worth large sums, too. A 1957 Chevrolet Bel Air fuel-injected convertible in excellent condition that cost $2,476 when it rolled off the assembly line commands $80,000 now. Other valuable cars include the 1969 Camaro, the 1955 Chrysler 300 and the 1964 Pontiac GTO. A Ford Thunderbird that went for about $4,000 in 1957 could have fetched $47,000 in mid-1992.

Not all cars of the 1950s and 1960s are valuable, of course. The ones that are represent a dramatic innovation in engineering or style. The closer a model is to its original condition, the higher the price it fetches. Ideally, a car should have all the same parts it had when it came out of the showroom, or it should be an exact reproduction with genuine, not after-market, parts.

Some of these machines sport protruding tail fins. Chrome drips off hoods and doors and dashboards light up like jukeboxes. To many people such excess was not Detroit's finest hour. But to others it is one more reason to own the cars they once drove only in their dreams.

Your Insurance

How Much Life Insurance Do You Need?

INSURANCE agents offer formulas for how much insurance you need, but the formulas may be flawed. The problem is that they cram many different kinds of people, with different requirements, into the same pigeonhole. How much coverage you really need hinges on what you want it to do for you. Do not make the mistake of expecting it to do too much. In fact, insurance should be designed to maintain, not to raise, the standard of living a family has achieved.

To figure out how much life insurance you need, estimate your family's living expenses. Then determine where that money will come from, if you should die. Include your Social Security benefits, savings, assets that can be sold and your spouse's income. The gap that's left between what costs you expect and what income you can count on is what you need to cover with life insurance. So, if you are a middle-income person with dependents, you are likely to need life insurance coverage in six figures. Instead of relying on any formula, ask a number of insurance agents to help you estimate how much life insurance you require. Then make sure an agent recommends the appropriate type of policy. Low-cost term insurance is usually the right policy for parents of young children.

Another approach is to go to a disinterested expert such as a fee-only practicing financial planner who does not sell insurance. Ask to have your insurance planned. Almost every planner has a computer program that can take in all important variables and generate a sensible answer.

You should use insurance *only* to protect dependents. Even if you are someone's provider, you may well need coverage for just a limited period, for example, until your children finish school. Or you may need it much longer — perhaps for the rest of your spouse's expected life. People without children often make the mistake of listening to agents who recommend buying policies while both the premiums and the risks of being medically uninsurable are low. Neither argument is convincing. If you cannot think of a beneficiary, you do not need life insurance.

When you are in the market for insurance, you can choose between two kinds of agents. The first is the captive agent; he or she is under contract to sell for just one company. The second is the independent agent; he or she can choose from among several companies to find a policy to suit each customer.

You might assume that an independent will get you the best possible deal. Don't count on it. Most independents, especially those who sell life insurance, represent only a handful of companies. And most companies pay higher commissions to agents who sell the most profitable policies. So you may be steered to a particular company even if it offers a less comprehensive or more expensive policy.

For that reason, when you want to buy insurance, let a planner guide you to the right *type* of policy and to an experienced agent for a top-rated company.

How Life Insurance Agents' Predictions Can Let You Down

THE return of interest rates to what once passed for normal is causing grief for many people who bought whole life or universal life policies in the past dozen years. For everyone who considers buying a whole life or universal life policy in the future, there's a lesson to be learned, or at least reiterated: numbers don't lie.

During the 1980s, when everybody came to expect high interest rates on investments, insurance companies stepped up the marketing of "interest-sensitive" policies. They ground out glowing illustrations showing that there would be no need to pay premiums after a few years even as their policies' cash surrender value and death benefits rose majestically. Those illustrations, known in the trade as ledger statements, have a capacity to mislead you badly if they are based on overly optimistic assumptions about various insurance costs and, most of all, the rate of return on the insurer's investments of policyholders' money.

In so-called vanishing-premium policies, you theoretically can pay large premiums for a few years and, by plowing all dividends back into additional insurance, generate enough internal tax-deferred earnings to pay for the policy for the rest of your life. But the dividends used to show how the premium can vanish are not guaranteed. Far from it. They are refunds paid out of surplus, which depends mainly on the company's return on investments.

In the heat of recent competition, sales-minded companies puffed up their policy illustrations. They did so by assuming that the high interest rates the companies were then earning on real estate loans and junk bonds would be available practically forever. Then came the recession. Commercial real estate values tumbled. Developers went into default on their mortgages. And the low-rated bonds of financially shaky companies sank in value as more and more borrowers failed to make their interest payments. Even insurers that had invested cautiously in government and high-quality corporate bonds had to reduce their dividends.

Responsible insurers may keep their sales illustrations within reasonable bounds. But that does not stop their agents from grinding out prettier numbers. Don Barnes, a veteran insurance journalist and columnist for the *National Underwriter,* wrote in 1992: "Now that agents have access to computer software, they can compose their own illustrations, which — quite naturally — tend to be totally optimistic and located on the sunny side of the street. . . . As interest rates sink, those remarkable projections made in the jolly days of the mid '80s look quite sour."

So cast a skeptic's eye on agents' numerology. Request, in writing, the internal rate of investment return on which the figures are based. Also, ask the agent to get you his company's data sheets from Moody's Industry Outlook–Life Insurance. If the agent refuses or equivocates, send him away. If he produces these documents, look at two telltale numbers:

Total investment return: Companies with the strongest growth of investment income will be best able to credit high interest to their policyholders.

Quality of investments: The percentage of holdings that are below investment grade indicates how much risk the company is taking in an effort to earn higher interest. Stay with insurers that get high grades for claims-paying ability from two or more independent rating services. Ratings are not ironclad. From November 1991 to February 21, 1992, two dozen companies were downgraded, including such stalwarts as Mutual of New York and Prudential. But the ratings are all you have to go on. The three best grades are A+ +, A+ and A from A.M. Best; AAA, AA+, and AA from Duff & Phelps and Standard and Poor's; and Aaa, Aa1 and Aa2 from Moody's.

What You Can Expect from Social Security

A VAST system of social insurance at any given time helps see one in six Americans through the hardships of death or illness or the expanding years of old age. You don't have to be poor or pass a means test to receive Social Security benefits. You just have to have worked in a covered occupation long enough — as briefly as 18 months in rare cases. Almost all occupations are covered.

When an American breadwinner dies, his or her dependent children up to college age are usually entitled to monthly income benefits. Similarly, benefits usually flow to a surviving spouse until the youngest child is 16. Widows and widowers can again get benefits at 60, this time for life. Parents under 29 earn the right to survivors' benefits for their families after paying Social Security taxes for a mere 18 months, provided they have been married for at least that period of time. Older people need more so-called work credits — up to ten years' worth for those born before 1930.

As generous as they may seem at first, survivors' benefits do not eliminate the need for life insurance in households with mid-size or higher incomes. For a 35-year-old parent with an annual income of $55,000 who died in 1992, survivors' benefits ranged up to $2,190 a month, the equivalent of $36,280 a year before taxes. (At most, only half of Social Security benefits are subject to income tax.) The survivors' benefits for the average family were much lower, $1,252 a month for a widow and two children. But like all other Social Security payments, survivors' benefits rise each January to match the increase in the cost of living during the 12 months through the previous September.

Children are eligible for survivors' income until their 18th birthday, with an extension to age 19 if they're still attending high school full-time. A child who becomes disabled before age 22 continues getting income for as long as the disability persists. So does a parent who takes care of the child.

A working parent, however, or a child who holds a job may lose some or all of his or her benefits by earning more than a limited wage. Here's how it works:

For every $2 earned above $7,440 in 1992 by a person under 65, Social Security took back $1 in benefits. So if your 1992 benefit was $12,000, earning $31,440 would have wiped out every penny of it. Starting at age 65, the penalty eases; in 1992 the earnings threshold was $10,200. Each $3 of higher earnings costs $1 of Social Security if you're between 65 and 70. There's no penalty after that. Then again, few folks that age still have school-age kids.

Social Security also pays income to disabled wage earners and their families. To qualify for this benefit, you must be a lot worse off than you would have to be to collect on a disability insurance policy. That is, you must be so severely disabled physically or mentally that you won't be able to do any kind of work for at least a year. Or else your doctor must attest that your illness is expected to end in death. If you lose your sight, though, you can work for limited pay and still collect disability income.

After 24 months of disability, beneficiaries become eligible for Medicare, Social Security's hospital and medical insurance plan designed primarily for retirees.

Disability coverage usually starts in the sixth month of disability and ends at age 65 if you live that long. Quite often, applications are rejected at first. They can be appealed, however, with some hope of reconsideration.

If you are under 24, you earn Social Security disability coverage after working for 18 of the previous 36 months. The work time expands with age, reaching five years (20 calendar quarters) for people age 31 through 42. But the longest anyone has to work to qualify is ten years.

Income extends to your spouse and one child, or to two children, under the same conditions as survivors' payments. The maximum benefit for a single disabled 25-year-old in 1992 was $1,266 a month; the benefit increased to $1,899 if the recipient had a spouse and children. The national average family benefit for 1992 was $1,056.

How to Cut Your Costs

SINCE 1987, consumers have been paying more for life insurance than they had for several years. Fortunately, though, there are ways to hold down your costs.

It is wise to remember that the premium alone is not totally reliable for comparing prices. There is a better way of stating your life insurance costs. It is called the interest-adjusted index, and all agents can quote it to you. This index takes into account three other variables that affect your real insurance prices. Those three are the dividends on the policy, its cash value and the interest you could have earned if you invested your money elsewhere. Ask your agent for the interest-adjusted cost index of your policy and then compare it with those of policies offered by competing companies. But compare only similar policies — term with term, whole life with whole life.

It pays to scout around for an insurance firm that provides special discounts. There are discounts for nonsmokers and for people who engage in regular exercise. (For more, see "Your Insurance: Discounts for Healthy Habits.")

Little-known discounts on other insurance can cut your bills. People who equip their homes with dead-bolt locks, smoke detectors and fire extinguishers pay about 5% to 10% less for homeowners insurance than their less vigilant neighbors. Allstate reasons that retirees 55 and older are often at home and gives them a 10% discount on homeowners insurance. And car owners who install antitheft devices can pay 5% to 10% less for auto coverage. (For more, see "Your Insurance: Auto Policies.")

Discounts for Healthy Habits

BEING conscientious about your health and fitness can trim not only your figure but also your insurance bill. For example, nonsmokers get 5% to 25% price breaks on their life, health and disability insurance.

To qualify for the lower rates, you may have to pass a medical exam certifying that your weight, blood pressure and cholesterol levels are normal. You also will have to declare on a questionnaire that you exercise regularly. Allstate Insurance's 10-year term life policies, for instance, are 15% to 30% cheaper for physically fit nonsmokers who say they exercise three to five times a week, use seat belts while driving and avoid excessive salt. But you must not have a high-risk occupation or hobby, such as automobile racing.

Prudential also offers premium discounts. One example: A 50-year-old man who smokes pays $2,376 a year for $100,000 worth of universal life insurance. But he will pay only $1,786 for the same premium if he does not smoke, does exercise regularly and is certified by a doctor as being physically fit. Manhattan Life ranks individuals on a healthiness scale. For $100,000 of universal life coverage, a 40-year-old male smoker pays $876 a year, versus $780 for a nonsmoker.

If you suffer from hypertension, you can cut your premiums by as much as half by taking steps to correct your condition. Compared with those who have normal blood pressure, hypertensive people pay an average of 50% more for term insurance and up to 25% more for health policies. Both costs can drop if the policyholder's blood pressure comes down. A 30-year-old man with moderately high blood pressure will pay $290 annually for a $100,000 renewable term life policy with Allstate. If he reduces his blood pressure to normal for a year or two while maintaining a healthy life-style, his premiums will sink to about $154. Insurers are willing to offer lower rates because people who reduce their high blood pressure with medication and diet have a near-normal mortality rate.

Such incentives are beginning to show up in health insurance policies, too. Blue Cross/Blue Shield offers plans in at least 10 states that give discounts for nonsmokers. And employers are beginning to reward their employees who have healthy habits by giving rebates, or paying for a greater percentage of their health bills.

Three Kinds of Life Policies

INSURANCE companies have a talent for thinking up new "products" to sell, but their most popular policies continue to be whole life, term and the relatively new universal life. Which of those three is best for you?

In pondering that question, bear in mind that you need life insurance early in your career, when your children are young and your assets are low. But if you plan properly as you grow older, your insurance needs should decline or even disappear.

The insurance that protects your family when you need it most for the lowest possible price is *term insurance*. Premiums are modest when you are young but advance along with your age. Rates go up every year in the simplest plan. That's annual, renewable and convertible term. If you want, you can convert it automatically into whole life insurance. In fact, fewer than 2% of all death claims are from term insurance.

According to Rick Lindgren of Coad Brokerage in Manhattan, a special need for term insurance may arise if you are engaged in a short-term business venture such as real estate holdings. Then, a term policy covering the life of the partnership might be advisable.

Whole life insurance premiums, by contrast, never rise. But whole life buyers start out paying several times as much as they would for term. At Equitable, $166 a year buys $100,000 worth of annual renewable term at age 40 for a man who does not smoke, and $152 buys that amount for a woman who does not smoke. By contrast, $100,000 of whole life costs $1,573 a year for nonsmoking males and $1,333 for nonsmoking females at age 40.

The excess premium goes into a whole life cash reserve. When you retire, you can surrender your policy and retrieve the cash in your reserve. If you have kept the policy 25 or 30 years and used dividends to increase the face value, its cash value will be about two-thirds the face value of the policy.

Whole life, thus, is a form of savings account. The tax-deferred earnings grow, but the policyholder usually collects just a modest interest rate on his savings. And whole life has other disadvantages. There are heavy sales charges, typically 50% of the first year's premium plus a small percentage annually for the next nine years.

You can withdraw some of your paid-in cash and still remain insured. You can also borrow against it, typically at 8% to 10% interest — or less if you bought the policy before 1980. You cannot easily vary the premium or freely increase the insurance protection to suit your changing situation, however.

But you can do all that and more with *universal life insurance.* This policy combines term insurance with a tax-deferred savings account that pays a variable interest rate. So if you want to protect your family and build up tax-deferred savings, one way to do it is to buy a universal life policy. Flexibility is the hallmark of universal life. You can skip a year's premiums and remain insured. You can reduce your coverage or, if you're healthy, increase it. And you are told what you're paying for insurance and the rate of interest on your savings in the policy.

One important warning: Although universal life can cost less than ordinary whole life, you have to shop for a policy with utmost care, because these policies too can carry large sale commissions, amounting to 50% or more of your first year's premium. Universal life does not always make sense for people who need less than $50,000 of insurance. It is often the case that the smaller the policy, the more burdensome the fees. And the guarantees are not as strong as they are with whole life. If you want a fully guaranteed policy, stick with whole life.

Variable Life Policies

VARIABLE life insurance is a relatively new type of policy that hitches an old-fashioned whole life policy to the unpredictable investment markets.

In many ways, variable life is like standard whole life. You pay fixed annual premiums. You can cash in your insurance anytime for its cash value. You can borrow against your policy at an interest rate stated in the contract. But unlike whole life, the cash value of your policy — and its death benefit — can sink as well as soar.

Why the difference? When you buy a whole life policy, part of your premium goes into investments chosen by the insurance company to yield at least a minimum *guaranteed* rate each year, usually 4% to 4½%. Not so with variable life. Here, part of your premium goes into managed investment pools that *you* select. Depending on the company, you can put your money into a stock fund, a bond fund or a money-market fund. Or you can put some in each. With some restrictions, you can switch among funds in search of the highest total returns.

If the investments behind your policy do well, the cash value of the policy rises — potentially much faster than that of a standard whole life policy. And the death benefit rises too, which it won't do in whole life unless you use the dividends to buy more insurance. Your gains, if any, are tax-deferred. If your investments lose value, so does your policy — although the benefit payable to your survivors will never fall below the amount of insurance you initially bought.

There is also a kind of life insurance called variable universal life, and it combines some of the advantages of universal life and variable life. Ordinary universal life offers you so-called flexible-premium features, which allow you to vary from year to year the amount of your premium going into insurance coverage and the amount going into investments. Variable life allows you to switch the money in your investment account among various investment funds.

Variable universal life insurance offers you *both* the flexible-premium features of ordinary universal life and the fund-switching privileges of variable life. It thus gives you maximum control over where your insurance money goes. About 30 companies sell variable universal life, including Chubb, Equitable and John Hancock.

As with all life insurance that combines insurance with investment, any earnings are tax-deferred until you cash in the policy. If your beneficiary receives the earnings, they are exempt from federal income taxes.

Is variable life sensible for you? The answer might be yes if you plan on keeping the policy for 10 years or more. Otherwise, high fees and commissions — especially at the front end — will eat into early cash buildup.

Avoiding Mistakes with Your Health Policy

How much should you be paying for health insurance, and what kind should you buy?

Unless you can join a group plan through your company or professional association, you will have to buy an individual policy. Each policy is custom-made according to age, health status, region and the deductible, so the costs may vary greatly. At Blue Cross/Blue Shield, for instance, a 35-year-old single man might pay anywhere from $950 to $4,100 a year, while a family of four might pay from $2,500 to $8,300. Policies that cost much less may provide poor coverage. Avoid insurance promising to pay a set amount each day in the hospital instead of a portion of total expenses. A policy that pays for a single disease is also a mistake; it won't cover you for most forms of costly illness.

The indispensable coverage for most people is a comprehensive major medical policy covering hospitalization, outpatient services and doctor bills. Such policies are available from Blue Cross/Blue Shield and insurance companies. The policies make you pay a maximum of 20% of most expenses in addition to a certain deductible, but no more than $1,000 in any one year. And the best plans place *no* ceiling on benefits. (For more, see "Your Health: Checking Up on Your Health Insurance.")

Long-Term-Care Insurance

A LONG stay in a nursing home can wipe out a lifetime of savings. Medicare pays for 100 days in a skilled nursing facility, but only after a stay in a hospital, and it pays nothing for long-term custodial care. Even care in your own home can reduce you to a pauper's level, though not quite as rapidly. Studies indicate that more than 40% of all Americans who turn 65 in 1992 will eventually enter a nursing home, and many others will require paid help to continue living at home. The numbers are bound to increase as the baby boomers grow older. More than one-fifth of all Americans will be over 65 in 2030.

Fortunately, the need for long-term-care coverage has become a major public issue. Congress and some state governments are considering legislation, and more than 100 companies and 26 Blue Cross plans are offering a number of types of long-term-care insurance. Some of these policies pay as much as $200 a day toward the cost of skilled nursing care provided by a nurse or other medical professional. They also cover custodial care — that is, if you do not need medical attention but you do require some help in dressing, eating and walking. The best policies include home care and day care as well. About 150 employers were offering long-term-care insurance in 1990, covering about 130,000 people, according to the Health Insurance Association of America.

When you buy it yourself, you will find that the cost of this insurance varies tremendously, from $100 all the way up to $15,000 a year. The price depends on your age when you buy the policy and the benefits you elect. Although long-term-care is generally not needed for people in their fifties and sixties, the price is far lower during those years than it is if you wait until you are seventy or over. For example, the average cost for a policy paying $80 a day for nursing-home care and $40 a day for home health care with a maximum coverage period of four years is about $480 a year at age 50. At age 65, the cost of such a policy is about $1,135, and at 79, it goes up to about $3,840. And with inflation protection, which ensures that you won't lose benefits as long-term-care costs skyrocket, prices rise to $660 at age 50, $1,395 at age 65 and $4,200 at age 79, as of July 1, 1992.

If you are interested in securing long-term protection, ask your insurance agent these key questions before you buy:

— Does the policy cover the whole spectrum of nursing care? Skilled care generally includes such services as giving injections that can be performed only by (or under the direct supervision of) nurses, physical therapists or other medically trained experts. Intermediate care must also be under the supervision of skilled medical personnel, but registered nurses are not required to be on 24-hour duty. Highly trained or licensed people are not required at all for custodial care. Most long-term nursing-home patients need custodial care, as do patients in their own homes. Day care is for people who live at home but need supervision, or company, while they are up and around. Look for a policy that provides all of these kinds of care, that will cover you even if you need *only* intermediate or custodial care and that allows you to enter a nursing home without a prior hospital stay.

— How generous is the daily benefit? It can range all the way from $25 (for at-home care) to $200 (for nursing-home care). The nationwide average for care in a nursing home is $30,000 to $40,000 a year. Home care including physical therapy, help with medication and preparation of food costs at least half that much.

— How long does a person have to be in a home before benefits begin? Some policies cover you from the moment you enter a nursing home. Others require that you be confined for a certain number of days, usually 20 to 100, before payments begin. You might want to remember that the longer the waiting period, the lower your insurance premiums will be. Avoid any policy that makes prior hospitalization or a stay in a skilled nusing home a prerequisite for coverage.

— How long do benefits last? Plans typically cover you for two to six years.

— Does the policy include protection against inflation?

— Are any illnesses, injuries or pre-existing conditions excluded from coverage? Don't buy a policy that excludes nursing-home stays due to mental or nervous disorders such as Parkinson's or Alzheimer's disease. And be sure the policy is guaranteed renewable.

Selecting the Best Disability Policy

THE biggest gap in many people's insurance protection is the absence of a disability policy.

Even if you are young and healthy, the odds are uncomfortably short that someday you may need such insurance. Almost half of all people now aged 35 will be incapacitated for three months or longer before they're 65. So, for protection in case you are laid up, it makes sense to buy a disability insurance policy. It can cost from a few hundred dollars to $1,500 or more a year.

In tailoring your policy, aim to replace 60% to 70% of your current earnings before taxes. That should be enough to maintain most of your spending power, because disability benefits are tax-free if you have paid for your own insurance. Don't rely on Social Security to replace your lost wages in case of serious illness or accident. As explained in "What You Can Expect from Social Security," you must be severely disabled for at least a year or be suffering from a fatal illness to get disability benefits from that source. Even then you will have to wait at least five months from the onset of the disability for payments to begin. The average benefit in 1991 was $1,022 a month for a family.

You are probably best off with coverage to the age of 65, but you can save hundreds of dollars a year in premiums by settling for five years of income instead.

An even better way to reduce premiums is to increase the number of weeks you must be disabled before the policy starts paying — the so-called waiting period. Take a man aged 35 who wants $1,000 a month in benefits. If they begin one month after he is disabled, his policy at Northwestern Mutual would cost him about $724 a year. But if he increases that waiting period to three months, the price falls to $388.

Disability-income policies offer more riders than a John Wayne Western. A few are worth a look.

To protect yourself against inflation, you can choose a rider that will increase monthly benefits automatically to a specified annual maximum. If you go all out, such a rider can push up your premium by 25% or more. Limit your cost-of-living boosts to a yearly 4% of your initial benefit — a simple rather than a compound increase.

One of the latest riders, available from the Guardian and a few other companies, actually lets you order up a large addition to your benefits during periods of extended disability. Called a Future Increase Rider, it can catch your income up to the raises you got before you were sidelined, as well as to inflation. But you may have to wait many months for the boost to take effect. Activation occurs after the next anniversary date of your policy, plus a waiting period equal to the one for regular benefits. The Guardian's Future Increase Rider adds 10% to your original premium.

Still another rider to consider insures your eligibility for long-term-care insurance. For the price of its basic policy bought before age 45, CNA, a leading writer of long-term-care insurance, lets you convert your disability coverage into a high-quality long-term-care policy anytime from age 55 to 72. Another approach, offered by UNUM, guarantees your right to add long-term-care insurance to your disability policy, often at a discount from the ordinary premium for people your age. This opportunity is restricted to four 90-day periods when you're 56, 59, 62 and 65.

Two things you don't want an insurer to do are to raise your premiums or cancel your coverage. Any disability contract worth considering should be at least guaranteed renewable. The *best* type of policy is called *noncancelable*. It both guarantees renewal and freezes the premium at its original level for as long as you keep the insurance. Above all, buy a policy that covers all types of disabilities and that also protects you if you are only partially disabled. Some weasel-worded contracts give the company an out by saying you are considered to be disabled only if confined to home.

The most important decision is to choose the right insurance company. If you become disabled you will be destined to have a relationship that may last for years. A few companies write most of the high-quality individual disability policies. The leaders include: Connecticut Mutual, Equitable, Massachusetts Mutual, Minnesota Mutual, Mutual of New York, New York Life, Northwestern Mutual, Paul Revere, Provident Life and Accident and UNUM.

Help for the Hard-to-Insure

PEOPLE with serious health problems or dangerous jobs are considered bad insurance risks, but if you are one of them, do not despair. Insurance companies are willing to take chances and sell you life, disability and health policies. The trouble is, they are so-called substandard policies. They cost you more, or give you less coverage than a regular policy. About 3% of all life insurance applicants may pay up to twice as much for protection as people who do not pose extra risks.

The easiest and least expensive way to get insurance, of course, is to work for a company that offers group coverage. If you are not protected by a group, ask an insurance agent to refer you to a broker who specializes in high risks. Brokers usually deal only through agents, and each is familiar with a number of insurers. Have your agent put *several* brokers to work for you — and see who comes up with the broadest coverage for the lowest cost. Fortunately, there is always room for negotiation.

Even for a hard-to-insure person, term life insurance — straight protection without any cash value — is less expensive than whole life. A 30-year-old diabetic man who does not smoke, for example, can buy $100,000 of term insurance from one company for $268 a year; were he not diabetic, the same coverage would cost him $132.

Another option is to buy what is called a graded-death-benefit policy. With it, the death benefit gradually increases over a period of years until it equals the face value of the policy. The disadvantage is that if you should die shortly after the policy is issued, your survivors will receive less than the policy's face value.

A word about disability insurance: If you are a high-risk person, you may not be able to get this kind of insurance at all. Although there are common standards that insurance companies follow, one person's medical problem may be viewed differently by various companies — with different conclusions. If you do qualify for a regular disability policy, expect to pay 20% to 100% more than the usual rate. You may be able to cut the premium cost by agreeing to accept lower monthly benefits, by waiting longer for benefits to begin and by collecting them for a shorter period of time. You may also reduce your premium by taking out a policy with a so-called limited exclusion rider that disallows benefits if the disability is caused by a condition that existed before the policy's purchase. This type of plan, which covers other disabilities, costs only as much as the coverage sold to people who are not high-risk.

Auto Policies

IN 1988, a fateful year in the auto-insurance business, the average premium jumped 23%, to $600. The figures varied widely by state, from a low of $337 in Nebraska to $845 in New Jersey. Automobile insurance became a consumer's cause célèbre that year when Californians put their votes where their voices were. What they wanted but did not get was a rollback in premiums.

In fact, premiums are generally on the rise, and careful shopping is as important as ever. You need to know what to look for. The standard policy contains six basic types of coverage: bodily-injury liability, property-damage liability, uninsured motorist, medical payments, collision and comprehensive.

Don't skimp on bodily-injury liability and property-damage liability coverage. If you or anybody driving your car with your permission is in an accident in which someone is killed or injured, bodily-injury liability coverage pays you for an attorney to defend against lawsuits by victims of the accident. It also pays other court costs and any judgments against you. Property-damage liability covers property that you do not own. The average driver should carry a policy that would pay up to $100,000 for a single injury, and up to $300,000 for all injuries in any one accident. It should also cover up to $50,000 in property damage. If you have substantial assets or a high salary that could be seized in a court to pay off a judgment that exceeds your auto coverage, raise your liability limits to $300,000 or $500,000. If you need further coverage, consider an umbrella policy. A $1 million umbrella policy costs about $150 to $200 a year in many states.

In some states, you are required to buy uninsured-motorist coverage. Buy some even if you don't have to. It pays you for injuries, pain and suffering caused by a hit-and-run driver or someone who cannot pay a judgment. If you have adequate health and disability insurance where you work, you may not need medical payments coverage. It may largely duplicate protection already supplied by your regular medical policy.

Many are the ways to save on your policy. According to the Insurance Information Institute, you should take as large a deductible as you can afford on collision and comprehensive, which covers fire, theft and vandalism. The deductible is the amount you agree to pay before the insurance kicks in. For instance, increasing the deductible to $500 from the common $200 may reduce your collision premium about 15% to 30%. A $1,000 deductible can save you as much as 40%. If your car is paid for or more than five years old, or if its value is under $1,500, consider dropping collision and comprehensive coverage altogether. It never pays more for repairs than your car is worth.

You can reduce your premium further through discounts. For example, companies may give you a discount if you have a good driving record, or 5% to 15% off the comprehensive premium cost if your car has antitheft devices. Driver training could cut as much as

15% off your premium. And people aged 50 and over often can get discounts of 10% to 20%.

Once you understand your options, start canvassing companies for price quotes. To get a benchmark price, call State Farm. It's the nation's largest auto insurer and, in many areas, one of the least expensive. You also will want to learn about a company's reputation for service. To do that, check with your state's insurance department. The larger states, including Illinois, New York and California, publish annual lists of companies with the highest and lowest percentage of consumer complaints.

As you survey the insurance companies, be sure to learn which are most forgiving if you have an accident. For example, if you are at fault for an accident that results in a payment of more than $400, then the Nationwide Insurance Company usually will raise your rates 30% for a period of three years, while State Farm may disqualify you for a discount, or if you already have one, may withhold it for three to six years. However, companies will also reward you for accident-free years. Nationwide, for example, does not raise your rates under the conditions mentioned if you have been a policyholder for at least five years and have not had an accident in the past three.

There are often significant differences in collision and comprehensive premiums for various car makes and models. So be sure to check this out when you buy a new car. Allstate, for instance, offers 10% to 45% discounts in most states on comprehensive and collision coverages for cars that are least likely to be stolen — usually full-sized sedans and mini-vans — and that are harder to damage and easier to repair.

Many states have drafted insurance companies into the war against auto theft. If you live in one of those states and you have installed special alarms or other antitheft devices, you can arrange for your premiums to be reduced. There are many other steps that drivers everywhere can take to improve their insurance against auto theft. (For more, see "Your Auto: Devices That Deter Theft.")

If you rent a car while waiting for the insurance settlement, you will probably have to bear some of that expense, too. Most policies pay about $15 a day toward a rental car. Renting is likely to cost you two or three times that much per day, and you may not get a settlement within a month. Thus, it is wise to buy a little-known rider, which at State Farm costs typically $15 to $40 a year, depending on your age and location, and extends your period and amount of coverage. The rider also pays up to $400 for meals, lodging and transportation while you are waiting for your own car and covers a substantial share of your policy's deductible if you have an accident driving the rental car.

Your insurance coverage for the theft of accessories or possessions you have in the car may not be as extensive as you expect. Some insurance companies that classify removable radios as a portable accessory do not cover their theft. If you have resorted to toting your expensive stereo or radio around when you are out of the car, consider buying a disguise for it instead. For about $20, a plain plastic front gives your equipment the look of an ordinary factory-installed radio.

Neither your auto policy nor any extra coverage applies to other things that a thief might steal from your car, such as a $1,000 set of golf clubs or a $400 designer blazer. But you are probably covered anyway. Most homeowners policies apply to anything taken by someone who breaks into your car. There is a hitch, though: you have to *prove* that the doors were locked at the time of the theft.

Whatever kind of insurance you are buying, you can save money and worry by remembering this: Never risk more than you can afford to lose. But don't pay to insure what you can afford to risk.

Homeowners Policies

E VERY owner of a house or apartment needs insurance to protect his or her residence and its contents against calamity, but how much coverage is enough? The amount you should have depends on the *replacement cost* of your house. That is, what you would have to spend to rebuild your castle as it now stands.

Insurance companies offer policies that cover your home and its contents for 100% of their replacement cost. Premiums are higher, of course, than for a standard homeowners policy. You also can add a package deal to a standard policy that guarantees replacement costs for home and contents. Extra coverage for the contents, for example, tacks only an extra dollar or two per $1,000 onto your annual premiums. But not all houses are eligible for total coverage. Most insurers won't guarantee the replacement cost of damage to older homes that have handiwork that would be expensive if not impossible to replace, and the construction of some older homes might not meet current fire codes.

Fortunately, total losses are rare and you may be adequately insured for partial damage with 85% of the replacement cost. Be sure that your policy indexes the replacement cost to inflation. And if you make a substantial improvement to your house, raise your coverage to reflect its new value.

Although standard homeowners policies cover your personal possessions, they set limits on what you can claim. Usually they reimburse you only for what you paid for the item — minus depreciation — and not for what it would cost to replace it today. That's why policies that cover replacement costs of contents have become so popular. Your yearly premium may go up about 10%, but the extra protection is worth it.

If you have a home-based business, you will need to add an *incidental business option* to your policy. It provides insurance for such property as personal computers or typewriters, plus important liability protection.

You can hold down your insurance costs by taking advantage of special deals offered by most companies. There are premium discounts of up to 20% on new homes, 5% for installing dead-bolt locks and smoke detectors and 15% if you put in an elaborate fire and burglar alarm. Increase your deductible to $500 from the standard $250, and you will save on your annual premium. How much depends on which company you select, the state you live in and the amount of insurance you purchase. But never scrimp on overall coverage just to keep costs down.

No homeowners policy covers all perils. The most popular, however, is called HO-3. Any endorsed HO-3 provides top-of-the-line coverage. It will reimburse you not only for fire and windstorm, but also if, for example, your water pipes freeze and burst. Yet even this policy does not protect you against floods or earthquakes. For that you need to seek extra coverage at higher cost.

If you live in an apartment, a co-op or condominium, you also need insurance to protect you from fire, burglary and even liability. True, landlords, co-op corporations and condo associations have insurance. But their policies cover only the building itself, and mishaps that occur in common areas. So you need your own policy.

It should cover excess living expenses. For example, if your apartment is damaged by fire, the insurance company will pay for your stay in a hotel. Your policy also should cover full replacement costs for articles that are stolen or destroyed. Apartment insurance, which only 26% of renters carry, generally costs anywhere from $90 to $200, with a standard deductible of $250.

Another point to remember is that homeowners and tenants policies set low limits on the payments for jewelry, furs, silverware and collectibles. But you can buy endorsements that protect your valuables at a small additional cost — for example, from $10 to $30 a year for $1,000 of value on jewelry, or $12.50 a year for $2,500 coverage on silverware.

Your homeowners policy does include some liability coverage. That pays your legal expenses to defend yourself in case you are sued for injuries to people on or off your property and pays the damages if you lose or settle the claim. But what if you get sued for ramming into a highly paid executive on a ski slope and crippling him for life? The possibility is remote, yet if you were hit by such a lawsuit, the $100,000 or more that most homeowners policies pay on such claims might not be enough. Ask your agent about higher liability limits.

Umbrella Insurance

ACCIDENTS can happen, and when they do, the law says that people who were to blame must pay the victims' financial losses. You can protect yourself against such damage suits by buying an umbrella policy. This supplements the protection you already have against injury claims as a standard part of your homeowners and automobile insurance.

Anyone could benefit from this extra protection. A judgment against you could lay claim to your future income for many years.

Liability policies cover you for accidents you might cause or be responsible for. You usually can buy a $1 million policy for $100 to $200 a year. But since the umbrella policy takes over where auto or homeowners insurance ends, insurers will issue it only if you already have substantial primary coverage.

The best contracts cover almost every kind of liability claim except those related to business activities. For example, they should protect you if you are sued for libel, slander or invasion of privacy, malicious prosecution, wrongful eviction, defamation of character or discrimination. Some policies insure against bodily injury or property damage resulting from your use of reasonable force to protect persons or property. A good policy also pays for most of your legal defense. Your policy should extend to everyone in your household who is related to you by blood, marriage or adoption. That includes children away at school.

Checking Your Insurer's Safety

You buy life insurance in case something happens to you. But what if something happens to your insurance company?

That's no idle question. In 1991 six major insurance organizations had to be taken over by state regulators — the Executive Life Insurance companies of California and New York, First Capital Life of California, Fidelity Banker's Life of Virginia, Monarch Life and Mutual Benefit Life. All except Monarch collapsed into insolvency because they were overloaded with junk bonds worth a fraction of their face value. In Monarch's case, the parent company went bankrupt. It was the biggest failure in the history of the life insurance industry. And it was followed by the failure of First Capital Life and its affiliates, in which American Express Corporation has a large ownership position. State regulators suspended payment of cash surrender values but not death and annuity benefits while state life insurance guarantee funds and the life insurance industry tried to patch together a plan to keep the promises made to the failed companies' policyholders.

The lesson is a grim one. If you worry that your insurance company may collapse, your only readily available checkpoints are four independent services that judge the ability of insurers to pay their claims. Yet until a little more than a year before it went under, Executive Life got top ratings from A. M. Best Company and Standard & Poor's.

Every year A. M. Best assigns insurance companies one of nine grades ranging from A++ to C−, depending on their financial status, to an F for firms in liquidation. A. M. Best bases its ratings on many factors affecting the insurer's financial stability, including policy renewal rates and the performance of the firm's investments. An A + + or A + (A + + was introduced in 1992) is supposed to give strong reassurance that a life-insurance company will not fail. Of the 1,341 companies Best reported on in 1991, 291 received an unqualified A +, and 576 did not even qualify for a letter rating.

While Best sizes up far more companies than any other service, several investment advisers to corporate-benefits departments find the ratings of three other firms — Standard & Poor's, Moody's Investors Service and Duff & Phelps — more thorough. S&P's top rating of AAA went to 218 companies out of 670 on its evaluation list of January 31, 1992. Moody's awarded its highest grade, Aaa, to 13 out of 98 companies as of April 3, 1990. Duff & Phelps gave its top rating of AAA to 24 out of 111 companies as of June 15, 1992.

You can get Best ratings by writing to the insurers you are interested in considering, or their agents. Or you can look up the ratings in *Best's Insurance Reports*, available at public libraries. For a second opinion, phone S&P at 212-208-1527, Moody's at 212-553-0300 or Duff & Phelps at 312-263-2610. And for a fee that depends on the extent of the request, you can get an opinion from Weiss Research (800-289-9222), the only ratings service that downgraded Executive Life before its troubles hit the headlines.

Making a Household Inventory

CLOSE your eyes and try to list all your living-room furnishings or the contents of your jewelry box. If you have trouble coming up with a complete tally, imagine how hard it would be when you are upset, after a fire or burglary. Making a written inventory of your household goods can be one of the best money-saving steps you can take. A list not only guarantees that any insurance claim you submit after a burglary or a fire will be complete, but it also assures you of a smooth claims process. Your insurance company probably can give you an inventory form to fill out. Also, the Insurance Information Institute offers a free pamphlet, *Taking Inventory*, which provides checklists for everything from serving tables to snowblowers. To order, call 800-942-4242.

Insurers are not likely to question claims based on such inventories, especially if you submit them along with photos, receipts or appraisers' statements for valuable items. You should leave a copy of your inventory of household goods with your insurance agent or in your safe-deposit box.

What should go into your inventory? Write down the date you bought each item of value in your name, plus its price. If an appraiser has estimated the value of any of your possessions, you should record the figure and the date. Make sure the appraisal is precise and explicit. Highly generalized descriptions will not back up a claim.

Describe each object as graphically as possible. Be sure to include its age, brand name, size, model number and other relevant details. For tableware, note the manufacturer, pattern and number of place settings. If your possessions are extensive and of particularly high quality, you might consider videotaping and recording your verbal descriptions of them.

In some categories of property, though, you may wish to lump together a number of articles and attach a single estimate of value. This is a particularly wise tactic with clothing. Unless you have closets full of designer evening gowns, there is no sense driving yourself crazy counting and describing everything in your wardrobe. Even a couple of priceless Hawaiian shirts should not be too hard to describe if an insurance company asks you to.

Your Personal Security

What to Do If You Are Ripped Off

WHEN your pocket has been picked, you are left with a purseful of problems. But there are ways to help your recovery from a rip-off.

Some 3.5 million Americans a year are victims of personal larceny. If you are one of them, chances are slim that your property will ever be recovered. Still, you should quickly inform the police about the theft. You will need a police report to prove your loss to the IRS, to your insurer and perhaps to your bank.

You also should immediately notify your bank and all of your credit-card issuers. A thief can swiftly begin using your checks and credit cards, and a few hours' delay increases the chances that he will get away with it. If you know the numbers of any stolen checks, your bank can stop payment. If not, you probably will have to close your account and open a new one. You are not liable for checks written by a thief, but if the signature closely matches your own, you will have to spend time proving to the bank it was a forgery.

Once you report the loss of your credit cards, you are not liable for any subsequent charges. If the thief gets away with using your cards before you report the loss, your liability is limited to $50 a card. But that amount adds up quickly if you have several cards. Many credit-card issuers have operators available around the clock. They also may provide toll-free numbers or accept collect calls.

One precaution is to sign up with a credit-card protection service offered through banks and credit-card firms. For $6 to $15 a year, a service will immediately contact all of your credit-card issuers after you notify it of the theft. The service pays any liabilities incurred after you call. Some services will even wire you money if you are robbed while traveling.

Another piece of plastic you may carry is a debit card used to operate the automatic teller machine at your local bank. If fraud is not involved, your liability is up to $50 if you notify the bank within two business days after finding false charges on your bank statement; it jumps to $500 if you take three to 60 days. After that, liability is unlimited.

But what if your bank or credit union sends you a renewal card and it gets lost in the mail? Even if someone charges up a storm on the card, you wouldn't have to pay a penny. Federal law says that you have to "accept" the card first before you become liable for bad purchases. And if you didn't receive the card, you didn't accept it.

If you have any problems, be sure to state your case to your card issuer in writing. If that doesn't clear things up, contact the Federal Reserve Bank nearest you or, if you have a card issued by a credit union, write to the nearest office of the National Credit Union Administration.

Keeping Records to Reduce Your Loss

N O ONE even wants to think about having his or her home burglarized. But if you confront the possibility beforehand, you can reduce your financial loss.

A burglary occurs every 10 seconds, according to the FBI. To prevent a burglary from leaving you broke, make an inventory of everything you have in your home. Your insurance company probably can give you a form to fill out. Then go through each room, opening drawers and cupboards and carefully listing every object of value. Record all identifying information, such as serial numbers of appliances and account numbers of credit cards. For tableware, note the manufacturers, pattern and number of place settings. Describe jewelry as fully as possible. It's also wise to photograph the contents of your house, item by item. Do this yourself with self-developing film that does not need to be processed by strangers. For art, antiques and family heirlooms you'll also need to cite estimates of each item's age and value. The best proof is an appraiser's dated statement. (See also "Your Insurance: Making a Household Inventory.")

Get receipts and appraisals for particularly valuable items. Without these documents, you will have to rely on what the insurance adjuster says your goods are worth. An appraisal must be precise and explicit to back up a claim. Don't accept any that give only highly generalized descriptions of your valuables.

Appraisers for your goods can be located through the American Society of Appraisers, 535 Herndon Parkway, Herndon, Virginia 22070. It publishes a free directory of those members who are personal property appraisers, plus a free pamphlet, *Information on the Appraisal Profession.* For $7, you can get its *Directory of Professional Appraisal Services,* which includes appraisers in all fields. (See also "Your Services: Appraisers.")

You might even videotape your possessions. This technique lets you zoom in on details of antiques and fine artworks, highlighting makers' marks and signatures while commenting on their value. Videotaping services will do the job for you. But before you hire anyone to videotape your belongings, check his or her reputation with the Better Business Bureau and the local police.

If your home is burglarized, you will need accurate records for both the IRS and the police. These records will help you reduce your losses.

After a burglary, the criminals often melt down the precious metals in their loot and break up the jewelry to prevent its being traced. But most other stolen merchandise winds up back on the market intact. Police sweeps of pawnshops and suspected fences and crooked retailers sometimes turn up stolen property.

You are allowed to deduct only those losses that exceed 10% of your adjusted gross income. And the loss must be figured as the lower of two amounts: the price paid for the item or its current value. So, if you lose something that is worth less today than when you bought it, you can deduct only its current market value. But if an item has grown in value since you bought it, you can deduct only its original, lower cost.

Protecting Yourself
with Locks and Alarms

Y OU can help make your home safe by installing the right locks and alarms, and it need not cost you a fortune or create a fortress. To stop a thief, first call the police — not for a squad car but for a free security checkup. Police departments often will send patrolmen to inspect your property and show you where it is vulnerable.

It is important to have reliable locks on all windows, since most burglars find it easier to break in through windows than to pick a lock on a door. Of course, do not forget to have strong locks on all doors, not just the front door. Crime prevention experts recommend replacing ordinary key-cylinder locks with pick-resistant ones. Quality pick-resistant locks are made by Schlage Lock Company and Medeco Security Locks, among others. Most good locks are secured by a rigid dead-bolt that extends at least one inch into the jamb.

For most residences, ultra-sophisticated locks that replace keys with magnetic cards, voice recognition or coded pushbuttons are expensive overkill. Homeowners who want more protection than locks give can choose one of several alarm systems. It pays to check out the craftsman who puts in the system, since alarms are only as reliable as the people who install them. Be sure to get competitive bids, to ask for and check references and call your local Better Business Bureau to see if there have been any complaints about installers whom you are considering. You should shop as warily for an alarm system as for a used car.

About 2,500 installers are members of either the National Burglar and Fire Alarm Association or the Central Station Alarm Association. Both are in Bethesda, Maryland, and the NBFAA will put you in touch with the state chapter, which will in turn provide you with a list of its members in your town. To check out these candidates, request that the contractors give you the names and phone numbers of several recent customers. Then ask your state or local consumer protection agency whether complaints have been filed against the contractors' companies.

Expect to spend at least $1,500 for a contractor-installed alarm system. You often can get discounts of up to 10% on your property insurance if you put one in. The standard setup deploys two lines of defense. First, door and window trip switches detect break-ins. Second, interior sensors react to an intruder's movements, body heat or noisy forced entry.

Many such alarms also send out alerts by phone or cable-TV lines to the alarm company's local 24-hour monitoring center. Its staff responds to alarms by calling the customer to confirm an emergency or by immediately notifying the police. The charge for this service averages $20 to $30 a month. Nationwide companies that sell systems with 24-hour monitoring services include ADT, Honeywell Protection Services, Westec and Rollins Protective Services.

If you want to secure your home for much less money, you can buy basic, off-the-shelf alarms for a few hundred dollars and hook them up yourself. You get them in consumer electronics stores, though you do have to be handy around the house to properly install and fine-tune them.

One good home security device is Radio Shack's $100 indoor infrared detector. Its built-in alarm is triggered by a burglar's body heat.

A new generation of wireless alarm systems has recently come on the market. Schlage Lock Company's Keepsafer system, soon to be sold under the label of Keepsafer by Linear, is one of the least expensive and easiest to install. The basic system costs around $150 and consists of a central control console that has a built-in alarm horn and is plugged into a regular household outlet. The package also contains two transmitter sensor switches that you put on doors or windows.

Weekend or vacation houses that are often unoccupied are particularly vulnerable to break-ins as well as electrical or plumbing breakdowns. Most alarm companies have developed attachments that monitor such problems. For example, Honeywell manufactures a temperature sensor that may be applied to most basic alarm systems. It is called a farm-a-stat, and it retails for $100.

Renting a Safe-Deposit Box

R ISING crime has made more people than ever look for a safe place to put their valuables, whether they are jewelry, collectibles or important papers. Almost invariably, the most economical place to store precious possessions is a bank deposit box. The smallest cost up to $50 a year and are large enough for documents, securities and real estate deeds and appraisals. If you have anything else, you probably will want a bigger box. Those larger boxes are in short supply and anyone with a lot of jewelry, a stamp collection or anything bulky may face a long waiting list.

One solution is to find one of the many private safe-deposit companies. They have no connection with banks, but they do have security. To get in, you usually need to pass a complicated screening process.

Commercial vaults offer anonymity. But once the government receives information from another source, the vaults are subject to the same regulations as those in banks.

The private vaults have the advantage of offering flexible storage space. Lockers can be fitted with special shelves and racks for stamp collections, rare books, wine, even computer tapes and disks. These tapes and disks fill more than half of all private vault space. Works of art can be kept in rooms that have temperature and humidity controls and special fire-fighting systems designed not to damage art.

These commercial bulk storage facilities are sensible for two-home families who wish to lock up valuables when they are out of the area. Owners of vacation homes, for example, may want to store special possessions during the off-season.

Private vaults can be more expensive than banks for small spaces, but they are often cheaper for bulky storage. A private three-by-three-by-two-foot locker costs on average about $50 a year.

For more information about private vault companies, write to the National Association of Security and Data Vaults, 3562 North Ocean Boulevard, Fort Lauderdale, Florida 33308.

Buying a Safe for Your Home

SINCE there are long waiting lists for safe-deposit boxes in banks, more and more people are searching for a secure place to store their valuables right in their own homes.

The biggest weakness of a home safe is its accessibility. If you take a weekend away from home, professional burglars have plenty of time to find and defeat your safe. So a safe-deposit box in a bank or a vault at a private safe-deposit company is the most secure place for jewelry, securities, coins and other valuables, but a home safe can be useful for documents and records.

When you buy a safe, be sure it has been rated by the Underwriters Laboratories for fire resistance. Say it is rated a class 150 two-hour safe. That means that temperatures inside will go no higher than 150 degrees Fahrenheit during a two-hour fire. A class 150 two-hour safe is a good one for protecting stamps and other expensive collectibles.

If you insist on keeping not only your documents but also tiaras and gold bullion in your home, then forget about a wall safe. A burglar can drill around the metal box and pull it free. What you will need is a so-called burglary-resistant safe. It should be anchored with bolts or embedded in a concrete floor and concealed by a rug. A floor safe the size of a file-drawer cabinet can cost from $850 to $2,000.

Fancier, stronger safes can go for more. You can easily pay over $2,500 for a medium-size model with inch-thick special alloy walls, and an inch-and-a-half-thick door, a special locking mechanism in the door and an Underwriters Laboratories label marked TL-30. The TL number is an index of resistance to burglars' tools. Be sure to check with your insurance company. Most policies will spell out for you what specifications your safe should have to meet your coverage.

If you do not have a safe, the best protection for your valuables is ingenuity. Avoid the more common hiding places, like the toe of a shoe or the bottom of a sugar canister. Some people have foiled burglars by using false-bottom books, sewing jewelry into stuffed toys or pillows or even freezing diamonds in the ice tray. Just be careful not to gulp them down in a martini.

Your Consumer Problems

Gaining Through Complaining

For customers bedeviled by faulty products, snarled-up bills or late deliveries, a few well-chosen threats can succeed when all else fails. You can gain by complaining shrewdly.

Any good gripe to a store or manufacturer, as writer Marlys Harris has observed, has five simple elements: a clear statement of the problem; facts that back up your story; a request for redress; a deadline by which the problem must be solved; and a threat that you are prepared to carry out if you do not get quick and complete satisfaction.

Many quite proper threats can produce results. For example, you can threaten to stop payment to the offending store or service person, to end your patronage or to tell other people how badly you have been treated. If all else fails, you can threaten a lawsuit. But use that as a last resort, for you often will have to be prepared to spend thousands of dollars on legal fees.

Face-to-face gripes frequently fail because you take out your anger on a clerk or bank teller who does not have the power to correct a problem. To get any results from an oral complaint, of course, you should ask to see the manager or whoever is in charge.

One successful face-to-face technique is called the broken record. It has been developed by specialists in assertiveness training. You drive your listener to distraction by tirelessly repeating your problem and your request for redress in a helpful and unctuous manner. Or you can take this technique another step by announcing, "I'm *not* moving until you straighten this out."

You may be tempted to make your gripe by telephone. That is less daunting than face-to-face complaining, but it often feels like punching a cloud. If you elect to fight that way, demand the name or employee number of the person with whom you speak. Write it down, along with any promises the complaint handler makes.

If the first person you speak with fails to solve your problem, ask to talk with a supervisor. Keep heading upward until you get some response. If you suspect a complaint handler is giving you the runaround by sending you to another department, threaten to get back to him. That is why you have asked for his name or number.

The telephone is particularly suited to solving delivery problems. You just threaten to call the dispatcher every 15 minutes until the truck arrives. After a few such distracting calls, he or she usually manages to work miracles.

If you have a gripe about snarled-up computers, immobile bureaucrats, snooty clerks or an unreliable product you have bought, the most effective way to complain is generally by writing a firm, effective letter. Aim your missive directly at the head of the company. Although he or she will probably pass it to a subordinate, the chief's interest is often enough to turn the laziest employee into a dynamo.

Since countless employees in large stores and companies must pore over letters that are usually boring, vague, abusive and lengthy, you have to make your letter stand out. One way to do that is simply to write plain, forceful English. The first paragraph should be brief — no more than two sentences of 10 or 15 words each. It should summarize the problem in a dramatic way — for example, "I'm very distressed by a billing problem that your company refuses to correct." And it should demand proper redress.

In the second paragraph pop a surprise: compliment the company. You might say that you have been delighted with its appliances over the years. In fact, those marvels have been joys to own. Then, in the next paragraph, go in for the kill. "So you can imagine my dismay," you might say, "when my latest purchase turned out to be a dud."

Move on to the facts, but omit unnecessary details. Since most people only scan letters you should state your demand twice — in the second sentence of the first paragraph and at the end. Also, try to establish a relationship with your reader to gain empathy. A businessman might say that he is in business, too, and would be upset to learn that one of his customers had been treated as poorly as he has.

A "P.S." is especially important. Tests have shown that a P.S. is one of the first things people read, so you want to make a statement that will get someone to read the rest of the letter. To a bank president, you might say you will be compelled to move your account elsewhere, notify the banking commission or take up the matter with your lawyer if you do not hear from the executive by a certain date.

If your complaint does not bring immediate results, step up your demands. Not only do you want your toaster replaced, but since you have had to put up with delay after delay, you think the company should throw in an electric can opener as well. When you keep raising the ante, management tends to become more eager to settle.

One further tip: The U.S. Office of Consumer Affairs has published a free, 92-page *Consumer's Resource Handbook*. It lists the names, addresses and phone numbers of consumer affairs directors at more than 700 corporations. If you do not get satisfaction from them, the booklet directs you to the addresses and phone numbers of other sources of help, such as local Better Business Bureaus and government consumer protection offices. To get the handbook, write to the Consumer Information Center–P, Pueblo, Colorado 81002.

Help from Better Business Bureaus

Now that the government has relaxed its regulation of business, where can consumers turn for help to settle their complaints against companies? More and more of them are relying on the Better Business Bureau.

The nation's nearly 160 Better Business Bureaus operate on funds contributed mostly by local firms. All the bureau members agree to respond promptly to consumer complaints, make fair adjustments when the customer has grounds for a gripe and advertise honestly. The most common complaints concern merchandise sold by mail, phone, radio or television.

How much a Better Business Bureau can help varies widely from community to community. For example, the Manhattan office, with a large full-time staff and budget, is one of the country's most pro-consumer bureaus. But some bureaus with smaller staffs spend less time on investigations.

Probably the best time to call for help is before you make a deal. The bureau will give you its report on the reliability of a company. If the report is satisfactory, the bureau will tell you so. If the company has an unsatisfactory report, the bureau explains why. But Better Business Bureaus won't ever give you lists of complaint-free companies. That's because recommendations of any kind are taboo. People who think they have been swindled or misled may get help, but it may take weeks to settle the case. It's best to put complaints in writing to give bureau specialists time to check out the facts.

Increasingly, the Better Business Bureau is resolving disputes by arbitration. All of its bureaus offer this service free to buyers and sellers willing to accept the results as legally binding. Most consumers who don't like an arbitrator's decision may have no further recourse, and in some states the courts will decline to hear their case. However, consumers who complain about their automobiles can reject an arbitrator's decision and go to court.

Your Retirement

Strategies to Start Saving Now

A LMOST everyone can look forward to an even longer average life span and better health than his or her forefathers. But if you are under 40, what you probably will not be able to do is retire as early as your parents could, or quit working completely when you do retire, or count on the government for as much of your support in your great age. Because you will have to do more to take care of yourself when you are old, you will have to start saving and investing while you are reasonably young.

Population trends will strain Social Security and private pensions, but only in the future. In the decade of the 1990s, the Social Security system will enjoy a huge surplus — some estimates run to *$1 trillion* by the year 2000. That is because the people who start retiring and tapping into Social Security benefits will come from the small generation that was born in the 1930s Depression. Meanwhile, the bulging generation of baby boomers born from the mid-1940s to the mid-1960s will be reaching their peak earning years and paying tremendous sums in Social Security taxes. Consequently, the Social Security system will have more than enough cash when today's 60-year-olds retire. It is *after* that that trouble may set in.

Today, less than 13% of America's population is over 65, but by 2030 that should rise to almost 22% as the 75 million baby boomers grow older. Although the primary reason for the aging of America is the increase in births in the years just before 1920 and after World War II, lengthening life spans are also a factor. If a man makes it to the age of 65 in the year 2010, he will have a 50-50 chance of living one to three years into his 80s; women will live even longer — into their mid-80s. With fewer young people and many more elderly, the few will have to support the many through Social Security taxes. The U.S. probably will have to scale back government-paid retirement benefits. They will be lower in real dollars, and they will start later in life. Thus, your private pension — from either your employer or your Individual Retirement Account and Keogh plan, or from both — will become relatively more important than such sources are for contemporary retirees.

The combination of your 1992 pension, your investment income and your Social Security benefits needs to add up to 70% to 80% of your last year's salary to maintain your standard of living. Take, for example, a single person who retired in 1992 and requires 75% of a $55,000 income before taxes to live comfortably. Figuring maximum Social Security of $13,056, that means the income from pensions and investments would have to be slightly over $28,000.

The highest private pension coverage is provided to employees in the automotive, chemical, petroleum, aircraft and public utilities industries. Retailing, food-processing and garment-manufacturing firms tend to have the lowest level of pensions. Some of the best pensions go to government employees — military personnel and federal and state civil servants. A cost-of-living escalator makes many of their retirement plans especially generous.

Happily, great new opportunities to save and invest for retirement are opening up. The number of tax-deferred corporate pension and savings plans has more than doubled since 1975. IRAs, which let your savings grow tax-free, are now available to everyone who works for money, although not everyone can deduct his or her contributions.

Qualifying for an old-fashioned lifetime pension is easier now than it once was. You have to work at the same company for only five years to become "vested." (Vesting means that you are guaranteed benefits when you retire.) Or employers can choose an alternative plan that stretches out the process to seven years, by vesting 20% of your pension benefits after three years and 20% in each of the subsequent four years.

In addition to formal pensions, many companies offer payroll-deduction savings plans such as 401(k)s. Eighty-five percent of 1,006 major corporations surveyed in 1991 by Hewitt Associates offered pension plans plus at least one and sometimes more than three payroll deduction plans for the purpose of savings and investment.

Even if you have only a meager company pension, there are ways to use whatever assets you have to achieve substantial gains.

You might start investing for retirement by putting a bit of money into a mutual fund that aims for growth. This type of fund invests in stocks of solid companies that offer better-than-average opportunities for capital appreciation. A mutual fund, of course, is an excellent place to put your yearly contribution to your Individual Retirement Account. You can find updated rankings of the best-performing mutual funds in the "Fund Watch" column of *Money* magazine.

You might further diversify your retirement fund by looking into real estate. Ask a stockbroker or financial planner to seek out real estate investment trusts (REITs). These are public companies that invest in apartments, health-care facilities and commercial developments. Be less eager to put your savings in real estate limited partnerships. Their track records during the 1980s were for the most part miserable. For most people, too, they violate a wise rule: Don't invest in anything you don't understand.

To be financially secure later on, you will have to concoct a recipe for retirement income that will not reduce your quality of life. The time to start saving and investing, of course, is now.

It is wise to get into the habit of investing in a tax-deferred savings plan, such as an IRA, beginning at age 30, so that time and compound growth can work on your behalf. Aim to save and invest 10% of your pre-tax income between the ages of 30 and 40. Then, increase that amount by one percentage point a year between the ages of 40 and 45. After 45, try to save 15% a year when you don't have college expenses.

If your employer offers you a savings or profit-sharing plan where the company kicks in 50 cents or more for every dollar you invest, that is an offer you should not refuse. There is, however, one exception. If the plan invests exclusively in the company's own stock and you are not confident about your employer's future, you might be wise to put your money elsewhere.

Nearly all companies with profit-sharing or savings plans let their vested employees leave with a lump-sum benefit. What comes next can be a real bonanza. The employee can take the employer's contributions plus any money that he has earned in the plan and defer paying taxes on the total by depositing all of it in an Individual

Retirement Account. There the money can be invested, just like a regular IRA, and will compound tax-free until it is withdrawn.

How Much Social Security Contributes

You don't have to be poor or pass a means test to receive Social Security benefits. You just have to have worked in a covered occupation long enough — as briefly as 18 months in some cases. Almost all occupations are covered. For an official estimate of your future benefits, just telephone 800-772-1213 and ask for Form SSA-7004-PC. Its questions are easy to answer, and a few weeks after returning the form you will receive an eight-page document called a Personal Earnings and Benefit Estimate Statement. You can ask for retirement amounts at various ages, from 62 to 70, the period during which benefits postponed rise handsomely in terms of monthly income. Just remember, the figures will be in today's dollars. The benefit estimate statement will also tell you not only what you will receive in retirement benefits but, in addition, the monthly amounts that your family would get if you died or that you and your family would get if you were disabled.

The payout for someone who retires at age 65 depends on that person's present age. If you were born in 1957, for example, Social Security's computer currently estimates that your maximum monthly benefit will be $1,662. If you were born in 1947, the benefit is put at $1,491. Those are 1992 dollars. Because actual payments are adjusted each year for inflation, you should view your future benefits in terms of their present buying power.

To qualify for amounts like these, you would have to have been earning for the past several years the full amount of income subject to Social Security tax, for example $51,300 in 1990, $53,400 in 1991 and $55,500 in 1992.

At best, the monthly benefits for a 35-year-old earning $60,000 in 1992 would add up to less than $20,000 a year in current buying power. So, obviously, Social Security won't replace most of your income from work. If your wages remain low most of your life, you and your spouse may get 65% of what you earned in your last few preretirement years. More likely, this government pension will provide 37% or less of a couple's eventual nest egg.

The youngest age at which you can retire and collect Social Security is 62. Retiring that young will cost you 20% of what you could have claimed at 65, which the Social Security System now considers "full" retirement age. That age is due to rise for today's younger folks. If you were born between 1943 and 1954, you'll have to wait until you're 66 to get the full benefit. If you were born after 1959, make that age 67. The cheerier news is that by staying on the job until you're 70, you qualify for benefits as much as 40% higher.

Unless you postpone this pension until age 70, it probably won't pay to work after your Social Security checks start rolling in. If you do, you will be docked for earning more than a minimal amount. In 1992 a 65-year-old flunked the so-called earnings test by making more than $10,200. For every three dollars above that, you would have been docked $1. If you were under 65, the earnings threshold was a mere $7,440, and the penalty for earning more was $1 for every $2 of paycheck.

No matter how old you are, you must pay income taxes on as much as half of your Social Security benefits if your other income pushes above fairly modest levels — $32,000 for married couples and $25,000 for singles. And for this test, the government counts as income half of your Social Security income and also tax-free interest on municipal bonds.

How to Plan at Different Stages of Life

R EGARDLESS of your age, now is the time to figure out how much you will need to make retirement secure — and where that cash will come from.

Your first step is to calculate your anticipated income and expenses during your post-employment years. Usually it is unrealistic to aim for an annual income equal to your pay in the last year before you quit. You most likely will not need that much anyway, because your work-related expenses will disappear and you won't be putting part of your income into retirement savings any longer. Your tax bill stands to decline, too, because at least half and at most all of your Social Security benefits will be tax-free. So you should work toward building retirement income of between 70% and 80% of your pre-retirement earnings, before taxes. Be aware that traditional pension plans often pay you only 30% of your final five-year average compensation if you retire at 60.

After figuring out how much you will require each year, you should estimate your life expectancy. Use the national mortality tables that you can get from your insurance agent. But to be sure you will not run out of money, you should add eight to 10 years to the number of additional years the tables say you can expect to live.

To determine where your retirement income will come from, start with the Social Security benefit that you can expect to get. The Social Security Administration has now greatly simplified the procedure for finding out. For details, see "How Much Social Security Contributes."

When you are in your 30s, start setting priorities for your spending, so that your major expenses will be paid off when you retire. At this age, it is a good time to buy a house or apartment, so your mortgage will also be paid off by the time you quit work. You should get into the savings habit. As mentioned earlier, try to save at least 10% of your pay. If you must, cut back on entertainment, travel and other discretionary expenses to find the extra money. It is when you are young that you should build an emergency fund equal to three to six months of living expenses. It should go into risk-free money funds or U.S. Treasury securities.

When you reach 45, aim to put away 15% of your income. Continue making the maximum contributions to tax-saving Individual Retirement Accounts, Keogh, SEP and 401(k) plans. Take full advantage of any of your company's savings and investment plans. If possible, do not switch jobs until you have worked for the same company long enough for your pension benefits to be vested.

Once you hit your 50s, try to continue to save 15% of your gross income, especially in tax-deferred plans. Your investments should now tilt conservatively. Look for blue-chip stocks, conservative mutual funds and fixed-income investments, such as bonds and GNMA mortgage funds.

When you reach your 60s, you probably soon will be collecting a Social Security check, and you should be aware of these points:

First, the government will not send you a check until you notify the local Social Security office that you are ready. So be sure to file an application three months before you want the first check to arrive.

Second, many couples do not realize that if only one spouse works for pay, Social Security will send you a monthly check amounting to about 1½ times the worker's entitlement.

Third, although Social Security docks your benefits if you earn more than a certain amount (see "How Much Social Security Contributes"), you can earn all the investment income you want and not be docked a dime.

Those GICs in Your Savings Plan

FEW people really understand guaranteed investment contracts. Yet employees saving for their old age have poured billions of dollars into them — about 65% of the more than $300 billion in 401(k)-type savings plans are in GICs. If you participate in one of those kinds of plans, the chances are better than one in three that you're putting some of your salary into GICs. But you probably don't know it, because these investment options usually have another name, such as "stable value fund," "guaranteed fund" or "capital preservation fund."

GICs are a type of security issued only by insurance companies and sold only to large financial institutions such as those that take custody of employee benefit funds. Over the term of the contract, usually one to five years, the insurer promises to pay a stated rate of interest. During that time the value of your investment, including its earnings, does not fluctuate.

GICs resemble bank certificates of deposit, but they have one big advantage over CDs: GICs generally do return at least two-thirds of a percentage point more than Treasuries of comparable maturities. GIC investors get the peace of mind that goes with owning something with constant value: GICs guarantee a set yield.

While only insurers can issue GICs, banks have got into the lucrative act by offering nearly identical bank-investment contracts, or BICs. Initially, BICs were covered by federal deposit insurance, but after the insurance industry cried "Foul!" Congress passed legislation eliminating BICs from the FDIC program.

Lately the safety of some GICs has come into question. They are not, of course, insured by the U.S. government, as CDs are. Insurance analysts and rating services have become concerned over the large volume of shaky junk bonds and unprofitable real estate in some insurers' investment portfolios.

In fact, GICs may prove to be only as safe as the insurance companies that issue them, and an insurer is only as safe as its assets and investments. The salary-withholding retirement plans of more than 20 companies and colleges were holding over $1 billion in GICs issued by Executive Life of California, Executive Life of New York and Mutual Benefit Life when the companies, loaded down with devalued junk bonds or bad real estate loans, were seized by state regulators in 1991. A few employers promptly announced they would make good any employee losses, but they were exceptions. While employees who invested in those GICs may eventually get their money out, it was frozen by most companies so that it could not be withdrawn or switched to other investment choices. Most states protect insurance policyholders from company bankruptcies to a certain extent through insurance-guarantee funds; the amount of coverage that GICs are accorded varies from state to state.

Junk bonds in insurance company portfolios aren't the only problem threatening GICs. Some insurers have perhaps unwisely boosted their interest rates — and their risk — in the battle for a larger piece of the retirement-plan business.

Banks, bond fund companies, money managers and some insurers are now promoting the so-called synthetic GIC. With this kind of investment, you still get the fixed interest rate of a traditional GIC, but your employer can choose the assets that back the contract. Rather than relying on all of an insurer's portfolio, for example, your plan manager could pick mortgages backed by Fannie Mae or Treasuries, which are virtually failsafe.

On balance, GICs deserve a place in your retirement savings and investment portfolio. But it is up to you to make sure that your money is entrusted only to healthy insurance companies. Your corporate benefits office should be able to name the insurers and give you their financial ratings. But in case you draw a blank there, ask for the name and phone number of the fund's trustee. Here's what you need to know:

— Is an investment adviser specializing in GICs screening the insurers for safety?

— Is the portfolio well diversified (that is, does it include GICs contracts from four to six insurers or banks)?

— Do all of the insurers have a top rating for claims-paying ability? Specialists in GICs prefer the evaluations of Standard & Poor's, Moody's or Duff & Phelps over those of A. M. Best, the industry's traditional rating firm. Look for a rating of AAA or AA, nothing less.

Annuities: Savings with a Tax Shelter

THE very mention of the word *annuity* may be enough to make your eyes glaze over. But consider these words: up to 7.5% interest, all of it tax-deferred; guaranteed principal; monthly checks for life. Now are you interested in annuities?

An annuity is a savings plan sponsored by an insurance company that offers some tax benefits. It is a contract promising to pay you a regular income, usually starting the day you retire and running for the rest of your life. Annuities are sold by brokers, bankers, financial planners and insurance agents. Contracts called single-premium annuities generally require a deposit of $5,000 to $10,000 or more, but others called flexible premiums allow you to start with as little as $250. The earnings on the money compound *tax-deferred*, just as with an IRA. And if you buy an annuity for your IRA, your contributions — up to $2,000 a year — may be *tax-deductible*.

The earnings on your annuity grow until sometime in the future, usually after you retire. Then you can either take one large lump sum or "annuitize" — that is, start collecting monthly payments that will continue either over a fixed period or for the rest of your life and perhaps your spouse's too. Each payment is considered to be partly a return of principal that will *not* be taxed, unless your annuity has been in an IRA, and partly your earnings or income on that principal (which *will* be taxed in any case). If you should die before you can begin collecting, the proceeds in most states go to your beneficiary and are not subject to probate.

After you buy a contract, the insurance company may let you withdraw up to 10% of the value of your annuity each year without any penalties. But you do have to pay income tax on your withdrawals, under a last-in, first-out rule that all withdrawals are considered interest until no more earnings are left. If you want to take out more than 10%, the company will also exact a surrender charge in the early years. Often it starts at 5% to 10% of the amount you are withdrawing during the contract's first year and declines until it disappears after five to 10 years. There are other fees as well. Many companies charge maintenance fees of $12 to $30 a year on fixed-rate and variable contracts. In addition, the IRS imposes a penalty of 10% if you withdraw money from your annuity before age 59½.

Because of those penalties, annuities are not for you if you are seeking a convenient place to park your spare cash for just a short period. Nor are annuities sensible for very young adults who cannot afford to tie up capital. But disciplined savers in their mid-30s or older who seek tax relief should seriously consider annuities.

Say, for instance, a 45-year-old man put a $100,000 inheritance into an annuity that paid an average of 7% interest over the years. By the time he reached 65, the tax-deferred buildup would be $386,968. If he then took monthly payments for life, he might draw $3,000 each month from an insurance company.

Different insurance companies make widely different monthly payments. Among various insurers, the lifetime payment for a man aged 65 ranges from $7.39 to $9.23 a month for each $1,000 of accumulated capital. For a woman aged 65, the range is lower due to a longer life expectancy — $6.77 to $8.98 per $1,000.

When you first buy a deferred annuity — that is, one in which to build up retirement funds — the sponsor of the annuity *guarantees* to pay you a certain interest rate on the money, generally for a year and sometimes up to ten years. After that, the rate moves up or down at the sponsor's discretion. Most insurance companies guarantee to pay you at least 3.5% to 5.5% a year, even if rates dip below that in the future.

The insurance company also guarantees to pay your heirs back all the money you put into a fixed annuity if you die before you can annuitize. So, you would be wise to deal only with major insurers. Look for ones rated A + + or A + by *Best's Insurance Reports,* which objectively analyzes the companies. You can find *Best's Insurance Reports* in public libraries and, sometimes, at insurance agents' offices.

Variable annuities are riskier than fixed ones because your principal is not guaranteed. With a variable, the insurance company invests your money in stocks, bonds or money-market securities — and most plans allow you to switch among them. Your returns fluctuate daily, along with their performance, and your monthly payments vary accordingly.

When shopping for a fixed annuity, do not give in to the temptation to buy the one that promises the highest interest. Many contracts dangle high rates before first-time buyers but slash the interest in later years. Before you buy any fixed-rate annuity, ask to see the interest rates that the insurance company has paid over the past 10 years.

Most companies offer an option that lets you pull out your money without paying an early-withdrawal penalty, provided the interest rate drops below a set level, such as one or two percentage points below the rate being paid when you bought the annuity. This so-called bailout clause usually comes at the cost of an initial interest rate of one-half to one full percentage point below those without escape clauses. If you bail out, you can transfer the money to another company and avoid paying taxes. But you're generally better off choosing a no-bailout annuity from a company that has paid consistently high rates.

Some company sponsors consistently outperform others in the surveys conducted by Lipper Analytical Services. The fixed-income leaders for A-rate investment-grade bond funds based on total reinvested rate of return for five years have been Aetna C Income Shares, Security Benefit 3 and Anchor 1 ICAP 2.

Leading the money-fund variable annuity rankings for five years are NW Mutual C, Security Benefit 4 and Aetna C Encore.

One research service that compares different insurers' ratings, interest rates and charges is U.S. Annuities (98 Hoffman Road, Englishtown, New Jersey 07726; 800-872-6684). It provides free quotes by telephone and publishes a quarterly, *Annuity & Life Insurance Shopper* (single issue, $20; one-year subscription, $45.)

How to Check Your Company Pension

I T IS too late to start preparing for your retirement on the day you pick up your gold watch. You should be looking into the pension plan that your employer provides right now.

Pension plans come in two kinds. First, there is the *defined benefit plan*. It promises you a fixed benefit upon retirement. Your pension is related to your salary and to the length of your employment, no matter what it costs the company to provide it. This means you can count on at least a certain minimum payment.

Second, there is the *defined contribution plan*. It permits you, your employer or both to invest a certain sum every year on your behalf before taxes. You are entitled to this money when you retire. Defined contribution plans are commonly company thrift or profit-sharing programs. Your employer may agree to match and invest a portion of your savings, or to set aside for you a percentage of profits pegged to your salary. Employee contributions and all earnings are tax-deferred. But if the plan's investments perform poorly, the losses eventually come out of your pocket. So it pays to monitor closely the rates of return in a defined contribution plan.

Hewitt Associates points out what a little foresight can do: Assume that a 30-year-old earning $40,000 a year puts only 1% of his pay in a 401(k) plan, and that his employer contributes 50 cents for each dollar he invests. If his salary rises 6% each year and his investments earn an average 8% a year, he could retire at age 60 with a nest egg of $129,600. With it he could buy an annuity from an insurance company based on a life expectancy of 79 years; the annuity would pay him $14,500 a year, or 7.5% of his final five-year salary.

But if he were to put away a full 6% of his salary, he could quit at 60 with $777,500. He could then purchase an annuity paying him $86,800 a year. That would be the equivalent of almost 45% of his final five-year pay.

Your pension is probably safer under a defined benefit plan than under a defined contribution plan. Even if your company runs into grave financial trouble, the Pension Benefit Guaranty Corporation, a government agency, insures defined benefit plans against termination. You are at least guaranteed to receive some pension. In 1992, the maximum insured benefit was $28,227 a year for a single-life annuity beginning at age 65.

Even if your pension plan is well managed and adequately funded, you may be in for a shock when you retire. Your monthly payments could be substantially less than your individual benefit statement has led you to expect. Only 3% of the companies surveyed by Hewitt Associates give cost-of-living raises to pensioners.

Typically, you will not get a company pension unless you work for the firm at least five years. Then you are vested. That means you are entitled to keep the benefits you have built up even if you quit the company before retirement age. If you work for the same company for many years, you probably will be rewarded with a better pension than if you move around a lot. Mobile workers cut their odds of lasting at a firm long enough to become vested. Employees at small companies often get less generous pensions than their counterparts at major corporations. At best, a pension will replace 60% of your pre-retirement income, and that will be the case only if you have worked for one of the more generous companies for at least three decades. If you retire at 60 instead of 65, many employers will cut your benefits by a third, and by half if you depart at 55.

If you are married, your original pension could well be 20% *less* than a single employee's. That is because employers pay insurance companies more for an annuity for a couple than for a single person, and the cost generally is passed on to the employee in the form of a smaller pension.

The best way to calculate your pension benefits is to read the summary plan description that your employer is obliged to give you once a year. Turn first to the summary plan's section on Social Security. You may discover that your company reduces your monthly pension benefit by a percentage of the amount you will receive from Social Security. That percentage could be as much as 83% on benefits accruing through the company plan's fiscal year that ends on or after December 31, 1988. Subsequent benefits will fall under a new rule of the Tax Reform Act that guarantees you half of your company benefit.

If you are married, check out the joint and survivor benefits section of the plan. Provided you are vested, the law requires companies to give your spouse at least one-half of your pension benefits after you die, unless he or she waives this right. Your monthly payment probably will be reduced while you are alive — if you and your spouse have elected to let the spouse receive the pension after you die. But another choice is becoming popular: the pop-up option. If your spouse dies first, your pension reverts to the higher monthly income for a single person.

If you are thinking of taking a leave of absence or quitting and coming back, you had better examine the provisions for interrupted service. You want to be sure you do not jeopardize your vesting.

If you want to know more about your pension than what you can see in the summary plan description, ask your company for a copy of the complete plan description, which enlarges on all categories in the summary and details the plan's investment strategy. You may also receive the pension fund's tax return, called Form 5500, by writing to the Department of Labor, PWBA Public Document Facility, 200 Constitution Avenue, NW, N5507 Washington, D.C. 20210. Officials will respond more quickly if you include your employer's identification number and the plan number, which your company can provide.

Once you have a copy of Form 5500, give it a careful reading. The first thing you want to know is, has the company told the IRS that it might terminate the plan? If so, the information will appear in item 9.

Item 34 lists the fund's assets and liabilities. Notice if considerable sums languish in non-interest-bearing bank accounts. Look for diversification and degree of risk. More than a third of the assets invested in a single kind of real estate, for example, could be a sign of unnecessary risk.

Item 21 will tell you if the company is up to date on its payments to the fund. If it is not keeping current with its obligations, the next step could be termination of the plan.

Your company's employee benefit managers should be happy to answer any questions you have about Form 5500. But if you get the feeling they are trying to hide something, take that as a warning about the future of your pension.

Should You Insure Your Pension?

COUPLES getting ready to retire on a pension face a tough choice: Should their monthly retirement income continue for as long as either of them lives, or should the money stop flowing after the death of the spouse who earned the pension?

The two-life option may seem like the best pick, until you discover that it will reduce your pension income by 20% — and perhaps much more if your spouse is several years younger than you. It's a dilemma tailor-made for insurance agents. Opt for the higher pension, they say, and protect your spouse by taking out an insurance policy on your life. The extra income you gain from the pension will more than pay for the premiums. And if your spouse dies first, you can surrender the policy, invest the cash value it has accumulated and have a full pension for the rest of your life.

In some cases, it might be smart to buy the insurance. But you can seldom be sure. The problem is that you're trading a sure thing for a gamble. If you do die first, the policy will certainly pay off. The gamble is whether the proceeds will do the job. Will this suddenly accessible lump of money generate as much income as the pension would have guaranteed?

The answer depends on events that you cannot possibly predict, such as how much income the insurance money would produce and for how long, how long you will go on living and how much the cost of living will rise. Remember, you'll be paying large amounts up front and betting that one or both of you will live long enough to make up the cost. At best, you won't come out ahead for many years to come.

You surely should not replace your spouse's benefit with insurance if your pension has built-in inflation protection or pays bonuses when investment returns exceed expectations. Don't do it, either, if your spouse is much younger than you are, because it will take an awfully large insurance policy to cover his or her long life expectancy.

The proper focus of the pension decision is not on insurance but on which of the many different and baffling income options is best for you. To tick off a few more choices:

— The joint-and-50%-survivor benefit. Here, your spouse gets half of your pension if you die first.

— Five, 10, 15 or 20 years certain. Your beneficiary continues to receive pension benefits for the specified number of years if you die first.

— The pop-up option. You choose a two-life income option. Then, if your spouse dies first, you collect the higher income available for a single person.

Should You Take Early Retirement?

COMPANIES are offering some tempting sweeteners these days to encourage employees to take early retirement. Rather than close plants or lay off people, hard-pressed corporations give financial inducements to employees who leave voluntarily, usually between the ages of 55 and 62. But you would do well to look hard before you leave. Early-retirement extras can carry you only so far. The pension that seems so high today may be gobbled up by inflation tomorrow.

Almost every company pension plan provides for early retirement. About 85% of major plans contain terms that cut early retirees' pension checks by *less* than the actuarial tables would mandate. Yet the difference in payments can be substantial. In some cases, if you quit at 55 — when your earnings may well be on the rise — you might get only 25% of the monthly pension you would have received had you worked to age 65.

When deciding whether to retire early, you have to figure out what you want to do and whether you can afford to do it. Sit down with a pencil and paper — or personal computer — and analyze expected income and outgo. Your company's personnel department should provide individual or group counseling to help you. But it's wise to beware of the arm-around-the-shoulder manner of some company-paid consultants. They may make retirement seem more flowery than it will be.

Most retirees need 70% to 80% of their pre-retirement salary to maintain their standard of living. To figure out how much money you'll need, draw up two scenarios — one assuming a relatively modest annual inflation rate of 3% to 4% and one with a rate of 6% or more. You can shade toward the lower end of that spectrum if your major outlays, such as your housing costs, children's education expenses and medical bills, are under control. If not, you will need more. In any case, if the combination of your pension and Social Security falls short of your requirements, you will have to make up the difference through savings and investments or a second career.

Social Security penalizes workers for early retirement. At age 62 — the earliest you can begin drawing benefits — the monthly payment is 20% less than it would be if it were started at age 65. And the gap is never closed. For 1992, the maximum annual benefit at 62 was $10,320 per worker, or $15,120 for a couple with a nonworking spouse also 62. However, if you are retiring early from one job but intend to keep working in another job, you can postpone receiving your Social Security benefits and thereby increase the size of checks when you start accepting them.

About 70% of pension plans permit you to take your pension in a lump, up front, and it's a good option. Quite often you also have the choice of taking any severance pay in installments or in a lump.

One appealing investment choice is to have the whole lump-sum payout, except for your contribution, transferred into a special rollover-type Individual Retirement Account. Employers can start doing that after January 1, 1993. (If you accept the lump sum in a check, though, your company will have to withhold 20% for tax purposes.) Having the money transferred to an IRA defers taxes on the money and its future earnings until you withdraw it later on. The

IRA rollover is particularly attractive for the many early retirees who find that their biggest nest egg is in their company's tax-deferred thrift or 401(k) plan.

But that is not your only tax-savings choice. You can take out all that money right away and cut the taxes on it by figuring them under the 5- or 10-year forward averaging method if you qualify. But unless you need a large chunk of money, you'll do best to let it compound untaxed even while you are retired.

Making the Most of Your Nest Egg

I F YOU are nearing retirement, it is time to think about the best way to minimize taxes and maximize the income you will collect on the money you have been saving. Your first decision is how best to withdraw your money from tax-deferred accounts. You may have several such plans, including an IRA, and a company-sponsored 401(k) or stock bonus program. Each presents its own special tax problems. So be sure to ask an accountant or a financial planner to guide you through the maze of regulations.

Most tax-deferred retirement accounts offer several choices of how you can withdraw your money.

If you take it all out in a *lump sum,* you often pay less tax than if you withdraw a series of smaller amounts. Most retirement plans, with the exception of IRAs, let you use forward averaging to calculate your taxes.

If you turned 50 years old by January 1, 1986, you can use either 10-year or five-year averaging. For example, if you received $200,000, you would pay $42,775 in taxes with five-year averaging and $36,920 using 10-year averaging.

You could get an even better tax break on a lump-sum withdrawal if you began participating in the plan before 1974. Before then, lump sums were taxed at low, long-term capital-gains rates. After 1974, you began paying ordinary income tax on the money. But you can divide the money according to how many years you participated in the plan before and after 1974. Say that you started just over 24 years ago, in 1969. Then about one-fifth of your retirement fund will qualify for capital-gains treatment, and four-fifths for forward averaging. Beginning in 1987, the low tax rates on your capital gains for the pre-1974 investments began to be phased out and they will be totally eliminated in 1993. But if you were 50 years old by January 1, 1986, you can still take advantage of the capital-gains rate on your pre-1974 portion.

Once you have your IRA, you will have to pay ordinary income taxes on the amount you take out. Withdrawals from your IRA can begin without penalty during early retirement (earlier than age 59½) if you take out enough each year to simulate an annuity. But starting at age 70½, the last deadline for IRA withdrawal, you must stick to a withdrawal schedule based on life expectancy. If your 70th birthday falls within the year, and you are a single man or woman, you would have to withdraw one-sixteenth of your total IRA money. A woman would have to withdraw one-fifteenth. A husband and wife, each 70 years old, would have to take out one-twenty-first. Each year after that, their life expectancy would change so the fractions would change. If you're single, you can slow your withdrawals by naming a beneficiary. If possible, choose someone 10 years younger than you are. Then the first withdrawal could be no more than 4% of your tax-deferred savings.

If you want open-ended growth in your retirement account, consider either a variable annuity or a mutual fund. Many mutual funds will arrange a systematic withdrawal plan or a payout schedule that meets tax requirements for IRAs.

Does It Pay to Work after You Retire?

THE word "retirement" is no longer automatically associated with golf carts and golden-years cruises. More and more people are deciding to find another job after they retire. But after all the taxes you have to pay and all the Social Security benefits you stand to lose, does it really pay to take a job after retirement?

Your income after you retire includes your pension, Social Security benefits and any money you collect from IRA and Keogh plans and your investments. As long as you are not earning any money from a job, you can keep all of this, less the taxes you must pay.

But if you are under 70 and start earning wages, you are in a different ball game. The more money you earn, the smaller your Social Security check will be. You will still have to pay Social Security taxes on your earnings. In 1991 retirees between the ages of 62 and 65 could make up to $7,080 without jeopardizing their payments; people aged 65 to 70 could earn $9,720. And don't forget: Your new salary will be taxed for Social Security and can also throw you into a higher income tax bracket and thus shrink the net return on your investments. Depending upon the amount of your adjusted gross income, you may indeed have to pay income taxes on part of your Social Security benefits. The good news is that after you are 70 years old, you collect your full Social Security benefit no matter how much you earn from a job.

If you plan to go on working after you retire, it is best to consult now with your company retirement counselor or an accountant and figure out how much you really will profit from your labors. Ideally, you also should start three years before retirement to investigate the job market, make contacts and take any necessary classes.

One excellent place to start a post-retirement job search is with Forty Plus, operating in 18 cities. These are self-help cooperatives staffed by job-seeking members. They run placement services, aid you in preparing your résumé and coach you in job-interviewing techniques.

If you do not want to work for pay but you do wish to keep busy, look for volunteer work. Two programs can help place you. One is the Retired Senior Volunteer Program, and the other is Voluntary Action. You can find them listed in the phone book or by calling your local Office for Aging. Also, check your city or county agency that directs services for the elderly; it may have lists of volunteer jobs for retirees.

Your Medical Care

O NE thing is sure about your health insurance when you retire: Medicare, which is Social Security's hospital-medical plan, will not be enough to see you through.

Medicare starts at age 65. Its hospital coverage, called Part A, covers almost every American. Part B, which pays doctors' bills, is optional but essential. Estimates vary, but it is safe to say that the two plans together reimburse an average of no more than $60 out of each $100 of total medical expenses.

Almost every retiree should get a policy to supplement Medicare, generally called Medigap. Most large corporations provide it after Medicare phases in, and many employers continue their regular group plan until then for early retirees, often at company expense. A new law says that, starting in 1992, you will have six months after retirement to buy any Medigap policy without having to undergo a medical exam or answer questions about your health. But new accounting rules requiring companies to put aside reserves for that coverage will eat so heavily into profits that future retirees will probably have to pay some or all of their own premiums. If your employer does not cover insurance costs for early retirees, the law guarantees you the right to continue your group coverage, at your own expense, for 18 months after you retire.

New Medigap regulations prescribe ten standardized policies, designated by the letters A through J (except in Massachusetts, Minnesota and Wisconsin, which have adopted different standardized plans). Seniors can choose a bare-bones plan — one that picks up the patient's 20% share of allowable doctor fees and the uncovered cost of hospitalization that lasts more than two months. Or they can tailor a policy to their needs and ability to pay. The premiums, by one insurance executive's estimate, may range from $600 a year for Plan A, the bare-bones basic coverage, to $2,500 for Plan J, the most nearly comprehensive one.

Plans H, I and J include some reimbursement for prescription drugs. You can choose a plan that pays for either $1,250 or $3,000 worth of pharmaceuticals per year, but that amount is payable only after a $250 deductible plus your out-of-pocket 50% share of bills above that. So a patient's annual pharmacy tab would have to reach either $2,750 or $6,250 to capture the full insurance benefit.

The new rules should protect you against overinsuring yourself. In the past, many Medigap policyholders were sold redundant additional policies. The fact is that except for long-term nursing-home coverage, which is not included in any supplemental plan, one Medigap policy is all anyone should need, and it is now illegal for agents to sell you more.

If your pocketbook permits, buy a plan with at least these features:

— Full coverage of doctors' bills. By far the largest loophole in Medicare is in Part B, the premium for which — $36.60 a month in

1993 — comes out of your Social Security check. Medicare pays 80% of doctors' fees, after a $100 yearly deductible, but only if a physician is willing to accept an "allowable" fee. Half of all doctors refuse to do so, however, because they charge more than Medicare is willing to pay. The excess, which can be up to 15% more than the allowed charge, needs to be separately insured.

— Full coverage of hospital bills after Medicare runs out. There is a sizable deductible for each hospital stay. It was $652 in 1992 and goes up from year to year. Medicare pays the rest for the first 60 days of a hospitalization. For the next 30 days, your share of the cost is $163 per day. In rare cases of even longer stays, you can draw on a lifetime reserve of 60 hospital days, for which your part of the bill is $326 a day. Add it all up, and your out-of-pocket bill could reach $25,178. Medigap insurance should reimburse you for all of that.

— Early coverage of existing illnesses. The best policies insure the patient immediately. Others put benefits for pre-existing illnesses on hold for one to six months.

— Guaranteed renewable coverage. Group Medicare policies covering retired members of professional societies, religious groups and other associations are seldom guaranteed renewable. The insurer can drop the whole group after reasonable notice. Some commercial policies are "conditionally" renewable. That means that if the company decides to pull up stakes in a particular state because it is losing money there, it can cancel all of its policies in that state. Make sure your policy is guaranteed renewable.

— Nursing-home coverage. The first 20 days of posthospital care in a skilled nursing home are Medicare's complete responsibility. The next 80 days cost the patient $81.50 each. A Medigap plan should take care of that. But don't expect any Medigap plan to pay for care in a custodial nursing home, where people with chronic illnesses spend the rest of their lives. That calls for a special long-term-care policy.

— Illnesses while you're out of the country. Even some otherwise comprehensive policies don't cover this circumstance.

To help you evaluate the new Medigap policies, United Seniors Health Cooperative has updated its booklet *Managing Your Health Care Finances* ($10, United Seniors Health Cooperative, 1331 H Street, NW, Suite 500, Washington, D.C. 20005). And consult the 1992 Medicare Handbook, free at Social Security offices throughout the U.S.

Your Housing

ONE of the major financial decisions you will face when you near retirement is what to do with your house. Do you sell it? Or stay in it and tap your home equity?

If you are 55 or older, you probably can take the once-in-a-lifetime exclusion that exempts you from taxes on the first $125,000 gain from selling your home. But if you don't want to sell, you can tap into the equity that you have built up in your house by getting a so-called reverse mortgage. As long as you remain in your home, you can collect monthly payments, tax-free, or, if you prefer, take the money as a lump sum or line of credit, or any combination of these options. Principal and interest are due only when you sell your house or die.

To meet the growing demand for reverse mortgages, private companies are offering an increasing variety of them, including one insured by the federal government. For a list of all reverse-mortgage programs, send a letter with a stamped, self-addressed envelope and $1 to the National Center for Home Equity Conversion, 1210 E. College Drive, Suite 300, Marshall, Minnesota 56258. A 352-page book, *Retirement Income on the House,* is available for $24.95 plus $4.50 for shipping from the National Center, or by calling 800-247-6553.

You also can sell your house and continue living there by using a sale-leaseback arrangement. For example, the buyer gives you a 10% down payment and you give him or her a 10- to 15-year mortgage at 9% to 10% interest. You also sign a lease granting you the right to rent the house for the rest of your life. During the term of the lease, the income from the mortgage should pay your rent and leave you with some extra cash, too. The buyer in a sale-leaseback deal is responsible for taxes, insurance and maintenance, which saves you money. Many parents have sold their houses to their grown children and then leased them back.

The American Association of Retired Persons staffs a home-equity-conversion clearinghouse and publishes *Home-Made Money,* a free 44-page *Consumer's Guide to Home Equity Conversion* (AARP, Home Equity Information Center, 601 E Street, NW, Washington, D.C. 20049).

Continuing-Care
Retirement Communities

IMAGINE yourself as a retired person enjoying safety and independence in comfortable surroundings with few worries about bills
for catastrophic illness. A dream? Yes, but one already coming true
for thousands of people who live in continuing-care communities.

There are now nearly 900 such communities in the United States,
many of them in Florida, California and Pennsylvania and almost all
sponsored by religious or other nonprofit organizations. For a
onetime payment plus monthly maintenance you can get a contract
that entitles you to an apartment, meals, medical service and, if
necessary, nursing-home care until you die. In 1991, the median
entrance fee for a one-bedroom unit was $70,529 with a median
monthly fee of $1,145. Costs are lower if you choose a contract that
covers less nursing-home care and still lower if you pay for medical
services as needed.

Continuing-care facilities are not new. The four oldest were
established before 1900. But the bulk of them have appeared since
1960, and it's estimated that they will increase in number by the
hundreds in the next ten years. Unfortunately, many of these
facilities fell into bankruptcy, or suffered severe financial difficulties,
in the 1970s and early 1980s. In the most egregious cases, the
operators were con men. Other communities were run by people
with the best of intentions but the worst of calculations. Victimized by
circumstances beyond their control, elderly residents failed to get the
homes and care for life that they had been promised. The money
they paid was gone.

Today's picture is far brighter. Thirty-six states now have laws
regulating continuing-care communities, including how they handle
their financial obligations. And the nursing-home industry itself has
tackled the job of inspection and accreditation. So far, 111 communities in 22 states have won approval from the Continuing Care
Accreditation Commission, an independent agency sponsored by the
American Association of Homes for the Aging. For a list of them,

send a stamped, self-addressed business-size envelope to the CCAC at 901 E Street, NW, Suite 500, Washington, D.C. 20004-2037.

If you are considering this kind of retirement, check out all aspects carefully. In a sense, you are choosing an insurance policy as well as a home. For starters, restrict yourself to communities whose financial stability has been studied by an actuary. Read a copy of his or her report. If you can't get one, or if it says fees may be raised to cover cash shortfalls, strike the place from your list. Think twice about high up-front fees and lack of escrow accounts.

Ask for the biographies of the community's principal owners and operators. They should have solid experience in similar developments. Request the names of residents of these communities and then make some phone calls to investigate whether the projects are financially sound and deliver what they promise.

If you are thinking about a new project that is financed with state revenue bonds, ask for a copy of the prospectus and study it closely. The developer should allot more than 50% of the bond sale proceeds to land acquisition and construction costs. If he is spending anything less than 50% on these basics, that is clear warning that the developer is skimping — or skimming.

For further information about continuing-care communities, write to the American Association of Retired Persons, 601 E Street, NW, Washington, D.C. 20049; or the National Consumers League, Suite 928, 815 15th Street, NW, Washington, D.C. 20005. The American Association of Homes for the Aging publishes *The Continuing Care Retirement Community: A Guidebook for Consumers*. It includes a consumer checklist and a financial worksheet to help you decide if you should sign a continuing-care contract. You can get it from AAHA Publications, Suite 500, 901 E Street, NW, Washington, D.C. 20004-2037.

Retiring to Foreign Countries

SOME 400,000 Americans have chosen to retire in a foreign country. Their reasons are varied, but perhaps the main one is the hope of living comfortably on a modest income in an ambiance of choice. Unfortunately, many people are learning that bargains do not come that easily.

Fluctuations in the dollar's strength against foreign currencies make it difficult to plan how far your money will go, especially in countries with strong currencies of their own. Furthermore, rising standards of living in many countries bring higher living costs. Even Mexico, a longtime favorite of Americans, has posed a problem with its mounting inflation (as well as pollution) in recent years. Nonetheless, more than 62,000 Americans have retired to Mexico, the largest concentration in and around Guadalajara in the state of Jalisco.

If you are considering a foreign address, you will be wise to approach your new life with an eye to detail instead of a faraway look. Jane Parker, former head of Retirement Explorations, cautions against cutting all ties until you have given your chosen spot a rehearsal living, at various seasons if necessary. Keep an open mind and be prepared for adjustments that can range from petty annoyances to downright disillusionment. You simply may not want to tolerate a different life-style in return for picturesque views.

Pick a country with topflight medical standards. Notable among them are Canada, Costa Rica, France, Germany, Britain, Sweden and Switzerland. Medicare does not extend beyond U.S. territory, but many private plans, including Blue Cross/Blue Shield, will cover you.

Local health insurance also is available. In countries with large expatriate enclaves you will find private health insurance programs, such as that of the American Society of Jalisco. Your best opportunity in some countries may be a government-sponsored health program. In Spain, Americans living on the Costa del Sol, for example, can make medical arrangements with the country's socialized medical plans.

On the matter of taxes, the U.S. Internal Revenue Service takes its cut of your income no matter where you go. You may also be subject to the taxes of the country where you live, although you usually need a substantial income, or business, to owe taxes to your adopted country. One comfort: The U.S. has tax treaties with many countries that let you credit one set of taxes against the other, so you don't pay twice. If you have questions about possible taxation, consult a tax lawyer of the country *before* you move there.

Should you keep your money in the local currency or in U.S. dollars? As long as the dollar is more vigorous than the local currency, expatriate retirees should keep their money mainly in greenbacks. Some countries allow you to maintain a local bank account denominated in dollars or in another foreign currency of your choice.

Wherever you settle, you should have two wills: one covering property in the U.S., the other for assets in the other country. And each should mention the other.

The monthly magazine *International Living* ($29 a year, $3 an issue) often discusses retirement abroad. Each year the January issue rates countries on their quality of life, weighing such factors as health, cost of living, culture and the economy. The editors have also written a book, *The World's Top Retirement Havens* (1991, $15.95). Both are available from Agora Inc., 824 East Baltimore Street, Baltimore, Maryland 21202; 410-234-0515 or 800-433-1528.

If you wish a personal contact, write or phone Richard Krueger, Lifestyles Explorations Inc., Suite 1900, 101 Federal Street, Boston, Massachusetts 02110; 508-371-4814 (24-hour service). Lifestyles Explorations was previously called Retirement Explorations, but demand was so big from nonretirees seeking overseas opportunities that the firm changed its name. It sets up one- and two-week group trips to countries that are popular with Americans who want to live abroad, particularly Costa Rica, Honduras, Ireland, Portugal, Uruguay and Canada. Each tour includes meetings with and lectures by local real estate brokers, business people and academics as well as transplanted Americans, both retirees and entrepreneurs.

Your Estate

Wills: Drafting Your
Most Important Document

THE prolonged, moderately growing prosperity that many fore-casters expect for the U.S. could have one unexpected conse-quence that would be a mixed blessing. It could swell the value of your investments, your company stock purchase and pension plans and your other assets so much as to create both a windfall and an estate tax headache for your heirs. In fact, you may have such a problem and not know it. Even if your income is modest, you may be building up great — and taxable — corporate benefits.

Because you will have more than you expected to leave to your heirs, it is increasingly important to put in writing just who will inherit your accumulated wealth. You can do one or more of four things:

— You can write a will, which leaves instructions for after your death about how the wealth is to be distributed. Your state officials will then see to it that your intentions are carried out, through a public process called probate.

— You can, in effect, attach labels to some types of possessions declaring who will own them when you die. With financial assets such as life insurance policies, bank and brokerage accounts and retirement plans, you do this by designating a beneficiary or co-owner. With real estate you do it by sharing the title of ownership jointly with the person who will inherit it by "right of survivorship." In either case, transfer of the property is a private affair. It is not subject to probate.

— You can create a trust and turn over to it the legal ownership of your worldly goods. In this document you declare, just as in a will, who is to inherit everything. Here, too, you cut the state out of the process. Such a trust is called a revocable living trust. By naming yourself as the trustee, you can keep complete control over your property, just as if you still owned it. In fact, you can regain ownership at any time by taking the asset out of the trust or by revoking it.

The pros and cons of wills and living trusts will be explored in the next section. Either is preferable to a fourth way of handing down property: doing nothing. In the absence of legally binding instructions, the law of your state determines who gets what — quite possibly not the heirs you would have named. Usually the state gives one-third to one-half of your after-tax estate to the surviving widow or widower and the rest to the children. If you have no surviving spouse or children, then your estate goes to your parents, brothers and sisters and other blood relatives — or if you have none, then to the state itself. Unless you make proper provisions, your legacy will not be passed on to a friend or live-in lover whom you might have preferred to make your heir.

Appallingly, nearly two-thirds of adult Americans leave matters to the state. Yet merely by putting the right words on paper and having them properly witnessed, you may save your survivors considerable bitterness. No family situation brings on more stress than divvying up Dad's or Mom's estate. One academic study shows that where no legally binding instructions were left behind, arguments among the heirs were four times as likely to occur. And more than mere wealth may be at stake. Only in a properly executed will or trust can you appoint a guardian for your children or make special provision for an aging relative or a handicapped child.

The desire to legitimately avoid death taxes often plays an overriding part in how people arrange their estates. The federal tax act of 1981 allows you to leave your entire estate tax-free to your spouse; there is now no limit on the so-called marital deduction. But when your widow or widower dies, the *total* amount that can go untaxed to your children or other heirs is limited. The maximum, spread out among all your heirs, is $600,000 tax-free. Even so, this limit is generous enough that the heirs to most estates will not have to pay any federal taxes on them.

But if you drew up your will before September 13, 1981, when the old law was still in effect, and if you used the conventional wording of that time, the probate court could interpret your will to mean that you wanted only 50% of your estate to go to your spouse. Unless you change the wording now, your estate could be taxed on the other 50%. A simple rewriting can reduce the tax to zero. So do not wait to write — or rewrite — your will or trust.

A valid, up-to-date will or trust can enable you to protect from the federal tax collector as much as $1,200,000. Instruct your executors or trustees to put as much money as can bypass estate taxes, currently the aforementioned $600,000, into a so-called bypass trust. Instruct the trustee to pay the income from investments in that trust to your spouse, as well as any principal that he or she requests. Your spouse can then accept the income as needed or leave it to pile up in the trust. Marvelously, it does not matter how large the funds in trust grow after your death. Every penny will escape federal estate tax. Leave the rest of your estate to your spouse directly or indirectly through a second trust, called a marital trust. Your spouse will be able to pass along another $600,000 to his or her heirs. An experienced lawyer can explain in detail how all this works and can tell you what kinds of trusts, if any, make sense for you. Then the lawyer can design your estate accordingly. (For more, see "Your Estate: The Advantages of Trusts.")

Many people think that writing a will or trust is unnecessary because their surviving spouse will automatically inherit everything. But this is true in only a few states, and only if the assets are acquired during the marriage and are not gifts to or inheritances of one spouse. In most states, the law will make your spouse share your estate with your children, siblings or parents. And since assets left to anyone other than a spouse are taxable if they are more than $600,000, the federal government can become an unintended heir to part of your estate. So even if you still think you would never be worth enough to worry about making a will or creating a trust, you had better visit a lawyer anyway to find out how your *state* taxes will cut into your estate.

Most states do not accept wills or trusts that have not been vouched for by witnesses. Don't ask a beneficiary to be a witness; the will may be legal, but the beneficiary could lose his or her legacy.

It is wise to have a lawyer draft your will — and your spouse's. Resist the temptation to write one yourself following the instructions in a how-to book or using official forms published by some states. A technical slipup could make your homemade testament worthless. Only a lawyer knows what constitutes a valid document in your state. Some lawyers at legal clinics will draw up your will for as little as $75, but $250 is average for a simple document. The cost rises with the complexity of your finances. Don't be shy about interviewing a prospective lawyer and getting the cost in writing.

Lawyers admit that wills are loss leaders, and they hope to be made executors for the estate. Fees for executors typically are 2% to 5% of the gross estate. But you are under no obligation to do more than pay your lawyer for the will.

Once the will is drawn, sign only one copy, preferably under the supervision and witness of your attorney, and leave it with him or her. You can make minor changes with amendments at any time. Don't put your will in a safe-deposit box. Some states require that safe-deposit boxes be sealed on the holder's death, and it takes time to get the will released.

When drafting a will, people often make the mistake of trying to control their beneficiaries after they themselves have gone. For example, some time ago, one man set up a trust in his will but specified that the trust could hold only assets that yielded 4% to 8%. That was a reasonable return when the will was written — and anything above 8% was considered dangerously speculative. But when interest rates roared up, the trust manager was forced by the terms of the will to sell off many sound and high-yielding investments.

A sensible guideline when making bequests in a will is to use percentages rather than dollar amounts. If you do not, a lot can go wrong. Take the sorry case of a man who had a $100,000 estate and left all of it to his beloved sister, except for $10,000 that he willed to his nephew. But when the man died after a long illness, medical bills had shrunk his estate to only $12,000. The nephew got his promised $10,000 but the unfortunate sister collected only $2,000. The man would have been far wiser to have left his nephew 10% of the estate. In that case, the sister would have collected $10,800.

Dissolution of a marriage cancels any rights your ex-mate might have to your estate. But should you die before a separation agreement is signed, your soon-to-be ex probably will still inherit. And people will think it was very sporting of you not to hold a grudge.

Review your will at least once every three years, or more frequently if there is major tax legislation, and keep it up to date. You may want to change some bequests, now that you can leave more money free of taxes. Be sure to revise your will if you move, particularly from a common-law state to a community-property state or vice versa. In a community-property state, any assets acquired during marriage are jointly owned by both partners — except for gifts and inheritances. But in a common-law state, assets are owned by whoever buys them.

You do not have to write a new will every time you want to make small changes, such as substituting a beneficiary or changing the amount of someone's bequest. In these cases, your lawyer usually will write a codicil, which must be witnessed and kept with your will. Whatever you do, don't write on the will itself. Such changes may invalidate it, reducing all your careful planning to ashes.

Finally, you may think a will or trust is a statement of who gets what. But it may be just as important to state explicitly who does not get what — and why.

In most of the world, custom and law dictate that children automatically receive most of the parents' wealth when they die. That is, unless the kids have committed some awful crime. Only Britain and her former colonies give people the freedom to leave their heirs whatever they deem appropriate. So leaving it to the kids or not leaving it to them is a choice Americans enjoy as a vestige of our colonial past.

Let's say you have decided to exercise your option — you are going to leave it all to your darling daughter — but you want to cut off entirely your unworthy son. You had better say so in no uncertain terms in your will or trust. If you simply omit any reference to a child, rather than specifically disinheriting him or her, that relative might be able to make a case that the drafting was flawed, that you "lacked testamentary capacity" or that people whom you left your money to exerted "undue influence."

Disenfranchised children are frequent will-challengers. One reason is that, if their claim is upheld in court, they stand to gain an inheritance equal to what state law provides if a parent dies intestate. That's usually one-half to two-thirds of the estate.

And squabbling is not limited to the rich. Fights over estates can be more a matter of frustrated expectations than anything else. One top estate lawyer tells the story of a widower who sought to leave 95% of his estate to his impoverished daughter and 5% to his son who was a wealthy doctor. The son challenged the will and settled out of court for another $5,000. Says the estate lawyer: "I guess he wanted to prove that Daddy loved him as much as his sister."

Two valuable books on drawing up wills and trusts are *Probate* by Kay Ostberg (McKay, $8.95) and Alexander Bove Jr.'s *The Complete Book of Wills & Estates* (Henry Holt, $10.95).

Wills Versus Living Trusts: The Pros and Cons

IN RECENT years millions of people have traded in their will for a living trust, largely to avoid the sometimes costly and time-consuming process of probate, the legal process by which the state oversees the carrying out of a person's wishes as set down in a will. A living trust is designed to do the same job that a will does. Whereas a will names an executor or executrix to carry out its provisions, a trust designates a trustee to do the same. But a will is probated publicly, while a trust is a private matter — unless some disgruntled heir challenges it in court.

In books and do-it-yourself manuals, advocates of trusts hold them out as the solution to all the problems of estate planning. It is true that a living trust can carry out your wishes in life and death while leaving you in charge of your wealth until the end. But according to its enthusiasts, a living trust can also speed the settlement of estates, liberate cash needed by survivors to pay the household bills, shield family assets from public scrutiny, fend off creditors and save legal fees.

As with all panaceas, the truth about trusts falls short of the claims. There's no disputing that they can do the job of a will and circumvent probate. But whether a trust will serve better than a will depends on its purpose, who creates it, where that person lives and what he or she hopes to accomplish. For example, a living trust is the document of choice for putting a professional in charge of your investments during your lifetime if and when you no longer are competent to manage your own money or interested in doing so. A trust can also continue to handle your investments after your death if you don't want your heirs to take on that responsibility.

A living, or *inter vivos*, trust used as a substitute for a will should be a revocable trust, one that can be readily changed or terminated by the person who created it (called the grantor in legalese). It must be signed, witnessed and notarized if it is to become an effective legal instrument. Typically, you transfer all your assets to the trust and name yourself the beneficiary of its income and principal. Then, as in a will, you specify who will inherit its assets, and under what conditions.

Laws governing living trusts differ markedly from state to state. For example, most states let you act as your own trustee, so you can continue to have full control of your investments. But in at least one state, New York, you cannot be the only trustee. Someone else must be named co-trustee. That means you must get the other trustee's signature every time you make an investment move or do anything else not specifically authorized in the trust document.

Advertisements soliciting business for lawyers who specialize in living trusts sometimes claim that they will save you money in taxes. That is just plain bunkum. Your estate is subject to the same taxes whether it is controlled by a will, a trust or the laws of your state.

Trusts do erect a privacy screen around your bequests, if that is important to you. Neighbors and the press cannot gain access to a trust as they can to a will that has been filed for probate. But wills do not give away precisely how rich you were, except to the extent that you make large specific bequests.

As money savers, living trusts make better sense in some states than in others. Massachusetts and California permit notoriously high legal fees for probating a will. There, trusts are becoming the document of choice for people of means. In many other states legal fees for settling an estate are the same whether it is controlled by a will or a trust. In some cases, trust estates have been more expensive to settle than probated estates.

Probate provides protections that trusts do not. The deadline for creditors to file claims against a probated estate and for disappointed heirs or disowned relatives to contest the will is generally three to six months after the will is filed for probate. No such time limit protects a trust. Further, estates governed by a trust can be tied up just as long as probate estates. The first stumbling block is the Internal Revenue Service. An estate must remain open until all the assets have been evaluated, and set down on a federal estate tax form, and the information filed with the IRS. Beyond that, the disposition of an estate depends on the dispatch with which your lawyer and accountant handle the case. Estates often get low priority on law-office calendars.

The Advantages of Trusts

Y ou probably think that trust funds are only for fabulously wealthy people, but you could easily be wrong. If you have children or substantial investments, you may be able to reduce your taxes by setting up a trust. The basic idea is simple: You transfer ownership of property or money to a trust on behalf of a beneficiary. Your beneficiary can be one or more persons — usually including your spouse or children. Or it can be an institution, such as a college or a church.

The person who contributes the assets is called the *grantor*. The grantor sets down instructions for the management of the trust and for passing out its income and principal. The grantor also chooses a trustee. That's a third party who holds title to the trust property and administers the trust. You can serve as trustee, or manager, of a trust you set up or you can name someone else to manage it for you. Of course, you will need to consult a lawyer about the proper way to establish a trust tailored to your needs.

There are two kinds of trusts. One is a *testamentary trust*. It is established in your will and starts paying off after you die. This trust is usually set up so a financially astute relative can manage the inheritances of youthful or potentially spendthrift heirs. Because testamentary trusts are part of your will, they do not avoid probate, which is the lengthy and sometimes expensive legal process by which estates are inventoried. The other kind of trust is a *living trust,* and it starts paying some income to your beneficiaries during your lifetime. After your death, the trust assets automatically pass to your chosen heirs — or remain in trust for their benefit. The assets also escape probate. That can be a big bonus in some states, notably California and Massachusetts. Estate administration can take months or years to complete, and the costs can be high. Lawyers' fees and probate expenses can slice 5% to 7% off a medium-sized estate that includes a house, some pension benefits and personal cash. Several computer software programs can help you set up a living trust. One is

TrustMaker (Legisoft, $99; 415-566-9136), which works for both Macintosh and IBM-compatibles. The same company also created WillMaker. At best, however, these programs produce boilerplate documents. Take heed of what attorney Alexander Bove says in *The Complete Book of Wills & Estates:* "Approach preprinted forms in the same way you would a cheap suit of clothes bought from a mail-order supply house. The price may be right, but you'd be a fool to think it will fit or be fit to wear."

If you are married, it is probably wise to have a lawyer set up what's called an irrevocable bypass, or credit shelter, trust. Here's how it works:

Suppose you and your spouse have $1 million in assets, which is not so unusual for couples who bought homes when real estate was cheap and who faithfully contributed to company retirement accounts. In your will, do *not* leave the entire sum to your spouse. If you do, then when your spouse dies, your heirs will have to pay a stiff tax on any amount over $600,000. To avoid that, arrange in your will to put $600,000 into a trust and give the remainder of your estate to your spouse. In this case, the remainder is $400,000.

While your mate remains alive, he or she can receive the income earned by the trust and some of the principal. Upon your spouse's death, the money in the trust goes to the other heirs whom you have named as beneficiaries. There would be *no* estate tax on any amount in the trust. Your heirs get the whole amount free of federal estate tax. (A note from the lawyers: The above discussion assumes that the ownership — jointly held beneficiary designations — of your assets has been structured to be subject to the terms of your will.)

Beyond the bypass, there are other trusts you should consider. If you and your spouse have large life insurance policies, you may want to transfer ownership of them to something called an irrevocable life insurance trust. This also alleviates estate taxes if you do it right. Giving away your policy will keep it out of your estate only if you live another three years and let the new owner pay the premiums. You must also be sure not to retain any powers to change the policy or reach its cash value. The surest way of getting immediate estate-tax shelter from an insurance trust is to have your heirs buy a new policy on your life. Under the tutelage of a skilled estate attorney, set up the trust and make a gift to it of enough money to pay the first annual premium. As beneficiaries of the trust, your heirs then can proceed to use the money to buy the insurance, although no words in the trust should dictate how the money is to be spent. Each year after that you make another gift to the trust to cover the next premium. But the decision whether to pay it must belong to the beneficiaries. A note of caution: An irrevocable trust, by definition, cannot be revoked or controlled by the grantor. If you desire to control the trust, give up the tax savings and make the trust revocable; never let a professional adviser talk you into making decisions for tax purposes if they do not coincide with your goals.

Minimizing Estate Taxes

L ET me tell you the true story of a millionaire who has set up his estate so that when he dies, his heirs will inherit his wealth without having to pay any taxes. You need not be a millionaire to learn a lesson or two for your own estate from Saul Jacobson.

An engineer from Delaware, who is now retired in Palm Beach, Florida, Jacobson is 79 and hopes to live to be at least 90. But just in case he doesn't, he has set up his estate so that his heirs will inherit it all — more than $1 million — without having to pay any taxes. He calls his planning "an enduring act of love."

Jacobson wisely sought advice from professionals — not just one but four of them: a financial planner, an accountant, a lawyer and a bank trust officer. All this cost him about $10,000, but he estimates that it will save his family at least half a million dollars.

His will states that half of Jacobson's assets will go directly to his son. The son could inherit up to $600,000 tax-free under federal law. To pay the taxes on any amount above that, Jacobson has bought life insurance.

In addition, he has set up what lawyers nickname a QTIP — that's a qualified terminable-interest property trust. The QTIP will provide for Jacobson's wife. If she survives him, she will collect the income from the QTIP for as long as she lives. When she dies, the money in the trust will go to Jacobson's two grandchildren. Only then will it be subjected to the estate tax. The QTIP defers the tax until the death of the second spouse.

You might be able to draw a lesson from Saul Jacobson and leave the largest possible tax-free estate for your spouse and any children or grandchildren. Just consult a seasoned lawyer and inquire whether it is worthwhile for you to set up a QTIP, a bypass or some other trust. If you get a QTIP like the one described here, a federal tax may be imposed because the terms of the trust call for skipping a generation.

Whatever you do, be sure you have a solid and up-to-date will or living trust. Remember to study the plan, trust instrument or will prepared by your professional advisers. Unless you strongly indicate otherwise, their proper goal will be to minimize your taxes. Only you know your true wishes — and maybe they will include giving an outright bequest of $10,000 to Aunt Mae or Cousin Charlie, with no strings attached.

Picking a Trustee

A NY trust needs a trustee who will take responsibility for the money. The trustee is both a watchdog and a safe-keeper. He or she protects the assets in the trust, collects any debts or dividends that are due and may pay a regular stipend to the heirs in accordance with the trust.

Very often people who write wills and set up trusts designate banks as the trustees. For honesty, impartiality and continuity, banks are hard to beat. The fees that trustees are entitled to collect vary from state to state and institution to institution. In New York, for example, the annual fee on assets of $1,000,000 is .0069%. Above that amount, the percentage of assets lost to fees is even less. But how well do bank trust departments really do in managing estates and in guiding assets to growth?

In an earlier era of money management, bank trust departments minded the wealth of millionaires' widows and the heirs to great fortunes. The trust departments placed caution above all else, and so they invested in top-grade bonds and conservative stocks in order to produce returns of 3% a year or so. That hardly seems acceptable today.

Most trusts designed to minimize estate taxes are irrevocable. Unless the trust specifically permits beneficiaries to switch banks, they can do little short of going to court, or threatening to do so, to upgrade performance or dismiss incompetent trustees. State and federal bank regulators are powerless to help. The courts can oust a trustee, but only on proof of fraud, incompetence or misappropriation of funds. So lawyers offer some advice to anyone putting a trust provision in his or her will:

First, give beneficiaries an escape hatch by specifying their right to replace trustees. Do not retain any such rights yourself. You would be taxed under the grantor trust rules of the Internal Revenue Code — effectively defeating your original intentions in establishing the trust.

Second, appoint a co-trustee, preferably a friend or relative whom the bank would have to consult before changing investments and who would serve without fee.

Finally, spell out the trust manager's responsibilities; they can range from simple caretaking to complete control.

Above all, investigate now whether your spouse, your children or your other heirs would benefit by your setting up a trust and getting a trustworthy trustee.

Becoming an Executor

IT SEEMS like such an honor. A relative or close friend asks you to be the executor of his or her estate. You are flattered to be so trusted. But be warned: Estate administration is tough, time-consuming and sometimes even risky. You could wind up spending months, or even years, worrying about death, taxes — and greed.

The first rule of being the executor, as writer Evan Thomas has noted, is not to be one in the first place. Tell Aunt Sadie to get a lawyer or a seasoned bank officer who knows how to administer an estate. The only problem is that such a professional costs money, and Aunt Sadie didn't get to be rich by spending a cent she didn't have to. If you refuse the job, then the fees for a professional executor will reduce the estate by 2% to 5%. Under most state statutes, the executor (professional or not) will be entitled to a fixed fee unless it is waived. Banks and trust companies may charge more than the amounts provided by state statutes.

If you do accept the request to become a nonprofessional executor, you will find that the job, for all its drawbacks, can be interesting. It is like having a person's life suddenly open before you. Of course, you may also find out a lot you didn't want to know.

Don't try to do the job by yourself. Get an expert lawyer to help, unless Aunt Sadie lived in Texas or one of the other few states that have fairly simple probate procedures. If the estate includes land, an ongoing business, a trust, substantial charitable bequests or anything else that could cause a tax problem, then whatever state you live in, hiring a lawyer is a must.

Finding that lawyer is not always easy. Start with the attorney who drafted the will. If he or she is not available, ask at your local bar association. Try to find a lawyer who is a fellow of the American College of Probate Counsel. The members of this organization have had at least 10 years' experience and are recommended by their peers.

When you become the executor of an estate, face up to the fact that you are going to be busy for quite a while. The very first thing an executor must do is find the will and read it. Next, have the lawyer whom you've hired get the will probated, that is, "proved" in the probate court as a valid will. The court will issue to you what's known as letters testamentary that give you authority as executor. You then have to notify all the heirs and any relatives who would have been entitled to inherit under state law if there had not been a will.

Your real chore will be finding and taking possession of the deceased person's property. Tangibles such as the house, car or jewelry should be locked up. An obituary is an advertisement for burglars. Buy or renew the insurance on all the property. If you don't, you could be personally liable for any loss.

Put any cash into a separate checking or savings account for the estate. Pay all the bills out of the estate checking account. Fortunately, it's usually the lawyer's job to pay any taxes, but you will need to give him a precise inventory of the assets and their value. And you — the executor — are responsible for seeing that the taxes are paid on time.

When the will has been probated and all taxes and debts have been paid, the executor prepares an accounting for the probate court of all assets received and sold, all claims and expenses paid and all amounts due to those who are to get the remaining estate. Then he is finally ready to distribute what is left to the heirs.

Sometimes the court will allow an executor to make distributions to needy heirs before the final accounting. Otherwise you allow at least four to six months for creditors to come forward before parceling out, say, the deceased person's pearls or the 300 shares of General

Motors. If you do not wait and there is not enough money left in the estate to satisfy creditors, you could be held personally liable.

Probably the most trying aspect of your job as an executor is keeping meticulous records of the estate's expenses and receipts. That means more than just filling up a shoebox with check stubs and random bank statements. It might be worthwhile to pay the minimum annual fee of around $750 to a bank trust department to act as custodian. The bankers will keep the records for you.

If the estate includes a large portfolio of securities, the executor will need astute investment advice to preserve and perhaps increase the assets before he or she hands them over to the heirs. Hiring a professional investment counselor means another fee, but may save the estate money in the long run.

Executors are held to a high standard of fiduciary responsibility. They run significant legal risks if they act in any way that could be considered contrary to the heirs' interests. So, there are a few things not to do. Don't deposit in your personal checking account any checks made out to you as executor, and never make yourself a temporary loan out of the assets of the estate. Also, you shouldn't buy anything from the estate without permission of all the other heirs and possibly the court.

Should you as the executor take a fee? In a few states, compensation is set by law — usually a onetime fee of 1% to 5% of the estate. In most states, though, an executor simply puts in for a "reasonable" fee and the court upholds it as long as no one objects.

For years it was traditional for executors who were family members to forgo a fee for their blood, sweat and tears. The fee might reduce the executors' own inheritance, and as ordinary income it would be taxed at higher rates than estate taxes. But now lawyers are urging executors to go ahead and take the money. Chances are, by the time you have made all the distributions and the court has discharged you from your responsibilities, you will have earned every cent.

Should You Leave It All
to Your Children?

NOWHERE but in America do so many parents enjoy the privilege of grappling with the question of what to leave their children. There are about 2 million U.S. households that enjoy a net worth of at least $1 million. Most of the millionaires inherited their wealth or built it on a business they founded. But plenty of corporate careerists also have created seven-figure estates by taking advantage of company profit-sharing, retirement savings and stock purchase plans. In short, estate planning is fast becoming a major concern of the middle class.

And nowhere is the feeling about inherited wealth so ambivalent as in the U.S. Many people worry that Commodore Vanderbilt's grandson was right when he declared that "inherited wealth . . . is as certain death to ambition as cocaine is to morality."

Fortune magazine surveyed 30 multimillionaires on the subject of what they plan to leave to their heirs. One-fifth of them said their children will be better off with only minimal inheritances. And almost half plan to leave at least as much to charity as to their heirs.

For example, Warren Buffett, chairman of Berkshire Hathaway, is worth more than $4 billion. After putting his children through college, Buffett contents himself with giving them several thousand dollars each at Christmas. He plans to leave most of his money to his charitable foundation. Buffett says that setting up his heirs with a "lifetime supply of food stamps just because they came out of the right womb" can be "harmful" for them and is "an antisocial act."

T. Boone Pickens, the rich and famous oilman, warns, "If you don't watch out, you can set up a situation where a child never has the pleasure of bringing home a paycheck."

Yet there are sensible ways of passing on what you have without depriving the kids of their own feeling of achievement. Estate experts have some tips.

First, don't be so secretive with your heirs. As soon as the children begin to mature, bring the family finances into the daylight, so they will know approximately what they will get some day and have some idea of how to hold on to it. They should also know, of course, if they will not be getting anything. Talks about family money, like those about sex, should begin as early as possible.

Second, shelve the silver spoon. No matter how well off you are, make sure your children go to work. Psychiatrists say that lack of work experience not only alienates heirs from humanity but also contributes to insecurity about their ability to survive without their inheritance.

Third, give later rather than sooner. Most estate advisers agree that the age of 21 is too early for children to reap a windfall. Businessman William Simon, the former U.S. treasury secretary, suggests that parents put a reasonable amount in a trust that starts paying interest only when the child reaches 35 and then allows him or her to tap into the principal in two installments, at 40 and 45.

Above all, put child-rearing above estate planning. Psychiatrists say that wealthy parents in particular often pay too little attention to child-rearing. As billionaire Warren Buffett advises: "*Love* is the greatest advantage a parent can give."

Widows: Managing When Alone

IT IS sad but true that more than 11 million American women are widows. Those who are in the best financial shape are not necessarily the ones with the largest inheritances. Rather, they are the women who regularly, thoroughly and candidly discussed family finances with their husbands and, more important, what to do with their legacies if their husbands died first.

Because women live much longer than men, widows outnumber widowers by five to one. In 1992 the average age of widows was about 72. At that point in their lives, quite a few may have been widowed for some years, and unless they have remarried or are still going to remarry, they could be looking forward to a decade or more of life on their own. Up to the time of their husbands' death, many of them had never thought much about how to handle the family's assets or how their own economic needs would be met.

By contrast, the widows who cope the best are those who taught themselves — well in advance — how to manage money. The *wrong* time to start asking about, say, the difference between money-market funds and stock-market mutual funds is when a woman has to start managing the family assets alone.

Wives should insist on periodically reviewing their family assets and liabilities with their husbands. Lynn Caine, author of the book *Widow,* suggests that a couple set aside an annual "contingency day" to assess what the surviving spouse would inherit and consider what he or she should do with it. They should discuss whether she or he ought to sell the major inherited assets, such as their house or art collection or business. The couple should also re-examine their wills *every* year and discuss where the widow or widower should seek financial advice.

Every married couple should update and put in writing all the information that can help the survivor and an executor settle the estate. This should include such basic facts as the names and phone numbers of the family attorney, accountant, stockbroker and insurance agent; also, the locations of bank accounts and safe-deposit boxes and important documents, such as wills, deeds and partnership agreements; and a list of assets and debts. Of course, all this information should be kept in one safe and convenient place.

Every married woman should regularly read the newspaper business pages and financial magazines. That is a necessary first step in planning for the possibility that someday she may have to direct her own financial affairs. A wife also should handle her own checking account, pay the bills periodically and take an active part in meetings with any of her husband's professional advisers, such as the stockbroker or insurance agent.

The first priority of a widow should be to preserve her inheritance. For instance, it may be foolish to sell off the family house, which is probably the best place for her to live today and may well be worth more tomorrow. She may be able to delay paying some bills so that the money can earn bank or money-fund interest. To guard against mistakes and con men, a new widow would be wise to double check whether questionable bills already have been paid.

She ought to wait six months or a year before considering investing her inheritance in anything that isn't safe and liquid. Her thinking may be clouded if she makes any immediate decisions. Until the widow seeks advice from professionals to decide how to diversify her investments, any insurance money and other inherited cash can be kept safely in certificates of deposit, money-market funds or those mutual funds that invest in conservative stocks.

A new widow or widower can get wise counsel from a booklet called *What Do You Do Now?* It is available for $2.50 with a $10.00 minimum-ordering requirement plus 15% of cost for shipping from the Life Insurance Marketing and Research Association (Order Department, P.O. Box 208, Hartford, Connecticut 06141). She or he also can get information on self-help groups in the United States and Canada by writing to the International THEOS Foundation, 1301 Clark Building, 717 Liberty Avenue, Pittsburgh, Pennsylvania 15212. Another source of support and financial information is the Widowed Persons Service, an AARP agency located at 601 E Street, NW, Washington, D.C. 20049. The service sponsors about 230 programs across the country and encourages widows or widowers to write for the nearest address.

Remember this: Eventually, a widow must assume responsibility for financial decisions. The sooner any married woman prepares for widowhood, the better. A much more secure legacy than money is knowing how to manage it.

Beware of State Taxes

A RE you planning to move to another state after you retire? If so, now is the time to confront the delicate subject of *state* death taxes.

As mentioned earlier, your estate can escape federal taxes if it is valued at $600,000 or less. But 25 states and the District of Columbia collect their own inheritance or estate taxes. For example, Ohio, Mississippi and South Carolina exempt anywhere from $25,000 to $400,000 from estate taxes. But the remainder is taxed at rates from 1.7% to 18.5%, depending on the estate's size.

Often the amount of the tax depends on whom you leave the money to. For example, if you are a Delaware resident and you leave your entire estate directly to your spouse, he or she owes no tax. But your child will pay tax on anything over $25,000. In Michigan, a child receives an exemption of $10,000 but only $100 is tax-free if the assets are left to a cousin or a friend.

More than one state can tax your estate. Stocks, bonds and other paper assets are taxed in the state where you legally resided at the time of your death. But real estate, jewelry, furniture and other so-called tangible assets are taxed where they're situated. Most states will consider you a resident if you pay income tax there, or if you vote, do your banking, register your car, get a driver's license or have your primary home there.

You can cut the bill by taking full advantage of deductions. State laws generally give your spouse, children and grandchildren the most generous exemptions and the lowest tax rates. So, the more you give or leave to your immediate family, the less is owed to the state taxman.

You can also cut estate taxes by giving money to your heirs while you are still alive. You can give as much as $10,000 a year tax-free to as many people as you want. Married couples jointly may bestow as much as $20,000 a year.

If you want to leave your entire estate to your spouse, you can do it in such a way that it will escape part or all of the state tax when he or she dies. To accomplish this, bequeath part of your property directly to your spouse and instruct that the rest be placed in an irrevocable trust from which your spouse can draw income after you die.

Most important, before making any estate-planning decisions, call your state tax department for detailed information. And be sure to consult an attorney.

Why Everyone Should Write a Living Will

A LIVING will (not to be confused with a living trust, described earlier) is a document that spells out any medical situations in which you would not want to be kept alive after becoming terminally ill. Everyone over 21 should consider drafting a living will, according to Giles R. Scofield, a fellow in bioethics at the Cleveland Clinic Foundation. "It doesn't matter how old or young you are," he says. "My recommendation: If you have ever thought about what you would want done, write it up." Recent Supreme Court decisions have held that a living will or some evidence of your intention regarding life-sustaining methods is necessary in order to allow a physician to stop such treatment.

You don't even need a lawyer. Groups such as Choice in Dying (200 Zarick Street, New York, New York 10014), a nonprofit educational council, can help you fashion a living will for yourself that will withstand most challenges. Choice in Dying will send you a set of forms at no charge, though it welcomes donations.

The kit also includes a form that you can fill out to create a "durable power of attorney for health care," also known as a "health-care proxy." This is a legal document in which you give your next of kin or another trusted person the power to decide, when you cannot, whether you should be kept alive by artificial or heroic means, such as heart resuscitation.

Pro-life advocates have strong reservations about living wills. "People signing them often contemplate circumstances far different from those being invoked," cautions David O'Steen, executive director of the National Right to Life Committee.

It is up to each person who writes a living will to make his or her wishes clear and explicit. If you agree with the right-to-life philosophy, you can express your desire to be kept alive under most circumstances. You might, for example, wish to reject only the kind of extraordinary treatment that is risky and therefore elective.

To give your living will maximum authority, sign it in the presence of two witnesses who are not your relatives, and have all signatures notarized. Robert Klein, business editor and Certified Financial Planner, sensibly advises you to take these other steps to strengthen your position:

— Choose a person to make medical decisions for you if necessary. There is no hard-and-fast rule, but a friend may be more persuasive to a judge than a relative who is also your heir. Discuss your feelings with this representative before signing your living will, and periodically afterward, to make sure you are both in accord. Give this person a copy of your living will.

— Give copies of the documents to members of your family, your physician, attorney and clergyman. Keep them informed of your wishes so that they won't interfere if the time ever comes to invoke your wishes. In particular, make sure that your doctor agrees with your decision and is willing to put a copy of your living will with your medical records. If he or she refuses, think about finding a more understanding physician.

— When choosing a hospital or nursing home, ask the institution to agree in writing to comply with your living will. If it will not, go elsewhere.

— Put your living will with other important papers or have your attorney put it in his vault along with your will. Do not keep it in your own safe-deposit box.

— Update your living will regularly. At least every five years sign it again before witnesses and a notary. Not only will a recent reaffirmation of your wishes carry extra weight with doctors, hospitals and judges, but it will also force you to reconsider your position. The idea of clinging to a life you cannot enjoy may be abhorrent to you now, but who knows? In 10 or 20 years, any thread of life may seem precious.

Postscript

A Look Ahead to the Next Ten Years

Readers of previous editions of this book will recall that I believe we Americans are living through an unprecedented period of rapid social and political change, and that the changes will have profound effects upon our economy and our personal fortunes. I have received many requests for reprints of these thoughts. Here, then, I repeat them, substantially expanded and updated.

A s an editor travels across this great country of ours — and it *is* a great country — one word keeps echoing in his mind. That word is *revolution*.

It is absolutely indisputable that we live in revolutionary times. Just consider the many social upheavals that we Americans have lived through in the last generation or so: the youth revolution, the black revolution, the sex revolution, the women's revolution and more. These upheavals have shaken our American society and economy so fundamentally that we shall never be quite the same again.

This should not surprise us overly much, because although we Americans are essentially a conservative people — we have had the same form of democratic government for more than two centuries — we are a people of the revolution. We were born of a rather long and violent revolution that began 217 years ago. Since then we have seen so many upheavals: the emancipation of the slaves, the enfranchisement of women, the rise to positions of power and influence of the later immigrants, the broad wave of education and affluence and culture that swept over our country during and immediately after World War II.

It should never be forgotten that we Americans have a proud history and heritage of revolution, that ours is the land of the *continuing* revolution. And it is this rare capacity to change, to grow, to reform from within — peacefully, in an enduring democracy — that makes us the envy of the rest of the world.

History's lesson is that it is precisely in times of wrenching change, such as the one we are now experiencing, that humankind makes its most significant advances, that the largest enterprises are created, that the richest personal fortunes are built, that the most enduring achievements are recorded. More than that, all of us — you and I — can effect change. We can make things happen; we can make things happen for the better.

My belief is that not only are we going through a series of revolutions that will significantly affect our lives and our livelihoods, but also in the immediate future the rate of change will accelerate and the degree of change will sharpen and in some cases become more shattering. If there is one certainty in our mercurial world, it is simply this: Those of us who anticipate the changes and who sensibly act upon them not only will survive but also will prosper. And those of us who attempt to ignore the changes and conduct our activities as before will stagnate and wither.

Business, in particular, must quickly and correctly discern the political, social and economic changes all around us — and act upon them. In this age of instant information and highly mobile technology, if you expect something to happen, it probably *will* happen — but much quicker than you anticipate. If we are to survive, let alone serve well and succeed in our jobs, all of us will have to create both a *mindset* to recognize change when it does occur, and a *mechanism* within our companies and organizations to act upon it. You would be surprised at how many business leaders fail to do that.

Speed will become an increasingly important competitive weapon. We will have to act — and react — faster to anticipate and respond to the developments all around us and to seize upon good ideas. *Fortune* writers know that it is much better to publish 80% of a story one day early — just so long as that 80% is accurate and fair — than 99% of a story one day late.

To appreciate the speed and magnitude of change, just consider how much our world has changed in only twenty years:

In the early 1970s, oil from Saudi Arabia cost $2.60 a barrel, a Chevy Malibu set you back $2,891 and a median-priced new house was $26,900. The Dow Jones industrials were heading toward their awesome closing high of 1051.7. Meanwhile, President Richard Nixon, having distanced himself from a third-rate burglary at the Watergate, was en route to reelection by a landslide.

Today's world is quite a different place. In the intervening period, we Americans have experienced five Presidents, four recessions, two bouts of double-digit inflation and one frightening flare-up of interest rates that pushed the prime beyond 20%. Think about what is now common but then did not exist: money-market funds, single-industry mutual funds, foreign-country mutual funds, tax-exempt bond funds and bond unit trusts, tax-sheltered variable annuities, stock futures contracts, asset-management accounts, junk bonds and discount brokers. In that almost ancient age of the early 1970s, if any casual acquaintance had asked you about your very intimate experiences with savings or mortgage rates, stocks or Treasury bills, you would have thought him gauche, gross or slightly mad. But money soon became the new sex, and such personal investing subjects came out of the closet. They are now the most intensely discussed topics among consenting adults.

People who consistently have anticipated the turns in the economy have usually managed to cope, and even prosper, better than those who have not. In the present uncertain era, when the only sure thing is that change will occur, nobody can anticipate precisely what the next 10 years may bring. But after weighing current trends and realities, we can make a fair estimate of the probable shape of at least some future developments.

We know, for example, that over the next decade some 75 million American baby boomers, now aged 29 to 47, will be passing through the time of life when people invariably spend the most for houses, cars, books, diapers and most other goods and services. So consumer demand stands to rise. We know that these young (or at least youngish) adults will continue to be a vigorous force in the economy and will make still larger contributions to the economy as they gain more experience and grow more skilled. Consequently, the economy's efficiency is likely to increase. There are still other, broader developments that you can discern, developments that perhaps you can act upon to increase your earnings, enrich your investments and enhance your career.

Given America's heritage of revolution and given the new power relationships in the world, let me suggest that there will be at least 10 major developments that will substantially change our country, our lives and our livelihoods in the next 10 years.

POINT ONE: In the U.S., we face a period of rather prolonged, sustained economic expansion.

True enough, we have never seen such a spotty, fractionated economy. Some communities and businesses are thriving; others are taking it on the chin. It is hard to talk about the total economy without first recognizing that there are, and will continue to be, sharply differing performances among its varied parts.

But taking it as a whole, the U.S. economy has been recovering, and I expect it to continue growing — albeit slowly and erratically — at least through the middle of 1993, which is as far as *Fortune*'s economists can foresee. They anticipate that the real gross national product, after inflation is subtracted, will grow by about 1.8% in 1992 and 2.7% in 1993. That would be nowhere near a boom, of course, but it would be much better than a recession.

The crash diet of cutbacks, spin-offs and restructurings that American business is going through is *permanently* changing the structure of our economy. Most of the *Fortune* industrial 500 companies have vigorously pursued the slimming-down process of the last few years. So far, the evidence overwhelmingly shows corporate restructuring, despite its regrettable human costs, to be a powerful force for economic improvement.

The most visible consequence is that after years of stagnation, U.S. manufacturing productivity has risen rather sharply. (Productivity growth in the services is sluggish, but that is another story.) The heroes are the smokestack industries — metals, textiles, tires — that were prematurely given up as dying or dormant several years ago.

We are benefiting from the combination of three factors: the spurt in manufacturing productivity, the decline in the value of the dollar and some wage concessions by labor. Measured in dollars, compensation per hour in U.S. manufacturing is 30% less than in Germany and only 7% higher than in Japan. After years of stagnation and decline, a number of U.S. industries rather suddenly have become quite competitive in global markets. The U.S. now holds the lead in quality and technology in aircraft, computers and software, pharmaceuticals, medical equipment, telecommunications equipment and

networking, farm equipment and pulp and paper. In other industries — such as cars, machine tools and steel — we are not the world
leaders, but our quality and efficiency are improving, and we can
look forward to increasing export gains.

Point two: The stock and bond markets in this environment
should do well — over the intermediate term and the long term. I
can absolutely guarantee you that at some point the market will
fall — quite possibly by 10%, 20% or perhaps more. The trouble is,
I cannot tell you when. As the economists say, "Give them a figure or
a date, but never both at the same time."

I do not know — and I do not know anybody who knows
— whether the stock market will be higher a week or a month from
today than it is today. I do not believe that it matters very much,
because almost all of us should be looking at the market from a
long-term point of view. But I believe that the market will be higher
two years from now, and significantly higher five years from now,
than it is today.

There are several reasons to expect that even if stocks fall
temporarily, the long-term bull market will resume: speculation in
the market is certainly not excessive; deep recession in the economy
is nowhere in sight; inflation and interest rates show no sign of
roaring up in the near future; and despite its surge since 1982, the
Dow Jones industrial average is still undervalued.

In terms of real purchasing power, in late 1992 the Dow was lower
than it was a generation ago. Merely to match the record that it
reached in 1965 in terms of real dollars — that is, after discounting
for inflation — the Dow would have to hit nearly 3500. Also, the
stock market in the U.S. over the past several years has risen much
less than stock markets in many foreign countries whose economies
are not as strong as ours. It is likely that U.S. stocks are due for a rise,
quite possibly a substantial rise over the long term.

Point three: We are entering a technology- and service-oriented
era.

The countries, the regions and the companies that master the new
technologies or that develop the information services and the financial services that productively enhance the new technologies — those
will be the countries, the regions and the companies that will prosper
economically, will dominate politically, will inherit the future.

By contrast, the regions and companies that will sink into deeper
trouble will be those that are unwilling to change and to modernize
but instead seek through artificial means — such as import tariffs or

quotas — to protect and prop up the outmoded and the inefficient industries. We will succeed only if we can outcompete lower-wage foreign producers, but we can do that only if we continue to invent, to innovate and to offer high quality and reliability, excellent service and appealing design.

In the next 10 years, the computer's middle-age spread will revolutionize our job opportunities and the way we work. As demands increase for services, notably information delivery, jobs by the millions will be created for computer programmers, systems analysts and other service workers as disparate as secretaries and paralegals, financial advisers and nurses. Demand will be intense for the skilled, whether they wear white, blue or pink collars. But many unskilled assembly-line workers will have to step down to the lower-paying levels of the services, accepting jobs as restaurant workers or janitors.

Industries based on resources — including energy — have been battered lately. But as the Western economies continue to expand, rising demand will revive many resource-based industries and the regions dependent on them. Thus, in the later 1990s we may be entering a period in which the major growth sectors will be not only high technology and services but also energy and some other resources.

One consequence will be a marked shift of power within the U.S. Already under way is a historic migration of jobs, and with it, a movement of people, and with that, a swing of economic and political power. The population is shifting to the West and parts of the South. Note that three of the four candidates for President and Vice President in 1992 came from those regions.

POINT FOUR: The American nation, and much of the rest of the world, is now going through a conservative revolution of remarkable depth and breadth. This revolution extends far beyond the economy and into society and politics. The trend will continue regardless of which political party controls the White House and the Congress. Furthermore, the revolution is only in its infancy. There is more to come.

The cause is clear: for the first time in history, after millennia of living as peasants or subsistence farmers, millions more people in many countries possess something in the way of material assets. They are struggling up into the broadening middle class. In the recent past, they have seen their assets eaten away by inflation, and so they are apprenhensively fighting above all else to *conserve* those assets. As a consequence, they are changing their politics, their attitudes and their life-styles. They are shifting to support conservative policies and they are electing conservative governments.

You don't have to be an American chauvinist, a jingoist or even a capitalist to recognize the many countries where free electorates in just the last few years have changed their governments and moved their economies from the left to the center. Voters have done so in a dozen nations, including Britain, Germany, Canada, the Netherlands, Belgium and, most recently and surprisingly, Sweden. Economic freedom is also spreading in Africa and Latin America. Most dramatically, peoples who have long been enslaved by Communist governments are racing to free up human enterprise.

Consider also: What if you and I were not Americans? What if we did not live in our home cities but instead in Caracas or Hong Kong? What would we be thinking? Somewhere in the back of our minds we would be wondering: How can I transfer some of my money to the United States, that island of political stability and economic vibrancy in an otherwise unstable, uncertain world? That, in fact, is the kind of thinking that is taking place throughout the world. It is certainly not because of attractive interest rates that investment capital continues to move into the U.S. The main reason is that however little they earn on their money, people know that so long as it is invested in the U.S. economy, it will be safe and secure.

In the U.S., a conservative revolution is obviously under way — in economics and in society at large. My estimate is that this trend will continue.

In economic policy it will take the form of more movements toward freedom and away from government control. New businesses will rise rapidly, and competition will heighten — both competition at home and competition from abroad. With rare unanimity, Democratic and Republican leaders alike are speaking up for the need to stimulate investment and enterprise to create jobs and economic growth.

A conservative revolution is also sweeping over, and sweeping up, our young adults, those in their twenties and thirties. Many of them grew up in a rare time of declining expectations, and an era — some years ago — of oppressive inflation and scary unemployment. Consequently, they value a job and put a premium on their careers.

In the nation's universities, young people no longer automatically expect to rise to higher stations in life than their parents or their older siblings. They recognize that they have to work for their advancement. Therefore, every freshman class is more conservative, more realistic, more moderate than the previous one. The students are more conservative than their instructors and professors. In the last several years, the whole situation on campus has been turned on its head.

POINT FIVE: The Cold War is over and we have won — and we should be doing more celebrating over that revolutionary reality. Communism has been dethroned and democratic capitalism has triumphed. The former Soviets, the other Eastern Europeans and many peoples of the Third World are rushing to join the capitalist parade, and China probably isn't too far behind.

As a result, commercial competition stands to replace 3,000 years of grand ideological confrontations. Free-for-all struggles for markets are likely to replace bloody wars for territory. Trade wars may well replace Star Wars. So we are entering an unprecedented era of global economic competition — and global *opportunity*.

In this new world of freer economies, what are some of the countries that we should keep our eye on for potentially spectacular growth and marketing opportunities and competition?

India, for one. Where is the world's second-biggest — or perhaps even very biggest — middle class? Not in Germany, not in Japan, not in Britain, not in France, but in India. Measured by its consumption patterns rather than by its dollar income, the certifiable middle class there numbers at least 100 million — by some measures it may be as high as 300 million — and is growing fast.

South Africa, loaded with minerals and strategically located, could turn out to be a global powerhouse when — not *if* but *when* — blacks are allowed to play a significant role in government.

Mexico shows great promise under President Salinas, whose government is doing all the right things to privatize inefficient and bureaucratic state-owned companies.

Chile, now that it has thrown off 16 years of dictatorship and embraced University of Chicago economics, likes to bill itself as the Switzerland of Latin America.

Indonesia is also cleaning up its act and may emerge as a significant market.

POINT SIX: A big issue of the 1990s, perhaps the biggest of all, will be the clash between the haves and the have-nots, between the world's rich and poor, between the affluent and the deprived, between the comfortable and the angry in our own country and in the world at large.

In global affairs, the major battles that America will face will not be the confrontation between East and West, the old Cold War, and not even the conflicts between West and West — that is, between the U.S. and Europe, or between the U.S. and Japan — though those may be acute. The hardest confrontations will be between the world's North and South, between the affluent, industrialized nations in what we may call the northern hemisphere and the yearning, the restless, the insistent countries clustered in the southern hemisphere, countries that are increasingly demanding larger shares of the wealth that has been laboriously built up over the centuries in the world's North.

In our own society and economy, we face the American dilemma of a Third World amid a First World. Millions of our fellow Americans are living under Third World conditions of nutrition and infant mortality and safety.

As our economy grows more competitive and complex, the U.S. is rapidly — and perhaps dangerously — becoming two nations. One America is educated, skilled, confident, secure, equipped to compete. Its people get jobs in the expansive new industries and services; they move to the growing regions; they put their money in all the fresh forms of high-reward investments, and their lives grow richer.

But the other America is uneducated, unskilled, demoralized. Its people — in the urban ghettos and the rural hollows — fall further and further behind. The recession of the early 1990s and the inflation of the early 1980s exacted their cruelest price on the people who were least prepared to cope: the poor. The good life, the American dream, has become ever more elusive for them. Surely one of the nation's most basic challenges in the 1990s, and beyond, will be to find means for the American underclass to lift itself out of its economic and educational slough.

Many of our government programs and institutions have failed. Our public schools in a distressing number of communities have produced a generation of semiliterates. Our public housing has created public slums. Our public welfare has created despair, dependence and hopelessness among millions of our fellow Americans.

So I believe that private enterprise — perhaps working with government tax incentives, credit and guarantees, but within the private economy — will have to take on more and more of the job of razing and then rebuilding the slums, of creating the factories and offices, and even, in some cases, of providing basic schooling to its employees. Surely all that will be a continuing challenge and opportunity for every American. We cannot allow ourselves to feel comfortable as long as so many of our fellow citizens remain so helplessly far behind.

POINT SEVEN: The fastest-growing socioeconomic problem in the U.S. will be education. Specifically, it will be the harsh reality that our public primary and secondary schools, particularly in the large cities but also in many suburbs and towns, are just not educating our young people to get jobs, or even to cope with the increasingly complex demands of the economy.

Consequently, business is more and more becoming the educator of last resort — teaching employees not only basic skills but also the three Rs, which the public schools are failing to teach them. In the years ahead, as it struggles to find enough able workers, business will become more deeply involved with education, teaching workers within companies, adopting schools within communities, lending managers and technicians to help with the job of education, and generally using its intelligence and influence to reform the school system.

We are not going to end this crisis simply by throwing money at it. But if you think we can solve it without spending more tax money, think again. We will have to lengthen the time that the schools are kept open, perhaps from 7:00 a.m. to 6:00 p.m. every working day, and for a full twelve months every year. We will have to do that to give all of those millions of latchkey kids a place to go and something constructive to do while their parents are at work. We will probably have to move to a system of school choice. We will have to raise teachers' pay, since we will be demanding so much of them. We will have to put a higher premium on being a teacher, and we'll have to give that job a loftier status, as it now has in Japan and Europe.

The computer, video and other forms of modern technology show tremendous potential as teaching tools. But the challenge is to make them as readily available to the poor as to the affluent. The affluent child is surrounded at home by computers — and by parents able to help teach him or her. But not so the deprived child of the central city. The profound irony is that the computer can become the great teacher and unifier, but unless we find a way to spread its mastery among the population, the computer will become the great divider.

In the 1990s and beyond, knowledge will be power. Unless we find means to bring knowledge to the deprived, then the gap between rich and poor, between majority and minority, will grow ever dangerously wider.

POINT EIGHT: The most important social development in the United States will be the continuing rise to positions of power and influence of the nation's most important majority: American women.

As an editor goes around this country and speaks with hundreds upon hundreds of women, he recognizes that this absolutely revolutionary movement has spread: it has spread from the coasts inland, from the North to the South, from big cities to small communities. The result is that there is literally no woman in the country — whatever her position on such controversial issues as abortion or affirmative action — who remains unaffected.

Already the women's movement has profoundly changed our thinking on our basic economic policy-making. Take, for example, the way we think about such a sensitive and human issue as unemployment. So many women have come flocking into the labor force lately — just over 73% of all American women aged 20 to 54 are today at work in the paid economy or actively seeking paying jobs — that even liberal economists now consider full employment to be not a 4% rate of unemployment but rather a 6% or even higher rate.

What the women's revolution portends is that future recessions will be milder and briefer than they otherwise would have been. That is because if one person in a household loses his or her paycheck, there is a much better than 50% chance that yet another person in that household will be bringing in full-time earnings. In part because we have so many multiple-earner families, purchasing power will continue to climb, and our buying of goods and services — particularly of quality goods and services — will be stronger than it otherwise would have been.

Young women who are members of multiple-paycheck families have a motivation to practice economic conservatism because they rather suddenly, surprisingly, find themselves quite affluent. It's not at all unusual for college-trained couples in their twenties or early thirties to be earning $40,000 or $50,000 a year or even more. They are the new elite — people who find themselves with assets — and they want to conserve those assets from the twin depredations of oppressive inflation and high taxation. So while women will remain a liberal force on social issues, it is quite likely that they will become a more conservative force on economic issues.

I cannot stress enough that the women's movement is a real revolution — and it is just beginning. In the past decade, the proportion of women among students graduating with master's degrees in business has grown from one in four to one in three; among law students it has increased from one student in three to two students in five. Women soon will be rising to much loftier positions of influence and power all around us. They will be knocking on the doors of real power.

Most important, their revolutionary rise of consciousness, of self-awareness, of ambition and of demand will give the U.S. a significant edge in the intensifying global competition of the next 10 years. Whatever our shortcomings as a nation may be, we are far ahead of our allies and competitors in Europe, let alone Asia, Latin America and the Middle East, in admitting large numbers of women to positions of economic power and decision-making. This will significantly expand our pool of talent and merit — the group from which we draw our business, our political, our societal, our academic leaders — in the next decade. In short, with a larger group to choose from, we shall select better leaders. We have long since passed the day when we could afford the brutal luxury of shutting out of positions of leadership more than one-half of our American population.

POINT NINE: There will be a dramatic expansion of the quality market for goods and services. We Americans are coming to appreciate, as Europeans and the Japanese have so long appreciated, that smaller can be better and that less can be more if the goods and the services that one buys deliver real value for money. We also shall adopt — indeed, we are rapidly adopting — a conservation ethic. You see this revolution going on in every aspect and facet of American life. You see people being more quality-conscious everywhere. They are not necessarily picking the fanciest designer label or paying the highest possible price, but they are showing a new, sophisticated awareness that high quality is more efficient and therefore more economical in the long run.

A remarkable change is occurring in American marketing. As you go across the country and study markets, whether markets for magazines or for cars or clothes or food, you see that the goods that are selling well are those that deliver real value for money: high quality, reliability, durability. And the goods that are selling poorly are those that do not have lasting value: the faddish, the flashy, the easily discarded goods.

We will buy fewer goods, but they will be better, higher-quality goods. We Americans shall adopt a European style of living, embracing the quality market. Our standards of living will not decline. Indeed, they will change, but they will rise. And business-people — entrepreneurs, manufacturers, brokers and bankers, among others — who produce and deliver quality goods and quality services will surely prosper.

Before I go on to my final point, let me give you my own short list of superlatives — what may be the biggest, the best, the worst, the most in the next 10 years.

Biggest-selling consumer goods: Anything that is of high quality; also, convenience goods and services.

Biggest dogs on the market: Anything that stresses low price over high quality.

Biggest-spending consumer group: The aging youth market, the maturing baby-boom kids, many of whom are coming perilously close to 40 years of age. We might call them the over-the-thrill crowd.

There will not be a new baby boom, but there will be a parenting boom, as more and more of the swelling generation of two-income working couples in their mid- to late thirties decide to have a child — only one child, Superbaby! — or at most two.

Most significant demographic change: The number of people who are 65 or 70 or older and retired will surge. There may well be sharp generational conflicts between the retirees and the baby boomers. For example, the elders will want to collect ever more generous Social Security benefits — including unlimited cost-of-living allowances — while the boomers will want to hold down the benefit payments and instead save and build up the funds for future years, so that there will be enough left for the boomers themselves when *they* start to retire, around the year 2010.

Strongest comeback by a currently depressed industry: Energy. It is ridiculous and dangerous to speak of an energy "glut" when the U.S. still must spend more than a billion dollars a week to import energy. Barring some unexpected breakthrough disovery, the world still will have only finite sources of liquid energy, and as industry expands around the globe, demand for energy once again will scrape up against the limits of supply. Thus, we should be taking every sensible step now to explore for and develop energy and conserve what we have.

Most promising energy source: Natural gas, because the U.S. possesses plenty of it, tucked away in relatively small but still economical pockets.

Least promising energy source: Solar power, a victim — so far — of extravagant hopes and disappointing performance.

Fastest-rising regions: Areas rich in technological enterprises, in services and, ultimately, in certain resources — specifically, the Southwest and the West for high-tech, for services and eventually, too, for energy; and the Southeast for much of the same, except energy.

Best investments: Growth stocks — and mutual funds concentrating on growth stocks. And in the longer term, land — land in areas that hold resources, including energy resources and even farmland, which is now undervalued.

Surest political trend: The swing away from the left and toward the center in many countries.

Biggest tax battle: Whether or not to introduce some form of broad consumption tax, such as a European-style value-added tax or a national sales tax. Speaking privately, the leaders of Congress — of both parties — say that such a tax is inevitable and desirable to finally balance our federal budget.

I take the contrarian view that Americans would be willing to accept a deficit-cutting program if it showed every sign of being fair, equitable and efficient; I believe that they are willing to accept sacrifices so long as they are convinced that *everybody* in our society will have to make some sacrifices.

Any new taxes should be leveled on consumption. People should be taxed less on what they put into the economy (in the form of work, saving and investment) and more on what they take out (in the form of consumption). So increases in taxes on whiskey, cigarettes and gasoline should be favored over growth-retarding increases in taxes on personal income and corporate profits. Ideally, every dollar of additional taxes should be matched by two dollars' of reduction in government spending.

The most indefensible spending is that for people whose incomes are above the national median. Spending of all kinds on the poor — for welfare, Medicaid, housing and food — adds up to about 9% of the budget. Although workfare can trim that, the poor need most of what they get. But spending for subsidies to farm operations with gross sales above $100,000 a year amounts to almost $7 billion. Medicare payments to people who are well off run to further billions. Those are luxuries that our nation no longer can afford.

POINT TEN: In conclusion, let me observe that we are entering an era when the countries that possess the rare combination of human and material resources will prosper and inherit the future.

The next 10 years will provide more dangers and yet more opportunities than the last decade. In negotiating this period, it might be wise to recall history's lesson: This country has the unique capacity to change and to amaze. Our nation also has the human *and* material resources to make life better.

The startling reality is that for all its blemishes, the U.S. possesses unique and sometimes undervalued assets. Foreigners often see these visible advantages more clearly than we do, and so they are investing in America as if it were a high-growth stock. Asians, Europeans and Latin Americans are putting billions into apartments in Florida, office buildings in California, beachfronts in Hawaii, factories in South Carolina, laboratories in Illinois and much more.

Increasingly, foreigners are also investing their lives in this country. Immigration visa applications are surging. The newcomers are not only the oppressed or the anxious from Russia and Cuba, Poland and China, Yugoslavia and Vietnam, but also educated, affluent people from all over. What these investors and immigrants are telling us should be clear: America is a stable, free land, and Americans who have some money to put aside might do well to invest in its future.

The nation's strengths range from enviable (and inexpensive) communications and transportation services to the world's most vigorous and most easily accessible venture capital markets. Beyond its resources of computers and other machines, the U.S. possesses fabulous amounts of raw materials — more, in many cases, than any other developed nation — and they are bound to pay rewards tomorrow to the investors of today.

It is not in industry or agriculture or the services that America has made its boldest advances; rather, it is in society, and that societal progress stands to enrich and enlarge the nation's human capital. About 7.7 million Americans between the ages of 18 and 24 are attending colleges and universities. This represents one in every 3.5 people in that age group. When they graduate, many of these students will go into business, industry and the sciences, and may well increase the value of your investments.

If I am right about our current problems (and they are many) as well as our future potentials (and they, too, are many), there will be five ingredients for the economic, the political and the social success of nations in the next 10 years. Societies, people, countries will do well if they have a number of the following five characteristics:

First, a rich, modern, highly productive agricultural base, giving a country the capacity not only to feed its own people but also to export food — for economic gain, occasionally for political leverage, certainly for humanitarian purposes.

Second, an abundant base of energy-bearing raw materials — not only oil and natural gas but also coal, hydroelectric power and all the rest.

Third, a vital, strong base of other, nonenergy raw materials: iron ore, copper, lead, phosphate, zinc and the like.

Fourth, an advanced, automated, highly developed technology and industry, including information and financial-services industries.

Fifth, and most important, an educated, motivated, well-informed, skilled, sophisticated population.

I have gone down the list of all the member nations of the United Nations — 178 at latest count. It is fascinating and revealing if you try to apply these five criteria. You very quickly see why, for all its vaunted military might, the former Soviet Union fell into such grave despair: it qualifies under at most two of the five headings. The Russians and the other former Soviets suffer from awful problems because of their totally inefficient, bankrupt agriculture, because of the erratic nature of their industry, and because of the questionable skills and education of so much of their population.

China has a brilliant future, but a distant one. It suffers from severe problems and shortages and will continue to do so for the rest of this century and probably well into the next.

Germany and Japan are fairly well off, but only fairly so, because they lack the food and the fuel to supply their own populations, let alone to export.

Britain has some significant problems at the moment, but given its advanced industries, its energy resources and its skilled, educated population, it faces a potentially very bright future — *if* it chooses the proper policies now.

But there are three, and only three, nations on the face of the earth that qualify by all five measures: rich agriculture, abundant energy and nonenergy resources, advanced industrial technology and skilled, educated populations. Those three — regardless of their problems now — are Canada, Australia and, of course, the United States.

What our nation *lacks* is also apparent. It is the will, the methods, the procedures and often the institutions to exploit those resources. It is the leaders with skill and vision to rally the people. It is the resolve to overcome individual interests for the benefit of all. But those are purely psychological and institutional constraints, and thus they can be surmounted. That is where *we* come in. Surely we — you and I — *can* make a difference.

The U.S. has no major physical or material limitations. That is quite a superlative, definitive statement, but it is indisputably correct. So despite all of our immediate and very visible problems, if we Americans follow sensible policies of government deregulation, of investment stimulation, of energy conservation and energy development, then the economic, the political and the social future of the United States in the rest of these very revolutionary 1990s will be absolutely *dazzling*.

Index